Tamar's Tears

Tamar's Tears
*Evangelical Engagements with Feminist
Old Testament Hermeneutics*

Edited by
ANDREW SLOANE

☙PICKWICK *Publications* • Eugene, Oregon

TAMAR'S TEARS
Evangelical Engagements with Feminist Old Testament Hermeneutics

Copyright © 2012 Wipf and Stock Publishers. All rights reserved. Except for brief quotations in critical publications or reviews, no part of this book may be reproduced in any manner without prior written permission from the publisher. Write: Permissions, Wipf and Stock Publishers, 199 W. 8th Ave., Suite 3, Eugene, OR 97401.

Pickwick Publications
An Imprint of Wipf and Stock Publishers
199 W. 8th Ave., Suite 3
Eugene, OR 97401

www.wipfandstock.com

ISBN 13: 978-1-60899-982-8

Cataloguing-in-Publication data:

Tamar's tears : evangelical engagements with feminist Old Testament hermeneutics / edited by Andrew Sloane.

xx + 378 pp. ; 23 cm. Includes bibliographical references and index.

ISBN 13: 978-1-60899-982-8

1. Bible. O.T.—Feminist criticism. 2. Women in the Bible. 3. Evangelicalism. 4. Violence in the Bible. 5. Bible. O.T.—hermeneutics. I. Sloane, Andrew. II. Title.

BS575 S56 2012

Manufactured in the U.S.A.

We thank the editors of Tyndale Bulletin for permission to use material from Robin Parry, "Feminist Hermeneutics and Evangelical Concerns: The Rape of Dinah as a Case Study," *Tyndale Bulletin* 53.1 (2002) 1–28; and Andrew Sloane, "Aberrant Textuality? The Case of Ezekiel the (Porno) Prophet," *Tyndale Bulletin* 59.1 (2008) 53–76.

Contents

Contributors / vii

Acknowledgments / ix

Introduction: Engagement not Conflict / xi

1. "And he shall rule over you": Evangelicals, Feminists, and Genesis 2–3—*Andrew Sloane* / 1

2. Feminist Hermeneutics and Evangelical Concerns: The Rape of Dinah as a Case Study—*Robin Parry* / 30

3. Hermeneutics by Numbers? Case Studies in Feminist and Evangelical Interpretation of the Book of Numbers —*Richard Briggs* / 65

4. Adding Insult to Injury? The Family Laws of Deuteronomy —*Jenni Williams* / 84

5. This Is Her Body . . . : Judges 19 as Call to Discernment —*Nicholas Ansell* / 112

6. Colliding Contexts: Reading Tamar (2 Sam 13:1–22) as a Twenty-First Century Woman—*Miriam Bier* / 171

7. Aberrant Textuality? The Case of Ezekiel the (Porno) Prophet—*Andrew Sloane* / 191

8. His Desire Is For Her: Feminist Readings of the Song of Solomon—*Grenville Kent* / 217

9. Justice at the Crossroads: The Book of Lamentations and Feminist Discourse—*Heath Thomas* / 246

10 Patriarchy, Biblical Authority, and the Grand Narrative of the Old Testament—*Junia Pokrifka* / 274

11 Can our Hermeneutics be both Evangelical and Feminist? Insights from the Theory and Practice of Theological Interpretation—*Todd Pokrifka* / 315

Concluding Reflections: Seeing Tamar's Tears / 352

Index / 355

Contributors

NICHOLAS ANSELL (MPhil, PhD) is Assistant Professor of Theology at the Institute for Christian Studies, Toronto, Canada.

MIRIAM J. BIER (BA, DipTchg, GradDipAppTheol, MTh) is completing her PhD on the book of Lamentations at the University of Otago, in Dunedin, New Zealand.

RICHARD S. BRIGGS (PhD) is Lecturer in Old Testament; Director of Biblical Studies and Hermeneutics at Cranmer Hall, St. John's College, Durham University, where he teaches the Old Testament. Richard lives in Durham, England, and is married to Melody, with three lively children.

GRENVILLE J. R. KENT (MA *Film*, MA (Hons) *Theol*, PhD) is Lecturer in Old Testament and Arts at Wesley Institute, Sydney. Based in Sydney, he is the besotted husband of Carla and proud father of five young children.

ROBIN A. PARRY (MA, PhD, PGCE) is an editor at Wipf and Stock Publishers. He has written books on Old Testament ethics, trinitarian worship, universalism, and a commentary on Lamentations. He is married to Carol and has two daughters, Hannah and Jessica. They live in Worcester, England.

JUNIA POKRIFKA (MDiv, STM, PhD) is Associate Professor of Old Testament at Azusa Pacific University (California, USA). Junia lives in Southern California with her husband Todd and two sons, Daniel and Immanuel.

TODD POKRIFKA (MDiv, STM, PhD) is Lecturer in Theology at Azusa Pacific University. He is the author of *Redescribing God: The Roles of Scripture, Tradition, and Reason in Karl Barth's Doctrines of Divine Unity, Constancy, and Eternity* (Wipf and Stock, 2010).

Andrew Sloane (MBBS, BTh, ThD) is Lecturer in Old Testament and Christian Thought at Morling College (affiliated with the Australian College of Theology). Andrew lives in Sydney with his wife Alison and three young adult daughters, Elanor, Laura, and Alexandra.

Heath Thomas (PhD) is Assistant Professor of Old Testament & Hebrew at Southeastern Seminary in Wake Forest, North Carolina and Fellow in Old Testament Studies at The Paideia Centre for Public Theology in Ontario, Canada. Heath lives in Wake Forest with his wife, Jill, and four children Harrison, Isabelle, Simon, and Sophia.

Jenni Williams (MA, PhD) is Tutor in Old Testament at Wycliffe Hall, Oxford. She lives in Oxford with her husband Jon, son Daniel, and daughter Elanor.

Acknowledgments

It is customary for academics to thank those who have helped make their work possible. Let me follow that custom, but note that this is not an empty form. Truly we acknowledge—and give thanks to God for—the many people who help and support us and the projects we work on.

So first, we would acknowledge the generous support of our families and friends, those who give us so generously of their time and love and forbearance, and who are willing to express (or kindly feign) interest in the strange worlds of ideas we inhabit.

We also thank our various institutions for the provision of study leave and working environments in which it is possible to pursue interests such as these, as well as the editorial staff at Wipf & Stock for all their hard work.

Andrew and Robin would also like thank the editors of *Tyndale Bulletin* for permission to use articles originally published in the *Bulletin* as the basis for their chapters (2 and 7) on Dinah and Ezekiel. They originally appeared as: Robin Parry, "Feminist Hermeneutics and Evangelical Concerns: The Rape of Dinah as a Case Study," *Tyndale Bulletin* 53.1 (2002) 1–28; and Andrew Sloane, "Aberrant Textuality? The Case of Ezekiel the (Porno) Prophet," *Tyndale Bulletin* 59.1 (2008) 53–76. In addition, Andrew expresses his gratitude to the Tyndale Fellowship for the invitation to present the 2010 Annual Old Testament Lecture, which formed the basis of his chapter (1) on Genesis 2–3.

As editor, Andrew would like to thank each of the contributors to the volume for their valuable feedback, reflections, and discussion on each of our pieces. These made it a truly collegial endeavour and one from which we all profited—and demonstrates the value of hospitable engagement between those who share common concerns but different perspectives.

Finally, in July 2010 most of the contributors to this volume met in Worcester for a symposium on evangelicals and feminist Old Testament hermeneutics. This was an invaluable (and very enjoyable) experience made possible by Robin Parry's generous assistance and the warm hospitality of his family and church (City Church, Worcester). It allowed us to present early versions of our papers, discuss the issues, note objections and possibilities we hadn't seen for ourselves and hang out with an excellent bunch of people. The story, of course, did not begin there; it began in 2008 when Robin contacted me about the possibility of our working together on this project. So, on behalf of all of us who have profited so much from our ongoing conversations: thanks, Robin, for making this possible and for lubricating the wheels of our common endeavour.

Introduction

Engagement Not Conflict

MUCH PUBLIC AND ACADEMIC discourse seems to be controlled by images of conflict: culture wars; remnants of class struggle; the clash between "progressive" and "conservative" political agenda; battles between rival schools of thought or disciplinary perspectives; the list goes on. So our imaginations and perceptions of interactions between alternative viewpoints are shaped; we come to see ourselves as manoeuvring through the frontlines, sniping at, ambushing, or directly assaulting the entrenched positions of our foes. Sometimes we do find ourselves embattled, defending the truth or seeking to establish or extend a bridgehead in hostile intellectual territory. But not all the time; at times a more irenic, a more conversational approach is appropriate. The contributors to this volume aim to exhibit just such a peaceable approach to the interface between evangelical and feminist approaches to OT interpretation. Of course, many evangelicals and many feminist biblical scholars would see this interface as a skirmish zone in a key conflict over the nature and use of the Bible. We beg to differ, seeking a more excellent way, a friendlier path through this territory that might prove fruitful for both evangelical and feminist biblical scholars.

But first we should perhaps explain how it is that evangelical and feminist interests are seen as being in essential conflict. Many feminists consider *evangelical* feminism to be impossible. They see the Bible as irredeemably patriarchal and, given their view of the priority of women's experience and their critique of patriarchy, they argue that one cannot, therefore, accept the Bible's authority and also embrace feminist perspectives. Many evangelicals consider evangelical *feminism* (or perhaps, being a *feminist* evangelical) to be impossible. They see the Bible as presenting a hierarchical (or complementarian) model of male-female relationships, and argue that to question that model on the basis of a feminist critique of patriarchy is to sell out the Bible and its authority.

We consider both claims to be wrong—and do so in part on the basis of *demonstration*: that is, we are evangelicals and we are feminists and so our very existence challenges those claims. This book, however, does not aim to address *this* question (many others have explored the question of whether it is possible to be both evangelical and feminist[1]); rather, taking it to be the case that it is possible to be evangelical and feminist, it seeks to address the issues that feminist biblical interpretation (specifically, Old Testament interpretation) raises for evangelical Christians who engage in the disciplines of biblical and theological scholarship. In so doing, we trust that this will show both that it is possible to be an evangelical feminist biblical scholar, and how it can be done.

What, then, are the key issues that feminist OT hermeneutics raises for evangelical interpreters? Here are some: is the text as a whole, or are particular texts, inherently oppressive? If so, how do we understand Scripture as God's word? If not, how do we understand the criticisms that have been levelled against it and the features of the text that generate those criticisms? How do we wrestle with the historical and cultural particularity of the text/s while maintaining it is the word of a God of freedom and fidelity; a God of love and justice? What do we do with texts that seem to deny women the dignity we believe is rightly theirs— and which have been used in such ways? How do we hear the voice of feminist criticism, learning from it, without denying our evangelical heritage? In particular, how do we affirm the Bible as the authoritative word of the God of life in the face of such critique? It is questions such as these that exercise the minds of the writers of the pieces that follow.

Before we outline where the individual pieces take us, it is worth clarifying a few things. First, we want to be clear that we recognise that both evangelicalism and feminism/ feminist interpretation are *pluralist* enterprises. While there is no need to present taxonomies of these movements here (which are, anyway, outlined in pieces such as Robin Parry's in this volume), it is worth noting the diversity that exists within them. Feminists range from those who see Scripture and the faiths informed by it as irredeemably patriarchal, inimical to women and their interests, to those who see Scripture and (elements of) the faiths informed by it as liberating and life-enhancing for all people, including women (at least when properly understood and appropriated). Evangelicals vary widely

---

1 See, for instance, Van Leeuwen, ed. *After Eden*; Pierce *et al*., eds., *Discovering Biblical Equality*.

on their views of Scripture (ranging from, say, strongly inerrantist views that tightly identify the words of Scripture with the Word of God, to infallibilist views and beyond, which see a more dynamic and complex relationship between them), their understanding of the theological task (ranging from, say, strongly propositionalist views that see theology as a matter of systematizing the truth claims of Scripture, to post-conservative evangelicalism, which sees theology as seeking to articulate the narrative identity which is ours in the gospel in particular cultural contexts). Of course, they also vary in their responses to feminism (ranging from those who see it as a fundamental challenge to our faith, to those—such as the contributors to this volume—who see it as presenting challenges to which we must respond and insights from which we must learn). All of this to say that in this volume we seek to both acknowledge and reflect a variety of sympathetic responses to a variety of feminist concerns, doing so within the "broad church" of evangelicalism. We should also note that we are all too aware that (ironically) most of the contributors to this volume are men. This was due in part to a relative dearth of women evangelical OT scholars who are interested in the issues (or at least of our knowledge of them). Perhaps this volume might help prompt the solution to this problem. And so, to the essays in the volume.

In the first piece, "'And he shall rule over you': Evangelicals, Feminists and Genesis 2–3," Andrew Sloane notes that Genesis 2–3 has prompted many feminist interpretations, ranging from those which seek to recover from it (or read out of it) an egalitarian understanding of male-female relationships to those that deconstruct and reject it as irredeemably patriarchal. He identifies key interpreters and interpretive perspectives (Phyllis Trible's now classic egalitarian, literary reading; Gale Yee's patriarchal, ideological reading; Mieke Bal's non-patriarchal, readerly perspective; and J'annine Jobling's post-Christian, post-feminist reading) and engages with their interpretations of Genesis 2–3. In doing so he seeks to analyze their underlying assumptions and methodologies and critically appraise their interpretation of the text from an evangelical point of view. He concludes with some reflections on evangelical feminist interpretation of Genesis 2–3. While he resists the claims of "suspicious" and "resistant" readings of the text, he argues that evangelicals need to listen carefully to feminist interpretations in order to identify where our uses of the text have distorted its meaning and been damaging to women and to ensure that they reflect God's liberating vision of human community.

Robin Parry's chapter, "Feminist Hermeneutics and Evangelical Concerns: The Rape of Dinah as a Case Study," begins by outlining the challenge feminist hermeneutics poses for traditional notions of biblical authority. In doing so he gives a brief introduction to the main lineaments of feminist hermeneutics (using, in part, Osiek's influential five-fold taxonomy: rejectionist, loyalist, revisionist, sublimationist, and liberationist). Genesis 34 is set out as a case study for displaying feminist interpretations that read with the narrator but against patriarchal interpreters and those which read against the narrator himself. He argues that a "high view" of Scripture can accommodate many of the concerns raised by feminist critics of biblical narrative, including those that note the narrator's focus on perspectives other than Dinah's. While this opens up the possibility of imaginative reflections on her, and other women's, experience in the text, these should not be considered as exegetical reflections. Furthermore, he maintains that an evangelical hermeneutic will not easily be able to endorse an interpretation that stands over against the stance of a biblical narrator.

The third chapter, "Hermeneutics by Numbers? Case Studies in Feminist and Evangelical Interpretation of the Book of Numbers" by Richard Briggs, claims that it is easy to treat both evangelical and feminist hermeneutics in an abstract and over-generalised way. His paper considers the two approaches by way of careful comparison of how self-defined writers in the two traditions offer comment on particular passages in the book of Numbers; in particular, passages which raise obvious gender-related matters (5:11–31; 12 and the story of Miriam; 27 and 36). From such a comparative study, it becomes apparent that both approaches to the biblical text highlight some features of it and leave others submerged, whether deliberately or inadvertently. This evaluation, however, accords differently with the declared aims of the two approaches. In particular, a key issue is the extent to which either of these approaches occupies themselves with probing and interacting with the theological subject matter of the text, an area in which there are weaknesses in each case. He also observes that there is almost no overlap at all between feminist and evangelical commentary on the book of Numbers, which itself suggests that there is scope for fruitful interaction between feminist and evangelical approaches in developing properly *theological* interpretations of Numbers.

In chapter 4, "Adding Insult to Injury? The Family Laws of Deuteronomy," Jenni Williams notes that Deuteronomy is often seen as the OT legal witness to social justice *par excellence*. Its unequivocal freeing of women debt slaves and its law protecting a "slandered virgin" are often pointed to as evidence of a growing respect for women as people in Old Testament thought and an emergence from the idea of woman as property. Recent feminist readings of Deuteronomy have thrown this comfortable understanding into considerable doubt, highlighting such phenomena as a rape victim who can be made to marry her attacker (Deut 22:28–29). Through close engagement with the work of Carolyn Pressler and Tikva Frymer-Kensky her chapter examines whether, as far as its treatment of women is concerned, Deuteronomy has deserved the praise given to it by some or the blame attributed to it by others, and asks whether both may have been premature. It also asks how evangelicals may benefit from feminist perspectives on the text, noting that, while the texts do not themselves encode an egalitarian view of women, they can be used in the construction of an egalitarian and liberating theological vision.

Chapter 5, "This Is Her Body . . . : Judges 19 as Call to Discernment" by Nicholas Ansell, responds to Phyllis Trible's claim that Judges 19 is a "Text of Terror" in a double sense; because it not only portrays events that are truly horrifying, but does so in a way that adds to the betrayal of the unnamed woman. Consequently, in Trible's view, God's call to compassion comes to us by means of a text that is itself in need of redemption. Building on one of Trible's underdeveloped insights, this essay explores the intra-textual relationship between Judges 19 and the Achsah-Caleb-Othniel paradigm of Judges 1 to see how Old Testament "wisdom thinking"—in which patriarchal gender symbolism is subtly yet powerfully undermined—can help us discern the redemptive-historical potential of this unnerving narrative. He argues that, far from being complicit in the woman's brutalization and silencing, the narrative requires that we hear her story as part of an unfolding canon that culminates in the person and work of Jesus Christ (and his suffering, rejection, betrayal, and death) and speak for her and other victims of (male) violence.

Miriam Bier's piece, "Colliding Contexts: Reading Tamar (2 Sam 13:1–22) as a Twenty-First Century Woman," grapples with the question of biblical authority in relation to difficult texts; a problem that has been identified as a key issue for evangelical feminist readings of the Hebrew Bible. She examines three phenomena in Hebrew narrative that offer difficulties and possibilities for reading Tamar's story in 2 Sam 13:1–22 in line with how the biblical narrative itself "works." The first is the "God's eye view" effect, and the difficulty this creates when the narrator's (androcentric, patriarchal) word is accepted as God's word. The second is the use of narrative techniques for evaluating characters and morality, and the possibility this creates for expressing a narrative and thus divine indictment of Amnon. The third is the narrative "gap" created by the absence and silence of God. This silence of God could be interpreted in at least two ways: tacit acceptance (or at the very least, ambivalence toward), or tacit indictment of the happenings of the chapter. In the face of God's silence, she argues, it is entirely appropriate for people wishing to remain faithful to the biblical text to "read the gap," and use their own voices to protest the treatment of Tamar by her brother Amnon. This will ensure that, despite male violence and divine silence, Tamar's voice continues to be heard.

Andrew Sloane's second piece, "Aberrant Textuality? The Case of Ezekiel the (Porno) Prophet," addresses a specific criticism of the prophets brought by some feminist interpreters. "Pornoprophetic" readings of the unfaithful wife metaphors in Hosea 1–3, Jeremiah 2 and 3, and Ezekiel 16 and 23 criticize them as misogynistic texts that express and perpetuate negative images of women and their sexuality. He seeks to present an evangelical response to Athalya Brenner and Fokkelien van Dijk-Hemmes' pornoprophetic reading of Ezekiel 16 and 23. He outlines their claims and supporting arguments, including their assertion that the texts constitute pornographic propaganda which shapes and distorts women's (sexual) experience in the interests of male (sexual) power. He argues that both their underlying methods and assumptions and their specific claims are flawed, and so their claims should be rejected. While acknowledging the offensive power of the texts, he concludes that alternative explanations such as the violence of Israel's judgment and the offensive nature of Jerusalem's sin account better for the features of the texts which they find problematic.

In chapter 8, "His Desire Is For Her: Feminist Readings of the Song of Solomon," Grenville Kent notes that the Song of Songs has been of great interest to feminist and womanist commentators, who have seen there a strong female voice and character and a relationship that approaches Edenic gender equality. Some recent oppositional readings have radically questioned this. His chapter surveys key feminist approaches, three that see equality and read with the text (Trible's rhetorical criticism, Brenner's politically savvy analysis of the text using critical theory, and Weems' womanist commentary), one that considers resistant readings but predominantly reads of equality (Exum's various contributions), and one resistant reading (Black's counter-reading and use of the grotesque). He argues that, while it may initially seem too good to be true, egalitarian readings of the Song are more persuasive than those that read against the grain of the text or seek to find hidden oppressive agenda in it, allowing us to hear in the Song authentic voices speaking of equality and delight for women and men, and finding in it glimpses of Edenic harmony restored in God's redemption of human love and sex.

Heath Thomas' piece, "Justice at the Crossroads: The Book of Lamentations and Feminist Discourse," observes that the little book of Lamentations has generated an extensive amount of interest from feminist readings in recent years. A central issue at stake in these readings is the notion of justice. His essay aims to assess feminist interpretation(s) of Lamentations and compare these renderings with an approach that interprets Lamentations within an OT theological context. He briefly assesses varieties of feminist interpretation as well as its deployment in Lamentations research, and queries the views of justice in Lamentations from feminist scholarship. He renders the conception of divine justice in Lamentations within the context of the larger OT, contrasting these findings against the view(s) of justice held up in feminist readings of Lamentations. As with other pieces in this volume, he demonstrates the existence of a variety of feminist approaches to the book. He concludes that wrestling with questions of justice in feminist discourse on Lamentations suggests that the book complexly affirms the justice of God explicitly through direct statements and implicitly through the very logic of lament prayer. This allows the writer/s of the text and its readers to both question and affirm the sovereignty and justice of God in openness to the possibility of a divine response.

The final two pieces by Junia and Todd Pokrifka differ in kind to the others in this volume: they deal with thematic and constructive theological work from the OT rather than specific texts or books that have been subject to feminist scrutiny. Junia's chapter, "Patriarchy, Biblical

Authority, and the Grand Narrative of the Old Testament," directly addresses the issues of patriarchy and biblical authority. She notes that many feminists have argued that the frequent and often pervasive presence of patriarchy in the Old Testament is incompatible with the idea that the Old Testament can speak authoritatively to women and to feminist concerns. She presents an alternative to this view that draws from a particular understanding of the grand narrative that unifies and underlies the various texts of the Old Testament. Beginning with Genesis 1–3, she outlines the way that the Old Testament narrative handles human relationships with God, with other humans, and with the creation. As she traces related themes through various phases of the Old Testament's story, aspects of Genesis 1–3 will become a hermeneutical key for a redemptive reading of the remaining stories of the Old Testament. She suggests that this way of reading helps to defray some of the feminist concerns regarding the presence of patriarchal aspects in the Old Testament, while maintaining the authority of the Old Testament.

Chapter 11, the last in the volume, "Can our Hermeneutics be both Evangelical and Feminist? Insights from the Theory and Practice of Theological Interpretation" by Todd Pokrifka, offers the outlines of a hermeneutic that is both evangelical and feminist, seeing it as an instance of evangelical theological interpretation of Scripture. After defining the essential terms, he argues for a hermeneutic that is feminist *because* it is evangelical. This conviction depends on a certain theological reading or construal of Scripture, one that regards Scripture as a narrative unity that is structured largely around redemption. He presents a critical defence of the redemptive-movement hermeneutic expounded by William J. Webb. The result is a hermeneutic that fully recognizes the cultural patriarchy and other oppressive elements in Scripture, but that is nonetheless able to embrace the supreme authority of Scripture in witnessing to God's redemptive and liberating justice for women.

Clearly, the pieces approach different texts and issues and do so from a range of perspectives that are both evangelical and feminist; indeed, there are matters of both method and substance on which the authors of this book disagree despite (sometimes even *because of*) our common commitment to being both evangelical and feminist. We trust that in the midst of this diversity there is a common commitment to friendly and faithful engagement with feminist OT hermeneutics from broadly evangelical points of view. We are, however, confident of one thing: this volume will not please everyone. We do hope it pleases some, who find in it perspectives and attitudes they share (or at least find compatible with a faithful reading of Scripture); we also hope that it challenges those it doesn't please, encouraging them to rethink their assumptions about the nature of feminist or evangelical biblical interpretation or both. Even so, we realise that some of our evangelical friends and colleagues will see us as selling our soul (or that of the Scriptures) to the spirit of the age. And some of our feminist friends and colleagues will see us as trapped in false ideas of authority and Scripture. So be it. At the risk of presumptuously claiming the moral high (and middle) ground, that is the doom of those who seek to moderate between extremes. We believe that we have negotiated this middle ground (seeing it as *middle ground* and not as "no-man's [*sic!*] land" or a demilitarized zone) without being unduly combative. We hope and believe that hasn't come at the cost of compromise: of *really* losing our evangelical uniqueness; of *actually* betraying our feminist concerns. But that is something for readers to judge as they engage with the pieces that follow.

BIBLIOGRAPHY

Pierce, Ronald W., et al., eds. *Discovering Biblical Equality: Complementarity Without Hierarchy*. 2nd ed. Downers Grove, IL: InterVarsity, 2005.

Van Leeuwen, Mary Stewart, ed. *After Eden: Facing the Challenge of Gender Relations*. Grand Rapids: Eerdmans, 1993.

1

"And he shall rule over you"

Evangelicals, Feminists, and Genesis 2–3

ANDREW SLOANE

INTRODUCTION

GENESIS 2–3 HAS PLAYED an important role in feminist theology and feminist Old Testament hermeneutics. (This is, no doubt, because of the role it has played in traditional readings of Scripture and the patterns of male-female relationships that they endorse.) It is also due to the crucial role these chapters play in "setting the scene" for the rest of Scripture and the conditions under which the rest of the story unfolds.[2] For evangelicals this is heightened because these chapters are generally taken as presenting God's intentions for humanity and the rest of creation, intentions which, after the "fall" are restored (and reaffirmed and transformed) in the *eschaton*.[3] It matters deeply, then, just what those

---

1. "Complementarian" is the preferred terminology of contemporary evangelical exponents of the traditional (hierarchical) view of gender relationships. See, for instance, Piper and Grudem, eds., *Recovering Biblical Manhood and Womanhood*. Others, who might be considered evangelical feminists or egalitarian in their view of gender relationships, see this terminology as misleading. See, for instance, Pierce et al., eds., *Discovering Biblical Equality*.

2. Note Barr and others who see it as marginal to the unfolding story, and the critique of that, variously, in Stordalen, *Echoes of Eden*; Mettinger, *The Eden Narrative*; Wright, *OT Ethics*; Wright, *The Mission of God*.

3. This receives a measure of dominical authorisation in Matt 19:1–12 where Jesus

intentions are, what the ordering of human relationships ought to be, and in what that vision of life as it is meant to be consists.

This has, as is (too) well known, generated significant controversy amongst evangelicals. Is this creation order one in which there is a natural and God-ordained hierarchy of men over women, with men and women being equal in being but having "complementary" roles in God's purposes for the species?[4] Or is it one of fundamental equality, which is marred by sin, so that hierarchy is a sign of disorder, of the disharmony that sin (is and) generates?[5] As an evangelical feminist, I take the latter to be the case: but this is not the occasion on which to *argue* for that view; my job is otherwise and there are many useful discussions of the issues. Besides, all too often we evangelicals get caught up in our own in-house debates and fail to address significant issues in the broader academy. So, my aim in this piece is, as an evangelical feminist, to engage with general feminist interpretations of Genesis 2–3, with a view to: understanding different perspectives; learning from them when I believe we can; identifying issues and questions that arise from them for evangelical understandings of Genesis 2–3 (and biblical interpretation more generally), as well as questions that we as evangelicals might put to feminist interpreters; and determining points of resistance and rejection, places where evangelical interpreters must part company with our feminist friends (especially, I suspect, in relation to matters of the authority and function of the Bible).

There is a bewildering array of feminist interpretations of Genesis 2–3, adopting an equally bewildering range of theological and interpretive viewpoints; certainly more than can be scrutinized in detail here.[6]

---

uses Genesis 2 as the basis for his rejection of (pharisaic patterns of) divorce. For the notion of the reaffirmation and transformation of creational purposes in the eschaton, see O'Donovan, *Resurrection and Moral Order*.

4. With "complementary" entailing relationships of superordination of men and subordination of women. So Stitzinger, "Genesis 1–3"; Hurley, *Man and Woman in Biblical Perspective*; Ortlund, "Male-Female Equality and Male Headship: Genesis 1–3"; Foh, "What is the Woman's Desire?"; Foh, *Women and the Word of God*; Collins, "What happened to Adam and Eve?"; Grudem, *Evangelical Feminism and Biblical Truth*.

5. This allows for a kind of "complementarity" of women and men that does not entail permanent hierarchical ordering of gender relationships. So Evans, *Woman in the Bible*; Griffiths, "Mankind: Male and Female"; Besançon Spencer, *Beyond the Curse*; Bilezikian, *Sex Roles*; Hayter, *The New Eve In Christ*; Tucker, *Women in the Maze*; Hess, "Equality."

6. They range from "maturation" readings, positive and negative (see Bechtel, "Rethinking the Interpretation of Genesis 2:4b—3:24," Bechtel, "Genesis 2.4b—3.24";

I will, therefore, need to be selective in my treatment of the subject, seeking to cover a few major points of view in some depth, rather than attempting an impossible comprehensiveness. (While a number of taxonomies of feminist interpretation are available,[7] my choice is driven by both methodological and substantive concerns: that is to say, I will attempt to give something of a feel for the interpretive approaches adopted and conclusions drawn in feminist engagement with these texts.) My exponents will be Phyllis Trible (an egalitarian, literary reading), Gale Yee (a patriarchal, ideological reading), Mieke Bal (a non-patriarchal, readerly perspective), and J'annine Jobling (a post-Christian, post-feminist reading). This is, of course, a highly selective portrayal of feminist hermeneutics;[8] I trust it is not tendentious. I will briefly outline the key contentions in each interpretation of the text, and seek to identify contributions and concerns for evangelicals in their points of view. In so doing, it will become apparent, I believe, that deeper issues of reading strategies and substantive commitments relating to God, humans and Scripture will be at least as significant as surface details of exegesis and the reading of texts. I will attempt to identify some of these, I trust the most significant of them, and discuss their implications for our engagement with, criticism of, learning from, and appropriation of feminist interpretation of Genesis 2–3.

Wolde, *Stories of the Beginning*, 34–73; Niditch, *Oral World and Written Word*, 30; Niditch, "Genesis"; Simkins, "Gender Construction"; Parker, "Mirror, Mirror"; Veenker, "Forbidden Fruit"; Day, "Wisdom and the Feminine in the Hebrew Bible") through (generally negative) structuralist and deconstructive readings (see Milne, "Eve and Adam"; Milne, "The Patriarchal Stamp of Scripture"; Pardes, "Beyond Genesis 3"; Slivniak, "The Garden of Double Messages"); Fewell and Gunn, *Gender, Power, and Promise*, 9–38; to (positive) "masculist" approaches (see Goldingay, "Masculist Interpretation"; Olson, "Untying the Knot?").

7. See, for instance, the five-fold taxonomy of Osiek, "The Feminist and the Bible"; and the (slightly different) three-fold taxonomies of Sakenfeld, "Feminist Uses of Biblical Materials"; Sakenfeld, "Feminist Perspectives on Bible and Theology"; and Abraham, *Eve*, 29–42.

8. I will not, for instance, examine in detail the work of Phyllis Bird or Carol Meyers, despite their importance for feminist interpretation of Genesis 2–3 because, while they differ in their methodologies and on the meaning of some details of the text, their basic understanding of Scripture and of the more-or-less egalitarian significance of Genesis 2–3 largely parallels that of Trible. See Bird, "Gen 1:27b"; Bird, *Missing Persons*; Bird, "What Makes a Feminist Reading Feminist?"; Bird, "Feminist Interpretation and Biblical Theology"; Meyers, "Genesis 3.16 Revisited"; Meyers, *Discovering Eve*. For an analysis of Meyers' and Bird's interpretations of Genesis, see Abraham, *Eve*, 139–88, 89–231.

PHYLLIS TRIBLE: A STABLE, EGALITARIAN TEXT

Let me begin, then, with the work of Phyllis Trible. Her pioneering interpretation of 2:4b—3:23 has changed the way the text is approached.[9] Her interpretation has generated significant debate, particularly over whether the text is, as she claims, fundamentally egalitarian in its orientation.[10] I will briefly outline her argument, noting in passing criticisms and defenses of her central claims, before analyzing its significance for evangelical interpretation of Genesis 2–3.

Trible presents a close reading of the text of Genesis 2–3 in which she seeks to demonstrate that, far from endorsing the subordination of women to men, it presents a vision of life in community fundamentally sympathetic to feminist concerns. She believes that the original created state of humanity was one of total harmony, of freedom (within limits) and delight, in which male and female were equal partners, finding satisfaction, intimacy and fulfillment in each other.[11] While an original hierarchy of humanity over the earth and animals was established, there was no hierarchy of male over female.[12] However, sin has entered the picture: it distorts relationships, and results in oppression and alienation between male and female.[13] Thus while sin and the hierarchies it creates are current realities, they are not inherent to God's creation order.[14] Genesis 2 encodes an egalitarian ideal for human relationships; Genesis 3 ascribes the loss of that ideal and the

---

9. Trible, "Depatriarchalizing"; Trible, *God and the Rhetoric of Sexuality*, 72–143. See the reflections on the significance of *God and the Rhetoric of Sexuality* arising out of the 2003 meetings of *SBL* on the twenty-fifth anniversary of its publication: Balentine, "A Tribute to Phyllis Trible," Wudel, "*God and the Rhetoric of Sexuality*: An Appreciation"; Koosed, "Coming of Age in Phyllis Trible's World"; Bellis, *Helpmates*, 39–42. This is in contrast to the assessment in Milne, "Eve and Adam," who (wrongly) sees her work as having had little impact on mainline biblical scholarship.

10. See particularly the critique in Clines, "What Does Eve Do to Help?," and the many influenced by it.

11. Trible, "Depatriarchalizing," 36–39; Trible, *God and the Rhetoric of Sexuality*, 73, 86–88, 90, 92, 96–97, 99–102, 105, 107, Trible, "Feminist Hermeneutics"; Trible, "Pilgrim Bible"; Trible, "Five Loaves and Two Fishes"; Trible, "Treasures."

12. Trible, *God and the Rhetoric of Sexuality*, 73, 75–76, 85–86, 90.

13. Trible, "Depatriarchalizing," 40–43; Trible, "Biblical Theology"; Trible, *God and the Rhetoric of Sexuality*, 112–15, 18, 23, 26–35, 37, 39, 201.

14. Trible, "Depatriarchalizing," 40–41; Trible, *God and the Rhetoric of Sexuality*, 112–15, 117–20, 132–34; Trible, "Pilgrim Bible," 6; Trible, "Five Loaves and Two Fishes," 291–92; Trible, "Treasures," 43.

coming into being of the current pattern of distorted relationships to human sin. Hierarchies, then, are not normative for gender relationships, despite the arguments of those who see this text as encoding and fostering patriarchy.[15] Thus Genesis 2–3 is a thoroughly egalitarian text that challenges all patriarchal relationships, including those of the societies that produced and read the text.[16]

Space does not allow a full and detailed appraisal of her interpretation of the text and the arguments for and against it.[17] I will, therefore, limit my analysis to three of her key arguments: the sexually undifferentiated nature of the human prior to the woman's creation; the nature of her creation as a "companion corresponding to" the human; and the role that naming plays in the narrative.

Trible claims that "the human" (הָאָדָם, *hā-ʾādām*) as initially created by God is asexual; only with the advent of the woman, and the resulting interplay of "man" (אִישׁ, *ʾîš*) and "woman" (אִשָּׁה, *ʾiššâ*) does sexuality come into being.[18] There is, then, a threefold use of "the human" (הָאָדָם, *hā-ʾādām*) in the narrative: initially it refers to the sexually undifferentiated human being; with the creation of the woman it refers ambiguously to the male human being, without thereby losing its original inclusive sense; in the final scene it refers again to the male creature, but in such a way that the female is eclipsed from the reference, becoming subsumed into the man's identity.[19] This is important for her argument that male and female are equal in creation, for if there is no male until there is female then there is no temporal or theological priority of the man over the woman, and nor is she derived from his being.[20] This claim has been questioned, on the basis of the normal use of "human" (אָדָם, *ʾādām*), and the absence of clear textual markers signifying the shifts in meaning of

---

15. Trible, *God and the Rhetoric of Sexuality*, 73.
16. Trible, "Depatriarchalizing," 47–48; Trible, "Biblical Theology," 8.
17. For this, see the analysis in chapter 8 of my ThD thesis: Sloane, "Wolterstorff, Theorising and Genesis 1–3," from which much of the following discussion has been drawn. See also Abraham, *Eve*, 45–112.
18. Trible, *God and the Rhetoric of Sexuality*, 80, 89–90, 94, 98–99, 102–3, 104, 107; Trible, "Five Loaves and Two Fishes," 291; Trible, "Treasures," 41–42; cf. her earlier view (in Trible, "Depatriarchalizing," 35, 37, now retracted) that the human in 2:7 was androgynous.
19. Trible, *God and the Rhetoric of Sexuality*, 80, 94, 98–99, 107, 134–35.
20. Ibid., 98–99, 100–103; Trible, "Five Loaves and Two Fishes," 291; Trible, "Treasures," 42.

the word that she suggests.²¹ Trible has sought to counter those criticisms: "Prior to the appearance of woman, *hā-'ādām* is the sexually undifferentiated earth creature. Only with the appearance of woman (i.e., with the introduction of a gender specific word) does the man appear."²² She also argues that the presence or absence of these markers is not a determinative indicator of a shift in usage: for in driving out the humans *hā-'ādām* is used (which she recognises is an inclusive use), but there is no marker for a shift back to generic use.²³ It seems to me that linguistic usage, allied with the ideal reader's expectations of the word's referent and the illocutionary force of the word in this narrative context indicates that Trible's suggestion fails.²⁴ This does not, however, warrant the "traditional" hierarchical inferences drawn from the text, as temporal priority does not indicate inferiority, and thus creation order cannot be used to justify the relational inferiority of women.²⁵

Another key to her egalitarian reading of the text is her understanding of the woman being created as a "companion corresponding to" the earth creature. Her argument is clear: the word עֵזֶר (*'ēzer*, help or helper) neither connotes nor denotes inferiority, especially given the frequency of its use with reference to God as help or helper of Israel or the needy. So too, the unusual compound preposition that qualifies it כְּנֶגְדּוֹ (*cěnegdô*, like opposite, or corresponding to) reinforces the equality of the one being described.²⁶ Furthermore, the lack which the

---

21. Gardner, "Genesis 2:4b–3"; Fretheim, "Genesis," esp. 353; Abraham, *Eve*, 76–81; Gellman, "Gender and Sexuality in the Garden of Eden"; Kawashima, "Revisionist Reading Revisited."

22. Trible, "Reflections" (the quote is from page 25).

23. Ibid., 25.

24. Lanser, "Genesis 2–3." I am not persuaded, however, that her reading of the text as patriarchy growing uncomfortable with its own assumptions adequately accounts for the larger pattern of dis/harmony that Trible has rightly noted controls the text. See also Kawashima, "Revisionist Reading Revisited," who adopts a specifically *realist* orientation to texts and interpretation.

25. Baldwin, "Women's Ministry"; Bilezikian, *Sex Roles*, 29–31; Evans, *Woman in the Bible*, 14–15; Griffiths, "Mankind: Male and Female"; Hayter, *The New Eve In Christ*, 96–98; Mickelson, "Egalitarian View"; Tucker, *Women in the Maze*, 36–37; Vogels, "Gen 2:18." Some of the broader issues at stake are discussed below.

26. Trible, *God and the Rhetoric of Sexuality*, 90; cf. Trible, "Depatriarchalizing," 36; Trible, "Biblical Theology," 8; Trible, "Feminist Hermeneutics," 117; Trible, "Five Loaves and Two Fishes," 291; Trible, "Treasures," 42. She cites Exod 18:4; Deut 33:7, 26, 29; Pss 33:20; 115:9–11; 121:2; 124:8; 146:5; in support of this claim.

woman eventually supplies is a relational lack—aloneness—not a functional quality. The recognition of the need for a suitable companion for the human, the delay in God's provision, the resolution of the narrative tension and the earth-creature's need in the creation of the woman, and the man's recognition of her as companion and mate all point to her significance and value in the narrative.[27] This description, then, far from entailing the woman's inferiority to the man, accents her equality with the man and the man's need for her. This claim has also been criticised, most trenchantly, perhaps, by Clines in his article "What does Eve do to help?"[28] His arguments are based largely on his perception of how the word "help" works in everyday *English* discourse and on the text's being too naïve to have such a subtle view of the man's plight as Trible suggests: rather, the man's need is for help in procreation and his agricultural labours.[29] Given the weakness of his case (and its dependence on subjective readerly responses), and the strength of Trible's interpretation (and its anchoring in the text), it seems to me that her claim stands.[30]

Finally, she argues that naming—and its absence—plays an important role in the narrative. She believes that naming is an expression of authority or a claim to power; thus when the man names his wife "Eve" in 3:20, he is violating their equality, asserting his patriarchal power over her.[31] It is important for her interpretation that this takes place only after they have sinned: hierarchy, and the subordination of the needs and very existence of the woman to the man, is not God's intention for relationships but an effect and instantiation of sin: "Ironically, he names her *Eve*, a Hebrew word that resembles in sound the word *life*, even as he robs her of life in its created fullness."[32] For this claim to work, however, naming must be a *post* sin act. Trible argues that 2:23 is not an example of the naming formula on the grounds that it does not contain all its standard

---

27. Trible, *God and the Rhetoric of Sexuality*, 90–94, 98, 102–4.

28. Clines, "What Does Eve Do to Help?" esp. 30–33; similar claims are made in Gellman, "Gender and Sexuality in the Garden of Eden," 330; for a mediating view, see Abraham, *Eve*, 81–84.

29. Clines, "What Does Eve Do to Help?" 33–37.

30. See, for instance, Vogels, "Gen 2:18"; Hamilton, *Genesis 1–17*, 175–76; Dennis, *Sarah Laughed*, 12–14; Fretheim, "Genesis," 352; Hartley, *Genesis*, 60–63; Hess, "Equality," 86–87; Jacobs, *Gender, Power, and Persuasion*, 32–41.

31. Trible, "Depatriarchalizing," 41–42; Trible, "Biblical Theology," 8; Trible, *God and the Rhetoric of Sexuality*, 133.

32. Trible, *God and the Rhetoric of Sexuality*, 133.

formulaic features. The verb קָרָא (*qārā'*, call) is not joined with שֵׁם (*šēm*, name); אִשָּׁה (*'iššâ*, woman) has been used previously in the narrative in relation to the woman, and so this is not an act of *re-naming*; אִשָּׁה (*'iššâ*, woman) is not a name *per se*, but a common noun. The absence of these typical features means that this is not an act of power of the man over the woman, but a recognition that at last he has met his counterpart.[33] Thus, the man does not name the woman until after the Fall. Patriarchal ordering of relationships is a mark and consequence of the Fall: it is not God's will for interpersonal relationships but a sinful distortion of it.[34] This, in my view, is one of the weakest aspects of her interpretation. First, her argument that 2:23 does not have all the features of a naming formula and so does not count as one fails to adequately account for the fluidity of naming formulae in the OT and ignores the illocutionary force of the words.[35] Second, it is, in fact, unnecessary to distinguish 2:23 from 3:20, with the latter being a "true naming" while the former is not, for naming is not in itself an act of dominion. It may be *used* in such contexts as an expression of an existing hierarchical relationship; it does not itself establish hierarchy. Naming is an act of *discernment*, by which the namer identifies a key characteristic of an entity or discerns its significance; it is not an act of power by which the namer claims authority over the named.[36] In each case the man perceives something significant about the

---

33. Trible, "Depatriarchalizing," 38–39; Trible, *God and the Rhetoric of Sexuality*, 99–100.

34. Trible, "Depatriarchalizing," 41–42; Trible, *God and the Rhetoric of Sexuality*, 133–34.

35. Ramsey, "Name Giving"; Lanser, "Genesis 2–3," 72–73; Abraham, *Eve*, 84–85.

36. Ramsey, "Name Giving," 35; cf. Otwell, *And Sarah Laughed*, 17–18; Hamilton, *Genesis 1–17*, 176–77; Dennis, *Sarah Laughed*, 14–15. While this is contrary to the opinion of a majority of OT scholars (see, for instance, Cassuto, *A Commentary on the Book of Genesis: Part One*, 130; Rad, *Genesis*, 82–83; Stitzinger, "Genesis 1–3"; Vawter, *On Genesis: A New Reading*, 74; Wenham, *Genesis 1–15*, 68; Clines, "What Does Eve Do to Help?" 37–40), Ramsey's case is compelling, especially in light of the use of the formula in its "purest" form in Genesis 16:13. This is disputed by Grudem, *Evangelical Feminism and Biblical Truth* (p. 33 n. 17). who argues that Gen 16:13 is a *private* name as opposed to "woman" which is a public (generic) name, and therefore is irrelevant to the status of naming in the OT. Similarly Gellman argues that only names that "stick" have authoritative force; Hagar's does not, therefore it does not count against naming being an authoritative act (Gellman, "Gender and Sexuality in the Garden of Eden"). There is, however, no indication in the text that Hagar's name for God is restricted to the private realm or is not meant to inform our understanding of God and God's character.

woman and her role in God's world; in neither case is she subordinated to or marginalized by the man. This, of course, is not to say that there is no evidence of hierarchical disordering of relationships after the "Fall"; it is simply to say that Gen 3:20 is not an instance of it.

Clearly, there are aspects of Trible's interpretation that are open to debate.[37] Furthermore, given that she sees clear evidence of an unacceptable patriarchal bias in Scripture, her view of the nature and authority of Scripture does not fit standard evangelical notions.[38] This does not, however, affect her reading of Genesis 2–3; indeed, her "close reading" of the text, now a common feature of literary-oriented interpretations of Scripture, fits well with classical evangelical commitment to the careful study of the text of Scripture as a way of unpacking its theological significance, as is evident in the impact her work has had on "evangelical feminists."[39] Her analysis has brought to light features of the text often overlooked in traditional exegesis, such as the significance of the man being "with her" throughout the woman's dialogue with the snake in 3:1–6.[40] As such evangelical interpretation of Genesis 2–3 is well served by Trible's interpretation of these texts.

GALE YEE: A STABLE, BUT OPPRESSIVE TEXT

Gale Yee presents a very different reading of the text. She believes that the Bible, including Genesis 2–3, expresses fundamentally negative attitudes to women, which she seeks to identify and expose.[41] She aims to "investigate the problem of the symbolization of woman as the incarnation of moral evil, sin, devastation, and death in the Hebrew Bible, and how this symbolization of a particular gender interconnects with the issues of race/ethnicity, class and colonialism during the times of its production." Holding man in thrall by her irresistible attractions, woman embodies all that is destructive in man's experience, seducing him away from God

---

37. This is also evident in the controversy surrounding her claim that the image of God includes male and female. See Trible, *God and the Rhetoric of Sexuality*, 12–23; and the critique in Bird, "Gen 1:27b," and Abraham, *Eve*, 70–73; 224.

38. Trible, "Depatriarchalizing," 30–31; Trible, "Women & the Word"; Trible, "If the Bible's So Patriarchal, How Come I Love It?"; Trible, *Texts of Terror*; cf. the critique of Abraham, *Eve*, 101–12.

39. See, for instance, Evans, *Woman in the Bible*, 11–21.

40. See Trible, *God and the Rhetoric of Sexuality*, 113–14.

41. Yee, "Genesis 2–3"; Yee, *Children of Eve*.

and a life of good down paths of moral perversity and entrapment."[42] She applies this to her analysis of Genesis 2–3.[43]

She believes that both class and gender relations are important in the text's presentation of "Eve as the vocal temptress,"[44] with the relationship of king to peasantry finding "its theological origin in the relationship between the divine and the human at the primordial beginning."[45] Furthermore, the woman is created "to serve the man as the man serves the deity in tilling the garden."[46] The story "legitimizes royal interests" and justifies "the current lower status of the peasant in the tributary economy" by shifting the conflict from the public (male) realm to "the more private domain of household relations between men and women" and further enhances the power of the monarchy by undermining existing power systems by "stressing the nuclear family and the marital bond."[47] The woman "mediates the fundamental contradictions in the story," and so highlights a gender conflict so as to mask the broader class interests of the text "which become mystified and concealed through the theological cover of a story about origins and 'the fall.'"[48] Through "ideological displacement" the text shifts attention from the "latent text" of class conflict to its "manifest text" of gender and subordination.[49] This manifest text is equally oppressive: "The woman becomes responsible for the man's violation of the single command imposed on him"; and so in the "politics of blame," the woman "becomes liable for the theological breach between the man and his God and the political breach between the peasant and his king."[50] Thus: "In the ideology of the text, the woman pays a big price. Renamed Hawwah/Eve by her husband, she becomes the mother of all living. She can only become mother, however, through suffering. For her role in the man's transgression, God punishes her by increasing the pain of her childbearing. Her husband will rule over her,

---

42. Yee, *Children of Eve*, 1.

43. Yee, "Genesis 2–3"; Yee, *Children of Eve*, 59–74. The latter is an expanded and updated version of her earlier article. Subsequent references will be to the latter piece.

44. Yee, *Children of Eve*, 77.

45. Ibid., 77–78.

46. Ibid., 78.

47. Ibid.

48. Ibid.

49. Ibid.

50. Ibid.

just as the king governed the peasant. Because her husband 'listened to her voice,' she becomes temptress, seducer and the downfall of men."[51]

Yee's reading utilizes the method and assumptions of ideological criticism. Hers is a "materialist-feminist reading of the text that understands literature as an ideological production of social praxis, which itself is governed by ideology."[52] In her hands this involves both "extrinsic" and "intrinsic" analysis of the text. Extrinsic analysis aims to shed light on "the sociohistorical circumstances of a text's production" and their ideological associations.[53] Genesis 2–3 is "correlated with the transition in Israel from a familial mode of production to a native-tributary mode of production," which took place in the early monarchy.[54] Intrinsic analysis "investigates the rhetorical strategies of the text itself to ascertain the different ways in which the text inscribes and reworks ideology."[55] Paradoxically, the absence of an obvious political agenda is a clue to its hidden presence: "Since it *seems* to be a story primarily about male-female relationships, Genesis 2–3 mystifies and conceals the class interests in the text."[56] This mysterious and hidden ideological agenda is encoded in a number of symbolic associations that she finds in the text: God represents the king, and God's relationship with the man that of the king to peasants in the emerging tributary system; the prohibition of one tree indicates the royal elite's concern to control knowledge, and so power; the planting of a garden represents claims that the royal elite provides for the peasants, who should acknowledge their largesse with appropriate subordination to them; the expulsion from the garden and the clothing of the couple after the "fall" both represent the cementing of distance and distinction between king and peasant, and so on.[57]

---

51. Ibid., 78–79.

52. Ibid., 9. This is driven by Marxist analysis, and draws heavily on the work of Eagleton and Jameson (see ibid., 9–24), as well as the earlier ideological reading of the text by Kennedy, "Peasants in Revolt."

53. Ibid., 5; 25–26.

54. Ibid., 67. This, of course, requires that the text be dated to that period of Israel's history, which is when she believes it (and the Yahwist source of which it is a part) was produced (see ibid., 60–67).

55. Ibid., 5; 27–28. This includes assessment of the "absences" in the text and the selection of genre, both of which expose its ideological concerns.

56. Ibid., 5–6, italics in the original.

57. Ibid., 67–77.

This narrative is, for Yee, particularly unfriendly towards women and their interests, given the way it encodes the increased stratification of gender roles in the monarchy.[58] The woman is created as agricultural and reproductive assistant to the man; he asserts his authority over her by naming her and controlling her sexuality (both before and after the "fall"); she is blamed as temptress and source of evil; and she is firmly placed under male control.[59] Moreover, the broader political agenda further demonises women as "the ones most susceptible to these forces [represented by the snake] that threaten the state,"[60] and, by identifying her primary role as childbearing in submission to her husband, mirroring that of the peasant to his king, Gen 3:16 legitimizes the king's use of power to keep peasants under control.[61] "The traditional interpretations of Genesis 2 that justify the subordination of women by appealing to this text are consistent with its thoroughgoing androcentrism."[62] Her conclusion matches that of Kennedy, whose work is an earlier mirror of hers: "The social values encoded in the text are anything but egalitarian. Overarching the subordination of the woman to the man is the subordination of the peasant couple to the royal élite."[63]

Such an approach to the text of Genesis 2–3, should it stand, poses serious problems for evangelicals and others committed to the authoritative status of the Bible as the word of a God of freedom and justice. While the analysis of her claims entails examination of her methodology and assumptions, once again, a detailed critical analysis of ideological criticism lies beyond the scope of this piece.[64] Nonetheless, there are crucial problems with this approach to texts. First, she does not explicate the mechanisms by which this story functions as an ideological expres-

58. Ibid., 70.
59. Ibid., 70–76.
60. Ibid., 74.
61. Ibid., 75.
62. Ibid., 70–71.
63. Kennedy, "Peasants in Revolt," 8.
64. I present a detailed analysis of James Kennedy's earlier ideological interpretation of Genesis 2–3, which is used extensively by Yee in her treatment of Genesis 2–3, in Sloane, "Wolterstorff, Theorising and Genesis 1–3," chapter 9; see also chapter 7 of this volume. For a positive appraisal of ideological criticism (in conjunction with reader-response criticism) see Davies, *The Dissenting Reader*. For positive appraisals of Yee's work, see Brenner, "Poor Banished Children of Eve"; Jobling, "Poor Banished Children of Eve"; Bellis, *Helpmates*, 53–54.

sion of monarchical power and the subordination of women) Kennedy, for instance, sees political allegory as the means by which textual transmutations are made;[65] Yee articulates no such mechanism, leaving me bewildered as to how she makes those associations.[66] Second, the symbolic connections seem curiously inconsistent. While God stands for the king and the man for the agrarian worker, the woman is just "woman." Why? Given that the surface "gender" story both conveys and obscures a deeper "political" story, it seems oddly arbitrary that the woman does not stand for some element of the political order. Third, she relentlessly adopts the most negative construal of the text, using the putative role of texts as bearers of oppressive ideology as justification. This, however, seems to be a case of assuming the conclusion: that is, she is using those features of the text to argue for her claim that the text is oppressive; but the grounds on which she identifies those features of the text as being oppressive rather than liberating is that the text is oppressive, and so these features of it are expressions of that oppression. This seems viciously circular.[67] Fourth, there are questions about the dating of the text and its traditions which, given the centrality to her argument of a particular moment of transition in Israel's political history, raises questions about her basic thesis.[68] Finally, it seems to me that her claim is self-referentially incoherent: if all texts are ideological, then so is hers (and so cannot be taken as a true articulation of the nature of texts, simply a disguised set of power claims); if only some are, then on what grounds do we establish that *this* text is ideological?[69] That then allows us to ques-

---

65. Thus God can *allegorically* stand for the king; the man for the peasant, and so on. See Kennedy, "Peasants in Revolt," 3–7.

66. Jobling, "Poor Banished Children of Eve," 360 who, while accepting the ideological nature of texts and the mystifying strategies writers use to exculpate themselves, raises questions about the cogency of her intrinsic reading of the text and the way if always generates a *political* reading.

67. It might work, perhaps, as a thought experiment: how would the text work if it were a species of political ideology? Like this . . . However, for that to be adopted as the best reading of the text, actual arguments must be adduced. And this, in my view, she has failed to do.

68. Brenner, "Poor Banished Children of Eve," 334, although she sees this as a relatively minor concern; cf. Bellis, *Helpmates*, 53–54. Indeed, dating Genesis to the Persian period (as is current scholarly consensus) results in a very different ideological reading of the text, for which see Brett, *Genesis*, esp. 1–35, 137–46.

69. Perhaps she might claim that *literary* texts are ideological while *theory* is not. But that seems absurd: it is hard to imagine more ideologically driven texts than, say,

tion her fundamental assumptions and the exegesis that arises out of them, leaving us free to present a more cogent explanation of the text and its main features which, in turn, functions as a further refutation of her claims.[70]

MIEKE BAL: AN UNSTABLE, NOT PARTICULARLY PATRIARCHAL TEXT

Let me turn now to those who are not so sanguine about the stability of texts and their interpretation. Mieke Bal has presented a reading of the text and its reception that seeks to incorporate aspects of feminist literary theory: indeed, she is primarily a literary critic, with no direct interest in the text as authoritative Scripture.[71] She explicitly rejects all realist notions of texts and their meanings: there is no fixed meaning of a text; rather, texts generate a multiplicity of readings in interaction with their readers, and the "meaning of the text" and the meanings it generates in the history of its reception cannot be distinguished.[72] She presents, then, hers as one reading of the text amongst others, in the hope that it might open up new possibilities for readers of the Hebrew Bible. Central to this reading is her view that the text has been misrepresented in the tradition. Despite the dominance of the misogynist readings of Paul and the author of the pastorals, amongst others, it does not subordinate women to a prior male, nor does it blame "Eve" for the advent of sin and evil.[73] Indeed, the text is not about sin and a "fall," but about the necessarily painful process of maturation, the emergence of true character in escaping from an illusory world of personal immortality into a world of responsibility and reproductive maturity.[74] In transgressing Yahweh's

---

Das Kapital or the "historical" works of David Irving, or mid-twentieth-century histories of European "settlement" of the "new world." I am not denying that some texts (including various kinds of "literary" texts) are ideologically driven; I am claiming that a case must be *made* for a particular text being ideologically driven, or we are left in an infinite regress of ideological claim and counter-claim.

70. See, for instance, Sloane, *At Home in a Strange Land*, 159–69, and the works cited in footnote 3 above.

71. Bal, *Lethal Love*, 1; cf. the generally appreciative comments in Jobling, "Mieke Bal on Biblical Narrative"; Bellis, *Helpmates*, 42–43.

72. Bal, *Lethal Love*, 1–4, 131–32.

73. Ibid., 104, 109–10, 130. I find this an odd claim in light of her rejection of the notion of a fixed meaning of texts.

74. Ibid., 119–25.

command, ("she did not exactly sin, she opted for reality" and Yahweh's response is best seen, not as punishment, but "as an explicit spelling out of the consequences of the human option, as another representation of the reality of human life."[75] While neither a feminist nor a feminine text, Genesis 2–3 is not as misogynistic as the tradition has made it out to be: indeed, while there are echoes of patriarchy in it, it is a patriarchy that undoes itself.[76] Central to this is her notion of the "emergence" of Eve (and of character) in the unfolding of the text: ("Eve' exists only at the end of Genesis 3, where her name is mentioned for the first time. What existed before was an earth creature, then a woman, next an actant, then a mother, and, finally, a being named 'Eve' . . . the development . . . of this character in Genesis displays a slow construction out of the continuous restriction of possibilities."[77] However, the establishing of fixed gender roles in Gen 3:16,[78] and the naming of the woman by the man, sees the emergence, not just of character, but of patriarchy.[79] Their relationship is no longer about sexual attraction (as celebrated in 2:23–24); rather, "Eve is imprisoned in motherhood."[80]

There are a number of issues with her "exegesis" of the text. First is the density and opacity of her work, and its dependence on (frequently assumed rather than articulated) elements of feminist literary theory.[81] This, it seems to me, is a common feature of post-structuralist literary criticism, but is a problem nonetheless. (Second, she sees the character of Yahweh as being at best dubious in the narrative, in part because she is not governed by theological interests but is willing to treat God as a character like any other in the text.[82] While such a view has support in the literature,[83] her particular construal depends on problematic an-

75. Ibid., 125.
76. Ibid., 110.
77. Ibid., 107–8.
78. Ibid., 126. She recognises that in Gen 3:16 the woman is not cursed; rather, it speaks of distribution of labour between female and male (the production of children and food, respectively—cf. Meyers, *Discovering Eve*, 72–121; Meyers, "Genesis 3.16 Revisited"). It does, however, establish the sexual roles that are so problematic for feminists.
79. Bal, *Lethal Love*, 126–27.
80. Ibid., 128.
81. So too, Jobling, "Mieke Bal on Biblical Narrative," 4, 7.
82. Bal, *Lethal Love*, 123–24.
83. See, for instance, Fewell and Gunn, *Gender, Power, and Promise*, 22–38, and Rooke, "Feminist Criticism of the Old Testament," who also see the text as demonstrat-

thropological speculations regarding food and sex and totemism and, furthermore, alternative readings of the text make better sense.[84] Her notion of the undifferentiated nature of "the human" (הָאָדָם, *hā-'ādām*) suffers from the same weaknesses as does Trible's. So too, her claim that "Eve" as a character emerges only at the end of the text and must not be read back into the earlier narrative fails to account for the illocutionary force of names and of character in texts.[85] Allied to this is her claim that the text deals with the maturation of the human couple (largely as a result of the moral agency of the woman) and not with "sin." This is a claim found frequently in the literature, in part in resistance to NT and later readings of the text, in part arising out of the perceived absence of the language of sin and punishment in the text.[86] This, however, fails to account for the use of the language of command and the clear elements of accountability found in 3:14–19.[87] So too, where Bal does address the "judgement" speech of Yahweh, she sees Yahweh's voice as contributing to the trapping of women in the social construction of gender roles, rather than recognising that Gen 3:16 deals with the consequences of sin, and Yahweh's ratification of those consequences in judgement.[88] It is no more an endorsement of those gender constructions as Yahweh's inviolable will for human community than 3:17–19 is an endorsement of frustrating agricultural toil and eventual death.

More significant, however, is her notion of the text and its instability and the way its meaning merges with the history of its reception. Such a perspective, with its associated radically reader-driven herme-

---

ing the inherent instability of patriarchy and the texts that seek to justify it. cf. Whybray, "The Immorality of God"; Barr, "Is God a Liar?" on more general issues relating to God's character.

84. Moberly, "Did the Interpreters Get It Right?"

85. Lanser, "Genesis 2–3," 73–74; but see Schneider, *Mothers of Promise*, 169–74, 97–205, who has a separate discussion of "Eve" and "the woman in the garden" which, while not citing Bal, seems to follow her approach to characterisation in narrative.

86. Dragga, "Genesis 2–3"; Korsak, "Genesis." See also Bechtel, *et al*, cited in footnote 6 above.

87. Brueggemann, *Genesis*, 40–54; Schüngel-Straumann, "Genesis 1–3"; Dennis, *Sarah Laughed*, 23; Vogels, "Like One of Us"; Stordalen, *Echoes of Eden*, esp. 473–74; Craig, "Misspeaking in Eden"; Mettinger, *The Eden Narrative*, esp. 123–35; Jacobs, *Gender, Power, and Persuasion*, 23–70.

88. Hamilton, *Genesis 1–17*, 201–2; Bledstein, "Are Women Cursed in Genesis 3.16?"; Dennis, *Sarah Laughed*, 28–30; Fretheim, "Genesis," 362–64, 69; Olson, "Untying the Knot?" 78–80; Vogels, "Power Struggle"; Hess, "Equality," 90–93.

neutic, is hard to reconcile with the more realist approaches to texts and their interpretations that typify evangelical engagement with Scripture.[89] Indeed, she notes the traditional criteria used to judge interpretations, but finds them inadequate as they are "based on conventional assumptions about literature."[90] This demonstrates that critiquing a particular interpretation requires careful understanding, analysis and critique of the underlying methodological and substantive presuppositions that control that interpretation.[91] This is the kind of analysis that evangelicals need to engage in if we are to come to grips with the possibilities and problems of feminist interpretations. I will turn to this below.

J'ANNINE JOBLING: A DECONSTRUCTED IRREDEEMABLY PATRIARCHAL TEXT

Texts and their interpretation become even more unstable in post-Christian, post-feminist criticism. Taking further Bal's commitment to plurality as the goal of interpretation, J'annine Jobling presents a reading, a re-reading and a subversion of that re-reading of Genesis 2–3.[92] Such an approach is broadly representative of post-Christian hermeneutics, with its commitment to radical readerly perspectives and the instability of texts and interpretive traditions, and the (almost) irredeemable androcentricity of the biblical traditions.[93] She states: "The aim is to challenge and disrupt more traditional readings and exemplify how alternative paradigms and methods of interpretations can lead to different theologi-

---

89. Osborne, *The Hermeneutical Spiral*; Vanhoozer, *Is There a Meaning In This Text*; Vanhoozer, *First Theology*; Vanhoozer, *The Drama of Doctrine*. For a perspective that, while locating meaning in the interaction of text and reader, still sees meaning in basically realist terms, see Callahan, *The Clarity of Scripture*.

90. Bal, *Lethal Love*, 13–14. These criteria are plausibility (conforming to the presuppositions of readers regarding the text), adequacy (dealing with those features of the text that the reader sees as important, the "facts" of the text), and relevance (fitting the reader's worldview).

91. For a detailed outline and application of this claim, see Sloane, "Wolterstorff, Theorising and Genesis 1–3."

92. Jobling, "Post-Christian Hermeneutics."

93. See Isherwood and McPhillips, "Introduction"; Wootton, "Who's Been Reading MY Bible?" noting that, in her view, this does not lead to interpretive anarchy, for readings arise out of and find their cogency in particular interpretive communities and their norms. For a (somewhat) dissenting voice, which sees the value and importance of key Christian claims (in this case resurrection—both Jesus' and ours) see Stuart, "The Return of the Living Dead."

cal accounts of the female subject . . . the reading given will itself then be deconstructed, highlighting the unstable nature of interpretation."[94] She argues that the biblical texts inscribe the dominant ideologies of patriarchy. Feminists seek to subvert and then reimagine the "powerful myths" of the Bible and set them to work in feminist frameworks. This is a "heterological" practice, which searches for and affirms the "other."[95] She notes feminist critique of the way the Genesis myth portrays the inherent weakness, subordination and defectability of women, but then attempts to "read Genesis 2–3 other-wise" (and then does so again to dismantle that reading in its turn). This first rereading shows the search for the other fails: "in the creation story, the woman is ultimately absorbed into male personhood, bone of his bone, flesh of his flesh. Upon her creation, she has no (articulated) desire; she has no voice." Her brief emergence into subjectivity in Genesis 2–3 leads to disaster and is speedily repressed. Ever forth, her desire shall be for her husband, who shall rule over her, and she shall bear the consequences of her actions in her own body with the multiplication of pain in childbirth."[96] Her attempt to dismantle this reading in light of narrative time results in an equally androcentric interpretation. The "lyric" (non-linear) pre-"fall" narrative submerges female subjectivity into the male, while the linear narrative that follows is essentially masculine in nature, a reassertion of the "phallogocentric economy" which effaces female desire and subjectivity.[97]

The inescapably androcentric nature of the (readings of the) text is not her primary concern. For her, the fact that there are multiple conflicting readings is the point, as interpretation then becomes a transgressive act in which the inherent tensions and contradictions of the texts are exposed, undermining oppressive claims to singular meaning and thus opening more creative possibilities.[98] She argues that the contrast between hermeneutics of resistance and of redemption is false; what we need is a "hermeneutics of destabilization," in which we recognize there is no fixed meaning, that there is otherness and difference, making possible reconfigurations in which the texts (and other potent symbols, memories and meanings) become used in the construction of our own

---

94. Jobling, "Post-Christian Hermeneutics," 90.
95. Ibid., 91.
96. Ibid., 98.
97. Ibid., 100.
98. Ibid., 100–101.

meanings.⁹⁹ Such a commitment to otherness, she believes, opens us to imagination, community and transformational love.¹⁰⁰

I find it hard to know what to say to such radical (and at times impenetrable) approaches to interpretation as those of Bal and Jobling. I wonder whether here, in these radically reader-driven textual subversions, we have less an interpretation of texts, and more a use of texts as (unstable and shifting) sites for the generation of new "meanings."¹⁰¹ What, then, is the point of engaging with these texts, other than as a catalyst for creative imagination? Perhaps just that others have taken them as meaningful and have used them in ways that these "interpreters" see as damaging to women; this deconstructive play is a way of undermining that meaning-full use so as to free up a space in which they (and others) can create new possibilities.¹⁰² It is hard to know what to say to that, as it operates within such a very different view of texts and authors and meaning—and, indeed, of human community and what makes it possible. Ironically, despite their commitment to the generation of more inclusive communities, I find it hard to see how such an approach allows for meaningful community and communication; it seems to leave us trapped in a text-filled silence in which significant relationships and the communication that underpins them is impossible—indeed, is subverted to that which undermines them. I wonder whether such a *reductio* is the best (perhaps the only?) response to such views, arising, as they do, from theories that disallow the possibility of reasoned argument against them on the basis of the text and its (more or less possible) meanings.

CONCLUDING REFLECTIONS

How, then, should evangelicals respond to these feminist interpretations of the text? Let me begin at the end. It seems to me that crucial questions arise out of the more "suspicious" readings I have discussed regarding

---

99. Ibid., 102–3.

100. Ibid., 103.

101. That seems to be the approach deliberately adopted in Boer, "The Fantasy of Genesis 1–3," who sees all texts and interpretations as unstable fantasies. On the other hand, Carr, "Politics of Textual Subversion," sees these instabilities as present in the text as a result of its pre-literary history and the subversion of an earlier more egalitarian vision by a later hierarchical (and anti-Wisdom) one.

102. Bal, *Lethal Love*, 1–8; 131–32; Jobling, "Post-Christian Hermeneutics," 100–103.

the nature of (biblical) texts and of (biblical) interpretation. (These remorselessly deconstructive or ideological readings of texts seem to leave little room for texts as instances of interpersonal communication: interpersonal power plays, yes; interpersonal communication, no.) There seem to me to be insuperable conceptual problems with such approaches to texts. [Either *critical* texts are privileged from these ideological or deconstructive interpretations, in which case they can be instances of meaningful communication (which seems arbitrary, or at least insufficiently justified to warrant acceptance); or they are not, in which case they are not primarily instances of interpersonal communication but are themselves ideological impositions on readerly freedom or subject to deconstruction (and so their claims about the nature and function of texts fail—or more strictly, they are self-referentially incoherent inasmuch as it is impossible in an act of communication to claim that such acts are illusory). Indeed, it seems (ironically) that in the interest of various versions of liberation, readers may become wielders of arbitrary power over texts and those who wrote them. Now these concerns are not confined to feminist interpretation; they are more general hermeneutical observations, as can be seen in both advocates and opponents of such perspectives.[103] (It does mean that in order to effectively engage with feminist (and other) concerns, evangelicals need to become more critically literate, hermeneutically aware and effective in communicating sophisticated notions of texts as communicative entities, lest these conversations bypass us entirely or come to surreptitiously control our or others' interpretive agenda.)

However, our response need not be entirely negative; indeed it should not be. We do need to be aware of the androcentric nature of

---

103. See Davies, *The Dissenting Reader* for a non-feminist appreciation of readerly hermeneutics of suspicion and the endorsement of this general strategy for biblical interpretation. For criticisms of these perspectives and defences of the claim that texts in general and Scripture in particular are instances of communication, see Greidanus, *The Modern Preacher and the Ancient Text*; Wolterstorff, *Divine Discourse*; Ward, *Word and Supplement*; Vanhoozer, *Is There a Meaning in This Text?*; Vanhoozer, *The Drama of Doctrine*; Osborne, *The Hermeneutical Spiral*; Brown, *Scripture as Communication*. Brown, Vanhoozer, Ward, and Wolterstorff in particular articulate a speech-act perspective on interpretation that, it seems to me, is a particularly fruitful one for evangelical hermeneutics in light of our desire to understand both the human and the divine discourse of Scripture. For the connection between human and divine communicative acts, see Barker, "Speech Act Theory, Dual Authorship, and Canonical Hermeneutics: Making Sense of *Sensus Plenior*."

much biblical literature; (whatever positive messages it may bear about women, it generally does so from the perspective of men and in relation to their interests.) These concerns are particularly acute in other texts and are best addressed in relation to them, but they need to be acknowledged here as well. They are, in my view, greatly mitigated by a sensitivity to the meaning of the text and, paradoxically perhaps, particularly to its not being a text primarily about gender and gender relationships. Let me briefly explore this claim.

While Trible's analysis has greatly enhanced our understanding of Genesis 2–3, her focus on issues of gender has distorted her reading in crucial ways and generated interpretive difficulties, such as the question of the sexually undifferentiated nature of the earth creature prior to the creation of the woman. (That is one instance, perhaps the clearest, of this unhelpful focus on gender.) It seems to me that the text is more about God's creation of human community, God's purposes for that community and the nature of community as intended by God, and the devastating effects of human sin on an initial condition of harmony. (Now, while an egalitarian understanding of gender relationships certainly best fits with that picture, and a "complementarian" (or hierarchical) one clashes with it, the text is not *about* gender relationships, except inasmuch as they necessarily reflect and have bearing on the fundamental nature of human community.[104]

Such a perspective helps us, I believe, understand better what is happening in the creation of the man (*hā-'ādām*). Trible is right that gender is not the concern here, and so claims of the temporal (and so relational) priority of male over female are misguided. That is not, however, because gender can be (almost arbitrarily) "written out" of the meaning of *hā-'ādām*, but because questions of gender have not yet been written into the text. The "not good" pertains, as is generally recognized, to the incompleteness of human community with the creation of an isolated individual. The delighted response of the man is, then, a celebration of the new goodness of completed human community. This community involves gender and relationships between the genders; and the equality, mutuality and delight of that community is certainly expressed in the sexual relationship of the man (as male) and the woman (as female). But that is a tangential "application" of the nature of God's intentions for

104. Westermann, *Genesis*, 20–22; Korsak, "Genesis," 49; Kimelman, "The Seduction of Eve"; cf. Abraham, *Eve*, 101–12; 233–45.

human community to marriage and human sexuality, as witnessed by the parenthetic nature of Gen 2:24 and the absence of sexual connotations in 2:25 (which is an expression, not of sexual innocence as is often claimed, but of the relative unimportance of concerns of sexuality at this point in the text). Thus, the perspective is not that of the *man*: it is *God's* perspective regarding human community; the man's eventual delight is an acknowledgement of its accomplishment. This is not an *androcentric* but a *theocentric* and *relationship-centered* text.

However, we can also learn from feminist interpreters such as Trible something of the liberating potential of this vision of community, and the prevalence and dangers of androcentric *interpretations* of the text. As evangelicals we need to acknowledge how our readings of the text and our traditions of interpretation can distort the text and damage people—and repent of the harm they can do lest we negate the *evangel* of Scripture we claim to champion. Feminist interpretation of Genesis 2–3 has demonstrated the patriarchal orientation of much of the Christian tradition. As we have seen, some feminists see that as arising out of the texts themselves; however, those perspectives are generally driven by understandings of the text and of Scripture as a (religiously authoritative) text that evangelicals (and others) can rightly reject. Other feminists see Genesis 2–3 as resisting, even subverting, such a patriarchal ethos. While many, if not most of these (non-evangelical) feminists see Scripture as a whole as deeply imbued with a patriarchal ethos, they see Genesis 2–3 as amongst the biblical texts and traditions that speak with another voice. While we as evangelicals may not accept their approach to (other elements in) Scripture, I see no reason to reject their reading of Genesis 2–3, and every reason to embrace and endorse their recognition that these early chapters of Scripture speak of God's good purposes for human community, in which women and men are called to share as equal partners and suffer, if not equally, then inescapably, the effects of human sin.

We who are both evangelical and feminist also need to show by our interpretation of the text that a commitment to God's word as true divine (and human) communication is consistent with a commitment to the liberation and equality of all women and men. This word is good news to women and others who have suffered as a result of the sinful distortion of relationships and the misuse of power. And we also need to acknowledge the many evangelicals (and others) who have shown that this text is a liberating text and learn from them.[105] Genesis 2–3 speaks of a God who graciously creates human community, acknowledging that the need for interpersonal relationships is written into the very fabric of (human) reality: aloneness is "not good"; human community requires the existence of a "partner as a counterpart" (2:18). The relationships established by this creative act of God are to be characterized by mutuality, equality, intimacy and delight (2:23, 25), and are the framework within which humans are called to enjoy the freedom-within-limits of God's good world (2:15–17). Sin distorts those relationships, resulting in humans heeding a voice other than God's in an act of fracturing moral autonomy and so suffering the tragic consequences of the alienation which is sin (3:6, 8–13). God acts in judgment, acknowledging the painful consequences of sin and ratifying them as punishments for human disobedience, and announcing their inevitable termination in death (3:14–19, 21, 22–24). Neither the circumstances of the woman's creation (better, the completion of the creation of the human community) nor the judgments of God establish a hierarchical ordering of relationships between women and men. Gen 2:18–25 speak a word of freedom and equality; Gen 3:16 speaks a word of fracturing and failure, a failure characterized by a mutual struggle for power, one in which, in the world as we know it, men tend to get the upper hand. But this is not God's perpetual will for human relationships which we defy to our peril. It is a "curse" to be combated even as we combat pain in childbearing and weeds in our fields. Genesis 2–3 does not inscribe a world of unequal power that we must accept as our Creator's will; it opens up a story in which we are called to renewed relationships that reflect our Creator's delight in persons and relationships of equality and joy. While he may, indeed, "rule over you," this is not God's final word for women—or for men.

---

105. What follows draws on the work of evangelical feminists such as: Evans, *Woman in the Bible*, 11–21; Van Leeuwen, ed. *After Eden*; Hess, "Equality," 82–95; "Women of Renewal: A Statement." I should note that this is one evangelical reading of the text that is consistent with feminist concerns. Others are certainly possible, especially given the pluriformity of evangelicalism and the polyvalence of texts and the under-determination of interpretations by the phenomena of the text.

BIBLIOGRAPHY

Abraham, Joseph. *Eve: Accused or Acquitted? A Reconsideration of Feminist Readings of the Creation Narrative Texts in Genesis 1–3*. Carlisle, UK: Paternoster, 2002.

Bal, Mieke. *Lethal Love: Feminist Literary Readings of Biblical Love Stories*. Bloomington, IN: Indiana University Press, 1987.

Baldwin, Joyce. "Women's Ministry: A New Look at the Biblical Texts." In *The Role of Women*, edited by S. Lees, 158–76. Leicester, UK: InterVarsity, 1984.

Balentine, Samuel E. "'It Is Not Too Late to Seek a Newer World': A Tribute to Phyllis Trible." *Lexington Theological Quarterly* 38.1 (2003) 3–9.

Barker, Kit. "Speech Act Theory, Dual Authorship, and Canonical Hermeneutics: Making Sense of *Sensus Plenior*." *Journal of Theological Interpretation* 3.2 (2009) 227–39.

Barr, James. "Is God a Liar? (Genesis 2–3)—and Related Matters." *Journal of Theological Studies* 57.1 (2006) 1–22.

Bechtel, Lyn M. "Genesis 2.4b—3.24: A Myth about Human Maturation." *Journal for the Study of the Old Testament* 67 (1995) 3–26.

———. "Rethinking the Interpretation of Genesis 2:4b—3:24." In *Feminist Companion to Genesis*, edited by Athalya Brenner, 77–117. Sheffield, UK: Sheffield Academic, 1993.

Bellis, Alice Ogden. *Helpmates, Harlots, and Heroes: Women's Stories in the Hebrew Bible*. 2nd ed. Louisville: Westminster John Knox, 2007.

Besançon Spencer, A. *Beyond the Curse: Women Called to Minister*. Peabody, MA: Hendrickson, 1985.

Bilezikian, G. *Sex Roles: A Guide for the Study of Female Roles in the Bible*. Grand Rapids: Baker, 1985.

Bird, Phyllis A. "Feminist Interpretation and Biblical Theology." In *Engaging the Bible in a Gendered World*, edited by Linda Day and Carolyn Pressler, 215–26. Louisville: Westminster John Knox, 2006.

———. "'Male and Female He created Them': Gen 1:27b in the Context of the Priestly Account of Creation." *Harvard Theological Review* 74.2 (1981) 129–59.

———. *Missing Persons and Mistaken Identities: Women and Gender in Ancient Israel*. Minneapolis: Fortress, 1997.

———. "What Makes a Feminist Reading Feminist? A Qualified Answer." In *Escaping Eden: New Feminist Perspectives on the Bible*, edited by Harold C. Washington, et al., 124–31. New York: New York University Press, 1999.

Bledstein, Adrien Janis. "Are Women Cursed in Genesis 3.16?" In *A Feminist Companion to Genesis*, edited by Athalya Brenner, 142–45. Sheffield, UK: Sheffield Academic, 1993.

Boer, Roland. "The Fantasy of Genesis 1–3." *Biblical Interpretation* 14.4 (2006) 309–31.

Brenner, Athalya. "Poor Banished Children of Eve: Woman as Evil in the Hebrew Bible." *Catholic Biblical Quarterly* 67.2 (2005) 332–34.

Brett, Mark. *Genesis: Procreation and the Politics of Identity*. London: Routledge, 2000.

Brown, Jeannine. *Scripture as Communication: Introducing Biblical Hermeneutics*. Grand Rapids: Baker, 2007.

Brueggemann, Walter. *Genesis*. Atlanta: John Knox, 1982.

Callahan, James. *The Clarity of Scripture: History, Theology & Contemporary Literary Studies*. Leicester, UK: InterVarsity, 2001.

Carr, David. "The Politics of Textual Subversion: A Diachronic Perspective on the Garden of Eden Story." *Journal of Biblical Literature* 112.4 (1993) 577–95.

Cassuto, Umberto. *A Commentary on the Book of Genesis: Part One.* Jerusalem: Magnes, 1961.

Clines, David. "What Does Eve Do to Help? And Other Irredeemably Androcentric Orientations in Genesis 1–3." In *What Does Eve Do to Help? and Other Readerly Questions to the Old Testament*, edited by David Clines, 25–48. Sheffield: Journal for the Study of the Old Testament, 1990.

Collins, C. John. "What Happened to Adam and Eve? A Literary-Theological Approach to Genesis 3." *Presbyterion* 27.1 (2001) 12–44.

Craig, Kenneth M., Jr. "Misspeaking in Eden, or, Fielding Questions in the Garden (Genesis 2:16—3:13)." *Perspectives in Religious Studies* 27.3 (2000) 235–47.

Davies, Eryl W. *The Dissenting Reader: Feminist Approaches to the Hebrew Bible.* Aldershot, UK: Ashgate, 2003.

Day, Linda. "Wisdom and the Feminine in the Hebrew Bible." In *Engaging the Bible in a Gendered World*, edited by Linda Day and Carolyn Pressler, 114–28. Louisville: Westminster John Knox, 2006.

Dennis, Trevor. *Sarah Laughed: Women's Voices in the Old Testament.* London: SPCK, 1994.

Dragga, Sam. "Genesis 2–3: A Story of Liberation." *Journal for the Study of the Old Testament* 55 (1992) 3–13.

Evans, Mary J. *Woman in the Bible.* Exeter, UK: Paternoster, 1983.

Fewell, Dana Nolan, and David M. Gunn. *Gender, Power, and Promise: The Subject of the Bible's First Story.* Nashville: Abingdon, 1993.

Foh, Susan T. "What is the Woman's Desire?" *WTJ* 37.3 (1975) 376–83.

———. *Women and the Word of God: A Response to Biblical Feminism.* Phillipsburg, NJ: Presbyterian & Reformed, 1979.

Fretheim, Terence E. "Genesis." In *New Interpreter's Bible*, edited by Leander Keck, 319–674. Nashville: Abingdon, 1994.

Gardner, Anne. "Genesis 2:4b–3: A Mythological Paradigm of Sexual Equality or of the Religious History of Pre-exilic Israel?" *Scottish Journal of Theology* 43.1 (1990) 1–18.

Gellman, Jerome. "Gender and Sexuality in the Garden of Eden." *Theology & Sexuality* 12.3 (2006) 319–35.

Goldingay, John. "Hosea 1–3, Genesis 1–4, and Masculist Interpretation." *Horizons in Biblical Theology* 17.1 (1995) 37–44.

Greidanus, Sidney. *The Modern Preacher and the Ancient Text.* Grand Rapids: Eerdmans, 1988.

Griffiths, V. "Mankind: Male and Female." In *The Role of Women*, edited by S. Lees, 72–95. Leicester, UK: InterVarsity, 1984.

Grudem, Wayne. *Evangelical Feminism and Biblical Truth.* Sisters, OR: Multnomah, 2004.

Hamilton, Victor P. *The Book of Genesis Chapters 1–17.* Grand Rapids: Eerdmans, 1990.

Hartley, John E. *Genesis.* Peabody, MA: Hendrickson, 2000.

Hayter, Mary. *The New Eve In Christ: The Use and Abuse of the Bible in the Debate About Women in the Church.* London: SPCK, 1987.

Hess, Richard S. "Equality With and Without Innocence: Genesis 1–3." In *Discovering Biblical Equality*, edited by Ronald W. Pierce, et al., 79–95. Downers Grove, IL: InterVarsity, 2005.

Hurley, James B. *Man and Woman in Biblical Perspective*. Leicester, UK: InterVarsity, 1981.

Isherwood, Lisa, and Kathleen McPhillips. "Introduction." In *Post-Christian Feminisms: A Critical Approach*, edited by Lisa Isherwood and Kathleen McPhillips, 1–10. Aldershot, UK: Ashgate, 2008.

Jacobs, Mignon R. *Gender, Power, and Persuasion: The Genesis Narratives and Contemporary Portraits*. Grand Rapids: Baker Academic, 2007.

Jobling, David. "Mieke Bal on Biblical Narrative." *Religious Studies Review* 17.1 (1991) 1–10.

———. "Poor Banished Children of Eve: Woman as Evil in the Hebrew Bible." *Journal of Biblical Literature* 124.2 (2005) 359–61.

Jobling, J'annine. "Post-Christian Hermeneutics: The Rise and Fall of Female Subjectivity in Theological Narrative." In *Post-Christian Feminisms: A Critical Approach*, edited by Lisa Isherwood and Kathleen McPhillips, 89–103. Aldershot, UK: Ashgate, 2008.

Kawashima, Robert S. "A Revisionist Reading Revisited: On the Creation of Adam and Then Eve." *VT* 56.1 (2006) 46–57.

Kennedy, James M. "Peasants in Revolt: Political Allegory in Genesis 2–3." *Journal for the Study of the Old Testament* 47 (1990) 3–14.

Kimelman, Reuven. "The Seduction of Eve and the Exegetical Politics of Gender." In *Women in the Hebrew Bible*, edited by Alice Bach, 241–69. New York: Routledge, 1999.

Koosed, Jennifer L. "Coming of Age in Phyllis Trible's World." *Lexington Theological Quarterly* 38.1 (2003) 15–19.

Korsak, Mary Phil. "Genesis: A New Look." In *A Feminist Companion to Genesis*, edited by Athalya Brenner, 39–52. Sheffield, UK: Sheffield Academic, 1993.

Lanser, Susan S. "(Feminist) Criticism in the Garden: Inferring Genesis 2–3." *Semeia* 41 (1988) 67–84.

Mettinger, Tryggve N. D. *The Eden Narrative: A Literary and Religio-Historical Study of Genesis 2–3*. Winona Lake, IN: Eisenbrauns, 2007.

Meyers, Carol L. *Discovering Eve: Ancient Israelite Women in Context*. New York: Oxford University Press, 1988.

———. "Gender Roles and Genesis 3.16 Revisited." In *A Feminist Companion to Genesis*, edited by Athalya Brenner, 118–41. Sheffield, UK: Sheffield Academic, 1993.

Mickelson, Alvera. "An Egalitarian View: There is Neither Male nor Female in Christ." In *Women in Ministry: Four Views*, edited by B. Clouse and R. G. Clouse, 173–206. Downers Grove, IL: InterVarsity, 1989.

Milne, Pamela J. "Eve and Adam: Is a Feminist Reading Possible?" *Bible Review* 4.3 (1988) 12–21, 39.

———. "The Patriarchal Stamp of Scripture: The Implications of Structural Analysis for Feminist Hermeneutics." In *A Feminist Companion to Genesis*, edited by Athalya Brenner, 146–72. Sheffield, UK: Sheffield Academic, 1993.

Moberly, R. W. L. "Did the Interpreters Get It Right? Genesis 2–3 Reconsidered." *Journal of Theological Studies* 59.1 (2008) 22–40.

Niditch, Susan. "Genesis." In *Women's Bible Commentary*, edited by Carol Newsom and Sharon H. Ringe, 13–29. Louisville: Westminster John Knox, 1998.

———. *Oral World and Written Word: Ancient Israelite Literature*. Louisville: Westminster John Knox, 1996.

O'Donovan, Oliver. *Resurrection and Moral Order: An Outline for Evangelical Ethics.* Leicester, UK, 1994.

Olson, Dennis T. "Untying the Knot? Masculinity, Violence, and the Creation-Fall Story of Genesis 2-4." In *Engaging the Bible in a Gendered World*, edited by Linda Day and Carolyn Pressler, 73–86. Louisville: Westminster John Knox, 2006.

Ortlund, Raymond C. "Male-Female Equality and Male Headship: Genesis 1-3." In *Recovering Biblical Manhood and Womanhood: A Response to Evangelical Feminism*, edited by John Piper and Wayne Grudem, 95–112. Wheaton, IL: Crossway, 1991.

Osborne, Grant. *The Hermeneutical Spiral: A Comprehensive Introduction to Biblical Interpretation.* 2nd ed. Downers Grove, IL: InterVarsity, 2006.

Osiek, Carolyn. "The Feminist and the Bible: Hermeneutical Alternatives." In *Feminist Perspectives on Biblical Scholarship*, edited by Adela Yarbro Collins, 93–105. Chico, CA: Scholars, 1985.

Otwell, John H. *And Sarah Laughed: The Status of Woman in the Old Testament.* Philadelphia: Westminster, 1977.

Pardes, Ilana. "Beyond Genesis 3: The Politics of Maternal Naming." In *A Feminist Companion to Genesis*, edited by Athalya Brenner, 173–93. Sheffield, UK: Sheffield Academic, 1993.

Parker, Kim Ian. "Mirror, Mirror on the Wall, Must We Leave Eden, Once and for All? A Lacanian Pleasure Trip through the Garden." *Journal for the Study of the Old Testament* 83 (1999) 19–29.

Pierce, Ronald W., et al., eds. *Discovering Biblical Equality: Complementarity Without Hierarchy.* 2nd ed. Downers Grove, IL: InterVarsity, 2005.

Piper, John, and Wayne Grudem, eds. *Recovering Biblical Manhood and Womanhood: A Response to Evangelical Feminism.* Wheaton, IL: Crossway, 1991.

Rad, Gerhard von. *Genesis.* Translated by John H. Marks. 3rd ed. London: SCM, 1972.

Ramsey, G. W. "Is Name Giving an Act of Domination in Genesis 2:23 and Elsewhere?" *Catholic Biblical Quarterly* 50.1 (1988) 24–35.

Rooke, Deborah W. "Feminist Criticism of the Old Testament: Why Bother?" *Feminist Theology* 15.2 (2007) 160–74.

Sakenfeld, Katherine Doob. "Feminist Perspectives on Bible and Theology: An Introduction to Selected Issues and Literature." *Interpretation* 42.1 (1988) 5–18.

———. "Feminist Uses of Biblical Materials." In *Feminist Interpretation of the Bible*, edited by Letty M. Russell, 55–64. Philadelphia: Westminster, 1985.

Schneider, Tammi J. *Mothers of Promise: Women in the Book of Genesis.* Grand Rapids: Baker Academic, 2008.

Schüngel-Straumann, Helen. "On the Creation of Man and Woman in Genesis 1-3: The History and Reception of the Texts Reconsidered." In *A Feminist Companion to Genesis*, edited by Athalya Brenner, 53–76. Sheffield, UK: Sheffield Academic, 1993.

Simkins, Ronald A. "Gender Construction in the Yahwist Creation Myth." In *Genesis: A Feminist Companion to the Bible (Second Series)*, edited by Athalya Brenner, 32–52. Sheffield, UK: Sheffield Academic, 1998.

Slivniak, Dmitri M. "The Garden of Double Messages: Deconstructing Hierarchical Oppositions in the Garden Story." *Journal for the Study of the Old Testament* 27.4 (2003) 439–60.

Sloane, Andrew. *At Home in a Strange Land: Using the Old Testament in Christian Ethics.* Peabody, MA: Hendrickson, 2008.

———. "Wolterstorff, Exegetical Theorising, and Interpersonal Relationships in Genesis 1–3." ThD diss., Australian College of Theology, 1994.

Stitzinger, Michael F. "Genesis 1–3 and the Male\Female Role Relationship." *Grace Theological Journal* 2.1 (1981) 21–44.

Stordalen, T. *Echoes of Eden: Genesis 2–3 and Symbolism of the Eden Garden in Biblical Hebrew Literature*. Leuven: Peeters, 2000.

Stuart, Elizabeth. "The Return of the Living Dead." In *Post-Christian Feminisms: A Critical Approach*, edited by Lisa Isherwood and Kathleen McPhillips, 211–22. Aldershot, UK: Ashgate, 2008.

Trible, Phyllis. "Biblical Theology as Women's Work." *Religion in Life* 44.1 (1975) 7–13.

———. "Depatriarchalizing in Biblical Interpretation." *JAAR* 41.1 (1973) 30–48.

———. "Feminist Hermeneutics and Biblical Studies." *The Christian Century* 99.4 (1982) 116–18.

———. "Five Loaves and Two Fishes: Feminist Hermeneutics and Biblical Theology." *Theological Studies* 50 (1989) 279–95.

———. *God and the Rhetoric of Sexuality*. Philadelphia: Fortress, 1978.

———. "If the Bible's so Patriarchal, How Come I Love It?" *Bible Review* 8.5 (1992) 44–47, 55.

———. "The Pilgrim Bible on a Feminist Journey." *Daughters of Sarah* 15 (1989) 5–7.

———. "Reflections on the 25th Anniversary of *God and the Rhetoric of Sexuality*." *Lexington Theological Quarterly* 38.1 (2003) 21–26.

———. *Texts of Terror: Literary-Feminist Readings of Biblical Narratives*. Philadelphia: Fortress, 1984.

———. "Treasures Old and New: Biblical Theology and the Challenge of Feminism." In *The Open Text: New Directions for Biblical Studies?*, edited by Francis Watson, 32–56. London: SCM, 1993.

———. "Women & the Word: A Choice for Faith." *Living Pulpit* 1.2 (1992) 9.

Tucker, Ruth A. *Women in the Maze: Questions and Answers on Biblical Equality*. Downers Grove, IL: InterVarsity, 1992.

Van Leeuwen, Mary Stewart, ed. *After Eden: Facing the Challenge of Gender Relations*. Grand Rapids: Eerdmans, 1993.

Vanhoozer, Kevin. *The Drama of Doctrine: A Canonical-Linguistic Approach to Christian Theology*. Louisville: Westminster John Knox, 2005.

———. *First Theology: God, Scripture and Hermeneutics*. Downers Grove, IL: InterVarsity, 2001.

———. *Is There a Meaning in This Text? The Bible, the Reader, and the Morality of Literary Knowledge*. Downers Grove, IL: Apollos, 1998.

Vawter, Bruce. *On Genesis: A New Reading*. London: Chapman, 1977.

Veenker, Ronald A. "Forbidden Fruit: Ancient Near Eastern Sexual Metaphors." *Hebrew Union College Annual* (2000) 57–73.

Vogels, Walter. "'It Is Not Good That the 'Mensch' Should Be Alone; I Will Make Him/Her a Helper Fit for Him/Her' (Gen 2:18)." *Eglise et Theologie* 9 (1978) 9–35.

———. "'Like One of Us, Knowing *Tôb* and *Ra'*' (Gen 3:22)." *Semeia* 81 (1998) 144–57.

———. "The Power Struggle between Man and Woman (Gen 3,16b)." *Biblica* 77.2 (1996) 197–209.

Ward, Timothy. *Word and Supplement: Speech Acts, Biblical Texts, and the Sufficiency of Scripture*. Oxford: Oxford University Press, 2002.

Wenham, Gordon J. *Genesis 1–15*. Edited by David A Hubbard and Glen W Barker. Word Biblical Commentary. Waco, TX: Word, 1987.

Westermann, Claus. *Genesis: A Practical Commentary*. Translated by David E. Green. Grand Rapids: Eerdmans, 1987.

Whybray, Roger N. "The Immorality of God: Reflections on Some Passages in Genesis, Job, Exodus and Numbers." *Journal for the Study of the Old Testament* 72 (1996) 89–120.

Wolde, Ellen van. *Stories of the Beginning: Genesis 1–11 and Other Creation Stories*. Translated by John Bowden. London: SCM, 1996.

Wolterstorff, Nicholas. *Divine Discourse: Philosophical Reflections on the Claim that God Speaks*. Cambridge: Cambridge University Press, 1995.

"Women of Renewal: A Statement." *First Things* 80 (1998) 36–40.

Wootton, Janet. "Who's Been Reading MY Bible? Post-Structuralist Hermeneutics and Sacred Text." In *Post-Christian Feminisms: A Critical Approach*, edited by Lisa Isherwood and Kathleen McPhillips, 71–88. Aldershot, UK: Ashgate, 2008.

Wright, Christopher J. H. *The Mission of God: Unlocking the Bible's Grand Narrative*. Nottingham, UK: InterVarsity, 2006.

———. *Old Testament Ethics for the People of God*. Leicester, UK: InterVarsity, 2004.

Wudel, B. Diane. "*God and the Rhetoric of Sexuality*: An Appreciation on the Twenty-Fifth Anniversary of Its Publication." *Lexington Theological Quarterly* 38.1 (2003) 11–14.

Yee, Gale A. "Gender, Class, and the Social-Scientific Study of Genesis 2–3." *Semeia* 87 (1999) 177–92.

———. *Poor Banished Children of Eve: Woman as Evil in the Hebrew Bible*. Minneapolis: Fortress, 2003.

2

Feminist Hermeneutics and Evangelical Concerns

The Rape of Dinah as a Case Study

ROBIN A. PARRY

> The biblical texts are entangled in a marginalization of women that in different ways and degrees encompasses the past, the present, and the foreseeable future . . . To speak of the Hebrew Bible/Old Testament as "holy scripture" is to accord it an authority and a prestige which ultimately transcends the feminist critique.
>
> —Francis Watson[1]

IT IS TRADITIONALLY ASSUMED by evangelical readers of the Bible that the narratives in the OT are ethically beneficial and that a Christian hermeneutic will be primarily a hermeneutic of faith and trust. However, things are not quite as simple as that, and recent feminist critics have been amongst those who have approached the biblical text first and foremost with a hermeneutic of suspicion. They consider the text of the Bible to be both patriarchal and androcentric and thus potentially harmful to women. Many would say that rather than uncritically opening ourselves to be shaped by the stories, we ought to expose some of them as oppressive and damaging even if they are, in other ways, liberating. This challenge cuts deeply, and simply cannot be ignored. The present chapter is an attempt to maintain the centrality of the canon in Christian ethics whilst trying to take the problems posed by androcentrism and

1. Watson, *Text, Church and World*, 187, 189.

patriarchy within the Bible seriously. The following reflections begin and proceed from within a fairly conservative Christian tradition. This interpretative community and its tradition forms the sedimentation upon which I hope that creative interpretative innovation can take place as that tradition comes into dialogue with feminist scholarship.

The focus will be on Genesis 34 but I shall have to set my reflections on that passage within a broader set of considerations. Section I gives a brief introduction to feminist interpretation whilst Section II outlines feminist concerns with Genesis 34 in particular. In Section III, I defend the continuing usefulness of Genesis 34 in Christian ethics whilst attempting to learn important lessons from feminist schools of thought. I believe that, although initially the various feminist hermeneutics of suspicion seem to undermine the *normative* use of Scripture in Christian ethics, they can open up fruitful ways of ethically reading stories which the Christian can welcome.

THE CHALLENGE OF FEMINIST HERMENEUTICS

Feminism is a broad family of related but different positions. Consequently, feminist readers of biblical texts are often at variance with each other both in terms of conclusions and methodology. However, according to Katherine Doob Sakenfeld, "the beginning point, shared with all feminists studying the Bible, is appropriately a stance of *radical suspicion*."[2] This is because women's experiences have been excluded (a) from the official interpretations of the Bible, and often (b) from the Bible itself, making the Bible a powerful tool in the oppression of women. Letty Russell writes that, "it has become abundantly clear that the Scriptures need liberation, not only from existing interpretations but also from the *patriarchal* bias of the texts themselves."[3] Similarly, Fiorenza thinks that the Bible is "authored by men, written in androcentric language,[4]

---

2. Sakenfeld, "Feminist Uses of Biblical Materials," 55.

3. Russell, "Authority and the Challenge of Feminist Interpretations," 11.

4. *Patriarchy* is a surprisingly difficult notion to pin down but it is usually seen as a dominance of men over women in the power-relations of a society as reflected in public institutions such as government, marriage, the law, religion, education, labor, and so on. This is seen by feminists as oppressive for women and necessarily evil in that it is a primary structure of human alienation and exploitation. *Androcentrism* is the claim that texts are written from the perspective of men. Clearly one could have texts which reflect patriarchal structures but which do so from women's perspectives. However, biblical texts usually discuss issues of war, or the royal court, or the Temple, which are

reflective of male experience, selected and transmitted by male religious leadership. Without question the Bible is a male book."[5]

Feminist interpreters have been keenly aware of the uses to which the Bible has been put and the problem of biblical authority has never been far from the surface. Ruether says: "The Bible was shaped by males in a patriarchal culture, so many of its revelatory experiences were interpreted by men from a patriarchal perspective. The ongoing interpretation of these revelatory experiences and their canonisation further this patriarchal bias by eliminating traces of female experience or interpreting them in an androcentric way. *The Bible, in turn, becomes an authoritative source for the justification of patriarchy in Jewish and Christian society.*"[6]

How can a text like *this* be authoritative? Christian and Jewish feminists have had to struggle with this question since the Bible is the foundational text for both faiths and cannot simply be dismissed.

Sakenfeld presents a typology of the views of feminist biblical scholars on biblical authority.[7] At one end of the spectrum she places Fiorenza who argues that the maleness of the Bible makes it impossible for it to form the basis for a transcontextual critical principle. That honor belongs to the experience of oppressed women according to which biblical texts are interpreted and evaluated. The Bible stands and falls as measured against this standard and cannot itself be considered authoritative.[8] At the other end of the spectrum are the evangelical feminists who wish to maintain as much of a traditional view of the Bible's authoritative status as possible.

---

the domain of men and it is not surprising to find that such texts are both patriarchal *and* androcentric. Thus the biblical text gives the impression that ancient Israel was far more oppressive of women than it actually was (so Meyers, *Discovering Eve*). Even when women come into the frame they are often seen from a male perspective and this may pose more of a problem than the patriarchal social structures themselves. My comments shall thus focus on androcentrism and only make passing reference to the problem of patriarchy.

5. Quoted in Thistleton, *New Horizons in Hermeneutics*, 442–43. The claim is not that the Bible sets out to *consciously* exclude women but simply that it reflects "a culturally inherited and deep-rooted gender bias" (Exum, "Murder They Wrote," 59).

6. Ruether, "Feminist Interpretation," 116 (italics mine).

7. Sakenfeld, "Feminist Perspectives on the Bible and Theology."

8. See Thistleton, *New Horizons*, 442–50, for a critique of Fiorenza.

Between the poles one could place Letty Russell,[9] Mary Ann Tolbert,[10] and Phyllis Bird[11] who see Scripture as authoritative *in so far as* it makes sense of their experience or mediates God's liberating word for the oppressed. Farley similarly argues that the truth-claims of the biblical witness simply cannot be believed unless they "ring true" to the experience of women.[12] The authority of Scripture is redefined by Russell, as the "authority to evoke consent" rather than as an extrinsic authority,[13] thus the locus of authority shifts from text to reader.[14] David Clines has even suggested that the notion of authority should be abandoned by feminists altogether because he sees it as a male notion ill fitted to feminist perspectives.[15] This would be a dramatic shift away from the Christian tradition and is going unnecessarily far for some Christian feminists.[16]

One useful typology of feminist responses to the Bible is that of Carolyn Osiek[17] who discerns five basic stances:[18]

(a) *The Rejectionist*. The Bible is rejected as authoritative perhaps along with Christianity itself (if the Christian tradition is seen as irredeemable).[19]

(b) *The Loyalist*. The Bible cannot be rejected under any circumstances. Two possibilities open up for the loyalist: one can reinterpret "oppressive" texts in non-oppressive ways, seeing the problem not with the text but with its readers,[20] or one could

---

9. See Russell, *Feminist Interpretation*.
10. See Tolbert, "Protestant Feminists and the Bible."
11. See Bird, "Biblical Authority" in Bird, *Missing Persons and Mistaken Identities*.
12. Farley, "Feminist Consciousness," 43.
13. Russell, *Feminist Interpretation*, 141.
14. Ibid.
15. Clines, "What Does Eve Do to Help?"
16. E.g., Bird, *Missing Persons*, 260–61.
17. Osiek, "The Feminist and the Bible: Hermeneutical Alternatives," 99–100. The typology is adopted by Schottroff, Schroer, and Wacker in chapter 2.
18. For a different typology see Sakenfeld, "Feminist Uses."
19. Osiek, "The Feminist and the Bible," 97–99. Mary Daly is the most obvious writer in this category.
20. This is the main strategy of evangelical feminists. For non-evangelical examples, see Meyers on Gen 3:16 (*Discovering Eve*, chapter 5); Trible on Gen 2 (Trible, *God and the Rhetoric of Sexuality*).

opt for the complementarian position which, strictly speaking, is not a feminist position.[21]

(c) *The Revisionist*. The Bible and the Christian tradition, it is argued, have been stamped by the patriarchal culture in which they arose but they are not *essentially* patriarchal and can be reformed. The "submerged female voices" of women hidden behind text and tradition can be recovered from scraps of linguistic, rhetorical, and narrative evidence. The intention is to reconstruct, as far as possible, the lives of ordinary Israelite women at different periods of the nation's history.[22] One may also try to bring to the surface often-ignored texts that present women in a more positive light.[23] The revisionist, along with the rejectionist and the liberationist, may also highlight the androcentric and patriarchal dimensions of biblical texts in order to show how women are often ignored or presented from men's perspectives.[24] Some put biblical texts under the critical eye of psychoanalytic theory to uncover subconscious themes.[25] The aim of such studies is often, at least partially, to subvert such texts and undermine their authority. Such studies may then "playfully" re-imagine the story from the perspective of the women.[26]

---

21. Osiek, "The Feminist and the Bible," 99–100.

22. Carol Meyers' magnificent study, *Discovering Eve* (1988) is a classic example of this approach. See too Phyllis Bird's, "The Place of Women in the Israelite Cultus" in Bird, *Missing Persons*.

23. For example, Exum, "You Shall Let Every Daughter Live." Exum still thinks that Exod 1–2 has a very positive portrayal of women yet she now thinks that this too supports patriarchy for the message sent out is: "Stay in your place in the domestic sphere; you can achieve important things there. The public arena belongs to men; you do not need to look beyond motherhood for fulfilment" (Exum, "Second Thoughts about Secondary Characters"). Exum goes too far here. The text does not *strongly subvert* patriarchy but neither does it set out to reinforce it. I simply cannot hear what Exum thinks she hears in the story.

24. Bach, *Women in the Hebrew Bible*, xiv–xv.

25. See for instance, Rashkow, *The Phallacy of Genesis* and Exum, "Who's Afraid of 'the Endangered Ancestress?'"

26. See e.g., Bach, "With a Song in Her Heart."

(d) *The Sublimationist.* The "feminine principle" of life-giving and nurturing are glorified and the tradition is scoured for feminine symbols of God and the church.[27]

(e) *The Liberationist.* To consider the Bible generally looking for theological perspectives which can be used to critique patriarchy (e.g., new creation, *shalom*, prophetic critique of oppression, *koinonia*). The central message of the Bible is seen to be that of human liberation motivated by eschatological hope. Letty Russell finds a biblical basis and motivation for her liberationist message "in God's intention for the mending of all creation"[28] and Ruether seeks strands of cultural critique from Israel's prophets with which to attack patriarchy.[29] Both, however, take the starting point of a feminist ideology that comes from beyond the text and is brought to it with the hope of correlating the feminist critical principle with one internal to Scripture.[30]

Clearly these strategies, or at least (b)–(e), need not be seen as in conflict and one could embrace some combination of them. I shall make use of selected strategies from the loyalist, the revisionist, and the liberationist, arguing that they not only contribute to reading the Bible ethically but that they are consistent with a "high" view of Scripture.

FEMINIST READINGS OF GENESIS 34: RESTORING DINAH'S HONOR

Feminists can read *with* the biblical text and against androcentric interpreters and/or against the biblical text itself. Both strategies have been used to attempt to restore both Dinah and her honor in recent work.

---

27. Osiek, "The Feminist and the Bible," 101–2. Mary Gray's book *Redeeming the Dream* which seeks for feminine metaphors of atonement in the tradition to replace dominant "male" ones could be seen as "sublimationist."

28. Russell, *Feminist Interpretation*, 138. A recent collection of essays in honor of Letty Russell picks up this new creation theme: Farley and Jones, *Liberating Eschatology*. See also my review of this book in *European Journal of Theology* 10.1 (2001) 76–77.

29. Ruether, *Sexism & God-Talk*.

30. Ruether, "Feminist Interpretation."

Reading with the Text but against the Classical Interpreters

On reading the history of the interpretation of Genesis 34 one is struck by the fact that an element of only minor interest to the narrator of the story, Dinah's "going out to see the daughters of the land," becomes a matter of central concern to both Jewish and Christian interpreters. Without doubt past interpretations of Genesis 34 have reflected the perspectives of the male interpreters, for "classical" readings of the story often blame Dinah for the massacre.[31] Consider Aalders' Christian commentary on Genesis where we read, "We can surmise that [Dinah] also had some natural desires to be seen by the young men of the city as well . . . It was disturbing that Dinah would so flippantly expose herself to the men of this pagan city . . . As a matter of fact, *Dinah was far more at fault for what had happened than anyone else in the City of Shechem.*"[32] All interpreters agree that Dinah was a young woman who went out alone in a dangerous place and that this was, at very least, unwise. Beyond that there is divergence. Some see Dinah as "asking for it" by being deliberately provocative[33] whilst others are more sympathetic towards her.[34] Some see Dinah's act as a rebellion against her parents[35] whilst others see her acting with parental permission.[36] Still others see her sin as enjoyment of the illicit sexual encounter with Shechem.[37] The morals drawn from the story are simple: first, parents should ensure that daughters

---

31. So *Genesis Rabbah* LXXX:II h–i, III f–g; Bernard of Clairvaux, *Selected Works*, 124; Ancrene Wisse in *Anchoritic Spirituality*, 68; Calvin, *A Commentary on Genesis*, 218. On the Christian interpretative tradition concerning OT rape stories from 150–1600 AD see now Schroeder, *Dinah's Lament*.

32. Aalders, *Genesis*, 154, 159 (italics mine).

33. So *Genesis Rabbah* LXXX:I; LXXX:IV.4–5; St Gregory's Pastoral Rule XXIX; *Ancrene Wisse*, 17, 67–68; Henry, *An Exposition of the Five Books of Moses*, 112, 114.

34. Luther, *Luther's Works*, 187–88, 192, 194. On Luther see especially Schroeder, "Luther's Interpretation."

35. So Luther, *Luther's Works*, 192–94.

36. *Genesis Rabbah* blames Jacob for letting Dinah go.

37. So *Glossa Ordinaria* (Schroeder, "Luther's Interpretation," 779–80); *Genesis Rabbah* LXXX:XI; Richard of Saint Victor (Schroeder, "Luther's Interpretation," 780); *Ancrene Wisse*, 68; Matthew Henry implies it (Henry, *Exposition*, 112). Luther took the opposite view—that the rape was not pleasurable for Dinah but was a crime against her.

stay in the home in safety;[38] second, women should avoid both curiosity and allowing men to see them.[39]

Two recent studies helpfully exemplify contrasting feminist attempts to read Genesis 34 *with* the text but *against* androcentric interpreters. The first is that of Dana Nolan Fewell and David Gunn (1991) whilst the second is that of Susanne Scholz (1998).

Fewell and Gunn criticise Meir Sternberg for reading the story through androcentric, "action-man" glasses.[40] He fails to see that the ideology of the reader plays a critical role in the sense that is made of a text.[41] Against Sternberg they propose a feminist reading of the text which makes as much, if not more, sense of it as his.[42] As far as Dinah is concerned they argue that the narrator in verse 2 may be storing up sympathy for her, the victim, rather than her brothers, as Sternberg thinks.[43] At the very least, as readers with a horror at the crime of rape, we cannot help but feel for Dinah.[44] However, Shechem in verse 3 calms her fears and, out of genuine love for her, he promises to take care of her. This is a surprising sequel to the rape and it complicates our response as the narrator "tips the balance in Shechem's favour."[45] Dinah herself, according to Fewell and Gunn, sees a marriage as the best way forward and that is what Shechem offers.[46] She chooses to remain in his house until

---

38. So Jerome, Letter CVII.6, XXII.25; Luther, *Luther's Works*, 93; Calvin, *Commentary*, 218; Babbington, *Works*, 139–40; Henry, *Exposition*, 112.

39. St Bernard, 124–25; *Ancrene Wisse*, 68–69.

40. To follow the whole debate one needs to read Meir Sternberg's original chapter in *The Poetics of Biblical Narrative*, chapter 12; Fewell and Gunn's response, "Tipping the Balance"; Sternberg's reply, "Biblical Poetics and Sexual Politics"; and Paul Noble's assessment, "A 'Balanced' Reading of the Rape of Dinah."

41. Fewell & Gunn, "Tipping," 194.

42. Ibid.

43. Ibid., 195.

44. Ibid.

45. Ibid., 196–97.

46. Ibid., 210, and Jeansonne, *The Women of Genesis*, 95, use Deut 22:28–29 to support Dinah's right to marry Shechem. There are, however, three problems with this. For a start, Deut 22:28–29 *may* not even refer to a rape case (so Hugenberger, *Marriage as Covenant*, 225–60). Second, the negotiations in Genesis 34 presuppose that the family of Dinah *can* refuse the marriage which indicates that a law more like Exod 22:15–16 than Deut 22:28–29 was at work. Finally, as Sternberg has shown ("Sexual Politics," 482–83), even if Deut 22 is about rape it would not, from a Mosaic perspective at least, be applicable to a Hivite. On this text see the excellent chapter by Jenni Williams in this volume.

the wedding.[47] The narrator is calling for a "compromised, but realistic, resolution."[48] In contrast to the reformed rapist we see the aggressive brothers of Dinah who care only for *their* honor (not hers). In mindless revenge they murder, plunder, and rape a whole city[49]—an act that is grossly disproportionate—and they cannot see that Shechem is trying to make restitution for his crime.[50] Having no concern about what is best for Dinah, they take her *against her will* from the house of Shechem and kill the reformed fiancé, the only person who will allow her a voice.[51] Dinah must be seen as a young woman with her own choices but the brothers only see a helpless girl needing to be rescued from herself and her fiancé.[52]

Scholz argues that Fewell and Gunn's approval of the marriage of the rapist to the rape-victim makes the status of their interpretation as a *feminist* reading of Genesis 34 suspect.[53] She claims that biblical texts are always read from some non-neutral perspective and that true feminist readings must be "from the perspective of the subjugated, that is the rape victim-survivor."[54] To illustrate how Genesis 34 has not been read from that perspective she argues that nineteenth-century German commentaries on Genesis 34 paralleled contemporary German medical attitudes towards rape. They marginalised it, distrusted and condemned the victim, and claimed that love can make rape "not so bad."[55] Thus the "commentaries of Genesis 34 were not developed from the perspective of Dinah. They reflected the perspective of the powerful."[56] She then rereads Genesis 34:1–3 from Dinah's perspective in such a way as to make the horror of rape the key focus.[57] Verse 2, she argues, emphasises

---

47. Fewell and Gunn, "Tipping," 200.
48. Ibid., 197.
49. Ibid., 205.
50. Ibid., 200–201.
51. Ibid., 211.
52. Ibid.
53. Scholz, "Through Whose Eyes?" For an excellent feminist critique of readings that interpret Genesis 34 as a seduction rather than a rape see now Blyth, *Terrible Silence, Eternal Silence*, chapter 2. Also Blyth, "Redeemed by His Love?"
54. Scholz, "Whose Eyes?" 151.
55. Ibid., 154–60.
56. Ibid., 159–60.
57. Ibid., 164–71.

Shechem's increasing use of violence against Dinah so that verse 2b describes the action of rape.[58] Her treatment of verse 3 is her most original contribution to the study of the chapter.[59] She argues that it is *not* intended to reflect positively upon Shechem. She reads it as follows: "His (sexual) desire (נפשׁו, *napšô*) stayed close to (בדינה, *bĕdînâ*) Dinah." The context then requires us to read the second line as "and he lusted after (ויאהב, *wayyeʾĕhab*) the young woman." Following Fischer she reads the final line as, "and he attempted to soothe the young woman (וידבר על־לב הנער, *wayĕdabbēr ʿal-lēb hannăʿarā*)."[60] In other words, he has to calm her because she does not consent. "This interpretation of Gen 34:1–3 indicates that several verbs describe the selfishness and the disregard Shechem held for Dinah. The interpretation confirms the notion of the Women's Movement that rape is *primarily* an act of violence rather than a sexual act. When rape is accentuated, love talk is not involved."[61]

58. Ibid., 165–68.
59. Ibid., 168–71.
60. Fischer, "Die Redewendung דבר על־לב im AT."
61. Scholz, "Whose Eyes?" 171. It is worth noting at this point a new interpretation of Genesis 34 by Joseph Fleishman ("Shechem and Dinah") and now by African OT scholar Daniel Hankore ("Reading and Translating"). Fleishman and Hankore argue that the Dinah story does not concern "rape" but the practise of "abduction marriage." Hankore explains:

> Abductive marriage is widely practiced among the Hadiyya people [of Ethiopia]. The particular nature of this practice is that it is violent—some girls may even lose their lives in an attempt to refuse, and it may spark fights between different groups because the Hadiyya people are a shame/honor conscious community. Thus, since the Hadiyya people are an exogamous community, shaming and restoring the threatened group honor is a very serious matter because abductive marriage is very humiliating for the girl and her family.
> According to this tradition the man who intends to marry a girl by abduction first spies out the scene and then kidnaps and abducts the girl with the help of his friends for the purpose of marriage; and then takes her to a hiding place (usually with another family), and has a sexual intercourse with her by force right away, and makes sure that her family will not find the place where he hides her at least for one week to a month, depending on the seriousness of the reaction of the girl's family. In the meantime the boy does all his best to convince the girl to consent to marry him. And then the family of the boy will plead with the family of the girl so that they will let their son marry their daughter.

Despite their stark differences, both these studies argue that the story must be read from the woman's perspective and that one can, to some extent at least, read *with* the text to restore Dinah's honor as a person with value and choices.

Reading against the Biblical Text

Within Genesis 34 both patriarchy and androcentrism are issues of concern to feminist readers. The problem with patriarchy is seen most clearly in the way in which marriages in Israel are arranged without any reference to the wishes of the girl involved. Genesis 34 reflects this widespread custom. Naomi Segal complains that "Dinah is an object of exchange so blank that to violate her is to enter nothing but instead to 'take' something—from whom? Not from her. The text is singularly clear in exposing the discursive economics of male sexuality, with its exchange of object-females among subject-males . . . The shared norm of all the

---

Abductive marriage can be aborted . . . However it will be endorsed in most cases . . . Sometimes it may provoke a serious fight between the two families, especially if the girl's family is very proud of their status in the community, which will make them very aggressive to restore their threatened honor. In such a case the family of the girl will feel humiliated and dishonored that they will do whatever they can in order to abort the marriage and bring the girl back home." Hankore, "Reading and Translating," ch. 6.

Hankore argues that abduction marriage is not classified by the Hadiyya as "rape." Rape does occur amongst the Hadiyya but in rape an individual "takes" a woman in secret with no intention of marrying her.

The proposal that Genesis 34 concerns abduction marriage is very plausible. It is also possible that abduction marriage would not have been conceptualized by ancient Israelites as "rape" in a straightforward sense, or, at least, as a "rape" *of the same kind* as a sexual attack that was not intended as an abduction marriage. But even if this is so, the feminist critique stands. In terms of how *we* conceptualize rape, *this is rape* because the woman did not consent to sexual intercourse (see Shemesh, "Rape is Rape is Rape"). And if seeing from the perspective of the victim concerns us at all—and it should—then this is a sexual assault that should be opposed. The distinction that the Hadiyya make between abduction marriage and rape does mark a distinction that we can recognize. However, it should be seen as a distinction *within the broader category of sexual assault*. It is a culturally specific *kind* of rape.

It is suggestive here to note the intertextual links between the Dinah story in Genesis 34 and the Tamar story in 2 Sam 13 (see Parry, *Old Testament Story*, 143–46). If the former concerns abduction marriage and the latter concerns rape, then, by means of these links, the biblical text invites us to see abduction marriage *as a kind of rape* or, at very least, as *morally akin to rape*. Either way, it is a sexual assault that is resisted by the texts.

men is expressed in the narrowly ambiguous pronoun that defines the crime as 'a disgrace to *us*.'"[62]

Perhaps more worrying seems to be the clear androcentrism of a story that, although it involves the rape of a woman, is all about men and their reactions.[63] The silence of Dinah is the central issue of concern for most feminist readers. Why is her view not directly represented? Why is she never consulted about what she would like to happen vis-à-vis marriage? The worry is that it is not simply biblical interpreters who ignore her perspective, but *the biblical narrator himself*.

Rashkow objects to the androcentrism reflected in the way that Dinah is defined in relation to men.[64] She is Jacob's *daughter*. She is the brothers' *sister*. Why is she never simply Dinah—a woman with her own identity?[65] We need to be careful here not to presuppose that people are only seen most fully as people when they are considered as isolated individuals who are fully "themselves" on their own. This notion of the solitary-self has been subjected to sustained criticism by philosophers and theologians in recent years. The "self" is a "self-in-relation": part of what it is for me to be me is to be someone's son, someone's brother, someone's father. Feminism itself has played an important role in re-discovering the crucial place of relationality in identity.[66] Thus Genesis 34 does not demean Dinah by referring to her as "Jacob's daughter" or "their sister." Now there is an issue of asymmetry in the biblical texts on this matter—in ancient Israel's patrilinear society, people were more often "identified" by their relations to men than by their relations to women—but things are more balanced in the Dinah story. In Genesis 34, the men are described as "*her* father" and "*her* brothers" indicating

---

62. Segal, "Review of *The Poetics of Biblical Narrative*."

63. Bechtel is the only feminist scholar I have come across who challenges this consensus ("What If Dinah Was Not Raped?"). I critique her view in my *Old Testament Story and Christian Ethics*.

64. Rashkow, "Daughters and Fathers in Genesis."

65. Ibid., 104–6. See too Segal, "Review," 248.

66. Kock ("A Cross-Cultural Critique") argues that western feminism has often made the mistake, among other things, of assuming that western views of individual autonomy are essential to the liberation of women. Feminists from non-western cultures have rightly objected and refused to see the necessity of abstracting women from the network of social relations within which they find their sense of identity. Western feminists have usually taken these criticisms seriously. It seems to me that Rashkow is stuck in an *Enlightenment*-Feminist mode of thought in her criticisms here.

that their identity is formed, in part, by their relation to her. Also she is related to her mother Leah (34:1)—a female—and thus it seems to me that Rashkow's criticism is not as powerful as it at first appears.[67] In fact, all the relational participant references Dinah receives reinforce her value. She is not just another woman to the Israelites but a *sister* and *that* is why they are so angry at the rape. Indeed, the text highlights the way in which rape is never simply a crime against an individual but it is rather a crime against an individual *and*, indirectly, a crime against those to whom that individual is socially bonded. This does not take anything away from our western appreciation of the importance of the individual but it does challenge our tendency towards individual*ism*.

Rashkow raises another objection to the narrator in Genesis 34 claiming that a repeated theme in biblical narratives is the daughter's transgression against her father and subsequent departure from the closure of the house. For example, Dinah "goes out," is raped (Gen 34:1–2), and is then "narratively banished from the text."[68] Rashkow here seems to accept the "classical" reading of Dinah's "going out" as an excursion condemned by the narrator. My first task in the next section will be to question this view but it seems appropriate, at this point, to make a preliminary criticism of Rashkow's argument, for she only gives two examples of this supposedly "repeated theme": the first is Genesis 34 and the second is Jephthah's daughter in Judges 11. Apart from the fact that two examples would not be enough to establish the claim, it seems to me that neither of the examples provides any evidence for the proposal. Jephthah's daughter does not transgress against her father in any straightforward sense and the text of Genesis 34 says nothing of Dinah's rebellion against Jacob. Nevertheless, Rashkow, in line with the classical interpreters, clearly thinks that Dinah's "going out" is condemned by the narrator and she subjects that condemnation to a feminist-psychoanalytic critique.[69]

---

67. The wider Genesis context of God's concern for Leah and her offspring, combined with the reminder that Dinah is Leah's daughter, may suggests that, though Dinah is abused by Shechem and, in a different way, by her family, she is cared for by God.

68. Rashkow, *The Phallacy of Genesis*, 67.

69. Another complaint about Genesis 34 is the way in which insult is added to injury by using Dinah's violation as an "excuse" for victimising Canaanites (Laffey, *An Introduction*, 41–44). Men typically use the rapes of women to justify wars and Genesis 34 is no exception (see Keefe, "Rapes of Women/Wars of Men"). I do not intend to take up this challenge in what follows for I argue in my *Old Testament Story and Christian Ethics* that the narrator is *not* trying to defend the massacre.

DINAH'S HONOR: SOME REFLECTIONS

Does the Narrator Disapprove of Dinah's "Going Out"?

Given the agreement between *some* feminist readers such as Rashkow and "classical" readers it is appropriate to begin with a reassessment of the view that the narrator condemns Dinah for "going out."[70]

Does יצא (yāṣā') Indicate a Narratorial Disapproval of Dinah?

The first thing to refute is Sarna's claim that the verbal stem יצא (yāṣā') can connote "coquettish or promiscuous conduct."[71] Jacob Neusner also comments that, "the verb 'go out' when associated with a woman carries the sense of 'awhoring.'"[72] Neither Sarna nor Neusner provide any evidence for this assertion. Wenham tentatively provides some support for the claim by observing that in the Laws of Hammurabi 141 the cognate Akkadian verb *waṣû* "describes a housewife who conducts herself improperly outside her home, and the targums translate 'cult prostitute' as 'one who goes out into the countryside.'"[73] However, that one example of a cognate verb can be produced in which a woman "goes out" in a dubious fashion is a very weak basis for the claim that the Hebrew verb itself carries bad connotations. For a start, we cannot make a simple transfer from Akkadian to Hebrew. Secondly, that a verb *in some contexts* can carry negative overtones does not suggest that the verb carries those connotations inherently. We shall see below at least one "whorish going out" in the Hebrew Bible, but this simply does not show that all women "going out" were viewed negatively. Even *if* the later Jewish targums spoke of cult prostitutes as women who "go out into the countryside"[74] that does not establish that the notion of women "going out" carried sexual overtones *whatever* the context, nor even that the sexual usage of יצא (yāṣā') goes back to the time when Genesis was written. We need to study the "goings out" of women in the Hebrew Bible itself. On inspec-

---

70. On the question of whether the narrator blames Dinah or not, see now Blyth, *Terrible Silence, Eternal Silence*, ch. 5.

71. Sarna, *Genesis*, 233.

72. Neusner, *Genesis Rabbah*, 146.

73. Wenham, *Genesis 16–50*, 310.

74. I say "if" because the whole notion that there was ever such a thing as cult prostitution in the ancient Near East has been seriously challenged by several recent scholars.

tion the Emperor's new prostitute vanishes into thin air. All the Qal uses of יצא (yāṣā') predicated of females can be categorised as follows:

- Genesis 24 is full of women who "go out" to collect water (vv. 11, 13, 15, 43, 45. See also 1 Sam 9:11) yet it certainly cannot be said that "coquettish or promiscuous conduct" is connoted.

- It seems to have been quite common for groups of women to "go out" in worship.[75] In none of these cases does the verb יצא (yāṣā') imply improper behaviour (Exod 15:20; Judg 11:34; 21:21; 1 Sam 18:6; Jer 31:4).

- Most of the 1,068 uses of the יצא (yāṣā') stem simply denote someone moving from one place to another. It is not surprising that it is used of women in this way (Ruth 1:7; 2:22; 2 Kgs 4:21, 37; 8:3).

- The OT often describes women who "go out" to meet people. This category includes Leah (Gen 30:16), Dinah (34:1), Jael (Judg 4:18, 22), and Michal (2 Sam 6:20). The only case in which a woman "goes out" as a prostitute is Proverbs 7:10, 15.

- Some miscellaneous examples of the verb יצא (yāṣā') predicated of females include "going out" in divorce (Deut 24:2), and in approved "romantic" contexts (Song 1:8; 3:11).[76]

- Women can also be freed ("go out") from slavery (Exod 21:3, 7, 11).

What we can say with certainty is that when the verb יצא (yāṣā') is used of women it does *not* carry any automatic negative connotations. The vast majority of the above women who "go out" are not being implicitly condemned for having done so. It all depends on what the women "go out" to do; thus Sarna and Neusner are simply wrong. The closest we get to support for the traditional view is Proverbs 7:10, 15 where a prostitute comes out to seduce a man.[77] Clearly *her* "going out"

---

75. See Meyers, "Miriam the Musician."

76. Other miscellaneous uses include Zech 5:9; Jer 29:2; 38:20–23; Mic 4:10 (the last three refer to "going out" into exile).

77. Possibly also Judg 4:18, as the account of Jael's "going out" to welcome Sisera seems to make use of sexual innuendoes; see Niditch, "Eroticism and Death in the Tale of Jael." However, her later "going out" to meet Barak does not seem to have such overtones.

is considered morally suspect but let us remember that Dinah did *not* go out to seduce men. She went out to see the *women* of the land and was raped!

The rabbis in *Genesis Rabbah* and later commentators such as Rashi saw a connection between Leah's "going out" to have sex with Jacob and Dinah's "going out": As Leah went awhoring so did Dinah.[78] The connection is less than convincing. Firstly, it is not fair to describe Leah's act as one of prostitution—she was *married* to Jacob.[79] Second, there is nothing sexual about the *verb* יָצָא (yāṣā') in Genesis 30:16. The proposal Leah made was sexual but her "going out" was merely a prerequisite for the making this proposal. Third, apart from the parallel phrases ("and Leah went out" // "and Dinah went out") the two events are not parallel at all. Leah went out to persuade her husband to impregnate her whilst Dinah went out to see the local women and was raped. One simply cannot read off a negative assessment of Dinah from this parallel. This strategy having failed another rears its head.

Hamilton translates verse 1 as "she went out *to be seen* [implied—'by the men'] among the daughters of the land."[80] As we have seen the idea that Dinah went out to get "picked up" by some dishy young bloke traces its roots way back into the history of interpretation. His reasoning is that the construction רָאָה (rā'â, to see) in the infinitive + בְּ (bĕ) is unique and thus he prefers to translate as a passive rather than an active form. However, out of 111 uses of the Qal infinitive construct of רָאָה (rā'â, to see) in the OT there is no clear example of a passive use ("be seen"). Every occurrence is most naturally read as active ("to see"). If the narrator had wanted to say that Dinah had gone to "be seen" he would have used the Niphal infinitive construct which always bears that sense.[81] Hamilton does add that "the active sense is possible only if one understands *be* partitively, that is, 'to see *some* of the women.'"[82] The weight of evidence would support *this* reading.

78. *Genesis Rabbah*, LXXX:I.Y.

79. And unlike a prostitute Leah paid Rachel in mandrakes for the privilege of sleeping with Jacob rather than seeking payment from her "client."

80. Hamilton, *The Book of Genesis*, 351; so too Aalders, *Genesis*, 154, and Kass, "Regarding Daughters and Sisters," 31.

81. There is some textual support for a Niphal in the Samaritan Pentateuch (followed by some of the Jewish *Midrashim*—see Salkin, "Dinah, the Torah's Forgotten Woman") but the MT and LXX support the Qal reading (as does Hamilton himself).

82. Hamilton, *Genesis 18–50*, 353.

Perhaps, the traditionalist may reply, women could "go out" acceptably in groups but to go out alone was seen as wrong. This is more plausible but unpersuasive. We note that Rebecca is not frowned upon in Genesis 24 for "going out" alone before all the other women to collect water. Similarly, Rachel kept her father's sheep, apparently alone, yet there is not obvious condemnation for that.[83] Having said this, I do think that it would have been considered unwise for a woman to go out alone into territory not her own. This is put very well by Naomi in Ruth 2:22, "It will be good for you, my daughter, to *go* with the girls, because in someone else's field you might be harmed." It is not that Ruth would have been seen as *immoral* in going out to someone else's field. Rather she would have put herself in possible danger and would be wise to find security in a group. The Dinah situation finds its most comfortable parallel with Ruth 2:22. Dinah was going out into dangerous territory—the land of the Canaanites. In doing so alone she may well have been considered to have acted naively but not necessarily promiscuously.

Does the Narrator Blame Dinah?

Given the mountains of blame heaped upon Dinah by classical interpreters, one is struck by the fact that at *no* point in the chapter is Dinah blamed for what has happened. Blame is always placed squarely on *Shechem's* shoulders. Shechem saw her, took her, lay [with] her, and shamed her (v. 2). Shechem "defiled" her (vv. 5, 13, 27[84]) and "did folly in Israel" (v. 7). Now it was perfectly possible for a woman to "do folly" by engaging in illicit sexual relations[85] but no mention is made of Dinah "doing folly." Shechem treated her as a prostitute (v. 31). No mention is made of Dinah *acting* like a prostitute and thus sharing in the blame. This is because in Israel women were not held responsible in cases of rape.[86]

Did Dinah know what would happen to her? Did she know that she would (or might) be raped? Could she have known how her rapist would react? Could she have anticipated her brothers' response? The only ac-

---

83. Gen 29:6–12.

84. Verse 27 actually says that "they [i.e., the now deceased men of Shechem] defiled Dinah." Nevertheless, no blame is attached to Dinah here.

85. Deut 22:21.

86. Deut 22:25–27.

tion for which she is responsible is her own "going out" and the only blame is any that may attach to her lack of wisdom.

Does Genesis 34 Support Locking up Our Daughters?

Interpretation is underdetermined by the text with regard to the restriction of daughters to the home. It could be used, as argued above, as evidence for Dinah's lack of wisdom in going out alone given the dangers. However, beyond that it cannot direct us. If one is already committed to the idea that women are vulnerable and best kept safe in the security of the home, as the classical readers were, then Genesis 34 certainly could be used to reinforce such a belief. Alternatively, if one was a feminist who was angered at the fact that women are preyed upon, one could equally use the text to support a campaign to "Claim Back the Night." The narrator is not especially concerned to address such issues. We may be, and we may use the text to inspire us in our reflections, but we cannot use it to settle the issue either way. Either readers' response could be a legitimate one *as far as doing justice to the text goes*.

The Problem of Patriarchy in Genesis 34

Patriarchy is simply *assumed* in Genesis 34 as in the rest of the Hebrew Bible where it is was neither justified nor critiqued. Does the fact that Israel was a patriarchal society make patriarchy a biblical norm for all cultures at all times? Not obviously. Let me make a few brief remarks in an attempt to set the problem posed by Israel's apparently male dominated social structures in some perspective.

First, Carol Meyers has urged great caution in this area. She argues that the concept of patriarchy needs to be nuanced to deal with differences across time and culture, maintaining that in ancient Israel, as in some contemporary peasant societies, women had a great deal of power even if they had little authority and would not have (usually) found their place in society as harsh or oppressive.[87] Biblical societies were strongly patrilinear[88] but "male dominance [was] . . . a public attitude of deference

---

87. Authority is a hierarchical arrangement that may be expressed in formal legal or juridical traditions (Meyers, *Discovering Eve*, 41).

88. Patrilineality refers to the tracing of group membership through the father's line. The inheritance of property is also through this line. Patrilineality has been explored by Steinberg in the Genesis stories (Steinberg, *Kinship and Marriage in Genesis*).

or of theoretical control but not a valid description of social reality."[89] Thus care ought to be taken when criticising ancient Israelite society, for it may not have been nearly *as* oppressive for women as it may at first look.[90] It remains the case that Israel's laws and social structures were dominated by men and can be termed patriarchal so long as care is taken when so doing.

Second, the biblical metanarrative of creation, fall, and restoration could provide the ground for a biblical critique of patriarchy.[91] In creation men and women are equally in God's image[92] and equally commissioned to fill and subdue the earth.[93] Francis Watson believes that "The Hebrew narrators [in Genesis 1–3] were somehow able to transcend the all-embracing, self-evident patriarchal context in which they no doubt lived and worked, in order to assert that 'in the beginning it was not so.'"[94] Genesis 3:16 seems to be a watershed in gender relations as sin could be seen as the origin of men ruling over their women.[95] If this is correct, then oppressive patriarchy could be rooted not in the creative intentions of God but in the fallenness of the world. Redemption then restores men and women equally[96] enabling men and women to receive both the Spirit and his gifts.[97] One could see the patriarchy of Israel along the

---

89. Meyers, *Discovering Eve*, 42.

90. Similar warnings are made by Schroer in Schottroff, Schroer, and Wacker, *Feminist Interpretation*, 89–91. Schroer writes that "one must warn against comparing ancient Israelite patriarchy with that of today's industrialised, technological, and individual-orientated societies. In an agrarian culture where they are part of the process of production, women are often in positions of equal power to men even when they are excluded, for example, from politics and public activities" (ibid., 90–91).

91. See Various, "Living between the Times"; Walsh and Middleton, *Truth Is Stranger Than It Used to Be*; Watson, *Text, Church and World*, chapter 11. See too the chapter in this volume by Junia Pokrifka.

92. Gen 1:26. There are many and diverse feminist interpretations of this crucial text. See the chapter in this volume by Junia Pokrifka.

93. Gen 1:28.

94. Watson, *Text, Church and World*, 194.

95. Gen 3:16 has generated many feminist studies among which are Bird, "Genesis 3 in Modern Biblical Scholarship," in Bird, *Missing Persons*, 174–93; Bledstein, "Are Women Cursed in Genesis 3:16?"; Meyers, "Gender Roles in Genesis 3:16 Revisited" (see too Meyers, *Discovering Eve*); Trible, *God and the Rhetoric of Sexuality*, 126–28. See the helpful chapter in this volume by Andrew Sloane.

96. Gal 3:28.

97. Acts 2:16–17; 1 Cor 11:3ff.

same lines as the divorce laws—not God's intention, but allowed due to sin-hardened hearts.[98] However, now that the new age has dawned such social structures are passing away.[99] This basic hermeneutic is that adopted by the majority of evangelical feminists as well as by many non-evangelical, Christian feminists. It has the benefit of allowing one to recognise the patriarchy of Israel without seeing it as normative. It also seeks out a critical principle with which to critique patriarchy that has genuine claims to be Christian and *internal* to the biblical canon rather than an alien principle rooted in secular ideology.[100]

The Problem of Androcentrism in Genesis 34

> [T]o call Genesis 34 a story about a woman's rape is to say something about the text that the author himself takes measures to exclude from representation. While without the rape event, there would be no story, the tale that is told is not *Dinah's* story; it is her father's story, her brothers' story, even her rapist's story. There is a pervasive narrative silence about this young woman's personal experience of her ordeal and a denial of, or at least a contextual disinterest in, the fact that Shechem's act of sexual assault was a forcible violation of her bodily integrity and that it would have been a source of immense physical, emotional, and spiritual distress for her. Dinah is a catalyst in this narrative, not a subject of consciousness; as an object, others act upon her and it is *their* actions that guide the unfolding sequence of events. The reader barely catches a glimpse of her; she is always just outside the field of vision, kept offstage, while the events to which she

---

98. Matt 19:4–9 pars.

99. The persistence of patriarchy in the NT could be seen in terms of the tension between the "now" and the "not yet" which marks the present experience of the Christian. The patriarchy of the NT is a radically Christianized and subversive form of patriarchy but it is patriarchy none the less. The question is: was the patriarchy of the NT merely a concession to culture or a norm for all Christians?

100. Thiselton criticises Fiorenza and Daly for finding their critical principle outside the biblical text and not being open to dialogue with the text from which one can learn. Instead one approaches the text with all the answers and simply measures the text against them (Thiselton, *New Horizons*, 442–50). Francis Watson finds the redemption of an otherwise oppressive Bible in the claim that the elements in the canon which resist oppression are not mere "scattered fragments" but belong to the "fundamental structure" of that very canon (Watson, *Text, Church, and World*, chs. 9–11). Thus the critical principle used to subvert many biblical narratives is not merely secular and external to the Bible but *also religious and internal to it* (ibid., 190).

is so consciously and painfully a participant in revolve around her. Furthermore, the space where her voice ought to have been heard is instead filled with other voices, male voices, while her exclusively female experience as a victim of sexual violence effectively remains little more than a narrative periphrasis. Unnoticed and ignored among the shadows of this story, Dinah's silence thus becomes nothing less than a form of oppression, the mark of her exclusion from honest representation within the text.[101]

It is indeed true that there is no *direct* indication of Dinah's perspective on the crime in Genesis 34. Before commenting on this it is worth pointing to some *indirect* indicators of how she felt.

First, we are told in 34:3 that Shechem "spoke to her heart" which clearly indicates that she was distressed and Shechem consequently took steps to calm her.[102]

Second, the sons (and Jacob?) saw the rape as an act in which Dinah is treated as a prostitute (v. 31) and is thus "defiled" (vv. 5, 13, 27). It is "folly in Israel" (v. 7). It is sometimes assumed that this is merely the men's view on the crime and not Dinah's. The marriage, we are told by the sons, is "a disgrace to us" and both Fewell & Gunn and Segal take the "us" here to refer to the sons *in contrast to* Dinah. Segal thinks that we ought to see the rape from Dinah's perspective—as her autonomy being cruelly violated.[103] However, it is most unlikely that Dinah would see her rape as modern western women would.[104] For us, rape is primarily a violation of a woman's autonomy and bodily integrity, but that is no reason to imagine that Dinah would see a violation of her autonomy as primary. It may be the case that the sons *imagine* that Dinah will see the rape from the same perspective as themselves and they cannot see that even if this is so it would be much more than that to her. They do fail to perceive *fully* her perspective and this is a weakness on their part. Nevertheless, I would imagine that she would perceive her rape in much

---

101. Blyth, *Terrible Silence, Eternal Silence*, 3–4.

102. Rightly, Scholz, "Whose Eyes?" Incidentally, Fewell and Gunn are quite wrong to take Shechem's speaking to Dinah's heart as a perlocutionary act which wins her over to his cause (Noble, "Tipping the Balance," 196). Sternberg has clearly demonstrated that it indicates *nothing* about Dinah's response to Shechem's soothing words (Sternberg, "Sexual Politics," 476–78). Thus the text does *not* indicate that Dinah came to love Shechem.

103. Segal, "Review," 247.

104. Rightly Keefe, "Rapes of Women," 79.

the same categories as her family: as "folly" and as "defiling."[105] Now they *are* presuming on Dinah here, for they have not actually consulted her (she was inaccessible at Shechem's house), but presumably she shares the basic Israelite perspectives on rape and exogamy—the same one her brothers would have.[106]

The considerations above suggest that if it is legitimate to re-imagine the story from Dinah's perspective, then care ought to be taken to avoid anachronism—to imagine that Dinah is a modern western woman with modern western values. We need to try to understand how the rape would be seen *within her Israelite worldview*. One could, with cogency, still argue that Dinah had internalised a *patriarchal* perspective on her rape—seeing it, as Tamar saw her rape, as a defiling act that degrades her social worth[107]—but even though that is likely the case, it would still remain a part of the warp and weft of *her* perspective. Whilst we should challenge such a patriarchal construal of rape, attempts to restore Dinah's voice must ring true to the ancient cultural context.

However, we are still left with the problem that the story, quite clearly, does not take Dinah's perspective into consideration and this raises the legitimate concern that the person most affected by the crime is silenced, not only by the men who negotiate over her fate, but also by the narrator himself. What can we say about this?

Let us first note that every story is told from some perspective. Any incident can be told from the perspective of any of the parties directly or indirectly involved. The Genesis 34 events could be narrated from the perspective of the Hivite town dwellers, Jacob, the sons, Shechem, Dinah, or from any number of other perspectives. Each version would be, to some extent, a different story. Every story is told for some reason. This leads to a selection and organisation of the material so as to make the desired point. Every telling of a story has to marginalize some characters and events so as to focus on whatever it is the storyteller wishes to focus on. That Dinah is marginalised in the plot need not imply that she

---

105. It presumably goes without saying that we do not conceptualize the crime of rape in exactly the same way as ancient Israelites (nor should we feel obligated to by some simplistic understanding of how biblical authority functions).

106. Incidentally, to imagine, as some have, that Dinah would enjoy the rape owes more to male fantasising than to textual evidence or studies of actual rape cases (on reading Genesis 34 in the light of actual rape testimonies see especially Blyth, *Terrible Silence, Eternal Silence*).

107. See Blyth, *Terrible Silence, Eternal Silence*, ch. 3.

is not morally relevant but only that *in the telling of this story* the rape is not the main focus of the plot. Unless one believes that every story which *includes* a rape must be a story *about* rape there is no *prima facie* problem with the narrator's strategy here. Nobody would suggest that the rape is not taken seriously in Genesis 34—it leads to a massacre!

Nevertheless, even though the rape is taken seriously it is done so *from a male angle*. Is Dinah's view of the crime seen to be irrelevant? To some extent it depends on whether one feels that the lack of a certain perspective in the biblical narrator's telling of a story rules out the legitimacy of that perspective. In this case, we could ask, "Does the fact that the narrator's chosen function for this story makes no use of Dinah's perspective rule out the legitimacy or relevance of Dinah's perspective?" Clearly that depends on what we mean by "relevance." Dinah's perspective is not relevant to the point our narrator wants to draw attention to in his telling of story (it is not a "gap" in the narrative that needs to be filled for a reader to make-sense of the text). This, however, is not to say that it is not relevant to *any* legitimate telling of the story, nor that it is in conflict with the narrator's point. Stories may be open to the possibility of a range of uses of, and perspectives on, the events so long as those perspectives cohere with their overall worldview. From the fact that Dinah's view is not found in Genesis 34 one cannot infer that Dinah's view does not matter, nor even that Dinah's view does not matter to the author.[108] One can only infer that Dinah's view is not relevant to the point that the narrator wants to make in his use of the story here.

It could be argued that the narrator *should* have set out to see her side of things. Her view may not suit his purposes but that is merely because his purposes, shaped by the ideology of patriarchy, are androcentric and so the feminist critique still has bite. However, although the task of presenting Dinah's view would be very worthwhile—indeed in certain contexts it will be a *moral imperative*[109]—why *must* the narrator do this? If the narrative somehow made Dinah's perspective illegitimate or irrelevant in a broader sense (rather than simply for the purposes in mind for his particular use of a story) then we have strong grounds for

---

108. I hesitate to say "narrator" as it seems to me that a narrator has no existence beyond the text and consequently one cannot talk of their holding views which are not expressed in the text (unlike authors who clearly can and do).

109. On the moral imperative see especially Blyth, *Terrible Silence, Eternal Silence*.

deep concern. However, as I have already said, we cannot infer from Dinah's silence that the views of the victims of rape do not matter.[110]

A deeper concern is that Dinah's silence is a manifestation of "the androcentric values and the androcentric worldview of the biblical narrative"[111] in which rape was considered a crime against men (husbands and fathers) and not women.[112] Consider Thistlethwaite's definition of rape in Israel: "Biblical rape is theft of sexual property."[113] Rape, on this analysis, has nothing to do with a crime against the woman herself. Thistlethwaite is correct, in my view, that rape in Israel was seen as a crime against the father (if the girl was unmarried) or the husband. Children were under the authority of their fathers and one was not allowed to engage in sexual relations with a daughter unless the father had given permission for marriage. However, she is, I suspect, wrong if she intends to imply that rape in Israel was *only* an offence against the father or the husband. Rape was also seen as wronging a woman herself. Consider the words of Tamar to Amnon in 2 Samuel 13:12–13 before the rape: "Don't force me . . . What about me? Where could I get rid of my disgrace?" Consider her words after he rapes her and then casts her out in verse 16: "Sending me away would be a greater wrong than what you have already done to me." Notice, the crime is, from her perspective,

---

110. There are possible explanations for Dinah's silence which do not reflect the view that her perspective is irrelevant because it is female. For instance, Sternberg ("Sexual Politics") has suggested that Israelite rules on exogamy would rule the marriage out of court and that, consequently, Dinah's views for or against the marriage were really irrelevant, *but then so too were those of any of the male characters*. It is not only Dinah's views but also Jacob's which are absent from the story. A fascinating alternative view on Dinah's silence is that of feminist scholar Alice Keefe (see Keefe, "Rapes of Women").

111. Exum, "Who's Afraid?" 145.

112. See for instance, Pressler, "Sexual Violence and Deuteronomic Law." Pressler argues that behind the laws on violence against women lies the assumption that "female sexuality is male property" (ibid., 112).

113. Thistlethwaite, "'You May Enjoy the Spoil of Your Enemies,'" 59. Rashkow similarly writes, "And as the Genesis 34 narrative of Jacob's daughter Dinah makes clear, rape is not considered a violation of the daughter so much as *a theft of property* that deprives the father and necessitates compensation to him" (Rashkow, "Daughters and Fathers," 70). Besides my comment above to the effect that rape was also a crime against women in Israel, I think that it is dubious to claim that there is any form of compensation to Jacob in Genesis 34. Shechem offers a generous but standard payment of a מוהר (*môhār*) for the marriage. There is no obvious compensation mentioned, except that Shechem offers an unusually generous amount—but that is presented as Shechem's desperate attempt to persuade Jacob to allow the marriage and *not a compensation*.

primarily against her and not her father.[114] Furthermore, it is misleading, in my view, to talk of wives in Israel as sexual property.[115] Nevertheless, in spite of all that I have said, it remains the case that Genesis 34, along with most OT narrative, is androcentric. As I consider Dinah and Leah's views to be valuable it is, *at very least*, inadequate for an analysis of sexual justice or the ethics of rape.

The outcome of this discussion seems to me threefold. First, the fact that Genesis 34 is told from a male perspective does not, in and of itself, make it illegitimate for such perspectives are surely relevant. Second, the androcentricity need not even make it problematic in *a strong sense* for such perspectives are not necessarily inconsistent with female ones and do not rule out the latter's legitimacy. Third, if we grant the legitimacy of a female perspective then we grant *that there is more to be said about the incident at Shechem than is said by Genesis 34*. This need not be a threat to Genesis 34 but it does point towards the legitimacy of some kind of re-imagining the story from the perspective of the women involved (Leah, Dinah, and the Hivite women). This leads me on to a hermeneutical proposal made by Richard Bauckham.[116]

Bauckham argues that the Bible contains several narratives, or parts of narratives, which are gynocentric (seen from a female perspective). He pays special attention to the book of Ruth demonstrating how it reflects female perspectives on its subject matter.[117] "The value of Ruth

---

114. It could be argued in response that 2 Sam 13 presents Tamar's personal female perceptions of her rape and not the public male perceptions embodied in law codes such as those Pressler discusses. This distinction is too sharp. Tamar's perceptions would reflect the social attitudes of ancient Israelite society which were broader than the law codes but which played an important role in Israelite personal and social ethics (on the complex and obscure relations between OT laws and social norms see Rodd, *Glimpses of a Strange Land*). Such social attitudes were admittedly shaped by Israelite patriarchy so that the crime against the woman was not primarily one of violence against her autonomy but a crime against her honor and her chances of marriage. Nevertheless, rape was still seen as an offence *against the woman* as well as her father or husband (contra Rodd, *Glimpses*, 263–69). See the chapters in the volume by Jenni Williams on Deuteronomy, and Miriam Bier on Tamar.

115. Hugenberger, *Marriage as Covenant*, ch. 6; Wright, *God's People in God's Land*, ch. 6.

116. Bauckham, *Is The Bible Male?*; Bauckham, "Book of Ruth."

117. Which is not to claim that it was written by a female (Bauckham, *Is the Bible Male?* 6–7; Bauckham, "Book of Ruth," 29–31) nor is it to claim that Ruth subverts the patriarchal structures of OT society for it does not. "Ruth is the paradigmatic upholder of patriarchal ideology" (Fuchs, "Status and Role of Female Heroines," 78). Fuchs sees

as women's literature is precisely that it renders visible what is usually invisible."[118] Now, that a book such as Ruth is included within the canon serves as a counterbalance to the majority of androcentric texts. But it does more than that: "By revealing the Israelite women's world which is elsewhere invisible in biblical narrative it makes readers aware of the lack of women's perspectives elsewhere and it also authorizes them to supply just such a women's perspective elsewhere, expanding the hints and filling in the gaps which they can now see to be left by the narratives written purely or largely from a male perspective."[119] He concludes, "Even though the majority of biblical narratives are androcentric, there are enough authentically gynocentric narratives to counteract this dominant androcentricity, provided we allow them to do so."[120] Bauckham is saying that the *biblical canon itself* could legitimize such an imaginative approach to its androcentric narratives.[121]

A traditional Christian will need to ask what the connection is between the voice of the narrative and the voice of God. Perhaps it would be better to speak of the *voices* of a narrative for biblical narratives draw in different voices and different perspectives. Genesis 34 is a case in point, for we can clearly distinguish the perspectives of Jacob, his sons, Shechem, Hamor, and the Hivite men. Sternberg has shown how the narrator skilfully brings all the divergent voices of the characters into play, mediating between them and leading the reader towards certain evaluations of those characters. That is to say that the narrator too has a perspective and a voice and he aims to lead the reader to share this view. Should we identify the narrator's perspective with God's?[122] Sternberg thinks that the narratorial voice is actually presented as a prophetic voice

---

the book of Ruth as a book *from* a man's world and *for* a man's world but, although she is correct in seeing the book as one which operates within the norms of patriarchy, she fails to appreciate the degree of gynocentrism observed by Bauckham and others. See Brenner, *A Feminist Companion to Ruth* for various essays highlighting the book of Ruth as "a female text" (ibid., 14), "a collective creation of women's culture" (ibid., 139) and "an expression of women's culture and women's concerns" (ibid., 143).

118. Bauckham, *Is the Bible Male?* 14.

119. Ibid., 17.

120. Ibid., 23.

121. And, of course, a male reimagining of the gynocentric sections of Ruth is also legitimized.

122. The notion that a God's-eye view is neutral in some way is not a Christian one. A God's-eye view would be one in full possession of the facts and pure in its moral judgements.

identified with God's.[123] However, this is highly questionable[124] and, even *if* Sternberg is right, from a canonical view God's perspective on any particular incident cannot be exhausted by that of a narrator, even if the narrator captures part of it. We could say then that the narrator's perspective is only "identified" with God's in this weaker sense. The canon of the Hebrew Bible and the New Testament both endorse multiple, authorized perspectives on the same events indicating that no single telling of the event claims to pick out *every* morally and theologically salient feature, and numerous different perspectives can stand side by side in harmony. What, for instance, is God's perspective on Jesus? That of some particular Gospel writer? Of Paul? Of Peter? Of Revelation? God's view cannot be exhausted by any one of their perspectives nor by their cumulative totality. Further, as Miriam Bier points out in her essay on 2 Samuel 13 (see ch. 6), even God's silence may be a *speaking silence*.

Nevertheless, for the traditional Christian, all the biblical narrators' perspectives are divinely authorised as appropriate ones and together they shape and inform readerly perspectives. None of them would be seen to *conflict* with divine perspectives[125] and God speaks through them to his people recommending ways of seeing situations. However, we should not infer from the authorized nature of biblical narratives that the narrator says all that is worth saying or exhausts the divine perspective. This seems to me to make imaginative retellings of Dinah's feelings unthreatening to the canonical account—at least in principle. So long as they are not thought by the Christian community to have the status of the canonical telling then the enterprise seems perfectly legitimate.

Some reflections on biblical authority may be in order here. One cannot move without thought from the claim that a particular biblical text was inspired by God to the claim that it is normative or authoritative. Classical Christian views of the Bible have seen divine authority

---

123. Sternberg, *Poetics*, ch. 2.

124. Wolterstorff, *Divine Discourse*, 245–52.

125. Perhaps Wolterstorff would nuance this to suggest that God would be saying what the narrator is saying *unless we have good grounds for thinking that God would not be saying that* (ibid., ch. 12). Exactly what would count as good reasons is then a crucial question as the door could be open to anybody to reject illocutionary stances of biblical narrators on the grounds that they think that God would never take such a stance. The whole notion that God appropriates human illocutionary stances could be ultimately undermined in this way. A canonical perspective could serve as a control and guide in such cases.

mediated through *the canon as a whole* rather than its individual parts in isolation.[126] The Bible is not normative because it is composed of normative parts as if normativity is found as much in those parts in isolation. Nor is normativity something which supervenes upon the complex intertextual links of the completed canon as if at some point the collection "went critical" and suddenly, as if by magic, the authority appeared. Rather, I suggest, each part of the whole is inspired and, in its original contexts, mediated some mode of divine authority.[127] However, when incorporated within the canon the way in which they are normative is modified by interactions with fellow texts. Thus any part of the Bible can *only* function normatively for the church *when seen within the context of the whole*. Clearly, as the canon has grown and the plotline has moved on, the way in which different texts function normatively changes.[128]

So, returning to feminist concerns, even if a biblical narrative sets out models for appropriate wifely behaviour (say) one cannot simply *assume* that those models are still normative today in the same way as they were when the texts were originally produced. It seems to me that the very nature of the canon invites a certain kind of relativizing of texts in light of the whole. Biblical narratives can, in principle, be supplemented and "relativized" by other biblical texts[129] and by archaeological finds without threatening their inspiration or their authority. In the context of gender issues the kind of relativizing that I am proposing does not

---

126. Some feminists see the canon itself as a patriarchal construction. For a brief but helpful critique see Bauckham, "Book of Ruth," 44–45.

127. Clearly different genres mediate divine authority in different ways (compare the Ten Commandments with Proverbs) and thus I speak of *modes* of authority. Further clarification is obviously required here. It may be that the notion of authority is not elastic enough to cover all the biblical texts and should be abandoned in some cases.

128. I am focusing in this chapter on the role of the canon in opening up and closing down various interpretations of the biblical text. But I am not suggesting that other factors do not play a similar regulative role. Theological beliefs (including christological beliefs), for instance, can guide readers in assessing the adequacy of interpretations as *Christian* interpretations. But space does not permit an exploration of such theological regulators.

129. I suggest that the biblical plotline itself prioritises certain key texts and themes theologically over others. For instance, Gen 1–2 has long been recognised by Christians as carrying a priority over Esther (say) or Deuteronomy in theological considerations of gender relations. This is because Gen 1–2 reflects the way God set things up in the beginning prior to sin's distortions (see Matt 19:1–8).

relativize the androcentric texts *in every respect* but simply in their androcentrism.[130]

Let me bring these reflections to Genesis 34 and briefly explore the limits and legitimacy of restoring the female perspectives. Genesis 34 simply does not provide the information from which to construct Dinah's viewpoint, let alone those of Leah or the Hivite women. In the story her view is not a gap that needs to be filled in order to make sense of the narrative but a blank—an information gap to which the narrator does not draw attention.[131] Herein lies the potential danger of "authoring the secret diaries of Dinah"[132]—"Anyone who wanted answers to these questions [about Dinah's view] would have no option but to invent their own."[133] One could invent a range of totally contradictory perspectives for Dinah and none of them could claim to be anything more than the imaginative reconstructions of the reader. This is only a problem if one thinks that one is finding the "right" answer given by the text rather than supplementing the text with informed yet *imaginative* stories. Some reflections are in order.

An *exegesis* of Genesis 34 should make no reference to Dinah's views as they are simply irrelevant to the storytelling of the chapter.[134] This does little for issues of women's justice or dignity, but I have attempted to argue that it need do nothing to harm them either *so long as* it does not legitimize the broader claim that Dinah's view does not matter *at all*.

If we grant, as we must, that the female views are not irrelevant, then we open up the legitimacy and possibility for imaginative, Midrashic reflections on how Dinah, Leah, or the Hivite women may have felt. Such reflections will not make the pretence to exegesis, but will simply claim the status of readerly reflections—using the text as a springboard—and not explanations of the narrator's interests.

Such readerly reflections must be grounded upon the text and a careful reading of it and they will never replace the text. Genesis 34 will be the basis for every fresh readerly reflection. Any reflection which misreads the actual text would thereby falsify itself. The biblical narrator

---

130. With Bauckham, "Book of Ruth," 44.
131. On gaps and blanks see Sternberg, *Poetics*, 235–58.
132. Noble, "Balanced Reading," 200.
133. Ibid., 198.
134. Rightly, Noble, "Balanced Reading."

may not share our concerns or interests but that need not stop us reading a text from the perspective of those concerns and interests. The narrator may say things which have a bearing on our concerns and provide fuel for our own reflections. Reflections on Dinah's view on her rape could draw on the story of the rape of Tamar in 2 Samuel 13 which, I would argue, deliberately alludes to Genesis 34. The narrator in 2 Samuel sees the importance of the view of the rape victim and a reader could thus claim scriptural support for reflecting on the Shechem incident from an imaginative reconstruction of Dinah's view. Schroer comments on 2 Samuel 13 that "a woman reading this text will note that the narrators of the story are on Tamar's side. They declare her to be free from any guilt, stress her wisdom and thoughtfulness, and feel sympathy for her. And this is how the story of a sexual assault at the royal court is at least snatched from the jaws of the final injustice, that of being silenced. In Israel, the victims of violence are remembered."[135] Perhaps a text like Psalm 55 could also be brought into intertextual relationship with our texts. Ulrike Bail has argued that it is a woman's complaint to God about a sexual assault by a man close to her.[136] Even if this is not correct the text could be *re*appropriated in such a way. Such can only enrich one's reading of Scripture.

Third, for readers who consider the biblical text inspired, readerly reflections will not be able to reject the narrator's perspective as false. This is not likely to impress some feminist readers. Alice Bach argues that feminist readers must suspect and resist the biblical narrator. Clearly, such a method *can* and *has been* applied to the Bible as to many texts but *prioritizing* an orientation of suspicion as opposed to one of trust in approaching the Christian Scriptures is alien to the Christian tradition.[137]

---

135. Schottroff, Schroer, and Wacker, *Feminist Interpretation*, 55. Judg 19 is often seen as a text that dehumanizes women in the grotesque brutality dealt to the Levite's concubine. However, the text very clearly presents the rape and murder of the woman as a dreadful deed indicating how serious the decline of Israel has become. In no way is the deed presented as legitimate nor is the Levite's shocking behaviour in throwing her out to be abused excused. Her story is told and must be retold *in memoriam* of women victims of violence (see the essay in this volume by Nik Ansell).

136. Bail, "Vernimm, Gott, Mein Geber."

137. I do not want to suggest that a feminist hermeneutic is one of suspicion *as opposed to* one of faith. It should be obvious from Section I that many feminists seek to *combine* both. My point is that a feminist hermeneutic will usually *begin* with suspicion and then see what is left for faith whilst a Christian hermeneutic will *begin* with faith and suspicion will play a role subsidiary to it. Alternatively one may tone this down

Feminists may often read the Bible in this way but to do so is not to read with a traditional Christian hermeneutic. Christian *Midrash* on OT narratives may see the women's view as either running along the grain of the text (in line with the narrator) or perpendicular to the text (neither with nor against the narrator[138]) or against the text.[139] However, if a woman's re-imagined perspective does run against the grain of the text it is *prima facie* subverted by the narrator who, for the Christian community, retains his "authorized perspective" which, whilst incomplete, will not—normally—be seen to be wrong. It may be felt that this hamstrings some important feminist critiques of the Bible and I am forced to agree. Nevertheless, I believe that to surrender the fundamental biblical hermeneutic of faith for one of suspicion is to pay a price too high.

---

and argue that any critique of the biblical narrators must be done by means of a critical principle *rooted in the biblical metanarrative itself* rather than one imposed from the outside (Watson, *Text*, ch. 11; Middleton and Walsh, *Truth*, ch. 8). However, pitting the whole *against* its parts seems at very least problematic as a method in conservative Christian hermeneutics. I can see that the whole can *complement or relativize* the parts but I am somewhat cautious about the idea that it can be used to *reject* the parts.

138. Much of the Dreamworks cartoon *The Prince of Egypt* would be what I call "reading perpendicular to the text."

139. One could imagine that "Telling Queen Jezebel's Story," say, would involve reading against the narrator. However, the traditional Christian will not want to subvert the narrator's condemnation of Jezebel even if they may seek to understand her in a more rounded way. The biblical narrator may not tell the *whole* truth about Jezebel but he does tell the truth.

BIBLIOGRAPHY

Aalders, G. C. *Genesis*, Volume 2. Translated by J. Vriend. Grand Rapids: Zondervan, 1981.

Anonymous. *Anchoritic Spirituality*. Translated by A. Savage and N. Watson. New York: Paulist, 1991.

Babbington, Gervase. *Works Containing Comfortable Notes upon the Five Books of Moses*. London, 1615.

Bach, A. "With a Song in Her Heart: Listening to Scholars Listening for Miriam." In *Women in the Hebrew Bible*, edited by A. Bach, 419–27. London: Routledge, 1999.

―――, ed. *Women in the Hebrew Bible: A Reader*. London: Routledge, 1999.

Bail, U. "Vernimm, Gott, Mein Geber: Psalm 55 und Gewalt gegen Frauen." In *Feministische Hermeneutik und Erstes Testament*, edited by H. Jahnaw et al., 67–84. Stuttgart: Kohlhammer, 1994.

Bauckham, R. "The Book of Ruth and the Possibility of a Feminist Canonical Hermeneutic." *Biblical Interpretation* 5 (1997) 29–45.

―――. *Is the Bible Male? The Book of Ruth and Biblical Narrative*. Cambridge: Grove Books, 1996.

Bechtel, L. "What if Dinah Was Not Raped (Genesis 34)?" *Journal for the Study of the Old Testament* 62 (1994) 19–36.

Bernard of Clairvaux. *Selected Works*. Translated by G. R. Evans. New York: Paulist, 1987.

Bird, P. *Missing Persons and Mistaken Identities: Women and Gender in Ancient Israel*. Minneapolis: Fortress, 1997.

Bledstein, A. "Are Women Cursed in Genesis 3:16?" In *Feminist Companion to Genesis*, edited by A. Brenner, 142–45. Sheffield: Sheffield Academic, 1993.

Blyth, C. "Redeemed by His Love? The Characterization of Shechem in Genesis 34." *Journal for the Study of the Old Testament* 33 (2008) 3–18.

―――. *Terrible Silence, Eternal Silence: A Consideration of Dinah's Voicelessness in the Text and Interpretative Traditions of Genesis 34*. PhD diss., University of Edinburgh, 2008. http://www.era.lib.ed.ac.uk/handle/1842/2593

Brenner, A., ed. *A Feminist Companion to Ruth*. Sheffield, UK: Sheffield Academic, 1993.

Calvin, J. *A Commentary on Genesis*. Translated by J. King. London: Banner of Truth, 1965.

Clines, D. J. A. "What Does Eve Do to Help? And Other Irredeemably Androcentric Orientations in Genesis 1–3." In *What Does Eve Do to Help?*, edited by D. J. A. Clines, 45–48. Sheffield, UK: Sheffield Academic, 1990.

Earl, D. "Towards a Christian Hermeneutic of Old Testament Narrative: Why Genesis 34 Fails to Find Christian Significance." *Catholic Biblical Quarterly* (forthcoming).

Exum, J. C. "Murder They Wrote: Ideology and the Manipulation of Female Presence in Biblical Narrative." In *The Pleasure of Her Text*, edited by A. Bach, 45–67. Philadelphia: Trinity Press International, 1990.

―――. "Second Thoughts about Secondary Characters: Women in Exodus 1:8—2:10." In *A Feminist Companion to Exodus to Deuteronomy*, edited by A. Brenner, 75–87. Sheffield, UK: Sheffield Academic, 1994.

―――. "Who's Afraid of 'The Endangered Ancestress?'" In *Women in the Hebrew Bible*, edited by A. Bach, 141–56. London: Routledge, 1999.

―――. "'You Shall Let Every Daughter Live': A Study of Ex 1:8–2:10." *Semeia* 28 (1983) 63–82.

Farley M. and S. Jones, eds. *Liberating Eschatology: Essays in Honor of Letty Russell.* Louisville: Westminster/John Knox, 1999.

Farley, M. "Feminist Consciousness and the Interpretation of Scripture." In *Feminist Interpretation of the Bible*, edited by L. Russell, 41–51. Philadelphia: Westminster, 1985.

Fewell, D. and D. Gunn. "Tipping the Balance: Sternberg's Reader and the Rape of Dinah." *Journal of Biblical Literature* 110 (1991) 193–211.

Fischer, G. "Die Redewendung דבר על־לב im AT: Ein Beitrag zum Verstandnis von Jes 40:2." *Biblica* 65 (1984) 244–50.

Fleishman, J. "Shechem and Dinah in the Light of Non-Biblical and Biblical Sources." *Zeitschrift für die Alttestamentliche Wissenschaft* 116 (2004) 12–32.

Fuchs, E. "Status and Role of Female Heroines in the Biblical Narratives." In *Women in the Hebrew Bible*, edited by A. Bach, 77–84. London: Routledge, 1999.

Gray, M. *Redeeming the Dream: Feminism, Redemption, and the Christian Tradition.* London: SPCK, 1989.

Hamilton, V. P. *The Book of Genesis: Chapters 18–50.* NICOT. Grand Rapids: Eerdmans, 1995.

Hankore, D. "Reading and Translating Genesis 28:10—35:15 as a Votive Narrative, with Special Reference to the Dinah Story." PhD diss., Africa International University, Nairobi, Kenya, 2010.[140]

Henry, M. *An Exposition of the Five Books of Moses.* London, 1725.

Hugenberger, G. P. *Marriage as Covenant: A Study of Biblical Law and Ethics Concerning Marriage Developed from the Perspective of Malachi.* Leiden: Brill, 1994.

Jeansonne, S. P. *The Women of Genesis: From Sarah to Potiphar's Wife.* Minneapolis: Fortress, 1990.

Kass, L. R. "Regarding Daughters and Sisters: The Rape of Dinah." *Commentary* 93 (1992) 29–38.

Keefe, A. "Rapes of Women/Wars of Men." *Semeia* 61 (1993) 79–94.

Kock, M. "A Cross-Cultural Critique of Western Feminism." In *After Eden: Facing the Challenge of Gender Reconciliation*, edited by M. S. van Leeuwen, 70–113. Grand Rapids: Eerdmans, 1993.

Laffey, A. L. *An Introduction to the Old Testament: A Feminist Perspective.* Minneapolis: Fortress, 1988.

Neusner, J. *Genesis Rabbah: The Judaic Commentary to the Book of Genesis.* 3 Vols. Atlanta: Scholars, 1985.

Luther, M. *Luther's Works.* Vol. 6. St Louis: Concordia & Philadelphia: Fortress, 1986.

Meyers, C. *Discovering Eve: Ancient Israelite Women in Context.* Oxford: Oxford University Press, 1988.

———. "Gender Roles in Genesis 3:16 Revisited." In *Feminist Companion to Genesis*, edited by A. Brenner, 118–41. Sheffield, UK: Sheffield Academic, 1993.

———. "Miriam the Musician." In *A Feminist Companion to Exodus to Deuteronomy*, edited by A. Brenner, 207–30. Sheffield, UK: Sheffield Academic, 1994.

Niditch, S. "Eroticism and Death in the Tale of Jael." In *Women in the Hebrew Bible*, edited by A. Bach, 305–15. London: Routledge, 1999.

Noble, P. "A 'Balanced' Reading of the Rape of Dinah: Some Exegetical and Methodological Observations." *Biblical Interpretation* 4 (1996) 173–203.

---

140. The thesis will be published in 2012 by Pickwick.

Parry, R. A. *Old Testament Story and Christian Ethics: The Rape of Dinah as a Case Study*. Milton Keynes: Paternoster, 2004.
Pressler, C. "Sexual Violence and Deuteronomic Law." In *Feminist Companion to Exodus to Deuteronomy*, 102–12. Sheffield, UK: Sheffield Academic, 1994.
Osiek, C. "The Feminist and the Bible: Hermeneutical Alternatives." In *Feminist Perspectives on Biblical Scholarship*, edited by A. Y. Collins, 93–106. Atlanta: Scholars', 1985.
Rashkow, I. *The Phallacy of Genesis: A Feminist-Psychoanalytic Approach*. Louisville: Westminster/John Knox, 1993.
Rashkow, I. 'Daughters and Fathers in Genesis . . . or, What Is Wrong with This Picture?' In *The New Literary Criticism of the Hebrew Bible*, edited by D. J. A. Clines and C. Exum, 250–65. Sheffield, UK: Sheffield Academic, 1993.
Rodd, C. S. *Glimpses of a Strange Land: Studies in Old Testament Ethics*. London: T. & T. Clark, 2001.
Ruether, R. R. "Feminist Interpretation: A Method of Correlation." In *Feminist Interpretation of the Bible*, edited by L. Russell, 111–24. Philadelphia: Westminster, 1995.
———. *Sexism and God-Talk: Towards a Feminist Theology*. London: SCM, 1983.
Russell, L. "Authority and the Challenge of Feminist Interpretations." In *Feminist Interpretation of the Bible*, edited by L. Russell, 137–48. Philadelphia: Westminster, 1995.
Sakenfeld, K. D. "Feminist Perspectives on the Bible and Theology: An Introduction to Selected Issues and Literature." *Interpretation* 42 (1988) 5–18.
———. "Feminist Uses of Biblical Materials." In *Feminist Interpretation of the Bible*, edited by L. Russell, 55–64. Philadelphia: Westminster, 1995.
Salkin, J. K. "Dinah, the Torah's Forgotten Woman." *Judaism* 35 (1986) 284–89.
Sarna, N. M. *Genesis*. Philadelphia: Jewish Publication Society, 1989.
Scholz, S. "Through Whose Eyes? A 'Right' Reading of Genesis 34." In *Genesis: A Feminist Companion to the Bible (2nd Series)*, edited by A. Brenner, 150–71. Sheffield, UK: Sheffield Academic, 1998.
Schroeder, J. A. "The Rape of Dinah: Luther's Interpretation of a Biblical Narrative." *Sixteenth Century Journal* 28 (1997) 775–91.
———. *Dinah's Lament: The Legacy of Sexual Violence in Christian Interpretation*. Minneapolis: Fortress, 2007.
Segal, N. Review of *The Poetics of Biblical Narrative* by Meir Sternberg. *Vetus Testamentum* 38 (1988) 247–48.
Shemesh, Y. "Rape is Rape is Rape: The Story of Dinah and Shechem (Genesis 34)." *Zeitschrift für die Alttestamentliche Wissenschaft* 119 (2007) 2–21.
Steinberg, N. *Kinship and Marriage in Genesis: A Household Economics Perspective* Minneapolis: Fortress, 1993.
Sternberg, M. "Biblical Poetics and Sexual Politics: From Reading to Counter Reading." *Journal of Biblical Literature* 111 (1992) 463–88.
———. *The Poetics of Biblical Narrative: Ideological Literature and the Drama of Reading*. Bloomington: Indiana University Press, 1987.
Thiselton, A. *New Horizons in Hermeneutics: The Theory and Practice of Transforming Biblical Reading*. Exeter: Paternoster, 1992, 442–43.
Thistlethwaite, S. B. "'You May Enjoy the Spoil of Your Enemies'—Rape as a Biblical Metaphor for War." *Semeia* 61 (1993) 59–75.

Tolbert, M. A. "Protestant Feminists and the Bible: On the Horns of a Dilemma." In *The Pleasure of Her Text: Feminist Readings of Biblical and Historical Texts*, edited by A. Bach, 5–23. Philadelphia: Trinity, 1990.

Trible, P. *God and the Rhetoric of Sexuality*. London: SCM, 1978.

Various. "Living between the Times: Bad News and Good News about Gender Relations." In *After Eden: Facing the Challenge of Gender Reconciliation*, edited by M. S. van Leeuwen, 1–16. Grand Rapids: Eerdmans, 1993.

Watson, F. *Text, Church and World: Biblical Interpretation in Theological Perspective*. Edinburgh: T. & T. Clark, 1994.

Walsh, B. and R. Middleton. *Truth is Stranger Than It Used to Be: Biblical Faith in a Postmodern Age*. London: SPCK, 1995.

Wenham, G. J. *Genesis 16–50*. Dallas: Word, 1994.

Wolterstorff, N. *Divine Discourse: Philosophical Reflections on the Claim That God Speaks*. Cambridge: Cambridge University Press, 1995.

Wright, C. J. H. *God's People in God's Land: Family, Land, and Property in the Old Testament*. Carlisle: Paternoster, 1990.

3

Hermeneutics by Numbers?

Case Studies in Feminist and Evangelical Interpretation of the Book of Numbers

RICHARD S. BRIGGS

ANY DISCUSSION OF HERMENEUTICS as it operates at the interface between evangelicalism and feminism invites the charge of being an elusive subject caught between two massively contested approaches, drowning under waves of abstraction and generalisation. Just defining these terms could keep us busy forever. So instead I shall examine three carefully focused case studies from the book of Numbers, in order to see what is involved in negotiating the claims of evangelical interpretation and feminist interpretation. The thesis, in due course, will be that both approaches to the biblical text highlight some features of it and leave others submerged, whether deliberately or inadvertently, though this evaluation accords differently with the declared aims of the two approaches. In particular, a key issue is the extent to which either of these approaches occupies themselves with probing and interacting with the theological subject matter of the text, an area in which there are weaknesses in each case.

THE TEXTS

Three texts, or complexes of texts, present themselves for consideration from the strange book of Numbers, a book perhaps more helpfully titled, in the Hebrew tradition, "In the Wilderness," and a book notoriously difficult to hold in a coherent interpretive perspective.[1] In canonical order the relevant passages for our enquiry are, first, the case of the woman suspected of adultery in 5:11–31, secondly the various texts relating to Miriam, in particular the tale of chapter 12, and thirdly, the two texts in 27:1–11 and 36:1–12 usually described as referring to the daughters of Zelophehad, and concerning the five named women Mahlah, Noah, Hoglah, Milcah, and Tirzah.

In fact this selection covers almost every mention of women in the book in any case. There are only three (or possibly four) other named women in Numbers. Two are mentioned in lists: Jochebed (26:59), in the midst of the second of the book's censuses doubtless because she was, as this verse states, "mother to Aaron, Moses and their sister Miriam"; and Serah (26:46), Jacob's granddaughter, named also in passing, though it is not clear why, in Genesis 46:17.[2] More significant in the narrative is "Cozbi daughter of Zut" (25:15, 18), the daughter of one of Midian's leaders who is caught up in the incident which sparks the plague of chapter 25, and is killed by Phinehas in the heat of the action, as it were (25:8). Verse 18 hints that she may be held responsible in some sense for seducing the Israelite man concerned, though this is not clear in the earlier narrative. A possible fourth woman is Zipporah, who may be the wife of Moses in view in 12:1, though this is a much-contested question, and will be noted briefly in the discussion of Miriam below. Beyond this there are even very few unnamed women in view: the occasional piece of legislation allows for "either a man or woman" (5:6; cf. also 6:2), and in a couple of cases women are clearly in view as part of the general discussion (18:11, for example) or as the subject of a legal ruling (chapter 30) although in chapter 30 the focus is partly the extent to which a husband might inadvertently ratify his wife's "thoughtless utterance" (v. 6). There are also mentions of Dathan's and Abiram's wives (16:27–33); the women of Moab at the beginning of the account of the plague in chapter 25, and some Midianite women in chapter 31, but that's it, as far as feminine presence in the book goes.[3] In general, English translations

---

1. The most influential proposal remains that of Olson, *The Death of the Old and the Birth of the New*, whose thesis is clear in his title: that the book sets up a fundamental contrast between the two generations subject to census in chapters 1 and 26.

2. Bronner explores the wide-ranging midrashim that sprung up around Sera(c)h in "Serach and the Exodus."

3. Much of the data for this survey is conveniently gathered, with brief comment, in Meyers *et al*, eds., *Women in Scripture*, 65, 103, 127–29, 154, 170–71, 216–22.

obscure the fact that even references to "Israelites" in the book are to "the sons of Israel" (*běnê-yisrāʾēl*), so that, for example, the ruling about wearing tassels on one's clothes (15:37–41), so public and prominent in later Jewish practice, is understood to apply only to men.[4] And more broadly, one might suggest that neither sex nor gender is a topic that looms large on the interpretive horizons of the book of Numbers.

As so often, one of the factors in the hermeneutical debate in and around feminist concerns is the interpretive significance of the absence of women, an observation always complicated by the conspicuous presence of a few women (most notably, here, Miriam). Such presences make it impossible to argue that the general absence was a non-ideological reflection of a world where such possibilities had not occurred to them. Clearly Israel could see that women could prophesy, take the lead in worship, and so forth, but such accounts remained minority reports. It is to the exceptions that we now turn, taking them in reverse order because this helps to clarify some of the issues. No attempt will be made to offer comprehensive analyses of the massive literature on all these passages, but rather a significant and representative set of voices from various relevant quarters will be brought into dialogue with each other.

THE DAUGHTERS OF ZELOPHEHAD

Katherine Doob Sakenfeld's Princeton inaugural address in the late 1980s took as its topic "Feminist Biblical Interpretation," and focused on this text about the daughters of Zelophehad as its case study.[5] The two relevant passages tell a story in two distinct movements. In chapter 27 the five women stand before Moses and before Eleazar the priest and explain that their father, who had no part in Korah's rebellion (chapter 16), has nevertheless died in the wilderness, with no sons. As a result, his inheritance will pass out of the family. Moses enquires of YHWH about the matter, and the result is a ruling that the inheritance should indeed pass to daughters in such cases. Somewhat unexpectedly, the issue recurs in the final chapter of the book, where the male leaders of Zelophehad's own tribe (the Gileadites of Manasseh) bring a complaint. As a result of this ruling, they point out, land can now pass out of the tribe, since

---

4. See, for example, Sakenfeld, *Numbers*, 96, who suggests that the text is not explicitly about men (given that "sons of Israel" could refer to all at the time), but that it is understood that way in the tradition.

5. See Sakenfeld, "Feminist."

if these women marry out of the tribe their land will pass to their new husbands. This time the ruling is that the women must "marry who they think best, only it must be into a clan of their father's tribe." (36:6) What do the various parties to our conversation make of this tale?[6]

Sakenfeld's account, summarized in her later commentary, actually operates by way of comparing and contrasting three diverse feminist approaches to this text, which she labels as follows. First there is the "formalist" and literary approach, focusing on the narrative received as a literary text, and famously exemplified in the careful exegetical work of Phyllis Trible. Secondly a "culturally cued literary reading" broadens its interpretive constraints compared to the first approach, looking for a sense of what was "imaginable or probable for speakers and hearers in a particular ancient patriarchal culture." This is the approach she herself prefers. Finally there is a more historical approach which seeks to reconstruct a plausible picture of women's life in ancient Israel less liable to be skewed by later Western constructions of male and female, an approach found in the work of, for example, Phyllis Bird.[7] This remains a helpful taxonomy. How does it work with Numbers 27 and 36?

Sakenfeld's own interpretation of these texts begins with the observation that the focal concern of both stories "is a problem faced by a male in a patriarchal culture," whether the problem of a man's dying with no sons, thereby losing his name, or the problem of losing land and the subsequent economic implications, with the daughters reduced to "little more than pawns."[8] In her subsequent commentary she notes that while the narrator presents the daughters as obedient (and thereby representative of the obedience of the "new" generation at the end of the book), and living happily ever after, the reader might pause a little and ask just how far this set of judgments served to rein in the women to the men's agenda.[9] Feminist scholars may be particularly predisposed to look at whether there is significance in the difference between Moses' enquiring of YHWH in the apparently priestly setting of 27:5, and the resolution passed down directly by the men (though reportedly from YHWH) who are meeting in the apparently non-sacral setting of chapter 36. Does the

---

6. Much of the scholarship on these texts is reviewed in Shemesh, "Gender Perspective."

7. Sakenfeld, "Feminist," 161.

8. Ibid., 157–58.

9. Sakenfeld, *Numbers*, 187–88.

text here hint that YHWH is somewhat more positive to women than Israel's male leaders?[10] In the words of Ankie Sterring, do we have here an inspiring tale in chapter 27, followed in chapter 36 by an account of the male backlash that accompanies women's achievement?[11]

What do evangelical commentators say (and what do they not say) regarding these texts?[12] Some say (relatively) little. Gordon Wenham describes chapter 27 as extremely interesting "from a legal point of view," a story that highlights the daughters' piety; while chapter 36, whose judgment is received at face value, celebrates "dutiful compliance" and is "a fitting conclusion to the book of Numbers itself."[13] What one might call "literary coherence" is a feature of evangelical interpretation of Numbers, keen to show that the book has a literary purpose and integrity. Such an emphasis is doubtless a riposte to the perceived "charge" that Numbers is a redacted collection of sources, as in Seybold's oft-quoted phrase that the book is the "junk room of the priestly code."[14] Ulrich, for instance, thinks that the two questions raised by chapters 27 and 36 are "why did the author separate them?" and "why did the author end the book with such a provincial ruling?," and when he has resolved these two points to his own satisfaction, the only comment on the substance of the text is that "Zelophehad's daughters exemplified the faith that tenaciously clung to the Lord despite adverse circumstances."[15] Other evangelical commentators also tend to be brief on these texts, arguing over questions of when it was written and how the texts relate to other texts on property rights, while engaging relatively little with the substance of the two judgments presented. Typical is Budd who stops at the point of asserting a theological emphasis on the rights of women in property law, exactly as the text relates the judgments, without actual evaluation of the case(s).[16] One place where one might look for an evangelical feminist

---

10. Shemesh discusses such views, though concluding that they have no basis in the text itself, "Gender Perspective," 93.

11. Sterring, "Daughters," esp. 98. Sterring notes that the daughters do eventually receive their inheritance in Joshua 17:1–7.

12. We restrict ourselves to works self-described as evangelical in some way, though we shall revisit this point in the conclusion.

13. Wenham, *Numbers* (1981), 191–94, 239–40.

14. Klaus Seybold, as cited in Wenham, *Numbers* (1997), 40.

15. Ulrich, "Zelophehad's Daughters," esp. 529, 538.

16. Budd, *Numbers*, 302–3. Budd's commentary is perhaps on the fringes of what might typically be thought to be an "evangelical" approach.

reading of these texts is in the entry on Numbers in IVP's *Women's Bible Commentary*. Here Dorothy Irvin offers some general thoughts on property rights, before suggesting that Moses' referral to the Lord rendered the judgments passed in these stories "divine and unquestionable." In conclusion: "we see that ancient Israel had legal provisions to ensure that women, with their different status under the law, were fairly provided for, as fairness was envisioned at that time."[17]

Even on a cursory survey it is striking how little engaged with the theological and ethical substance of the text much of this evangelical commentary is. At the risk of generalization, we find self-described evangelical commentary concerned primarily with the tasks of (a) accounting for the text in literary and historical terms, and (b) defending the judgments of the text. The first of these points typically leads to a focus on matters of literary coherence and historical appropriateness (e.g., several comment on why a law about land distribution should be discussed at a point in the biblical narrative where Israel is in the wilderness). The second incorporates a great exegetical strength, at least when done well, which is the careful elucidation of what judgments are in fact present in the text.[18] Nevertheless, theological and ethical comment is a little thin, and where ethical issues are in view at all the argument is generally that these texts are self-evidently just and are also good for women. In fact surprisingly little is made of the apparent conclusion that the daughters of Zelophehad get a counter-culturally strong deal in ancient legal terms,[19] and none (that I encountered) thought that chapter 36 in any way undermined the settlement of chapter 27. One would not guess, from reading evangelical works, that Numbers 27 "has become a cultural model of a struggle to obtain one's rights under both divine and human morality and justice."[20]

By way of an interim conclusion, let me suggest that both feminist and evangelical approaches successfully highlight certain features of these texts. The former engage with the theological and ethical is-

---

17. Irvin, "Numbers," 81.

18. An interesting case study might be how Numbers 36:4 relates to the Jubilee, cited as an irrelevant addition by Noth (*Numbers*, 257), where evangelicals (among others, of course) pay careful attention to how this reference might be designed to function.

19. Though this is noted as part of a general argument in this direction by Webb, *Slaves, Women and Homosexuals*, 77.

20. Shemesh, "Gender Perspective," 80, with an impressive list of examples.

sues, though their "gender perspective" typically leads to what Shemesh describes as an ill-fated attempt to turn the daughters of Zelophehad into forerunners of modern feminism.[21] As Shemesh rather interestingly notes, perhaps picking up on a certain individualism prominent among interpreters today, "Feminist scholarship has, of course, been bothered by the restriction placed on Zelophehad's daughters' freedom of choice; but there is no proof that it troubled the daughters themselves."[22] The counterweight to such feminist suspicion is the evangelical tradition, which evidences no sign of hermeneutical suspicion with regard to the judgments of Moses. We shall see, in due course, that such suspicion is inextricably related to construals of the text's authority, but first we turn to the other case studies.

MIRIAM

"Buried within Scripture are bits and pieces of a story awaiting discovery. It highlights the woman Miriam." Thus wrote Phyllis Trible in her influential article "Bringing Miriam Out of the Shadows," a parade example of Sakenfeld's first kind of formalist-literary feminist scholarship.[23] It remains the best introduction to a close reading of the Miriam texts, which begin, without Miriam being named, in Moses' birth narratives in Exodus 2; incorporate the famous Song of the Sea in Exodus 15; and which culminate (canonically) with a reference to Israel's three-fold leadership of Moses, Aaron and Miriam as divinely appointed to lead in Mic 6:4.[24] In Numbers, Miriam's complaint about Moses and subsequent punishment occupies chapter 12, and notice of her death is given at 20:1.[25]

The narrative of Numbers 12 sees Miriam and Aaron speak against Moses "because of the Cushite woman whom he had married" (v.1), though in fact the account rapidly devolves on to questions of prophetic legitimacy, as a follow on to the story of prophecy in the camp

---

21. Ibid., 80–95, especially 82.

22. Ibid., 94.

23. Trible, "Shadows," cited here from the reprint in Brenner, ed., *Feminist Companion*, 166.

24. For all these texts see also Burns, *Miriam*, and the incisive analysis of Gafney, *Daughters of Miriam*, 76–85.

25. She is also listed in the genealogy of 26:59; see Burns, *Miriam*, 85–90, highlighting that the memory of her thus lives on in priestly circles.

in 11:24–30. Angered by the complaint, YHWH inflicts leprosy on Miriam, before Moses intercedes on her behalf, and she serves seven days punishment outside the camp. The story is a flashpoint of feminist and other criticism, in part due to the difficulty of discerning whether the Cushite woman is Zipporah, or a second wife, and what implications that has with regard to questions of how Moses is treating women, and then whether the complaint is related to her black skin color, Cush being modern-day Ethiopia.[26] It is relevant to note (a) the plural subject, Miriam and Aaron, making the complaint in verse 1 but with a feminine singular verb (*wattĕdabēr*, spoke, v. 1); (b) the punishment being inflicted on Miriam only (v. 10); (c) the fact that Miriam's skin is "white as snow" standing in antithesis to the black skin of Moses' wife; and (d) that in Scripture Miriam is only ever called a prophet (*nĕbîʾâ*, prophetess) in Exod 15:20, in respect of which Burns concludes that the biblical portrait of Miriam is in fact of a leader, and the label "prophetess" in Exodus is a loose marker of identity rather than a description of her role in particular.[27]

Feminist commentary on Miriam and her significance extends down through the centuries from early Jewish sources to a veritable explosion of writing in recent decades.[28] Much of this writing is in the mode of hermeneutical recovery, *à la* Trible, or in other words is seeking to dig behind the canonical presentation of Miriam to find a more significant figure than the final text seems to present, hence "bringing Miriam out of the shadows." The argument is that even the best efforts of patriarchal redactors have been unable to erase the trace of her remarkable influence, whether as putative originator of the Song of the Sea now attributed to inarticulate Moses, or as a female leader now obscured by her two famous brothers.[29] The evident injustice of her suffering leprosy when Aaron does not is felt to be neither explained nor excused by the observation of the feminine singular verb in 12:1, as if that were to indicate that Aaron simply accompanied his upstart sister. And matters are compounded by the spectacle of Miriam arguing over her brother's

---

26. These options are explored in my *The Virtuous Reader*, 55–59; cf Gafney, *Daughters of Miriam*, 81–82.

27. Burns, *Miriam*, 46–48 and *passim*.

28. See the helpful overview of Trevett, "Wilderness Woman."

29. Trible ends her article with the striking "midrash": "Sing to the Lord . . . Patriarchy and its horsemen God has hurled into the sea"; "Shadows," 183.

choice of wife, especially if the complaint is over skin color. In one particular interpretive *tour de force*, Irmtraud Fischer seeks to demonstrate that Miriam was right with regard to the substance of her objection (at least in the eyes of the text's priestly redactors), but mistakenly did not take account of Moses' unique standing before God as it is explained in verses 6–8.[30] It is hard to avoid the conclusion that Miriam is a figure both of immense potential for a feminist reading of scripture but also a focal point of a good deal of problematic material. In a fine account of just the kinds of issues we have considered, Susan Ackerman notes that the results of (and prospects for) positive reconstructive scholarship regarding Miriam, and others, are mixed, and that what such scholarship has recovered is exclusion and marginalization as often as it is significance.[31]

Turning from this to the world of evangelical scholarship feels like entering an almost unrelated discourse. Consider, for example, the question of whether there is something amiss with the punishment of chapter 12 going only to Miriam, and not to Aaron. Budd essentially explains this on literary-critical grounds (different traditions, if not sources); Ashley thinks it is explained by noting that Miriam "took the lead" in the complaint of verse 1; Gane likewise concludes that Miriam "apparently was more at fault than Aaron"; while for Wenham it is perhaps due to Aaron's role as high priest, which is probably the most plausible view, and is a point noted also by Bellinger, who does however add the single evaluative comment: "that seems unjust."[32] Elsewhere, the absence of any comparable hinterland of self-described evangelical articles or books on Miriam sounds a deafening silence in comparison to the tidal wave of feminist scholarship. Even Dorothy Irvin's brief discussion, fair as it is with regard to several points, is unduly vague on specifics, and ends up suggesting that the punishment of 12:10 is sufficiently explained by Miriam's being "the stronger character and . . . the prime mover."[33] Although Miriam often receives passing mention in the context of the

---

30. Fischer, "Authority of Miriam." I have discussed Fischer's reading in *The Virtuous Reader*, 56–59.

31. Ackerman, "Is Miriam Also among the Prophets?," esp. 47–48.

32. See, respectively, Budd, *Numbers*, 133; Ashley, *Numbers*, 227; Gane, *Leviticus, Numbers*, 591; Wenham, *Numbers* (1981), 113; Bellinger, *Leviticus, Numbers*, 226.

33. Irvin, "Numbers," 81–84, here 83. Cf. the notion of the confirmed justice of her punishment in Branch, "Miriam," 569.

vexed evangelical question about women's leadership, such mentions are rarely engaged with biblical scholarship.[34] In short, for evangelical commentators, Miriam remains very much in the shadows.

Space precludes much examination of the fascinating history of interpretation of Num 20:1, Miriam's death notice. Suffice it to say that most commentators—feminist, evangelical, or neither—tend to find this an innocent piece of reportage, perhaps with the passing comment that here was a woman whose death (conspicuously?) merited a mention.[35] Largely ignored is the fascinating Jewish history of interpretation which took seriously the juxtaposition of verse 1 with the lack of water experienced by the wandering congregation in verse 2, the beginning of the story of Moses' striking the rock and thereby failing to enter the land. Thus *Targum Neofiti* 21.1 observes that with the death of "Miriam the prophetess, for whose merits the well used to come up for them" the well had been removed; and Pseudo-Philo notes "the three things that God gave to his people on account of three persons," the first of which is "the well of the water of Marah for Miriam" (*LAB* 20:8). The resultant tradition of "Miriam's well," which travelled in the wilderness to provide water for the Israelites, eventually becomes "the spiritual rock that followed them" in 1 Cor 10:4.[36] All that can be said here about this set of traditions is that it offers insights—which appear not to have been particularly embraced—on a whole range of matters, from the merits of Miriam (congenial to feminist scholars?) to the interpretive and arguably typological frameworks of the apostle Paul (congenial to evangelical scholars?).[37] Might this in part be because the two hermeneutical approaches under discussion are preoccupied with questions of their own to such an extent that the benefits of considering other approaches can be obscured?

THE WOMAN SUSPECTED OF ADULTERY

Our third text, Num 5:11–31, is the startling and problematic legislation concerning a jealous husband who suspects his wife of adultery, a text often referred to as the *sotah* text from the verb for "turning" (*sth*), since the woman concerned is one who is suspected of "turning aside"

34. An exception, though still brief, is Scalise, "Women in Ministry."
35. E.g., Sakenfeld, *Numbers*, 112; Wenham, *Numbers* (1981), 149.
36. On "Miriam's well" see Ginzberg, *Legends*, 50–54.
37. See the helpful discussion of Enns, "Moveable Well," though this is a rare approach in evangelical circles.

or "going astray." The text in fact incorporates two parallel scenarios, as a careful reading of verse 14 indicates: the spirit of jealousy may rush upon the man either because his wife has been unfaithful or because he is simply jealous of her (though she is in fact innocent). In either case, he is to take her before the priest, who shall make her swear a curse, which is then written down and dipped into a mysterious drink ("the water of bitterness," v. 24) which is mixed also with dust from the tabernacle floor (v. 17). The logic of the passage is that if she is innocent then nothing will happen as a result of this ordeal; but if she is guilty, she will suffer "bitter pain, and her womb shall discharge, [and] her uterus drop." (v. 27) The passage ends by saying that the man will suffer no penalty for bringing any unjustified charge should she turn out to be innocent.

There are few texts in the whole of scripture as difficult as this. I have written elsewhere on the various hermeneutical issues at stake in this passage and in most attempts to interpret it, so shall restrict myself to a brief summary of points of relevance to our present task.[38]

Feminists are (rightly, I would say) deeply troubled by this text. The passage serves as a "case history" of interpretation in the anthology *Women in the Hebrew Bible: A Reader*, edited by Alice Bach,[39] and Bach herself offers as strong an account as a feminist will likely be able to manage concerning how one might read this "glass half empty" text as a "glass half full" one. The outcome, she suggests, is that the text "reflects the potency of male imaginings," and all a reader can do is jump from this to the recognition that there are other ways of looking at things than the supposedly universal or normative male perspective herein assumed. At best, perhaps, the awfulness of the procedure described in Numbers 5 might backfire on the male perspective, and allow the female voice to emerge in critique.[40]

Numbers 5 provokes even evangelical commentators to take up a certain critical distance from the text. "Modern practice of the ordeal would obviously be indefensible," says Budd; Ashley talks about "the unjust treatment of women that this passage prescribes"; while Bellinger

---

38. See my "*Sotah* Text." On the details and early history of interpretation see Grushcow, *Wayward Wife*. For a recent thorough exegetical analysis see Lipka, *Sexual Transgression*, 102–21, arguing that the text "presents adultery as a crime that violates both religious and communal boundaries" (ibid., 121).

39. Bach, ed., *Women*, 461–522, incorporating 5 significant articles.

40. See Bach, "Good to the Last Drop," esp. 52.

concludes that in comparison to defenses of the procedure "a more honest approach to this text is to admit the gender inequity here" and search elsewhere for a more "appropriate" gender perspective.[41] Yet even here focus on background issues remains quite striking, as in Ronald Allen's "The text is of special interest to those who search for what they believe to be remnants of primitive rites within the books of Moses."[42] And much in evidence is the strong desire to find enduring theological value in the framework of judgments which go to make up the case. Thus Ashley includes in his discussion the thought that the limitation to the punishment of any woman here is "an operation of divine grace"; Irvin, who acknowledges that the passage seems "peculiar and harsh," goes on to remark that "this law must have been reassuring to women in those days"; and perhaps the most striking example, a little over-stated I think, is Gordon Wenham's comment that "Numbers 5, Paul and Revelation make the same point: unfaithfulness in marriage is incompatible with membership of the people of God."[43]

Nevertheless, in contradistinction to our other two case studies, we do find at least some evangelicals operating with caution about simply appropriating the presenting intentions of this text. It is one of the oddities of this particular text and its reception that in fact here, where one might expect to find feminists at their most strident in denouncing the text, one encounters instead a whole raft of feminist approaches wondering what to do with this passage without simply abandoning it.[44]

My own view, defended elsewhere, is that this text is fundamentally about the problem of unchecked suspicion rather than gender, and indeed that there are reasons to suspect that the reader is supposed to be suspicious of this passage.[45] It is, I think, to be noted that the man's accusation of the woman can proceed without witnesses, which marks the text out as unusual in the Old Testament; that the ritual described looks more like ancient Near Eastern practices than any other Old Testament text; and that the result of the ritual—the forced abortion—is self-evidently deeply problematic within the overall scriptural framework.

---

41. Budd, *Numbers*, 67; Ashley, *Numbers*, 122; Bellinger, *Numbers*, 198.

42. Allen, "Numbers," 744.

43. Ashley, *Numbers*, 124; Irvin, "Numbers," 77 noting, oddly, that "this ordeal seems to be slanted in favor of the woman"(!); Wenham, *Numbers* (1981), 85.

44. See my survey in Briggs, "*Sotah* Text," 302–6.

45. Briggs, "*Sotah* Text," esp. 306–11, much of which I summarize here.

Such observations should make the reader wary. But furthermore, the suspicion at work in the text links in strikingly with the prominence of the theme of trust (and the disastrous failure to trust) which recurs at key moments in the book of Numbers, particularly at the turning points of the reviewing of the land before entry (cf. 14:11) or the forewarning of the death of Moses (cf. 20:12).[46] My own conclusion: this unusual text "celebrates the untamed exercise of suspicion, in ways which are morally and theologically problematic, and yet also canonically evaluated as inadequate."[47]

HERMENEUTICAL CONCLUSIONS

Our three case studies in the book of Numbers suggest that we might draw the following conclusions.

Feminist interpretation brings to the text questions driven by the existential concerns of women, as readers and more generally as part of the community of faith perceived to be in some sort of continuity with that of ancient Israel. Such questions typically relate to whether the judgments in the text about women are in themselves just, or perhaps appropriate in comparison to judgments relating to men. There is a willingness to exercise hermeneutical suspicion, given that the text may be arriving in its final form at the mercy of various male shapers and redactors along the way. In limiting cases, such as with Numbers 5, there is the hope that we the readers may learn to live and act more wisely than the unreflected male practice to which the text still bears witness. Nevertheless, there is underneath all this the assumption that this text is worth persevering with; that even the book of Numbers might yet play its part in resourcing the faithful living of women today; and that it is worth taking the time to learn from Miriam, whether as she is portrayed in the text or as we might reconstruct her historically, or from Mahlah, Noah, Hoglah, Milcah, and Tirzah. In the extreme case, we must not forget the nameless female victims of the ordeal legislated in Numbers 5, and we must learn to conceive of male-female relationships better than that. There is a strong urge to write and reflect on women in scripture, and the kinds of questions brought to the table are circumscribed quite

---

46. 14:11 and 20:12 both use the vocabulary of a lack of 'ĕmunâ, trust, which resonates strongly with the inverse language of suspicion (qānā', translated as being "jealous" in the NRSV) which is so prominent in chapter 5.

47. Briggs, "*Sotah* text," 311.

often by a limited range of issues relevant to modern feminism. The attendant risk is that the shape of the life-giving witness of the text is predetermined to fit within a narrow range of categories, even where there may be other resources available upon deeper exploration (as in the case of Miriam's well).

Evangelical interpreters hold more tightly to the conviction that this text will nourish the lives of the faithful today, and that there is some kind of continuity between the judgments of the faithful in ancient Israel and the way in which readers should live today. Within this framework it is felt appropriate that considerable energy should be given to matters of literary coherence and, in some cases, the plausibility of a face-value historical reconstruction of the world behind the text. Concomitantly, it is rare to find evangelicals hermeneutically suspicious, except in limiting cases where (to some at least) the text seems to be simply so far outside the bounds of faithful practice as evangelicals understand it that some measure of caution may be admitted. It is surely the case that matters of existential relevance drive evangelical interpretive engagement with scripture, ranging from convictions about the God to whom the book of Numbers witnesses through to the belief that the faithful understanding of the text will be life-giving, though as a matter of observation it is striking how little space is given to such matters in the evangelical commentaries surveyed. Evangelicals write engagingly and often about life with God, but they seem to do it less in their biblical commentary than feminists do, at least with regard to the book of Numbers. They also, in fact, seem to write relatively little on women in Scripture.

Thus far I have attempted to address our topic, which offers so much general scope for unfounded accusation and counter-accusation, by way of exploring the actual practice of interpreters, and deducing hermeneutical conclusions from the specifics of textual engagement rather than making grand claims about what is or must be the case. Let me conclude briefly with a few broader-brush strokes, highlighting some similarities between the two approaches as well as some revealing differences.

First, both feminists and evangelicals give a strong sense of already knowing what they want to talk about when they come to Scripture. The former care less whether it is their own agenda foist upon the text, and sometimes (though not always) it is. The latter, I think, care deeply about whether an agenda is foist upon Scripture, but think that they are not guilty of such a charge. The main way in which evangelicals avoid such a practice appears to be by sidelining matters of existential import. They are, as a result, more likely to talk about the text than the subject matter of the text. While this is undeniably in one sense "safer," it is both something of a failure of theological nerve, and also, ironically, is still the foisting of a reader's agenda on the text, simply not a theological agenda. But in principle there is no reason why there should not be a major evangelical study of Miriam as a figure of faith (to whatever degree); or an evangelical study which finds Numbers 27 interesting more for what it says about female initiative and justice rather than legal procedures; or an evangelical engagement with Numbers 5 which will follow up Bellinger's hints of critique rather than get excited over Mosaic literary deposits. The significant hermeneutical point is that the scriptural text invites engagement with the reality to which it witnesses, and that the more the interpreter is involved in the task of trying to live in a way appropriate to the text, the better placed that interpreter will be for the very practices of faithful reading which they seek. This hermeneutical point has been widely and persuasively made in recent years by many writers, and is currently bearing fruit in the rising interest in "theological interpretation."[48] To oversimplify, feminists and evangelicals both, in different ways, bring some aspects of the text to life, and obscure others. They are also both, in their different ways, better at providing interpretive accounts which focus on providing answers to their own questions rather than allowing their questions to be refocused and their agendas challenged—which is in turn part of the emphasis of much recent theological interpretation. It would take us too far afield to ask how one might best pursue the subject matter of the text as comprehensively as possible, but might one at least wonder whether an interpreter alert to both evangelical and feminist insights might not be better placed than one who has only one or the other agenda?

Secondly, both kinds of approach draw their interpretive moves from a powerful governing view of authority. For evangelicals, the prevailing view of authority is often undeclared in commentaries, but in practice, especially with an Old Testament book like Numbers, it can function to collapse any sense that there might be a relevant canonical or Christological framework that will require the interpreter to do more than state what the text is saying. The result is commentaries that stick

---

48. For programmatic explorations in this area see Lash, "Martyrdom," and the essays gathered in Davis and Hays, eds., *The Art of Reading Scripture*.

to a limited range of issues, and eschew probing and thoughtful engagement with the subject matter of the text. It seems to me that there is an important difference here between trusting the text and thinking that one should not ask existentially demanding and difficult questions of it. This point may be illuminated by way of comparison with feminist views of authority. In Sakenfeld's inaugural lecture she argued that "the methods that Christian feminist interpreters are choosing may well have a great deal to do with our understanding of how the Bible may become the Word of God for the community of faith in our day."[49] The difference is that feminists will factor in hermeneutical suspicion as a key part of that issue. In the process, they engage vigorously with the subject matter of the text, sometimes (but not in fact always) by way of contesting it. At times, it seems, evangelicals and feminists can tend towards representing the two poles of Ricoeur's famous maxim, that hermeneutics is "animated by this double motivation: willingness to suspect, willingness to listen; vow of rigor, vow of obedience."[50] Again, one may wonder whether there is not scope for a more helpful cross-fertilisation of insights here.[51]

But finally, this last reflection brings me to a question. In writing this paper I had anticipated that there would be a considerable divergence between the two kinds of interpretation discussed here, but I was unprepared for the almost complete chasm that separates feminist and evangelical modes of commentary (at least on the book of Numbers). Yet I wonder now how far this is a result of the decision to limit attention to works self-described as evangelical? My impression, informal and anecdotal as it may be, is that there are many Old Testament scholars who would, in some sense or other, be willing to own both the labels "evangelical" and "feminist," but when they come to write on, say, Miriam, or Numbers 5, they do not in fact appear to see any purpose served by classifying their concerns as evangelical (or indeed, feminist). The kind of theologically constructive commentary offered by Dennis Olson's *Interpretation* volume, for example, needs neither label to go about its task, though the alert reader will recognize that it operates down-stream of Brevard Childs' canonical approach to Christian Old Testament in-

---

49. Sakenfeld, "Feminist," 163.

50. Ricoeur, *Freud and Philosophy*, 27.

51. As one example, I have considered the possibly constructive role of suspicion in "Juniper Trees and Pistachio Nuts."

terpretation.[52] Much of the current work in theological interpretation could be understood likewise. And my question is: does this matter? Does it matter whether an interpretation is evangelical or feminist? Or is it enough that it engages, carefully and probingly, with the subject matter of the text?

---

52. Olson, *Numbers*. Olson's *Death of the Old* (n. 1 above) was his Yale PhD thesis under the supervision of Childs.

BIBLIOGRAPHY

Ackerman, S. "Is Miriam Also among the Prophets? (and is Zipporah among the Priests?)." *Journal of Biblical Literature* 121 (2002) 47–80.

Allen, R. B. "Numbers." In *The Expositor's Bible Commentary Vol. 2*, edited by F. E. Gaebelein, 655–1008. Grand Rapids: Zondervan, 1990.

Ashley, T. R. *The Book of Numbers*. NICOT. Grand Rapids: Eerdmans, 1993.

Bach, A., ed. *Women in the Hebrew Bible: A Reader*. London: Routledge, 1999.

Bach, A. "Good to the Last Drop: Viewing the Sotah (Numbers 5.11–31) as the Glass Half Empty and Wondering How to View it Half Full." In *The New Literary Criticism and the Hebrew Bible*, edited by J. C. Exum and D. J. A. Clines, 26–54. JSOTS 143. Sheffield, UK: JSOT, 1993.

Bellinger, W. H. *Leviticus, Numbers*. NIBCOT 3. Peabody, MA: Hendrickson, 2001.

Branch, R. G. "Miriam." In *Dictionary of the Old Testament: Pentateuch*, edited by T. Desmond Alexander and David W. Baker, 568–70. Downers Grove, IL: InterVarsity, 2003.

Bronner, L. L. "Serach and the Exodus: A Midrashic Miracle." In *Exodus to Deuteronomy: A Feminist Companion to the Bible* (Second Series), edited by A. Brenner, 187–98. Sheffield, UK: Sheffield Academic, 2000.

Briggs, R. S. "Juniper Trees and Pistachio Nuts: Trust and Suspicion as Modes of Scriptural Imagination." *Theology* 112 (2009) 353–63.

———. "Reading the Sotah Text (Numbers 5:11–31): Holiness and a Hermeneutic Fit for Suspicion." *Biblical Interpretation* 17 (2009) 288–319.

———. *The Virtuous Reader. Old Testament Narrative and Interpretive Virtue*. Studies in Theological Interpretation. Grand Rapids: Baker Academic, 2010.

Budd, P. J. *Numbers*. WBC5. Waco, TX: Word, 1984.

Burns, R. J., *Has the Lord Indeed Spoken Only Through Moses? A Study of the Biblical Portrait of Miriam*. SBLDS 84. Atlanta: Scholars, 1987.

Davis, E. F. and R. B. Hays, eds. *The Art of Reading Scripture*. Grand Rapids: Eerdmans, 2003.

Enns, P. "The 'Moveable Well' in 1 Cor 10:4: An Extrabiblical Tradition in an Apostolic Text." *Bulletin for Biblical Research* 6 (1996) 23–38.

Fischer, I. "The Authority of Miriam: A Feminist Rereading of Numbers 12 Prompted by Jewish Interpretation." In *Exodus to Deuteronomy. A Feminist Companion to the Bible* (Second Series), edited by A. Brenner, 159–73. Sheffield, UK: Sheffield Academic, 2000.

Gafney, W. C. *Daughters of Miriam: Women Prophets in Ancient Israel*. Minneapolis: Fortress, 2008.

Gane, R. *Leviticus, Numbers*. NIVAC. Grand Rapids: Zondervan, 2004.

Ginzberg, L. *The Legends of the Jews. Vol. 3*. Philadelphia: Jewish Publication Society, 1911.

Grushcow, L. *Writing the Wayward Wife: Rabbinic Interpretations of Sotah*. AJEC 62. Leiden: Brill, 2006.

Irvin, D. "Numbers." In *The IVP Women's Bible Commentary*, edited by C. C. Kroeger and M. J. Evans, 70–87. Downers Grove, IL: InterVarsity, 2002.

Lash, N. "What Might Martyrdom Mean?." In *Theology on the Way to Emmaus*, 75–92. London: SCM, 1986.

Lipka, H. *Sexual Transgression in the Hebrew Bible*. HBM 7. Sheffield, UK: Sheffield Phoenix, 2006.

Meyers, C. et al, eds. *Women in Scripture*. Grand Rapids: Eerdmans, 2000.
Noth, M. *Numbers*. OTL. London: SCM, 1968.
Olson, D. T. *The Death of the Old and the Birth of the New: The Framework of the Book of Numbers and the Pentateuch*. BJS 71. Chico, CA: Scholars, 1985.
———. *Numbers*. Interpretation. Louisville: John Knox Press, 1996.
Ricoeur, P. *Freud and Philosophy: An Essay on Interpretation*. New Haven: Yale University Press, 1970.
Sakenfeld, K. D. "Feminist Biblical Interpretation." *Theology Today* 46 (1989) 154–68.
———. *Numbers: Journeying with God*. ITC. Grand Rapids: Eerdmans, 1995.
Scalise, P. J. "Women in Ministry: Reclaiming our Old Testament Heritage." *Review & Expositor* 83 (1986) 7–13.
Shemesh, Y. "A Gender Perspective on the Daughters of Zelophehad: Bible, Talmudic Midrash, and Modern Feminist Midrash." *Biblical Interpretation* 15 (2007) 80–109.
Sterring, A. "The Will of the Daughters." In *A Feminist Companion to Exodus to Deuteronomy*, edited by A. Brenner, 88–99. FCB 6. Sheffield, UK: Sheffield Academic, 1994.
Trevett, C. "Wilderness Woman. The Taming of Miriam." In *Wilderness: Essays in Honour of Frances Young*, edited by R. S. Sugirtharajah, 26–44. LNTS 295. London: T. & T. Clark, 2005.
Trible, P. "Bringing Miriam Out of the Shadows." In *A Feminist Companion to Exodus to Deuteronomy*. FCB 6. Edited by A. Brenner, 166–86. Sheffield: Sheffield Academic, 1994.
Ulrich, D. R. "The Framing Function of the Narratives about Zelophehad's Daughters." *Journal of the Evangelical Theological Society* 41.4 (1998) 529–38.
Webb, W. J. *Slaves, Women & Homosexuals: Exploring the Hermeneutics of Cultural Analysis*. Downers Grove, IL: InterVarsity, 2001.
Wenham, G. J. *Numbers*. TOTC. Leicester, UK: InterVarsity, 1981.
———. *Numbers*. OTG. Sheffield, UK: Sheffield Academic, 1997.

4

Adding Insult to Injury?

The Family Laws of Deuteronomy

JENNI WILLIAMS

ETAN LEVINE ONCE MADE a telling comment on the behavior of David in 2 Sam 20:3. David had left ten concubines behind to look after his affairs when he fled from Absalom. Absalom's first act was to sleep with the concubines (2 Sam 16:21–22), as an expression of seizing power. When David returned, these poor women, sexual victims of a power play between two men, are shut up: provided for, but denied any further sexual relationships and forced to live as *'almanot*.[1] Levine commented: "David's act is as sinfully wrong as it is legally exemplary (i.e., 'summum ius, summa iniuria')."[2]

The idea that a law, whether civil or criminal, could be a source of injury rings false to us. We expect our own laws to be just, to protect the vulnerable, the exploited, and the underprivileged. We expect them to be a source of healing, not injury. And evangelicals expect biblical law to do this, yes, and even more so. Any evangelical commentary on Deuteronomy will speak of its concern for social justice and for the poor.[3]

---

1. This Hebrew word has overtones of powerlessness, loss of status and disadvantage that cannot be conveyed by the English word "widow." These women are indeed disadvantaged.

2. Levine, "On Exodus 21,10," 152. The law in question is Deuteronomy 24, whereby a wife cannot return to her first husband after being divorced by a second. Presumably, David has elaborated this to fit the case of his abused concubines.

3. For example, Christensen, *Deuteronomy 1–11*, 208 "God loves the stranger, the

There is the repeated focus on the alien, the widow, and the orphan, which underpinned the social agenda of the prophet-reformers from Micah to Malachi. Yet a close look at some of the laws in Deuteronomy may leave us feeling uncomfortable about the way they deal with vulnerable women. When honestly looked at, they could indeed be called "summa iniuria," and indeed might be better named "adding insult to injury." The discussion begins with this uneasy possibility.

In terms of taxonomy, this discussion does not use one text that is "positive" to women to counter one which is "negative." Nor does it primarily approach the text to see what can be offered to women in oppressed situations, although this is explored briefly in the final section.[4] Both these are honorable approaches and vital to the hermeneutical task. But the approach taken here is to look at the family laws in Deuteronomy and ask whether they are oppressive or liberating to women in themselves.

Given the large amount of varied material available in Deuteronomy, it is worth explaining why these laws are a useful place to focus: "Through a culture's laws, we can see its values and some of its basic ideas about the world."[5] There has been discussion about whether the laws in Deuteronomy are law as we understand it, that is, a series of regulations, codes and guidelines designed to be implemented in an existing society.[6] However, whether they are concrete laws or theological desiderata makes no difference to our analysis, since even an ideal law tells us a great deal about how people were regarded in the legislator's society and in their thinking.

These particular laws were chosen because they speak about women who are put in an equivocal position by men, and as such, are a useful source for understanding how Deuteronomy addresses the problems faced by such women. It is hoped this will give a useful "broad" perspective on women in Deuteronomic law, although, as Pressler observes: "Discussions of the Deuteronomic view of women are distortive when

---

widow, and the orphan, and, therefore, his people, if they truly love God, must also be concerned for justice and righteousness in relation to their neighbours."

4. I have used Sakenfeld's three categories here: "Feminist Uses of Biblical Materials," 55–62.

5. Frymer-Kensky, "Law and Philosophy," 239. For a more extended discussion, see Walton, *Ancient Near Eastern Thought*.

6. Blenkinsopp, "The Family," 61. In fact, the English word "law" does not fully cover the idea of "Torah," which has clear overtones of teaching in it.

they fail to take into consideration the categories of laws in which the references to women are found and the roles played by the woman discussed in those laws."[7] Clearly, then, the most that this study can claim to be is an examination of Deuteronomy's view of an Israelite woman's life *within a family*, not of an Israelite woman's life *in toto*.

A series of studies by Christian and Jewish scholars in the late twentieth century wrote of Deuteronomy's "equality of the sexes,"[8] of the non-hierarchical character of relationships between men and women in the Israelite family,[9] and even that Deuteronomy is especially concerned with women.[10] Specialists in Hebrew Bible/Old Testament law observed that Deuteronomy was the first law to treat women as legal persons.[11] Weinfeld, in his *Deuteronomy and the Deuteronomic School*, for example, cites the lack of distinction between male and female slaves and other laws, which are not found in the older Covenant Code. He illustrates this with case law such as that which protects the property rights of the firstborn even when the mother is unloved (Deut 21:15–17), and the explicit inclusion of women in the cult, festivals and feasts (Deut 12:12–13). Most delightfully of all, he identified Deut 24:5 as "consideration for a woman's intimate feelings."[12] Immediately relevant to our discussion here, he holds that the law pertaining to the "seduced maiden" of 22:28–29 is not primarily concerned with the financial restitution but "the moral and personal wrong," which he contrasts to the parallel law in the Covenant Code Exod 22:16–17 (15–16 MT) which does not show the same concern for the woman.[13] In the case of the law of the "slandered virgin" he argues that the law's concern is about the wife's reputation.[14] Weinfeld attributes the inclusion of this material in Deuteronomy, with its "humanitarian" concerns, to Deuteronomy's twin influences of Torah and Wisdom.[15]

---

7. Pressler, *View*, 2.
8. Weinfeld, *Deuteronomy and the Deuteronomic School*, 291.
9. Steinberg "Adam and Eve's Daughters are Many," quoted in Pressler, *View*, 5.
10. Goldingay, *Theological Diversity*, 138.
11. Phillips, *Ancient Israel's Criminal Law*, 180
12. Weinfeld, *Deuteronomy and the Deuteronomic School*, 291.
13. Ibid., 285.
14. Ibid., 291.
15. Ibid., 294.

Comforting as these reflections are, a sustained challenge has been mounted against some of them by feminist scholars, arguing that the position of women is at once more nuanced and less favorable than the scholars above had considered. This chapter will examine these challenges, looking at two scholars in particular. Carolyn Pressler explores how women are seen within the whole nexus of family laws found in Deuteronomy 21, 22, 24, and 25.[16] Her approach begins from the belief that the order and stability of the family is both fundamental to the laws and built on gender asymmetry. She explores the consequences of this need for order and stability for women. The second approach is that of Tikva Frymer-Kensky, using two articles. The first article explores what the laws can tell us about understanding of human sexuality.[17] The second article discusses the importance of preserving virginity.[18] We will examine their approach to some of the laws in Deuteronomy, and then we will consider how their observations improve exegesis. Finally we will ask if there is a way to incorporate these insights into a hermeneutic that is at once feminist and evangelical.

CAROLYN PRESSLER: AUTHORITY AND THE LAW

Gender Asymmetry

Pressler begins from the basis that, so far from seeking to challenge patriarchal authority,[19] "the Deuteronomic family laws presuppose and undergird male headed and male defined hierarchical family structures, in which women hold subordinate and dependent status."[20] In one sense, such a position is not unexpected; the patriarchal character of Israelite

---

16. Pressler, *View*.
17. Frymer-Kensky "Law and Philosophy."
18. Frymer-Kensky, "Virginity."
19. Both Meyers (*Discovering Eve*, 30) and Pressler (*View*, 79), among others, have noted the misuse of the word "patriarchal" in the feminist context, where it has been equated with de facto oppression of women and systematic, intentional misogyny. Meyers in particular pleads for a technical understanding of the word, which means in anthropological terms, a society where visible authority is organised around men. Pressler in speaking of patriarchal authority also adopts this understanding. We should not understand that she is trying to portray institutionalised misogyny, although obviously, she sees a male-dominated authority structure as a state of affairs intrinsically undesirable and more difficult for women.
20. Pressler, *View*, 5.

society has been widely recognized.[21] The challenge to those who hold a high view of Scripture is the idea that Deuteronomy actively supports such patriarchy. Pressler argues that a woman's status within the household can vary, but it is essentially subordinate to a greater or lesser degree. For example, the focus for daughters is on chastity and the head of the household's "unilateral and absolute claim over her sexuality."[22]

One of the most useful parts of Pressler's evidence for her basic thesis is her examination of the imbalance between genders in each of the roles that people play: parent, child, and spouse. In this way she is able to categorize everyone's place in the visible authority structures, which in turn helps understand the thinking that underpins each law. She begins with the mother, and notes that one law in this corpus allows parity of status for the mother with the father since she takes the rebellious son to judgment (with his father), and speaks as a witness. Part of the complaint is the son's rebellion against her authority as well as his father's (Deut 21:20). On the other hand, in the law of the "slandered virgin" (Deut 22:13–21), the mother is a silent witness only (Deut 22:15–16). Pressler suggests this is because minors owed obedience to their own mother, but in inter-family disputes (as 22:13–21), the law pertains to offences against the head of household.[23] It is, of course, a very nice question to discern whether the head of house represents the family and is therefore the visible spokesperson,[24] or whether he is the plaintiff because he is the head of the house. There is certainly a clear logic to this at a procedural level: in this way a female complainant cannot be stymied by an opponent arguing she does not have the authority to deal with the issues. But is this simply a question of representation in a patriarchal reality,[25] or a deeper intention that only a man has a right to be involved in legal dispute? The discussion deals with this issue further below. For the moment, it is enough to observe that the male head of household has the legal authority in the community.

Pressler argues that a daughter, like a son, must obey her parents (there is a certain parallel between Deut 21:18–21 and 22:21), must

21. Ibid., 5.
22. Ibid., 113.
23. Ibid., 84–85.
24. As, for example, Perriman's discussion of male pre-eminence (*Speaking of Women*, chapter 1).
25. As argued by Perriman, in ibid., 36.

mourn for them (Deut 21:13), and is apparently a person of value to her family since the execration texts threaten the loss of daughters as well as sons (Deut 28:32, 41). However, unlike her brother, the offences for which a daughter is punished are based on her exercising her sexuality at her own choice, or her failure to protect her sexuality for her future husband. The son, on the other hand, is punished for excess and disobedience. A daughter cannot inherit, hence the need for the levirate law that provides for a widow with daughters: a further piece of evidence for gender disparity, this time between daughters and sons.[26]

Pressler categorizes asymmetry between wife and husband under three headings: economic control, marriage and divorce, and male possession of female sexuality.[27] In the laws under consideration, the first category deals with the question of damages, which are always offered to the male head of the household. "Based on other biblical texts, we would expect that the father typically controls the family's resources. Such evidence as Deuteronomy offers confirms that expectation."[28]

In the second category Pressler argues "the laws depict men as the agents and women as the objects of both marriage and divorce."[29] She also argues that the ease with which a man could procure a divorce is indicated by Deut 24:1–4. She also notes two cases we will examine below where he is prevented from divorcing his wife (Deut 22:19, 29) which suggest divorce was easily practiced unless the law prevented it. She argues that the grounds for divorce in Deut 24:1 cannot mean a serious offence, and that the pronouncement of 22:19 and 29 is intended to prevent the man acquiring an otherwise easy divorce.[30] The case for 24:1 illustrating how easy divorce is, is clear. However, if it is so easy, why would the husband go to all the bother of a false accusation (Deut 22:19)? The third category is the question of male possession of female sexuality. We will explore this is some detail when looking at Deut 22:13–29.

This analysis of asymmetry allows us to examine some underpinnings of law in Deuteronomy.

---

26. Pressler, *View*, 85–86.
27. Ibid., 86.
28. Ibid., 87.
29. Ibid., 88.
30. Ibid., 89–90.

The Authority of the Head of the Household

Pressler argues that the sexuality of women in a household belongs to the male head of the household. Her evidence comes from the law dealing with a recently married girl who is discovered not to have been a virgin when married (22:20–21). The rationale under which the girl proven adulterous is to be punished is that she threatens the social order by flouting her father's authority: "she has committed a disgraceful act in Israel by prostituting herself in her father's house" (Deut 22:21).[31] Pressler argues that it is not just against her head of household at the time of the offence that the girl has offended: "The husband's claim over his wife's sexuality is retroactive; it extends to the period before their betrothal."[32] This somewhat unusual idea comes from the basis that a man has a right to expect that his new wife should be a virgin. She observes that the later law of 22:28–29 shows that sex between a man and a woman before marriage is not a capital offence unless the girl then marries someone else.[33] In other words, the claim of her husband is somehow contemporaneous with that of her father in the matter of her sexuality. Whilst I agree that a man would indeed have believed he had the right to a virgin wife, I find it implausible that this right would have been articulated in terms of retroactive control. More likely it was articulated in terms of being cheated by a father-in-law who was not doing his job properly. After all, the law is framed in terms of the girl's offence against her father, not her husband. "This asymmetry shows that the issue was not protection of intimacy in marriage, or of chastity, *per se*. Rather, what was at stake in the laws concerning adultery was the authority of the male head of the household. This in turn was likely to have been a matter of paternity—the imperative need, in a patrilineal society, for a father to be certain that his sons were his own."[34]

We will explore further below the question of inheritance, but it should be noted here that what I understand Pressler to mean is that being sure a man has a son of his blood was an underlying reason for male authority. This in itself is interesting since Pressler has categorized male authority as a functional, rather than ontological, necessity, and

---

31. Ibid., 31.
32. Ibid., 26.
33. Ibid., 31.
34. Ibid., 42.

this itself will be useful when we come to consider what it means to be male and female in these laws.

Pressler observes that if the wife's sexuality and reproductive capacity was under her husband's control, that is still not same as saying that the women herself is the property of her husband. She notes that the woman has rights concerning her sexuality: the captured "foreign" woman, once she has entered a sexual relationship with a man, must be treated as a wife and cannot be disposed of as if she were still a captive of war (Deut 21:14).[35]

Another way of illustrating the authority of the head of household idea is to identify the person whom the law judges to be the aggrieved or the victim in any infraction. In the laws pertaining to the slandering of a virtuous wife (the "slandered virgin"[36] law), Pressler argues that the aggrieved party is the father as the head of household as well as the girl herself.[37] One piece of evidence for this is the penalty. On the face of it, this law prevents a man from an easy divorce from a girl of whom he has tired, hence the enthusiasm of many commentators for finding this a legal protection for women. But examination of the penalty shows he must *first* pay damages to the father and *then* be bound to his wife for life, even though the explanation is the insult to a virgin of Israel. The payment is to compensate the head of her former household for the grave insult to his honor. Indeed, Pressler quotes Phillips who argues that the primary offence is against the father: that accusing the woman is a way of perpetrating a fraud against her father (who will have to return the bride-price) rather than a genuine attempt to have her put to death.[38] But when her father is awarded damages, this now actually works against her: "Indeed, the father is compensated at the girl's expense; the damages paid to her father are taken from the household to which she is

---

35. Ibid., 102. In the matter of wife as property, one of the more intriguing readings of Deut 24:1–4 is that of Calum Carmichael, who attaches laws to patriarchal narratives. He argues that this law is to prevent a man from pimping his wife for some benefit for himself, as Abraham did twice with Sarah (Carmichael, *Women*, 10–13).

36. Despite Wenham's explanations in his important article on the meaning of *betulah*, and how well he proves his case in certain other texts, it seems the only possible understanding here of the issue is virginity ("Betulah," 326–48).

37. Pressler, *View*, 29.

38. Ibid., 25.

now permanently attached. The law apparently views the father and his household as an injured party."[39]

Nevertheless, this law does protect the woman, but Pressler seems to suggest this is only secondarily: "The law also prohibits the husband from ever divorcing his spurned wife, and thus provides her with some social/economic security. Since Israelite men apparently could divorce their wives at will, the prohibition is to be seen as a penalty imposed on the husband that protects the wife. The laws thus also treat the girl as an injured party."[40] Pressler also observes dryly that even this benefits the father who will no longer have to provide for the girl![41] Nevertheless, from this we can see that Pressler's analysis is nuanced and does not assume this is a legal system with total disregard for the unfortunate girl.

The Legal Status of Women

As we noted above, Pressler considers that a woman does have some legal standing: she is legally liable and can be a plaintiff along with her husband. Nevertheless, she argues that the laws appear to be addressed to men, and whether a man or woman's actions are culpable are defined by obligations to husband, father or father-in-law.[42]

Many scholars have noted that one effect of the Deuteronomic laws was to remove some of the male head of household's power or rather to give him a circumscribed authority underneath the law. So, for example, in the law concerning the rape of the unattached girl, in the Exodus version (Exod 22:16–17) the father is entitled to refuse to allow his daughter to marry her attacker. In the Deuteronomic version (Deut 22:28–29) there is no record that he has that right. The effect of this idea is to put women under the legal authority of the community rather than the head of the household, and this is significant. It should, to a certain extent, protect a woman from the arbitrary justice of the male head of house, since the law envisions that the best thing for the rape victim is to be married and secure. The issue such a "best thing" raises will be discussed further below.

Pressler observes, "The laws do not assume that the power and authority of the male head of household is unlimited. Dependent members

39. Ibid., 29.
40. Ibid.
41. Ibid.
42. Ibid., 43.

of the family, including women, are subject to the laws and judicial processes of the community, not the private justice of the father or husband. They are guarded by protective laws and customary rights. Nonetheless, the laws do assume a hierarchically structured family in which primary authority is vested in the male head of household and which is defined in terms of the man."[43] So the question of being legally "equal" does not detract from the essential dependency of women on the (male) authority structure. In the case of the "slandered virgin," Pressler believes the situation arises because the parents bring the case as plaintiffs rather than the husband. This suggests, she argues, that the concern is with "protecting the woman and her family from slander and dishonor, rather than protecting her from false charges."[44]

Whose Rights, Whose Consent?

By far the most challenging aspect of these laws is when they deal with rape (Deut 22:22–29). In Western society, consent to a sexual act is material. Pressler argues that in these laws, consent only pertains in the case of a woman who is betrothed,[45] where the sexual act is an infraction against another man's rights (logically, therefore, although Pressler does not say this, the woman is required to refuse consent). In this case, Pressler argues the place where the act happened is used to define whether there has been consent (because the woman could have cried out in the city, and if she did not, the law understands that she consented), and consent is used to define whether or not adultery has occurred.[46] If the woman is unbetrothed, Pressler argues that even if, as some scholars have said, the corresponding law in Exodus deals with seduction whilst this law in Deuteronomy deals with rape, the difference is "legally immaterial" as the girl's consent is not a defining factor in either example.[47] Pressler

43. Ibid., 113.
44. Ibid., 104.
45. Ibid., 32.
46. Ibid.
47. Nevertheless, Pressler still debates the meaning of the word used to describe what the man does (*taphash*, different from the verb in Exodus *patha*) and argues that when applied to people, it means "involuntary seizure." Pressler translates the phrase: "If a man overtakes . . . takes hold of and lies with . . ." However, the question of how words are nuanced is a huge minefield. Pressler agues that *taphash* is used thirty-two times, and only once (Ezek 29:7) with a non-violent meaning. I content myself here with observing that the most vital issue is what Deuteronomy means by this word.

argues that if the redactor of the passage wanted consent to be material, he would have included both cases, consent given and consent withheld, as he did in Deut 22:23–27:[48] "the comparison with Deut 22:22–27 and Exod 22:15–16 (Eng. 22:16–17) suggests, the woman's consent or lack of consent to sexual intercourse was a negligible factor in determining the gravity of a sexual offense."[49]

The Purpose of the Laws

Pressler comes finally to what she perceives to be the purpose of the Deuteronomic family laws. This can be summarized as the support of "hierarchical, patrilineal family structures,"[50] and protection of dependent family members. Overall Pressler resists the view of Weinfeld and Steinberg that the laws in Deuteronomy are particularly humane towards women or even endorse the equality of men and women. The protection offered by the laws to women is the protection offered to a dependent: "Indeed, these protective laws are necessary precisely because family relationships were understood to be hierarchical; the weaker members were vulnerable to the stronger members."[51] She argues that these laws in their context are set within a body of laws that affirm the authority of the male head of the house and do not challenge "the traditional structures of authority and control."[52] We will explore below how this acceptance of traditional structures impacts our hermeneutics.

TIKVA FRYMER-KENSKY: SEXUALITY IN THE LAW

Frymer-Kensky concentrates on what the Old Testament and its laws say about human sexuality, as a way of folding in questions of authority. She believes, as many scholars have argued, that the law of the "slandered virgin" (Deut 22:13–19) was not expected to be implemented since the evidence would be so startlingly easy to fake. "But the law certainly lays down a theoretical principle very important to Israel, *viz.*, that a girl is

---

48. As, for example, Middle Assyrian Law does: 55 deals with no consent and 56 with consent.
49. Pressler, *View*, 6.
50. Ibid., 96.
51. Ibid., 106.
52. Ibid., 107.

expected to be chaste while in her father's house."[53] In this she has a different understanding from Pressler who, as we have seen, foregrounds the question of authority which underlies the expression of sexuality. Frymer-Kensky foregrounds the concern for appropriate sexual expression itself. This is an interesting and useful difference in approach.

She argues that the nature of the God portrayed in the Hebrew Bible/Old Testament makes it difficult to formulate a coherent treatment of sexuality, since the God of the Old Testament does not model sexuality: "There is no vocabulary in the Bible in which to discuss such matters, no divine image or symbolic system by which to mediate it. God does not model sex, is not the patron of sexual behavior . . . Our only indication that the Bible considers sex as a volatile, creative, and potentially chaotic force is from the laws themselves. These laws of control reveal a sense that sexuality is not really matter-of-fact, that it is a two-edged sword: a force for bonding and a threat to the maintenance of boundaries."[54]

Therefore, sexuality finds itself in the area of law, the social realm. "On the surface, sexuality is treated as a question of social control: who with whom, and when."[55] The laws, therefore, concerned themselves with boundaries, and although there is "an inevitable double standard" since adultery means sex with a woman who is attached to someone else, she observes that men are also bound by the laws. In the case of homosexual expression, only the men are bound: lesbian sex is not considered. She argues that the laws of adultery are formulated in terms of a threat to the idea of "household" or "family." Thus, sex with a prostitute is not a threat and is not legislated against. The unevenness in the adultery laws has been defined as the epitome of male control over female sexuality[56] and is probably also a desire to be sure of paternity.[57] Frymer-Kensky also observes significantly: "Within Israel this treatment of adultery is not examined: it is part of Israel's inheritance from the ancient Near East

---

53. Frymer-Kensky, "Law and Philosophy," 243.

54. Ibid., 250. As Andrew Sloane commented, both these aspects are found in the Song of Songs and Proverbs.

55. Ibid., 249.

56. Whilst it is true that male sexuality is to some extent constrained, it is only constrained insofar as it relates to invading another man's rights: a man does not, at least not in the Deuteronomic legal material, commit adultery against his wife.

57. Ibid., 242.

and, like slavery and other elements of social structure, it is never questioned in the Bible."[58] We will return to this important observation when reflecting on what this means for Christians.

The Father's Honor

Frymer-Kensky considers the issue of female chastity, and its importance for the male head of the house. She uses Dinah (Gen 34) as an example of sexual abuse as a background to the laws of Deut 22:22–29.[59] She comments on the very first line of Dinah's story: "The very first word, 'out went' can strike terror into the mind of any patriarch. 'Out' means leaving the family domain, leaving both the protection and control of the head of the household. We often talk about the vulnerability of women who go out without protection. But rarely is it mentioned that when a woman goes out, she leaves her family vulnerable to any disgrace her actions may bring upon them."[60] The question of Dinah's story is discussed by Robin Parry elsewhere in this volume.[61] For the moment, we should note that foregrounded here for Frymer-Kensky, and for many commentators, is the shame a daughter can bring on her father by transgressing sexual boundaries. As has been seen, the law as formulated emphasizes this shame ("in her father's house") as well as the affront to the community ("disgraceful act in Israel"). "The honor of the family is at stake, for real men have the strength and cunning to protect and control their women. The defilement of the females unmans the men."[62] In a society where shame is such a powerful function of social control, an unruly member of the household must have been a source of considerable anxiety to the head of the house.

---

58. Ibid., 243.

59. One of the strengths of Frymer-Kensky's work is the interweaving of biblical narratives with laws as a way to understand the laws. It seems obvious to say that laws do not grow up ex nihilo: they grow up out of concern to address certain situations (case law) or to set up an ideology (apodictic laws). But they also grow up in a culture whose thought is shaped by its narratives (witness the French law whose name is the Good Samaritan law). These narratives in turn become a key by which we can interpret the law's intent. Feminist hermeneutics, with its emphasis on literary observation, can benefit from this type of cross-interpretation.

60. Frymer-Kensky, "Virginity," 86.

61. See chapter 2 of this volume.

62. Frymer-Kensky, "Virginity," 84.

Frymer-Kensky also considers a possible power play between two males. "By eloping with a girl, a man both eliminates competing suitors, and demonstrates her father's inability to control his own daughter."[63] The net result of this may be that the father will be able to ask less for the bride price of compensation since the girl is now not so marriageable. This indeed may be the understanding upon which the bride price is fixed in 22:28–29. Only total control of the girl can protect the father from this and, as Frymer-Kensky observes, protect both the father and the girl from gossip that will also hurt her marriageability.

Frymer-Kensky argues that the law dealing with the "slandered virgin" is concerned primarily with the honor of the father or the family. Unless the parents can prove their daughter's virginity at marriage, they face one of two unpalatable alternatives: either the family did not control its daughter or they conspired with her in a fraud.[64] Whichever it is, their honor is lost. Frymer-Kensky compares the situation here to that of Judah and Tamar (Gen 38). When Judah's family honor is apparently besmirched by his daughter-in-law, he simply decrees she shall die an exemplary death (Gen 38:24). In Deuteronomy, as Frymer-Kensky and other scholars note, the law steps in to limit the power of the father in addition to resolving the intolerable situation for the head of the household's honor. He cannot, as Judah attempts to, pass summary judgment on his daughter. Frymer-Kensky argues that the no-divorce provision, which is "odd to our modern sensibility," is a deterrent to the husband making false accusations. Yet its primary focus is on the man: "Still, the law ignores the girl's wishes or her prospects for a more congenial marriage in its concern to assure that men cannot use this method of ridding themselves of unwanted wives."[65] Here is an important perspective: where there is a tension between what may be best for a woman and the status quo of the male authority system, her individual well-being will be subordinated to the patriarchal communal well-being. She observes that, in the case that the woman was indeed not a virgin on her wedding night, the power, although not the authority, shifts away from the community. The woman's parents may, if they wish, preserve her from the penalty by faking the sheet or they may be so angry with her they will refuse to help: "In the final analysis, the fate of the girl rests with her

63. Ibid., 85.
64. Ibid., 93–94.
65. Ibid., 94.

parents."⁶⁶ This is therefore a note of caution to be sounded when reflecting on how the law limits the power of the male head of the family, as it may well do in theory. In practice the power to kill his daughter or allow her to live may remain still with the father. Nevertheless, this is not what the law envisions.

Consent

Frymer-Kensky has a different perspective from Pressler on the consent or otherwise of the woman in 22:28–29. She argues that the previous law deals explicitly with rape since it envisions the possibility of crying for help. But "the verb 'grab' in the law of the unwed virgin, seen from the perspective of the girl's family, could simply means he grabbed what he wanted without showing respect for the family's honor and the protocols of propriety."⁶⁷ The underlying consideration for whether the case deals with rape or seduction without proper overture to the family depends on our understanding of what Deuteronomy believes is at stake. For Frymer-Kensky, the father's right to dispose of his daughter's sexuality and his requirement to do it right in the eyes of the community is paramount. It is not just his pride: it is the doing of things decently and in order. For Pressler, the question of control of female sexuality as an expression of authority is paramount.

Overall, Frymer-Kensky's analysis of the laws starts not from how they are structured, but what they intend to address: the threat to the well being of the family when its sexual boundaries are breached. She, like Pressler, explores how the laws seek to ensure that patriarchal authority should not be undermined, or at least should be restored if breached. However her exploration comes from the direction of observing how the community manages its sexual life with appropriate boundaries.

REFLECTIONS

This section addresses two issues: it examines the clearer understandings these two scholars brought to the exegesis of Deuteronomy's family laws, and then considers how Christians can deal hermeneutically with the issues raised.

---

66. Ibid., 95.
67. Ibid., 92.

Deepening Exegesis

While I found my encounter with Pressler and Frymer-Kensky was rather astringent, their basic theses are helpful. Firstly, Pressler's observation about asymmetry is entirely fair, but requires a little qualification, based on something she observes herself: "The Deuteronomic family legislation is not interested in 'women' *per se*. Rather, the laws refer to women in terms of their roles of mother, daughter, and wife. In each of these, the woman's status is defined in relationship to the family, and especially in relationship to the male head of the family."[68] It is entirely fair to observe that, within the roles, there is certainly what we might call role asymmetry: sons have inheritance rights; daughters (in Deuteronomy) apparently do not. Husbands, certainly in the pre-exilic period, may express their sexuality as they please (except if they infringe another husband's rights),[69] wives may not, and so on. The head of the family is conceived as male (although the Deuteronomic narratives of Samuel and Kings tell us of differing cases, they also usually speak in those cases of poverty, vulnerability and helplessness, for example 1 Kgs 17:8–12). Ancient Israel as portrayed in Deuteronomy is a male hierarchy. So it is indeed asymmetric. But I argue that it is not, if it can be expressed this way, an ontological asymmetry, merely a societal or organizational one. So I accept Pressler's observation with the minor qualification of "role" rather than "gender" asymmetry.[70] I consider that the father's regulation of his household's sexuality is not a question of some theological metastructure about gender. "The Deuteronomic family laws examined have as their primary focus neither women, per se, nor men, per se, but the family."[71] This idea of differentiating roles from person is, of course, an entirely anachronistic construct. There is no evidence that Israelite so-

---

68. Pressler, *View*, 82.

69. Andrew Sloane pointed out Wenham's assertion that laws are "floor" requirements (Wenham, *Story as Torah*, 80), but I have been arguing in this piece that laws reflect how a society sees appropriate behaviour. If, in the post-exilic period, as evidenced by the wisdom writings (possibly Job 31:1 and Mal 2:15), a more clearly developed covenantal understanding of marriage and chastity is in evidence, I argue that there is no evidence for it in the time of the Deuteronomists. See below for the question of a trajectory in sexual morality.

70. I'm grateful to Andrew Sloane for pointing out that the control a man apparently had over his slaves' sexuality (Exod 21:2–6) and the control of both father and mother over their sons' behaviour (Deut 21:18–21) strengthens the "role" perspective.

71. Pressler, *View*, 102.

ciety conceived of any difference between gender and role, nor indeed much evidence that the Deuteronomist subjected traditional patriarchal structures to a thoroughgoing theological critique.[72] So I am not arguing that any Israelite man would have thought, "I only hold this role of authority because this is how we happen to structure our society." Nevertheless, I believe that my observation about role as opposed to person may have a contribution to make at the hermeneutical level. It insists that we only ask the text questions it can answer, rather than the questions we want to put to it. These texts answer questions about how Israelite society organized itself. This society organized itself within a patriarchal paradigm it inherited, largely uncritically, from its ancestor nations. The laws, which are Yahwistic in their theological basis and articulation, seek to control and manage. The laws do not answer the question "Why this way?" Nor do they explain what it means to be male and female. Only in the later text of Genesis 1 do we have a clearly articulated theological statement on male and female.

Secondly, Frymer-Kensky's observations about sexuality are helpful because they explain why this issue is so vital. The Deuteronomic laws do not rule on the goodness or otherwise of sex but attempt to keep it within clearly defined boundaries. From reading Frymer-Kensky it seems to me that the issue is not so much one of control of a person by controlling their sexuality, but preserving a society's well being, by circumscribing a force that can be injurious to the community's wellbeing socially and even theologically. There must be clarity of paternity, as will be discussed below with reference to virginity. Legally and theologically, sexual infringements are polluting, an offence against YHWH himself, hence the re-iterated phrase "You shall purge the evil from among you." Deuteronomy contains the re-iterated warnings to keep the covenant "that it may go well with you" (Deut 6:1–3). Adultery is not just an individual sin, an infraction of tort law.[73] It is a corporate calamity. In this sense, then, the father's role is essentially one of responsibility as well as

---

72. Deut 17, for example, simply articulates series of measures designed to prevent abuse by a king (eerily redolent of the abuses of Solomon), but does not attempt a theologically particular "Yahwistic" view of what it means to be a king. Such reflections are found scattered through the Old Testament, of course, but never systematised, hence the apparent tension between Deut 17 and 1 Sam 8.

73. For a discussion of this issue, see the debate between Phillips, "Another Look at Adultery," 3–25, and McKeating, "Sanctions against Adultery in Ancient Israelite Society."

authority, and this explains the question of honor and shame. For it is his shame if his negligence brings about a communal disaster, which could bring down the wrath and judgment of YHWH. I found the work of Hilary Lipka on sexual transgression and religious boundaries particularly helpful in understanding this. She argues that in the Deuteronomic material, adultery is a crime against YHWH and against the community, as is indicated by the penalty of stoning which is reserved only for the gravest infractions to the community's well-being.[74] She argues that, although the offence is against the husband, it also belongs in YHWH's province as author of and authority behind the laws. Lipka describes this as an intertwining of religious and communal conceptions.[75] Thus YHWH warns that they must "purge" the evil, as multiple places in Deuteronomy emphasize the keeping of the laws as the way to remain in the land (4:40). Thus I disagree with Pressler that the laws do not concern themselves primarily with morality. On the contrary, I tend to think, with Frymer-Kensky, that issues of male authority and honor are consequent on the gravity of the moral issue.

This is also why the laws we examined require that the slandered wife or the betrothed rape victim be exonerated publicly. Since the act of which they are accused is a pollution to the community and an offence to YHWH, they must be cleared publicly in order to restore both the woman herself and her community. This may also underlie the peculiar oath-ritual of Num 5:12–31 discussed in this book by Richard Briggs: nothing less than the vindication of heaven can free the woman and her children from accusations and doubt about inheritance.[76] In other words, not only are women legal persons, but theological persons. They are not independent, true. They have no equality, also true. But they have personhood. Therefore, although authority (and power) is vested in the male head of the household, that power and authority are by no means so absolute or monolithic as might be thought.

---

74. Lipka, *Sexual Transgression*, 122.

75. Ibid., 122.

76. See chapter 3 of this volume. Certainly public restoration seems to be vital in the case of Jesus healing with woman with a gynaecological disorder. His deliberate address of "daughter" (Mark 5:34) restores her to full status in the covenant community, from which she has been disbarred by the law (Lev 15:25).

These two ideas of role asymmetry and sexual boundaries can inform readings of these laws in three areas which we may find difficult: male headship, sexual morality and consent.

Male Headship

As Pressler and Frymer-Kensky have shown us, there are limitations to male headship. I contend that this is because, although Deuteronomy's legislation has its roots in tort law, it is actually not tort law. No woman is the whole possession of a man in these laws.[77] The restoration of the community to what are perceived as right relationships overrules a man's wishes. Middle Assyrian Law 55 provides a talion law that the father of a rape victim may rape the attacker's wife. Such an idea is unconscionable in Deuteronomy. Women can (albeit through parents) appeal to the community when their own well-being is damaged by slander (Deut 22:13-19). Indeed, this appeal actually goes around the male head (the husband). Their right not to be abused without consequence is supported by the community. If, as remains possible, the law in 22:28-29 is a man and a woman simply getting a little ahead of themselves, the law prevents the woman from being denied the man she wants by her father's arbitrary tyranny. If, on the other hand, it is indeed a case of rape, and the perceived best thing to be done for the woman is to marry her off, her father's hurt pride cannot prevent this.

Sexual Morality

To our modern ears this whole area of sexual expression, where a man may have (heterosexual) sex before marriage, but a woman must be a virgin when married, smacks of nothing more or less than the most sexist hypocrisy. But we need to ask the question about why virginity is so important in parts of the Hebrew Bible.[78] Interpreters have often understood a girl's virginity on her wedding night to be the vindication of her father's success as head of household. My contention is that the sole advantage of virginity is neither the vindication of the male head of the household, nor the ego issue of being the one to take her virginity, but

---

77. Blenkinsopp ("The Family," 62) observes a similar nuance in the Deuteronomic Decalogue, where the wife is removed from the itemised list of Exod 20, where she actually appears after the house! In Deuteronomy this separation may indicate "a slight raising of consciousness."

78. Clearly not all of it since there are laws in Leviticus dealing with priests marrying sexually experienced women.

firstly a clear indicator of non-pollution in the community and secondly, and more immediately, a simple and practical guarantee of one thing which seems vitally important to the Old Testament: paternity. For some reason the biological link of father to son is vital. This absolute necessity is evidenced by the startling lack of adoption formulae in respect of families,[79] and the lengths to which men would go to get biological offspring. There is evidence that adoption was freely practiced in other cultures around Israel, but almost none in Israel itself. The reason is unclear but seems to be linked to such ideas of immortality (or perhaps better 'continuance') as Israel had and also to clarifying inheritance. This in turn has close links to covenantal theology. Marrying a virgin means a man can be absolutely sure that any child who appears in the next few months is biologically his. It is not a glorification of female virginity as such, but a marker of practical morality and clarity of paternity. I am in no way seeking to argue that this is fair—it is, after all, the tyranny of biology—merely seeking to understand the thinking behind this insistence on female virginity.

Consent

In the matter of consent, which is perhaps the place above all where the laws lay themselves open to accusations of gender (as opposed to role) asymmetry, the question is more difficult. Yet Pressler is not quite right to say that consent is no part of the laws, since consent is the measure by which, in the case of an "attached" woman, an adulterer is defined and a victim exonerated. But for the girl herself, her emotional and psychological well-being is subordinated to the demands of her community and her menfolk. There is no help for it: she must marry her attacker. Maybe the loss of virginity as the loss of marriageability is what underlies the idea that an unattached girl must marry her rapist. There may even be the idea that, in the face of events, this is better than the alternatives facing the victim, and that at least she has some degree of status in the community: "Taken together, the various laws that treat of extramarital sex evidence a strong feeling in Israel that sexual intercourse should properly be confined to marriage, of which it was the es-

---

79. That adoption as a concept is not unknown is evidenced in Hosea's extended metaphor, in the divine adoption of the king (Ps 2) although not in Abram's despairing cry (Gen 15:2), nor yet with Jacob and Joseph's blessing of their own descendants (Gen 48:12; 50:23) which deal with inheritance issues.

sence (Gen 2:24) and the principal sign. Thus the victim of rape, the slave girl, or the female captive taken for sexual pleasure must become, or must be treated as, a wife."[80] Both Pressler and Frymer-Kensky note that one of the secondary reasons for making the attacker marry the girl is "protection" for her. She might otherwise be left like Tamar, daughter of David, desolate and alone (2 Sam 13:20).[81] Indeed, Absalom removes Tamar from the household of David to his own. Is this because a raped daughter is a reproach to her father's honor, a living reminder of his failure? The woman married off would at least be spared that: she would not have to be desolate, she could build a life. Indeed Tamar, desperate, tries to persuade Amnon to keep her after the rape: it seems that she understands only too well that he, her rapist, is now her only way to avoid the fate which overtakes her (2 Sam 13:16).

Lest we treat the idea that sex ought to be in marriage as an indication of some sort of equality of relationship, however, it is important to note that, as Bird observes, the law makes provision still for polygyny and if prostitution is frowned on (and it is hard to find a positive reference to the practice in the Old Testament), it was the prostitute who was the social outcast and not her male clients. Nevertheless, the useful perspective is what we might call the "regularizing" position: that if a man had sex with a woman, it ought, wherever possible, to make a marriage.

Whilst I vigorously resist the idea that the only issue here is a violation of tort law, it is true that the offence against the sexual self is not articulated or at least is not taken into account in the judgment. We must be honest about this and say clearly that Deuteronomy's treatment of a rape victim is one we would consider inappropriate to her well-being now. However the message to the man who rapes (if this is what it means) an unmarried woman is clear: what he has done is a very serious wrong. Granted, the infringement is phrased in terms he can understand: that is, the pollution to his community (which has

---

80. Bird, "Images of Women in the Old Testament," 24–25.

81. This poor girl is the epitome of virtue (she does not "go out," she obeys her feckless father's thoughtless command, she cries out and tries to prevent the pollution) and the antithesis of a disobedient member of the household, and yet a truly terrible fate comes upon her, inflicted from beginning (David sending her to her half-brother's bedroom) through middle (Amnon's rape and abandonment) to the end (Absalom's fatuous comfort and her complete seclusion). For more on this episode, see Miriam Bier's discussion in chapter 6 in this volume.

contaminated the community's peace) and the affront to another man's rights. But this at least can be said: he has been told that what he has done is catastrophically wrong and has consequences that will reverberate for the rest of his life. He cannot gratify his own desires with a woman who cannot (betrothed) or does not (single) consent and expect to walk away scot free.

In contrast to Frymer-Kensky's reading of Genesis 34, I believe that the emphasis on determining rape in the countryside (Deut 22:25) demonstrates that there is no idea of a woman 'asking for it' by putting herself in an unprotected environment. Deuteronomy does not ask what on earth she was doing out there in the first place: it doesn't matter: there is no excuse for rape.

The Challenges for Hermeneutics

We need now to consider the hermeneutical question. It is difficult to see how we could claim that these laws embody the equality and mutuality that is the biblical ideal, offered from creation (Gen 1:27; 2:18). I am perfectly content to accept that ancient Israel was a patriarchal society where men's rights are the group's rights and women take their place in the hierarchy below men. But how do we understand these laws that perpetuate such a structure as the word of God, living and active? Surely the word of God must aspire beyond the limitations of the society it speaks to?[82]

One possible way of understanding is explored by John Goldingay. He starts, as most scholars do, with ancient Near Eastern comparisons, and notes that Israel's laws had to begin with where Israel was. He gives the classic New Testament example of Jesus affirming that Deuteronomy allows divorce (Mark 10:5), not because it was what God wanted, but because of the people he was dealing with. In the same way he argues Deuteronomy is dealing with a patriarchal society from within: "Formally, it [Deuteronomy] accepts many features of that social order yet its creative, egalitarian, and liberating dynamic explicitly undermines other aspects that it formally leaves untouched."[83] It remains one of the God-given paradoxes of biblical hermeneutics that those who

---

82. Kroeger and Evans, *The IVP Women's Bible Commentary*, for example, merely comments ruefully that the thinking behind the law seems to be "Any marriage is better than no marriage" (102).

83. Goldingay, *Theological Diversity*, 165.

sought to bring an end to slavery in Britain did so on the basis of a sacred document that never explicitly condemns slavery and indeed provided laws for its regulation and implementation. Since this is so, might we also argue for employing the Deuteronomy laws in the same way? Male headship of the family is a given in ancient Israel and is therefore regulated and guided in Deuteronomy. Liberation readings of all kinds suggest a Christian hermeneutic should cry out against structural sins, and therefore we must find a way to enfold the patriarchal status quo in a hermeneutic which will ultimately deconstruct it.

As we have seen, many of ancient Israel's organizing principles were inherited practices from ancestor nations. From this, I want to suggest that the way Israelite society organized itself, as recorded in the Deuteronomic laws, is not mandated for us. Although Deuteronomy does not attempt a thoroughgoing critique of its society, it does lay down principles by which oppression may be deconstructed. These principles must form the basis for how the church understands the significance of Deuteronomy for today. For example, Deuteronomy 15 attempts to provide against poverty by certain practices. It does not mandate a philosophical, social, or political system that will bring this about. But its principle is clear: God does not want people to be poor, or to be rich at the expense of others. Such principles are articulated at the broadest level by the apodictic laws. In this case we could point to Deuteronomy 5–11 as an articulation of the theological principles by which the case laws are to operate. The case laws implement these principles on the ground. Therefore, the following seem to me to be some "on the ground" principles in the family laws:

1. whoever bears authority answers for it to the community and cannot exercise it in any arbitrary or tyrannical way;
2. women are persons: socially, legally, theologically;
3. *women do not "ask for it," and forcing sex on a woman who cannot or does not consent is a very serious offence;*
4. *sexual boundaries are vital for the well-being of the whole community and its relationship with God.*

The next question for the church is how we apply a theological understanding of how Deuteronomy deals with men who abuse women, and discern what, if anything, can be the significance for us. "God is always having to choose between the least calamitous courses of action."[84] It is not an easy idea to deal with, but frequently in the Bible, the sinfulness of humanity forces God into "least worst" choices. In a fallen world, sometimes this is the best outcome for which one can hope. The instance of a woman marrying her attacker might be another of these "least worst" scenarios. In our society, this no longer pertains: we interpret (in no small measure through the Bible's understandings of human dignity) rape as an offence against the wholeness of another human being. Women have choices now if this appalling thing should happen to them. "The intent of the law was the laudable one of guaranteeing the woman's economic security, but the modern reader would tend to think of it as resulting in a thoroughly bad situation for everyone involved except the father, and especially bad for the victim of sexual aggression—one of the many examples of the social and psychological gap between text and reader."[85] To Western society, to sacrifice the well-being of an individual to a perceived damage to the community is an alien way of thinking. No doubt my reaction to forcing a girl to marry her rapist is conditioned by my cultural inheritance, but I think I must say that there are things that are just plain wrong. Moreover, we do our hermeneutics in the community of our culture, and it is to that community that the church must find an answer to questions about women in the Bible. Having said that, the idea of affront to the community as part of the crime and restoration to the community *in addition to* the restoration to the individual is an idea we have lost in Western society to our great detriment. So, to Deuteronomy's concern for restoration of the community, I add the imperative and overruling need to heal female sexual well-being (which I take from Scripture itself), and thus consider it is in no way appropriate to ask a woman to marry her attacker: on the contrary, it reinforces the violation.

This exploration also offers the theologically difficult but true thought that living the godly life does not necessarily mean life will consists only of blessings. It hurts us to think this, as it hurt Job's friends, because it tells us of a God who is sovereign and yet allows these things to happen and sometimes—often—does not intervene. Yet we dare not refuse its truth, and it may be some comfort to those who are victims of

---

84. Goldingay, *Walk On*, 45.
85. Blenkinsopp, "Family," 60–61.

other people's violence to know that the Bible assures them they did not bring it on themselves.

Overall then I have tried to argue that the laws in Deuteronomy work within their society to try to make things better for women within the existing, deeply patriarchal, structures. All this is by no means to speak of equality. Deuteronomy is no text of liberation for women, any more than for slaves or foreigners. But it is possible to understand Deuteronomy as part of the trajectory, through the later prophetic insistence on marriage as covenant (Mal 2:14), through intertestamental reflections on marriage, through development of beliefs in Jewish thought about sexual rights of women, and above all through Jesus' teachings and attitude to women, to the truly egalitarian idea expressed by Paul that not only is the wife's sexuality her husband's, but the husband's sexuality is his wife's (1 Cor 7:4).

CONCLUSION

This chapter has explored with Pressler and Frymer-Kensky the nature of how family life was regulated in the Deuteronomic law code. It has found that the laws presume a male authority structure and do not question it, nor do they question the right of the male head of household to implement the asymmetric regulation of sexuality established by the law. But the chapter also questioned whether this is really a basis on which to formulate a theological view of men and women. Instead, the laws seem to regulate roles within the existing structure. By themselves, they do not legislate for equality between men and women even if it can be argued that they do at least try for restoring some of the damage caused by sexual sin and rape. But they do proclaim women to have theological and legal personhood, and as such are part of the trajectory in Israelite thinking towards marriage as covenant and the gravity of violating a person.

I described my encounter with Pressler and Frymer-Kensky as astringent. But, if I may push the metaphor a little, an astringent has a positive effect on skin. It removes the things that prevent the skin from breathing properly and being healthy. If astringents sting, they also cleanse. This encounter had a similar effect. I encountered issues I did not expect. I began my study by thinking that Deuteronomy had a very positive view of women. But I could not find liberation within Deuteronomy, merely the improvement of a patriarchal structure. But

I also found that my hermeneutical skin breathes a little more easily. It breathes more easily because I needed to ask better questions about what Deuteronomic law has to say to the church, and how, if not a text of liberation itself, it can be part of a broader witness that can be a liberation to women. And (even if I was not entirely persuaded by some of their analyses and conclusions), I have Tikva Frymer-Kensky and Carolyn Pressler to thank for that.

BIBLIOGRAPHY

Bellis, Alice Ogden. *Helpmates, Harlots, Heroes.* Louisville: Westminster John Knox, 1994.

Bird, Phyllis. *Missing Persons and Mistaken Identities: Women and Gender in Ancient Israel.* Philadelphia: Fortress, 1997.

Blenkinsopp, Joseph. "The Family." In *Families in Ancient Israel*, edited by L. G. Perdue et al., 48–103. Louisville: Westminster John Knox, 1997.

Brenner, Athalya. *The Intercourse of Knowledge: On Gendering Love, Desire, and "Sexuality" in the Hebrew Bible.* Leiden: Brill, 1997.

Carmichael, Calum M. *Women, Law and the Genesis Traditions.* Edinburgh: Edinburgh University Press, 1979.

Christensen, Duane L. *Deuteronomy 1–11.* WBC 6A. Waco, TX: Word, 1991.

———. *Deuteronomy 21:10—34:12.* WBC 6B. Waco, TX: Word, 2002.

Craigie, Peter C. *Deuteronomy.* NICOT. Grand Rapids: Eerdmans, 1976.

Emerson, Grace I. "Women in Ancient Israel." In *The World of Ancient Israel*, edited by R. E. Clements, 317–94. Cambridge: Cambridge University Press, 1989.

Frymer-Kensky, Tikva. "Law and Philosophy." In *Studies in Bible and Feminist Criticism*, 239–54. Philadelphia: Jewish Publication Society, 2006.

———. "Virginity." In *Gender and Law in the Hebrew Bible and the Ancient Near East*, edited by V. H. Matthews et al., 79–98. London, T. & T. Clark, 2004.

Goldingay, John. *Walk On: Life, Loss, Trust, and Other Realities.* Rev. ed. Grand Rapids: Baker, 2002.

———. *Theological Diversity and the Authority of the Old Testament.* Grand Rapids: Eerdmans, 1987.

Kroeger, Catherine Clark, and Mary J. Evans, eds. *The IVP Women's Bible* Commentary. Nottingham, UK: InterVarsity, 2002.

Levine, Etan. "On Exodus 21,10 'Onah and Biblical Marriage." *Zeitschrift fur Altorientalische und Biblische Rechtgeschichte* 5 (1999) 133–64.

Lipka, Hilary. *Sexual Transgression in the Hebrew Bible.* Sheffield, UK: Sheffield Phoenix, 2006.

McKeating, H. "Sanctions against Adultery in Ancient Israelite Society." *Journal for the Study of the Old Testament* 11 (1979) 57–72.

Meyers, Carol L. *Discovering Eve.* Oxford: Oxford University Press, 1988.

Niditch, Susan. *War in the Hebrew Bible.* Oxford: Oxford University Press, 1993.

Perriman, Andrew. *Speaking of Women: Interpreting Paul.* Leicester, UK: Apollos, 1998.

Phillips, Anthony. *Ancient Israel's Criminal Law: A New Approach to the Decalogue.* Oxford: Blackwell, 1970.

———. "Another Look at Adultery." *Journal for the Study of the Old Testament* 20 (1981) 3–20.

———. "The Decalogue—Ancient Israel's Criminal Law." *Journal of Jewish Studies* 34.1 (1983) 1–20.

Pressler, Carolyn. *The View of Women Found in the Deuteronomic Family Laws.* Berlin: de Gruyter, 1993.

Sakenfeld, Katharine D. "Feminist Uses of Biblical Materials." In *Feminist Interpretation of the Bible*, edited by Letty M. Russell 55–64. Oxford: Blackwell, 1985.

Walton, John. *Ancient Near Eastern Thought and the Old Testament.* Grand Rapids: Baker Academic, 2006.

Weinfeld, Moshe. *Deuteronomy and the Deuteronomic School.* Oxford: Oxford University Press, 1972.

Wenham, Gordon. "Betulah 'A Girl of Marriageable Age.'" *Vetus Testamentum* 22 (1972) 326–48.

———. *Story as Torah.* Grand Rapids: Baker Academic, 2000.

5

This Is Her Body . . .

Judges 19 as Call to Discernment

NICHOLAS ANSELL

TEXTS OF TERROR

"THE BETRAYAL, RAPE, TORTURE, murder, and dismemberment of an unnamed woman is a story we want to forget but are commanded to speak. It depicts the horrors of male power, brutality, and triumphalism; of female helplessness, abuse, and annihilation. To hear this story is to inhabit a world of unrelenting terror that refuses to let us pass by on the other side."[1] With these words, Phyllis Trible begins her study of Judg 19:1–30, her last phrase deliberately alluding to the parable of the Good Samaritan. What makes this a "text of terror" for her is not just that a woman gets subjected to horrific violence on the way from Jerusalem to Jericho (so to speak) but that the priest and Levite who fail to respond to her suffering (cf. Luke 10:31–32) represent not only the characters in the story, but also the author or editor of the Book of Judges itself. The role of tending to her wounds, putting her on a donkey and taking her to the nearest inn must fall to the reader. "Truly, to speak for this woman," Trible writes, "is to interpret against the narrator, plot, other characters, and the biblical tradition because they have shown her neither compassion nor attention."[2]

1. Trible, *Texts Of Terror*, 65.
2. Ibid., 86.

Judges 19:1—21:25: A Summary

Before examining why Trible reaches this conclusion, and before exploring how the narrative may speak "for" this unnamed woman in ways that have been overlooked, it may help to re-familiarize ourselves with this horrific story. A Levite from Ephraim takes a young woman, or "girl,"[3] from Bethlehem as his concubine or secondary wife. Yet by the end of the second verse, she has returned to her father's house, where she stays for several months before the Levite travels south to see if he can get her back. While some translations preface her departure by telling us that she was "unfaithful to him" (19:2, NIV), or had "played the harlot against him" (NKJV, ASV), others say that she "became angry with him" (NRSV, NLT) or simply "left him" (Douay-Rheims, reflecting the *reliquit* of the Vulgate). As much will depend on how we interpret this verse, we will return to the exegetical and text critical issues in some detail below.

When the Levite decides to travel south in order to get her back, she has been in Bethlehem for "four months," a period of time that will be associated with safety later in the narrative.[4] After what seems like the beginning of a reconciliation between them—for he had decided to "speak to her heart" (v. 3a),[5] while she, for her part, brings him into her father's house (v. 3c, NIV)—, the Levite is detained by his father-in-law for five days by his repeated offers of hospitality. The four times that the Levite is encouraged to "fortify" himself and "enjoy" himself before leaving (vv. 5, 6, 8, and 9, NRSV) are, in Hebrew, references to strengthening his "heart" and staying so that it might be well with his "heart" (KJV), this fourfold repetition of a key term from verse 3a indicating that he has yet to "speak tenderly to" his concubine (19:2, NRSV). What to a modern interpreter might look like "male bonding" between the father and his son-in-law is revealed as a father's attempt to promote genuine reconciliation and thus offer protection to his daughter.[6]

---

3. In Judg 19:3–9, she is repeatedly called a *naʿara*, "girl," as in the NRSV—the translation I will cite unless otherwise stated.

4. The only other reference to "four months" occurs in 20:47 when the 600 Benjaminites escape death before eventually reconciling with the Israelites who are, at this point, annihilating the rest of their tribe. This precarious safety may thus be contrasted with the temporary safety of the unnamed woman.

5. Trible, *Texts of Terror*, 67. Cf. Lapsley, *Whispering the Word*, 38–40.

6. Trible sees "male bonding" here in *Texts of Terror*, 68 while Fewell, in "Judges," 81, also blames the father for delaying their departure and thus putting them in danger. But see Lapsley's excellent narrative analysis in *Whispering the Word*, 40–41.

When the Levite finally leaves with his concubine and servant, it is almost evening. Refusing to stop at the foreign city of Jebus (later called Jerusalem, 19:10, cf. 1:7, 8, 21), he decides that they will spend the night at the Benjaminite city of Gibeah. No one offers them shelter except for an old man, also originally from Ephraim, who knows that it is not safe for them to stay in the city square. Men soon begin pounding on his door, demanding that the Levite come out so that they might "know" him (19:27, KJV, RSV). Interpreting their intentions as sexual and violent, the old man, here identified as the "master" (*ba'al*) of the house (19:22, 23), offers his own virgin daughter and the Levite's concubine instead. Before the mob can respond, however, the Levite intervenes to push his concubine out of the door, across the threshold from hospitality to hostility.

What happens next is matched in horror only by the crucifixion for she is "trapped in a world of men . . . [and] has nowhere to go but back to the husband who threw her out, only to find that the door of hospitality and safety is still closed against her."[7] As a consequence of being pushed outside, she is raped and abused by the mob until dawn. The man who remains safe indoors and who finds her the next morning "lying at the door of the house, with her hands on the threshold" (19:27) is no longer her husband according to the narrator but "her master," *'adônêhā* (in its plural form in 19:26 and 27) partly echoing the way he refers to his concubine as a "female servant," *'āmâ*, before entering the old man's house in 19:19 (NKJV).[8] When she fails to respond to his command that she "Get up" (19:28), he loads her onto one of his donkeys and returns home. Then, foreshadowing the way in which Saul will summon the people to war by dividing up a yoke of oxen (1 Sam 11:7),[9] and echoing the way Abraham "took the knife" to slay Isaac (Judg 19:29a/Gen 22:10)[10]—for the narrative has not told us that she is dead[11]—the Levite seizes his con-

---

7. Fewell, "Judges," 81.

8. Perhaps the *ba'al* of the house is included in the plural *'adônêhā* of 19:26–27. In addition to the Levite's reference to her as the old man's female servant in 19:19, the Hebrew in 19:25 can, at a stretch, be read as saying that the old man pushes her out of the door.

9. See Trible, *Texts Of Terror*, 80.

10. Trible, in ibid., 80, observes that "in all of scripture only these two stories share that precise vocabulary."

11. See Polzin, *Moses and the Deuteronomist*, 200–202. Here the LXX (in both recensions) differs from the MT by stating that she is dead in 19:28. This (no doubt later)

cubine once again (19:29, cf. 19:25[12]) and cuts her up to disperse her twelve parts throughout Israel.[13]

In response, 400,000 soldiers assemble before Yahweh at Mizpah, a place otherwise associated with the story of Jephthah the Gileadite (10:17; 11:11, 29, 34) and the tragic sacrifice of his daughter (11:29–40). Incensed by the Levite's account, which focuses on his own plight while masking his betrayal (see 20:4–5[14]), the tribes demand that the Benjaminites surrender those responsible for this awful crime. When they refuse, the Israelites ask God which tribe should attack them first. Judah (the woman's own tribe) is chosen but the Israelites are heavily defeated twice in a row, losing 40,000 men before finally striking down 25,000 Benjaminites. While the remaining 600 men flee, the Israelites put their towns to the sword, killing women, children, and even animals.[15]

The victory is hollow, however, as the remaining tribes become distressed that one of their number will soon be history. Because of an oath the Israelites have taken never to give their daughters in marriage to the Benjaminites—a vow made at Mizpah like the fatal promise of Jephthah in 11:30—the remaining 600 men are unable to leave any descendants. Though a loophole is found on this occasion, the result is still deadly. Realizing that no one from Jabesh-gilead has taken part in the civil war or the vow, the Israelites send 12,000 men to this city to kill every male, and every female who is not a virgin, thus securing 400 wives for the tribe. The Israelites advise the remaining Benjaminites to abduct 200 of the young women who are dancing in the annual festival to Yahweh at Shiloh, also persuading their fathers and brothers not to seek further retribution. The Book of Judges then concludes with the words, "In those days there was no king in Israel; all the people did what was right in their own eyes" (21:25).

---

insertion "adopt[s] the Levite's point of view as expressed in Judg. 20.5," as Müllner notes in "Lethal Differences," 133.

12. The NJB, which says that the Levite "took hold of his concubine" in 19:25 and 29, is one of the few translations to reflect the fact that the same verb in used in both passages.

13. It is noteworthy that all six references to "cutting" that use *nth*, the verb we find in Judg 19:29 and 20:6 and in the thematically related 1 Sam 11:7, refer to the priestly activity of preparing sacrifices. See Exod 29:17; Lev 1:6, 12; 8:20; 1 Kgs 18:23, 33.

14. Cf. the literal translation of Lapsley, *Whispering the Word*, 51: "The lords of Gibeah rose against *me* and they surrounded *against me* the house at night. *Me* they devised to kill. My [concubine] they raped/humiliated until she died" (her emphases).

15. See nn. 4 above and 61 below.

"The Challenge to Redeem Scripture"

Trible's insightful and often moving rhetorical analysis of this dreadful narrative draws our attention to many of its subtleties that are otherwise obscured in our English translations. For example, after the Levite has sent out the pieces of the concubine's body to the tribes, the *New Jerusalem Bible* has the Israelites exclaim, in 19:30, "Put your mind to this." Trible, however, notes that the Hebrew should be rendered "Direct your heart to her," thus echoing the Levite's intention in 19:3 to persuade his concubine to come back by "speaking to her heart."[16]

Trible argues that in 19:3, this phrase connotes reassurance, comfort, loyalty, and love as it brings to mind Yahweh's promise in Hos 2:14 to woo Israel in the wilderness. Yet if this puts the Levite in a good light at the beginning of the narrative, it also highlights the extent to which he betrays his concubine after he has her back. The tribes also fail to direct their hearts to her. "Outrage erupts at the harm done to a man through his property," Trible notes, "but ignores the violence done against the woman herself."[17] Furthermore, in securing wives for the Benjaminites, "[w]hat these men claim to abhor, they ... reenact[] with vengeance." By the time we reach the end of this tale of terror, she writes, "The rape of the one has become the rape of six hundred."[18]

No one denies that the characters in the story commit atrocities that cannot be defended, even if interpreters disagree about whether the author of Judges, or the God of the narrative, should be exempt from criticism. Thus, in a work that can be fairly described as an exercise in evangelical apologetics, Alden Thompson admits that this is "the worst story in the Old Testament."[19] Focusing on the four-fold refrain that de-

---

16. Trible, *Texts Of Terror*, 81. Cf. 67. Cf. Pressler, *Joshua, Judges, and Ruth*, 246: "the last half of verse 30 literally means 'Direct your heart to her. Take council. Speak out.'" Szpek, however, notes in "The Levite's Concubine," 128–29, that compared to 19:3, "the idiom has been truncated [as] the word 'heart' *leb* has been omitted. The Levite has most subtly omitted his heart, his compassion, his love for the concubine." Block, *Judges, Ruth*, 548 n. 286, prefers to call this an "abbreviation." Much depends on who is speaking. The NRSV and NJB, which follow the LXX^A at 19:30, ascribe these words to the Levite. But the MT, which is to be preferred, sees these words coming either from those who see the dismembered body (NIV, NET, KJV) or from the narrator, thus Block, ibid., 548 and Butler, *Judges*, 410. The heart of the reader, therefore, cannot be omitted or abbreviated but must be supplied.

17. Trible, *Texts of Terror*, 82.

18. Ibid., 83.

19. This is the title to Thompson, *Who's Afraid of the Old Testament God?*, chapter 6.

clares that "in those days, there was no king in Israel" (17:6; 18:1; 19:1; 21:25),[20] two instances of which closely frame these chapters, he writes that the Book of Judges "was probably put in its present form sometime during the monarchy, apparently by someone who firmly believed that a good king was one of the greatest blessings that could happen to a land." Taking this as a "clue to the author's attitude towards his story and the reason for its inclusion in Scripture," Thompson concludes that this "tragic tale of human wantonness and disregard for law and order . . . illustrate[s] the great depravity that can pollute a land in the absence of a proper king."[21]

Trible also sees the book's own perspective as favoring the monarchy. "The lack of a king," she writes, "is a license for anarchy and violence. So the editor uses the horrors he has just reported to promote a monarchy that would establish order and justice in Israel. Concluding not only this story but the entire book of Judges with an indictment, he prepares his readers to look favorably upon kingship." Noting the irony of the fact that Saul comes from the tribe of Benjamin and establishes his capital in Gibeah, she suggests that "undercutting Saul to advocate the Davidic monarchy may be precisely what the author intends."[22]

For Trible, however, this perspective is woefully inadequate. Advocating the Davidic monarchy is no solution as "[t]he reign of David brings its own atrocities. David pollutes Bathsheba; Amnon rapes Tamar; and Absalom violates the concubines of his father." "In those days," Trible notes sharply, "there was a king in Israel, and royalty did the right in its own eyes. Clearly, to counsel a political solution to the story of the concubine is ineffectual. Such a perspective does not direct its heart to her."[23]

This failure to direct one's heart, this failure to show her "compassion" and "attention,"[24] is, for Trible, the heart of the matter. Commenting on his all-too-brief portrayal of the gang rape, Trible claims that "if the

20. The first and last occurrences add the phrase "all the people did what was right in their own eyes" (NRSV). The final phrase actually means "in his own eyes" (KJV, NKJV, ASV). This may not be a time to impose inclusive language on the text. As Trible notes in *Texts of Terror*, 84, this echoes the words of the old man in 19:24: literally, "Do to them the good in your own eyes."

21. Thompson, *Who's Afraid of the Old Testament God?*, 107–8.

22. Trible, *Texts of Terror*, 84.

23. Ibid., 84.

24. Ibid., 86, as cited above.

storyteller advocates neither pornography nor sensationalism, he also cares little about the woman's fate . . . Appearing at the beginning and close of *a story that rapes her*, she is alone in a world of men."[25]

Trible is more positive about the shapers of the canon, noting that the next story we encounter in the Hebrew Bible, at the beginning of 1 Samuel, is the story of Hannah, a woman of faith whose worth is appreciated by a loving husband, Elkanah, and by Eli, the priest who blesses her. Similarly, the Septuagint (LXX), like the Christian canon which adopts its ordering of the Old Testament, follows the tale of terror with the story of Ruth who also experiences hospitality during the days when the judges ruled (Ruth 1:1). In this way, a canon-sensitive reading may speak for the unnamed woman rather than against her. That said, the combination of both positive and negative elements in Trible's hermeneutic is nowhere more evident than when she observes, "Alongside the concubine, the women of Benjamin, the young women of Jabesh-gilead, and the daughters of Shiloh stand Hannah, Naomi, Ruth, and the women of Bethlehem. Though the presence of the latter group cannot erase the sufferings of their sisters, it does show the Almighty and the male establishment a more excellent way. To direct the heart of these stories to the concubine, then, is to counsel redemption."[26]

While the immediate canonical context may counter the violence, the response of the rest of Scripture, in Trible's judgment, consists of two "meagre" memories of the crimes of Gibeah in Hos 9:9 and 10:9, thus leaving the responsibility for showing compassion to those of us who are "the heirs of Israel."[27] The Scriptures may have failed; but the imperative to "direct our hearts to [this unnamed woman], take counsel, and speak" (19:30) still calls us to confess the present reality of such male violence, insist that this story he retold but never be repeated, and finally "*repent*."[28]

Trible's approach to Judges 19, it is fair to say, utilizes a hermeneutic of suspicion that is not evident in her earlier work on Genesis, Ruth, and the Song of Songs found in *God and the Rhetoric of Sexuality*. But it is important to emphasize that she would not wish to cut this narrative out of the canon. These tales of terror, even in their biblical form, must not be forgotten. The faithful struggling with the Hebrew

---

25. Ibid., 76 and 80, my emphasis.
26. Ibid., 85.
27. Ibid., 86.
28. Ibid., 87, my emphasis.

Bible/Old Testament that she advocates—in which "to counsel redemption" involves embracing what she calls "the challenge to redeem Scripture"[29]—can be contrasted with the approach of Rosemary Ruether in this context. While Trible says that to hear and tell these tales is "to wrestle demons in the night,"[30] Ruether wants to bring this conflict to an end and banish the darkness. To this end, she includes Judges 19 in a rite of exorcism for offensive biblical material in which the community of faith is invited to cry in unison, "Out, demons, out . . . These texts and all oppressive texts have lost their power over their lives. We no longer need to apologize for them or try to interpret them as words of truth, but we cast out their oppressive message as expressions of evil and justifications of evil."[31] For Trible, by contrast, texts of terror are still occasions for a hermeneutic of retrieval or redemption. The call to "direct our hearts" to the unnamed woman is a call to compassion and repentance that is heeded neither by her Levite master, the editor of Judges, nor the rest of the canon. Nevertheless, she would still say (if I hear her correctly) that this is a call that comes to us *from* and *through* the text of Scripture as well as *in spite of* it.

The Heart of the Matter

Should we "try to interpret [the words of Judges 19] as words of truth"? Or is there a more conflicted relationship between the Word of God and the words of men? Normally, evangelical approaches to Scripture would be expected to side with the first of these perspectives. In the context of the present discussion, therefore, it is important to realize that Trible does not adopt the second outlook because of a theological *a priori*. It is not that she has low expectations about finding the Word of Life in Scripture. The problem, we might say, is ethical rather than theological. And our reading of Judges 19 will have to address this if it is to attend to the heart of the matter.

This focus can also help us appreciate why Richard Middleton and Brian Walsh, who may be located theologically at the progressive end

---

29. Here I am connecting *Texts of Terror*, 85 (as cited above) with "If the Bible's so Patriarchal, How Come I Love it?," 55—an essay in which Trible reflects on the difference between *God and the Rhetoric of Sexuality* and *Texts of Terror*.

30. Trible, *Texts of Terror*, 4.

31. Ruether, *Women-Church*, 137. On Ruether's approach to Scripture, see Ansell, *The Woman Will Overcome the Warrior*, chapters 2–3.

of the evangelical spectrum, adopt a hermeneutical strategy that is very close to Trible's in this context. Because, in their view, the texts of terror "stand in significant tension with the overwhelming ethical trust of the biblical story,"[32] and because, in the case of Judges 19, this tension cannot be resolved from within the canon as there is no "inner-biblical critique" available,[33] they, like Trible, finally appeal to the role of the reader in his/her calling to indwell and continue the biblical drama. "The story," in their view, "*cries out* for resolution . . . But this is a resolution that occurs—if it occurs at all—*outside* the parameters of the biblical text."[34]

While appealing to a redemption that lies beyond the Bible is itself a thoroughly biblical idea, as the story the Scriptures tell does not end with the formation of the biblical canon, the problem for Middleton and Walsh is not the incomplete nature of the biblical witness in Judges 19, but the way in which that narrative seems to close down the Word of Life. Like Trible, therefore, Middleton and Walsh attempt to exercise what we might call a biblically faithful hermeneutic of suspicion towards the Bible. They are unwilling to simply write off the biblical tradition as oppressive. But they are not content to say that the problem lies in our interpretation rather than in Scripture itself.[35] "There is a sense," they admit, "in which genuine faithfulness to the authority of Scripture means that we must go not only beyond the biblical text but sometimes even *against* it."[36]

Here, then, is the dilemma: Does a deeply biblical desire to *stand with* the widow, the orphan, and the stranger (Deut 10:18; 24:19–21; 27:19; Pss 94:6; 146:9; Jer 7:6; 22:3; Ezek 22:7; Zech 7:10; Mal 3:5) mean that, in the case of Judges 19, we must *stand against* the text? The issue that Trible, Walsh and Middleton put before us is not a choice "for" or "against" the Bible; it concerns what it means to be biblical in the deepest sense.

---

32. Middleton and Walsh. *Truth Is Stranger Than It Used to Be*, 178.

33. On what they call the "explicit inner-biblical critique of earlier totalizing readings of the metanarrative," see also ibid., 187.

34. Ibid., 181. Their emphases.

35. See ibid., 178.

36. Ibid., 184. Their emphasis.

Narratives of Redemption

One way to explore this important, complex question is to try and characterize the kind of ethical sensitivity that Trible, and those who sympathize with her position, would like a narrative such as Judges 19 to exemplify. To that end, we might take as a starting point a footnote very near the end of her essay, in which she refers to a report in the *New York Times* of a then recent two-hour gang rape of a young woman that took place in a Massachusetts bar in 1983.[37] A few years after the publication of *Texts of Terror*, the 1988 film, *The Accused*, brought this horrific incident to the attention of the wider world. Although not unproblematic or beyond criticism,[38] we might still look to this film as illustrating the kind of narrative strategy that many feminist interpreters would like to have found in the Book of Judges. For while the violence is shown in some detail, the film not only condemns what it portrays but, thanks in large part to Jodie Foster's Oscar winning performance, does much to reclaim the agency and subjectivity of the woman whom the rapists and the male onlookers were intent on turning into an object. Susanna Moore's novel, *In The Cut*[39] and Joyce Carol Oates' novella, *Rape: A Love Story* are just two of the more recent examples of what we might call narratives of redemption in this context. To portray a woman or a young girl as a victim of male violence and to stop there runs the risk of merely evoking our pity; to portray her agency and to reveal her subjectivity despite the forces that would negate her is to engage in an act of resistance that calls forth compassion.

Judged in this light, the story of the unnamed concubine strikes many contemporary readers as a portrayal of violence that does nothing to reclaim the voice of the one who has been silenced. As such, it continues to reflect the perspective of the oppressors. The *events* cry out for our compassion. The *story* does not. Or so it seems. This is the cognitive and ethical dissonance that is so troubling to the contemporary reader. And this is what we must try and address.

---

37. See *Texts of Terror*, 91 n. 66. For the media coverage, see Benedict, *Virgin or Vamp*, chapter 4.

38. Although inspired by rather than strictly based on the events of 1983, *The Accused* did aim to deal with the legal and ethical issues surrounding the original case. For some feminist responses to the film, see Horeck, *Public Rape*, chapter 4.

39. Jane Campion's 2003 film of the same name, while a worthy interpretation in many ways, significantly alters the plot.

In the re-reading of Judges 19–21 that follows, I hope to show that Trible, and others (like Middleton and Walsh) who have developed a similar perspective, have significantly underestimated the redemptive potential of these chapters. This is not a (flawed) ethical tale that proposes a (superficial) political solution. That reading, I will suggest, owes much to a hermeneutic that cuts these chapters off from the rest of the book. Once it is read as part of a long and complex faith narrative that intends to disclose the depth meaning and ultimate horizons of the events it portrays, however, the final section of Judges evidences a spiritual discernment that allows us to see the unnamed concubine's story in a new light. This will go some way towards reclaiming her subjectivity—which I take to be an extremely important contemporary concern that may open up (and thus contribute to) the meaning of the text. For this reason, the dynamic, intertextual hermeneutic that I wish to develop will remain restless until the woman who falls, silent, in Judges 19 finds a way to speak.

Reading Ethically

Before turning to matters of exegesis, there is one other hermeneutical issue that should be addressed if we are to approach Judges 19–21 as the call to discernment that I believe it is intended to be. This concerns allowing Scripture the freedom to address ethical concerns in its own way; which brings us to what is sometimes called the "kerygmatic" nature of biblical discourse. Because it is a text of faith, the act of "reading Old Testament narrative ethically,"[40] which I take to mean reading it for its ethical implications, requires that we attune ourselves to what we might call its "more than ethical" character. As a radically religious text that seeks to give spiritual (re-)direction to the whole of life, the Bible is a book *for* ethics, *for* the development of ethical sensitivity, rather than a book *of* ethics; just as it is a book *for* political discernment and *for* scientific wisdom rather than a book *of* politics or a book *of* science.

This distinction is as subtle as it is important. There is nothing wrong with describing the Bible as a "political" book, for example, if what we mean is that it addresses political concerns and projects a vision that has socio-economic ramifications. It certainly does! But that does not mean that we should read the Bible as a good, or bad, example of po-

---

40. This is the subtitle to Wenham, *Story as Torah*, which focuses on Genesis and Judges.

litical discourse.[41] Thus, by analogy, to characterize Scripture as having an "overwhelming ethical thrust" (as Middleton and Walsh put it),[42] as if this focus best describes the particular angle of vision that we (should) find in the Bible, risks fostering an impatience with biblical narratives which, typically, do not "spell out" the ethical implications of their own message.[43]

A viable biblical hermeneutic, in other words, should be attentive to the dangers of reductionism. If a narrowly ethical (mis)construal of biblical discourse is wedded to feminist concerns, we will most likely foreclose on the interpretive process before the Scriptures can gain our trust,[44] and before we may sense their power to transcend and undercut their own (patriarchal) culture.[45] Ironically, it is only when we stop reading the Book of Judges as a good or bad example of direct ethical commentary, I suggest, that the way the text exhorts us to "direct our hearts" to the unnamed woman can become available to us. In this context, those who lose their ethics will find them.[46]

---

41. Bauckham, in *The Bible in Politics*, 6 (a book subtitled: "How to Read the Bible Politically") comments, "while the law and the prophets cannot be *instructions* for our political life, they can be *instructive* for our political life." His emphasis. This helpful distinction, I suggest, is not required simply because of a change in historical context. The Israelites who were first exposed to the Decalogue, the Jubilee, or the preaching of Amos did not receive political instructions as such, but exhortations in the language of faith that were politically instructive.

42. Middleton and Walsh, *Truth Is Stranger Than It Used to Be*, 178, as cited above.

43. I would rather speak of Scripture having an "overarching" and "central" "*certidudinal* purpose . . . thrust . . . [and] focus" to echo Olthuis, *A Hermeneutics of Ultimacy*, 25, 41, and 45. My emphasis. Middleton and Walsh recommend (but here do not follow) this work's insight into the "nature of confessional language" in *Truth is Stranger*, 233 n. 36. On the refusal of Judges to address ethics other than indirectly, thereby deepening and strengthening the call to ethical wisdom, see Lapsley, *Whispering the Word*, 42 and 36: "The narrator gently guides the reader, helping to create a moral space into which she may enter, and from which she may begin to make some ethical and theological judgments about what is happening in the story." It is precisely the faith focus and "more than ethical" character of the writing, in my view, that allows it to open up this "moral space."

44. On the danger of foreclosure in some feminist approaches to Scripture, see Thiselton, *New Horizons in Hermeneutics*, 439–52. Hermeneutical openness is closely related to the role of trust.

45. For all interpreters who see the origin of patriarchy in the fall, it follows that the Bible must have the capacity to transcend and undercut patriarchal culture if it is to be the Word of God.

46. See Matt 10:39 and 16:25.

JUDGES 19–21: TOWARDS A RE-READING

In the following discussion, Trible's approach to this text of terror will function as a point of departure in a double sense, as the alternative that I wish to propose will build upon two of her own suggestions and observations that I think need to be developed further. These "friendly amendments" to her position will lead to an exploration of some connections between the Book of Judges and Israel's "wisdom thinking"[47] which, to the best of my knowledge, have not been pursued before in feminist (or non-feminist) approaches to the book's final chapters.

The first of Trible's observations that I think can be developed in more depth concerns the connections she makes between the horrendous plight of the woman and the betrayal and crucifixion of Jesus. Thus with an explicit reference to Mark 14:41, she writes, "The woman is betrayed into the hands of sinners."[48] Later, she weaves together biblical allusions from Luke 22:19, 1 Cor 11:22, and John 15:13 to observe that "Her body has been broken and given to many. Less power has no woman than this, that her life is laid down by a man."[49] The words of Jesus in Matt 25:40

---

47. While Murphy, in *Wisdom Literature*, 3, restricts "wisdom literature" to Job, Proverbs, and Ecclesiastes, he claims that "wisdom thinking . . . was shared by all Israelites in varying degrees." Thus although "wisdom narrative" is a contentious category (see Gordon, "A House Divided," 94–96), I would maintain that biblical narratives typically engage in "wisdom thinking," even though, unlike Proverbs, Job, and Ecclesiastes, they do not engage in 'wisdom thinking about wisdom.' Cf. n. 136 below.

I take "wisdom thinking" (within and beyond Proverbs, Job, and Ecclesiastes) to be discernment that finds the way to "life" (Prov 3:18, 22; 4:13, 22–23; 8:35; 10:17; 11:30; 14:27, Deut 30:15–20; 32:47) via attunement to the spirituality of existence. Such wisdom begins with "the fear of [Yahweh]" (Prov 1:7; 9:10; 15:33, cf. Ps 111:10 and Job 28:28)—the "fear" without "fear," according to Exod 20:20, that signifies the presence of the sacred in the light of which creation is revelation. Hence the kind of writing we find in Prov 30:18–19 (NET):

"There are three things that are too wonderful for me,
four that I do not understand:
the way of an eagle in the sky [*baššāmayim*],
the way of a snake [serpent] on a rock,
the way of a ship in [the heart of] the sea [*beleb-yām*],
and the way of a man [*geber*] with [within] a woman [*be'almâ*]."

One reason there is "wonder" at the fact that the eagle, serpent, ship, and lover all find their way (see Murphy, *Proverbs*, 235, and Van Leeuwen, "The Book of Proverbs," 254) is because the "way[s]" of existence in Proverbs are not patterns by which we may plan and control our lives. For a critique of an exegetical fixation on "order" in this context, see Murphy, "Wisdom and Creation" and Ansell, "For the Love of Wisdom."

48. Trible, *Texts of Terror*, 76.

49. Ibid., 81. Cf. ibid., 64.

can also be heard in her claim that "Inasmuch as men have done it unto one of the least of women, they have done it unto many."[50] Here Trible is not suggesting that the death of the concubine points typologically towards the cross. This is, rather, a consciously retrospective reading in which the call to "remember" Jesus' death, which is explicit in two of the texts cited above (Luke 22:19 and 1 Cor 11:22), is extended back in time so that it may embrace someone whom Scripture would otherwise seem to forget. While I certainly support a Christocentric hermeneutic that is retrospective as well as anticipatory, my argument below will find additional and stronger intertextual connections between Jesus and this unnamed woman that are inspired less by "the challenge to redeem Scripture" (in Trible's sense) than by the desire to develop a deepened and expanded redemptive-historical hermeneutic.[51]

Trible's second undeveloped suggestion may be found in a footnote towards the end of her essay, where she refers to "illuminating parallels" that exist between the story of Caleb, Achsah, and Othniel, as portrayed in Judg 1:11–15, and other father-daughter and husband-wife relationships that we encounter later in the book, including those of the unnamed concubine. When these relationships are viewed in sequence, Trible suggests, the ensuing "progression from domestic tranquility to utter degradation . . . symbolizes the story of premonarchic Israel itself. Indeed, the concubine is Israel ravished and cut apart."[52] This is an extremely important observation, I believe, and it is a shame that it has not been integrated into her exegesis of the book's final chapters. The connection, and the contrast, between the unnamed woman and Israel will be one of the foci in the following discussion.

The fact that Trible's observation, insightful as it is, functions more or less as an aside highlights a fundamental weakness in her hermeneutic: in her reading, the story of the unnamed woman and the events that her death sets in motion are separated from the wider narrative of the Book of Judges in which they are situated. So this is where we should begin in sketching an alternative approach. For when the basic literary

---

50. Ibid., 83–84.

51. See Todd Pokrifka's discussion of a "redemptive-movement" hermeneutic in chapter 11 of this volume.

52. Ibid., 90 n. 52. Here Trible refers to an unpublished essay by E. T. A. Davidson which bears the same title as her recent, full-length study *Intricacy, Design, and Cunning in the Book of Judges*.

structure of the book is discerned, the implications for interpreting the story of the unnamed woman are significant.[53]

Literary Structure

It is widely recognized that Judges can he divided into a prologue (1:1—3:6), a main body (3:7—16:31), and an epilogue (17:1—21:25). The prologue and epilogue, each of which consists of two episodes (1:1—2:5 and 2:6—3:6; 17:1—18:31; and 19:1—21:25), contain many deliberate parallels. The main body of the text is also carefully structured. If we focus on the major judges, a thematic chiasm is visible. Following the brief Othniel cycle (3:7-11), which sets out the basic narrative form and provides us with a reference point by which to judge the stories that follow, there are five cycles which can be read as centered on the story of Gideon, who comes closest after Othniel to being an ideal judge, and his son Abimelech, the anti-judge (6:1—9:56). This central section is framed by the stories of Deborah and Jephthah who come, in turn, from Ephraim and Manasseh, the two tribes of Joseph (viewed as the "house of Joseph" in 1:22-23, 35). The outer frame is provided by the stories of Ehud and Samson, who deliver Israel from the east and west respectively.[54]

An alternative way of understanding the main body of the book includes the Othniel narrative in the overall chiastic structure thereby allowing for a number of positive/negative contrasts to be made: between Othniel and Samson (3:7-11; 13:1—16:31), Ehud and Jephthah (3:12-30; 10:6—12:7), and Deborah and Abimelech (4:1—5:31; 8:33—9:57). In addition to highlighting several striking internal parallels,[55] this approach places the Gideon cycle at the midpoint of the chiasm in a way that allows the distinction between his stand against, and subsequent lapse into, idolatry to come to the fore (6:1-32; 8:22-32). The central juxtaposition of the Gideon cycle and of Judges as a whole, in which

---

53. Feminist interpreters who read Judges 19–21 in the light of the whole include: Klein, *The Triumph of Irony*; Fewell, "Judges"; and Schneider, *Judges*.

54. For this overall perspective, see Davis and Wolf, "Judges," 327-28.

55. The Deborah and Abimelech narratives, for example, each contain a story of a woman crushing the skull of a male, the second of these being that of Abimelech himself. Also the direction that Othniel receives from Achsah (see below) may be contrasted with the direction Samson receives from his wives. For further details, see Dorsey, *The Literary Structure of the Old Testament*, 114–15, which draws on Gooding, "The Composition of the Book of Judges," as does Webb, *The Book of the Judges*, 34–35.

his conflict with the Midianites (6:33—7:25) is followed by a period of intertribal warfare (8:1–21), can then be related to the beginning and end of the book, the former conflict echoing the way the opening section looks back to the time of Joshua, the latter conflict anticipating events that culminate in the civil war of the book's closing chapters.

In each of these approaches to the book's literary structure, kingship emerges as a central theme in the book's central section. Although "Abi-melech," the name Gideon gives to his son, means "my father is king,"[56] thus raising questions about his own royal aspirations, Gideon resists considerable political pressure from the Israelites to declare that neither he nor his son would rule over Israel (see 8:23). In the mouth of such a central character, this assertion strongly suggests that the fourfold refrain in the epilogue which states that "In those days there was no king in Israel" (17:6; 18:1; 19:1; 21:25) is not advocating the monarchy as a solution to the preceding events.

As it is sometimes claimed that Judges 17–21 form a pro-monarchy appendix to what might otherwise be viewed as an anti-monarchical book, it is important to see how themes from the central section are present in the epilogue. Thus just before we are told that the old man offers his virgin daughter and the Levite's concubine to the mob, 19:22–23 tells us twice in two verses that he is the "master" or *ba'al* of the house. Not only should this remind us of the repudiation of the ways of Baal in 2:10–15; 3:7; 6:25–32; 8:33–35; and 10:6–10, but it is also intended to call to mind the numerous references to the "lords" or *ba'alei* "of Shechem" in Judges 9 who make Abimelech king in 9:6, following his slaughter of the seventy sons of "Jerub-baal"—the name given to Gideon in 6:32 as the one who contends with Baal. It is this atrocity, for which Abimelech had been paid "seventy pieces of silver out of the temple of Baal-berith" (9:4), that provokes the monarchy-denouncing parable of Gideon's youngest son Jothan in 9:7–20. The fact that the description of the old man as the *ba'al* of the house in 19:22–23 is deliberately designed to recall the events of Judges 9 is reinforced by what the Levite says in 20:5: "The lords [*ba'alei*] of Gibeah rose up against me, and surrounded the house at night. They intended to kill me, and they raped my concubine until she died."

The association between idolatry, violence, and kingship established in Judges 9 is thus clearly present in Judges 19 also. Furthermore, the *intra*textual connection between the *ba'alei* of Gibeah and Shechem

---

56. As noted by Gunn, "Joshua and Judges," 114. See also Judg 8:18–19.

is complemented by an important *inter*textual connection between the books of Judges and Genesis. For Shechem, the Canaanite prince after whom the city of Shechem is named (see Gen 33:18–19), is known to us from Gen 34:2 as the man who raped Jacob and Leah's daughter, Dinah. In retrospect, therefore, we can see that the connections that may already be discerned in Judges 9 not only between monarchy and idolatry, but between monarchy, idolatry, and rape are reiterated and intensified in Judges 19 and 20. In this light, the claim that the final chapters of Judges are part of a pro-monarchy epilogue that counters the central section of a text to which it has somehow been appended is untenable. And so too is a superficial, decontextualized interpretation of the refrain of 17:6, 18:1, 19:1, and 21:25.[57]

This does not mean that Judges must be read as utterly rejecting all notions of monarchy. If we are to resist an oversimplified reading of the refrain, then we must remember that this can cut both ways. Thus there is no need to deny that the book can be seen to reflect God's favoring of David over Saul in the way it portrays the events of Bethlehem and Gibeah, as Trible and others have pointed out. And there is no need to see its vision as opposed, in principle, to the alternative form of kingship that we find in Deut 17:14–20 (cf. 1 Sam 8:4–22) in which a king who becomes wise through the study of Torah is not set over against the tribes but, as one chosen "from among [his] own brothers" (Deut 17:15, NIV), represents the kinship/kingship that should exist between them. If Judges is read within the canon (as part of the former prophets of the Christian Bible or as part of the *Nevi'im* of the Hebrew Bible), then this kind of looking back and looking forward is natural. The same goes, *mutatis mutandis*, for a reading that would situate Judges within what scholars call the "Deuteronomic History" of Joshua through 2 Kings and the "Primary History" of Genesis through 2 Kings.[58]

While Judges is not at odds with its canonical setting, however, it does not simply express a uniform "Deuteronomic" theology but remains a distinct work with its own voice. Thus there is no sense in

---

57. Other interpreters who see that the refrain does not advocate monarchy include Fewell, "Judges," 82; Klein, *The Triumph of Irony*, 141; Webb, *The Book of Judges*, 201–3; and Dumbrell, "In Those Days There Was No King in Israel."

58. The Deuteronom(ist)ic History includes Joshua, Judges, 1–2 Samuel, and 1–2 Kings, but excludes Ruth, which does not follow Judges in the Hebrew Bible. For a careful study of the Deuteronomic History that recognizes the integrity of the books within it, see McConville, *Grace in the End*. On the "Primary History" (Pentateuch plus Deuteronomic History), see Freedman, *The Unity of the Hebrew Bible*, 1–40.

the narrative that Gideon should have embraced the kind of rule we see envisioned in Deuteronomy 17 in any formal sense. The peril and promise of kingship, transformed by Torah or not (cf. the "like the nations" theme of Deut 17:14 and 1 Sam 8:5), lies in the future. As for the era of the Judges prior to Samuel, the perspective on kingship at the centre and heart of the book bears a complex relationship with the closing refrain. For the fact that there was no king—or King—in, or over, Israel in those days underlines even as it contradicts Gideon's words found at the very centre point of the book in 8:23: "I will not rule over you, and my son will not rule over you; [Yahweh] will rule over you."[59] God's *absence* in Judges 19—situated as it is between the third and fourth occurrence of the kingship refrain—and the way in which this divine withdrawal is revealed in the story of the unnamed woman, and not just evidenced by it, is a theme to which we shall return.

A comparison between the opening and closing episodes of the book (as set out below) suggests that God's withdrawal from Israel, as summarized in 21:25, also finds expression in God's refusal to drive out the former inhabitants of the land, as articulated in 2:3, this being related, in turn, to the fact that the Israelites have entered into covenant with them and have failed to tear down their altars (see 2:2). God's refusal to drive out the Canaanites is reiterated in 2:21, where it becomes clear that this is a withdrawal with a purpose, as Israel's commitment to and participation in the covenant as given through Moses will now be tested (2:22; 3:4). That this is no mere test of obedience but involves a call to discernment and wisdom is another theme to which we shall return.[60]

Figure 1

Judg 1:1—2:5	Judg 20:1—21:25
(1:1a) After the death of Joshua,	(20:1–17) After the death of the unnamed woman, the people of Benjamin refuse to hand over the men of Gibeah to the tribes who are intent on "purg[ing] the evil from Israel."

---

59. The NRSV has God ruling "over" the people in 8:23 and a king "in" Israel in the final refrain. But the Hebrew uses the same preposition (*mšl* plus *b* or *melek* plus *b*) throughout.

60. Cf. the testing language of Gen 22:1. For a reading that sees this as a test of Abraham's discernment, see Ansell, "Commentary: Genesis 22:1–16."

Judg 1:1—2:5	Judg 20:1—21:25
(1:1b) the Israelites ask of Yahweh, "Who shall go up first for us against the Canaanites, to fight against them?"	(20:18a) Consequently, the Israelites ask of Yahweh, "Which of us shall go up first to battle against the Benjaminites?"
(1:2) Yahweh replies, "Judah shall go up. I hereby give the land into his hands."	(20:18b) Yahweh replies, "Judah shall go up first." [No victory promised until v. 28!]
(1:3) Judah suggests teaming up with Simeon—"his brother"—against the Canaanites.	(20:19-20) All the other tribes of Israel are united against the Benjaminites.
(1:4-11) Victory against the Canaanites and the Perizzites. Judah takes Jerusalem, puts it to the sword, and sets it on fire. [1:6-7: the dismemberment of Adoni-bezek, cf. 19:29]	(20:21-48) Heavy losses to both sides in the civil war. Towns of Benjamin (of "the children of my brother Benjamin" in 20:28, NKJV) are put to the sword and set on fire.
(1:12) Caleb promises, "I will give . . . my daughter Achsah as wife" to whoever attacks and captures Kiriath-sepher.	(21:1-3) We learn that the Israelites, to their regret, had promised at Mizpah, "Not one of us will give his daughter in marriage to Benjamin."
(1:13-18) Caleb gives his daughter to Othniel and grants Achsah's request for land, made via Othniel, followed by her direct request for springs. Judah continues to be victorious, "devot[ing]" Zephath "to destruction" (with "his brother Simeon") and taking Gaza, Ashkelon, and Ekron, with their territories.	(21:4-12) 400 virgins for the Benjaminites are taken by force from their part of the land to the camp in Shiloh "which is in the land of Canaan." The civil war thus continues as all the other inhabitants of Jabesh-gilead are "devote[d] to destruction."
(1:19-36) The victories come to an end, except for those of Caleb in 1:20—the only example of a successful "driving out" of the land's inhabitants—and the house of Joseph, which puts Bethel/Luz to the sword. The tribes fail to "drive out" the Amorites, Canaanites, and Jebusites, and so end up living alongside them (cf. the intermarriage theme of 3:6).[61]	(21:13-24) The civil war comes to an end. Peace is made with the Benjaminites. The vow not to give them their daughters in marriage is circumvented as the Benjaminites are encouraged to abduct 200 young women who are dancing in the yearly festival of Yahweh at Shiloh. Their fathers and brothers are persuaded not to seek retribution.

61. It would be a mistake in my view to see everything that Israel does in the left-hand column from 1:1 to 1:18 as endorsed by the narrative. It is telling that God does

Judg 1:1—2:5	Judg 20:1—21:25
(2:1–3) The angel of Yahweh, who led the people out of Egypt (cf. 19:30), confronts Israel for "mak[ing] a covenant with the inhabitants of this land" and failing to "tear down their altars." Consequently, the angel of Yahweh declares, "I will not drive them out before you; but they shall become adversaries to you, and their gods shall be a snare to you." Cf. 2:11—3:6	(21:25) "In those days there was no [K]ing [over] Israel; all the people did what was right in their own eyes."
(2:4–5) The Israelites (seem to) lament and repent.[62]	How will the readers respond to the preceding events, given the call to wisdom/discernment in 19:30?: "Has such a thing ever happened since the day that the Israelites came up from the land of Egypt [cf. 2:1] until this day? Consider it, take counsel, and speak out."

not confront the people in 2:3 and 2:21 for failing to subject the Canaanites to the *ḥerem*, but instead says that their failure to keep the covenant will result in the former inhabitants not being driven from the land. This suggests that God's judgment was to have been a driving into *exile*, analogous to the exile already on the horizon for Israel according to Deut 4:26–27 and 28:64. Read in this light, being driven out of the land is not unique to the Canaanites, just as the experience of exodus—see Amos 9:7!—is not unique to Israel. The people chosen to bring salvation to the nations, it would seem, cannot do so without experiencing exodus, exile, and return on behalf of the nations.

That God's judgment was intended as an expulsion emerges from a close reading of Judges 1–2. Here God's decision not to "drive out" the former inhabitants in 2:3 (*gāraš*, cf. Judg 6:9 and Josh 24:12, 18) and in 2:21 (*yāraš*, cf. Josh 23:13) is seen as a refusal to make up for Israel's failure to drive them out in the preceding chapter (reiterated in 1:21, 27, 28, 29, 30, 31, 32, and 33!). It is telling that *yāraš* is used not only for Judah's possession of land in 1:19a, but also for Caleb's victory in 1:20 (cf. Josh 15:14)—this being the only clear example in Judges of a successful "driving out" of the land's former inhabitants! The contrast between the driving out associated with Caleb, who is held in high regard in Judges, Numbers, Deuteronomy, and Joshua, and the repeated acts of annihilation associated with an Israel not noted for its faithfulness to the covenant, is very significant. This subtle but powerful critique of judgment as *ḥerem* should play an important role in how we judge events in each of the columns set out in figure 1.

62. This weeping can be compared to /contrasted with the weeping of 21:2.

Other comparisons (as briefly indicated above) are also highly revealing. Yahweh's agreement that Judah should go first in the conflict with the Benjaminites in 20:18, for example, when contrasted with what God promises in the opening chapter, is hardly a straightforward expression of God's will, as what initially sounds like a repetition of 1:2 is cut short, omitting any assurance of victory. Far from telling us that "Yahweh also joins the fight against Benjamin,"[63] as Trible puts it, as if the text has confused the Spirit of God with the spiral of violence, the events that unfold reveal that the Word of God cannot be subjected to Israel's agenda. If the narrative is read carefully, with attention to irony, one can see that the Israelites, in seeking the divine will by means of the oracle at Bethel, receive an answer that has been shaped and determined by their own question. That "Judah shall go up first" is said to be Yahweh's response, so its meaning cannot be entirely reduced to self-deception. But the heavy defeats that the Israelites suffer as a consequence of acting upon the revelation they receive here in 20:18 and again in 20:23 show us that the Word of God is not what they think it is.[64]

Revelation is thus not subject to human control. But its ironic character is not a paradox to mystify Israel or the readers of Israel's Scriptures so much as a call to wisdom. Commenting on the fact that all the people in 20:1 "gather as 'one man . . . to the Lord at Mitzpah,'" Trible observes, "[e]ven God, who has been absent altogether from the preceding act, participates as four hundred thousand soldiers demand an explanation from the Levite."[65] This is true enough. But *how* does God "participate" in the events that follow? If Trible's reference to "Yahweh . . . join[ing] the fight against Benjamin" reflects her concern that the God of the narrative has become caught up in the "holy" war that ensues, simply saying that God fights on both sides of the civil war, and not only "against Benjamin," will do little to distance the text from the myth of redemptive violence! So how should we understand God's presence here?

One way forward, I suggest, is to interpret these events in the light of God's refusal to bless Israel's response to the death of the unnamed woman; this refusal being related, in turn, to God's sovereign refusal to be King/king (17:6; 18:1; 19:1; 21:25). God's presence/absence in

---

63. Trible, *Texts of Terror*, 83.

64. The reply to their second question in 20:23 is far more ambiguous than they realize, as Lapsley notes in *Whispering the Word*, 54–55. Cf. Fewell, "Judges," 82.

65. Trible, *Texts of Terror*, 82.

Scripture is far more complex than most of our theologies will allow. And so too is the restless character of revelation. Judges 21:25 is thus not a conclusion as such. This "wickedness, stupidity, madness, and folly," to borrow the language of Eccl 7:25 (NJPS), is hardly the voice of Wisdom. And yet this non-revelation of God is a revelation, and thus an exposure, of patriarchy in which what is now "the rape of six hundred"[66] points us back to the call to discernment in 19:30.[67]

Finally, this way of comparing the beginning and ending of the book of Judges brings the brief but significant Achsah narrative to the fore (1:12–15 cf. Josh 15:16–19), for not only does Caleb's promise to give her in marriage stand in direct contrast to the vow of the Israelites not to allow their daughters to marry the Benjaminites, but the way in which she requests springs and land from her father stands in sharp contrast to the fate of the 400 virgins of Jabesh-gilead who are abducted into marriage and thus taken from their tribal land by force.

The story of Achsah has interesting parallels and contrasts with many of the episodes involving women throughout the Book of Judges.[68] For our present purposes, the contrasts between her story and that of the unnamed woman are especially pertinent.[69] In 1:14, for example, we are told that Achsah journeys to see her father and gets down from her donkey so fast that it sounds as if she falls to the ground,[70] even though the request she makes is assertive and "respectfully confrontational."[71]

---

66. Ibid., 83: "The rape of the one has become the rape of six hundred," as cited above.

67. My claim that God's judgment and God's revelation do not stop with the final verses of Judges but refer us back to the revelation of the unnamed woman is tied to my conviction that all judgment in Scripture is "judgment unto salvation"—on which see Ansell, "Hell: The Nemesis of Hope?," 208–10. For a similar approach to Judg 2:6–3:6, see Fretheim, *Deuteronomic History*, 87–98.

68. Klein notes the general pattern of Achsah "as paradigm woman" in "The Book of Judges," 60 and 70, and in *The Triumph of Irony*, 14 and 33–34. She comments on the contrasts that are thus established with the stories of Samson and Delilah in ibid., 121, 128, and 132 and of the abductees in ibid., 190. On the contrasts with the story of Jephthah's daughter, see Bal, *Death and Dissymmetry*, 49, 62, 148–49, and 165, and Fewell, "Judges," 82.

69. See Klein, *The Triumph of Irony*, 172–74 and Bal, *Death and Dissymmetry*, 156–57.

70. Klein, who speaks of her "prostrating herself" in "The Book of Judges," 59, notes, "The Hebrew is so concentrated that it almost sounds like Achsah falls off her donkey." Cf., *The Triumph of Irony*, 25–26, and "Achsah," 24.

71. Thus Fewell, "Judges," 82. Achsah's assertiveness in Judg 1:5 is stressed in *The Message*: "She said, 'Give me a marriage gift. You've given me desert land; Now give

While this may seem puzzling when taken in isolation, it establishes a thematic connection to and contrast with the donkey of 19:28 onto which the unnamed woman, who lies all-but-dead on the ground, has to be lifted.[72]

There are several other contrasts established between these two women within the space of these four verses. Achsah's request for life-giving water is granted, for example, while the unnamed woman's final request for life, symbolized by her hands that reach out for the threshold, is completely ignored. Achsah speaks boldly to her father in 1:15 and to her husband in 1:14 (tellingly "corrected" by the LXX which has him speaking to her)[73] while the unnamed woman (whatever her actions may say) does not speak a single word.[74] Achsah's story begins with her leaving her father, Caleb, to be married to Othniel, through whom she requests land before returning to her father to request water. The story of the unnamed woman begins with her leaving her "husband" to return to the safety of her father's house; it ends with her being transported back to the house of her "master" before her body is dispersed throughout Israel.

If Achsah is compared with the unnamed woman, therefore, her husband, Othniel, finds his counterpart in the Levite, while her father, Caleb, is compared to the father of the unnamed woman and contrasted with the old man from Ephraim who offers the unnamed woman hospitality before suggesting that she be betrayed to the mob along with

---

me pools of water!'" Cf. Bal, *Death and Dissymmetry*, 155: "The request itself creates an opposition between what Caleb had given her and what she wants. He gave her the land *negev*, translatable as Negev, as 'south' or 'dry.' The latter translation introduces the opposition: Achsah is not satisfied with a useless piece of dry land; therefore she wants the wells. Conceived of in this way, her request comes closer to a claim." Fewell's phrase, however, integrates the respect shown in her descent from the donkey. For the latter as a decisive way of establishing a face-to-face encounter with her father, see Fewell, "Deconstructive Criticism," 130.

72. This is noted by Hamlin in *Judges*, 166, McCann in *Judges*, 131, and by Fewell in "Judges," 82 and in "Deconstructive Criticism," 130. Bal, in *Death and Dissymmetry*, 153, has Achsah addressing her father "from upon her ass." Cf. LXX[A] on which see Butler, *Judges*, 6. But this too would point to a contrast with/connection to 19:28.

73. See Klein, *The Triumph of Irony*, 26, idem., "The Book of Judges," 57, and Bal, *Death and Dissymmetry*, 29, 149, and 153–54.

74. All the characters of Judges 19 speak—the Levite, the woman's father, the old man of Gibeah, the men of Gibeah, even the Levite's servant in verses 11 and 13—except for the old man's daughter who appears briefly in 19:24 and the unnamed woman who is present yet silent throughout.

his own daughter. Even the way this character is introduced in 19:16—"[and look, *wehinnê*[75]] there was an old man coming from his work in the field"—refers us back to the introductory chapters as his age would seem to put him, together with Caleb, in the generation of "the elders who outlived Joshua, who had seen all the great work that [Yahweh] had done for Israel" (2:7), while "the field" from which he returns is another echo back to 1:14. The contrast between these narratives from the book's opening and closing sections is often striking, therefore. But the positive connections between them can be even more revealing, as we shall see.

The Achsah-Caleb-Othniel Paradigm

Awareness of the Achsah-Caleb-Othniel paradigm can play a key role in the interpretation of the story of the unnamed woman, as I hope to show. But it can also close down our understanding if a misread pattern from Judg 1:11–15 is read into Judges 19 and is then mirrored back and forth between the two narratives. As a case in point, there is a tendency amongst interpreters who recognize that there is a connection between Achsah and the unnamed woman to see both women as representing Israel as the bride of Yahweh. This latter claim needs to be evaluated carefully as it combines genuine insight with an identification that is extremely misleading.

The Bride and the Concubine

That the unnamed woman represents Israel is made appallingly clear in the way she is cut into twelve pieces to be sent to the twelve tribes. When the prophet Ahijah rips his cloak into twelve pieces in 1 Kgs 11:30, the division between Judah and Israel is imminent. Similarly, in the final chapters of Judges, it looks as though Israel will not survive as a unified people given the huge casualties of the civil war and the near eradication of the tribe of Benjamin. Presumably the Levite does not see himself as engaged in the same kind of symbolic action that we recognize in Ahijah. But as a deliberate call to war ostensibly comparable to Saul cutting up a yoke of oxen to be sent throughout Israel in 1 Sam 11:7, the Levite's dismemberment of the unnamed woman comes close to being a self-fulfilling prophecy.

---

75. This is identical to the demonstrative particle in Judg 19:27, commented on below.

Interpreters who see the unnamed woman not only as Israel but as Israel the bride or wife of Yahweh, often distinguish between Achsah as faithful Israel and the unnamed woman as an Israel which has broken the covenant. This latter identification is invariably connected to seeing the MT of Judg 19:2 ("But she was unfaithful to him," NIV) as the preferred reading over against the LXX and other witnesses. Thus Lillian Klein writes,

> It has been suggested that Achsah is not only a wife to Othniel but also serves as a symbol of Israel, bride to Yahweh. She represents faith (she "asks" [1:15]) and fertility (she provides fields and water). Counter to Achsah, the concubine can be understood as a symbol of dishonored Israel. Neither faithful nor fertile ... [she] is sacrificed to her own passion, be it sexual or merely "doing what is right in [her] own eyes," and ... is literally reduced to pieces. The threat is implicit: Yahweh's bride, Israel, will be divided, reduced from a functioning whole to its "dead" components. It must cease its "whoring."[76]

One virtually unavoidable consequence of this interpretive stance is succinctly articulated by Barry Webb, who notes, "At the beginning of the episode the concubine 'plays the harlot' ([*znh*]); at the end she becomes the common property of the men of Gibeah (19:2, 25). The grim irony suggests that from the narrator's point of view there was an element of justice in the concubine's fate."[77] While Webb attempts to qualify what he has just said by stressing that this does not imply "moral approval of those responsible for her fate" and by suggesting that the woman's infidelity consists in nothing more than her "walking out on her husband,"[78] there is no getting the narrator off the hook. The irony is indeed grim. In a "Narrative Judgment" such as this, writes Cheryl Exum, we are dealing with "rape *in* a narrative and *by means of* a narrative."[79]

---

76. Klein, *The Triumph of Irony*, 173.

77. Webb, *The Book of the Judges*, 188. Hebrew transliterated.

78. Ibid.

79. Exum, *Fragmented Women*, 184, her emphases. Cf. Trible, *Texts of Terror*, 80 as cited above. Exum has in mind a parallel to the unnamed woman/Achsah contrast postulated by Klein. Cf. idem., "Feminist Criticism," 84: "If we understand [the unnamed woman's] abuse as her narrative punishment, then the sparing of the [old man's] virgin daughter makes sense: she is not mistreated because, unlike [the unnamed woman], she has not committed a sexual offense against male authority."

The alternative to this understanding of the unnamed woman's symbolic significance that I wish to propose will involve challenging this construal of Judg 19:2. But quite aside from matters of textual criticism, to which we shall return, the reason we can be confident that the unnamed woman does not symbolize Israel as the wife of Yahweh is that that the language used of her repeatedly, and thus emphatically, asserts that she is a "concubine" or secondary wife—language that is never used of Israel in relation to God. That the Hebrew term, *pîlegeš*, does refer to a kind of wife, and that the narrator fully believes that she should be treated as a spouse, can be inferred from the references to "father-in-law" and "son-in-law" in 19:4–9. But the English translations do a good job of conveying the fact that the term "wife" ("his woman" in Hebrew) does not occur.[80] Although it may come as no surprise that the Levite consistently avoids referring to her as a spouse, in keeping with his character(ization), it would not have been hard for the narrator to have countered this if Israel as wife were part of the intended meaning. The fact that the Levite is called "her husband" in 19:3 and 20:4 does not detract from this point but reinforces it.

Daughter of Yahweh

This does not mean that we have to abandon the idea that Israel is symbolically present in Judges 1 and 19 as the covenant between God and Israel can also be portrayed as a father-daughter relationship. That Achsah can be read as representing Israel in the way she relates to her father Caleb can be seen in the "respectfully confrontational" way she makes her request in 1:15,[81] the assertiveness of her approach being very much in keeping with the spirituality of the Psalms. Caleb, for his part, is well placed to represent God not only because of his high standing in Numbers, Deuteronomy, and Joshua, as well as in Judg 1:14–15 where he provides both land and springs of water, but also because his victory in 1:20 is the only instance in the entire book of a successful driving out of the land's former inhabitants, an expulsion that God had promised in Josh 23:5 but which is retracted after 1:20 in 2:3 and 21 (cf. Josh 23:13).[82]

---

80. *Contra* Fewell, "Judges," 83. Here the KJV, ASV, NJB, and NET are especially precise at 19:27.

81. See n. 71 above.

82. See n. 61 above. Josh 23:5 uses *yāraš*, the verb present in Judg 1:20.

The fact that the father of the unnamed woman may also be seen as imaging the God of the covenant may be obscured by commentators who accuse him of "male bonding" and of an excessive display of hospitality. But once we see that he is reminding the Levite of his intention to speak to his daughter's heart, as noted in the summary above, his actions can be interpreted in a different light.[83] The contrast between this father and the old man of Ephraim/Gibeah who would surrender the young woman together with his own daughter cannot be emphasized enough. If the father shows us what the God of Israel is like, the old man of 19:22-23 is the "*baʿal*" of his household.

Because it is uncommon to read the relationship between the unnamed father and daughter of Judges 19 as symbolizing and embodying God's desire to protect Israel, it is important to note that God's covenant love is seen in terms of a father-daughter relationship elsewhere in the Old Testament. As an explicit term for God, "father," while not common prior to the New Testament, can nevertheless be found in Deut 32:6; Isa 63:16 [twice], 64:7; Jer 31:9; Mal 1:6; and 2:10. One way in which the daughter of God theme comes to the fore involves the description of Jerusalem and her people (and perhaps Judah) as "daughter Zion." Usually, it is assumed that this has little if anything to do with parental imagery for God, either because most translations refer misleadingly to the "daughter *of* Zion" (see Isa 1:8; 52:2; 62:11; Jer 4:31; Lam 2:13; Mic 4:10; and Zech 9:9 in the NIV, RSV, and KJV) or because referring to a city as "daughter X, Y or Z" is classified as a common ancient Near Eastern convention. But while personification of this kind was known outside Israel, what has been overlooked is the unique way in which God as father and Jerusalem as "daughter Zion" become connected in the prophetic tradition. Thus Christl Maier in her recent study of gendered space in the Hebrew Bible refers to the implicit "father-daughter relationship" that exists between God and Israel in Isaiah 1–39 (before the well-known metaphors of bride and wife come to the fore in the second half of the book).[84] She also argues that both Isaiah and Jeremiah "de-

---

83. See also n. 6 above. This perspective counters the charge of "thoughtlessness" and "seductive hospitality" as proposed by Wilcox, in *The Message of Judges*, 167 and Hamlin, in *Judges*, 161, not to mention the parallel Ackerman, in *Warrior, Dancer, Seductress, Queen*, 238, tries to draw between the fathers of Bethlehem and Gibeah.

84. Maier, *Daughter Zion, Mother Zion*, 186–87.

scribe female Zion as a daughter whose bodily integrity is endangered and in need of protection by God in the role of the divine father."[85]

An appeal to God in precisely this role would explain the very high instance of daughter language in the aptly named book of Lamentations.[86] The references to daughter Zion's bruised and abused body throughout are especially poignant in 1:8–10 as "the city as woman shares the experience of her female inhabitants whose rape is stated in Lam 5:11." Given its liturgical character, which is accentuated within the Megillot (the five festal scrolls, which in the Masoretic order of the canon are: Ruth, Songs of Songs, Ecclesiastes, Lamentations, and Esther[87]), Maier is absolutely right at the exegetical level to extend this suffering-with to the "many other women who are victims of sexual violence in the context of war."[88] If we can discern the presence of God in the covenant between father and daughter in Judg 19:2–10, that will have very positive implications for how we may experience the rest of the chapter and the accounts of female abduction that follow in Judges 20–21.

THE SEARCH FOR WISDOM

Important as this is, if we were to conclude that the daughter of God theme in the Old Testament is primarily connected to Israel's need for protection against male violence, this might be seen as still falling within a paternalistic conception of the divine. So in order to explore the counter-patriarchal potential of the daughter of God theme in the Achsah-Caleb-Othniel paradigm in further depth, it will be instructive to take note of another instance of daughter of God imagery in the Hebrew Bible: the portrayal of Wisdom as divine offspring in Proverbs 8.

As Prov 8:22 may refer to God "fathering" her (*qānâ*, cf. Deut 32:6), while Prov 8:24 and 25 clearly imply that God is the mother who gave

85. Ibid., 7. Here she is anticipating chapter 3, which focuses on Isaiah 1–39 and Jeremiah 4–6.

86. Hilliers, in *Lamentations*, 30–31, notes that twenty of the approximately sixty-five OT occurrences of the "daughter X" and "virgin daughter X" pattern are found in this short book, and that the traditional "daughter *of*" translation is misleading. Sadly, however, he omits most instances in his translation since he sees them having a primarily metrical function. But see the NRSV at 1:6; 2:1, 4, 8, 10, 13, 18; and 4:22.

87. This is the order found in the *Biblia Hebraica Stuttgartensia* (hereafter, *BHS*), for example. In modern Hebrew Bibles, Lam becomes the central book as the scrolls, in the order Song of Songs, Ruth, Lamentations, Ecclesiastes, and Esther, come to reflect the order of the annual festivals with which they are associated.

88. Maier, *Daughter Zion, Mother Zion*, 149.

birth to her (*hûl*, cf. Deut 32:18),[89] it might be more appropriate if we were to speak here of a "daughter of 'God/ess'" theme, as "God" is a male word.[90] While a discussion of the issues surrounding gendered language for the divine exceeds the scope of the present paper, I will indicate the need for such a discussion by referring to God as "God/" in the following pages.

Among the many significant features of Proverbs is the fact that Wisdom, the daughter of God/, is described as a mother who thus represents God/-as-mother in relation to her own children.[91] In this context, it is very interesting that she is portrayed as relating to her male and female children quite differently. For although in her calling out to creation (8:1, 4; 9:3), she gives guidance to kings (8:15-16) and gives "instruction" to her other "sons" (8:10, 32-33, NIV), she is *made present* by her daughters. Thus while Prov 9:1 tells us that "Wisdom has built her house [*ḥākemôt bāneta bêtâh*]," this being a reference to the macrocosmic Temple of creation of 3:19-20, Prov 14:1 tells us that "Wisdom of women builds her house [*ḥakmôt nāšîm bāneta bêtâh*]" (NRSV, margin), her daughters here extending both her work and her reality.[92] This incarnational, embodied understanding of the dynamic and expanding presence of Wisdom in our world is especially evident, I suggest, in the

---

89. Proverbs 8:30 may look back to a time when Wisdom was a "little child" (NRSV margin). For a succinct discussion of 8:22, 24-25, and 30, see Perdue, *Wisdom Literature*, 55-56 and 361-62 nn. 90, 91, and 96. While Walke, in *Proverbs 1-15*, 417-22, has a different proposal for Prov 8:30, he supports Perdue's translation of 8:22, 24-25 in ibid., 408-13. While I accept the daughter of God theme, I think 8:22 refers (at least primarily) to God acquiring/embracing wisdom (given the meaning of this verb elsewhere in Proverbs). Cf. Ansell, "The Embrace of Wisdom."

90. Cf. Ruether, *Sexism and God-Talk*, 46: "God/ess [is] a written symbol intended to combine both the masculine and feminine forms of the word for the divine while preserving the Judeo-Christian affirmation that divinity is one. The term is unpronounceable and inadequate. It is not intended as language for worship . . . [but] serves here as an analytic sign to point toward that yet unnamable understanding of the divine that would transcend patriarchal limitations and signal redemptive experience for women as well as men."

91. Because Wisdom, the daughter of God/, represents God/ as mother, this explains why there is no sense in the imagery that her children are God/'s grandchildren. Wisdom's children are God/'s children.

92. Cf. n. 106 below. On the linguistic connection between 9:1 and 14:1, see Van Leeuwen, "The Book of Proverbs," 138. The divine/human parallel between 9:1 and 14:1 can be related to the divine/human parallel between 3:19-20 and 24:3-4, on which see the helpful discussion in ibid., 101.

"song of the valiant woman" that closes the final chapter.[93] And this is why Wisdom, who is herself described as a lover and kindred spirit in Prov 7:4, may be known by the man who is faithfully "intoxicated" by a woman's love (5:19).[94]

Although the book of Judges has been all but ignored in textbook discussions of wisdom literature,[95] there has been enough scholarly recognition of wisdom themes in the Samson cycle and elsewhere,[96] I suggest, to justify re-reading its complex, interconnected narrative in the light of the sapiential gender symbolism identified above. While even a cursory glance at the almost twenty references to women or groups of women in the book would go beyond the confines of the present essay, we will look at the Achsah-Caleb-Othniel paradigm in some detail to see how it may help us read the final section of Judges as a call to discernment.

---

93. For a form-critical analysis and survey of the history of interpretation, see Wolters, *Song of the Valiant Woman*, 3–14 and 59–154.

94. The "sister" imagery in Prov 7:4 (we would say "kindred spirit") is reminiscent of Song 4:9–12 and 5:1–2. It is also instructive to compare Prov 5:15–18 with Song 4:15, and Prov 5:19 with Song 2:7 and 3:5.

95. For passing references at best, see, e.g., Clifford, *The Wisdom Literature*; Crenshaw, *Old Testament Wisdom*; Hunter, *Wisdom Literature*; Murphy, *The Tree of Life*; and Perdue, *Wisdom Literature*.

96. For the Samson cycle as a kind of wisdom literature, see Perry, *God's Twilight Zone*, chapter 4, and the linguistic and thematic arguments summarized by Brettler, *The Book of Judges*, 50–54. Olson, in "The Book of Judges," 787, suggests "Mother in Israel," Deborah's title in 5:7, "may represent the place and office of a wise woman prophet who delivers divine oracles to resolve disputes." Fontaine, in "Wisdom in Proverbs," 103–4, sees the wisdom of the elders at work in Judg 8:5–6, 14, 16; 11:5–11. She also refers to Gideon's "proverb performance" in Judg 8 and to "[c]lan wisdom" operating within and between groups in Judg 8:21. Mathews, in *Judges and Ruth*, 105–15 and 160 n. 360, associates Jothan's parable in Judg 9:8–15 with "wisdom literature." Cf. ibid., 53, 147, and 203. Schroer, in "Wise and Counselling Women in Ancient Israel," 73, notes the wisdom of Manoah's wife in Judges 13. That said, apart from the Samson cycle (see n. 95 above), sustained attention to wisdom motifs in Judges has been minimal, despite the case made by Weinfeld, *Deuteronomy and the Deuteronomic School*, Part 3, for what we might expect from books within the Deuteronomic History, and despite the increasing recognition of the wisdom-sensitive redaction of works that are not wisdom literature *per se*, on which see, e.g., Sheppard, *Wisdom as a Hermeneutical Construct*, chapter 6, Sailhamer, "A Wisdom Composition of the Pentateuch?" Sailhamer, *Introduction to Old Testament Theology*, 240–52, and many of the contributions in Day et al., eds., *Wisdom in Ancient Israel*; Gammie et al., eds., *The Sage in Israel*; and Perdue, et al., eds., *In Search of Wisdom*.

It is important to emphasize that reading the stories of Judges in the light of gendered wisdom motifs should be sharply distinguished from allegorical exegesis (or eisegesis). In allegory, characters and the stories in which they appear typically refer us to a higher, essentially disembodied realm of moral or theological truths. Such an interpretation, or rather negation, of symbolic meaning is foreign to biblical narrative. Because the New Testament emphasizes the uniqueness or singularity of Jesus, we may readily grant that when the language of Hos 11:1, in which God/'s "son" Israel is called "out of Egypt," is used of Jesus in Matt 2:15, the Gospel writer is not telling us that Jesus' life merely illustrates motifs and patterns that have played out before as if his story were nothing more than a cipher for the story of Israel. But by the same token, the narrative is not claiming that the exodus has meaning only as a type or foreshadowing of the life of Christ. Rather, Jesus as God/'s "son" here symbolizes and represents Israel by participating in Israel's history and by recapitulating it in his own life so that its ongoing exilic state may now be brought to an end in what the prophets describe as a second exodus (see Isa 11:15–16; 40–55; Jer 16:14–15; 23:7–8).

On this reading, a symbol does not convey its truth by pointing to another more important reality but by participating in the meaning that is revealed.[97] In non-allegorical narratives that are rich in symbolic significance, therefore, female and male characters are not treated as a means to an end, but are seen to embody, disclose, participate in, and bring about the wider and more specific meanings that their lives symbolize and constitute. The woman with whom the man of Prov 5:19 is intoxicated does not point him (or the reader) to universal truths or timeless generalities that he could know in principle if he possessed what we (mistakenly) call a "God's eye view"! She is wisdom in flesh and blood, a wisdom that is the very meaning of the world of our experience and desire.

The biblical antipathy to idealized abstraction, in this and other contexts, may be seen in the way Prov 31:10 raises the question, "Who can find a [valiant] woman [*ēšet-ḥayil*]?" (KJV) at the beginning of the song that closes the book.[98] Because Woman Wisdom declares in 3:13,

---

97. This is emphasized in Tillich, *Dynamics of Faith*, 42.

98. The KJV rightly does not narrow "woman" to "wife" here. The word for her valor is the same as that used of Gideon when he is addressed as a "mighty warrior" (*gibbôr heḥāyil*) in Judg 6:12.

"I love those who love me, and those who seek me diligently find me" and because the second half of 31:10 so closely echoes the description of Wisdom in 3:15 and 8:11, we might conclude that this is a song in praise of Her. But even if that were so, this would not mean that we were being presented with an unattainable ideal or hypostatized divine attribute. Compelling evidence that this song is (at least in part) about the human incarnation of Wisdom is found barely a page later in the Masoretic version of the Hebrew canon, when Boaz answers the question of Prov 31:10 with the words "*ēšet ḥayil 'āte*," literally "woman of valor you," when Ruth approaches him in the middle of the night (Ruth 3:11). As this is the only instance of this phrase outside Proverbs, this is a good example of a verbal cue that can alert us to a wisdom motif that we might otherwise overlook.[99]

The presence of a "female embodiment of Wisdom" theme, often coupled with the assertive inflection it receives in Proverbs 31, can be traced throughout the Megillot, the five festal scrolls that Ruth introduces in the Masoretic canon.[100] Even more significant from a canonical point of view is the way Ruth 3:11 echoes the Genesis narrative. For although Boaz sees Ruth as the answer to Prov 31:10, so to speak, he does not have to "*find* a [valiant] woman," as he wakes up to discover that she has come to him—this being the experience of Adam when he first encounters Eve in Gen 2:21–23.

---

99. The only other reference to a woman of valor occurs in Prov 12:4. In saying that she will be recognized "in the gates" (Ruth 3:11), Boaz's words join the opening phrase of the poem (Prov 31:10) to its closing phrase (Prov 31:31) as noted by Christensen, *Deuteronomy 1:1—21:9*, 344–45 and Sailhamer, *Introduction to Old Testament Theology*, 213–14. Sakenfeld, in *Just Wives?*, 126–27, notes several ways Ruth embodies the qualities of Prov 31:10–31 towards Naomi. Ruth may also be connected to the house-building theme of Prov 14:1 discussed above, as this language is used in the blessing of Ruth 4:11.

100. In the Masoretic canon, Ecclesiastes is the central book of the five, while Ruth and Esther form an *inclusio*. The wisdom focus I am proposing is supported by Bartholomew's claim, in *Ecclesiastes*, 265–68, that Woman Wisdom is referred to in Eccl 7:28. Noting that Qoheleth is a feminine singular noun, Sailhamer remarks in *Introduction to Old Testament Theology*, 214 n. 28, that the books of the Megillot "are the only books in the Hebrew canon that have a feminine singular subject throughout"— a canonical grouping he thinks is inspired by the theme of wisdom as a young woman found in e.g., Prov 8:31. Longman, in *Proverbs*, 540, speaks of an assertive/valiant woman theme extending from Proverbs 31 to Ruth and to Song of Songs. Many scholars see the Megillot as a late, post-Christian canonical grouping. But see Christensen, "Josephus and the Twenty-Two-Book Canon," and his more recent *Deuteronomy 1:1—21:9*, lxxxvii–xcii and *The Unity of the Bible*, chapter 4.

Given the strong connection between wisdom and kingship in Prov 8:15, 2 Sam 14:7, and 1 Kgs 3:9, and given the fact that humanity's royal presence as *imago Dei* in Gen 1:16–18 introduces the wisdom-rich narrative of Genesis 2–3,[101] it is well worth considering whether the reason God/ says, "It is not good that the man should be alone; I will make him a helper ['ēzer] as his partner" in Gen 2:18 is because the man (representing not "humanity" so much as "humanity in need") lacks the wisdom to guide creation in history. It is no coincidence, on this reading, that 'ēzer refers elsewhere in the Pentateuch only to God/ (see Exod 18:4; Deut 33:7, 29).[102] Once we realize that the lack of a partner also reveals the need (to search) for wisdom, we can understand why the two references to Eve as 'ēzer in Gen 2:18–20 frame the account of Adam naming the animals of the field and the birds of the air that are brought to him. For not only is such naming an exercise in discernment, but the wild animals in particular have their own wisdom according to 3:1, even though it is only the man's encounter with the woman in 2:21–22 that can elicit the "at last" of 2:23.[103]

The interrelatedness of the search for wisdom and for a life partner can also help us appreciate the depth meaning to the restless, non-patrilocal pronouncement of Gen 2:24: "Therefore a man leaves his father and his mother and clings to his [woman], and they become one flesh." The reversal of patriarchal (divine as male) gender symbolism continues as the verb that is used for the man clinging to the woman, *dābaq*, is frequently used of humanity clinging to God/ (see Deut 10:20; 11:22; 13:4; 30:20; Josh 22:5; 23:8; 2 Kgs 18:6; Jer 13:11; Ps 119:31). Later in the narrative, when we are told that "Adam knew Eve" (Gen 4:1), such knowing (*yāda'* as in Gen 3:5, 7, 22) is clearly connected to the wisdom that is celebrated in Prov 30:18–19.[104] Because gender difference

---

101. As only the kings of the ANE were seen as imaging the god/s, Genesis 1 democratizes this understanding. For wisdom motifs in Genesis 1–3, see Ansell, "The Call of Wisdom/The Voice of the Serpent"; Ansell, "The Embrace of Wisdom"; and Sailhamer, "A Wisdom Composition of the Pentateuch?," 26.

102. In addition, the verbal form appears in Gen 49:25, where it refers to God/, and in Deut 32:38, where it refers sarcastically to false god/s doing what God/ alone can do.

103. The wisdom of the wild animals is implied in Gen 3:1. That the serpent is the wisest (not craftiest) among them coheres with how *'ārûm* as is understood in Prov 12:16, 23; 13:16; 14:8, 15, 18; 22:3; and 27:12. Cf. Ansell, "The Call of Wisdom." While animals are wise according to Prov 30:24–28, they do not know the path to the source of Wisdom according to Job 28:7–8, 11. Hence one dimension of the "at last" of Gen 2:23.

104. See n. 47 above.

and authentic sexual desire participate in the call to wisdom, they may symbolize it, allowing the biblical writers to address the central issues of human existence in a focused way.

One of the biggest obstacles to a wisdom-sensitive reading of Gen 2–3 is the way a traditional understanding of Eve's role in the fall has so dominated exegesis that her relationship to the creational and redemptive dimensions of the narrative has gone largely unnoticed. But if Eve, "the mother of all living" (Gen 3:20, cf. Prov 3:18; 8:35; 16:22),[105] is seen as a daughter of Wisdom given to help Adam shape history and thus realize the blessing of Gen 1:28, and if, to make explicit the intertextual relationship with Ezek 10:19 and 43:1–5, she is also seen to represent God/'s Glory accompanying Adam into exile in Gen 3:22—4:1,[106] then the way we are introduced to this counter-patriarchal way of symbolizing the covenant between God/ and humanity right at the beginning of the canon can alert us to the fact that this kind of wisdom thinking might show up almost anywhere in the Hebrew Bible.[107]

In the case of Judges, this canonical possibility makes sense because the Adam and Eve narrative forms the introduction to the Primary History, which runs from Genesis to 2 Kings. But an argument for the presence of this gendered, sapiential theme can also be made via the close relationship that comes to exist between the book of Judges and

---

105. As Eve, whose name, *ḥawwâ*, probably means/connotes Life (see BDB, 295, cf. LXX, *Zōē*), is referred to as "mother of all living" *before* giving birth (Westermann, *Genesis 1–11*, 267–68, is right to highlight this), her Life-giving may be seen to have Wisdom connotations that precede/exceed biological mothering.

106. As Ezek 10:19 portrays the Glory of God/ leaving the Jerusalem Temple via the east gate, to return the same way in Ezek 43:1–5, this means that the Glory, which becomes identified with Wisdom in the later Jewish idea of the *Shekinah*, did not return to heaven but went with Israel into exile. It is most interesting that while only the man is expelled from the Garden in Gen 3:22–24, to head east of Eden, Eve nevertheless accompanies him (see 4:1). Here, I suggest, Adam represents not humanity so much as fallen humanity, while Eve represents God/'s Glory going into exile. Cf. the discussion of Wisdom's sons and daughters in Proverbs above, and Ansell, "Creational Man/ Eschatological Woman," especially 16–21.

107. This is not to deny that Eve is also caught up in the dynamics of the fall. If, near the beginning of the biblical narrative, Eve is seen, in part, as an estranged daughter of Wisdom (cf. the "strange" woman of Prov 2:16; 5:3, 20; 7:5; and 22:14, KJV), this may be related to the "aversion to mixed marriage" theme in Neh 13:23–27 (cf. 1 Kgs 11:1–8) in the penultimate verses of the Masoretic canon. In distinction from the identification of women with spirit-negating matter in the Greek philosophical (wisdom) tradition, this recognizes the reality of female leadership, even though such leadership may go awry.

the book of Ruth. For in the Christian canon, which follows the LXX, not only has the *Kethuvim* been placed before the latter prophets, but the Megillot has been broken up,[108] Ruth and Lamentations now being positioned, respectively, after Judges and Jeremiah.

Although this represents a loss to the Writings section, we should not forget Trible's claim that there is redemptive significance in the fact that Ruth has come "[a]longside" the unnamed woman.[109] Furthermore, we can also say, on the basis of the intertextual relationship between Prov 31:10–33 and Ruth 3:11, that Ruth brings the "valiant daughter of Wisdom" motif with her into that part of the canon that tells of "the days when the judges ruled" (Ruth 1:1). In this, she does not introduce a new theme into the Deuteronomic History so much as echo and help us recognize the presence of another wise woman of valor who already stands alongside the unnamed woman on the other side of Judges 19.

Achsah and the Disclosure of Wisdom

If we return to look at the Achsah-Caleb-Othniel paradigm in the light of the "female embodiment and disclosure of Wisdom" theme that we have been exploring, Judg 1:14a emerges as a very significant text. On the surface, this half-verse may seem uneventful. In the NRSV, it reads: "When she came to him [i.e., to Othniel], she urged him to ask her father for a field." But as was the case with 1:14b–15 (which we looked at in terms of the daughter of God/ theme that may be discerned in the Caleb-Achsah relationship), there is a great deal of meaning here compressed into just a few words.

In Klein's analysis of the Hebrew, Achsah's coming to Othniel [*bebôāh*], which immediately follows her being given to him as a life partner, has sexual connotations (cf. the use of *bô'* in Gen 19:34) that flow into the meaning of this urging "for a field—a place to plant his seed." But while this is thematically related to the way this "young bride dramatically, but not seductively, asks for a source of water to make sure the seeds will grow"[110] in verse 15, it is important to realize that

---

108. Some would speak instead of the non-formation of the Megillot. But see n. 100 above. At very least, the connection between Prov 31:10, 31 and Ruth 3:11 strongly suggests that Ruth's placement next to Judges, however meaningful and fitting, is secondary not primary, *contra* the scholars cited by Brueggemann, *An Introduction to the Old Testament*, 322–23.

109. Trible, *Texts of Terror*, 85, as cited above.

110. Klein, *The Triumph of Irony*, 26. For the sexual connotations of her coming to

although she is making an indirect request to her father in verse 14a, her "urg[ing]" that Othniel ask for this land is not itself a request in either a direct or an indirect sense. In this respect, verses 14a and 14b–15—Achsah's interaction with Othniel and her interaction with Caleb—refer to separate activities each of which has its own symbolic meaning. While Achsah is "respectfully confrontational" towards her father, as explored above, her approach to Othniel has a different character and significance altogether.

To grasp the distinction, it is important to stress that the phrase that is used of her "urg[ing]"—"*wattesîtêhû*"—is far more powerful and directive than the English translations are able to convey. While the verb, *sût*, may be negative (it describes the Satan's attempted influence in Job 2:3), it is also used three times of God/: once by David in 2 Sam 26:19, when he seems to grant Saul the possibility that "it is [Yahweh] who has stirred you up against me," once in Job 36:16, where Elihu claims God/ "drew [Job] from the mouth of distress to a wide space," and once in 2 Chr 8:31, where the narrator, using a verbal form of *'ēzer*, says that God/ "helped" [*'azārô*] the king of Israel and "drew [the powerful enemy chariots] away from him." The "urg[ing]" of Judg 1:14a is no mere asking, no matter how assertively this is construed. If Klein is right to see Achsah as "an ideal image of Yahwist womanhood" here,[111] it is because this daughter of Yahweh is a daughter of Wisdom who gives fundamental (i.e., religious) direction to her life partner. And this means that Israel, as recipient of and respondent to God/'s revelation, is symbolized in this context not by Achsah, but by Othniel.[112]

This understanding of the gender symbolism in Judges 1, in which the female represents the divine while the male represents the creaturely, has direct implications for how we may understand the counterpart to the Achsah-Caleb-Othniel paradigm found in Judges 19 as this suggests that the Israel that does not live by divine Wisdom is represented by the Levite, not by his concubine. Instead of seeing Achsah and the unnamed woman as symbolically opposed to each other as contrasting images for Israel, therefore, we are now free to explore whether these two women have a positive connection via the presence of Wisdom.

---

his house, see Klein, "The Book of Judges," 56–58.

111. Klein, *The Triumph of Irony*, 26.

112. Fewell, in "Deconstructive Criticism," 133, wonders if Othniel rather than Acsah might represent Israel but does not develop this.

JUDGES 19 AS CALL TO DISCERNMENT

To fully disassociate the unnamed woman from an unfaithful Israel that does what is "right/wise in [its] own eyes" (Prov 3:7; 16:2; 26:5, 12; 30:12; Judg 17:6; 21:25), we will first need to look at whether Judg 19:2 claims that she was unfaithful to the Levite as is maintained by the NIV, KJV, NKJV, ASV, and WEB. As we shall see, this is not simply a matter of translation but involves the art and science of textual criticism. There is much at stake here. Siding with the NRSV or the NIV at this point will determine whether the relationship between wisdom and the unnamed woman is positive or negative.

Textual Criticism

The main argument in favor of the NIV (and similar translations) is that it represents an essentially correct understanding of the Hebrew phrase *wattizneh ālāyw* as found in the MT of Judg 19:2. Although this is probably more accurately translated by the NKJV which reads, "and [she] played the harlot against him," this only emphasizes the reference to sexual infidelity that the NIV wishes to convey.

As for the NRSV, which together with the RSV, NLT, NET, and NJB speaks of the unnamed woman's anger rather than infidelity, there are at least two arguments that are commonly put forward in its favor. One is that the Hebrew verb *zānâ* may have a second root that is cognate with *zenû*, an Akkadian word for anger or hatred.[113] The other is that the LXX[A], a recension of the LXX which refers very clearly to anger and not infidelity, represents a textual tradition that is superior to the MT at this point. Although there are other arguments in support of the NRSV here (such as the absence of any other reference to infidelity in the rest of the narrative), it is probably fair to say that the translators of the NRSV, and of the other versions which support it at 19:2, have come to their conclusions on the basis of one or both of these considerations.

My own view is that although the NRSV is extremely unconvincing as a translation of the extant MT of Judg 19:2, it is to be preferred over the NIV as the latter is untenable on text critical grounds. I would hasten to say that I am not basing this conclusion on a preference for

---

113. This claim is found in, e.g., *HALOT*, 275, *TLOT*, 388, *ad loc* and *NIDOTTE*, 1100. Its acceptance by Barthélemy, *Critique Textuelle*, 116, has also been influential. But see n. 118 below.

the LXX over the MT as such. Consequently, I do not think that the NRSV translation (which seems to be based too straightforwardly on the LXX[A]) is fully adequate. But I am thankful that the NRSV, together with its precursor, the RSV, and the contemporary evangelical NLT, alert the English reader to the fact that the NIV and other traditional versions can be challenged at this point.

My own argument concerning the best way of interpreting 19:2 will be based on what I take to be the most likely reading of the text in its earliest proto-Masoretic form. Thus rather than seeing the LXX as representing an earlier or superior textual tradition (a view that was popular among OT scholars before the discovery of the Dead Sea Scrolls[114]), I see the LXX in both its major recensions (LXX[A] and LXX[B]), together with the Vulgate, the surprisingly literal translation of Targum Jonathan, and the extant MT, as a witness to the earliest proto-Masoretic form of the biblical tradition. This allows for a proper respect for the MT as a textual tradition of enormous value,[115] without fixating on the extant MT, which in itself can at best only take us back to the "unified" consonantal text of the late first century AD.[116]

So if the phrase that is under dispute is *wattizneh ʿālāyw*, what form did it most likely take in the earliest proto-Masoretic version of Judg 19:2? Following the text critical work of Emanuel Tov, I propose that the key verb was *wtznḥ*, this being the consonantal form of *wattiznaḥ*, meaning "and she rejected [him]."[117] At some point in the four hundred years or so between the earliest proto-MT of the third century BC and the unified text of the proto-MT, this became *wtznh* and thus *wattizneh* when the vowel points were added many centuries later. While the substitution of a *he* for a *ḥet* represents a small change in one part of one

---

114. See Wolters, "The Text of the Old Testament," 23–25.

115. See ibid., 28–31 for what appears to be a growing scholarly consensus concerning the special status of the proto-Masoretic textual tradition. Methodologically, however, one may still distinguish the earliest "canonical" text (my focus) from the earliest text *per se*. Cf. Schenker, ed., *The Earliest Text of the Hebrew Bible* and Tov, "The Status of the Masoretic Text."

116. See Tov, *Textual Criticism of the Hebrew Bible*, 29–35, and Wegner, *A Student's Guide to Textual Criticism of the Bible*, 58–78. Cf. ibid., 34 and 139 for timelines that place the "unified" proto-MT soon after the destruction of the Second Temple.

117. See Tov and Polak, eds., *The Revised CATSS Hebrew/Greek Parallel Text*, ad loc. Meyer's proposal along these lines is found in BHS, *ad loc*. On this as the *lectio difficilior*, see n. 141 below.

Hebrew consonant (an easy to imagine error for a scribe copying a text in post-exilic script), the change in meaning (from rejection to infidelity or harlotry) is huge.

The original reading that I am proposing is not a wild conjecture but can be seen to lie behind a wide variety of independent witnesses, all of which go back to a Hebrew base text that is far earlier than the extant MT of our Hebrew Bibles. If we look at the occurrences of *zānaḥ* elsewhere in the Old Testament, we can see that God/'s rejection of Israel in particular is frequently paired with anger (see Hos 8:5; Pss 60:1 [MT 60:3; LXX 59:3]; 74:1 [LXX 73:1]; and 89:38 [MT 88:38; LXX 88:39]). This (and not a highly conjectural second root for *zānâ*) makes excellent sense of the LXX[A] translation "*ōrgisthē autō*" (she became angry with him, cf. NRSV, etc),[118] and also makes very good sense of the LXX[B] translation, "*eporeuthē*" (she left him),[119] together with the translations found in the Aramaic Targum Jonathan, "*ûbasarat 'elôhî*" (and she despised him),[120] and the Latin Vulgate, "*quae reliquit eum*" (and she left him). When one adds to this that the extant form of the MT also helps

---

118. While several commentators assume that LXX[A] here translates a second root for *zānâ*, the lexica on which they rely (see n. 113 above) only ever cite Judg 19:2 as an example. This alleged second root, which is not recognized by BDB and is explicitly rejected by *TWOT*, 563c, would appear to rest entirely on the alleged Akkadian cognate. To judge by the earliest source cited by *HALOT* and *TLOT* (cf. Barthélemy, *Critique Textuelle*, 116), it would seem that the lexica reflect a conjecture, first put forward in 1947 by G. R. Driver, in "Mistranslations in the Old Testament," 29–30, that attempts to explain the divergence of LXX[A] from the MT at Judg 19:2. This is entirely circular. Furthermore, we should note that it is *zānaḥ* and not *zānâ* that is most likely cognate with Akkadian *zenû*, as recognized almost fifty years ago by Yaron, "The Meaning of [*zānaḥ*]," 237–39, cf. Erlandsson, "*zānāh*," 99 and Ringgren, "*zānach*," 105–6 (although anger should not thereby displace rejection as the central meaning, on which see Broyles, *The Conflict of Faith and Experience in the Psalms*, 67–69). Barthélemy, ibid., defends the MT by harmonizing it with LXX[A] via the arguments I am here rejecting. Although this more or less exonerates the concubine, his discussion seriously muddies the waters. Textual criticism must contend with the conflict between the extant MT and LXX[A]!

119. Niditch, *Judges*, 189, notes the similarity between *poreuō* (go) and *porneuō* (fornicate). To argue that LXX[B] is corrupt here would align it to the extant MT. But besides being conjectural, the other textual witnesses remain united in their opposition.

120. On the "clear coherent" nature of TJon as a translation, see Smelik, *The Targum of Judges*, 641. Smelik's judgment that proto-TJon predates the Bar Kokhba revolt (AD 132–36) (see the summary of ibid., 642) is consistent with a Hebrew *Vorlage* predating the "unified" proto-MT. Certainly, its translation of 19:2 would cohere well with *zānaḥ* being cognate with Akkadian *zenû* (meaning hate) as suggested in n. 118 above.

us work back to *znh* as the original verb, the case against the NIV is formidable.[121]

The argument from immediate context is also strong. For while neither *zānâ* nor *zānah* are construed with the versatile preposition *'al* elsewhere, "*wattiznah 'ālāyw*" (she rejected against him) makes excellent sense in 19:2 as the grammatical and thematic counterpart to the Levite's decision in 19:3 to speak *'al-libbâh*" (to her heart) in 19:3. Thus, I will proceed to explore the story of the unnamed woman on the assumption that 19:2 intends to tell us that she rejected the Levite before returning to her father's house.

The Rejection of Wisdom

But how are we to interpret this rejection? If we continue to explore the narrative of Judges 19 in the light of the Achsah-Caleb-Othniel paradigm, then the language of 1:14a (as analyzed above) suggests a parallel and contrast: the young woman who has been *taken* in marriage in 19:1 (*wayyiqqah-lô 'iššâ pîlegeš* cf. Gen 6:2; 34:2, 4; 2 Sam 11:4; 12:4; 12:9–10), unlike the woman given in marriage in 1:13, rejects the Levite's advances and refuses to consummate the relationship.

This proposal (which is close to how Josephus seems to have interpreted the story[122]) fits well with the way the narrative refers to her as

---

121. See also the reference to Josephus' paraphrase in n. 122 below. The NIV is supported by the Peshitta. But given its date, it is not at all surprising that it should reflect the late, unified text of the MT. What is surprising is the departure of the Vulgate from the latter. Thompson, in *Reading The Bible With The Dead*, 194–95, comments, "it is a mystery beyond explanation that Jerome, who translated the Vulgate from what he liked to call the 'Hebrew truth,' seems to have preferred the Greek reading here." But rather than assume that he has followed LXX[B], why not entertain the possibility that the Hebrew scholars with whom he consulted pointed him to a Hebrew text that differed from (and I would add: was superior to) the "unified" form of the MT? The use of *reliquit* in Judg 19:2 connotes or implies the concubine's rejection of the Levite. Although it is a far weaker translation of *zānah* than *proiciet*, which is used for God/'s rejection of Israel [Hebrew *zānah*] in Hos 8:5 and Ps 59:3 [ET 60:1; MT 60:3; LXX 59:3], the latter verb responds to and is paired with *dereliqueris* (forsake) in 1 Chr 28:9.

The Vulgate ensured that the corruption of the MT did not affect the Christian reading of Judg 19:2 prior to the sixteenth century. For the history of interpretation, see Gunn, *Judges*, 243–75, Schroeder, *Dinah's Lament*, chapter 3, and Thompson, *Reading the Bible with the Dead*, 193–98. (For a helpful survey of recent feminist interpretation, see Scholz, *Sacred Witness*, 139–55.)

122. See Josephus, *Antiquities*, 5:136–37. His paraphrase of Judges 19–21 continues until 5:174. Although he would have been conversant with Judges 19 in Hebrew as well as in Greek, he clearly does not accept what is for us the MT of 19:2.

a "girl" (*na'ărâ*) no fewer than six times in 19:3, 4, 5, 6, 8, and 9. As the seventh and final use of *na'ărâ* in Judges occurs at 21:12, this establishes a connection between the unnamed young woman and the "four hundred virgins [*na'ărâ betûlâ*] who had never slept with a man" but who will soon be abducted to Shiloh in Canaan. If the young woman who is taken in marriage from Bethlehem to Ephraim in 19:1 is still seen as a virgin daughter when she leaves her father's house a second time to arrive in Gibeah in 19:15, this strengthens the connection that virtually every commentary recognizes between Judg 19:16–26 and Gen 19:1–11, as she and the virgin daughter of the old man from Ephraim now enter the narrative space occupied by Lot's two virgin daughters in Gen 19:8.

The intertextual relationship between Genesis 19 and Judges 19 is complex.[123] In the Genesis narrative, the men of Sodom reject Lot's offer of his two daughters, becoming more intent on violating Lot than the two strangers who are initially the object of their hostility. In fact it is their aggression towards Lot, as the one who "came here as an alien, and ... would play the judge" (Gen 19:9), that prompts the strangers, who are also God/'s messengers and who thus represent the true "judge," to blind the men of Sodom so that they cannot find the door to the house. In the Judges narrative, the old man from Ephraim takes on the role of Lot in offering hospitality, while the Levite is the stranger the men of Gibeah are intent on violating. Although the old man, like and unlike Lot, will offer his daughter and the unnamed young woman to the mob, there is no redirection of hostility towards him in this version as the intervention of the Levite occurs earlier than that of the messengers of Genesis. Far from blinding the men of Gibeah with God/'s Glory (assuming that *bassanwērîm* in Gen 19:11 means "with dazzling"[124]), the way he keeps them from entering the house is by forcing his concubine out of the door in his place. This act of self-serving substitution utterly separates him from the messengers of Genesis 19, while forcing the unnamed woman into the space of the stranger-messenger who represents God/.

In what emerges as a deep, yet complex, narrative coherence, the end leads us back to the beginning, as the possibility that the unnamed

---

123. Here Block, *Judges, Ruth*, 532–34, sets out the parallels very clearly, while Brettler, *The Book of Judges*, 86–87, helpfully summarizes the arguments for Genesis 19 being a basis for Judges 19.

124. See *HALOT*, 761, s.v. *sanwērîm*, which suggests dazzling. If this is correct, the unnamed woman in Judges 19 takes the place of God/'s Glory in Genesis 19. On the Glory/Wisdom connection, see n. 106 above.

woman represents (the rejection of) Yahweh here fits with the way her rejection of the Levite can be seen as Yahweh's rejection of Israel, the verb of 19:2 (as reconstructed above) also occurring in the context of Yahweh's rejection in Hos 8:5; Zech 10:6; Pss 43:2; 44:9, 23 [MT 44:10, 24]; 60:1, 10 [MT 60:3, 12]; 74:1; 77:7 [MT 77:8]; 88:14 [MT 88:15]; 89:38 [MT 88:38]; 108:11 [MT 108:12]; Lam 2:7; 3:31; and 1 Chr 28:9.[125] At the end of the story, therefore, having failed to speak to her heart despite the repeated prompting of her father, the Levite's betrayal of the unnamed woman represents Israel's betrayal of God/ and its utter rejection of divine Wisdom as way of life and way to Life (Gen 2:9; 3:22; Prov 3:18; 11:30).

Appeals to symbolic representation and to intratextual parallels with the Achsah paradigm, which have been central to the above discussion, are potentially compelling for those who trust the narrative logic that is often at work in the Old Testament. But such evidence can strike the contemporary reader as rather "indirect." While it is precisely the indirect nature of this approach that is consonant with the allusive nature of the wisdom tradition, I suggest, it may still be asked whether more "direct" evidence is available to show that Judges 19 has been consciously written with a wisdom theme in mind. I will bring this section to a close, therefore, by looking at some examples of wisdom-related terminology in this chapter. This focus on specific terms will lead to a discussion of the symbolic meaning of the unnamed woman's final action in Judg 19:27.

COUNSEL

Appropriately enough, the clearest example of direct linguistic evidence can be found in 19:30, where many have detected the voice of the narrator.[126] Here, immediately following the dismemberment of the unnamed woman, we hear the words, "'Has such a thing ever happened since the day that the Israelites came up from the land of Egypt until this day? Consider it, take counsel [*'uṣû*], and speak out [*dabbērû*].'" The reference to the exodus is a significant part of the call to discernment, and we shall

---

125. Of the 19 uses of *zānah* in addition to Judg 19:2 (as reconstructed), fifteen of these (listed above) refer to God/'s rejection of Israel. Apart from 1 Chr 28:9 (which is in the Hiphil), these are all in the Qal, as Judg 19:2 would be. The remaining references (in which God/ is not the subject) are Hos 8:3; Lam 3:17; 2 Chr 11:14; and 29:19.

126. See n. 16 above.

return to this below. I have already noted that the phrase "Consider it" can be translated "Set your heart on her." So how is the unnamed woman related to the "counsel" that the people need to take to heart before they speak out?

A major argument for seeing the unnamed woman as embodying Woman Wisdom here is that the verb translated as "take counsel," *'uṣû*, is cognate with *'ēṣâ*, one of the most important terms in wisdom discourse. Significantly, *'ēṣâ* itself is used in 20:7 when the Levite, probably despite his own intentions, reiterates the call to discernment of 19:30 by saying, "So now, you Israelites, all of you, give your advice [*dābār*] and counsel [*'ēṣâ*] here." He is thus asking them to speak out with wisdom, which according to 19:30, may occur only if they have first oriented their hearts to her and thus received wisdom.[127]

That *'ēṣâ* may refer to a wisdom that is revelatory is clear in 2 Sam 16:23, where we are told that "in those days the counsel that Ahithophel gave was as if one consulted the oracle of God." In the prophetic writings, Isa 11:2 and 28:29 employ this term when they speak of God/'s own wisdom, while the claim made in Jer 18:18, that "instruction shall not perish from the priest, nor counsel from the wise, nor the word from the prophet," would seem to refer to three identifiable offices, analogous to the well-known distinction between prophet, priest, and king. Here *'ēṣâ* is the key term for the office of the wise person.

In the wisdom literature itself, *'ēṣâ* appears frequently. In Job it refers to God/'s wisdom in 12:13; 29:21; 38:2; and 42:3 and to the fallible or false wisdom of human beings in 5:13; 10:3; 18:7; 21:16; and 22:18. In the later chapters of Proverbs it is also prominent (see 12:15; 19:20–21; 20:5, 18; 21:30; and 27:9). But most significant for the purposes of the present study is its emphatic use by Woman Wisdom herself in 1:25, 30, and 8:14.

The Doorway and the Threshold

One way to test whether turning our hearts to the unnamed woman and opening our hearts to the voice of Wisdom are connected in the call to discernment of 19:30 and 20:7 is to pay very close attention to what

---

127. The only other instance of *'uṣu* is in Isa 8:10 where it appears side by side with *'ēṣâ*. As this occurs as part of a quoted false prophecy ("God is with us") that the people trust because of their hostility to Assyria, this may be thematically related to the self-deception of Judg 20:18, as discussed above. On the way wise speech comes from a receptive heart, by contrast, see Ansell, "Jesus on the Offensive," on 1 Kgs 3:9.

she may be saying. Here, I suggest, we should not look for some kind of "message" that the unnamed woman consciously intended to convey so much as concern ourselves with the wisdom that she evokes and provokes in and through the body language of her final action.

And there is also the wisdom of the way the narrative has been structured to consider. Thus before exploring the significance of the unnamed woman's hands on the threshold in 19:27, we should note the way the narrator emphasizes her proximity to the "doorway" [*pêtaḥ*] of the house when she collapses, as this is repeated twice in 19:26 and 27b. While *pêtaḥ* is a common term for an entrance, doorway or opening, here it also serves to reinforce the significance of the reference to the "counsel" we may receive if we turn our hearts to her (19:30), as the doorway is often portrayed as the place where Woman Wisdom may be heard (see Prov 1:21; 8:3, 34).

Because the reference in Prov 8:34 refers to the doorway to Wisdom's own house, while the references in Prov 1:21 and 8:3 refer to her calling out in public spaces (the first in judgment and the second in invitation) the present setting outside a private house may be thought to rule out the idea that a daughter of Wisdom is being portrayed here. But we must not overlook (a) the way in which the house or world of Wisdom is extended through the activity of her daughters (cf. the discussion of Prov 9:1 and 14:1 above) and (b) the very public connotations of the doors that are closed against her. This latter consideration will be especially important.

This brings us to the unnamed woman's final action, conveyed to us as readers/hearers by the use of a demonstrative participle right in the middle of Judg 19:27. Once added to the NRSV, this reads: "In the morning her master got up, opened the doors [*daltôt*] of the house, and when he went out to go on his way—*and look [wehinnê]!*—there was his concubine lying at the door[way] [*pêtaḥ*] of the house, with her hands on the threshold [*weyādêhā 'al-hassap*]."

Texts that draw explicit attention to a woman's hands are rare in the Hebrew Bible, but here one may certainly think of daughter Zion stretching out her hands in Jer 4:31 and Lam 1:17. Also very striking in this context is the poetic portrayal of the wise woman of valor in Prov 31 as her acts of compassion are emphasized by a "*yādêhā . . . wekappêhā; kappâh . . . weyādêhā*" (hand/palm; palm/hand) construction in verses 19–20 near the centre of the alphabetic acrostic that closes the book (cf.

vv. 16 and 31). This might seem to be irrelevant to Judges 19, but as Hatton notes perceptively, there are numerous contrasts between what he calls "the Reintegration of Wisdom" in Prov 31:10–31 and the jarring language of Prov 1:20–33, in which Wisdom refers, with considerable anguish and anger, to the way her calling out and her outstretched hand ("my hand," 1:24 cf. Isa 65:2) have been persistently ignored.[128] Contrary to the orderly image she has in many a scholarly discussion of Proverbs, Wisdom, according to her opening speech, is introduced as isolated, marginalized, and rejected!

So what is the significance of the unnamed woman's hands touching the "threshold" in Judg 19:27? Although the equivalent Hebrew term, *sap*,[129] makes the first of its more than two dozen appearances here according to the English versions, there is reason to believe that it also occurs in Exod 12:21–23—a passage to which we shall return in due course. The next of its five other occurrences in the Deuteronomic History, in 1 Kgs 14:1–18, is of particular interest given the thematic connection with the present narrative. In this passage, Jeroboam's son Abijah falls ill, so the king sends his wife to learn of the future from Ahijah, the prophet who had ripped his cloak into twelve pieces before handing ten of them to Jeroboam with the promise that he would rule over Israel (1 Kgs 11:30–31, cf. 14:1–3). Here, however, the ripping of the cloak takes on a different meaning as we learn that Israel will now be uprooted from the land and scattered beyond the Euphrates. As for the child, Jeroboam's wife learns that because the boy has found favor with God/, he will be buried and his death mourned, unlike all the other males of the household who will be consumed because of the king's idolatry. Although Jeroboam's wife is told that her son will die upon her return to her own city ("Shechem in the hill country of Ephraim," 1 Kgs 12:25, cf. Judg 19:1, 16), 1 Kgs 14:17 tells us that the young boy [*naʿar*] actually dies "[a]s she came to the threshold [*besap*] of the [royal] house."

The four remaining references in the Deuteronomic History (in 2 Kgs 12:9; 22:4; 23:4; and 25:18) and the two found in Jeremiah (Jer 35:4 and 52:24) all refer to the high-ranking guardians or keepers of the

---

128. Hatton, *Contradiction in the Book of Proverbs*, 77. On Wisdom's displacement here, see ibid. 62–63 and 77–81. The prophetic language that Murphy notes in *Proverbs*, 10–11 fits a call from the margins.

129. A synonym, *miptān*, appears in 1 Sam 5:4, 5; Ezek 9:3; 10:4, 18; 46:2; 47:1; and Zeph 1:9.

threshold of the Temple. Significantly, the Temple thresholds are also in view in the remaining references in the prophets or *Nevi'im* (see Isa 6:4; Ezek 40:6–7; 41:16; Amos 9:1) with the apparent exception of Zeph 2:14, which may refer to a threshold within a palace in the desecrated city of Nineveh, and the partial exception of Ezek 43:8, which refers to God/'s anger at the fact that the Temple and the Royal House have been built side by side, "their threshold by my threshold."

Apart from the description of the thresholds of Solomon's temple being inlaid with gold in 2 Chr 3:7, the fact that thresholds have their guardians is a recurring feature of the references in the Writings or *Kethuvim* section of the Hebrew Bible, this extending to the thresholds in the Persian palace that are safeguarded by the eunuchs in Esth 2:21 and 6:2. Of the four remaining passages in 1–2 Chronicles, it is of special interest that the lower order of officials who are guardians of, or gate-keepers at, the thresholds within the Tent/Tabernacle in 1 Chr 9:19 and 22, and the gatekeepers and keepers of the threshold within the Temple in 2 Chr 23:4 and 34:9 are identified as Levites.

So how might this relate to the threshold of Judg 19:27? A recurring theme in almost all of these passages is the fact that the threshold represents a boundary either within sacred space (or would-be sacred, royal space) or between what is and what is not sacred.[130] In 1 Kgs 14:17, which, as noted above, is thematically linked to the narrative under investigation, the boundary that separates the inner from the outer is also the distinction between life and death as the wife of Jeroboam seems to bring the prophet's fatal judgment with her as she returns to the royal house. In Judges 19, by contrast, a woman's desire to live leads her to return to a house from which she has been expelled by a Levite who is intent on keeping the forces of death outside.

While the presence of a threshold in and of itself may not be enough to place the Levite within the boundaries of the "sacred" here, a close reading of the MT at 19:18, which introduces this part of the narrative, strongly suggests that Temple connotations I have been highlighting are intended. To adapt the NRSV, the Levite tells the old man, "We are passing from Bethlehem in Judah to the remote parts of the hill country of Ephraim, from which I come. I went to Bethlehem [*ad-bêt leḥem*] in Judah; and I am going *to the house of Yahweh* [*'et-bêt yhwh*] *and no man*

---

130. See Meyers, "Threshold," 544–45.

has brought me to the house [*'ôtî habbāyetâ*]."[131] When we read, in 19:21, that the old man brings the Levite into his house [*lebêtô*], we should notice the parallel between these three phrases. The Levite going to the house of YHWH is now the Levite in the house of *ba'al* (cf. 19: 22, 23 and the way the movement from field-to-"temple" in 19:16–21 mirrors the field-to-temple movement in 9:27).

Building on the narrative of the priestly Levite in the first part of the epilogue (17:1—18:31), this devastating account of the Levitical misconstrual of sacred space reaches its darkest point when we realize that his betrayal of an unnamed daughter of Wisdom represents, exemplifies, and constitutes nothing less than Israel's attempt to expel the divine presence. Her voice at the doorway is never heard because the "Temple" doors (the common term, *daltôt*, appears in a sacred setting in 1 Sam 3:15; 1 Kgs 6:31–32, 34; 7:50; 2 Kgs 12:9; 18:16; Ezek 41:23, 24, 25; Mal 1:10; Neh 6:10; 2 Chr 3:7; 4:22, 28:24, 29:3, 7) are closed. The line that is drawn here between the sacred and the profane has never been more violent.

Before we leave this discussion of the intertextual significance of the doorway and the threshold, we should note that because *sap* has a homonym in Hebrew, which is typically translated as basin,[132] this may have led to a misinterpretation of Exod 12:21–23, the passage in which Moses gives instructions about the slaughtering of the Passover lambs and the marking of the entrance to the house with blood. If the more common meaning of *sap* is retained, the hyssop would be dipped in the blood that had drained into a container in the threshold so that it might also be spread from there to the lintel and doorposts thus covering all four sides to the doorway. While no contemporary translation understands verse 22 in this way, the LXX and the Vulgate both witness to this reading.[133] It certainly coheres with the idea of the threshold as a liminal space between life and death as found in 1 Kgs 14:17.

---

131. The NRSV, following the LXX, has "I am going to my home." While Tov, *Textual Criticism of the Hebrew Bible*, 256–57, favors the LXX here, his argument being identical to that of Moore, *Judges*, 415–16, and Soggin, *Judges*, 287, see, e.g., Butler, *Judges*, 408–9, for a defense of the MT.

132. See 2 Sam 17:28; 1 Kgs 7:50; 2 Kgs 12:13 [MT 12:14]; Jer 52:19; and Zech 12:2.

133. For a discussion of Exod 12:22 as reflecting and transforming a threshold ritual, see Propp, *Exodus 1–18*, 408, Durham, *Exodus*, 161–63, and Levinson, *Deuteronomy and the Hermeneutics of Legal Innovation*, 58–60.

The reference to the threshold in Judg 19:27 occurs between the Levite's betrayal of the unnamed woman in 19:25 and his dispersal of her body in 19:29. That the Levite engages in nothing less than human sacrifice is clear in this latter text as it uses language that is drawn from the binding of Isaac narrative, as noted above. If there is also a reference to the Passover sacrifice, then the original order of events—slaughter, safety within from the forces of death, division of the lamb for the members of the household—is still present except that the Levite's departure from Gibeah for Ephraim relocates the division of the body inside his own home. This extends the sacrificial death of Exodus so that the slaughter now occurs in three stages: as betrayal to the mob, as rape, and as dismemberment.

It is the Levite's utter desecration of the Passover, I suggest, that explains why the call to discernment in Judg 19:30 begins by asking, "Has such a thing ever happened since the day that the Israelites came up from the land of Egypt until this day?" The task of bringing these two "days" together—as Exod 12:22/Judg 19:27 (cited below)—has been left to the reader so that the intertextual impact may be devastating and the nonchalance of the Levite beyond belief: "'Take a bunch of hyssop, dip it in the blood that is in the [threshold, *bassap*], and touch the lintel and the two doorposts with the blood in the [threshold]. None of you shall go outside the door of your house until morning' . . . In the morning her master got up, opened the doors of the house, and when he went out to go on his way, there was his concubine lying at the door of the house, with her hands on the threshold."

Narrative Resolution?

While the "daughter of Wisdom" theme found in Proverbs and present in Judges goes a long way towards clarifying how seriously the unnamed woman's life and death are taken by Scripture, the depth meaning of her betrayal analyzed above makes this more of a "Text of Terror" than ever. It is only right, therefore, that we draw this discussion to a close by focusing once more on Trible's serious claim that the narrative adds to her abuse because it shows her "neither compassion nor attention."[134]

In the above exploration, which has been written with the assumption that the Bible is a book *for* ethics rather than a book *of* ethics, I

---

134. Trible, *Texts of Terror*, 86, as cited above.

have tried to show that the narrative in question is focused less on showing compassion than on calling for/th compassion. It is the "indirect" pedagogy of wisdom thinking, I suggest, that can strike a contemporary reader as far more detached than it really is. Thus in Judg 19:30, we receive a call to discernment towards the end of a narrative that has tried to encourage both the Levite and the reader to direct their hearts, our hearts, to the unnamed young woman. But we do not find the narrator commenting on her fate in a way that parallels 11:40, where s/he tells us that "for four days every year the daughters of Israel would go out to lament the daughter of Jephthah the Gileadite" (11:40). For readers who believe that ethical sensitivity demands something analogous at the end of Judges 19, the reference to there being no king (especially when read as a monarchy-endorsing solution) is bound to be experienced as a let-down if not an assault.

But while the sentiments of Judg 11:40 must be supplied by the reader on this occasion, to conclude that the narrator "cares little about the woman's fate"[135] is to misconstrue the space we are given to respond. As the book of Judges is supposed to be read/heard as a whole, this narrative presupposes the story of Jephthah's daughter. It is not as if we are given no guidance. But at this stage of the narrative, our caring is provoked and evoked, rather than prescribed or even modeled, precisely because it must be fully our own. Wisdom calls for/th wisdom.[136] In this sense, the narrative is incomplete without our response. But when it comes, the Word of God/ is a part of us.

This perspective can help us evaluate Middleton and Walsh's claim that "The story *cries out* for resolution . . . But this is a resolution that occurs—if it occurs at all—*outside* the parameters of the biblical text"?[137] For if there is no "text" in any meaningful sense without readers, our role in responding to the call for discernment—which differs from re-

---

135. Ibid., 76, as cited above.

136. One reason why Proverbs, Job, and Ecclesiastes do not explicitly refer to Israel's salvation history is because wisdom involves owning one's own sense of the way existence reveals the way to life. One cannot hide behind the discernment of others. Cf. 1 Kgs 3. This characterizes "wisdom thinking" wherever it is found. Cf. n. 47 above. Thus wisdom's pedagogy cannot simply be described as "didactic," *contra* Crenshaw, *Old Testament Wisdom*, 32, 71, 84, and 100 as it has an indirect, evocative/provocative character. Here Seerveld, "Proverbs 10:1–22" is most helpful.

137. Middleton and Walsh, *Truth Is Stranger Than It Used to Be*, 181, their emphases, as cited above.

deeming a text that does not call for/th wisdom—is not "outside" the "con-text" of textual meaning. This does not mean that we supply the meaning or "redeem Scripture" so much as bring the text, with its restless, redemptive-historical message, to fulfillment. This is the meaning of Isa 55:10–11: the Word made flesh.

The failure of the text to provide resolution, therefore, is not a weakness but a strength. Here, it would seem, Trible agrees. To read intertextually, with Ruth and Hannah alongside the unnamed woman and the daughters of Shiloh, she says, is to "counsel redemption." Because Ruth and Hannah cannot "erase the sufferings of their sisters" in this context,[138] what she means by "redemption" is not "resolution." In fact, her own account of Judges 19–21 would suggest that it is precisely the attempt to find resolution in the form of retribution that results in the rape of the one becoming the rape of the six hundred.

To take this critique of resolution one step further, it is highly significant that the narrative does not suggest that the problem lies in the Israelites not following through and totally eradicating the tribe of Benjamin, as if they really should have "purge[d] the evil from Israel" (20:13) in this way. Here it seems, we have a narrative that has begun to discern what Jesus sees so clearly in John 8:2–11: God/'s call in the law of Moses to meet sin with a retributive justice-unto-death was always meant to self-deconstruct![139]

But if resolution is not redemption, we do still desire healing. And this surely includes a desire that the unnamed woman find a voice. So we may reframe the question and ask: Is this affirmation of her subjectivity only to be found through the reader? Or does the biblical witness itself somehow allow her to speak?

Finding a Voice

As this question concerns affirming both the agency and subjectivity of the unnamed woman, it is well worth reiterating that her story is not an allegory that points to a more real, more divine, meaning "above" but is the story of Wisdom in flesh and blood, her own actions and experiences, her subjectivity and her objectification, participating in God/'s presence with and absence from Israel. Having been taken in marriage,

---

138. Trible, *Texts of Terror*, 85, as cited above.
139. See Ansell, "Life After the Law?"

which in a patriarchal world is the correlate of being given in marriage,[140] her rejection of the Levite's desire coupled with her return to her father's house in 19:2 not only discloses Wisdom's refusal to be possessed by Israel but actually *constitutes* the withdrawal of Her presence. Similarly, the negation of her very flesh and blood desire to live, evident in her hands reaching out for the threshold, is the way of death and the path to exile (see Judg 19:27; 1 Kgs 14:17; 14:15; 14:7–8; 11:30; Judg 19:29).

The rejection of the unnamed woman at the beginning and her negation at the end are connected through the male desire to know her without love (*contra* Prov 4:6; 8:17, 35–36), without speaking to her heart (Judg 19:3–29), without mercy. The story of Wisdom and the stories of the daughters of Wisdom cannot be separated. Neither can meaning and vulnerability.

In rejecting male power/knowledge, the unnamed woman risks being read as unfaithful, as a harlot, or worse. When *wtznḥ/wattiznaḥ*, the phrase that was deliberately chosen by the final author/editor of the book to highlight this risk (Would Israel accept the valiant wisdom of her actions?), was misread as *wtznh/wattizneh*,[141] this (patriarchal) misconstrual becoming inscribed into the Masoretic text, then the Bible itself, in one of its central textual traditions, became wounded and in need of redemption.[142] Scripture's own vulnerability needs to be honored if its wisdom is to be heard.

Because Wisdom and her daughters, power and knowledge, truth and vulnerability cannot be separated, it is no coincidence that the New Testament begins in a way that refuses to hide the philosophy of violence towards the daughters of God/. On the first page of the First Gospel, we read of Tamar, Rahab, Ruth, and Bathsheba (Matt 1:3, 5, 6): Tamar who is to be burned alive until Judah admits she is more righteous than he

---

140. This patriarchal form of being given is also present in the Achsah narrative. Although the Achsah/Othniel marriage is a positive paradigm that is negated in varying degrees by other relationships in Judg, it reflects the patrilocal view of marriage that is absent in Gen 2:22, as discussed above.

141. In my view, this is not an innocent mistake but results from misconstruing the daughter of Wisdom as the Israel of Judg 2:17; 8:27 and 33, where *zānâ* does occur. Cf. Brown, "Judges," 275–76, who rightly sees *zānah* as the harder (and thus correct) reading in 19:2.

142. Here, it seems to me, even a conservative evangelical approach to textual criticism and biblical inspiration can embrace Trible's language about "the need to redeem Scripture" as cited above.

is (Gen 38:24, 26); Rahab who would have been subjected to the utter annihilation, or *ḥerem*, that was inflicted on Jericho if the spies had not kept their word (Josh 6:17); Ruth who is protected from sexual harassment and violence in the fields due to the intervention of Boaz (Ruth 2:9, 15[143]); and finally an unnamed Bathsheba ("the wife of Uriah") who, if the slaughtered lamb imagery of Nathan's parable is taken seriously (2 Sam 12:4), not only faces the threat of violence like Tamar, Rahab, and Ruth, but is raped by King David (2 Sam 11:4).

In Matthew's account of Jesus' conception, Mary and the Spirit are placed in parallel, both grammatically and theologically, with these foremothers of the Messiah (see Matt 1:16, 18, 20[144]). In Luke's account the theme of solidarity is also present, coming to the fore in the Magnificat, which draws on Hannah's prayer in 1 Sam 2:1–10. This can be seen in the way that Mary, in Luke 1:48, celebrates the fact that God/ "has looked with favor [*epeblepsen*] on the lowliness of his servant [*epi tēn tapeinōsin tēs doulēs autou*]" as if she sees her own vindication and blessing as answering Hannah's request to God/ in 1 Sam 1:11, which begins by saying "if only you will look [*epiblepōn epiblepsēs*] on the misery of your servant [*epi tēn tapeinōsin tēs doulēs sou*, LXX] . . ."

The extent to which Mary stands in solidarity not only with Hannah but with all the "lowly" whom God/ has now "lifted up" (Luke 1:52) can be appreciated best if we note that in the LXX and Greek New Testament, the word that the NRSV translates as "misery" in I Sam 1:11 and as the "lowliness" of the "lowly" in Luke 1:48 and 52, is *tapeinōsis*, which means humiliation rather than humility.[145] In its verbal form, it is used in the LXX for the rape of Dinah in Gen 34:2, the rape of Tamar in 2 Sam 13:12, 14, 22, and 32, and the rape of the women of Zion and the virgins of Judah in Lam 5:11.

Most significant for the present discussion is that the same term is used of the rape—the violation of the sacred—that is proposed by the old man and enacted by the mob in Judg 19:24 and 20:5.[146] As a central

---

143. Although one can easily overlook this because of the English translations, *ngʽ* ("bother" in Ruth 2:9, NRSV) is sexual in Prov 6:29 and violent in Gen 32:25, 32, while *taklîmû* ("reproach" in Ruth 2:15, NRSV) means to humiliate or abuse.

144. See Gundry, *Matthew*, 650 n. 18. Although he stresses this point in critique of Schaberg, *The Illegitimacy of Jesus*, connecting the Spirit to conceiving rather than to begetting could strengthen her thesis.

145. See Wengst, *Humility: Solidarity of the Humiliated*, chapter 4, especially 44.

146. This is the case in LXX^A and LXX^B.

theme of the Magnificat is the apocalyptic reversal that will lead to the vindication of the humiliated, it is in Mary's song that the unnamed woman finally gets to speak!

In the narrative of the unnamed daughter of Wisdom in Judges 19, we have the strongest example of incarnation and the clearest anticipation of crucifixion in the Hebrew Bible. For this reason, we must be crystal clear about the fact that there is nothing voluntary about her death. She is not the suffering servant of Isaiah. But as the theme of utter betrayal is so often eclipsed in Christian understandings of the cross, this is an important argument for reading her death alongside the death of Jesus.[147] For it is in the continuity and discontinuity between them that we may understand how Wisdom in the New Testament becomes suffering love as "Christ crucified" both reveals and re-constitutes "the [W]isdom of God" (1 Cor 1:23–24).

On the night he was betrayed, he took the bread and broke it into twelve pieces for his disciples with the words "This is my body, which is given for you. Do this in remembrance of me."[148] After the night she was betrayed, the body of the unnamed young woman was cut into twelve pieces and given to the tribes of Israel that they might direct their hearts to her, take counsel, and speak. As we read these texts of terror today in the light of their ultimate horizons, we remember two of the darkest moments in an ongoing story of oppression, compassion, and liberation in which we are called to find Wisdom and live. Open to the Light that shines in the darkness, we may even hear the words "This is her body . . ."[149]

---

147. In this context, Dyke, *Crucified Woman* is a helpful resource.

148. Luke 22:19. For the Wisdom background, see Prov 9:5.

149. Special thanks to AJ, and to Al Wolters, Aron Van de Kleut, Cal Seerveld, Jeff Hocking, Jim Olthuis, and Jon Stanley for their comments on this work in progress.

BIBLIOGRAPHY

Ackerman, Susan. *Warrior, Dancer, Seductress, Queen: Women in Judges and Biblical Israel*. ABRL. New Haven, CT: Yale University Press, 2009.

Ansell, Nicholas. "All in Good Time: Re-imagining Sexuality in God's Future." Unpublished paper.

———. "The Call of Wisdom/The Voice of the Serpent: A Canonical Approach to the Tree of Knowledge." *Christian Scholar's Review* 31.1 (2001) 31–57.

———. "Commentary: Genesis 22:1–16." *Third Way* 27.3 (April 2004) 16.

———. "Creational Man/Eschatological Woman: A Future for Theology." Inaugural address. Toronto: ICS, 2007. Online: http://www.icscanada.edu/events/20060526cn/inaugural_may2006.pdf

———. "The Embrace of Wisdom: Prov 8, Gen 1, and the Covenantal Dynamics of Existence." Unpublished paper.

———. "For the Love of Wisdom: Scripture, Philosophy and the Relativization of Order." Unpublished paper.

———. "Hell: The Nemesis of Hope?" In *Her Gates Will Never Be Shut: Hope, Hell, and the New Jerusalem*, by Bradley Jersak, 191–210. Eugene, OR: Wipf and Stock, 2009.

———. "Jesus on the Offensive." *The Banner* 143.10 (2008) 44–45.

———. "Life After the Law? Rethinking Truth in the Light of John's Gospel." Unpublished paper.

———. *The Woman Will Overcome the Warrior: A Dialogue with the Christian/Feminist Theology of Rosemary Radford Ruether*. Lanham, MD: University Press of America, 1994.

Bal, Mieke. *Death and Dissymmetry: The Politics of Coherence in the Book of Judges*. CSJH. Chicago: University of Chicago Press, 1988.

Barthélemy, Dominique. *Critique Textuelle de l'Ancien Testament*. Vol. 1: *Josué, Juges, Ruth, Samuel, Rois, Chronique, Esdras, Néhémie, Esther*. Göttingen: Vandenhoeck & Ruprecht, 1982.

Bartholomew, Craig G. *Ecclesiastes*. BCOTWP. Grand Rapids: Baker, 2009.

Bauckham, Richard. *The Bible in Politics: How to Read the Bible Politically*. 2nd ed. London: SPCK, 2010.

Benedict, Helen. *Virgin or Vamp: How the Press Covers Sex Crimes*. Oxford: Oxford University Press 1992.

Biblia Hebraica Stuttgartensia, edited by K. Elliger and W. Rudolph. Stuttgart: Deutsche Bibelgesellschaft, 1997.

Boling, Robert G. *Judges: A New Translation with Introduction and Commentary*. AB 6A. New York: Doubleday, 1975.

Block, Daniel I. *Judges, Ruth*. NAC 6. Nashville: Broadman & Holman, 1999.

Brenner, Athalya, ed. *A Feminist Companion to Judges*. FCB 4. First series. Sheffield, UK: JSOT Press, 1993.

———, ed. *Judges: A Feminist Companion to the Bible*. FCB 4. Second series. Sheffield, UK: Sheffield Academic Press, 1999.

Brettler, Marc Zvi. *The Book of Judges*. OTR. London: Routledge, 2002.

Brown, Cheryl A. "Judges." In *Joshua, Judges, Ruth*, edited by J. Harris et al., 121–290. NIBCOT 5. Peabody, MA: Hendrickson, 2000.

Brown, Francis, S. R. Driver, and Charles A. Briggs. *A Hebrew and English Lexicon of the Old Testament*. Peabody, MA: Hendrickson, 1985.

Broyles, Craig C. *The Conflict of Faith and Experience in the Psalms: A Form-Critical and Theological Study*. JSOTSup 52. Sheffield, UK: JSOT, 1989.

Brueggemann, Walter. *An Introduction to the Old Testament: The Canon and Christian Imagination*. Louisville: Westminster John Knox, 2003.

———. *Theology of the Old Testament: Testimony, Dispute, Advocacy*. Minneapolis: Fortress, 1997

Butler, Trent. *Judges*. WBC 8. Nashville: Nelson, 2009.

Clifford, Richard J. *The Wisdom Literature*. IBT. Nashville: Abingdon, 1998.

Christensen, Duane L. *Deuteronomy 1:1—21:9*. WBC 6A. 2nd ed. Nashville: Thomas Nelson, 2001.

———. "Josephus and the Twenty-Two-Book Canon of Sacred Scripture." *Journal for the Evangelical Theological Society* 29.1 (1986) 37–46

———. *The Unity of the Bible: Exploring the Beauty and Structure of the Bible*. New York: Paulist, 2003.

Crenshaw, James L. *Old Testament Wisdom: An Introduction*. 3rd ed. Louisville, KY: Westminster John Knox, 2010.

Davidson, E. T. A. *Intricacy, Design, and Cunning in the Book of Judges*. Bloomington, IN: Xlibris, 2008.

Davis, John J., and Herbert Wolf. "Judges: Introduction." In *The NIV Study Bible*, edited by Kenneth L. Barker *et al.*, 326–29. Rev. ed. Grand Rapids: Zondervan, 2003.

Day, John *et al.*, eds. *Wisdom in Ancient Israel: Essays in Honour of J. A. Emerton*. Cambridge: Cambridge University Press, 1995.

Dorsey, David A. *The Literary Structure of the Old Testament: A Commentary on Genesis–Malachi*. Grand Rapids: Baker Academic, 1999.

Driver, G. R. "Mistranslations in the Old Testament." *Die Welt des Orients* 1 (1947) 29–30.

Dumbrell, W. J. "In Those Days There Was No King in Israel; Every Man Did What Was Right in his Own Eyes: The Purpose of the Book of Judges Reconsidered." *Journal for the Study of the Old Testament* 25 (1983) 23–33.

Durham, John I. *Exodus*. WBC 3. Nashville: Thomas Nelson, 1987.

Dyke, Doris Jean. *Crucified Woman*. Toronto: United Church Publishing, 1991.

Erlandsson, S. "*zānāh*." In *Theological Dictionary of the Old Testament*, vol. 4, edited by G. Johannes Botterweck and Helmer Ringgren. Translated by David E. Green, 99–104. Grand Rapids: Eerdmans, 1980.

Exum, J. Cheryl. "Feminist Criticism: Whose Interests Are Being Served?" In *Judges and Method: New Approaches in Biblical Studies*, 2nd ed., edited by Gale A. Lee, 65–89. Minneapolis: Fortress, 2007.

———. *Fragmented Women: Feminist (Sub)versions of Biblical Narratives*. Valley Forge, PA: Trinity, 1993.

Fewell, Donna Nolan. "Deconstructive Criticism: Achsah and the (E)razed City of Writing." In *Judges and Method: New Approaches in Biblical Studies*, 2nd ed., edited by Gale A. Lee, 115–37. Minneapolis: Fortress, 2007.

———. "Judges." In *Women's Bible Commentary*, expanded ed. with Apocrypha, edited by Carol A. Newsom and Sharon H. Ringe, 73–83. Louisville, KY: Westminster John Knox, 1998.

Fontaine, Carole R. "Wisdom in Proverbs." In *In Search of Wisdom: Essays in Memory of John G. Gammie*, edited by Leo G. Perdue *et al.*, 99–114. Louisville, KY: Westminster John Knox, 1993.

Freedman, David Noel. *The Unity of the Hebrew Bible*. Ann Arbor, MI: University of Michigan Press, 1993.

Fretheim, Terrence E. *Deuteronomic History*. IBT. Nashville: Abingdon, 1983.

Gammie, John G., and Leo G. Perdue, eds. *The Sage in Israel and the Ancient Near East*. Winona Lake, IN: Eisenbrauns, 1990.

Gooding, D. W. "The Composition of the Book of Judges." *Eretz-Israel* 16 (1982) 72–79.

Gordon, Robert P. "A House Divided: Wisdom in Old Testament Narrative Traditions." In *Wisdom in Ancient Israel: Essays in Honour of J. A. Emerton*, edited by John Day et al., 94–105. Cambridge: Cambridge University Press, 1995.

Gundry, Robert H. *Matthew: A Commentary on His Handbook for a Mixed Church under Persecution*. 2nd ed. Grand Rapids: Eerdmans, 1994.

Gunn, David M. "Joshua and Judges." In *The Literary Guide to the Bible*, edited by Robert Alter and Frank Kermode, 102–21. Cambridge: Harvard University Press, 1987.

———. *Judges*. BBC. Oxford: Blackwell, 2005.

Hamlin, E. John. *Judges: At Risk in the Promised Land*. ITC. Grand Rapids: Eerdmans, 1990.

Harris, R. Laird et al., eds. *Theological Wordbook of the Old Testament*. Chicago: Moody, 2003.

Hatton, Peter T. H. *Contradiction in the Book of Proverbs: The Deep Waters of Counsel*. SOTSMS. Aldershot, UK: Ashgate 2008.

Hilliers, Delbert R. *Lamentations: A New Translation with Introduction and Commentary*. AB 7A. 2nd ed. New York: Doubleday, 1992.

Horeck, Tanya. *Public Rape: Representing Violation in Fiction and Film*. London: Routledge, 2004.

Hunter, Alistair. *Wisdom Literature*. London: SCM, 2006.

Jenni, Ernst, and Claus Westermann, *Theological Lexicon of the Old Testament*. Translated by Mark E. Biddle. 3 vols. Peabody, MA: Hendrickson, 1997.

Josephus, *The Works of Flavius Josephus: Complete and Unabridged*. Translated by William Whiston. New updated ed. Peabody, MA: Hendrickson, 1987.

Klein, Lillian R. "Achsah: What Price This Prize?" In *Judges: A Feminist Companion to the Bible*. FCB 4. Second series. Edited by Athalya Brenner, 18–26. Sheffield, UK: Sheffield Academic, 1999.

———. "The Book of Judges." In *A Feminist Companion to Judges*. FCB 4. First series. Edited by Athalya Brenner, 55–71. Sheffield, UK: JSOT, 1993.

———. *The Triumph of Irony in the Book of Judges*. JSOTSup 68. Sheffield, UK: Sheffield Academic, 1988.

Koehler, Ludwig et al. *The Hebrew and Aramaic Lexicon of the Old Testament*. Translated and edited by M. E. J. Richardson et al. 5 vols. Leiden: Brill, 1994–2000.

Lapsley, Jacqueline E. *Whispering the Word: Hearing Women's Stories in the Old Testament*. Louisville, KY: Westminster John Knox, 2005.

Lee, Gale A., ed. *Judges and Method: New Approaches in Biblical Studies*. 2nd ed. Minneapolis: Fortress, 2007.

Levinson, Bernard M. *Deuteronomy and the Hermeneutics of Legal Innovation*. Oxford: Oxford University Press, 1998.

Longman, Tremper. *Proverbs*. BCOTWP. Grand Rapids: Baker Academic, 2008.

Maier, Christl M. *Daughter Zion, Mother Zion: Gender, Space, and the Sacred in Ancient Israel*. Minneapolis: Fortress, 2008.

Matthews, Victor H. *Judges and Ruth*. NCBC. Cambridge: Cambridge University Press, 2004.

McCann, J. Clinton. *Judges*. IBC. Louisville, KY: Westminster John Knox, 2002.

McConville, J. Gordon. *Grace in the End: A Study in Deuteronomic Theology*. SOTBT. Grand Rapids: Zondervan, 1993.

Meyers, Carol. "Threshold." In *Anchor Bible Dictionary* 6, edited by David Noel Freedman et al., 544–45. New York: Doubleday, 1992.

Middleton, J. Richard, and Brian J. Walsh. *Truth Is Stranger Than It Used to Be: Biblical Faith in a Postmodern Age*. Downers Grove, IL: InterVarsity, 1995.

Moore, George Foot. *Judges*. ICC. New York: Scribner, 1906.

Moore, Susanna. *In the Cut*. New York: Knopf, 1995.

Müllner, Ilse. "Lethal Differences: Sexual Violence as Violence against Others in Judges 19." In *Judges: A Feminist Companion to the Bible*. FCB 4. Second series. Edited by Athalya Brenner, 126–142. Sheffield, UK: Sheffield Academic, 1999.

Murphy, Roland E. *Proverbs*. WBC 22. Nashville: Nelson, 1998.

———. *The Tree of Life: An Exploration of Biblical Wisdom Literature*. 3rd ed. Grand Rapids: Eerdmans, 2002

———. "Wisdom and Creation." In *Journal of Biblical Literature* 104.1 (1985) 3–11.

———. *Wisdom Literature: Job, Proverbs, Canticles, Ecclesiastes, and Esther*. FOTL 13. Grand Rapids: Eerdmans, 1981.

Niditch, Susan. *Judges: A Commentary*. OTL. Louisville, KY: Westminster John Knox, 2008.

Oates, Joyce Carol. *Rape: A Love Story*. New York: Carroll and Graf, 2004.

Olson, Dennis T. "The Book of Judges: Introduction, Commentary, and Reflections." In *New Interpreter's Bible*, vol. 2, edited by David L. Petersen et al., 721–888. Nashville: Abingdon, 1998.

Olthuis, James H. et al. *A Hermeneutics of Ultimacy: Peril or Promise?* Lanham, MD: University Press of America, 1987.

Perdue, Leo G. et al., eds. *In Search of Wisdom: Essays in Memory of John G. Gammie*. Louisville, KY: Westminster John Knox, 1993.

———. *Wisdom Literature: A Theological History*. Louisville, KY: Westminster John Knox, 2007.

Perry, T. A. *God's Twilight Zone: Wisdom in the Hebrew Bible*. Peabody MA: Hendrickson, 2008.

Polzin, Robert. *Moses and the Deuteronomist: A Literary Study of the Deuteronomic History. Part One: Deuteronomy, Joshua, Judges*. New York: Seabury, 1980.

Pressler, Carolyn. *Joshua, Judges, and Ruth*. WBC. Louisville, KY: Westminster John Knox, 2002.

Propp, William H. C. *Exodus 1–18: A New Translation with Introduction and Commentary*. AB 2. New York: Doubleday, 1999.

Ringgren, Helmer. "zānach." In *Theological Dictionary of the Old Testament*, vol. 4, edited by G. Johannes Botterweck and Helmer Ringgren. Translated by David E. Green, 105–6. Grand Rapids: Eerdmans, 1980.

Ruether, Rosemary Radford. *Sexism and God-Talk: Toward a Feminist Theology*. With a New Introduction. Boston: Beacon, 1993.

———. *Women-Church: Theology and Practice of Feminist Liturgical Communities*. San Francisco: Harper and Row, 1985.

Sailhamer, John H. *Introduction to Old Testament Theology: A Canonical Approach.* Grand Rapids: Zondervan, 1995.

———. "A Wisdom Composition of the Pentateuch?" In *The Way of Wisdom: Essays in Honor of Bruce K. Waltke,* edited by J. I. Packer and Sven K. Soderlund, 15–35. Grand Rapids: Zondervan, 2000.

Sakenfeld, Katharine Doob. *Just Wives? Stories of Power and Survival in the Old Testament and Today.* Louisville, KY: Westminster John Knox, 2003.

Schaberg, Jane. *The Illegitimacy of Jesus: A Feminist Theological Interpretation of the Infancy Narratives.* Expanded 20th Anniversary ed. Sheffield, UK: Sheffield Phoenix, 2006.

Schenker, Adrian, ed. *The Earliest Text of the Hebrew Bible: The Relationship between the Masoretic Text and the Hebrew Base Text of the Septuagint Reconsidered.* SBLSCS 52. Atlanta: Society of Biblical Literature, 2003.

Schneider, Tammi J. *Judges.* BO. Collegeville, MN: Liturgical, 2000.

Scholtz, Susanne. *Sacred Witness: Rape in the Hebrew Bible.* Minneapolis: Fortress Press, 2010.

Schroeder, Joy A. *Dinah's Lament: The Biblical Legacy of Sexual Violence in Biblical Interpretation.* Minneapolis: Fortress, 2007.

Schroer, Silvia. "Wise and Counselling Women in Ancient Israel: Literary and Historical Ideals of the Personified ḥokmâ." In *A Feminist Companion to Wisdom Literature.* FCB 9. First series. Edited by Athalya Brenner, 67–84. Sheffield, UK: Sheffield Academic, 1995.

Seerveld, Calvin G. "Proverbs 10:1–22: From Poetic Paragraphs to Preaching." In *Reading and Hearing the Word: From Text to Sermon: Essays in Honor of John H. Stek,* edited by Arie C. Leder, 181–200. Grand Rapids: Calvin Theological Seminary/CRC, 1998.

Sheppard, Gerald T. *Wisdom as a Hermeneutical Construct: A Study in the Sapientializing of the Old Testament.* BZAW 151. Berlin: de Gruyter, 1980.

Smelik, William F. *The Targum of Judges.* OtSt. Leiden: Brill, 1995.

Soggin, J. Alberto. *Judges: A Commentary.* Translated by John Bowden. OTL. Philadelphia: Westminster, 1981.

Szpek, Heidi M. "The Levite's Concubine: The Story That Never Was." In *Re-Imagining Eve and Adam and Other Brief Essays,* 119–32. San Jose: Writers Club, 2002.

Thiselton, Anthony C. *New Horizons in Hermeneutics: The Theory and Practice of Transforming Biblical Reading.* Grand Rapids: Zondervan, 1992.

Thompson, Alden. *Who's Afraid of the Old Testament God?* Grand Rapids: Zondervan, 1989.

Thompson, John L. *Reading the Bible with the Dead: What You Can Learn from the History of Exegesis That You Can't Learn from Exegesis Alone.* Grand Rapids: Eerdmans, 2007.

Tillich, Paul. *Dynamics of Faith.* New York: Harper and Row, 1957.

Tov, Emanuel. "The Status of the Masoretic Text in Modern Text Editions of the Hebrew Bible: The Relevance of Canon." In *The Canon Debate,* edited by Lee Martin McDonald and James A. Sanders, 234–51. Peabody, MA: Hendrickson, 2002.

———. *Textual Criticism of the Hebrew Bible.* 2nd rev. ed. Minneapolis: Fortress, 2001.

———, and Frank Polak, eds., *The Revised CATSS Hebrew/Greek Parallel Text.* Jerusalem, 2009. Module in the Accordance computer program. Electronic text hypertexted and prepared by OakTree software, inc., version 1.2.

Trible, Phyllis. *God and the Rhetoric of Sexuality.* OBT. Philadelphia: Fortress, 1978.

---. "If the Bible's So Patriarchal, How Come I Love It?" In *Bible Review* 8.5 (1992) 45–47, 55

---. *Texts of Terror: Literary-Feminist Readings of Biblical Narratives*. OBT. Philadephia: Fortress, 1984.

VanGemeren, Willem A, ed. *New International Dictionary of Old Testament Theology and Exegesis*. 5 vols. Grand Rapids: Zondervan, 1997.

Van Leeuwen, Raymond C. "The Book of Proverbs: Introduction, Commentary, and Reflections." In *New Interpreter's Bible*, vol. 5, edited by David L. Petersen *et al.*, 17–264. Nashville: Abingdon, 1997.

Waltke, Bruce K. *Proverbs 1–15*. NICOT. Grand Rapids: Eerdmans, 2004.

Webb, Barry G. *The Book of the Judges: An Integrated Reading*. Eugene, OR: Wipf & Stock, 2008.

Wegner, Paul D. *A Student's Guide to Textual Criticism of the Bible: Its History, Methods and Results*. Downers Grove, IL: InterVarsity, 2006.

Weinfeld, Moshe. *Deuteronomy and the Deuteronomic School*. Oxford: Oxford University Press, 1972.

Wengst, Klaus. *Humility: Solidarity of the Humiliated: The Transformation of an Attitude and Its Social Relevance in Graeco-Roman, Old Testament-Jewish, and Early Christian Tradition*. Translated by John Bowden. Philadelphia: Fortress, 1988.

Wenham, Gordon J. *Story as Torah: Reading the Old Testament Ethically*. Grand Rapids: Baker Academic, 2004.

Westermann, Claus. *Genesis 1–11: A Continental Commentary*. Translated by John J. Scullion. Minneapolis: Fortress, 1994.

Wilcox, Michael. *The Message of Judges: Grace Abounding*. BST. Downers Grove, IL: InterVarsity, 1992.

Wolters, Al. *Song of the Valiant Woman: Studies in the Interpretation of Proverbs 31:10–31*. Carlisle, UK: Paternoster, 2001.

---. "The Text of the Old Testament." In *The Face of Old Testament Studies: A Survey of Contemporary Approaches*, edited by David W. Baker and Bill T. Arnold, 19–37. Grand Rapids: Baker, 1999.

Yaron, R. "The Meaning of *zānaḥ*." *Vetus Testamentum* 13.2 (1963) 237–39.

6

Colliding Contexts

*Reading Tamar (2 Samuel 13:1–22)
as a Twenty-First Century Woman*

Miriam J. Bier

LOCATION: MY CONTEXT

Permit me, for a moment, to locate myself. I am a Kiwi, a Pākehā New Zealander born and raised in Aotearoa-New Zealand in the eighties and nineties. My parents met and got to know each other through evangelical organizations like Scripture Union, Inter School Christian Fellowship, and Tertiary Students' Christian fellowship. My brothers and I were strongly influenced by our own involvement with these organizations, and by the evangelical youth groups, camps, and conferences we attended as teenagers and young adults. We all continue to be actively involved in evangelical churches and actively support various evangelical mission agencies. Evangelicalism is in my blood.

When I began studying theology at an evangelical Baptist college in 2005, I started to confront, in a more intentional manner, biblical texts that I had always found challenging and disturbing. As I did so I found myself beginning to feel some affinity with various feminist perspectives: perspectives that resisted aspects of Scripture, read "against the grain," and some of which went so far as to question, or even reject, the Bible's authority. Suffice to say, these perspectives did not always sit well within my evangelical community, for many of whom the notion of *sola scrip-*

tura remains non negotiable. And so my initial response to feminist Old Testament biblical criticism was to throw my hands up in despair: how could I ever reconcile a faith in the (murderous, sexist, abusive) God I found in the biblical text, with my commitment to justice and equality for all people?[1] Further, in my current context as a beginning scholar, preacher, and teacher of the Hebrew Bible, how do I marry my continuing conviction of the usefulness and relevance of the Bible as "Word of God," with an appropriately critical stance toward the patriarchal and oppressive character of (much of) the biblical text?[2]

Of course, I am not the first to wrestle with these issues. Many women (and men) who have gained a feminist consciousness have identified the cognitive dissonance that results from recognizing that the text that is so integral to their faith tradition is also so thoroughly patriarchal and androcentric.[3] Responses to the biblical text and its authority once this issue has been identified have been documented in various taxonomies.[4] These need not be repeated in great detail here,

---

1. This paper draws on a paper written at a crisis point in my wrestling with this question as a Masters student in 2007 (Bier, "Is there a God in this Text?" 48–60). While drawing on the narrative critical theory and exegetical work contained in that paper, the current paper offers a somewhat different perspective, several years on.

2. Initial feminist approaches attempted to demonstrate that the text itself is not necessarily the problem, but that it was a matter of centuries of male translation and interpretation that lead to much of the patriarchal rhetoric around the Bible. Some still argue that if the Bible is read with a "proper" hermeneutic, patriarchal bias can be eliminated, (eg., Talbert-Wettler, "Proper Hermeneutical Methods," 53–69). Attempts have been made to reread parts of the Bible in ways that reveal a positive intent for women (eg. Trible, "Depatriarchalizing in Biblical Interpretation," 36), to identify strands of liberative tradition within the Bible that provide a hopeful view (Radford Ruether, Russell), or to read with a hermeneutical key that elevates one text or another as the lens through which the rest of the text should be read (eg., reading in light of Gal 3:28), in order to show that the Bible is not as patriarchal and androcentric as it appears. These attempts to "rescue" the content of Scripture are ultimately unsatisfying, as it becomes increasingly difficult to defend the Bible against the charge of being a patriarchal, androcentric text, produced by a patriarchal, androcentric society or societies. The question, then, is what to *do* with the text once this has been recognized.

3. For various statements of the problem see Osiek, "Hermeneutical Alternatives," 101; Camp, "Feminist Theological Hermeneutics," 155; Trible, "How Come I Love It?," 55; Tolbert, "Protestant Feminists and the Bible," 5; Sakenfeld, "Feminist Uses of Biblical Materials," 55; and Bird, *Missing Persons and Mistaken Identities*, 249.

4. For a helpful summary and an overview of Sakenfeld and Osiek's typologies see Parry, "Feminist Hermeneutics and Evangelical Concerns," 2–6; and chapter 2 of this volume.

except to say that for many feminists, alternatives such as rejecting parts or all of Scripture as authoritative, formulating a canon within a canon, gathering other authoritative voices from outside the canon, making women's experience authoritative over the text, and highlighting liberating strands within the Bible are some of a number of possible and constructive ways forward. But for evangelical women, anything that threatens the concept of biblical authority will not do.[5] Thus the crucial issue emerges as a question of authority: how is one to construe the authority of the biblical text, once its harmful ideologies of patriarchy and androcentrism have been exposed?[6] It seems to come down to a simple choice: either "accept the Bible as the word of God and submit to it, or reject it as the word of men."[7]

This is a "Clayton's choice" for evangelical women, however.[8] How can I accept an ancient patriarchal text as authoritative over my life, as though its patriarchy and androcentrism constituted the Very Word of God? Yet equally impossible is the notion of rejecting sacred Scripture, by which I am nurtured, guided, and encouraged; and further, angered and goaded to action. Must the text's patriarchy and androcentrism be accepted as integral to the status and authority of the Bible as *Scripture*, or else the Bible rejected entirely? Are these the only two options, or might the authority of the text be somehow construed anew?[9]

---

5. Cf. Hoggard Creegan and Pohl's observation that "for many feminists, the core Scripture can be culled, the wheat can be taken from the tares, and readers need not restrict themselves to the canon but can also add liberating voices from the tradition on an equal footing. *This stance toward scripture is clearly problematic for many evangelical women*" (Hoggard Creegan and Pohl, *Living on the Boundaries*, 164; italics mine).

6. Cf. Tolbert, "Protestant Feminists and the Bible," 11; Bird, *Missing Persons and Mistaken Identities*, 250; Sakenfeld, "Feminist Uses of Biblical Materials," 64; David Scholer offers some possibilities for evangelical feminist readings in Scholer, "Feminist Hermeneutics and Evangelical Biblical Interpretation," 407–20.

7. Bird, *Missing Persons and Mistaken Identities*, 252.

8. The term "Clayton's choice" is an Australasian idiom defined by the New Zealand Oxford English Dictionary as "existing in name only; not genuine, worthless"; with its origin "from the proprietary name of a soft drink marketed as 'the drink you have when you're not having a drink.'" A Clayton's choice is thus no real choice at all. I have elected to retain this idiomatic expression as a reflection of the Aotearoa-New Zealand context out of which I write.

9. While the concept of "authority" itself has been recognized as problematic, and perhaps not even a particularly helpful category, (Clines, *What Does Eve do to Help?*), there is still a question as to what an evangelical high view of Scripture is to make of troubling passages and features of the biblical text. Wright insists that the authority of

And so my original question becomes a little more nuanced: when I read and interpret the Bible in the church and in the academy, how do I manage to be *both* faithfully evangelical (upholding Scripture as the inspired word of God) *and* feminist (upholding the value of women as persons of equal worth to men) all at the same time?[10] When I turn to a particular text (2 Sam 13:1–22), identified by feminist readers as a "text of terror," how do I recognize and respond appropriately to the violence dealt to Tamar while still, somehow, holding *this* text as sacred, inspired by God, and "useful for teaching, for reproof, for correction, and for training in righteousness" (2 Tim 3:16)? And why would I even want to?! One might very well ask what possible use there might there be in a story of rape, power, and violence in the Christian church. It's hardly inspirational Sunday morning sermon fodder. And yet, as long as rape, violence, and power play exist in the church and in the world, we need texts like these before us. For these are the texts that confront us, and force us to face humanity's darkness. These are the texts that put the issues of violence, abuse, and power squarely on the agenda, and will not let the hard questions be ignored. My response, then, to those feminists who argue that such texts are inimical to the feminist task, serving no "useful feminist purpose," is that these texts *must* be engaged, and indeed must be engaged by *feminist* interpreters.[11] Otherwise, victims such as Tamar continue to be subjected to the same centuries-old patriarchal interpretations; which is to say, they are for the most part ignored. Further, these texts must be engaged by *evangelical* interpreters, who take seriously the notion that somehow, God still speaks through the biblical Word; and are willing to sit under Scripture as under the

---

Scripture must be thought of as the authority of God exercised *through* Scripture, but this leaves us still questioning as to *how* this authority is understood and enacted when it comes to actually reading the biblical texts (Wright, *Scripture and the Authority of God*, 17). A working understanding of authority (from Heath Thomas), as the affirmation that the biblical text is somehow God's word, a good word, and has a claim on the life of the Christian, is adopted for the time being; although Jenni Williams has suggested that authority in relation to Scripture might simply mean as little as "God would like me to hear this." This would allow the "vileness" of the text to stand, without the temptation to somehow "rescue" the text from its very terribleness.

10. Perhaps the more pertinent question might be whether such a thing is even possible!

11. Against Milne, who states unequivocally that "feminists need to ask if the Bible serves any useful feminist purpose. My answer to this question is a resounding no." (Milne, "No Promised Land," 49).

authority of God and hear what God might still speak through it to the church today.

Thus, while I do not claim to have discovered a foolproof evangelical-feminist approach to the text, I offer here some reflections on Tamar and her story in 2 Sam 13:1–22. I suggest that by paying attention not just to *what* the text says, but to *how* it says, some light may be shed on what seems to be an impossible hermeneutical task.

In examining "how" the text says, my reading will reflect on three phenomena in biblical narrative and the difficulties and possibilities each raises in relation to reading 2 Sam 13:1–22 as an evangelical feminist. First to be explored is the phenomenon of the "disappearing narrator," who speaks omnisciently and whose perspective is often, therefore, equated with the divine or "God's eye" view. This notion that the narrator is implicitly understood to speak for God leads to the difficulty of realizing that if read according to the narrative perspective, Tamar is merely incidental to the story. This possibility is not especially hopeful for Tamar or for women in general, if the narrator's story is indeed the "authorized" version of events.

Second, narrative techniques for expressing moral evaluations of characters and events will be explored in relation to 2 Sam 13:1–22. As a further consequence of the narrator's omniscience and "God's-eye view," the narrator's opinions and evaluations of the story's characters are usually unquestioningly accepted by readers as fair and objective, "correct" views. In 2 Sam 13:1–22 this leads to agreement with the narratorial (and thus, presumably, divine) indictment of Amnon as a cad, and the portrayal of Tamar as the innocent victim who presents the wise voice of reason. This is perhaps a little more hopeful stance. It acknowledges, after all, that no one is for a moment suggesting that what happened to Tamar is to be admired or emulated. There is still the difficulty, however, of what *purpose* the narrator's approval of Tamar and disapproval of Amnon serves in the greater narrative context. In exploring the possible purpose we shall see that, if 2 Sam 13:1–22 is read in light of the purposes of the wider narrative context, Tamar again disappears from view.

Third, the phenomenon of narrative "gaps" and the resulting ambiguity of interpreting these gaps will be discussed. When attention is paid not only to what is *said*, but also to what is *not* said; not only to who is *present*, but also to who is *absent*, a range of possibilities emerge. When it is observed that God neither appears nor speaks (whether directly or by proxy) in 2 Sam 13:1–22, the question of why this should be the case is necessarily raised.

These possibilities and difficulties are premised on my understanding that Scripture should be approached on its own terms, again, paying attention not just to *what* it says, but also to *how* it says. In the case of the first phenomenon mentioned above, this means being cognizant of the (human) narrator and the way he manipulates his readers (whether one chooses to submit to his machinations or not). In the second case, this means attending to clues that might express a moral stance in the text to guide readerly evaluation of characters and their actions. In the third case, this means attending to the gaps and silences in the text and questioning what remains unspoken. It is these narrative gaps and silences in the text that offer the most potential for a reading of Tamar's story that responds appropriately to *both* the sacred nature of the text *and* the atrocity of the story that is told. And so, to Tamar.[12]

> And so it was, after all this happened, that Absalom, son of David, had a sister, a beautiful sister, whose name was Tamar, and Amnon, son of David, loved her.[13] Amnon was distressed to the point of making himself ill because of Tamar his sister, because she was a virgin and in the eyes of Amnon it was impossible to do anything to her. Now Amnon had a friend whose name was Jonadab, son of Shimeah, David's brother, and Jonadab was a very clever fellow. And he said to him, "Why are you so poorly, son of the king, morning after morning? Will you not tell me?" And Amnon said to him "Tamar, the sister of Absalom my brother, I love."
>
> So Jonadab said to him, "lie down in your bed and make yourself ill, and when your father comes to see you say to him 'get my sister Tamar to come down and I'll eat some food; let her prepare the food while I watch so that I see it, and I will eat from her hand.'"[14]

---

12. My reading of Tamar owes a great deal to Phyllis Trible's now classic reading (Trible, *Texts of Terror*, 37–63).

13. Although a little unwieldy in translation, I have chosen to keep the proper names in the order in which they occur in the Hebrew here. Also note that while the translation of *'hb* has been retained as "love," it very quickly becomes apparent that this is nothing more than sexual obsession.

14. Does this not strike anyone else as an odd request? In which case, might David be implicated right from the word go? Was he really an unwitting agent, or actually a tacit accomplice?

So Amnon lay down and made himself ill[15] and the king came to see him. And Amnon said to the king, "get Tamar my sister to come down and make some cakes while I watch, two cakes, and I will eat from her hand." So David sent to Tamar at home and said "Please go to the house of Amnon your brother and make some food for him."[16]

So Tamar went to the house of Amnon, her brother, where he was lying down. And she took dough, and kneaded it, and made cakes while he watched, and she cooked the cakes. Then she took the pan and offered it to him but he refused to eat. And Amnon said "everyone get out of here!" and everyone got out of there. Then Amnon said to Tamar "come, bring the food into the bedroom and feed it to me." So Tamar took the cakes that she had made and went to Amnon her brother in the bedroom. She approached him to feed him and he grabbed her and said to her "come lie with me my sister." And she said to him "Don't, my brother, don't afflict me, for such a thing is not done is Israel; don't do this disgraceful/foolish thing. And where would I go with my shame? And you would be like one of the disgraced/fools in Israel. Please speak to the king for he will not withhold me from you."[17]

But he would not listen to her voice and he grabbed her and raped her.[18]

Then he hated her, Amnon, with a great hatred, and that great hatred with which he hated her was far greater than the love with which he had loved her and he said "get up, get out!"[19] And Tamar

---

15. Ironically, given he had already gotten to the point of making himself "ill" (*ḥlh*) with lust.

16. Is this David giving permission, choosing to close his eyes and ignore what was going on; or actually being so stupid as not to recognize his own downfall—lust and the abuse of sexual power—in his own son?

17. Note the fourfold negative: this is a clear no, such that Tamar is no means implicated as a guilty party (cf. the question over whether Dinah was complicit in the Shechem episode, Genesis 34, discussed in chapter 2 of this volume). Tamar's words both before and after her violation shatter two rape myths that are prevalent even today; first, that "she was asking for it;" and second, that "she'll be grateful later."

18. Note that two verbs are used here to signify rape: oppressed/humiliated (*'nh*) and lay with (*škb*). (Gravett, "Reading 'Rape' in the Hebrew Bible," 279–99.). It is important to appreciate the nuance of humiliation here, for this relates to is a feud between brothers, and their attempts to insult each other; again shadowing David's own exertion of power by way of sexual dominance over a woman.

19. Again, this translation is a little unwieldy, but I wanted to capture the repetition of "hate" words (from the root *śn'*) to emphasize the contrast from Amnon's so-called love (*'hbh*; which NRSV rightly translates, after the event, as "lust") to his all consuming

said to him "no, because this is a greater evil than the other you did to me, to send me away." But he would not listen to her.

He called the servant he had sent away and said "send this thing outside, away from me and lock the door after her." (Tamar was wearing a coloured tunic for this was how the king's virgin daughters were customarily dressed). And he made her go out and locked the door behind her.

So Tamar put ashes upon her head and went on her way, lamenting.[20] And Absalom her brother said to her "Has Amnon your brother been with you? Now my sister, be silent; he is your brother, don't set your heart to speak of the thing."[21] So Tamar dwelled, desolate, in her brother Absalom's house.[22]

David the king heard about all these things and was exceedingly angry.[23] But Absalom said nothing to Amnon, neither bad nor good, for Absalom hated Amnon because of the thing that he did, he humiliated[24] Tamar his sister.[25]

THE AUTHORITATIVE NARRATOR

The first narrative technique to be examined is the phenomenon of the "disappearing narrator." In Hebrew biblical narrative narrators are generally understood to be omniscient, thus presenting what appears to be the "God's-eye view" on events and cleverly receding into the background such that this version of events is accepted unquestioningly by unsus-

---

hate. Unfortunately this does mean losing the spareness of the Hebrew.

20. Ritual signs of mourning, indicating that she has entered the realm of the dead (cf. Anderson, *A Time to Mourn, A Time to Dance*).

21. Goldingay has, to my mind, the best evaluation of Absalom's speech when he summarizes it as "spectacularly useless male advice" (Goldingay, *Men Behaving Badly*, 268).

22. This seems far too convenient to me. How did Absalom just happen to be coming along when Tamar was thrown out? Did he suspect all along? Or did Amnon plan it that way, to ensure Absalom was aware of her shame? In a simple, unsuspicious reading of the plot, Absalom appears as the "good" brother, conveniently coming along to give comfort to his sister. But a deeper reading will ask whether *both* Absalom *and* Amnon might have been scheming all along: Amnon to humiliate Tamar and thus his brother Absalom; and Absalom in order to have reason to kill Amnon. These deeper questions demonstrate again that sex and politics are inextricably intertwined in this latter part of David's kingship.

23. David, although angry, does nothing. He is, ironically, impotent.

24. *'nh,* the same verb as used at the climax (v. 14).

25. Translation mine.

pecting readers and hearers. Narrators can thus recruit readers to their interests and way of thinking, presenting their perspectives and telling the story in a way that might seem objective, natural and true; and, most importantly, in a way that is assumed to align with the divine omniscient view. Accordingly, if the narrator makes a statement or expresses a perspective, it is presumed to cohere with what God also deems to be true. The narrator's reliability, omniscience and point of view are thus taken as equivalent to God's; and accepted as such by readers.[26] This trusting stance towards biblical narrators has been critiqued in some feminist readings of the Hebrew biblical texts. Alice Bach proposes that instead of reading with the biblical narrators, readers should take up "a mode of reading in which one imagines the biblical narrator as a storyteller with whom the reader must contend, as s/he does with characters within the story."[27] This allows Bach to re-imagine female characters from a perspective other than the narrator's, resisting the narrative portrayal and perspective of those characters.[28] While this may be a helpful stance to take for a feminist interpreter, it is rather more problematic for evangelicals. As Parry has argued, "an evangelical hermeneutic will not easily be able to endorse an interpretation that stands over against the stance of a biblical narrator."[29]

Thus if we are indeed to trust the narrator, then in the context of Tamar's story, what would he have us believe?[30] How has he framed Tamar's story to achieve and communicate his purposes for including this episode of rape in the narrative? I suggest two possible scenarios, based on the position of 2 Sam 13:1–22 in the greater context of the narrative; and the way in which Tamar's story is introduced as a story in the lives of Amnon, Absalom, and David.

---

26. Sternberg, *Poetics*, 128; cf. Amit, *Reading Biblical Narratives*, 97; Powell, *What is Narrative Criticism?*, 24; Berlin, *Poetics and Interpretation of Biblical Narrative*, 55; Greidanus, *Modern Preacher and Ancient Text*, 207; Alter, *Art of Biblical Narrative*, 157.

27. Bach, "Signs of the Flesh," 351.

28. See Bach's reading of Bathsheba (Bach, "Signs of the Flesh," 357).

29. Parry, "Feminist Hermeneutics and Evangelical Concerns," 1; cf. chapter 2 in this volume.

30. I use the pronoun "he" for the biblical narrator advisedly.

The Authoritative Narrator and the Context of the Succession Narrative

The first context is that of the succession narrative, in which the rape of Tamar is understood as a demonstration of Amnon's unsuitability for the throne and a justification for Absalom's later murder of Amnon.[31] Read in this light, the events of chapters 13 and 14 demonstrate how first one son of David, then another, makes an ultimately unsuccessful bid for power. The rape of Tamar thus becomes an episode demonstrating the power play between the two brothers, Amnon and Absalom. Amnon rapes Absalom's sister (and his own half sister) in an act that does not merely fulfill his own lust, but is also intended to humiliate Absalom.[32] Absalom bides his time and waits for his revenge, contriving an opportunity to kill Amnon two years later (2 Sam 13:38–39). The narrator states explicitly that this is because he hated Amnon for raping his sister, Tamar (2 Sam 13:23–39). Thus the narrative sets readers up to consider Amnon not at all suitable for the throne, justifying Absalom's later actions, and using Tamar's humiliation to do so.

This reading of the narrative context is supported by the introduction of Tamar in a string of family names: "Absalom son of David had a sister, a beautiful sister, whose name was Tamar, and Amnon, son of David, loved her." It is no accident that Absalom is mentioned first in the Hebrew, although he then disappears out of the narrative until much later (v. 20). Tamar's story is intended by the narrator to be understood as part of Absalom's story. Further, in the opening string of names, Tamar comes *between* Absalom and Amnon—an indication, perhaps, of the way in which the sister will be the opportunity for struggle between the two brothers.[33] Absalom also frames the narrative structure of the

---

31. 2 Samuel 9–1 Kings 2 has been generally accepted as "succession narrative" since Rost's 1926 study arguing that the Samuel material forms that background to the question of who will take the throne after David, with the culmination in Kings when Solomon is crowned (Rost, *The Succession to the Throne of David*).

32. Note that *'nh*, used to indicate rape in 2 Sam 13:14 reappears when Absalom reappears in verse 22, "for Absalom hated Amnon, because he had raped/humiliated his sister Tamar;" and again in the summary for the next episode, verse 32, "Amnon alone is dead. This has been determined by Absalom from the day Amnon raped his sister Tamar."

33. See Trible's analysis of the ring structure of 13:1–3; and her explanation of the way in which Tamar is surrounded by her brothers in the text (Trible, *Texts of Terror*, 38–40, 53).

unit by appearing at the very beginning (v. 1) and the very end of the narrative (v. 20, 22). Just as his appearances at the start and end of the narrative encompass Tamar's intervening humiliation, so he will be the one to encompass her in the story world, taking her into his home and thus gaining sympathy from readers as the "good" brother.

In this context of succession to the throne, it reads as though the narrator includes Tamar's story simply to advance the plot of political intrigue between brothers.[34] If the narrator speaks for God, is this political plot also God's word on the matter? Does God allow the violation of Tamar in order to demonstrate how Amnon is not worthy of the throne? It disturbs me that a story of lust and rape could be used in the context of demonstrating the male struggle for power, while the sister who is raped, violated, humiliated, and silenced, becomes an incidental plot device. And yet, if the narrator is understood to present the God's-eye perspective, will my evangelical commitment to the authority of Scripture require me to assent to the narrator's version of events? Must I accept the story as the narrator tells it, with neither narrator nor God explicitly objecting to this treatment of Tamar?

The Authoritative Narrator and the Context of David's Sin

There is a second possible narrative context to consider, and that is that rather than being an episode in the succession narrative, Tamar's story serves to demonstrate the outworking of David's sin in his family (cf. 2 Sam 12:7–12).[35] For while Tamar is introduced in relation to her brothers, her father David is also in view, in the initial ascription of Absalom and Amnon as sons of David.[36] Further, the chapter begins with the connecting phrase, "after all this happened." When glancing backwards to

---

34. Cooper-White, *The Cry of Tamar*, 5; Davies, *The Dissenting Reader*, 59; Brueggemann, *First and Second Samuel*, 177.

35. Gillian Keys argues, against Rost, that rather than a succession narrative, 2 Samuel 10–20 is an independent unit demonstrating primarily the theme of sin and punishment of David (Keys, *Wages of Sin*, 126). On reading 2 Samuel 13 as an outcome of David's sin see also Long, "Wounded Beginnings: David and Two Sons, 26–34; Propp, "Kinship in 2 Samuel 13," 39–53; Bar-Efrat, *Narrative Art in the Bible*, 282; Amit, *Reading Biblical Narratives,* 127; and Firth, *1 & 2 Samuel*, 434.

36. Note though, that while Amnon and Absalom are identified as David's sons, Tamar is identified as Absalom's *sister*, and not David's *daughter*. She is already a step removed from the king and his care; already a distant victim in the chain of consequences of David's sin.

see what has "happened," the story of David's adultery with Bathsheba in 2 Samuel 11 and 12 is immediately apparent. In this narrative context, Tamar's story becomes an instant illustration of the ongoing ramifications of David's sin. More than being simply an unwitting (or otherwise) accomplice to Amnon's plans, David himself is the reason for Tamar's humiliation. Seen from this perspective, Tamar is no longer a pawn/porn[37] in the power play between brothers tussling for the throne, but is instead an innocent victim of the curse on David, her father, the king (2 Sam 12:9–12).

Does this let God "off the hook," so to speak, if Tamar's misuse is seen not merely as an incidental plot device in various episodes on the way to the crowning of God's chosen king; but rather as an obvious and tragic outcome of David's sin? If, instead of seeing the narrator and God as complicit in manipulating events to get the right guy onto the throne, this is a valid reminder that all human sin has consequences?

I am not convinced: if the narrative perspective serves to show the terrible consequences of David's sin, then, worse even than being a simple plot device pawn/porn, Tamar is now the innocent victim of male sin at least three times over. First, she suffers as a direct outcome of her father's sin; second, she suffers as a result of Amnon's lust as he follows in his father's footsteps; and third, she remains the victim of male interpretations that have unquestioningly accept the playing out of male sin on a female victim without so much as a comment as to what it might mean for *Tamar*.[38]

While God is silent in 2 Sam 13:1–22, we may look back to 2 Sam 12:7–12 where God is the one who has pronounced the curse on David (via Nathan the prophet). This begs the question as to whether Tamar's experience is *intentionally* part of the horrifying "achievement of Yahweh's purpose" in punishing David.[39] Does this then make God directly *complicit* in Tamar's suffering?

---

37. The homonyms pawn/porn used together capture both the use of Tamar as an object (pawn); and the voyeurism of the passage, where Tamar is presented throughout as a sexual object to be seen (porn).

38. See for example, Firth's recent commentary, in which he notes both the contexts of David's sin and of "fraternal conflict between brothers," without commenting at all on the seriousness of the situation for *Tamar* (Firth, *2 Samuel*, 438).

39. Goldingay, *Men Behaving Badly*, 257. Cf. Firth, the characters "fulfil Yahweh's stated purpose in David's punishment," (Firth, *1 & 2 Samuel*, 435)

I am left with the difficulty regardless of which narrative context I take. Either way, Tamar's story remains that of the innocent victim who finishes up voiceless and vanquished as her male relatives' stories progress. Either way, Tamar is inconsequential. Either way, Tamar is an incidental character who, from the narrative perspective, is included in the biblical record to serve a purpose in male plot lines. Do I trust the narrator's version of events and equate that perspective with divine consent?[40] Must I read with the narrator and accept the portrayal of God as either absent, sitting back and letting an innocent woman suffer, just to show how dastardly her brother is; or worse, as complicit in commanding such an outworking of her father's sin? As an evangelical, wishing to approach the text on its own terms and uphold its integrity as *Scripture*, what other option do I have?

I am forced to look more closely, for hints that the narrator, and therefore God, is not so conspiratorial in the male plot against Tamar as it initially seems. What other clues might there be in the text as to a divine evaluation of the situation? This brings me to the second narrative technique to be discussed in relation to 2 Sam 13:1–22, the way in which biblical narrators subtly express opinions and evaluations of characters and morality.

EVALUATING MORALITY: DISCERNING THE NARRATIVE PERSPECTIVE

The second feature of biblical narrative to be examined in relation to Tamar is the way in which biblical narrators express value judgments in the text. In our narrative Tamar is clearly regarded positively by the narrator and thus, if we are going to read with the narrator, presumably by God. She is described as beautiful (13:1) and expresses a clear and rational moral position in protesting against Amnon's actions (13:12–13, 16). Tamar speaks eloquently on her own behalf and it is in her two extended speeches that the narrator's true feelings on the happenings of 2 Sam 13:1–22 are expressed.[41] Amnon is "vile," a "scoundrel;" such a thing is "not done in Israel." Amnon is very much in the wrong, and it is

---

40. Cf. Parry, "the narrator . . . has a perspective and a voice and he aims to lead the reader to share this view. Should we identify the narrator's perspective with God's?" (Parry, "Feminist Hermeneutics and Evangelical Concerns," 24).

41. Cf. Brueggemann, *First and Second Samuel*, 177; Conroy, *Absalom Absalom!*, 23 n. 16, 24; Bar-Efrat, *Narrative Art*, 277.

clear that the narrator's sympathy lies with Tamar. By virtue of the way in which the narrator is understood to speak objectively, and for God, the reader accepts this judgement as the authoritative position on the matter, sympathizing with Tamar and despising Amnon. By characterizing Tamar purely positively, the narrator inclines us to agree with Tamar's (and thus the narrator's, and presumably God's) assessment of Amnon. Clearly Amnon is the "bad" brother, and Tamar herself expresses the narratorial and divine indictment of his actions in her words.[42]

There is some hope then, some possibility that God is not so complicit in the violence against Tamar after all. There is a clear moral stance in the text, which the narrator intends readers to understand as the divine evaluative perspective on Amnon and his actions. But while the narrative's moral perspective (and so God's) might well indict Amnon, there is still a question as to what *purpose* this indictment serves. Is this ultimately to let Tamar's voice be heard, in what might be considered a proto-feminist voice in Scripture; or is it instead to vindicate *Absalom*, as the "good" brother who cares for his sister? In gaining sympathy for Tamar, is the narrator really looking for sympathy for *Absalom*, and justifying the future murder of Amnon?[43] Conroy maintains that "the outstanding point here is the way in which the reader's sympathies are alienated from Amnon and gained for Tamar (*and therefore for Absalom*)."[44] This makes sense in the ongoing scheme of things, for as soon as Tamar leaves Amnon's house, Absalom meets, silences, and subsumes her; only to take vengeance on his brother in the very next episode in the narrative context (2 Sam 13:23–38). Tamar is thus left desolate, swallowed up in Absalom's house, while the narrative continues telling *Absalom's* story. She has served her purpose. Although she has indeed voiced her reproach, this reproach remains subservient to the patriarchal interests of the narrative. And so I am back to square one, where Tamar is a pawn/porn in a power play between brothers; an extra in an all-male cast. To find some hope for Tamar it seems I must now turn from what the narrator says, to what is *not* said.

---

42. Cf. Amit, *Reading Biblical Narratives*, 130; Davies, *The Dissenting Reader*, 58; Fuchs, *Sexual Politics*, 202.

43. So Conroy, *Absalom Absalom!*, 23.

44. Ibid., 23; emphasis mine.

NARRATIVE GAP: THE ABSENCE AND SILENCE OF GOD

Thus the third phenomenon of Hebrew narrative to be examined in relation to Tamar is that of the narrative "gap" of God's absence as a character, and silence as a speaker, in this text. This silence may be the most hopeful possibility in the entire episode. For, while it is understood that the biblical narrator indirectly presents the divine, God's-eye view in his telling of events; it is significant that the *character* God never appears in this narrative. God never speaks, and nor does any divinely appointed representative of God. This time there is no prophet Nathan sent to call David or Amnon to account, no defense of the innocent lamb Tamar, no "thus sayeth the LORD" (cf. 2 Sam 12:1–14). This goes against the norm of Hebrew narrative in which God often appears as an actor in the narrative, or the narrator explicitly tells his audience of God's pleasure or displeasure.[45] Perhaps this divine silence is intentional, and even ominous–and to what effect? There are, I contend, at least two ways of reading God's absence and silence in 2 Samuel 13.

God's Absence and Silence as Complicity with the Male Plot against Tamar

First, the absence and silence of God as character in the narrative could be taken as tacit complicity, with everything that needs to be gleaned of the divine perspective discernible from the narrative techniques discussed above. That is, the narrator himself speaks for God, and expresses judgements that are accepted by readers as the divine perspective. If the narrator's view is simply equated with the divine view, then in the narrative context the story of Tamar serves little more than the plot lines of the men. God seems content to let the narrator tell the story, there is no intervention on behalf of Tamar. God's silence and absence are read as complicity with the male narrator and his patriarchal agenda.[46]

---

45. Significantly, God remains silent throughout much of the remainder of 2 Samuel, being conspicuously absent in 2 Samuel 13–20. Cf. the closing chapters of Judges, where God is also conspicuously absent, in another situation of rapid moral deterioration.

46. Cf. Trible, "Silence covers impotence and complicity" (Trible, *Texts of Terror*, 86).

God's Absence and Silence as Indictment of the Male Plot against Tamar

However, while God *is* clearly absent from the text of 2 Sam 13:1–22, I question whether this absence and silence necessarily connotes tacit *complicity*, or whether it might be indicative of something quite different going on. The second way this silence could be understood is as God choosing to have no part of such a terrible situation. Perhaps the absence of God as a character from the narrative at this point *removes* God from complicity in the episode. Perhaps, as Andrew Sloane has suggested, God's absence and silence does *not* imply concession or complicity, but rather "shouts condemnation of David as the kind of man who makes possible, even necessitates, this kind of behaviour."[47] As Mark Gray has asked, "how long can a holy God of justice insinuate God's self in the machinations of a regime plunging headlong to squalid immorality in all its varied private and public forms?"[48] Is God necessarily implicated in the violence against Tamar, or has God simply withdrawn, not deigning to dignify this behavior by even offering a presence in the narrative? Perhaps, God's silence speaks volumes, as God refuses to take any part in these particular machinations of men.

To return to my initial readings then; when I now read the narrative in light of the succession to the throne of David, might I read God's silence not as assent to, but rather as a *withdrawal* from, the dirty politics of power played out between brothers? For while it was noted that nowhere did the narrator or God explicitly *object* to the treatment of Tamar as a political pawn/porn; *neither do either explicitly endorse* this treatment. The narrative "gap" thus allows space for the silence to be read either way.

When I now read the narrative in light of the unfolding consequences of David's sin, it is perhaps more difficult to make this case in defense of God's silence, for, as we saw, there *was* an *explicit* word from the prophet Nathan as to how things were to play out (2 Sam 12:7–12). And yet this prophetic word speaks nothing of Tamar specifically. David and his sons still have free choice, and it is the former's inaction and the latters' actions that will ultimately cause Tamar to suffer.[49] Thus, while

---

47. Sloane, personal communication 12 Feb 2009.

48. Gray, "A Chip off the Old Block?" 53.

49. Cf. Firth, "Through it all David is a bit-part player who sends Tamar to help her brother, is angry about the rape, sends Amnon to the fateful feast and mourns

punishment may have been earlier pronounced by the prophet, by the time we reach Tamar, God has already withdrawn.

Further, when I now read Tamar's speech of courageous resistance against all the odds, I find an example of a voice of protest to be employed by God's people when God is silent. Even if it is a voice raised for the primary purpose of raising Absalom's profile in the eyes of the reader; and even if it is quickly silenced, Tamar's voice still stands. This is perhaps surprising, given the propensity to silence women in the biblical text. Tamar's protest is thus significant as a present minority voice, providing a precedent for further voices of protest to be raised.

CONTEXT AND RESPONSE: READING WITH TAMAR IN THE TWENTY-FIRST CENTURY

Narrative gaps invite reflection and response. The absence of the omnipresent God is a gap that calls for comment.[50] I have suggested two possible ways of reading this gap, as divine *complicity* or divine *indictment*. The latter possibility provides a more hopeful stance: perhaps God has nothing to do with author-izing Amnon's treatment of Tamar. Perhaps divine silence is indicative not of lack of care, but of righteous anger. Perhaps, in the absence of a divine voice for Tamar, it is up to me to speak into the silence. As noted above, generations of (predominantly) male interpreters have been complicit in the silencing of Tamar by focusing on the continuing plot lines of either Absalom and Amnon; or David. By taking Tamar's own voice of protest as my cue, and speaking out into the silence, I might perhaps draw Tamar and her plight into the light and out of the shadows of her male relatives.

Is this gap-filling and protest permissible, within an evangelical hermeneutical framework? My evangelical concern is to honor the integrity of the text as Scripture. This reading does so by working with the way the text itself works. It attends to what the narrator (and so God?) says but *also* to what *is not* said. It attends to the discomfiting gap of

---

for his son. David sends and becomes emotional, but nothing else. Is he accepting his punishment, or is he so bound by his own sin that he cannot act? Within the chapter's artistry this is perhaps a false dichotomy. David's sons make free choices and so resolve David's punishment, and David's failure to act is both a free choice and the means of his punishment. David's sin may not have been terminal, but sin's effects linger" (Firth, *1 & 2 Samuel*, 441).

50. Sternberg, *Poetics*, 251.

God's presence, and responds to the invitation to fill that gap by exploring the ambiguous absence and silence of God. It attends to the way in which the voice of protest is expressed, but notes how this is ultimately silenced in the narrative. In the absence of God's voice for Tamar and the silencing of Tamar's own voice of protest, it is *entirely* appropriate for people of God to speak up and express outrage at this text. This honors the integrity of the text because it is a response made precisely in keeping with the way the narrative itself "works." By the very structure of the text there is a gap, a space for a spokesperson for Tamar. Could it be the responsibility of interpreters to be that spokesperson? To speak up for justice when victims are silenced and when God appears absent?

In reading with the way the text "works" my feminist concerns are also addressed. This reading reveals the power dynamics at play. It questions the normalisation of violence against women and the stance that allows this violence to go unremarked in the biblical narrative while male interests are pursued in the ongoing story. It calls for protest against the injustice perpetrated against Tamar, finding in the narrative gap of divine absence and silence a space into which this protest may be spoken; and in Tamar's intelligent resistance a precedent for doing so.

And so I propose a further context for Tamar's story: the context of a God who is sometimes, on the surface, silent; but who nevertheless speaks. This is the context of a God who speaks and continues to speak *with* and *by* and *through* and *for* people. In this context, it is God's people who must now speak into the gaps and speak out in protest. Only by doing so might we ensure that Tamar's voice continues to be heard and is not buried forever in the basement of her brother Absalom's house. May Tamar continue to speak.

BIBLIOGRAPHY

Alter, Robert. *The Art of Biblical Narrative*. New York: Basic, 1981.
Amit, Yaireh. *Reading Biblical Narratives: Literary Criticism and the Hebrew Bible*. Translated by Yael Latan. Minneapolis: Fortress, 2004.
Anderson, Gary A. *A Time to Mourn, A Time to Dance: The Expression of Grief and Joy in Israelite Religion*. University Park, PA: Pennsylvania University Press, 1991.
Bach, Alice. "Signs of the Flesh: Observations on Characterization in the Bible. In *Women in the Hebrew Bible: A Reader*, edited by Alice Bach, 351–65. New York: Routledge, 1999.
Bar-Efrat, Shimon. *Narrative Art in the Bible*. Translated by Dorothea Shefer-Vanson. Sheffield, UK: Almond, 1989.
Berlin, Adele. *Poetics and Interpretation of Biblical Narrative*. Sheffield, UK: Almond, 1983.
Bier, Miriam J. "Is There a God in This Text? Violence, Absence, and Silence in 2 Samuel 13:1–22." In *Reconsidering God and Gender: Evangelical Perspectives*, edited by Myk Habets and Beulah Wood, 148–60. Eugene, OR: Pickwick, 2010.
Bird, Phyllis A. *Missing Persons and Mistaken Identities: Women and Gender in Ancient Israel*. Minneapolis: Fortress, 1997.
Brueggemann, Walter. *First and Second Samuel*. Louisville: Knox, 1990.
Camp, Claudia. "Feminist Theological Hermeneutics: Canon and Christian Identity." In *Searching the Scriptures: A Feminist Introduction*, vol. 1, edited by Elisabeth Schüssler Fiorenza, 154–71. New York: Crossroads, 1993.
Clines, D. J. A. "What Does Eve Do to Help? And Other Irredeemably Androcentric Orientations in Genesis 1–3." In *What Does Eve Do to Help?*, edited by D. J. A. Clines, 45–48. Sheffield, UK: Sheffield Academic, 1990.
Cooper-White, Pamela. *The Cry of Tamar: Violence against Women and the Church's Response*. Minneapolis: Fortress, 1995.
Davies, Eryl. *The Dissenting Reader: Feminist Approaches to the Hebrew Bible*. Aldershot, UK: Ashgate, 2003.
Goldingay, John. *Men Behaving Badly*. Carlisle: Paternoster, 2000.
Gray, Mark. "A Chip off the Old Block? Rhetorical Strategy in 2 Samuel 13:7–15." *Journal for the Study of the Old Testament* 77 (1993) 39–54.
Hoggard Creegan, Nicola, and Christine D. Pohl. *Living on the Boundaries: Evangelical Women, Feminism and the Theological Academy*. Downers Grove, IL: InterVarsity, 2005.
Keys, Gillian. *The Wages of Sin: A Reappraisal of the "Succession Narrative."* Sheffield, UK: Sheffield Academic, 1996.
Long, Burke O. "Wounded Beginnings: David and Two Sons." In *Images of Man and God*, 26–34. Sheffield, UK: Almond, 1981.
Milne, Pamela J. "No Promised Land: Rejecting the Authority of the Bible." In *Feminist Approaches to the Bible*, edited by H. Shanks, 47–73. Washington: Biblical Archaeology Society, 1995.
Osiek, Carolyn. "The Feminist and the Bible: Hermeneutical Alternatives." *Religion and Intellectual Life* 6.3-4 (1989) 96–109.
Parry, Robin A. "Feminist Hermeneutics and Evangelical Concerns: The Rape of Dinah as a Case Study." *Tyndale Bulletin* 53.1 (2002) 1–28.
Powell, Mark. *What is Narrative Criticism?: A New Approach to the Bible*. London: SPCK, 1993.

Propp, William H. "Kinship in 2 Samuel 13." *Catholic Biblical Quarterly* 55.1 (1993) 39–53.

Rost, Leonhard. *The Succession to the Throne of David*. Translated by Michael D. Rutter and David M. Gunn. Sheffield, UK: Almond, 1982.

Sakenfeld, Katharine Doob. "Feminist Uses of Biblical Materials." In *Feminist Interpretation of the Bible*, edited by Letty Russell, 55–64. Oxford: Blackwell, 1985.

Scholer, David M. "Feminist Hermeneutics and Evangelical Biblical Interpretation." *Journal of the Evangelical Theological Society* 30.4 (1987) 407–20.

Sternberg, Meir. *The Poetics of Biblical Narrative: Ideological Literature and the Drama of Reading*. Bloomington, IN: Indiana University Press, 1985.

Talbert-Wettler, Betty. "Can Use of Proper Hermeneutical Methods Transcend Gender Bias in Interpretations?" *Journal of the Evangelical Theological Society* 43.1 (2000) 53–69.

Tolbert, Mary Ann. "Protestant Feminists and the Bible: On the Horns of a Dilemma." In *The Pleasure of Her Text: Feminist Readings of Biblical and Historical Texts*, edited by Alice Bach, 5–23. Philadelphia: Trinity, 1990.

Trible, Phyllis. "Depatriarchalizing in Biblical Interpretation." *Journal of the American Academy of Religion* 41.1 (1973) 30–48.

Trible, Phyllis. "If the Bible's So Patriarchal, How Come I Love It?" *Bible Review* 8.5 (1992) 44–47, 55.

———. *Texts of Terror: Literary Feminist Readings of Biblical Narratives*. Philadelphia: Fortress, 1984.

Wright, N. T. *Scripture and the Authority of God*. London: SPCK, 2005.

7

Aberrant Textuality?

The Case of Ezekiel the (Porno) Prophet

Andrew Sloane

INTRODUCTION[1]

THE OLD TESTAMENT PROPHETS have been an important resource in Christian ethics, particularly in relation to understanding God's passion for justice—and God's corresponding passion that God's people reflect that in the conduct of their lives and the patterns of their communities. A recent movement of evangelicals engaging with social justice and advocacy on behalf of the poor derives its name from Micah's call to justice (Mic 6:6–8).[2] Ezekiel's vision of a new Jerusalem is a vital resource in Revelation's vision of the new heavens and earth where, in the words of Peter, righteousness is at home (2 Pet 3:13).[3] What are we to do, then, when the very ethics of the prophets is called into question or when they are criticized as oppressive, violent, misogynist and abusive? Such charges, if substantiated, would vitiate their use in Christian ethics and call into question evangelical views of the nature and func-

---

1. An earlier version of this chapter appeared in *Tyndale Bulletin* 59.1 (2008) 53–76.

2. The Micah Challenge and associated Micah Network. Details can be found on their respective websites, <http://www.micahnetwork.org/> [accessed 17/08/2007] and <http://www.micahchallenge.org/> [accessed 17/08/2007].

3. It is also interesting to note in this regard that his description of Sodom's sin in Ezek 16:49–50 focuses on abuse and neglect of the poor.

tion of Scripture. Athalya Brenner and Fokkelien van Dijk-Hemmes' pornoprophetic critique of Ezekiel (and Hosea and Jeremiah) present a substantial challenge to (evangelical) Christian use of the prophets as a resource in Christian ethics. And theirs are not isolated voices. Their views are either reflected and endorsed or echoed in the work of many others,[4] and have been echoed in the responses of "ordinary readers" to the texts.[5] Thus, whilst evangelical scholars have not extensively analyzed their work, it is important to do so, lest we neglect important issues in Old Testament interpretation and Christian ethics and fail to address significant ministry issues.[6] In this paper, then, I will begin by outlining Brenner and van Dijk-Hemmes' case, paying particular attention to Ezekiel 16 and 23. This will entail presenting their main conclusions and identifying what they take to be the justification of their position. I will then present an analysis of their claims, dealing with their assumptions and methodology, as well as their key evidence and arguments. In so doing I will appraise them from an evangelical perspective, present alternative explanations of key aspects of the texts and note in passing implications for our dealing with texts such as these.

ATHALYA BRENNER, FOKKELIEN VAN DIJK-HEMMES AND PORNOPROPHETICS

Their Case

The metaphors of the adulterous wife in Ezekiel 16 and 23 confront us with a shocking depiction of the sinful rebellion of God's people. Given

---

4. For the endorsement of their views, see Bal, "Foreword" [a glowing endorsement of the book]; Exum, "The Ethics of Biblical Violence Against Women"; Gordon and Washington, "Rape as a Military Metaphor in the Hebrew Bible"; cf. Magdalene, "Ancient Near Eastern Treaty-Curses"; Bird, "Poor Man or Poor Woman"; Guest, "Hiding behind the Naked Woman"; Yee, *Children of Eve*. For analyses of these texts that, while not specifically citing their work, clearly echo their methods and conclusions, see, Darr, "Ezekiel's Justification of God: Teaching Troubling Texts"; Pope, "Mixed Marriage Metaphor in Ezekiel 16"; Weems, *Battered Love*; Dempsey, "The 'Whore' of Ezekiel 16"; Shields, "Gender and Violence in Ezekiel 23"; Shields, "Multiple Exposures."

5. For instance, my eldest daughter, Elanor (then 15) found the metaphors offensive and misogynistic on first reading.

6. Wright, *OT Ethics*, 448n.13, has noted the need for a careful evangelical study of these issues (admittedly, specifically referring to Cheryl Exum's work cited above). Brief discussions of pornoprophetics can be found in Ortlund, *Whoredom*, 177–85; Block, *Ezekiel 1–24*, 467–71, neither of which adequately addresses underlying methodological and hermeneutic issues.

the explicit nature of Ezekiel's language, it is not surprising that readers, especially women, might be offended by the text. Brenner and van Dijk-Hemmes argue that our reaction should go beyond shock and offence to outright rejection of the text. Texts such as Ezekiel 16 and 23 are examples of what could be called "aberrant textuality"—texts that express and foster misogynist views of women and their sexuality and perpetuate sexual violence against them. They are *pornographic* in their presentation of women and women's sexuality and as such are not worthy to be treated as sacred Scripture—indeed they must be resisted as damaging to women and their interests. For instance, Brenner claims that "the twin image of the divine husband (YHWH) and his errant, promiscuous wife ... is a propaganda device which is pornographic in nature because of the female exposure and sexual violence against women that it builds on and even advocates, and because of its methods of persuasion."[7]

Texts such as these are damaging to women in the ways in which they function in religious communities. Brenner states: "Biblical pornography has been utilized as an extremely effective vehicle for the fossilization of gender roles because it carries a unique authority even when not acknowledged as such."[8] These texts, furthermore, address women in particular (harmful) ways, and in a manner distinct from how they address men. Van Dijk-Hemmes argues that while the metaphor in Ezekiel 23 humiliates both men and women, men are given a way of escape by means of identification with either the husband, Yahweh, or the righteous men of verse 45. This route is not available to women, who are specifically and directly spoken against at the end of the text which thereby both misrepresents women's experience and distorts their sexuality.[9]

In the same vein Brenner claims that the "prophetic" metaphors (including Ezekiel's) are the ultimate expression of fantasies of male domination with God, the male, being in absolute authority over the totally submissive female. Because of its psychological origins in male insecurity, this is not "just" a metaphor, but is an expression of a pornographic vision.[10] "A (male) fantasy of (male) domination is acted out by equating divine authority with male power. The (male) fantasy

---

7. Brenner, *The Intercourse of Knowledge*, 7.
8. Brenner, "Introduction," 12.
9. Van Dijk-Hemmes, "Metaphorization," 176.
10. Brenner, "Poetics of Pornography," 189.

of (female) submission becomes definitive. It is easily legitimized by a two-way application of the analogy: when God is imaged as a human male, human males can be viewed as divine... Metaphor creates its own "reality," its own frame of reference, not to mention hierarchy."[11]

This is a dangerous and destructive reality, one abusive of women: "This propaganda cleverly constructs a stereotype: everywoman, especially everywife, is a potential deviant and should therefore be tightly controlled. By males, of course. Wife-abuse and rape should be directly linked to the worldview which makes such prophetic propaganda acceptable. Religious-political propaganda can lead to wholesale rape of women: read the news about Bosnia."[12] She concludes "that whoever composed those passages perceived women and men—not to mention God—and gender relations in a certain way. That vision, that male fantasy of desire which presupposes a corresponding and complementary mythical fantasy of female desire, is pornographic. As a reader, I can resist this fantasy by criticism and reflection."[13]

Their Evidence and Arguments

Their primary evidence comes from an interpretation of the text driven by a particular interpretive stance.[14] The influence of that stance, particularly on what counts as evidence from the text to support their conclusions, is evident in relation to the "pornographic" elements in the text. Brenner argues that the very language used in the metaphors is problematic, given the associations of the root זָנָה (*zānâ*, to be [sexually] unfaithful) "the use of the same verbal sequence for designating female prostitution and promiscuity on the one hand, and for designating male illegitimate religious beliefs and practices on the other hand, estab-

---

11. Brenner, "On Prophetic Propaganda," 270–71. This is a slightly modified later version of "Poetics of Pornography" cited above.

12. Brenner, "On Prophetic Propaganda," 273.

13. Brenner, "Poetics of Pornography," 193. This is their conclusion both severally and together; in their joint conclusion to their work on pornoprophetics they claim that biblical pornography is potentially more dangerous than other forms of pornography inasmuch as the male vision of the text can be covertly equated with God's own view of women and their sexuality, requiring our resistance to such violent authoritarian control. See Brenner and Dijk-Hemmes, "Afterword."

14. Of course, all reading comes from an interpretive point of view; my criticism below is in relation to the nature and validity of the "pornoprophetic" point of view, not the fact that they have one.

lishes an unmistakable association that is hardly complementary [*sic*] to women and their sexual behavior."[15] She asserts, furthermore, that the "textual voice" is gendered as a male voice, which speaks to human social and sexual relations. "The message, although indirect, is clear. 'Wifely' loyalty is to be learnt through re-education and punishment, including exposure and public shaming."[16] Indeed, this male voice is also the voice of God, demonstrating "male authority as symbolized by and symbolizing divine authority."[17]

She makes similar points about the treatment of the male and female body, especially in the prophets. She argues that circumcision establishes a clear connection between the penis and the divine so that: "women are excluded a priori from this symbolic order . . . bonding with the (male) god is stamped on the (male) body."[18] Furthermore, the penis is afforded protection not offered the female body in the "so-called prophets" where female bodies are repeatedly exposed and threatened.[19] In the "'prophetic' vision" in Ezekiel 23, "the elusive demarcation lines between metaphor and 'reality' break down and the two worlds, the divine/human and the social, blur into one gendered schism."[20] "What we, all of us, ultimately see in the woman-community of the divine husband/human wife metaphor is not just a metaphorical woman but a *naked* woman—silent, accused of prostitution, framed for sustaining male violence."[21] She rejects this "pornographic fantasy of male desire."[22]

Their reading of Ezekiel also draws on their analysis of other "pornoprophetic" texts. For instance, van Dijk-Hemmes sees Hosea as "extolling an ideal patriarchal marriage in which the woman has to submit to her husband and remain faithful to him,"[23] which informs her reading of Ezekiel 23. The latter text also "speaks not only *of* women, but also—albeit indirectly—specifically *to* women."[24] It refers not only (or even

15. Brenner, *The Intercourse of Knowledge*, 148.
16. Brenner, "Pornoprophetics Revisited," 253.
17. Ibid., 266.
18. Ibid., 269.
19. Ibid., 266–71.
20. Ibid., 272.
21. Ibid., 272.
22. Ibid., 273.
23. Van Dijk-Hemmes, "Metaphorization," 168.
24. Ibid., 169, 70.

primarily) to the religious and political condition of Israel around the time of the exile, but to Israelite social and sexual realities. Thus, references in the text to the treatment of the *metaphorical* women become references to the expected treatment of *actual* women in the social world of ancient Israel: the deity's control over the city in grace, indictment, punishment and restoration reflects and endorses the control that *men in Israel had (and should have) over women and their sexuality*.[25]

Related to this is their understanding of the role of gender and sexuality in ancient Israelite society and the Hebrew Bible. Brenner sees desire and sexuality as strongly "gendered" in the Hebrew Bible, as reflected both in linguistic and textual data.[26] "The Hebrew word for 'male' ... is זכר [z-k-r], apparently from a root denoting 'to remember' ... A female... is designated by נקבה [n-q-b-h], derived from a consonantal sequence designating 'pierce, make a hole' (Qal) and formally constituted as the grammatical F formation of נקב [n-q-b], 'hole,' 'cavity,' 'opening,' 'orifice.'"[27] Etymology informs meaning and so: "A 'female' is sexed rather than gendered: she is an 'orifice'; orifices and holes require that they be filled. A 'male' is gendered: he is the carrier of memory, the one 'to be remembered,' thus a social agent. The female is there to be penetrated and to be receptive ... socially, there is no difference between her biological and social function. The male agent carries the burden of social continuity, of culture ('remembrance'); he is there to 'give,' that is, penetrate the female 'hole' or receptacle."[28]

This is precisely the picture that also emerges from the key texts relating to love and desire and male and female sexuality.[29] Their view of sexuality and gender in the Hebrew Bible in which women and their bodies are marginalized, subject to male power and control, informs their reading of the "prophetic" texts and, indeed, is taken to support their conclusions. Nonetheless, the strength of their case is tied to their underlying assumptions and the methodology that informs their analysis,[30] as are many of its key components. It is to those assumptions and methods that we now turn.

25. Ibid., 173, 75.
26. Brenner, *The Intercourse of Knowledge*.
27. Ibid., 11–12.
28. Ibid., 12.
29. Ibid., 13, 178.
30. Technically, these are "data-background" and "control" beliefs, following the

Their Methodologies and Assumptions

A key to their methodology is the use of *gendered* readings of biblical (and other) texts, associated with a key assumption that texts are the product of societies with particular (generally patriarchal) ideologies and that these ideologies are reflected in, perpetuated by and propounded in the text.[31] For instance, the "pornoprophetic" passages reflect M [masculine] voices, being "assigned to male speakers, even specifically to the supreme authority of a male God," and expressing male "fantasies about and against women."[32] Thus texts will knowingly or unknowingly expose the gender assumptions and gender-driven power relations of the people and communities that produced them. This belief in the inherently androcentric and oppressive nature of Israelite society and the texts it produced is so pervasive as to control their reading of the texts, including how they deal with alternative interpretations of key texts.

These assumptions and strategies are clearly associated with, and perhaps entail, a corresponding theological assumption: that these texts are not the authoritative word of God. For instance, Brenner chooses to designate the "pornographic" texts in Jeremiah as poetry rather than prophecy in order to undermine their authority.[33] Further, this is associated with a privileging of women's experience over the biblical text, as seen in her determination to "problematize the Jeremiah texts in which the husband-wife metaphor features and regard them as pornography," and to resist the text and its pornographic "male/poet/God's viewpoint."[34]

Related to this is their understanding of the nature and function of *pornography*, which is clearly crucial to a pornographic *reading* of these texts. This is derived from the work of Setel on Hosea,[35] who sees "pornography as both a description of and tool for maintaining male domination of female sexuality . . . through the denial, or misnaming

---

analysis of Wolterstorff, *Reason Within the Bounds of Religion*. I will, however, use the looser terminology of methods and assumptions in this paper.

31. Brenner, "Introduction," 13. The Bible is "a political document," containing "ideologies of specific interest groups" (Brenner, "On Prophetic Propaganda," 256; cf. Brenner, *The Intercourse of Knowledge*, 3–4).

32. Brenner, "Introduction," 12.

33. Brenner, "Poetics of Pornography," 179.

34. Ibid., 179, 92–93. See also Brenner, "Pornoprophetics Revisited," 273–75.

35. Setel, "Prophets and Pornography"; cf. Van Dijk-Hemmes, "Metaphorization," 170–71; Brenner, "Poetics of Pornography," 181.

of female experience."³⁶ All of this is apparent in Hosea's use of female sexual imagery,³⁷ which, in turn, makes it a pornographic view of female sexuality. Citing Setel, Brenner claims that pornography expresses "the objectification and degrading of 'woman' in a manner that makes abuse of females acceptable or even commendable; that it restricts female sexual choice to an actual state of slavery; and that it stresses the nature and meaning of male power (Setel 1985, 88) . . . Thus pornography preserves and asserts male social domination through the control of female sexuality."³⁸ This is true, whatever the cultural context of the production of the texts, as contemporary and biblical pornography are significantly similar.³⁹ "Hence, the relevant biblical texts can be problematized as follows. If contemporary pornographic literature is found to contain anti-female bias, the same should apply to pornographic biblical literature."⁴⁰

A similar move is made in relation to the texts' function as pornographic propaganda. Brenner's "minimalist" definition of propaganda is "a transaction of verbal (rhetorical) communication designed by its initiator(s) to persuade the recipients of communication to accept its message(s), then formulate new opinions, then act on the newly acquired position."⁴¹ Her definition of pornography is similarly minimalist: namely, "the representation of sexual acts that arouses sexual excitement."⁴² She identifies key (manipulative) rhetorical techniques at work in propaganda and argues that they are clearly evident in the "so-called prophetic books."⁴³ Given the sexual nature of the prophets' propaganda, this is pornographic propaganda.⁴⁴ "There is no doubt that, unlike modern pornography, the pornoprophetic passages are *not* intended as depictions of male desire *per se* . . . That, however, is small consolation. The ideology of male supremacy is indispensable to the husband/wife metaphor: without this ideology the metaphor will not be

---

36. Setel, "Prophets and Pornography," 87.
37. Ibid., 94.
38. Brenner, "Poetics of Pornography," 185–86.
39. Ibid., 181.
40. Ibid.
41. Brenner, "Pornoprophetics Revisited," 255.
42. Ibid., 257; note the absence of questions of authorial intent.
43. Ibid., 262.
44. Ibid., 265–66.

understood, even less be acted upon."⁴⁵ Her aim is to expose and censure such violent misogynistic representations as both propaganda and pornography.⁴⁶

The combination of gendered reading, ideological analysis and the identification of these texts as pornography shapes their understanding of Ezekiel 16 and 23. For instance women's experience is misnamed in Ezekiel 23:3, where women are blamed for being sexually abused in Egypt.⁴⁷ Van Dijk-Hemmes states: "Israel's sin in Egypt actually consists of its being oppressed . . . Within an androcentric framework women can easily be seen as guilty of their own abuse. Hence, the imagery of women is indispensable for conveying a message which is a contradiction in terms: the people are guilty of their own past enslaving inasmuch as women are, by definition, guilty of their own sexual misfortunes."⁴⁸ Their enjoyment of their violation and desiring more of it aims to convince the audience "that both metaphorical women, so perverse since their maidenhood, deserve the utterly degrading and devastating treatment to which they are to be exposed."⁴⁹

Their assumptions and methods lead to some surprising conclusions. The metaphors, while addressing Israel's religious and political faithlessness, also speak directly of women's sexuality. Van Dijk-Hemmes states: "Both women are degraded and publicly humiliated in order to stress that their sexuality is and ought to be an object of male possession and control."⁵⁰ Indeed, the religious and sexual functions of the text are linked:

> The androcentric-pornographic character of this metaphorical language must indeed be experienced as extremely humiliating by an M [male] audience forced to imagine itself as being exposed to violating enemies. Nevertheless, it is exactly this androcentric-pornographic character which at the same time offers the M audience a possibility of escape: the escape of the identification with the wronged and revengeful husband; or, more modestly, identification with the righteous men who, near the end of

45. Ibid., 266.
46. Ibid., 274.
47. Van Dijk-Hemmes, "Metaphorization," 172–73.
48. Ibid., 173.
49. Ibid., 173–75, quote from page 175.
50. Ibid., 175.

the text, are summoned to pass judgment upon the adulterous women (v. 45)... No such possibility of escape is left to F readers. In respect to them, the metaphorization of woman in Ezekiel 23 performs first and foremost a violent speech act which is even more offensive than the Hosean version: it simultaneously shapes and distorts women's (sexual) experience.[51]

Brenner, similarly, argues that the "prophetic" metaphors (including Ezekiel's) are the ultimate expression of fantasies of male domination: God, the male, is in absolute authority over the totally submissive female.[52] Indeed, because "the metaphor's ideology cuts both ways, accepting the metaphor entails endorsing patriarchy in both divine and human realms."[53] Hence, the use of pornographic propaganda "validates the metaphorized relationship between God and his community... by appealing to a familiar male view: women are by nature promiscuous, hence in need of containment."[54] This "political and personal fantasy of controlling the female body, and female sexuality," is even more dangerous in the Bible than in general Western culture and must be resisted:

> The utilization of this acceptable vision for religious purposes, the fact that female sexuality in it is not a target *per se*, may obscure the vision's origins while, simultaneously, lending it additional weight. Biblical pornography is therefore perhaps more dangerous than modern pornography. Almost imperceptibly we come to identify message and messenger, alleged author and authority—so much so that we have to recall contemporary analogues in order to resist the authority and violent control advocated in order not to be duped by the text's authoritative command... Exposure is a step towards undermining authority.[55]

ANALYSIS

Their Assumptions and Methods

Brenner and van Dijk-Hemmes' ideological-critical perspective, including their belief that the Bible has significantly contributed to Western

---

51. Ibid., 176.
52. Brenner, "Poetics of Pornography," 189.
53. Brenner, "On Prophetic Propaganda," 264.
54. Ibid., 266; cf. 70–73.
55. Brenner and Dijk-Hemmes, "Afterword," 194.

society's limitation and distortion of women's experience, is an expression of their feminist perspective. It is, however, neither typical of feminist biblical scholarship, nor necessary to it. Feminist scholars have helped to expose the masculine bias of traditional biblical scholarship, including the way that biblical texts have been *used* against women and their interests; but they do not all believe that the Bible is itself misogynistic.[56] Nonetheless, ideological approaches such as Brenner and van Dijk-Hemmes' have made a significant impact on contemporary biblical scholarship.[57] This makes it important to examine their perspective on the Bible and its interpretation, as does the fact that it is clearly contrary to central evangelical commitments—the most notable being the idea that the Bible is the authoritative word of God, and that this God is a God of liberation, love and justice.

Central to ideological criticism of the Bible is the claim that, whatever texts *purport to be about*, they actually encode the systems of domination and control of the cultures or cultural groups that produced them. These ideologies are primarily political and economic in their interests and the texts serve to both reflect and propagate those power systems. A concern for liberation and freedom, then, is best served by exposing these ideologies and resisting their force.[58] In such a resistant "reading against the grain" of the text, the intent of the biblical author governs neither the interpretation nor use of the text, as evident in Brenner and van Dijk-Hemmes' work on pornoprophetics.

---

56. Feminist positions range from the acceptance of traditional construals of the Bible's authority of evangelical feminists, to the outright rejection of the Judeo-Christian tradition and its Scriptures of Post-Christian feminists. See Trible, "Treasures"; Sakenfeld, "Feminist Perspectives on Bible and Theology"; Scholer, "Feminist Hermeneutics"; Thiselton, *New Horizons in Hermeneutics*, 430–39. Pierce et al., eds., *Discovering Biblical Equality* present a good selection of evangelical feminist scholarship. Trible, *God and the Rhetoric of Sexuality* positively interprets a number of OT texts, including Genesis 2–3, for which see my discussion in chapter 1 of this volume. For a taxonomy of feminist approaches, see Robin Parry's discussion in chapter 2 of this volume.

57. See the works cited above in fn. 3, along with the pioneering study of Galambush, *Jerusalem in the Book of Ezekiel*.

58. For these claims, see, Jameson, *The Political Unconscious*, 17–20, 74–102; Jameson, "The Symbolic Inference"; Thompson, *Studies in the Theory of Ideology*; and in relation to biblical studies, Kennedy, "Peasants in Revolt."

Large scale interpretive and epistemological ideas are implicit in this perspective, analysis of which would take us too far afield.[59] Ideological readings are, however, subject to serious question. For instance, Walhout has presented cogent arguments for the weakness of such a hermeneutic and the political presuppositions which nurture it.[60] Similarly, while all texts may encode an agenda, it is not clear that all such agenda are *political* in nature.[61] They may well be religious, artistic, philosophical, scientific, ethical, and so on; but to claim that such concerns are essentially and necessarily either intrinsically or instrumentally political in nature is either question begging or reductionist. Such agenda may well serve to foster the interests of a particular group, but this must be demonstrated rather than assumed, and it must be shown that this political agenda is either the real agenda which the other serves to mask, or a necessary correlative of it which exhaustively explains its origin and function.[62] This has not been done in relation to the Bible or the book of Ezekiel in particular.

As (evangelical) Christians, furthermore, we are entitled to reject their theories just because they conflict with our understanding of Biblical authority. Now, this needs to be understood carefully. We are not entitled to casually disregard or reject any theory that we take to be inconsistent with our view of Scripture: for that view could be wrong, and there have been many instances where Christian views of Scripture have needed to change in light of other evidence.[63] However, our beliefs that God speaks through Scripture and the human author's communicative actions, that the God who speaks is a good God, and so on, function legitimately as central assumptions in our scholarship and our living.[64] As such, beliefs that conflict with them may be rejected on the grounds of that conflict, unless the nature and cogency of those beliefs require

---

59. I have outlined such an analysis of an ideological reading of Genesis 2–3 in Sloane, "Wolterstorff, Theorising and Genesis 1–3," ch. 9, and (more briefly) in chapter 1 of this volume. See also the critique of ideological criticism and the hermeneutics of suspicion in Thiselton, *New Horizons in Hermeneutics*, esp. 410–70; Vanhoozer, *Is There a Meaning in This Text?*, esp. 148–95, 367–452.

60. Walhout, "Marxist and Christian Hermeneutics."

61. See Sternberg, *Poetics of Biblical Narrative*, 35–37, 41, 44–45.

62. Similar points are made in Riggs, *Whys and Ways of Science*, 136–70 regarding reductionist (ideological readings of the) sociology of science.

63. See Sloane, *On Being a Christian in the Academy*, 240–44.

64. See Wolterstorff, *Divine Discourse*.

that we adjust those prior beliefs. Furthermore, if we have good reason to question those challenges to our central assumptions, then we are entitled, even obliged, to maintain those assumptions and reject what conflicts with them.[65] That is the case in regard to Brenner and van Dijk-Hemmes' pornoprophetic reading of the prophets.[66] It also means that we are entitled to adopt an alternative hermeneutical perspective, one, not of suspicion towards texts and their ideologies, but of critical trust which examines the texts, for all their multivalence, for what God said and is saying by way of the text.

This brings us to the question: given its potential to shock and offend (female) readers, why do the prophets use the metaphor of an adulterous wife at all? On the basis of their ideological reading of the Bible, Brenner and van Dijk-Hemmes believe that a key reason is the inherently misogynistic nature of Israelite society. This is unfounded, for a number of reasons. First, the metaphor finds its ultimate origin in the nature of the covenant and its call to exclusive allegiance.[67] Israel is claimed by God as God's own "possession"; as such, God has exclusive rights over "her" and her loyalty.[68] It is Yahweh who takes initiative in the relationship, has the resources and power to "claim" Israel, and provides for "her" in her life and flourishing.[69] In light of this, as well as the relative roles of men and women in Israelite social and economic systems and the predominantly masculine language used for God, it is to be expected that Yahweh should be depicted as the *husband* in the marriage relationship.[70] This is reinforced by the nature of covenant, which is probably best understood as a way of extending the kinship system to include those who are not biologically part of the family structure.

---

65. For a detailed articulation and defense of these claims, see Wolterstorff, *Reason within the Bounds of Religion*; Sloane, *On Being a Christian in the Academy*.

66. For a similar argument from a Roman Catholic perspective, see Patton, "Should Our Sister Be Treated Like a Whore?"

67. Hall, "Origin of the Marriage Metaphor"; Greenberg, "Ezekiel 16."

68. I use "scare quotes" advisedly, as, while the language of possession is frequently used with reference to both God and Israel and husbands and wives, the primary issues relate, not to ownership and control, but to commitment and exclusivity. For refutation of the idea that men had 'property rights' in respect of their wives, see Wright, *God's People in God's Land*, 183–221.

69. For the clear elements of grace in Yahweh's choice of Israel, see Coleson, "Israel's Life Cycle from Birth to Resurrection"; Swanepoel, "Ezekiel 16."

70. See also Renz, *Rhetorical Function of Ezekiel*, 77.

In entering into "covenant" with Israel, Yahweh is "extending Yahweh's kinship network," with the associated rights and obligations, to cover a nation which has no natural calls on Yahweh's protection.[71] Once again, given the theological and social worlds in which this notion operated, it makes best sense for Yahweh to be presented as the *husband* and for the people's failure to be described as זָנָה (*zānâ* [sexually] unfaithful). This is reinforced by the tradition, current in both ANE and Old Testament literature, of the city as the (chief) deity's consort.[72] The metaphor is driven, then, not by misogynistic views of women's sexuality, but by a theological understanding of the nature of Jerusalem and of the relationship between God's people and their covenant lord.[73]

So too, Brenner and van Dijk-Hemmes' claims regarding the misogynistic nature of ancient Israelite society are implausible. Brenner's linguistic arguments are unsound, in the first instance because, as is now well known, etymology is generally an unreliable guide to meaning. Meaning is determined by linguistic usage which, in this instance, demonstrates that נְקֵבָה (*nĕqēbâ*, female) is simply used to specify a female creature or image, in the same way that זָכָר (*zākār*, male) specifies a male one.[74] However, even if etymology were a guide, as is occasionally the case with rare forms, the etymological data would undermine her case.[75]

---

71. For this, see Hahn, "Covenant."

72. Block, *Ezekiel 1–24*, 468–69; Carroll, "Desire under the Terebinths," 299; Galambush, *Jerusalem in the Book of Ezekiel*, 23–35.

73. See Ortlund, *Whoredom*. This perspective is also adopted, despite his distaste for Ezekiel, by Carroll, "Desire under the Terebinths," 283, 88–89, 99. He is more accepting, however, of Brenner and van Dijk-Hemmes' reading of the metaphor in later work. See Carroll, "Whorusalamin," esp. 76–77.

74. See the discussion of etymological fallacies in Barr, *The Semantics of Biblical Language*; Carson, *Exegetical Fallacies*, 27–64; Osborne, *The Hermeneutical Spiral*, 82–112. The majority of the 22 uses of נְקֵבָה (*nĕqēbâ*, female) are found in the Pentateuch where it is paired with זָכָר (*zākhār*, male), the one clear exception being Jer. 31:22. This, and other searches, were conducted using Gramcord (Bible Companion 1.6.4; GRAMCORD Morphological Search Engine 2.4cx; Loizeaux Brothers and The GRAMCORD Institute, © 1988–1998 and 1979, 1999).

75. Of the eighteen uses of the verb root נקב (*n-q-b*) in both Niphal and Qal, seven mean "pierce" or "make a hole"; the rest mean "designate" or "name," including five in Qal. The noun occurs rarely, and is of uncertain meaning, perhaps "socket" (Ezek 28:13, the NRSV translates it "settings"). Cf. Holladay, *Lexicon of the Old Testament*, 244, who identifies two uses of the noun, the other being Josh 19:33, where, however, it is most likely a place name. Would this derivation then mean that women are those "designated," rather than orifices?

Her cultural analysis of Israelite sexual ideology is similarly flawed: recent social scientific work on women in Israel suggests that the picture is much more variegated than Brenner and van Dijk-Hemmes claim, and that women's bodies played a positive as well as a negative role in the symbolic world of the OT.[76] Given the importance of this linguistic and cultural context for her understanding of individual texts, these flaws significantly undermine her argument.

Finally, Brenner's claim that pornography, understood as any sexual representation of the (female) form, is inherently patriarchal and misogynistic, is open to question. Apart from the theoretical weaknesses of her arguments,[77] the very existence of both male and female homosexual pornography demonstrates that it cannot be understood just as an expression of *male* domination of *females*.[78] Now, let me make it clear: I abhor pornography in all its forms. It demeans and objectifies men and women and belittles the gift of human sexuality. Equally, most pornography is produced by men for men and expresses and perpetuates a view of women which sees them as *objects* of male sexual desire and control. Unfortunately, objectifying depictions of female sexuality are not restricted to "pornography" but are prevalent in many cultural depictions and descriptions of women and their bodies, to the detriment of both women—especially young and adolescent women—and men.[79] In that respect feminist critique of pornography is on the mark. Where Brenner and van Dijk-Hemmes go wrong, however, is in their refusal to allow the intent of the (biblical) author any role in determining whether it counts as pornography or not, that being determined purely by its (possible)

---

76. See Keefe, "Stepping In / Stepping Out." Now I must acknowledge that Keefe sees these more positive images as belonging to the pre-monarchic period; later depictions of women and their bodies she sees as much more negative and even misogynistic, of which Ezekiel is a clear instance. I am not convinced of the validity of some of her assumptions and methods and, as I shall argue below, a cavalier ascription of misogyny to Ezekiel such as hers is flawed; nonetheless, her more general point about the range of representations of gender in Israel and OT texts stands.

77. See Carroll, "Desire under the Terebinths," esp. 280–81, 87; Carroll, "Whorusalamin," 78–80. It is worth noting that Carroll is sharply critical of the book of Ezekiel and its "appalling representations of YHWH," for which see, Carroll, "Whorusalamin," 77–78; Carroll, "Desire under the Terebinths," 284, 92, 300.

78. See Wikipedia; <http://en.wikipedia.org/wiki/Lesbian_pornography>; <http://en.wikipedia.org/wiki/Gay_pornography> [accessed Friday, 7 April 2006].

79. See Van Leeuwen, ed. *After Eden*, especially Part III. As the father of three adolescent women, these are messages I seek to expose and resist and counter.

effects.[80] This means any representation of the naked human form in art or literature is pornographic if it prompts sexual arousal (or can be envisaged as doing so). Given human predilections, this means that life drawing and surface anatomy texts can be lumped together with *Playboy* in the one amorphous conceptual category "pornography." That is not only an analytical confusion; it renders the notion of pornography void for vagueness. The purpose of a work must be a factor in determining whether it counts as a pornographic depiction of the female form. But as Brenner acknowledges, such was not Ezekiel's intent, which seriously undermines their counting Ezekiel 16 and 23 as *pornographic* texts with, in turn, significant implications for their general argument.[81]

Their Arguments and Evidence

Let us now turn to their arguments and evidence, beginning with van Dijk-Hemmes' claim that Ezek 23:3 is reminiscent of child sexual abuse. While it is understandable that this reference to childhood sexual activity raises the specter of child abuse, such a reading would be foreign to both Ezekiel and his audience. One reason we find child sexual abuse so horrendous is the clear power differential between perpetrator and "victim," and the inability of the child to make an informed and morally responsible decision about his or her sexuality. Whatever power differential existed between Israel and Egypt, however, has no bearing on this aspect of the metaphor, and Israel is presented as morally responsible from the beginning of her existence. We need to remember that metaphors are complex uses of language that do not map precisely onto their referents: central to their function *as metaphors* is the "is and is not" nature of the language; and a key to their interpretation is figuring out *how* the metaphor does and does not refer, as well as how it shapes a view of reality.[82] The notion that Israel's infancy was one of abused moral "innocence" or immaturity requires the illegitimate "mapping" of the metaphor onto Israel's history contrary to Ezekiel's intention and his audience's expecta-

---

80. This is consistent with their broader interpretive strategy, which can be characterized as a reader-oriented reading "against the grain" of texts (including cultural artefacts) that say see as inimical to women and their interests. As noted above, such readings necessarily diminish or discount the role of authorial intent.

81. I shall discuss the purpose of the graphic language of Ezekiel 16 and 23 below.

82. McFague, *Metaphorical Theology*; Stiver, *Philosophy of Religious Language*, 112–33.

tions. Ezekiel's concern is not, at this stage, with Israel's being burdened by slavery in Egypt, but with her history being shot through with infidelity from start to finish. This repeated motif in the book of Ezekiel would be familiar to his original audience and the book's original readers, as would Ezekiel's use of deliberately shocking language.[83] Furthermore, the prophet's description of Israel as sinful from the beginning is true to the account as we find it in Exodus, including flagrant idolatry (Exod 32; Num 25) and a desire to depend on Egypt's strength rather than Yahweh (Num 11).[84] Ezekiel is claiming that the nation Yahweh rescued from Egypt was a *sinful* nation, exemplifying from her origins the sins of which she is now guilty. The metaphor speaks, not of innocence abused but of sinfulness expressed. Child sexual abuse, then, does not pertain.

What clearly does pertain, however, is the claim that the language of Ezekiel's metaphor is crude and offensive. This is something that most translations sanitize—understandably so given the difficulty of rendering Ezekiel's language in a way that would be acceptable in a church context. He speaks, for instance, of Jerusalem as having "spread her legs" [וַתְּפַשְּׂקִי אֶת־רַגְלַיִךְ *watĕpaśĕqî 'et-raglayik*] (or, perhaps, "opening her vagina," depending on the force of רֶגֶל [*regel*, foot, leg] in this instance) to every passer-by (16:25).[85] He also talks of her "juices being poured out" [הִשָּׁפֵךְ נְחֻשְׁתֵּךְ *hiššāpēk nĕḥuštēk*],[86] a graphic portrayal of sexual arousal (16:36).[87] It is not surprising that, given their experience of patriarchy in society and the church, many women find this offensive, even pornographic, hearing echoes of male sexual abuse and exploitation of women. However, contrary to the pornoprophetic critique, this shock-

---

83. See his "call" and the description of Israel as a "rebellious house" (Ezek 2:9, etc.) and his characteristic use of "negative salvation history" in which stories that were traditionally used to speak of Yahweh's grace towards needy Israel are used to portray Israel's irremediable sinfulness (Ezek 20). For this, and the distinction between audience and readers, see Renz, *Rhetorical Function of Ezekiel*, esp. 41, 55, 72–93.

84. Coleson, "Israel's Life Cycle from Birth to Resurrection," 242.

85. The Hebrew word רֶגֶל (*regel*) meaning "foot" or "leg" can be used as a circumlocution for "genitals" (Holladay, *Lexicon of the Old Testament*, 332).

86. The word translated here "juices" [נְחֻשָׁה *nehôšâ*] is a *hapax legomonon*. I am following the translation of Greenberg, *Ezekiel 1–20*, 271, 85–86, as does Block, *Ezekiel 1–24*, in his comments on the verse (page 500), although he "euphemistically" translates it as "passion" (page 498).

87. The NRSV and NIV margin render this rather delicately as "your lust was poured out." Block, *Ezekiel 1–24*, 500, (overly) tactfully calls this "almost pornographic" language.

ing imagery is not designed to titillate a male audience with a voyeuristic display of female nudity and sexual activity.[88] Rather, the audience in Ezekiel 16 is consistently addressed directly;[89] Ezekiel 16 aims to shock, not titillate. Patton states, with reference to (other) pornoprophetic interpretations: "Although these readings help to reveal why this text is so easily misread, they conceal the awareness of and horror at sexual violence in the original text."[90] She goes on to say that "the metaphor of the punishment, the sexual violence that Shields and Weems find so offensive, also works only in a culture in which men are also horrified by the image. This is not a text that portrays sexual violence against women as a good thing. The metaphor would not work if the male audience were not shocked."[91] This does, of course, create problems for interpreters and especially translators—how can they render deliberately shocking and offensive language in a non-offensive manner?

For the audience to hear itself being described as "spreading their legs" and "pouring out their juices" on all manner of passers-by would have the same dramatic and shocking impact as Amos' turn to Israel in chapter 2, or Nathan's confronting "you are the man" in 2 Samuel 12.[92] Renz argues that the rhetoric of the metaphor confronts its exilic readers with Jerusalem's abhorrent behavior, inviting them to distance themselves from sinful Jerusalem and agree with Yahweh's judgment on the city, and so themselves.[93] With reference to the original audience, Patton argues: "The metaphor works as part of Ezekiel's theology because the audience is forced to recognize their own responsibility, in the author's view, for this defeat, for these rapes and mutilations. In part, the author tells the male audience that [because of their sin] they are the agents of the rapes of their own wives, sisters, mothers. If that is not shocking, then the prophetic message fails."[94] Perhaps we need to reconsider our

---

88. Smith-Christopher, "Ezekiel in Abu Ghraib," esp. 146.

89. With the exception of verse 45 Ezekiel 16 consistently uses 2fs forms in referring to the woman.

90. Patton, "Should Our Sister Be Treated Like a Whore?," 228.

91. Ibid., 233.

92. Cf. Bird, "To Play the Harlot," who makes a similar point in relation to the use of זָנָה (zānâ, [sexually] unfaithful) for the people's sin.

93. Renz, *Rhetorical Function of Ezekiel*, 77–78; cf. 88–89, 92–93, 144–45, once again drawing on the rhetorical distinction between audience and readers which is central to his argument.

94. Patton, "Should Our Sister Be Treated Like a Whore?" 233.

implicit belief that the Bible is a "nice" and "comfortable" book, fit at all times for polite society. Sometimes it is not; when it deals with shocking and offensive realities, the text may embody that offence. We ought not to sanitize it or render it innocuous, but rather to ensure that its offence is rightly directed—here, not against women and their sexuality, but the people of God and their (our) flagrant infidelity to their (our) covenant partner.[95]

Similar observations apply to the violence that the texts also embody. Here, again, we need to look squarely at the texts, see their stark, brutal violence and its association with female nakedness (Ezek. 16:37-42 and 23:22-28, 45, 46-47). This nakedness and violence, however, is neither pornographic voyeurism nor a means of expressing male domination;[96] rather it reflects the very real horror of exile as both experienced and anticipated by Ezekiel.[97] As Daniel Smith-Christopher notes, "The 'humiliation' of 'Jerusalem' as female must be directly connected to the ideology of, and practice of, Assyrian and Babylonian warfare . . . that suggested the imagery of stripping, and not a generally practiced punishment of adulterous women in Israel."[98] Similarly, Peggy Day argues that the stripping and execution of the "whore" of Ezekiel 16 (and similar texts) does not represent the normal treatment of an adulteress, but refers to the punishment of covenant violation; failure to recognize this results from a misunderstanding of both the biblical and ANE evidence and the working of the metaphors and their rhetorical intent.[99] Thus the violence of the texts reflects not standard patterns of behavior in Israel, but the violent realities of war and exile, and is meant

---

95. Contra Tiemeyer, "To Read—Or Not to Read—Ezekiel as Christian Scripture."

96. As claimed by Brenner, van Dijk-Hemmes and others. See, for instance, Brenner, "Pornoprophetics Revisited," 253, 66, 72; Van Dijk-Hemmes, "Metaphorization," 173, 75; cf. Exum, "The Ethics of Biblical Violence against Women," 248-49, 55-56; Gordon and Washington, "Rape as a Military Metaphor in the Hebrew Bible," 325; Magdalene, "Ancient Near Eastern Treaty-Curses," 334-40, 47.

97. Smith-Christopher, "Ezekiel in Abu Ghraib," 141-57.

98. Ibid., 153.

99. Day, "Adulterous Jerusalem's Imagined Demise"; Day, "The Bitch Had It Coming to Her"; Day, "Metaphor and Social Reality." She specifically refutes the dominant tradition of interpretation which sees the woman as receiving the normal punishment meted out to an adulteress in Israel, as reflected in Swanepoel, "Ezekiel 16," 98; Zimmerli, *Ezekiel 1*, 346; Klein, *Ezekiel*, 85; Cooper, *Ezekiel*, 174; Block, *Ezekiel 1-24*, 502-3; and even Renz, *Rhetorical Function of Ezekiel*, 146, 93, 96-97, although he believes there is a mix of the literal and metaphorical in the description of Jerusalem's destruction.

to generate a horror in the readers corresponding to the horror of exile.[100] Hence pornoprophetic interpretations misread the metaphor in seeing it as *justifying* this as appropriate (sexual) violence in Israel's social world, rather than reflecting the historical realities of judgment on Israel's sinful violation of that world.

This raises the question of to what the metaphor refers. It seems to me that Brenner and van Dijk-Hemmes implicitly or explicitly see Israelite sexual ideology as a key referent of the text.[101] The text refers to this patriarchal ideology either indirectly, by way of its influence on the metaphors and their workings, or directly, by way of its calling for women to submit to men in the same way that the city is meant to submit to her "male" overlord, Yahweh. The validity of that claim, in turn, depends on whether the text does, in fact, directly address women and their sexuality, and in a manner different to the way it addressed men. So, finally, let me address the claim that the metaphors (say in Ezek 23:10 and 48) do directly address women and their sexuality, and allow an "escape" for men that is not available to women. Corrine Patton identifies three key flaws in the case, the last of which is our focus: the "assumption that the female object is controlled," the failure to address the historical context of the language and metaphor, and the idea that verses 10 and 48 show that "this text is also being used to substantiate treatment of real women".[102] She argues that verses 10 and 48 do not address real women in Israelite society but the metaphorical woman—the (predominantly male) audience—confronting them with their own sin. This, far from allowing them to displace their shame onto women and so escape the indictment of the text, is a particularly confronting and humiliating way of presenting to the men in the audience their responsibility for the violence the city endured.[103] Furthermore, we need to recognize the

---

100. Smith-Christopher, "Ezekiel in Abu Ghraib," 155.

101. *Pace* Carroll, "Whorusalamin," 70, who argues that 'postmodern' readings such as theirs focus on the *signifier* not the *signified*. Rather, their concern is with both, but they focus on the signified as a sexual ideology rather than those historical phenomena that are the main concern of "modernist" historical-critical scholarship.

102. Patton, "Should Our Sister Be Treated Like a Whore?" 228.

103. Ibid., 231–32; see also Renz, *Rhetorical Function of Ezekiel*, 89. This issue of shame, whilst raised by Brenner and van Dijk-Hemmes, is a major focus of Galambush's analysis of Jerusalem in the book of Ezekiel, which informs their work. She argues that Yahweh's honor is impugned by the "infidelity" of the city, which, in turn, threatens all men with shame. The pornographic depiction of the violent treatment of the city

significance of Ezekiel's context. His ministry, coming as it does after the first deportation, follows a long history of recalcitrance and resistance to the prophets. Indeed, these metaphors are placed after his visionary encounter with the flagrant sins of Jerusalem in, say, Ezekiel 8. In light of that context perhaps Ezekiel needed to shock his audience in an attempt to awaken them to their plight.[104]

Thus we have seen that the main lines of argument used to support pornoprophetic readings of Ezekiel 16 and 23 fail. This, coupled with crucial problems with methodology and assumptions underlying the claims, undermines the force of their case. We have also seen that the texts are deliberately shocking in their portrayal of Jerusalem's sin, an uncomfortable reality that we must address. One way we must do so is to seek to ensure that their offence is rightly directed. While an ideological reading of these texts is unfounded, it should alert us to the possibility of our ideological distortion of these texts. Ezekiel 16 and 23 could, I suppose, be *used* to victimize and stigmatize women, although I have found no evidence of this.[105] We need to be careful, not just to avoid such misogynistic abuse of the texts, but also to ensure that our audience does not misunderstand them as being misogynist. This may be a difficult task, especially given the deliberately shocking nature of the material, but is necessary if these powerful texts are to confront the people of God today.[106]

---

serves to re-establish his control and shore up the threatened patriarchal order. See Galambush, *Jerusalem in the Book of Ezekiel*, esp. 23–35, 83–88, 102–5, 109, 117, 120, 124–25, 156–57, 159–63. Patton's rejection of this understanding of shame and its relation to the metaphor is reinforced by Odell, "The Inversion of Shame and Forgiveness in Ezekiel 16.59–63"; Keefe, "Stepping In / Stepping Out"; Stiebert, "Shame and Prophecy"; Lapsley, "Shame and Self-Knowledge."

104. Wright, *The Message of Ezekiel*, 127–29. Alternatively, reading it from the point of view of an exilic readership, the shock and outrage that the texts evoke calls them to judge their own behavior and accept Yahweh's judgment as just (Renz, *Rhetorical Function of Ezekiel*, 77–78, 144–45), *pace* Tiemeyer, "To Read—Or Not to Read— Ezekiel as Christian Scripture."

105. The claim, reiterated by Brenner and van Dijk-Hemmes, that these texts and the religious ideology they express foster (sexual) violence against women is akin to the unsubstantiated claim that (conservative) religion is to blame for the violence and wholesale slaughter of the last century, a claim clearly refuted in Guinness, *Unspeakable*, 34–46. This is not to say that biblical texts have not been illegitimately used to foster patriarchal interests. Clearly they have; but I have found no evidence that *these texts* have been so used.

106. We do need to recognize, however, that some people may find the sexually

CONCLUSIONS

The nature of the pornoprophetic criticism of Ezekiel—the claim that Ezekiel 16 and 23 are examples of "aberrant textuality" promulgating violent, misogynistic views that must be resisted and rejected—is clear. It is also clear that, while Brenner and van Dijk-Hemmes' arguments may work within a particular interpretive framework, they are only justified from within that perspective. Given, then, that their methods and assumptions are open to serious criticism, there is no good reason to accept their pornographic reading of texts such as Ezekiel 16 and 23. Indeed, given the implausibility of Brenner and van Dijk-Hemmes' key claims when assessed independently of their flawed methods and assumptions, we have good reason to reject their pornoprophetic reading of the metaphors. The texts do not articulate and perpetuate misogynistic sexual politics; they certainly give no comfort to contemporary abuse of women or domestic violence. They are violent and offensive texts, but that violence is not directed against women, but serves to highlight the offensiveness of sin and the reality of judgment. Texts such as these were used by God to confront God's erring people with the horror of their sin and its consequences. Read in that light, avoiding the errors of either wrongly directing the texts' indictment to women and their sexuality, or seeking to soften and sanitize deliberately appalling texts, we too are confronted with the horror of sin and its consequences. These texts, far from vitiating the value of the prophets for Christian theology and ethics, demonstrate that value with their uncomfortable and confronting rhetoric. I am not sure that my analysis will convince any proponents of "porno-prophetics." I hope that it allows us, if not to *like* the texts, at least to understand them and what they are about. And that, perhaps, is the best that any of us can hope for.

---

explicit and violent nature of the texts deeply problematic—so much so that hearing them expounded from the pulpit may be counterproductive. So, just as we may be willing to affirm the importance of addressing God as 'Father' but allow that this might not be helpful for all people in all circumstances, so we might wish to 'warn' people of the nature of the texts they are about to hear expounded, should we preach a text like this. I did something along those lines when preaching Ezekiel 16 as part of series on the book of Ezekiel in our local church, warning the congregation both in advance and at the time that this would be an "adults only" text and sermon and, that, having read the text, should they feel it might be overly difficult for them to hear a sermon on it, they should absent themselves from the sermon.

BIBLIOGRAPHY

Bal, Mieke. "Foreword." In *On Gendering Texts: Female and Male Voices in the Hebrew Bible*, edited by Athalya Brenner and Fokkelien van Dijk-Hemmes, ix–xiii. Leiden: Brill, 1993.

Barr, James. *The Semantics of Biblical Language*. Oxford: Oxford University Press, 1961.

Bird, Phyllis A. "Poor Man or Poor Woman? Gendering the Poor in Prophetic Texts." In *On Reading Prophetic Texts*, edited by R. Becking and M. Dijkstra, 37–49. Leiden: Brill, 1996.

———. "'To Play the Harlot': An Inquiry into an Old Testament Metaphor." In *Missing Persons and Mistaken Identities: Women and Gender in Ancient Israel*, 219–36. Minneapolis: Fortress, 1997.

Block, Daniel I. *The Book of Ezekiel: Chapters 1-24*. Grand Rapids: Eerdmans, 1997.

Brenner, Athalya. *The Intercourse of Knowledge: On Gendering Desire and "Sexuality" in the Hebrew Bible*. Leiden: Brill, 1997.

———. "Introduction." In *On Gendering Texts: Female and Male Voices in the Hebrew Bible*, edited by Athalya Brenner and Fokkelien van Dijk-Hemmes, 1–13. Leiden: Brill, 1993.

———. "On 'Jeremiah' and the Poetics of (Prophetic?) Pornography." In *On Gendering Texts: Female and Male Voices in the Hebrew Bible*, edited by Athalya Brenner and Fokkelien van Dijk-Hemmes, 177–93. Leiden: Brill, 1993.

———. "On Prophetic Propaganda and the Politics of 'Love': The Case of Jeremiah." In *A Feminist Companion to the Latter Prophets*, edited by Athalya Brenner, 256–74. Sheffield: Sheffield Academic, 1995.

———. "Pornoprophetics Revisited: Some Additional Reflections." In *The Prophets: A Sheffield Reader*, edited by P. R. Davies, 252–75. Sheffield: Sheffield Academic, 1996.

Brenner, Athalya, and Fokkelien van Dijk-Hemmes. "Afterword." In *On Gendering Texts: Female and Male Voices in the Hebrew Bible*, edited by Athalya Brenner and Fokkelien van Dijk-Hemmes, 194–95. Leiden: Brill, 1993.

Carroll, Robert. "Desire under the Terebinths: On Pornographic Representation in the Prophets—A Response." In *A Feminist Companion to the Latter Prophets*, edited by Athalya Brenner. Sheffield: Sheffield Academic, 1995.

———. "Whorusalamin: A Tale of Three Cities as Three Sisters." In *On Reading Prophetic Texts*, edited by Bob Becking and M. Dijkstra, 67–82. Leiden: Brill, 1996.

Carson, D. A. *Exegetical Fallacies*. 2nd ed. Carlisle: Paternoster, 1996.

Coleson, Joseph E. "Israel's Life Cycle from Birth to Resurrection." In *Israel's Apostasy and Restoration: Essays in Honour of Roland K. Harrison*, edited by A. Gileadi, 237–50. Grand Rapids: Eerdmans, 1988.

Cooper, Lamar. *Ezekiel*. Nashville: Broadman & Holman, 1994.

Darr, Katherine Pfisterer. "Ezekiel's Justification of God: Teaching Troubling Texts." *Journal for the Study of the Old Testament* 55, (1992) 97–117.

Day, Peggy L. "Adulterous Jerusalem's Imagined Demise: Death of a Metaphor in Ezekiel XVI." *Vetus Testamentum* 50, (2000) 285–309.

———. "The Bitch Had It Coming to Her: Rhetoric and Interpretation in Ezekiel 16." *Biblical Interpretation* 8.8 (2000) 231–54.

———. "Metaphor and Social Reality: Isaiah 23.17-18, Ezekiel 16.35-37 and Hosea 2.4-5." In *Inspired Speech: Prophecy in the Ancient Near East*, edited by J. Kaltner and L. Stulman, 63–71. London: T. & T. Clark, 2004.

Dempsey, Carol J. "The 'Whore' of Ezekiel 16: The Impact and Ramifications of Gender-Specific Metaphors in Light of Biblical Law and Divine Judgment." In *Gender and Law in the Hebrew Bible and the Ancient Near East*, edited by Victor H. Matthews, et al., 57–78. Sheffield: Sheffield Academic, 1998.

Exum, J. Cheryl. "The Ethics of Biblical Violence Against Women." In *The Bible in Ethics*, edited by John W. Rogerson, et al., 248–71. Sheffield: Sheffield Academic, 1995.

Galambush, Julie. *Jerusalem in the Book of Ezekiel: The City as Yahweh's Wife*. Atlanta: Scholars, 1992.

Gordon, Pamela, and Harold C. Washington. "Rape as a Military Metaphor in the Hebrew Bible." In *A Feminist Companion to the Latter Prophets*, edited by Athalya Brenner, 308–25. Sheffield: Sheffield Academic, 1995.

Greenberg, Moshe. *Ezekiel 1–20*. Anchor Bible. New York: Doubleday, 1983.

———. "Ezekiel 16: A Panorama of Passions." In *Love and Death in the Ancient Near East: Essays in Honour of Marvin H. Pope*, edited by J. H. Marks and R. M. Good, 143–50. Guildford, CT: Four Quarters, 1997.

Guest, Deryn. "Hiding behind the Naked Woman: A Recriminative Response." *Biblical Interpretation* 7 (1999) 413–48.

Guinness, Os. *Unspeakable: Facing Up to Evil in an Age of Genocide and Terror*. New York: HarperCollins, 2005.

Hahn, Scott. "Covenant in the Old and New Testaments: Some Current Research (1994–2004)." *Currents in Biblical Research* 3 (2005) 263–92.

Hall, Gary. "Origin of the Marriage Metaphor." *Hebrew Studies* XXII (1982) 169–71.

Holladay, William. *A Concise Hebrew and Aramaic Lexicon of the Old Testament*. Grand Rapids: Eerdmans, 1971.

Jameson, Frederic. *The Political Unconscious: Narrative as Socially Symbolic Act*. Ithaca, NY: Cornell University Press, 1981.

———. "The Symbolic Inference; or, Kenneth Burke and Ideological Analysis." In *The Ideologies of Theory: Essays 1971–1986, Vol 1; Situations of Theory*, 137–52. London: Routledge, 1988.

Keefe, Alice A. "Stepping In / Stepping Out: A Conversation between Ideological and Social Scientific Feminist Approaches to the Bible." *Journal of Religion & Society* 1 (1999) 1–14.

Kennedy, James M. "Peasants in Revolt: Political Allegory in Genesis 2–3." *JSOT* 47 (1990) 3–14.

Klein, Ralph. *Ezekiel: The Prophet and His Message*. Colombia: University of South Carolina Press, 1988.

Lapsley, Jacqueline E. "Shame and Self-Knowledge: The Positive Role of Shame in Ezekiel's View of the Moral Self." In *The Book of Ezekiel: Theological and Anthropological Perspectives*, edited by M. S. Odell and J. T. Strong, 143–73. Atlanta: SBL, 2000.

Magdalene, F. Rachel. "Ancient Near Eastern Treaty—Curses and the Ultimate Texts of Terror: A Study of Divine Sexual Abuse in the Prophetic Literature." In *A Feminist Companion to the Latter Prophets*, edited by Athalya Brenner, 326–52. Sheffield: Sheffield Academic, 1995.

McFague, Sallie. *Metaphorical Theology: Models of God in Religious Language*. London: SCM, 1983.

Odell, Margaret S. "The Inversion of Shame and Forgiveness in Ezekiel 16.59–63." *Journal for the Study of the Old Testament* 56 (1992) 101–12.

Ortlund, Raymond C. *Whoredom: God's Unfaithful Wife in Biblical Theology*. Leicester, UK: Apollos, 1996.
Osborne, Grant. *The Hermeneutical Spiral: A Comprehensive Introduction to Biblical Interpretation*. 2nd ed. Downers Grove, IL: InterVarsity, 2006.
Patton, Corrine L. "'Should Our Sister Be Treated Like a Whore?': A Response to Feminist Critiques of Ezekiel 23." In *The Book of Ezekiel: Theological and Anthropological Perspectives*, edited by M. S. Odell and J. T. Strong, 221–38. Atlanta: SBL, 2000.
Pierce, Ronald W., et al., eds. *Discovering Biblical Equality: Complementarity without Hierarchy*. 2nd ed. Downers Grove, IL: InterVarsity, 2005.
Pope, Marvin H. "Mixed Marriage Metaphor in Ezekiel 16." In *Fortunate the Eyes that See*, edited by Astrid B. Beck, et al., 384–99. Grand Rapids: Eerdmans, 1995.
Renz, Thomas. *The Rhetorical Function of the Book of Ezekiel*. Boston: Brill, 2002.
Riggs, P. J. *Whys and Ways of Science*. Carlton: Melbourne University Press, 1992.
Sakenfeld, Katherine Doob. "Feminist Perspectives on Bible and Theology: An Introduction to Selected Issues and Literature." *Interpretation* 42.1 (1988) 5–18.
Scholer, David M. "Feminist Hermeneutics and Evangelical Biblical Interpretation." *Journal of the Evangelical Theological Society* 30.4 (1987) 407–20.
Setel, T. Drorah. "Prophets and Pornography: Female Sexual Imagery in Hosea." In *Feminist Interpretation of the Bible*, edited by Letty M. Russell, 86–95. Philadelphia: Westminster, 1985.
Shields, Mary. "Gender and Violence in Ezekiel 23." In *SBL Seminar Papers no. 37, part 1*, 86–105. Atlanta: Scholars, 1998.
———. "Multiple Exposures: Body Rhetoric and Gender Characterization in Ezekiel 16." *Journal of Feminist Studies in Religion* 14.1 (2004) 5–18.
Sloane, Andrew. *On Being a Christian in the Academy: Nicholas Wolterstorff and the Practice of Christian Scholarship*. Carlisle, UK: Paternoster, 2003.
———. "Wolterstorff, Exegetical Theorising, and Interpersonal Relationships in Genesis 1–3." ThD diss., Australian College of Theology, 1994.
Smith-Christopher, Daniel. "Ezekiel in Abu Ghraib: Rereading Ezekiel 16:37–39 in the Context of Imperial Conquest." In *Ezekiel's Hierarchical World: Wrestling with Tiered Reality*, edited by S. L. Cook and C. L. Patton, 141–57. Atlanta: SBL, 2004.
Sternberg, Meir. *The Poetics of Biblical Narrative: Ideological Literature and the Drama of Reading*. Bloomington, IN: Indiana University Press, 1985.
Stiebert, Johanna. "Shame and Prophecy: Approaches Past and Present." *Biblical Interpretation* 8.3 (2000) 255–75.
Stiver, Dan. *The Philosophy of Religious Language: Sign, Symbol and Story*. Cambridge: Blackwell, 1996.
Swanepoel, M. G. "Ezekiel 16: Abandoned Child, Bride Adorned or Unfaithful Wife?" In *Among the Prophets: Language, Image and Structure in the Prophetic Writings*, edited by P. R. Davies and David J. A. Clines, 84–104. Sheffield, UK: JSOT, 1993.
Thiselton, Anthony C. *New Horizons in Hermeneutics*. Grand Rapids: Zondervan, 1992.
Thompson, J. B. *Studies in the Theory of Ideology*. Cambridge: Polity, 1984.
Tiemeyer, Lena-Sofia. "To Read—Or Not to Read—Ezekiel as Christian Scripture." *Expository Times* 121 (2010) 481–88.
Trible, Phyllis. *God and the Rhetoric of Sexuality*. Philadelphia: Fortress, 1978.
———. "Treasures Old and New: Biblical Theology and the Challenge of Feminism." In *The Open Text: New Directions for Biblical Studies?*, edited by Francis Watson, 32–56. London: SCM, 1993.

Van Dijk-Hemmes, Fokkelien. "The Metaphorization of Woman in Prophetic Speech: An Analysis of Ezekiel 23." In *On Gendering Texts: Female and Male Voices in the Hebrew Bible*, edited by Athalya Brenner and Fokkelien van Dijk-Hemmes, 167–76. Leiden: Brill, 1993.

Van Leeuwen, Mary Stewart, ed. *After Eden: Facing the Challenge of Gender Relations*. Grand Rapids: Eerdmans, 1993.

Vanhoozer, Kevin. *Is There a Meaning in This Text? The Bible, The Reader, and the Morality of Literary Knowledge*. Leicester, UK: Apollos, 1998.

Walhout, Clarence. "Marxist and Christian Hermeneutics: A Study of Jameson's *The Political Unconscious*." *Faith and Philosophy* 3.2 (1986) 135–56.

Weems, Renita J. *Battered Love: Marriage, Sex, and Violence in the Hebrew Prophets*. Minneapolis: Fortress, 1995.

Wolterstorff, Nicholas. *Divine Discourse: Philosophical Reflections on the Claim That God Speaks*. Cambridge: Cambridge University Press, 1995.

———. *Reason within the Bounds of Religion*. 2nd ed. Grand Rapids: Eerdmans, 1984.

Wright, Christopher J. H. *God's People in God's Land: Family, Land, and Property in the Old Testament*. Grand Rapids: Eerdmans, 1991.

———. *The Message of Ezekiel: A New Heart and a New Spirit*. Leicester, UK: InterVarsity, 2001.

———. *Old Testament Ethics for the People of God*. Leicester, UK: InterVarsity, 2004.

Yee, Gale A. *Poor Banished Children of Eve: Woman as Evil in the Hebrew Bible*. Minneapolis: Fortress, 2003.

Zimmerli, Walther. *Ezekiel 1: A Commentary on the Book of the Prophet Ezekiel, Chapters 1–24*. Philadelphia: Fortress, 1979.

8

His Desire Is For Her

Feminist Readings of the Song of Solomon

GRENVILLE J. R. KENT

"Majestic as Lebanon stately as cedars
His mouth so delicious his fragrance so pleases . . .
Say I delight in his love.
Say he's the one my soul was."

—Sinead O'Connor, "Dark Am I Yet Lovely" (2007)

"This is the Song of Solomon.
Here's a woman singing . . .
And I'll do it for you,
I'll be the rose of Sharon for you."

—Kate Bush, "Song of Solomon" (1993)

THE SONG OF SOLOMON was among the first biblical texts to receive scholarly attention from feminists.[1] It seems an obvious site for the project, with a confident female voice, unmediated by a (male) narrator, with its own perspective and subjectivity; a large cast of female characters, including the daughters of Jerusalem in a chorus role; an egalitarian relationship without male dominance, despite patriarchal social structures (and possibly kingship) in the background; and positive men-

---

1. See Bass, "Women's Studies," 6–12; Brenner, "Feminist Criticism of the Song," 28–31.

tions of motherhood[2]. Yet while early studies "tended to praise the Song for its non-sexism, gender equality, and foregrounding of the woman," Exum observes that "dissenting voices" are increasingly heard.[3] Black also notes that there "have recently been a few who have started to ask difficult questions of the Song, and our numbers seem to be growing."[4] This paper will consider feminist readings with and/or against the text and critiques of them, and will dialogue with these from one evangelical point of view, recognizing that there are evangelicalisms just as there are feminisms.

I acknowledge that males can be regarded, as Fuchs puts it, as "interlopers in a field that was created specifically so as to evade male judgment, authority, and hegemony."[5] Yet Bird thinks feminism "should make sense to men as well,"[6] Nolan Fewell calls it a "stimulating mode of analysis for men as well as women,"[7] and Exum welcomes "more male scholars" into gender studies and into "dialogue between male and female readers on the subject of gender construction."[8] I write in this spirit, claiming no high ground.

PHYLLIS TRIBLE

For the pioneering Trible, feminism disturbs easy assumptions from a patriarchal[9] church, synagogue, and academy. Trible sketches three feminist approaches to hermeneutics. A first uncovers "the inferiority, subordination and abuse of women in Scripture"[10] and, in some cases, attempts re-interpretation. A second looks within Scripture for women's voices and stories and for feminine images of God, counter-texts that provide "a critique of patriarchy."[11] A third approach "retells biblical stories of terror *in memoriam*, offering sympathetic readings of abused

---

2. Cf. McCall, "Feminist/ Womanist Contributions," 420–21.
3. Exum, *Commentary*, 81.
4. Black, "Beauty or the Beast?" 308.
5. Fuchs, "Men," 93–114.
6. Bird, "What Makes a Feminist Reading," 130.
7. Nolan Fewell, "Feminist Criticism," 249.
8. Exum, "Developing Strategies," 225.
9. Trible seems to use the term in the broad sense. For a tight definition see Robin Parry's chapter in this volume (chapter 2).
10. Trible, "Biblical Studies," 3.
11. Ibid., 4.

women."[12] These approaches are not incompatible: Trible uses the first two on the Song, and the third on other texts.[13] She finds some texts "pose the question of authority,"[14] and is very clear that her feminist biblical theology "recognizes that, despite the word, *authority* centers in readers. They accord the document power even as they promote the intentionality of authors."[15] She sees the Bible as offering options, setting "before the reader life and good, death and evil, blessing and curse"[16] and asking us to choose the good. "Within this dialectic movement, feminism might claim the entire Bible as authoritative, though not necessarily prescriptive." For Trible, feminist hermeneutics must wrestle with the text and, Jacob-like, not let go without a blessing of "a theology that subverts patriarchy."[17]

Trible's treatment of the Song finds gender equality.[18] She identifies the speakers as one woman, one man and "a group of women," with the woman "most prominent" and "dominant." The woman "opens and closes the song," a "structural emphasis by which her equality and mutuality with the man is illuminated."[19] Trible's primary move is to make inter-textual comparisons: "Genesis 2–3 is the hermeneutical key with which I unlock this garden."[20] In the Song, the garden is no longer the site of fall and tragedy, but of delight. The woman herself is the garden (Song 4:12), and invites the man to her garden to eat the choicest fruits, willingly also becoming his garden (4:16; c.f. 5:1), a delightful statement of "mutual habitation and harmony,"[21] as both belong to each other in a "mutual possession formula" (2:16; 6:3).[22] The five senses, once fallen to the temptation of forbidden fruit, are now serving love: tastes (2:3; 4:16; 5:1, 13), scents (2:13; 3:6; 4:11; 5:13; 6:2), touch (1:2; 2:3–6; 4:10, 11; 5:1; 7:6–9; 8:1, 3), sights (4:9; 6:13), and sounds (5:2). Plants are no longer

12. Ibid.
13. Trible, *Texts of Terror*.
14. Trible, "Overture," 406.
15. Ibid., 407.
16. Ibid., 408.
17. Ibid.
18. Trible, "Love's Lyrics Redeemed," 144–65.
19. Ibid., 145.
20. Ibid., 144.
21. Ibid., 153.
22. Ibid., 159.

a source of temptation, but are pleasant as originally in Eden (Gen 2:9) the lily (Song 2:1–2), apple trees (2:3–5), other pleasant plants (7:13; 2:13; 4:3, 13; 6:7; 5:15; 7:8; 4:14). There is no "tree of disobedience."[23] Their garden is watered (4:15, 12), as was Eden (Gen 2:6, 10–14). There is no serpent (cf. Gen 3:14), and animals are "synonyms for human joy"[24] (Song 2:8, 9, 17; 8:14; 5:11–12; 4:1–2, 5; 1:9; 2:12; 4:8). Love can even capture the spoiling little foxes (2:15). Work—originally a delight in Eden, until disobedience brought thorns and thistles, pain and sweat (Gen 2:15; 3:16, 18–19)—is transformed from pain (Song 1:6) into pleasure (1:7; 2:16; 6:3), and "sexual play intertwines with work, redeeming it beyond the judgments of Genesis 3:16–19."[25] Birth is beautiful (Song 6:9; 8:5), a reversal of pain in childbearing (Gen 3:16), and motherhood receives seven positive mentions (Song 1:6; 3:4; 3:11; 6:9; 8:1; 8:2; 8:5) with no mention of any father, suggesting "the prominence of females."[26] The Genesis curse that the woman's desire would be for her husband and he would rule over her (Gen 3:16) is now reversed by her statement that "His desire is for me" (7:10). Trible interprets: "in the Song, male power vanishes. His desire becomes her delight. Another consequence of disobedience is thus redeemed through the recovery of mutuality in the garden of eroticism."[27] "Male dominance is totally alien to the Canticles. Can it be that grace is present?"[28] "A new context marks a new creation."[29]

> They are naked without shame; they are equal without duplication... Animals remind these couples of their shared superiority in creation... If the first pair pursue the traditional occupations for women and men, the second eschews stereotyping... As equals they confront life and death. But the first couple lose their oneness through disobedience. Consequently, the woman's desire becomes the man's dominion. The second couple affirm their oneness through eroticism. Consequently, the man's desire becomes the woman's delight... Paradise lost is Paradise Regained.[30]

23. Ibid., 155.
24. Ibid., 156.
25. Ibid., 157.
26. Ibid., 158.
27. Ibid., 160.
28. Trible, "Depatriarchalizing," 47.
29. Trible, "Loves Lyrics Redeemed," 160.
30. Trible, "Depatriarchalizing," 47.

Even in the back-to-Eden world of the Song, the consequences of the fall are still visible. The lovers face threats like winter, foxes that spoil vineyards, angry and domineering brothers, abusive watchmen, jealousy and anxiety, and yet love is as strong as death.

Trible's reading has been very influential. Exum recognizes this but calls Trible's work "mainly descriptive" of positive and negative texts, claiming that Trible's "method, rhetorical criticism, does not allow her to step outside the ideology of the text to interrogate it."[31] I would counter that Trible has shown herself quite capable of using rhetorical criticism to step outside the ideology of texts and vehemently challenge them: take her treatment of Judges 19–21 for example.[32] She does interrogate the Song and, having done so, finds it egalitarian, reversing the post-fall curse and patriarchy, a text in line with her feminist concerns. Why then would she wish to step outside its worldview?

Jobling claims the discipline has moved on and Trible is "no longer by any means the paramount figure."[33] She rather dismisses Trible's work as a mere "salvage operation" on Scripture and faults Trible's method of rhetorical criticism, particularly her quest for "proper" readings determined by what the text itself supports or does not support. Jobling argues that this begs important questions of what is "proper," and that it feels too controlling, imposing extra-textual criteria on a supposedly text-driven reading.[34] So Jobling's first criticism is that Trible presumes that she reads from a stable text. However the logical alternative is an unstable text that can generate an enormous variety of postmodern readings without textual controls. Jobling's second critique is that Trible's attempt to read this text is inconsistent or self-deceived because she has imposed alien criteria on the text while claiming to work with what the text supports. Yet Trible is quite clear that it is a feminist concern that she brings to the text, and that in this instance (though certainly not in others) she finds that concern mirrored in the text. Trible's criterion for arbitrating between competing readings is the text itself (which overlaps with a standard evangelical approach), but Jobling finds this provides no way of distinguishing between the text and "text as interpreted."[35] One response

---

31. Exum, "Developing Strategies," 214.
32. Trible, *Texts of Terror*, 65–91.
33. Jobling, *Interpretation*, 60.
34. Ibid., 65–67.
35. Ibid., 67.

is that, while there are a number of ways that "Moonlight Sonata" can be interpreted, a pianist who makes it sound like "Chopsticks" has gone beyond interpreting the score. This, of course, presumes some kind of realist notion of texts and meaning (or at least "performance") and an ethics of interpretation that seeks to honor the integrity of texts and/or author's intentions.

Jobling finds Trible's stable categories of "male" and "female" restrictive, ignoring the social construction of gender.[36] She calls Trible's descriptions of mother love "romanticized," claiming they will collapse into a phallocentric worldview.[37] To my knowledge Jobling has not offered alternatives or her own sustained reading of the Song.

More fundamentally, Fuchs undercuts the entire enterprise of attempting to rescue the Bible from sexism. She claims that "neoliberal ideals" ("equality, independence, rationalism, individualism, competitiveness, and power over others") are "projected on biblical women in an attempt to recuperate and reappropriate them as feminist models."[38] She finds the search for "strong" women is sexist because it demands women prove themselves to be like men to be accepted into the system.[39] Fuchs prefers "deconstruction" and "a critical reading in light of poststructuralist concepts of ideology, power, and politics," and the method of "reading as a woman," which means "reading from the margins, against the grain"[40] in a way that is not naïve about power and language.[41] She aims to avoid essentialism, considering gender as a social construct.[42] For Fuchs, neoliberals are not suspicious enough of "totalizing narratives" and "coherent truths," and thus they allow hegemonies that may in time take feminism back to male-dominated literary practices and male constructs. For her, "the goal of poststructural criticism is for the most part revisionist and transformational."[43] Fuchs also finds the acceptance of Trible and others by male feminists in the academy is itself sexist. "Once women are made to express their compliance with the authority of the

36. Ibid., 69.
37. Ibid., 70.
38. Fuchs, "Reclaiming," 45.
39. Ibid., 63.
40. Ibid., 47.
41. Ibid., 64.
42. Ibid., 65.
43. Ibid., 64.

Bible, they can safely be accorded legitimacy. The Father's authority . . . is embodied not only in the Bible but in the traditional academic field of biblical studies."[44] This does not seem quite accurate. Many scholars, including evangelicals, have welcomed Trible's solid challenge to their own long-held interpretations, even though her nuanced description of the Bible's authority as discussed above hardly portrays her as weakly "compliant." One could also question whether most readers really respect the authority of God primarily on the basis of male gender, or on the basis of divinity and its attributes and a character of love, with God's "gender" only as part of a metaphor. Most scholars would clearly differentiate the authority of Scripture itself from "the academic field of biblical studies" with its many competing views. Trible has earned an influential position in the academy (for example, serving as president in 1994 of the Society of Biblical Literature), yet it is implausible to argue that the academy requires acceptance of biblical authority as the basis of legitimacy. In fact, it seems at times that the test of compliance with biblical authority is a test that has to be failed before a scholar is granted legitimacy. And if it is sexist to accept Trible, what should a biblical scholar or a scholarly organization do with her work? Is it not legitimate to welcome her ideas and the influence they are gaining in the academy and, one hopes, society?

Pardes finds Trible's basic approach convincing, but nuances it. For example, Pardes does not find the Song idyllically free of patriarchalism. She sees it in the background in ancient society (in the watchmen and brothers, for example) but not in the lovers' relationship, thus making a text with a "rare antipatriarchal bent."[45]

I would argue that evangelicals may with integrity appreciate Trible's literary approach and her determination not to let an apparently sexist Scripture be the last word but to look for other ways to interpret it. Evangelicals are likely to assume that the text was inspired by a good God and therefore would not be contrary to the interests of half of God's children. They would tend to resist the assumption that any biblical text would be hopelessly patriarchal in its message, and welcome the idea that the text should be the controlling factor in its interpretation, not wishing to grant themselves the authority that "centers in readers."[46] While Trible does grant herself that authority, her reading of the Song

---

44. Ibid., 96.
45. Pardes, "I Am A Wall," 126.
46. Trible, "Overture," 407.

proves to be neither an uncontrolled reader response allowing the text to become almost infinitely elastic, nor a determinedly oppositional reading, but rather a canonical or inter-textual reading in light of Genesis 2–3. Her approach has been epoch-making, and is followed by many others,[47] including evangelicals.

ATHALYA BRENNER

Brenner defines feminism as the recognition that women are subordinated to men, and an advocacy of a "transformation of this social situation." Literary criticism is part of this project, as it deals with "cultural myths we live by."

> The Bible . . . has largely been viewed as a predominantly male textual document, read for centuries as if it had been mostly composed and edited by males. It has been interpreted and transmitted as such within male-centered communities for thousands of years, and has been enlisted to promote and justify the social order it by and large reflects. Its interpretation and teaching have been performed almost exclusively by males, and exploited to further the gender-specific interests of their dominant social group. Retrieving a biblical text by and for a woman reader is therefore a formidable task.[48]

Aware of the "politics of exegesis,"[49] and seeing biblical women as "always subordinate, often misrepresented,"[50] Brenner's interest is applying "feminist critical theories" to the Bible and theology, analyzing patriarchy, androcentrism, and phallocentrism within biblical texts, exposing "sexual politics in the literary characterization of female individuals and female types," reclaiming the "female heritage" often masked by male texts, and recovering "female institutions, social activities, status, self-image and literary activities," examining the place of women in

---

47. To cite but a few, Davidson structures *Flame of Yahweh* around the back-to-Eden paradigm: "Sexuality in Eden: The Divine Design," "Sexuality outside the Garden," and "Return to Eden." Landy, *Paradoxes*, builds upon it. See also Huwiler, "Song," and Bergant, *Song*. Noegel and Rendsburg, *Solomon's Vineyard*, 156, build on Trible's notion of reversal in arguing that the male lover looking in through the window at the female lover is an expression of his desire for her, and that this reverses the common biblical motif of a woman gazing out a window.

48. Brenner, *Feminist Companion*, 14–15.

49. Brenner, "Whose Love?" 265.

50. Brenner, *Israelite Women*.

monotheistic and other religions, and attempting to "re-write biblical interpretation . . . in a manner that will contribute towards the correction of the historical and social balance between the sexes."[51]

The Song interests Brenner[52] as a feminist because of "possible female authorship of the book or parts thereof"; "the lack of sexism" or "social prejudice against women"; "equality in the love relationship"; "predominance of the female figures"; "elements of matristic practices" (putting social power in the hands of women) and "matrilineal practices" (tracing inheritance and kinship on the distaff side); the possibility of "gender analysis of female and male discourse, that is, the defining of the emotional and psychological attributes that society expects of its male and female members"; and the potential fruitfulness of comparing the Song "with love lyrics of cognate Near Eastern cultures" and with love-themes elsewhere in the Hebrew Bible.[53]

In the Song, Brenner sees autonomous figures in a world free of "patriarchal bias." People are linked to mothers (3:4; 6:9; 8:1–2) and brothers are called mother's sons (1:6; 8:1–9). She argues that the female scorns social mores on "virginity," "segregation of women," and "the patriarchal code on female modesty" when she roams the streets at night looking for her lover (3:1–3; 5:7). Females co-operate in her search (2:7; 3:5; 5:8–9; 6:1; 8:4).[54] Brenner assigns around 53 percent of the text to the lead female voice(s), 34 percent to the lead male voice(s), with 7 percent debatable and 6 percent for choruses.[55] She sees "pronounced gynocentrism"[56] in the Song. "Female figurations are the dominant actors . . . strong, articulate, outspoken, active; in fact, much more so than their male counterparts. There is no equality of the sexes in the Song, which is how Trible describes the situation. There is female superiority."[57]

Brenner argues that possible "female authorship—perhaps enveloped by male editorship, like the rest of the Hebrew Canon—should be

---

51. Brenner, *Song*, 87–88.
52. One could broadly group with Brenner the approach of Fokkelien Van Dijk-Hemmes, "Traces"; "Structure of the Song of Songs"; "Imagination of Power."
53. Brenner, *Song*, 88.
54. Ibid., 90.
55. Brenner, "Women Poets," 89.
56. Brenner, "Whose Love?" 265.
57. Ibid., 273.

considered for the SoS or most of it."[58] She acknowledges that a male author with a good ear could "recreate an authentic representation of female emotion through his psychological and poetic insights. However, some passages are so typically feminine that female authorship is a distinct possibility."[59] The dream sequences (3:1–4; 5:2–7) are threatening and troubling, but Brenner finds them "'typically female' in terms of modern psychology,"[60] exploring the inner world of a woman: "female dreams representing female inner psychological reality and fears within the social reality."[61]

Brenner's later work complicates the notion of authorship, considering that a female character created by a male or female author could narrate a male character's story. She argues for "reading the SoS or portions thereof as female *and* male texts, a dual reading with the two possibilities put forward side-by-side, without looking to privilege the one reading over the other."[62] Noting early feminist interest in "women's experience" as a category, the later Brenner modifies this in the light of pluralism and social location, which have complicated the "universal sisterhood" concept almost beyond usefulness, and encouraged "personal/ autobiographical criticism." And so she writes her own history,[63] with a section exploring what has shaped her as a person and a reader of the Song. She also writes in the character of Shulamith, a dancer.[64]

One could question details of Brenner's reading. For example, it is not clear that the female chorus show co-operation with the woman's search: they seem like competitors. Merkin observes that "these unwilling soul sisters are as likely to jeer at the Shulamite's advice as to applaud it."[65]

Brenner's comments on the politics of exegesis are a very valuable corrective for anyone who has been to evangelical and other academic conferences in the U.S. or Europe and noticed just how male they tend

---

58. Brenner, *Feminist Companion to the Song*, 257.

59. Brenner, "Women Poets," 97.

60. Ibid., 90.

61. Brenner, *Song*, 89.

62. Brenner, "Gazing Back," 295–300.

63. Brenner, "'My' Song of Songs." Fontaine, "The Voice of the Turtle: Now It's My Song of Songs," 169–84.

64. Brenner, "Anonymous Woman from the Song," 163–90.

65. Merkin, "The Woman In The Balcony," 241.

to be (not to mention white, middle-class, and middle-aged—or "male, pale, and stale" as a friend jokingly put it). One test for people like me (who could fit all those categories) may be how we consider a new reading or approach on its own merits rather than leaning on groupthink. Along this line, Brenner's autobiographical approach is potentially helpful. While its I-voice still sounds like a scholar rather than truly getting into the character of the dancing girl as a novelist could, the method can offer a way of declaring one's biases[66] and one's intention to reconstruct creatively and read behind the text.

Some commentators will have none of the notion of female authorship: Clines, for instance, sees a male writer and readership, and the woman as a fantasy figure reflecting male desires.[67] Yet there are many possibilities for co-authorship or, if not sit-down co-authorship, then the literary borrowing or recording by a writer of the voice of another. Brenner's notion of dual authorship is creatively used by Exum in her commentary. There is little doubt that the woman speaks most and, I would add, has some of the wisest comments about love (e.g., Song 8:6–7), and yet how this equates to "female superiority" is not shown.

Overall, Brenner's readings seem so convincing because they are clearly based in the text, and reveal concepts and fresh angles that previous exegetes (usually male) have not seen. Evangelicals can welcome the challenge of Brenner's readings and her approach of reading with the text rather than against it.

RENITA J. WEEMS

Weems' womanist project is "to combine the best of the fruits of feminist biblical criticism with its passion for reclaiming and reconstructing the stories of biblical women, along with the best of the Afro-American oral tradition, with its gift for story-telling and its love of drama."[68] Weems does not have an evangelical high view of Scripture: she disowns any "naïve attachment to the principle of *sola scriptura* or a slavish belief in

---

66. Cf. Patte, "Male European-American," "Some (calling on Bultmann) denounce personal voices as preunderstandings and presuppositions to be overcome. Others (including feminist and other advocacy scholars) applaud them as manifestations of valuable interests and concerns." "I have been trained to mute my personal voice." (ibid., 13). See also the personal narrative of Dant, "Growing Up," 493–97.

67. Clines, "Why Is There a Song of Songs?" 99.

68. Weems, *Just a Sister Away*.

these texts as the divinely revealed word of God, the sole authority in all matters religious."[69] An "important part of womanist biblical criticism involves empowering readers to judge the biblical texts, to not hesitate to read against the grain of a text if needed, and to be ready to take a stand against those texts whose worldview runs counter to one's own vision of God's liberation activity in the world."[70] Weems argues that "it is not texts *per se* that function authoritatively. Rather, it is reading strategies."[71]

For her, "feminist scholars . . . have convincingly demonstrated that specific texts are unalterably hostile to the dignity and welfare of women."[72] And so for Weems the feminist reader can even alter the functional canon. "Part of rereading androcentric texts can entail choosing not to read them at all."[73]

Yet Weems does not deploy these oppositional strategies in the sunny garden of the Song. She says it "reclaims human sexuality and celebrates female sexuality," while "embodying gender balance and mutuality."[74] It "helps us to model and celebrate intimacy that does not abuse power . . . love without domination," and sex as "communion . . . without the diminishment of oneself."[75] Weems hears a predominant female voice, "the only unmediated female voice in all of Scripture. Elsewhere, women's perspectives are rehearsed through the voice of narrators, presumably male . . . But in Song . . . the experiences, thoughts, imagination, emotions, and words of this anonymous black-skinned woman are central." "[U]nlike many women of the Bible, she is assertive, uninhibited, and unabashed about her sexual desires."[76] Weems is challenged by Song 5:2–8, the scene in which the woman is beaten by night watchmen. This is often taken as a dream sequence, as is the related scene in 3:1–4. Yet Weems wonders "what and how does the protagonist's beating contribute to the book's general meaning?"—especially with such a "playful and seductive" mood in the rest of the book. She

---

69. Weems, "Re-Reading for Liberation," 33.
70. Ibid., 37.
71. Weems, "Reading *Her* Way," 64.
72. Ibid., 57.
73. Weems, "Liberation," 35.
74. Weems, "Commentary," 366.
75. Ibid., 408, 423.
76. Ibid., 364. See also Weems, "Song of Songs," 156. Walsh, "Woman's Voice," argues similarly.

asks why biblical narratives so often portray brutality to women,[77] and yet she lifts that weight off this passage, seeing instead a woman who is willing to suffer to be with her lover. "[T]his passage is clear: With love comes suffering and disappointment."[78] There is a "cost lovers must pay for defying social customs."[79]

For Weems, the woman of the Song is not the passive object of the male gaze, but in 5:10–16 produces an erotic and intimate "paean to male beauty [that] is the only one of its kind in the Bible. It represents our only look at the male body through the eyes of a woman. It is a woman's subjective construction of male beauty."[80]

Weems sees the female character as forcing a re-examination of prejudices "in a culture that ranks skin color," and "women on the low end of the economic totem pole who have to do . . . menial work," who nonetheless "tell it like it is" and "pursue their desires."[81] Theoretical hermeneutics aside, then, Weems as a determined oppositional reader finds little of concern in the Song.

Exum claims Weems has been "taken in" by an "illusion,"[82] because the Song is edited (by an "androcentric narrator") and so there cannot be an unmediated female voice, and so the "woman" is an artistic construct. Yet did Weems really forget about writers (and possibly redactors and scribal copyists and translators) and claim the woman's text was absolutely and totally unmediated, or did her comment mean the woman is unmediated within the world of the text? Whoever has handled "her" words since, she speaks freely within the diegesis or narrative world of the Song.

One could ask whether the woman in the Song is really black like an African or more likely of Middle Eastern appearance. Her "black and beautiful" comment (Song 1:5) has been understood as describing class, not ethnicity. For example, Dobbs-Alsopp has argued that a "luminous and ruddy complexion was stereotyped as the normative image of health and beauty for the day (cf. 1 Sam 16:12; 17:42; Song 5:10; Lam 4:7)"[83]

77. Weems, "Commentary," 413.
78. Ibid.
79. Ibid., 434.
80. Ibid., 415.
81. Weems, *What Matters Most*, 2–3.
82. Exum, "Ten Things," 27.
83. Dobbs-Allsopp, "Black *and* Beautiful," 129.

and lightness may have been "an image of beauty" derived from "an elite culture" who did not have to perform outdoor work.[84] Yet this is hardly a fundamental critique of Weems' hermeneutic—indeed, it fits within it, as she is concerned to speak not just for women, but for any who are marginalized on the basis of their social location (including their role as "menials" in various modes of economic production).

Weems's quest for equality is admirable, and her commentary ends up demonstrating (perhaps unconsciously) that, in the Song at least, one does not need to lessen the authority of scripture to achieve an egalitarian reading. It could even be argued that allowing the Song to have more authority could give it greater traction in moving readers towards its egalitarian ideals, since readers who regard it as (part of) "the word of God" may be even more likely to let it influence their culture towards the ideal of human equality.

J. CHERYL EXUM

Exum's years of study have produced various layers of reflection on the Song. She began with a "'straight' (i.e., not marked as feminist)"[85] literary and structural analysis of the Song, and then commenced a feminist quest for "positive portrayals of women," and "strong countercurrents of affirmations of women" among "the admittedly patriarchal context of biblical literature,"[86] suggesting women had significant roles and showed independence and initiative. More recently Exum argued that one "promising strategy for getting at a woman's perspective in androcentric texts is to look for the alternative, competing discourses within the text,"[87] thus allowing women not to read against their own interests. She sees a way forward for feminism in "investigations of the ideology and interests that motivate biblical representations of women and . . . developing ever more sophisticated methods for exposing traces of the problematic of maintaining patriarchy."[88] Exum has used Bal's approach to "reveal how patriarchal texts undermine themselves."[89]

84. Ibid., 129 n. 5.
85. Brenner, "On Feminist Criticism," 34, referring to Exum, "Literary and Structural Analysis."
86. Exum, "Let Every Daughter Live," 63–82.
87. Exum, "Developing Strategies," 217.
88. Ibid., 225.
89. Ibid., 215.

She observed that, uniquely in Scripture, the Song's "text foregrounds a woman's speech, and it is through speech that subjectivity is most readily conferred,"[90] and yet she advocates more study on "the nature and limits of her autonomy." Exum wonders whether the male and female characters are constructs: "Might the man who is conjured up by a woman be a man who is conjured up by a woman constructed by a man? In other words, is the woman of the Song the construct of an androcentric narrator . . . ?"[91] She wonders, "Does male focalization deconstruct the female voice?"[92]

Exum declares her motives for this more questioning enquiry: "I am cautious in principle about seeing this text as an anodyne to other, androcentric biblical writings where woman is coded as other . . . It seems too good to be true."[93] She declares mixed motives: "I want to be seduced by the Song of Songs, to enter into its idyllic world of eroticism, and, as a critic and a feminist, I want to be a resistant reader, asking whether the Song really challenges the biblical gender status quo or not . . . As a postmodern commentator I want to problematize the text, not in an abstruse way that confuses the reader, but in a way that reveals a multiplicity of meanings . . ."[94]

More recently[95] Exum has set out to "problematize certain interpretive issues." In a provocative article that seems to emphasize a contrarian aspect of her views, she questions the assumption that the Song is a woman's text. Yes, female desire is celebrated, the woman transcends social norms, initiates sex, and so on, and critics praise the Song "for its nonsexism, gender equality, and gynocentrism,"[96] but Exum discounts this praise by arguing that the text can turn "the most hardened of feminist critics into a bubbling romantic."[97] "Readerly desire seems to play a particularly important role in the interpretation of this book about desire, more so than for other Biblical books."[98] Women "want to believe

---

90. Ibid., 226.
91. Ibid., 229.
92. Ibid., 230.
93. Ibid., 228.
94. Ibid., 248–49.
95. Exum, "Ten Things," 27.
96. Ibid., 24.
97. Ibid., 25.
98. Exum, *Commentary*, 85.

that erotic love transcends gender interests, and so that is what we find in the Song."[99] Women identify too closely with the woman. Exum wonders whether the Song presents a male fantasy of a woman, as Clines argues,[100] or a woman's fantasy, and concludes, after Brenner, that it can be read twice. She claims, "There is no gender equality," citing the man's elusiveness as a lover, bounding off over the hills with an autonomy and sexual freedom the woman does not possess.[101] She claims there is "gender bending," as imagery is applied to male and female alike, and some gendered imagery is applied to the other gender. On the beating scenes, Exum sees one possible message is that "bad things happen to sexually active, forward women,"[102] though she acknowledges that the mistreatment may be in a dream sequence, and that the woman keeps on with her search afterwards. Exum claims "the female body is on display," and there is something wrong with the female body; it is not a complete woman but "a collocation of body parts." Yet she finds the poetry "seductive." She finds it allows women to "identify with an object of desire, but also with a desiring subject."[103] And she finds that feminists "don't have to deny ourselves the pleasure of the text. All we need to do is misread it (. . . in a positive, Bloomian sense) . . . Why should an ancient author's intention matter? . . . Feminist readers . . . might do well to say to the ancient authors and traditionists who preserved it for us, 'thanks for your text, and I'll decide how to read it.'"[104]

Yet in her commentary, Exum reads the Song as a unified love song that "looks at what it is like to be in love from both a woman's and a man's point of view" using dialogue without intruding narration.[105] Both voices are "in complete accord, both desirous, both rejoicing," and "they merge into one, creating the poetic equivalent of their sexual union," yet they have "different perspectives," a feature that reveals "the poet's remarkable sensitivity to differences between women and men—differences that, in turn, reflect cultural assumptions about gender differences

---

99. Exum, "Ten Things," 26.
100. Clines, "Why Is There a Song of Songs?"
101. Exum, "Ten Things," 30.
102. Ibid., 30.
103. Ibid., 35.
104. Ibid., 35, citing Harold Bloom, *A Map of Misreading,* New York: Oxford University Press, 1975, and attributing the final quote to a Mieke Bal lecture.
105. Exum, *Commentary,* 1.

and roles," while challenging these as well.[106] "She expresses her desire and explores her feelings for him, and his for her, through stories" in which both play roles, "as themselves (2:8–17; 3:1–5; 5:2—6:3) or in fantasy guises (3:6–11)." "The man does not tell stories. His way of talking about love is to look at her and tell her what he sees and how it affects him." "The man constructs the woman . . . through the gaze . . . The woman constructs the man primarily through his voice. She quotes him speaking to her (2:10–14; 5:2), but he never quotes her."[107] She speaks of her feelings of being in love as feeling "faint" (2:5; 5:8). He describes what she has done to him in terms of "conquest, of power relations: "*you* have captured my heart" (4:9)." This (and 6:5) is a man who usually feels "in control" but is now "powerless to resist; his autonomy is challenged." He speaks of being captured, and "she speaks of surrender to him (8:10)."[108] He "deals with his anxiety about her effect on him by distancing himself from the whole person through the breakdown of her body into parts—eyes, hair, teeth,"[109] etc. She does the same to him (5:10–16), "but the fact that she too owns the gaze is an extraordinary feature of the Song, for traditionally woman are looked at and men do the looking." This is "mutual pleasure in visualizing the beloved's body."[110] "She treats his [body] by parts to cope with his absence and to conjure him up through the evocative power of language."[111]

Exum raises the question of whether the man's looking is erotic or a voyeuristic gaze: "is this looking loving, or is it objectifying and controlling, or something of both?" She distinguishes between voyeuristic gaze, "looking that intrudes upon that which is seen" and erotic "looking that participates in that which is seen . . . Nor is the one who looks, the subject of the gaze, automatically in a position of power over the one seen (we need only recall that looking at his lover makes the man feel he has lost control)."[112] In the Song the look "preserves the mystery," and it is

106. Ibid., 14.
107. Ibid.
108. Ibid., 15.
109. Ibid., 17.
110. Ibid., 20.
111. Ibid., 21.
112. Ibid., 22–23.

"reciprocal," and the man "always puts himself in the picture, participating in what he sees."[113]

Exum's reading is sophisticated and nuanced, and demonstrates commendable openness to new approaches. One could question details of the argument. For example, does describing parts of a beloved's body necessarily equate to breaking it down? Some feminist critiques of contemporary pornography have objected to the visual dismemberment which removes (parts of) the head and face from the body, but the Song features the verbal equivalent of close-up shots which track from foot to head (7:1–5) or head to foot (5:10–16), and depict desirable parts in the context of a beautiful body and a love for a person holistically. Both the man and the woman do this. If this is potentially objectionable, lovers could find it hard to move past meaninglessly bland comments like, "I like your body overall."

Exum has frankly declared the thinking, the inner arguments, behind her more recent suspicious approach: she feels a duty as a feminist to be a resistant reader. And yet she fair-mindedly asks whether the Song deserves to be resisted, that is, whether it really promotes patriarchy or gender equality. One wonders what the test of this could be. If a postmodern reader-response interpretation concludes that the Song is sexist, would this demonstrate sexism in the text itself or merely reveal the ideology that one particular reader brings to the text?[114] Could this then make the case that the Song itself is sexist? How well resistant readings will work on the Song is yet to be seen, though one will be explored below, but what if feminist analysis finds that the text of the Song itself presents an egalitarian ideal? Will further resistance be needed? Exum's commentary is not blind to dark moments in Song and new theoretical means to push back against the text, but in the end does not really need to use them.

---

113. Ibid., 23.

114. In a witty and quirky article, Merkin, "The Woman in the Balcony," 250, is commendably frank about this issue: "I am writing out of my idiosyncratic tastes." Merkin concludes, "in the end, the song throws one . . . upon oneself as Author." By contrast, evangelicals have seen Scripture as having an intended message (however imperfectly it is sometimes understood).

FIONA C. BLACK

Black's method is resistant reading,[115] seeking to problematize the text in whole or in parts.[116] She proposes a reading strategy based on postmodern "resistance to coherence (or an emphasis on counter-coherence or difference); a recognition of marginal voices; an acknowledgement or encouragement of plurivocality in readers and their texts; and a promotion of intertextuality." She decides against any attempt to "settle the meaning of my chosen text, or even to make it cohere with the rest of the book."[117] Beginning "by intending a counter-coherent reading," Black decides that "therefore its end surely should remain as resistant to resolution and coherence as its beginning."[118]

To describe her readerly relationship with the text, Black uses Roland Barthes' metaphor of "the erotic, textual body."[119] She finds imagery that attracts and repels, discomforts and brings bliss, seducing the reader into a "coital quest . . . where the excitement builds to a satisfying climax."[120] Black uses this concept to explain why many readers of the Song are "blind to its faults," showing "loyalty" and "acclamations of the text's charms." The text is not authoritative: readers as lovers "are subject to the desires and whimsy of the text, which teases them by play at display and hiding" but "they respond with their own demands and restrictions, so that there is constant dialogue and negotiation between the two."[121]

---

115. Black, "Allegorical and Feminist Readings," 104–29, also considers allegorical readings, but I lack the space for analysis of feminist allegorical readings of the Song. Most have avoided the allegorical method, perhaps due to their place in interpretive history. Indeed, Bekkenkamp and van Dijk, "Women's Cultural Traditions," 80–81, have argued that a strong, independent female character may have driven male interpreters to seek a non-literal interpretation. Yet see Cainion, "An Analogy," 219–59, and Butting, "Women Rewrite the Scriptures," 130–51. Ostriker, "Holy of Holies," 50, views the Song as an allegory of a love relationship with God without hierarchy.

116. Exum, *Song*, 83, lists as other resistant readers Clines, "Why is There A Song of Songs?" and Polaski, "What Will Ye See in the Shulammite?" Polaski uses Foucault's image of the panopticon, a prison designed so that prisoners are always seen, and claims the woman is trapped in a male gaze which she has internalized and cannot escape (unlike the male), and so must always view herself through patriarchal eyes and values.

117. Black, "Nocturnal Egression," 94.

118. Ibid., 104.

119. Black, "Erotic Reading," 36.

120. Ibid., 43.

121. Ibid., 50.

Black and Exum jointly advocate "the importance of a counterreading of the biblical text in which the picture of love is not so rosy as many commentators would have it," challenging "comfortable assumptions" and highlighting what scholars have been "reluctant to see."[122] And so they argue that many scholars de-emphasize the scenes of violence in the Song: "What would happen to the place of honour held by the biblical Song of Songs if, rather than suppressing these recalcitrant details, we foregrounded them?"

Black takes the scene of the woman being beaten (Song 5:7) as a "challenge to the woman's autonomy,"[123] one that produces "the decentering—the abjecting—of the woman."[124] It is a lesson intended by the watchmen: "If she will not contain herself, they will." These supposed "keepers of order and preventers of violence" use "disorder and violence to repress the actions of the woman." Yet the woman's acts are "transgressive," "and this appears to be the reason for her treatment": she has left the house, "the 'proper' environ for women in the patriarchal order," and she is "reminded" that she should stay covered and "guard the borders of her body and its desires. She is pushed from the center of the song where she was a speaking, loving subject."[125] Black found herself "tempted to find a way to recover the woman's position, or somehow recover the loss from my own "negative" ending by appealing to the rest of the book," yet "that kind of ending did not sit well either, especially since it must be through violence that the woman maintains her important role in the social order."[126]

Elsewhere, Black chooses to apply theory on "the grotesque," a mix of the comic and terrifying, in order to unsettle "coherent readings" and "to explore the threat to order" in the Song. She comments: "An ostensibly perverse intromission of the grotesque serves here as a heuristic for viewing bodily imagery and readerly desire."[127] As Black "unleashes the grotesque,"[128] the woman becomes "ill-proportioned, odd-looking and impossible. A giant, her head is as massive as Mt. Carmel . . . And

---

122. Black and Exum, "Semiotics," 342.
123. Black, "Nocturnal Egression," 95.
124. Ibid., 98.
125. Ibid., 102.
126. Ibid., 104.
127. Black, "Beauty or the Beast?" 304.
128. Ibid., 308.

the tower which is her nose juts out awkwardly and unbalances... The woman is like a biblical Barbie—though much less alluring—for she appears so ill-proportioned that she could not stand."[129] Wine flowing over lips and teeth becomes a "bleeding vagina," and "mouth and vagina become one, suggesting the provocation of oral engagement and the horror of *vagina dentata* in one fell swoop." Thus Black problematizes the "supposedly complimentary body descriptions." She argues that the man's body has "less textual space devoted" to it, and certain features are "not as grotesque." He may "represent the classical body against which Bakhtin defines grotesque figuration."[130] By contrast, the woman may be ridiculed because of "the lover's unease" at "this sexually autonomous woman" who is a threat to patriarchy. And so Black finds the Song may be after all "a paradigmatically patriarchal text... The grotesque reveals that it is difficult to sustain a feminist reading of the Song, and, in fact, that the Song may confound or resist gender-critical readings."[131]

Black is to be commended for calling attention to the darker sections of the Song, aspects that are often neglected but that are important to its nuanced themes.[132] Yet it is possible to over-state the importance of two brief dark passages in an overwhelmingly sunny and positive text, which could replace one imbalance with another. If the Song is unified in some sense, at the very least functioning as a collection of disparate poems edited into a final form, then someone intended that its parts should interconnect in some way artistically and thematically and should inform one another. Plurivocality can produce valuable insights, but it should be careful of unplugging literary connections and assuming, despite contrary evidence, that various voices are unrelated. The "Song of Songs" may well be composed of a plurality of "Songs," but it still titles itself as a "Song."[133]

Black's description of the abjection of the woman may very well expose injustice and patriarchy in the watchmen, which works as a barrier the woman overcomes in her quest for autonomy and mutuality, but that does not mean that the writer sides with these characters who function as mere foils. The wish to make abjection the final word requires, as

129. Ibid., 311–12.
130. Ibid., 315–16.
131. Ibid., 316–17.
132. As I briefly suggest in "Preaching the Song of Solomon," 128–29.
133. It is recognized that the title can be variously understood.

Black acknowledges, that elements of the text be ignored, and not just distant sections but the immediate structure of the nighttime sequences as narrated by the woman herself. How can one conclude that the woman is removed as a speaking subject when she is in fact telling the story (3:1–4; 5:6–8), and goes on speaking and loving afterwards? Black's cuts seem arbitrary and without warrant in the text, apparently a personal choice driven by a wish to be oppositional. This is akin to re-cutting someone else's film: it may produce an interesting text but it may have little to do with the original one. Put another way, re-writing *Much Ado About Nothing* or *When Harry Met Sally* so that the dark plot turns fill most of the narrative would not leave a comedy. Black's method is more like re-writing than commentary on an existing text, and is one without invitation in that text: a poem does not ask to be read as a choose-your-own-adventure novel.

Furthermore, her "intromission" of grotesque theory seems arbitrary and imposed upon the text. Why *that* theory? Why not any other?[134] Black traces its cultural history to the Renaissance[135] but makes no attempt to demonstrate its existence as a mode of expression in the world of the writer of the Song. Nor is it demonstrated that the bodily descriptions would have been taken as grotesque by the Song's original culture.[136] The text itself often praises the woman's beauty (and the man's), and it is hard to believe that a lover would shift from love and affirmation to ridicule and back so quickly. Black claims that the "grotesque reveals that it is difficult to sustain a feminist reading of the Song," and yet feminists have generated many and varied readings. All that is really demonstrated

---

134. One could also ask why Burrus and Moore, "Unsafe Sex," 24–52, use feminism alongside Queer Theory and sadomasochism, viewing the Song as pornography. Others have read contemporary pornography into the Song. See Boer, "Solomon Meets Annie Sprinkle," 151–82; "Pornography and the Song," 53–70; "The Second Coming," 276–301. Also Moore, "History of Sexuality," 28–49. On pornography see also Setel, "Prophets and Pornography," 143–55. For a Queer reading, see King, "Song of Songs," 356–70.

135. Black, "Beauty or the Beast?" 309.

136. Yarber, "Our Dancing Bodies," 477–78, responding to different writers, makes a similar point: "Perhaps these feminists are projecting contemporary standards of beauty back onto this dancer . . . [In the Song] voluptuous and curvy women were described as beautiful . . . Furthermore, curvy and full-figured women are the norm in belly dance. Quivering bellies, trembling thighs, shaking buttocks, and shuddering breasts are precisely the point. Contemporary American culture may not see the Shulamite's dancing body as beautiful, but her lover certainly did."

is that it is difficult using grotesque theory to sustain a feminist reading of the Song, but this need not trouble feminists.

Black's resistant readings are fascinating examples of reception history, yet it can be argued that they say less about the text than about the theories the reader may choose to intromit. Evangelicals may find resistant readings of value in that their imaginative and provocative claims motivate a re-examination of the text.

CONCLUSION

Feminist scholars have traditionally seen the Song of Solomon as a text reversing the Genesis curse of harsh male domination by portraying gender equality, strong female characters, and a strong female voice (possibly unmediated, possibly authorial in some sense), and by featuring female heritage and social and literary activity.

Trible is willing to take up hermeneutical arms against patriarchalism where she perceives it in Scripture,[137] yet she finds the Song a private garden of love and gender equality in a world (and even a canon) where this is not always the case. Weems, by no means a submissive reader, does not feel the need to deploy her reading-as-resistance firepower on the Song, but rather finds it a city of peace. Brenner, using various innovative methods of analyzing the text, finds it free of patriarchal bias and reads of feminine equality or even more. Exum, eternally vigilant against being a soft touch, seeking new theoretical challenges and constantly cross-checking her conclusions by considering other ways of reading, nonetheless hears male and female voices with unique perspectives becoming one, in a manner reminiscent of Genesis. Each of these commentators, from their various perspectives and with some disagreement on details, sustains an egalitarian reading from the text of the Song.

Some recent feminists seem to feel almost duty-bound to read against the grain and to discover patriarchalism in the Song. So far only a few oppositional readings have been generated and one must remain open to further attempts, and yet Black's reading, while creative and potentially catalytic, seems to import pre-existing conclusions and to ignore key textual data, rather than making its case from the themes and emphases of the text itself.

---

137. The book of Judges provides half of Trible's examples in *Texts of Terror*, 65–116.

Egalitarian readings currently seem much more persuasive. Could this be because the Song is after all promoting gender equality? Must that be too good to be true?

BIBLIOGRAPHY

Ayo, Nicholas. *Sacred Marriage: The Wisdom of the Song of Songs.* New York: Continuum, 1997.

Bass, D. C. "Women's Studies and Biblical Studies: An Historical Perspective." *Journal for the Study of the Old Testament* 22 (1982) 6-12.

Bekkenkamp, Jonneke, and Fokkelien van Dijk. "The Canon of the Old Testament and Women's Cultural Traditions." In *The Feminist Companion to the Song of Songs*, edited by Athalya Brenner, 67-85. Sheffield, UK: Sheffield Academic, 1991.

Bergant, Diane. *The Song of Songs.* Collegeville, MN: Liturgical, 2001.

Bird, Phyllis. "What Makes a Feminist Reading Feminist? A Qualified Answer." In *Escaping Eden: New Feminist Perspectives on the Bible*, edited by Harold C. Washington, Susan Lochrie Graham, and Pamela Thimmes, 124-31. New York: New York University Press, 1999.

Black, Fiona C. "Beauty or the Beast? The Grotesque Body in the Song of Songs." *Biblical Interpretation* 8 (2000) 302-23.

———. "Nocturnal Egression: Exploring Some Margins of the Song of Songs." In *Postmodern Interpretations of the Bible—A Reader*, edited by A. K. M. Adam, 93-104. St. Louis, MO: Chalice, 2001.

———. "Unlikely Bedfellows: Allegorical and Feminist Readings of the Song of Songs 7.1-10." In *A Feminist Companion to Reading the Bible: Approaches, Methods and Strategies*, edited by Athalya Brenner and Carole R. Fontaine, 104-29. London: Dearborn, 2001.

———. "What Is My Beloved? On Erotic Reading and the Song of Songs." In *The Labour of Reading: Desire, Alienation and Biblical Interpretation*, edited by Fiona C. Black et al., 35-52. Atlanta: Society of Biblical Literature, 1999.

Black, Fiona C., and J. Cheryl Exum. "Semiotics in Stained Glass: Edward Burne-Jones's Song of Songs." In *Biblical Studies/ Cultural Studies: The Third Sheffield Colloquium*, edited by J. Cheryl Exum and Stephen D. Moore, 315-42. Sheffield, UK: Sheffield Academic, 1991.

Boer, Roland. "King Solomon Meets Annie Sprinkle." *Semeia* 82 (1998) 151-82

———. "Night Sprinkles: Pornography and the Song of Songs." In *Knockin' On Heaven's Door: The Bible and Popular Culture*, 53-70. London: Routledge, 1999.

———. "The Second Coming: Repetition and Insatiable Desire in the Song of Songs." *Biblical Interpretation* 8.2 (2000) 276-301.

Brenner, Athalya. "Aromatics and Perfumes in the Song of Songs." *Journal for the Study of the Old Testament* 25 (1983) 75-81.

———. "'Come Back, Come Back The Shulammite' (Song of Songs 7:1-10) A Parody of the *Wasf* Genre." In *On Humour and the Comic in the Hebrew Bible*, edited by Yehuda T. Radday and Athalya Brenner, 251-75. Sheffield, UK: Almond, 1990.

———. "Gazing Back at the Shulammite Yet Again." *Biblical Interpretation* 11 (2003) 295-300.

———. *The Intercourse of Knowledge: On Gendering Desire and "Sexuality" in the Hebrew Bible.* Leiden: Brill, 1997.

———. *The Israelite Woman: Social Role and Literary Type in Biblical Narrative.* Sheffield, UK: JSOT, 1985.

———. "Love Me Tender, Love Me True . . . : I Am an Anonymous Woman from the Song of Songs." in *I Am . . . Biblical Women Tell Their Own Stories*, 163-90. Minneapolis: Fortress, 2005.

———. "'My' Song of Songs." In *A Feminist Companion to Reading the Bible: Approaches, Methods and Strategies*, edited by Athalya Brenner and Carole R. Fontaine, 154–68. London: Dearborn, 2001.

———. "On Feminist Criticism of the Song of Songs." In *A Feminist Companion to The Song of Songs*, edited by in Athalya Brenner, 28–31. Sheffield, UK: Sheffield Academic, 1993.

———. *The Song of Songs*. Sheffield, UK: Sheffield Academic, 1989.

———. "To See Is To Assume: Whose Love is Celebrated in the Song of Songs?" *Biblical Interpretation* 11.3 (1993) 265–84.

———. "Women Poets and Authors." In *A Feminist Companion to the Song of Songs*, edited by Athalya Brenner, 86–97. Sheffield, UK: Sheffield Academic, 1993.

Brenner, Athalya, and Fokkelien van Dijk-Hemmes. *On Gendering Texts: Female and Male Voices in the Hebrew Bible*. Leiden: Brill, 1993.

Burrus, Virginia, and Stephen D. Moore, "Unsafe Sex: Feminism, Pornography and the Song of Songs." *Biblical Interpretation* 11.1 (2003) 24–52.

Butting, Klara. "Go Your Way: Women Rewrite the Scriptures (Song of Songs 2.8–14)." In *A Feminist Companion to Reading the Bible: Approaches, Methods and Strategies*, edited by Athalya Brenner and Carole R. Fontaine, 130–51. London: Dearborn, 2001.

Cainion, Ivory J. "An Analogy of the Song of Songs and Genesis Chapters Two and Three." *Scandinavian Journal of the Old Testament* 14 (2000) 219–59.

Clines, David J. A. "Why Is There a Song of Songs and What Does It Do to You If You Read It?" In *Interested Parties: The Ideology of Writers and Readers of the Hebrew Bible*, 94–121. JSOTSup205. Sheffield, UK: Sheffield Academic, 1995.

Dant, Jim. "Growing Up With Solomon's Song: Song of Songs 7:1–9." *Review and Expositor* 105 (2008) 493–97.

Davidson, Richard M. *Flame of Yahweh: Sexuality in the Old Testament*. Peabody, MA: Hendrickson, 2007.

Deckers, M. "The Structure of the Song of Songs and the Centrality of *Nepeš*." In *A Feminist Companion to the Song of Songs*, edited by Athalya Brenner, 172–96. Sheffield, UK: Sheffield Academic, 1993.

Dobbs-Allsopp, F. W. "'I am Black *and* Beautiful': The Song, Cixous and *Écriture Féminine*." In *Engaging the Bible in a Gendered World: An Introduction to Feminist Biblical Interpretation in Honor of Katharine Doob Sakenfeld*, edited by Linda Day and Carolyn Pressler, 128–40. Louisville: Westminster John Knox, 2006.

——— "The Delight of Beauty and Song of Songs 4:1–7." *Interpretation* (2005) 260–77.

Exum, J. Cheryl. "A Literary and Structural Analysis of the Song of Songs." *Zeitschrift für die alttestamentliche Wissenschaft* 85 (1973) 47–49.

———. "Asseverative *'al* in Canticles 1:6?," *Biblica* 62 (1981) 416–19.

———. "Developing Strategies of Feminist Criticism/ Developing Strategies for Commentating on the Song of Songs." In *Auguries: The Jubilee Volume of the Sheffield Department of Biblical Studies*, edited by D. J. A. Clines and S. D. Moore, 206–49. JSOTSup260. Sheffield, UK: Sheffield Academic, 1998.

———. "How Does the Song of Songs Mean? On Reading the Poetry of Desire." *Svensk Exegetisk Årsbok* 64 (1999) 47–63.

———. "In the Eye of the Beholder: Wishing, Dreaming and *Double Entendre* in the Song of Songs." In *The Labour of Reading: Desire, Alienation and Biblical Interpretation*, edited by Fiona Black et al., 71–86. Atlanta: Society of Biblical Literature, 1999.

———. "Seeing Solomon's Palanquin (Song of Songs 3:6–11)." *Biblical Interpretation* 11 (2003) 301–16.

———. *Song of Songs: A Commentary.* Louisville: Westminster John Knox, 2005.

———. "Ten Things Every Feminist Should Know about the Song of Songs." In *The Song of Songs: A Feminist Companion to the Bible*, edited by Athalya Brenner and Carole R. Fontaine, 24–35. Sheffield, UK: Sheffield Academic, 2000.

———. "'The Voice of My Lover': Double Voice and Poetic Illusion in Song of Songs 2:8—3:5." In *Reading from Left to Right: Essays on the Hebrew Bible in Honour of David J. A. Clines*, edited by J. Cheryl Exum and Hugh G. M. Williamson, 141–52. London: T. & T. Clark, 2003.

———. "You Shall Let Every Daughter Live: A Study of Exodus 1:8—2:10." In *The Bible and Feminist Hermeneutics*, edited by in M. A. Tolbert, 63–82. Chico: Scholars, 1983.

Fontaine, Carole R. "The Voice of the Turtle: Now It's My Song of Songs." In *The Song of Songs: A Feminist Companion to the Bible*, edited by Athalya Brenner and Carole R. Fontaine, 169–84. Sheffield, UK: Sheffield Academic, 2000.

———. "Watching Out for the Watchmen (Song of Songs 5.7): How I Hold Myself Accountable." In *The Meanings We Choose: Hermeneutics, Ethics, Indeterminacy and the Conflict of Interpretations*, edited by Charles H. Cosgrove, 102–21. London: T. & T. Clark, 2004.

Fuchs, Esther. "Biblical Feminisms: Knowledge, Theory and Politics in the Study of Women in the Hebrew Bible." *Biblical Interpretation* 16 (2008) 205–26.

———. "Men in Biblical Feminist Scholarship." *Journal of Feminist Studies in Religion* 19.2 (2003) 93–114.

———. "Reclaiming the Hebrew Bible for Women: The Neoliberal Turn in Contemporary Feminist Scholarship." *Journal of Feminist Studies in Religion* 24.2 (2008) 45–65.

Huwiler, Elizabeth. "The Song of Songs." In Murphy, Roland E., and Elizabeth Huwiler, *Proverbs, Ecclesiastes, Song of Songs.* Peabody, MA: Hendrickson, 1999.

Jobling, J'annine. *Feminist Biblical Interpretation in Theological Context: Restless Readings.* Aldershot, UK: Ashgate, 2002.

Kent, Grenville J. R. "Preaching the Song of Solomon." In *"He Began with Moses . . .": Preaching the Old Testament Today*, edited by Grenville J. R. Kent, et al., 128–29. Nottingham, UK: InterVarsity, 2010.

King, Christopher. "Song of Songs." In *The Queer Bible Commentary*, edited by Deryn Guest *et al.*, 356–70. London: SCM, 2006.

Landy, Francis. *Paradoxes of Paradise: Identity and Difference in the Song of Songs.* Sheffield, UK: Almond, 1983.

McCall, Robin C. "'Most Beautiful Among Women': Feminist/ Womanist Contributions to the Reading of the Song of Songs." *Review and Expositor* 105 (2008) 417–33.

Merkin, Daphne. "The Woman in the Balcony: On Rereading The Song of Songs." In *Out of the Garden: Women Writers on the Bible*, edited by Christina Büchmann and Celina Spregel, 238–51. New York: Ballantine, 1995.

Meyers, Carol. "Gender Imagery in the Song of Songs." *Hebrew Annual Review* 10 (1986) 209–23.

———. "'To Her Mother's House': Considering a Counterpart to the Israelite *Bêt 'āb*." In *The Bible and the Politics of Exegesis: Essays in Honor of Norman K. Gottwald on His Sixty-Fifth Birthday*, edited by David Jobling, *et al.*, 39–51. Cleveland, OH: Pilgrim, 1991.

Moore, Stephen D. "The Song of Songs in the History of Sexuality." *Church History* 29 (2000) 328–49.

Noegel, Scott B., and Gary A. Rendsburg. *Solomon's Vineyard: Literary and Linguistic Studies in the Song of Songs.* Atlanta: Society of Biblical Literature, 2009.

Nolan Fewell, Dana. "Reading the Bible Ideologically: Feminist Criticism." In *To Each Its Own Meaning*: An Introduction to *Biblical Criticisms and Their Application,* edited by Steven L. McKenzie and Stephen R. Haynes, 268–82. Louisville: Westminster John Knox, 1999.

Ostriker, Alicia. "A Holy of Holies: The Song of Songs as Countertext." In *A Feminist Companion to Reading the Bible: Approaches, Methods and Strategies,* edited by Athalya Brenner and Carole R. Fontaine, 36–54. London: Dearborn, 2001.

Pardes, Ilana. "'I Am a Wall, and My Breasts are Like Towers': The Song of Songs and the Question of Canonization." In *Countertraditions in the Bible: A Feminist Approach,* 118–43. Cambridge: Harvard University Press, 1992.

Patte, Daniel. "The Guarded Voice of a Male European-American Biblical Scholar." In *The Personal Voice in Biblical Interpretation,* edited by Ingrid Rosa Kitzberger, 12–23. London: Routledge, 1999.

Polaski, Donald C. "What Will Ye See in the Shulammite? Women, Power and Panopticism in the Song of Songs." *Biblical Interpretation* 5.1 (1997) 64–81.

———. "Where Men are Men and Women are Women? The Song of Songs and Gender." *Review and Expositor* 105 (2008) 435–51.

Raphael, Melissa. "'Refresh Me with Apples, For I Am Faint with Love' (Song of Songs 2.5): Jewish Feminism, Mystical Theology and the Sexual Imaginary." In *The Good News of the Body: Sexual Theology and Feminism,* edited by L. Isherwood, 54–72. Sheffield, UK: Sheffield Academic, 2000.

Setel, T. Drorah. "Prophets and Pornography: Female Sexual Imagery in Hosea." In *A Feminist Companion to the Song of Songs,* edited by Athalya Brenner, 143–55. Sheffield, UK: Sheffield Academic, 1993.

Trible, Phyllis. "Depatriarchalizing in Biblical Interpretation." *Journal for the American Academy of Religion* 41 (1973) 30–48.

———. "Feminist Hermeneutics and Biblical Studies." *Christian Century,* Feb 3–10 1982. Page numbers are from www.religion-online.org/showarticle.asp?title+1281. Accessed 10 June 2010.

———. "Fives Loaves and Two Fishes: Feminist Hermeneutics and Biblical Theology." *Theological Studies* 50 (1989) 279–95.

———. "Love's Lyrics Redeemed." In *God and the Rhetoric of Sexuality,* 144–65. Philadelphia: Fortress, 1978.

———. "Overture for a Biblical Feminist Theology." In *Old Testament Theology: Flowering and Future,* edited by Ben C. Ollenburger, 399–408. Winona Lake, IN: Eisenbrauns, 2004.

———. *Texts of Terror: Literary-Feminist Readings of Biblical Narratives.* Philadelphia: Fortress, 1984.

van Dijk-Hemmes, Fokkelien. "The Imagination of Power and the Power of Imagination: An Intertextual Analysis of Two Biblical Love Songs: The Song of Songs and Hosea." *Journal for the Study of the Old Testament* 44 (1989) 75–88.

———. "Traces of Women's Texts in the Hebrew Bible." In *On Gendering Texts: Female and Male Voices in the Hebrew Bible*, edited by Athalya Brenner and Fokkelien van-Dijk Hemmes, 17–112. Leiden: Brill, 1991.

Walsh, Carey Ellen. "Woman's Voice in the Canon: 'A Mare among Pharaoh's Chariots': Locating Female Desire in Androcentric Texts: Constrictions and Escape Valves." In *Exquisite Desire: Religion, the Erotic, and the Song of Songs*, 135–58. Minneapolis: Augsburg Fortress, 2000.

Weems, Renita J. *Just a Sister Away: A Womanist Vision of Women's Relationships in the Bible,* San Diego: LuraMedia, 1988.

———. "Reading *Her* Way through the Struggle: African American Women and the Bible." *Stony the Road We Trod: African American Biblical Interpretation,* edited by Cain Hope Felder, 57–77. Minneapolis: Fortress, 1991.

———. "Re-Reading for Liberation: African American Women and the Bible." In *Voices from the Margin: Interpreting the Bible in the Third World*, 3rd edn., edited by R. S. Sugirtharajah, 27–39. Maryknoll, NY: Orbis, 2006.

———. "Song of Songs." In *Women's Bible Commentary (expanded edition)*, edited by Carol A. Newsom and Sharon H. Ringe, 156–60. Louisville, KY: Westminster John Knox, 1998.

———. "The Song of Songs: Introduction, Commentary, and Reflections." In *The New Interpreter's Bible*, vol. V, 362–434. Nashville: Abingdon, 1997.

———. *What Matters Most: Ten Lessons in Living Passionately from the Song of Solomon.* West Bloomfield, NY: Warner, 2004.

Yarber, Angela. "Undulating the Holy? Returning the Sacred to Our Dancing Bodies: Song of Songs 7:1–4." *Review and Expositor* 105 (2008) 471–80.

9

Justice at the Crossroads

The Book of Lamentations and Feminist Discourse

HEATH A. THOMAS

INTRODUCTION

THE ISSUE OF JUSTICE lies at the heart of the theology of Lamentations, and it is here that feminist approaches engage the book. Although it should be borne in mind that there is no one feminist interpretation, but rather diverse feminist *interpretations*, Doob Sakenfeld rightly notes, "A feminist, broadly speaking, is one who seeks justice and equality for all people and who is especially concerned for the fate of women—all women—in the midst of 'all people.'"[1]

This definition is not exhaustive, and at present in the discipline there is a drive to expand the horizons and semantics of "feminist analysis," differentiating objectives on the basis of class, ethnicity, and social location, amongst other categories. This is true especially in literary theory, social theory, political theory, and some forms of biblical interpretation.[2] Feminist scholarship on Lamentations generally lacks such detailed critical discussions. Rather, these works tend to relate patriarchal oppression in the text or explore women or women's voice in Lamentations.[3]

1. Doob Sakenfeld, "Feminist Perspectives on Bible and Theology," 5.

2. Cf. "Feminist and Womanist Criticism," in *The Postmodern Bible*, 225–71.

3. Meyers, ed., *Women in Scripture*, 214–15, 284, 316, 328, 333–34, 340, 518–20, 538.

Nonetheless, these studies still exhibit a concern for "justice" and "equality" delineated in Doob Sakenfeld's definition. Implicitly they ask a set of interrelated theological questions: "Is the presentation of God patriarchal and so unjust in Lamentations?" "Has God acted in a just manner towards his people in punishing them for their sins?" "Is the presentation of the feminine just in Lamentations?" Answers to these questions remain contentious due in part to the variety of feminist approaches on the one hand and the complexity of Lamentations' poetry on the other. Both will be explored below.

A further complication lay in the meaning of "justice" intended in Doob Sakenfeld's definition. What does this term intend in feminist discourse, how is it measured, and what is its goal? Proper thinking here remains crucial for rightly establishing criteria for virtues like "justice" in critical discourse and in practice. As Gardner and MacIntyre maintain, for any discussion of "justice" in today's world, when the very meaning of the term as a theoretical concept remains underdetermined and contested, any concord on agreed upon rules for establishing or questioning justice in practice is impossible.[4]

I wish to press this point a bit in the course of this essay. Doob Sakenfeld, Schüssler Fiorenza, and Tolbert all agree that for feminist interpretation to proceed, "the place of women's experience" plays a crucial role in articulating the substance of feminist critique and plays a vital role for constructing a notion of justice.[5] For in/justice to be identified in the Bible, it must first be encountered and experienced by women.[6] But on what definition, criteria, or end-goal is this construction formulated and given currency? If Lamentations' notion of justice is not endorsed by feminist discourse, then is it the fault of the biblical text or is it simply a necessary outcome of pre-determined philosophical underpinnings deriving from another ground of rationality by feminist interlocutors?[7] Moreover, who adjudicates which understanding of justice is the right one? Or in light of potential options for justice as a concept in the bibli-

---

4. Gardner, *Justice and Christian Ethics*, 13; MacIntyre, *Whose Justice? Which Rationality?*, 1–11, 349–403.

5. Doob Sakenfeld, "Feminist Perspectives," 6–9; Schüssler Fiorenza, *In Memory of Her*, 32; Tolbert, "Defining the Problem," 119–21.

6. The same could be said of any marginalized reader. See *The Postmodern Bible*, 226–27.

7. The substance of MacIntyre's project in *Whose Justice* applies to the questions raised here.

cal text and/or feminist discourse, is one simply left to choose which conception is useful, workable, or virtuous in the marketplace of ideas?[8]

Once upon a time theological and/or philosophical prolegomena were commonplace in biblical studies, although this is not the case today. Yet philosophical thinking needs to be re-habituated to a degree, so that differences or agreements in principle between the biblical text and feminist interlocutors on concepts like justice may be clarified at root and branch. Only then is it proper to speak of in/justice in the biblical text, and the consequent adoption or rejection of such conceptions by the interpreter.[9] Such thinking will be done in this essay by grounding our understanding and end-goal of the meaning of justice from the context in which the book of Lamentations lives and breathes—the Old Testament.

This essay aims to assess feminist interpretation(s) of Lamentations and compare these renderings with an approach that interprets Lamentations within an OT theological context. The rationale behind the structure of this assessment lies in an evangelical hermeneutic that sees the Bible (even the difficult bits) as a word from that engages and confronts the reader as a good word.[10] As such, it is sensible to engage feminist analyses alongside the conception of justice found in the broader OT and Lamentations. In what follows, I shall briefly assess varieties of "feminist interpretation" as well as its deployment in Lamentations research, and query the views of justice in Lamentations from feminist scholarship. It will then be in place to render the justice of God in Lamentations within the context of the larger OT. I shall then contrast these findings against the view(s) of justice held up in feminist readings of Lamentations. From this basis I shall offer some concluding thoughts concerning the nature of justice in feminist discourse on Lamentations.

VARIETIES OF FEMINIST APPROACHES

To begin it may prove useful to distinguish between "feminist," "female," and "feminine," for these three terms are not coterminous. Moi explains

---

8. These represent three major philosophical strands in the construction of a concept of justice. Cf. Sandel, *Justice*.

9. John Barton makes a similar point on feminist analysis in *The Nature of Biblical Criticism*, 159–61.

10. Cf. the discussion on Calvin and Barth on Scripture in MacDonald and Trueman, eds., *Calvin, Barth, and Reformed Theology*, 149–77.

that the first represents a political position, the second is a matter of biology, and the third is a social and cultural construct; collapsing the second and third terms comprises substance for some feminist discourse.[11] Each of these terms has a part to play in the discussion. For example, Barry argues that feminist criticism of the 1970s especially exposed "mechanisms of patriarchy, that is, the cultural 'mind-set' in men and women which perpetuated sexual inequality."[12] The mind-set as well as social structure of sexual inequality is deemed as unjust and follows the rationality of Doob-Sakenfeld's understanding of equality and justice above. This perspective espouses a democratic pluralism where humans are seen to be of equal value and have equal rights to habits of life. Experiences of inequality or injustice that arise when reading the Bible thus provides a foundation from which one may launch a feminist critique.

Second, feminists may critique the thought that what is culturally reckoned to be "feminine" ought to be equated with the biological designation "female." For example, conventions of women engaging in household duties are equated with a biological reality—to be a "female" is to work in the home. This conflation may come with disastrous effects, namely the degradation, subjugation, or oppression of women. Schüssler Fiorenza, whose outline for feminist biblical interpretation springs from the experience of women's liberation from oppression, recognized this particularly in terms of patriarchal coercion in biblical and theological discourse.[13] Feminist approaches are figured as inherently *liberative* from injustice(s), and accord with Trible's designation of feminism. Rather than a narrow focus upon women as such, feminism (and thereby feminist interpretation) remains inherently social and political, functioning as "a critique of culture in light of misogyny [hatred or distain for women, whether implicit or explicit]."[14] A feminist approach in this vein then redresses such degradation or eclipse and works to enact justice and liberate the woman's perspective from oppression. In this thread of feminist interpretation, the experience of injustice lay central—the interpreter perceives misogyny in a biblical text or in the reception of a biblical text that has led to the eclipse, obfuscation, or

11. Moi, "Feminist, female, feminine," 115–32.
12. Barry, *Beginning Theory*, 122.
13. Schüssler Fiorenza, *In Memory of Her*, 32.
14. Trible, *God and The Rhetoric of Sexuality*, 7.

oppression of women or women's voices. Feminist critique then, works to counteract this unjust eclipse and construct a new reality.

Whilst the above description remains viable, it should not be transformed into a caricature of *all* feminist approaches. Some feminist analysis investigates the place of women writers in the academic guild (and women's place in the literary canon). Others explore distinctive characteristics of women's creativity, style, and imagination. Finally, some feminist studies endeavor to formulate distinctively feminine theories of text and gender-based textualities.[15]

It is in place now to move to feminist readings of Lamentations. At once one may see the different threads identified above. In terms of Lamentations research, some interpreters work to identify misogyny (latent or explicit forms of hatred of women) in the book and explicitly read against the text, working to excise such oppression from cultural currency as a form of injustice (Guest and Seidman, below). Still others simply hear from feminist approaches, allowing the political edge that arises from them to inform their reading of Lamentations as a whole (O'Connor, Mandolfo, and Maier). One also may note an approach that reads the biblical text with fidelity, from the standpoint of a believing "woman's perspective" (Snow-Flesher).[16] Neglected feminine images and metaphors are explored more fully and integrated into a more coherent interpretation of the book. Snow-Flesher, O'Connor, Mandolfo, and Maier attempt to rehabilitate Lamentations as a just word from God, albeit starting from different theological/philosophical starting points and adopting different critical approaches. These threads of feminist interpretation shall be explored before situating Lamentations within its Old Testament context.

---

15. Richter, "Feminist Literary Criticism," 1063–64. Richter states that these three approaches are considered by some to present an evolutionary sequence, the last of which representing the last phase of development. He rightly argues, however, that this developmental view remains deficient on a number of grounds ("Feminist Literary Criticism," 1064). The history of feminist approaches is less tidy than this. Brenner and Fontaine, eds., *A Feminist Companion to Reading the Bible*.

16. So argue Clark Kroeger and Evans, "Preface: Why a Woman's Bible Commentary?," xiii. Inevitably, this enterprise becomes problematic, as a "woman's perspective," identified as such, becomes a boundary marker that may serve to solidify inherent patriarchal norms—this is at least a critique from a distinctive feminist ideology. Moreover, the notion of "woman" can easily be reduced to naïve essentialism. See the recent work by Moi, "'I am not a woman writer'," 259–71.

LAMENTATIONS: AN UNJUST GOD, AN UNJUST TEXT

Some explicitly feminist interpretations exemplify highly political readings of its poetry, reading against the text and advocating that the poetry stands as unjust and immoral literature. The logic follows that reading against the (Hebrew) Bible is necessary because: it exploits and abuses the feminine in its poetry, or it promotes an ideology that justifies and exemplifies female abuse via the (Hebrew) Bible's place as holy scripture in both Jewish and Christian traditions. Such exploitation and abuse become, in effect, "God's Word." Feminist approaches resist and contravene this unjust divine vindication.

Seidman's Jewish exploration of Lamentations resists the book's message and theology. Divine complicity in the violent destruction of feminine city of Jerusalem leads her to state of God: "If we forgive him, it is because we are too exhausted to do otherwise."[17] She does not want to forgive God but, in a sense, to abandon him. Seidman's perception that Lamentations justifies divine abuse (via theodicy)[18] leads her to wish for a bonfire in which all the books of destruction and abuse—the book of Lamentations included—could be thrown. From this she gains the title of her essay, "Burning the Book of Lamentations."

One notes a lack of rigorous scholarly and feminist engagement from Seidman, but this is not necessarily a drawback as hers is a testimony of a Jewish woman dealing with the liturgy of Tisha b'Ab and the text of Lamentations. Thus "feminist discourse" expands beyond scholarly boundaries. However, congruent with feminist approaches, Seidman exposes gender inequality and subjugation—she exposes a Jewish woman's experience of injustice wrought through the text of Lamentations.

Guest's scholarly analysis of theology in Lamentations derives from her concern to counter what she sees as a cycle of degradation of the feminine in the book. The justification of divine violence (theodicy), as well as masculine concealment behind the naked, abused, raped, and humiliated image of the woman, persists in the ideology of the author of Lamentations, the history of (mostly male) commentary of the book, as well as in God himself. This must be contravened.[19] Hers is an addition to the well-known discussion of porno-prophetics, and Guest traces how

---

17. Seidman, "Burning the Book of Lamentations," 288.

18. Theodicy is a constructed defense of God's actions towards his creation. For a fuller explanation as it relates to Lamentations, see below.

19. Guest, "Hiding Behind the Naked Women in Lamentations," 413.

personified Jerusalem is depicted as battered and the object of blame in Lamentations: she is raped (Lam 1:10), she is accused of guilt (Lam 1:5, 8), and she confesses guilt (Lam 1:14, 18, 20). Lamentations confirms the image of a battered woman to advance its rhetoric about Jerusalem's sin.

She sees that mostly male commentators have reduced the pain and violation of the feminine, especially the rape in Lam 1:10, to advance the theology of just punishment. Jerusalem got what she deserved because of her sin. God too is implicated in abusing the feminine to advance the rhetoric of the city's sinfulness. Within the account of rape of Lam 1:10, Guest argues that God is implicated in this violation and justified for it through a form of theodicy. YHWH is justified, even in rape, because the city deserved punishment for sin.

Justified violence toward the feminine leads Guest to read against the text, invalidating its claims. She argues that "an appropriate response to the personification of Zion/Woman in Lamentations is one of resistance to the text and a female solidarity" with ancient women in the situation of oppressive abuse.[20] She reads against those who created the metaphor of a personified city as female because she feels that these patriarchal "masterminds" justify their own oppressive worldview at the expense of the female, making "Zion/Woman the elected victim, the offering given up on their behalf" in Lamentations.[21] This abuse of the female can then extend outward, to those who read and comment on the text. As a result, Guest concludes that the image of Jerusalem as a battered and abused city, the very personification itself, "must be rejected: literary oppression of women should not be continued."[22]

Guest rightly brings attention to the pain and destructiveness presented in the book. However she paints far too monochrome a portrait of the book's theology. For instance, Guest under-reads the complexity of the issue of blame by placing it *directly* upon the female scapegoat, Jerusalem personified. She is certainly correct that Lamentations 1–2 present the feminine personification of the city as battered, isolated, and abused.

Even so, if one evades blame by hiding behind the female figure in Lamentations, then there are other persons behind whom the poet hides as well. Blame for the disaster is spread around quite a bit and the

20. Ibid., 427.
21. Ibid., 430.
22. Ibid., 444.

feminine is not singled out. The man (*geber*) of Lamentations 3 is also to blame for the punishment, especially in 3:39: "Why should a living human being, a man [*geber*], complain about his punishment for sin?" Lee argues that this works to implicate the man in blame for the punishment of exile.[23] Lee further argues that Lam 4:13–15 contains an extended tirade against the leaders of Jerusalem, the priests and prophets, who are defiled and impure because they shed innocent blood, enraging the deity. The poetry blames the male leadership for the downfall of Jerusalem here.[24] A similar critique is leveled at the male prophets in Lam 2:14, in which they have "seen for you [Jerusalem] false and deceptive visions; they did not expose your iniquity so as to restore your fortunes. They saw oracles that were false and misleading." Thus blame is spread around, not completely isolated to the female figure, though the female figure of Dear Zion certainly is implicated. So if one argues oppression and abuse as something to be excised, one must discard a good deal more than what Guest demands.

In addition, the theological presentation of theodicy is not as straightforward as Guest supposes. The Lord is not necessarily justified *carte blanche* at the expense of the feminine. Rather, as noted in the introduction to this essay, a strong protest element functions in the poetry of the book. Lamentations 2:20 sees Dear Zion confronting God in his activity. The protest impulse weaves into the fabric of verse and raises questions about the justice of God rather than simply or niavely affirming it. The poetry is not so unequivocally oriented towards theodicy that the feminine city must be "re-membered" as Guest suggests. Whilst helpfully elucidating the pain witnessed in Lamentations as well as a masculine bias in the commentary tradition, Guest obscures the complexity and ambiguity of the book's theology.

And yet both Guest and Seidman's interpretations are figured to be in some way liberative and accord with resistant feminist interpretations, as discussed above. On this reading the politics and social dynamics at work in the creation and reception of Lamentations create an oppressive situation for women, a situation that must be contravened by surfacing the subjugation. The desire to expose this, however, may come at the price of under-reading the poems and censoring their ambiguity and force *qua* poetry.

23. Lee, *The Singers of Lamentations*, 175.
24. Ibid., 186–89.

Moreover, one may press what is the end-goal of this conception of justice. What is its aim and along which lines of rationality is it established? In the discussion of Lamentations within its canonical framework, the cries of Zion are answered by God, and he is proven to be loving and just, at least according to the logic of Isaiah[25] and Zechariah. Seidman and Guest provide neither the rationality nor the context of their thinking on polarities like justice/injustice which gives rise other questions about the rational framework on which their interpretations of Lamentations rest.

Even if one wants to argue that the recognition of "injustice" in Lamentations arises from women's experience of reading it, one must still supply rationality to the very conception of justice that habituates the critique. Neither Guest nor Seidman, to my mind, have accomplished this. This is not to say that their interpretations are necessarily out of bounds *per se* even though I have highlighted some of their weaknesses above. But it nonetheless is true that these readings remain deficient by resting upon an unstated rationality and understanding of justice. Further, on the logic of the prayers of Zion, the feminine voice contests the very kind of simplistic theodicy advocated by Guest and Seidman for Lamentations, raising questions about the cogency of their interpretations.

LAMENTATIONS: GRASPING FOR A (JUST) WORD FROM GOD

Other contributions in Lamentations research are concerned with recognizing gender bias and the implications that arise hermenetuically and theologically therefrom (O'Connor), learning from feminist criticism and incorporating it into their own fabric of analysis (Mandolfo), or simply trying to read Lamentations with a "women's perspective" and from the perspective of (evangelical) Christian faith (Snow Flesher).[26] With the exception of the monographs of Mandolfo and O'Connor, these works do not carry the level of sophistication of Guest's article nor do they evince critical awareness of feminist discourse. This is, of course, an immediate drawback, but to be fair they do not aim (except

---

25. Maier, *Daughter Zion, Mother Zion*, 158–80.

26. O'Connor, "Lamentations," 187–91; O'Connor, *Lamentations and the Tears of the World*; Mandolfo, *Daughter Zion Talks Back to the Prophets*; Snow Flesher, "Lamentations," 392–95.

in the case of the monographs) at the level of scholarly critical discourse. O'Connor's and Snow Flesher's articles appear in one-volume women's Bible commentaries, where brevity is a necessity. The monographs, however, present an interesting mix of receptions of feminist discourse. O'Connor's *Lamentations and the Tears of the World* is clearly aware of feminist discourse, but does not demonstrate resistant feminist analysis in the vein of Guest. Rather, she reads Lamentations critically, but with fidelity. Theology may only be constructed after working through the feminine voice and its abuse in Lamentations.

O'Connor warns readers to be aware that in the book's imagery and in its structure Lamentations exhibits biases against women. Futher, these biases reflect and affirm an inherent subordination of women. One example demonstrates her view. Lamentations' favourite term for Jerusalem is "Daughter Zion," a personfication of the city as a woman. This term occurs pervasively in Lamentations and conveys overtones of dignity (associated with the loftiness of the capital city and temple therein), but also conceptually subordinates the female city to the male deity (whether as daughter or as wife). Furthermore, in Lamentations, Daughter Zion is scorned, raped, and said to be complicit in these experiences. These features, argues O'Connor, remain inherently harmful for women.[27]

Further, O'Connor sees in the structure of Lamentations gender bias. In its poetry, the concept of hope necessarily filters through a prism of masculinity and androcentrism. She argues that where the masculine figure of the "suffering/strong man" of Lamentations 3 appears and speaks (the central chapter of the book), hope begins to surface in the poetry. Likewise, when the community speaks in Lamentations 5 (the final chapter of the book), the feminine voice of Lamentations 1–2 recedes. Here O'Connor sees an inherent gender prejudice that stifles feminine voices in Lamentations.[28]

Despite these indications, O'Connor is able to develop a theology of "witness" from Lamentations, especially from the voice of Daughter Zion. In *Lamentations and the Tears of the World*, she argues the poetry begs God to witness their pain and situation of disaster. O'Connor marks Lam 2:20, where Daughter Zion stridently questions and protests God's

---

27. O'Connor, "Lamentations," 188–89.
28. Ibid., 189–90.

justice in his acts of slaughter and punishment. Far from allowing what she terms as Jerusalem's "abuse" to go unchecked, O'Connor argues that

> the book's speakers stand up, resist, shout in protest, and fearlessly risk further antagonizing the deity. They do not accept abuse passively. They are voices of a people with nothing left to lose, and they find speech, face horror upon horror, and resist unsatisfactory interpretations offered by their theological tradition. From the authority of experience, they adopt a critical view and appraise and reappraise their situation. The result is a vast rupture in their relationship with God, yet they hold on to God, and in that holding they clear space for new ways to meet God.[29]

The fearless contestation of Daughter Zion against the LORD's activity provides the means by which modern women may pray and use Lamentations. In contrast to Guest and Seidman, O'Connor attempts to rehabilitate Lamentations into the life of faith via her theology of "witness" through the voice of Daughter Zion. In this way, hers is not a *resistant* interpretation of Lamentations, but rather an approach that attempts to critically read the book with fidelity, arrived at only and through a reading that accounts for the abuse and possibilities of the feminine voice in the book.

Maier's approach that sees Zion as a mode of resistance generally coheres with the analysis of O'Connor, but Maier explores the presentation of Daughter Zion in Lamentations on the basis of sacred space, gender, and the body. She discovers that Lamentations' deployment of the feminine personification effectively serves as a medium to mourn the destruction of the city, to engage God through prayer (in the voice of Daughter Zion), and to pave the way for the city as a positive symbol which the people might embrace. Maier sees that the historical reception of the image of Daughter Zion, especially on display in Lamentations, is transformed into a mother for her abused people especially in Isaiah 40–66. Now while it may be argued that there is an inherent subordination of the female to the male in this imagery, it is nonetheless the true that the abused woman in Lamentations *is* addressed in restoration. Further, for Maier, the presentation of Zion as a mother is not a subordination-image as much as it is a religious symbol that depicts care, welfare, refuge, and glory. The mother image in the texts that receive Lamentations'

---

29. O'Connor, *Lamentations and the Tears of the World*, 123. See also O'Connor, "Lamentations," 190–91.

feminine imagery becomes a symbol of the vital body for the people where they are fed and find a space of rest.

Effectively, then, in the reception of Lamentations, the prophets especially transform the chastened "whore" of Lamentations into an expanded female image, with new roles and a glorified image. The canonical and historical presentation of Lamentations in the OT depicts Lamentations' moment of pain as one stop along the journey in relationship with God—from suffering to glorification.[30] Because Zion as a battered mother cries out to God on behalf of her children (people), "The wounded body of Jerusalem" serves as a signal against the hopeless situation of exile and "an unwillingness to surrender."[31] Although she is wounded and broken, she lives on. As she lives, she clears space for a broken people to live before God.

Mandolfo does not attempt to apply a feminist hermeneutic to her interpretation of Lamentations, but rather learns from the political edge of feminist analyses to inform her reading. In this way, feminist approaches are her conversation partners in the attempt to elucidate "dialogic theology" in Lamentations.[32] Mandolfo employs the literary theory of Russian theorist Mikhail Bakhtin, who argued that texts speak beautifully when they speak with many voices (polyvalence) rather than with one voice (monologism). The interaction of the many voices in a work of art is "dialogism."

Mandolfo teases out how this dialogic quality might be worked out in the prophets (Ezekiel, Jeremiah, Isaiah 40–66), who speak for God (the father/husband), and Lamentations 1–2, whose speech is that of Daughter Zion (the daughter/wife). She says, "If we care about justice, we must be careful not to approach the Bible, in Bakhtinian terms, as the monologic 'word of the father' that in the end justifies divine violence."[33] Lamentations provides a counter-voice to the divine violence in the prophets through its feminine, resistant voice against God (e.g., Lam 2:20). Her aim is not to overturn the Bible or do away with it *per se*, but rather to refigure concretized, essentialist, notions of justice and contest them through the voice Daughter Zion's protestation.

---

30. Maier, *Daughter Zion, Mother Zion*.
31. Ibid., 152.
32. Mandolfo, *Daughter Zion Talks Back to the Prophets*, 3.
33. Ibid., 5.

Mandolfo explores, like O'Connor, the use of the marriage metaphor in Lamentations, its tacit power relations (male subjugates female), and ultimately aims to dethrone biblical authority as presently construed as the "Word of God" and reify a new vision of biblical authority as the "words of God."[34] Divine silence to the cries of Daughter Zion marks Lamentations 1–2, as explored above. Rather than simply affirming this reality, Mandolfo figures Lamentations as Daughter Zion's response to God's voice heard in the prophets that accuse her of wantonness and sin. By attending to the feminine voice in Lamentations in dialogic interaction with the prophets, a full-fledged voice is constructed and "woman" reclaims her agency. Daughter Zion in Lamentations then, subverts the voice of God in the prophets, exposing the unjust construction of Zion therein and challenging it.[35] Mandolfo effectively destabilizes the objectification of "woman" and restores "woman" to a cogent subject, a responsible agent.[36]

Although dependent upon Mandolfo's insights and agreeing that Lamentations speaks back to the prophets as a kind of dialogic counter-testimony, Tiemeyer construes her hermeneutic framework differently than Mandolfo. Hers is broadly evangelical, and thereby she reads the Bible—the whole of it—as God's word and therefore authoritative for life and practice. But Tiemeyer is nuanced. She, too, learns from the political edge of feminist and even post-Holocaust hermeneutics, but finds in them a means to surface resistant readings in the text that the text itself authorizes. In this, she reads with the grain of the text rather than against it. In her analysis, Lamentations is a resistant voice that counterbalances the horrific imagery of divine violence in Ezekiel. She finds Lamentations authorizes a counter-testimony to the theodicy presented in the prophets . . . but this resistant voice also is authorized by God as a good word.[37]

Finally, one may see a rather different kind of feminist analysis in Snow Flesher's work on Lamentations. Hers comports broadly with evangelical hermeneutics. The commentary in which Snow Flesher writes is "written by women of faith who believe that all Scripture is

---

34. Ibid., 3–28.

35. Ibid., 81–102.

36. Ibid., 82–83. For corollary in feminist discourse, see Castelli, Moore, Phillips and Schwartz, eds., "Feminist and Womanist Criticism," 234–44.

37. Tiemeyer, "To Read—Or Not to Read—Ezekiel as Christian Scripture," 481–88.

inspired by God and given for the benefit of humanity. The contributors have examined the difficult texts from a 'hermeneutic of faith,' a conviction that the Scriptures are meant for healing rather than hurt, for affirmation of all persons, especially those who are oppressed."[38]

From this perspective, the differences between this work and those of Mandolfo, O'Connor, Guest, or Seidman become apparent. Yet with a concern for a commentary written with the chosen perspective of that of "women," the editors (Clark C. Kroeger and Evans) immediately fragment naïve essentialism to a degree, emphasizing the different *kinds* of voices present in "women's perspective": different social locations, ethnicities, and ecclesiastical backgrounds. Thus theirs cannot be identified as naïve, but rather guided by a view of the Bible that sees it as fundamentally helpful as a good word from God, especially when received in the context of (a community of) women and interpreted in that light.

Snow Flesher, like O'Connor, takes note of the feminine imagery in Lamentations. However, she argues differently that the imagery of Daughter Zion in Lamentations is a means to persuade God to deliver Jerusalem from distress, rather than a means to shame the people to repentance (as in the prophets).[39] Counter to Guest and Seidman in particular, Snow Flesher reads Lamentations as a means of fidelity to God: faithful interpretation of Lamentations *reads with* Daughter Zion and *cries out* to God on behalf of sufferers—even if/when the deity has caused the suffering. However, whilst Guest and Seidman reject such masculine abuse, Snow Flesher's conclusion is akin to, though not identical with, O'Connor's. Her approach runs counter to Mandolfo's program, for Snow Flesher embraces the biblical text of Lamentations as authoritative and helpful *as it is*, whilst Mandolfo wants to *recast* Lamentations' (and the prophets') "word of the father" and its nature as biblical authority, but without discarding them as does Seidman. Snow Flesher's analysis comes closer to Tiemeyer but in my estimation does not share the nuance of Tiemeyer's dialogic reading.

LAMENTATIONS AND JUSTICE IN AN OT CONTEXT

One notes in the analysis above a variety of feminist readings of Lamentations. On the one hand, Lamentations is decried as unjust by

---

38. Clark Kroeger and Evans, "Preface: Why a Woman's Bible Commentary?" xiv.
39. Snow Flesher, "Lamentations," 392.

Guest and yet affirmed by Tiemeyer and Snow Flesher. On the other hand are the mediating voices of O'Connor and Mandolfo that affirm the text of Lamentations as Scripture, but attempt to rehabilitate it with the perceived violence and injustice recalibrated. Ironically, despite the richness of the conversation in feminist hermeneutics, it is possible to lose the voice of Lamentations in the discussion. Further, it is essential to rightly delineate the theological presentation of justice both in the book and in its larger OT context. It is to this I now turn.

To address Lamentations' presentation of justice, it is in place to explain what is intended here by the very term itself. Justice here intends a double focus and derives from the OT. Its very meaning is consequent upon God and his actions towards his created order, and secondly upon humans' actions towards God and others within his created order. Gardner rightly suggests that "In Judaism and Christianity, God is just and righteous. Not only is he just in his relationships with humankind; he also requires justice in the human, earthly community."[40] Justice intends the right dealings of God towards his creation (humanity included), with so that his purposes of a peaceful and righteous society living before him might be achieved.

On this understanding, the meaning of justice is at once theocentric and active. Justice is a matter of judicial enactment in which God sets order to the world and maintains that order.[41] The OT presents justice as derivative from the person of God—justice cannot be understood or embraced without God, for "The LORD is known by his justice" (Ps 9:17); "For the LORD is a God of justice" (Isa 30:18b).

Likewise, the theocentricity of justice entails within it a relational aspect.[42] Justice is a manifestation of God's right dealings between himself and his creation, thus justice is *enacted*. "The LORD loves righteousness and justice; the earth is full of his unfailing love" (Ps 33:5). "Righteousness and justice are the foundation of your throne; covenantal loving-kindness and faithfulness surround your presence" (Ps 89:15). This last verse is situated within a hymn that extols God's ordinance of creation, including those who relate to God well in his created order. The language here should not be confused with abstract divine attributes,

---

40. Gardner, *Justice*, 5.
41. O'Donovan, *The Desire of the Nations*, 37–41.
42. Gardner, *Justice*, 48–9; Bovati, *Re-Establishing Justice*, 19–20.

but rather summary statements of real "earthy" manifestations of God's right dealings with humanity in creation.

Further, when it appears that the relationship between God and his world is amiss, the deity is addressed directly in order to set the just world right again, or re-establish justice. "You have seen O YHWH, my wrongs; judge my cause!" (Lam 3:59). In this last verse, the same Hebrew root for the word "justice" (špṭ) is employed in the appeal, signifying in part the belief that God will respond in justice: "judge (špṭ) my cause (špṭ)!"[43] The theocentric, active aspect of justice is important for the meaning intended here.

But in addition to the theocentricity of justice, one must also include a communal facet, as indicated by Gardner.[44] The reality of God's justice is, for the OT, to be extended outward to human community. Human interaction with others in community should be reflective or imitative of the justice God exerts in his creation. Community should live well into the order that God has established in justice. This human enactment of justice toward God and others may be administered in and through wise actions in a rather informal way (biblical wisdom), through proper enactment of the cultic life (sacrifices), or through proper adherence to God's instruction including adherence to law (legal codes). At any rate, for the OT the whole of life is the arena for just action, not simply the legal sphere.[45]

Further, enacting justice is achieved through societal structures functioning rightly. Judges will avoid bribes and pursue justice alone (Deut 16:19–20). Kings will adhere to God's teaching (Deut 17:18–20) and request divine wisdom to rule righteously (Ps 72:1–2; 1 Kgs 10:9; 2 Chr 9:8). The people writ large will pursue right relationships with one another (Ps 112:5; Prov 21:15; 29:7) and live well upon the land that God has given them. Justice is required in all segments of society, as God is just in all of his doings (Isa 1:17; 5:16; 56:1; Hos 12:6; Amos 5:15, 24; Zech 7:9). Each of these "administrations" of justice, when properly enacted, reflect divine justice and endorse a life of blessing, goodness, and peace.[46]

---

43. See the comments of O'Donovan on prayer and its relationship to justice in *The Desire of the Nations*, 38.

44. Gardner, *Justice*, 29–53, esp. 49–50.

45. McConville, *God and Earthly Power*, 94–96.

46. Gardner rightly affirms that this life of blessing, goodness, and peace is one in which God reigns supremely in society, one in which one loves one's neighbor, and

From this backdrop it is in place to return to the question of Lamentations and justice. Does Lamentations present a theology of justice? Yes. On its own testimony Lamentations affirms God's just activity in relation to his people. Lamentations 1:5 clearly states, "Her [Jerusalem's] foes have become her head; her enemies rest easy. For YHWH made her suffer on account of the greatness of her criminal acts." Here, the term "criminal acts" (*pĕšāʿêhā*) indicates a willful breach of normative rule and supplies evidence that God's actions ("YHWH made her suffer") represent just punitive action against her, albeit cast in the emotive terminology of suffering (*hôgāh*). Further, Lam 1:18 affirms, "YHWH is in the right (*ṣaddîq*), for I rebelled against his mouth." This language spoken by Daughter Zion, specifically the through the term *ṣaddîq* "just/righteous/in the right," implies that God's activity—both his rights to enact punishment against his people as well as the mechanism or process by which he did so—stands as just. God has acted within a frame of just action.[47] Other passages within Lamentations confirm this view as well (e.g., Lam 1:3, 8–9, 20; 2:14; 3:39; 4:13; 5:7).

On this theology, God's justice stands affirmed through a covenantal-punitive scheme, informed theologically by the warnings of the prophets which called upon God's people to return to YHWH, else destruction would come.[48] Because God elected this people for a purpose, namely to be a "holy nation" and a "royal priesthood" (Exod 19:5–6),

---

one in which all humanity shares in a responsible life before God, especially the poor, weak, and enslaved. Gardner calls this last point the "equalitarian" or "inclusive" aspect of covenantal justice in the OT (*Justice*, 49–50). The only caveat that needs to be added here is that "equality" and "inclusivity" is permitted so long as those who are included (esp. the weak and powerless) rightly habituate themselves under God. One may object to this suggestion citing the example of resident aliens and/or foreign slaves in the Pentateuch. Although not covenant people, foreign slaves in Deuteronomic law receive a unique place in society (Deut 24:16–18) and were permitted to live upon the land, even if (presumably) they did not adhere to Yahweh worship. They may still follow other gods. But this point neglects the larger point that God's ultimate aim for the nations, according to the broad sweep of the OT, is that they would come to know God and live in a society of righteousness under his rule (cf. Isa 45:22–33; 55:3; 56:6–8). See Gardner, *Justice*, 34–48. Thus "inclusivity" and "equality" as concepts still entail certain limits.

47. It is a typical feature of guilty characters in biblical texts to employ a nominal phrase with the term *ṣaddîq* "just/righteous/in the right," to confess to covenantal breach. E.g., Exod 9:27; 2 Kgs 10:9; Ezra 9:15; Neh 9:33; Dan 9:14; Deut 32:4–5. See Bovati, *Re-Establishing Justice*, 103–4.

48. Renkema, *"Misschien is er Hoop"*, 156–77; 273. So too House, *Lamentations*.

Israel had a responsibility for holiness before God and faithful love and service to him and the nations.[49] Their rebellion against God's word (or "mouth" in Lam 1:18) marred their holiness and impeded their priestly responsibility to the nations. The result of this, inevitably, was punishment for transgression and sin, as the pre-exilic prophets had warned.[50] In short, Lamentations provides internal evidence that God is justified in his actions, which remain punitive, because the people had sinned against him.[51]

Moreover, within a canonical framework, Lamentations comprises part of a larger testimony of God's justice. As recent research has ably demonstrated, a variety of texts in the OT engage the theology of Lamentations and affirm that God is in control of his people, that he loves them, and that the punitive actions on display in Lamentations must be understood as only a moment in the full-sweep of Israel's history. The reversal of Lamentations in Zechariah 1–2 through inter-textual evocations reinforce the theological point that God reverses his people's despoliation and restores them in justice.[52] Further inter-textual connections between Lamentations and Isaiah confirm the justice of God in a broad canonical frame. As Tiemeyer affirms, "[A]s Lamentations speak [sic] from the heart of the people of Jerusalem, so the response in Is. xl–lv seeks to comfort them."[53]

Interaction between Lamentations, Isaiah and Zechariah reveals that within canonical presentation of God in his relationship to his people, YHWH is shown to be kind and restorative in and through judgment. He punished them to restore them into a faithful life before him and a re-established form of justice and peace between them. On

49. McConville, *God and Earthly Power*, 50–73.

50. For discussion, see Renkema, "*Misschien is er Hoop.*"

51. It is true that some may find this kind of reasoning on the concept of justice rather circular: God himself determines categories by which his own actions are judged. And yet it is in place to note that there is no value-neutral construal of justice that can be brought to bear in the discussion (we all must begin somewhere) and further that the circularity of the argument can be understood as "virtuous" rather than "vicious" on a full account. This is so because, as will be demonstrated below, the full OT presentation of justice reveals that there are moments when God himself actually may be called into account (as in Lamentations). Divine justice is not quarantined from critical scrutiny in the Bible (as Tiemeyer maintains in "To Read"). Criteria exist by which God may be called into account—in terms of his actions against other nations or even Israel.

52. Stead, "Sustained Allusion in Zechariah 1–2," 144–70.

53. Tiemeyer, "Geography and Textual Allusions," 367–85, esp. 385.

this understanding, "Lamentations, then, is not the final stop along the journey, but only a dark night before the dawn" in Israel's relationship with God.[54] The larger canon unequivocally confirms that God's activity towards his people and city indeed are rightly punitive in nature, but not final. Punitive action remains a step towards reconciliation and re-established justice between God and his people in the world.[55]

These indicators within the broader context of the OT provide a frame by which to define Lamentations' concept of justice. First, Lamentations' internal evidence affirms God's justice—both in his essence and the way that he enacts his punishment for sin. One way around this internal evidence has been to subdue its potency by emphasizing Lamentations' propensity for complaint language.[56] Whilst it is incontestable that Lamentations recurrently complains about God and enemies (Lam 1:9c, 21–22; 2:20–2; 3:19, 43–50, 59–66; 5:1–22), sometimes the complaints raised derive from distress over sin with the hope that God would see and relieve or forgive the petitioner (Lam 1:11a, 20a–b; 3:39–42).[57] Confession of human breach in sin reinforces divine justice.

Second, Lamentations' conception of justice is anchored within a larger biblical story in which God punishes and restores his people to reorient them into faithful life before him. Removing Lamentations from this hermeneutical and canonical context may artificially warp the essential historical and theological interaction set on display in the canonical form of the OT. Reading Lamentations apart from its canonical context, in fact, denies it of its proper reception history within the canon and truncates its voice.

And yet, as quickly as one recognizes this view of divine justice in Lamentations, the poetry tempers its force. Lamentations 2:20; 3:42; 3:59 amongst other texts in their own way question the integrity of God's dealings with his people. Lamentations 2:20 reads, "Look, O LORD, and consider to whom you have done this! Is it right that mothers consume

---

54. Thomas, *"Until He Looks Down and Sees,"* 18. Both Jewish and Christian receptions of Lamentations evince this impulse: ibid., 6, 20–21.

55. Bovati, *Re-Establishing Justice*, 30–61.

56. See esp. Middlemas, *The Troubles of Templeless Judah*, 197–228.

57. For Lam 1:11a as a confession of sin, see Thomas, "The Meaning of *zōlēlâ* (Lam 1:11c) One More Time." For Lamentations' prayer in general, see Renkema, *Lamentations*, 69–71, 337–43.

their own fruit, little ones raised to health? Is it right that priests and prophets be killed in the sanctuary of the LORD?" Daughter Zion here raises fundamental questions about God's interaction with his people. She protests that God has acted in such a way that cannibalism and slaughter is the outcome. Lamentations 3:42 goes a bit further in affirming that God's people have sinned, but contends that God has not done what he *should* have done—namely to forgive the people because that is his very nature as a forgiving and compassionate god. The man/community prays to God, "We have transgressed and rebelled, (but) You have not forgiven" (Lam 3:42).[58] Here one finds an alternative theological impulse to theodicy. Braiterman and Dobbs-Allsopp identify it as "antitheodicy," or refusing to justify the ways of God to his people.[59]

These are lament prayers, a form of speech that is prevalent in the OT. Job, Lamentations, Habakkuk, Jeremiah, and many of the prayer-forms in the Psalter all evince such lament to God. These prayers cry out to God about a situation of distress that, by all counts from the perspective of the petitioner, is out of joint with the way things ought to be. This situation raises fundamental questions about God's justice in ordering the world.[60] So the kind of speech that we find in Lamentations is typical in complaint prayer to God.[61] The prayers of Lam 2:20–22; 3:42; 3:59 are on par with the confrontational force of Job 3, Pss 44 and 88—strident prayer indeed.

In line with this logic, divine justice may be seen to be questioned, protested, or denied. From the perspective of feminist analysis, Zion's speech underscores the reality that the victim is not silent because the poetry *authorizes* her resistance through lament. Or in O'Connor's analysis, the voice of (feminine) Zion is a testimony of resistance. But not only is it *her* lament, on the logic of the personification of Zion in Lamentations, it is the speech of the broken community, comprised men and women, children and elders, young men and maidens. Each of these is represented in the book. Here the voice of the woman is privileged, then, over and against a distinctively masculine voice (e.g., Lamentations

---

58. See the helpful discussion of Dobbs-Allsopp, *Lamentations*, 123.

59. Braiterman, *(God) After Auschwitz*; Dobbs-Allsopp, *Lamentations*.

60. Job 3; 9:28–31; 10:2–22; 13:17–28; 14:1–22; 17:4; 30:20—31:40; Hab 1:2–4, 12–17; Jer 12:1–4; 15:10–14, 15–21; 17:14–18; 18:18–23; 20:7–18; Pss 17; 22; 44; 74; 88; 94; 109; 130.

61. Miller, *They Cried to the Lord*, 55–134.

3, with the voice of the man). This fact speaks against, or at the very least complicates, the interpretations of either Guest or Seidman delineated above.[62]

But what is the function of Zion's lament prayer? One may argue that it serves to sever the tie between God and justice, and to create space to not only protest against God but perhaps even slander him, using the descriptor of *theo-diabole* ("God-slander") by Middlemas.[63] But when rightly understood, lament prayer does quite the opposite.

Miller beautifully captures the essence of lament prayer when he argues that it is rhetorical speech designed to move God to respond and that leans upon a theology of divine justice to empower the appeals uttered.[64] The tacit belief in the justice of the Lord as the righteous judge of the earth enables his covenant people to challenge him on areas they perceive to be fundamentally unjust in life, as lament prayer often implies.[65] For lament prayer to function it tacitly depends upon the very covenant faithfulness and (theocentric) justice of God as described above to undergird its rhetoric. If God is not just or powerful to deliver and re-order creation in a good way, why pray to the deity at all? The world may be perceived as being disordered, but lament prayer depends upon the justice of God to set the world to rights once again.

As one considers the function of lament prayer as found in Lamentations, the perspective of this kind of speech becomes apparent. Lament prayer is *subjective* speech written from the viewpoint of the sufferer rather than an objective position outside the situation of distress. Differentiation between these perspectives remains crucial. If lament is indeed *objective* speech, then it functions as an indictment against God from the perspective of one who sees his or her situation objectively (and Middlemas is right—this is "God-slander"). This stance then provides the foundation that warrants protest (or indictment) against the Lord. The lamenter *knows* God's action or inaction is somehow unjust. But lament simply does not embody this objective perspective. It functions as subjective speech—grounded in a tacit belief in divine goodness, justice, and power—represented internally from the perspective of the sufferer.[66]

62. For a different view, see Frymer-Kensky, *Reading the Women of the Bible*, 335–38.
63. Middlemas, *The Troubles of Templeless Judah*, 212.
64. Miller, *They Cried to the Lord*, 57, 126.
65. Brueggemann, *Theology of the Old Testament*, 235–36.
66. See Westermann, *Die Klagelieder*, 84–89.

One may note that interrogatives appear frequently in the lament form, and are indicative of this limited position of knowledge.[67] Raising a question is not the same kind of speech-act as indicating something with full knowledge of a situation. Lament raises questions, admitting the limited knowledge and perspective. But even if the lament form uses indicative statements or imperatives to demand things of God, it still does so with the expectation of divine response, implying its persuasive aim.[68] Rhetorically, then, even when it does offer statements or demands, lament still depends upon a logic of divine response. Lament's hope for divine encounter—*the* objective response—depends upon God rather than stands over and against him.[69]

To the best of human understanding, the lamenter presents a situation of distress to God in hopes that he will change it. And from the lamenter's perspective, the world *is* out of joint, but it is up to God to set it right: to correct any error of the petition, to change the lamenter's perspective, to deliver one from distress, but ultimately to enact justice. Divine justice and order in both creation and God's relationship with his people comprise the ground and substance of faith and hope in lament prayer. *So the subjectivity of the lament coupled with its rhetorical aim, grounded in a tacit belief of divine justice, reveals that even when Lamentations decries the justice of God in prayer, the very justice of God remains the ground upon which this prayer depends.*

This ambivalence between speech that affirms and questions God's justice should be understood as fundamental to the way the poetry is constructed to draw its readers into worship and prayer before the LORD rather than inherently contradictory speech. Diversity in speech to God is multiform due to the inherent fragmentation of the era in which it was created and provides distinctive avenues for its readers to actualize in worship to their Lord. The diverse prayers in Lamentations are grounded on the (tacit) view that God is indeed a trustworthy Lord, but they contain demands that his goodness, trustworthiness, and mercy be made real in the present world. The prayers of Lamentations are

---

67. Interrogatives in the complaint against God are common within community laments but also appear in individual laments (Ps 22:1; Hab 1:2, 13; Gen 25:22; Job 13:24).

68. Westermann, *Praise and Lament in the Psalms*, 177; see also 181–88.

69. For a somewhat different view see Brueggemann, *The Message of the Psalms*, 51–122.

designed to move God to respond to the petitioners precisely out of his (known) justice and mercy.

So does Lamentations present a theology of justice? One does not find a simple "yes" or "no" answer. The poetry at once affirms the fair dealing of God in concord with the meaning of justice outlined above. Direct statements confirming the deity's justice as well as statements affirming the peoples' sin (Lam 1:18) indicate the world is ordered in a proper way and that God exercises his administration of his creation—his people included—in a way that is right and just. This fact gives purchase for some feminist interpretation to reject the theology of the book—and God—as profoundly unjust as it vindicates God at the expense of an abused woman (Zion). Further, the interaction between Lamentations and the prophets confirms the LORD's justice from a broad canonical perspective. From this standpoint, God's justice as restoration through judgment becomes apparent and may yet provide further fuel for feminist fodder.[70]

But the poetry also makes space for God's activity to be questioned, pressing for the deity's justice to be made manifest in response to prayer. It may be that this is a place where a feminist critique may read *with* rather than *against* the grain of the biblical text and find a voice. O'Connor and Maier in particular highlight the fecundity of this interpretative vein in Lamentations but do little to tease out its implications in life before God. That is to say, the prayers of Lamentations—especially through the embodied voice of feminine Zion—create space for a distinctively human cry to God, recognizing ultimate dependence upon him but nonetheless highlighting discordance in the created order.

CONCLUSION

This exploration on "justice" in feminist discourse and Lamentations highlights a number of difficulties. In the first place, it is clear that nature of feminist discourse in general is broad indeed. Aims and methods vary, and with this diversity it becomes apparent that a set of pre-theoretical philosophical and theological constructs affect outcomes. Mandolfo's concern for justice is admirable in her interpreta-

---

70. This perspective is consistent with God's message of judgment and restoration in the prophets as well as the process of re-establishing justice when covenant relations are breached. Bovati, *Re-Establishing Justice*, 30–61. For a feminist response to the justice-through-judgment theme, see Baumann, *Liebe und Gewalt*.

tion of Lamentations. But the meaning of "justice" remains contested in feminist discourse, especially in light of the difference between hers, Tiemeyer's and Snow Flesher's deployments of feminist analysis. Guest's approach assumes that Lamentations is destructive and harmful, while Clark Kroeger, Evans, and Snow-Flesher assume that the Bible promotes help and healing. O'Connor and Tiemeyer's approaches, too, read the text with critical fidelity and may be contrasted against Guest's. Each of them have in common a view that reading Lamentations generates an experience of reflection on the in/justice of God. What they do with this experience, however, is different based upon a constellation of different pre-commitments.

Thus it becomes clear that there is no one "feminist" approach that has cogently addressed the issue of justice from a systematic perspective. One may press feminist analyses by asking whether this general feminist orientation adequately addresses the presuppositional elements at play in its formulation, particularly on the question of the meaning of, and *telos* of, "justice."

It has been demonstrated that within the canon, Lamentations' conception of the justice of God remains coherent, but complex. Lamentations affirms the justice of God explicitly through direct statements and implicitly through the very logic of lament prayer. Some feminist analysis (O'Connor, Maier, Mandolfo, and Tiemeyer) has ably highlighted the prayers of Lamentations and the discordant voice of Daughter Zion in Lam 2:20–22. The rhetorical force of the prayer must be taken into account and the feminine portrayal serves to underwrite its potency. Other feminist analysis (Guest and Siedman) strangely evade the strong prayers of the woman Zion preferring to locate the force of the poetry in its abusive qualities and decry it as unjust and unsalutary.

Feminist analysis generally does not take account adequately of the *telos* of justice for Lamentations either. Maier is an exception. Justice comes in the full sweep of the reception of Lamentations in the OT when Zion is transformed into a woman/mother who provides a refuge for her suffering and broken people. She has expanded roles and a glorified image. Maier's analysis complicates an overly positive or negative take on the feminine imagery of Zion in Lamentations or the OT in general. As such, Maier's analysis helpfully touches upon the "yes" and "no" on the issue justice in Lamentation advocated in this essay.

Further, Tiemeyer rightly exposes the resistant voice that Lamentations presents in the biblical canon. This is far from marginal speech that should be silenced. As she holds, this is authorized speech—the very word of God. In this way, Lamentations is a text to which some prophetic texts respond (Isaiah and Zechariah) but also it is a text that gives strident response to God and his actions (as Tiemeyer reveals in Ezekiel). In this way, Tiemeyer is right to say that in light of the issue of divine justice in texts like Ezekiel and Lamentations, "[A] Christian response, holding all of Scripture to be of equal authority, is to tread a fine line between accepting God's sovereignty, and holding him accountable for it."[71]

It is precisely in prayers of Lamentations, to my mind, where the justice of God can be affirmed and questioned in an almost paradoxical double-movement. The "yes" and "no" of the justice of God for Lamentations is advocated in its prayers. By praying, the petitioner affirms God is just and has created an ordered world so that he responds to injustice. But by praying, the petitioner rhetorically may call into question specific realities that, on the perspective of the petitioner, are seen to be out of joint. This disjuncture leaves open the possibility of divine response.

So a Janus-like threshold is created in which the prayers of Lamentations tacitly affirm, and depend upon, a logic and experience of God's justice, whilst the appeals raised explicitly question that self-same justice. Ironically, even in the appeals, on the basis of their rhetorical force, God's justice is expected in the immediate future and, I would argue, both expresses the relationship under negotiation and gives God the opportunity for his "response." It is in the appeals of Lamentations where the readings of O'Connor, Maier, Mandolfo, and Tiemeyer have well-served Lamentations' poems. And it is here, to my mind, is one place where the crossroads of feminist and evangelical interpretation of Lamentations may intersect productively.

---

71. Tiemeyer, "To Read," 488.

BIBLIOGRAPHY

Barry, Peter. *Beginning Theory: An Introduction to Literary and Cultural Theory*. Manchester: Manchester University Press, 1995.

Baumann, Gerlinde. *Liebe und Gewalt: Die Ehe als Metapher für das Verhältnis JHWH–Israel in den Prophetenbüchern*. Stuttgarter Bibelstudien 185. Stuttgart: Katholisches Bibelwerk, 2000.

Barton, John. *The Nature of Biblical Criticism*. Louisville, KY: Westminster John Knox, 2007.

Berlin, Adele. *Lamentations*. Old Testament Library. Louisville, KY: Westminster John Knox, 2002.

Bovati, Pietro. *Re-Establishing Justice: Legal Terms, Concepts and Procedures in the Hebrew Bible*. Translated by Michael J. Smith. JSOTSupp 105. Sheffield, UK: Sheffield Academic, 1994.

Braiterman, Zachary. *(God) After Auschwitz: Tradition and Change in Post-Holocaust Jewish Thought*. Princeton: Princeton University Press, 1998.

Brenner, Athalya. "Pornoprophetics Revisited: Some Additional Reflections." *Journal for the Study of the Old Testament* 70 (1996) 63–86.

Brenner, Athalya, and Carol Fontaine, eds. *A Feminist Companion to Reading the Bible*. Sheffield, UK: Sheffield Academic, 1997.

Brueggemann, Walter. *Theology of the Old Testament: Testimony, Dispute, Advocacy*. Minneapolis: Fortress, 1997.

―――. *The Message of the Psalms: A Theological Commentary*. Minneapolis: Augsburg, 1984.

Castelli, Elizabeth A., Stephen D. Moore, Gary A. Phillips, and Regina Schwartz, eds. "Feminist and Womanist Criticism." In *The Postmodern Bible: The Bible and Culture Collective*, 225–71. New Haven: Yale University Press, 1995.

Dobbs-Allsopp, F. W. *Lamentations*. Interpretation. Louisville: John Knox, 2002.

Fiorenza, Elizabeth Schüssler. *In Memory of Her: A Feminist Theological Reconstruction of Christian Origins*. London: SPCK, 1983.

Flesher, Leanne Snow. "Lamentations." In *The IVP Women's Bible Commentary*, edited by Catherine Clark Kroeger and Mary J. Evans, 392–95. Downers Grove, IL: InterVarsity, 2002.

Frymer-Kensky, Tikva. *Reading the Women of the Bible: A New Interpretation of Their Stories*. New York: Schocken, 2002.

Gardner, E. Clinton. *Justice and Christian Ethics*. New Studies in Christian Ethics. Cambridge: Cambridge University Press, 1995.

Guest, Deryn. "Hiding Behind the Naked Women in Lamentations: A Recriminative Response." *Biblical Interpretation* 7.4 (1999) 413–48.

Kroeger, Catherine C. Clark, and Mary J. Evans, eds. "Preface: Why a Women's Bible Commentary?" In *The IVP Women's Bible Commentary*, xiii–xv.. Downers Grove, IL: IinterVarsity, 2002.

Lee, Nancy C. *The Singers of Lamentations: Cities under Siege, from Ur to Jerusalem to Sarajevo*. Biblical Interpretation Series 60. Leiden: Brill, 2002.

MacDonald Neil B., and Carl Trueman. *Calvin, Barth, and Reformed Theology*. Paternoster Theological Monographs. Milton Keynes, UK: Paternoster, 2008.

MacIntyre, Alasdair. *Whose Justice? Which Rationality?* Notre Dame, IN: University of Notre Dame Press, 1988.

Maier, Christl M. *Daughter Zion, Mother Zion: Gender, Space, and the Sacred in Ancient Israel*. Minneapolis: Fortress, 2008.

Mandolfo, Carleen. *Daughter Zion Talks Back to the Prophets: A Dialogic Theology of the Book of Lamentations*. Semeia Studies. Atlanta: Society of Biblical Literature, 2007.

McConville, J. Gordon. *God and Earthly Power: An Old Testament Political Theology*. New York: T. & T. Clark, 2006.

Meyers, Carol, ed. *Women in Scripture: A Dictionary of Named and Unnamed Women in the Hebrew Bible, the Apocryphal/Deuterocanonical Books, and the New Testament*. Grand Rapids: Eerdmans, 2001.

Middlemas, Jill. *The Troubles of Templeless Judah*. Oxford Theological Monographs. Oxford: Oxford University Press, 2005.

Miller, Patrick D. *They Cried to the Lord: The Form and Theology of Biblical Prayer*. Minneapolis: Fortress, 1994.

Moi, Toril. "Feminist, female, feminine." In *The Feminist Reader: Essays in Gender and the Politics of Literary Criticism*, edited by Catherine Belsey and Jane Moore, 115–32. London: Macmillan, 1989.

———. "'I am not a woman writer': About Women, Literature and Feminist Theory Today." *Feminist Theory* 9.3 (2008) 259–71.

O'Connor, Kathleen. "Lamentations." In *The Women's Bible Commentary*. Expanded Edition. Edited by C. A. Newsom and Sharon Ringe, 187–91. Louisville: Westminster John Knox, 1998.

———. *Lamentations and the Tears of the World*. Maryknoll, NY: Orbis, 2002.

O'Donovan, Oliver. *The Desire of the Nations: Rediscovering the Roots of Political Theology*. Cambridge: Cambridge University Press, 1996.

Renkema, Johan. *"Misschien is er Hoop . . ." De Theologische Vooronderstellingen van het Boek Klaagliederen*. Franeker: Wever, 1983.

———. *Lamentations*. Historical Commentary on the Old Testament. Leuven: Peeters, 1998.

Richter, David H. "Feminist Literary Criticism." In *The Critical Tradition: Classic Texts and Contemporary Trends*, edited by David H. Richter, 1063–78. Boston: Bedford, 1989.

Sakenfeld, Katherine Doob. "Feminist Perspectives on Bible and Theology: An Introduction to Selected Issues and Literature." *Interpretation* 42.1 (1988) 5–18.

Sandel, Michael. *Justice: What's the Right Thing to Do?* New York: Farrar, Straus, and Giroux, 2009.

Seidman, Naomi. "Burning the Book of Lamentations." In *Out of the Garden: Women Writers on the Bible*, edited by Christina Büchmann and Celina Spiegel, 278–88. New York: Columbine, 1995.

Stead, Michael. "Sustained Allusion in Zechariah 1–2." In *Tradition in Transition: Haggai and Zechariah 1–8 in the Trajectory of Hebrew Theology*, edited by Mark Boda and Michael Floyd, 144–70. Library of Hebrew Bible/Old Testament 475. London: T. & T. Clark, 2008.

Thomas, Heath. "The Meaning of *zōlēlâ* (Lam 1:11c) One More Time." *Vetus Testamentum* 61.3 (2011) 489–98.

———. *"Until He Looks Down and Sees": The Message and Meaning of the Book of Lamentations*. Biblical Series 53. Cambridge, UK: Grove, 2009.

Tiemeyer, Lena-Sophia. "Geography and Textual Allusions: Interpreting Isaiah xl–lv and Lamentations as Judahite Texts." *Vetus Testamentum* 57 (2007) 367–85.

———. "To Read—Or Not to Read—Ezekiel as Christian Scripture." *Expository Times* 121 (2010) 481–88.
Tolbert, Mary Ann. "Defining the Problem: The Bible and Feminist Hermeneutics." *Semeia* 28 (1983) 113–26.
Trible, Phyllis. *God and the Rhetoric of Sexuality*. Overtures to Biblical Theology. Minneapolis: Fortress, 1978.
Westermann, Claus. *Die Klagelieder*. Neukirchen-Vluyn: Neukirchener, 1990.
———. *Praise and Lament in the Psalms*. Translated by Keith R. Crim and Richard N. Soulen. Atlanta: John Knox, 1981.

10

Patriarchy, Biblical Authority, and the Grand Narrative of the Old Testament

JUNIA POKRIFKA

INTRODUCTION

The Problem with Metanarratives

MANY FEMINISTS BELIEVE THAT the Old Testament cannot speak authoritatively to feminists and feminist concerns due to the pervasive presence of patriarchy within it. I would like to explore a "grand narrative" or metanarrative that unifies and underlies the various texts of the Old Testament, including those texts that seem to promote patriarchy, as a way to overcome the suspicion that the Old Testament not only embodies but condones and perpetuates patriarchy.

To find a solution to the problem of patriarchal oppression in a metanarrative (or *grand récit*) runs directly against some of the root tendencies of postmodernity, which increasingly pervade feminist biblical interpretation. Jean-François Lyotard's now-famous definition of the postmodern clarifies the nature of the challenge: "Simplifying to the extreme, I define postmodern as incredulity toward metanarratives."[1] For Lyotard, the postmodern condition causes "the narrative function" to lose the essential qualities that make it function meaningfully, namely "its great hero, its great dangers, its great voyages, its great goal."[2] Although

1. Lyotard, *The Postmodern Condition*, xxiv.
2. Ibid., xxiv.

this may well be a simplification of what is involved in postmodernity, I believe that it is typical for postmoderns—including postmodern feminists and biblical interpreters—to assume that all metanarratives are inherently problematic and oppressive. The reason is that metanarratives legitimate a particular way of life and its corresponding social institutions, forms of belief, and practices. Legitimating a way of life against possible alternatives leads to oppression of alternative narratives. So, it is thought, all metanarratives are inherently oppressive and exclusive.

Certainly, some construals of the biblical grand narrative have been oppressive, confirming Lyotard's representative postmodern view of metanarrative. However, this does not mean that all versions of the biblical grand narrative are oppressive, for at least two reasons. First, there is a contrast between modern metanarratives, which are intellectually totalizing, and the "non-modern metanarrative"[3] found in the Bible, which retains a place for the weakness and vulnerability of all humanity before God's unique mystery and power. In modern metanarratives, the rational comprehension and technological mastery of the world and its (non-Western) peoples are employed for the sake of a particular understanding of human progress. In biblical metanarrative, no such rational explanation of all reality is offered.[4] Second, the non-modern biblical metanarrative is marked by ethical features that militate against its being used for the oppression of one group by another. These characteristics include God typically siding with the oppressed and against the powerful, frequent ethical denunciations against oppressors, and statements of intended redemptive outcomes (even for oppression and suffering) that are global in scope. These liberating features of the Old Testament are arguably central to understanding the Old Testament as a narrative whole.[5] These factors render problematic any view that treats *all* metanarratives as oppressive.

In this chapter, I hope to show that it is precisely the presence of the biblical metanarrative, rightly understood, that enables women and men alike to have a hope for an ultimate and just end to oppression.

3. This phrase, with an illuminating explanation of it, is found in Richard Bauckham's *Bible and Mission*, 90ff.

4. Ibid., 90–91. Within the biblical framework, only God could offer such an explanation, and even when we acknowledge the reality of divine revelation, God, and much of God's creation remain mysterious.

5. Ibid., 100–103. See also the instructive comments about Scriptural "metanarrative" found in Bartholomew and Goheen, "Story and Biblical Theology," 65–71.

This grand narrative uniquely confronts and undermines the totalizing claims of all human cultures and their oppressive metanarratives, including those of Israel itself. Picking up on Lyotard's language, God is the great hero of this narrative, sin and death pose the great dangers, redemptive history provides its great voyages, and the consummation of God's just and loving reign is its great goal. In this grand narrative, both women and men can become heroes alongside God, who calls and graciously empowers them to participate in the divine redemptive work.

But it is only when the Old Testament is understood as a whole, and not merely as a collection of diverse and contradictory parts, that we can conceive of a grand narrative that is consistently liberating for both women and men. Accordingly, throughout this study, I will employ a canonical approach to biblical interpretation influenced by Brevard Childs. As such, I will interpret the final canonical form of the text in its literary context.[6] In the context of that canonical theological approach, I will draw on a kind of intertextual interpretation in which I bring texts from various parts of the Old Testament into mutually illuminating theological relationships with one another.

The Problem of Patriarchy and Patriarchal Metanarratives

There are obvious challenges to this canonical analysis of the grand narrative of the Old Testament. First of all, this collection of writing is clearly marked by patriarchal and androcentric features, which appear to be rather deeply imbedded and pervasive. Yahweh is named the God of the patriarchs—Abraham, Isaac, and Jacob. The legal codes of Israel treat women largely from the perspective of men and represent a social world in which women are seen as less valuable than men. Wisdom literature frequently speaks of the dangers of women to its implied readers, who are assumed to be male. Some texts appear to be patently misogynist. These problematic features cannot be denied or minimized.

Feminist biblical interpreters have developed various strategies to deal with patriarchy in the Old Testament. The "rejectionists" reject the Old Testament altogether, while the "loyalists" embrace the Old Testament as a whole. The "revisionists" reject some parts of the Old Testament and uphold other parts.[7] I do not think any of these respons-

---

6. I will also modify Childs' approach somewhat, not least by integrating it with a narrative approach that Childs does not employ.

7. These are the first three of five hermeneutical alternatives presented by Carolyn Osiek in "The Feminist and the Bible." Among the many sources that use or modify

es is entirely adequate. The rejectionists, who include post-Christian feminists and many postmodern feminists, focus too exclusively on the presence of patriarchy and misogyny in the Bible, dismissing the entire Bible as hopeless and unredeemable.[8] The opposite camp of the loyalists tent to deny or minimize the extensive patriarchal and androcentric elements of the Old Testament.[9] The revisionists in all their variety (including those who promote liberationist readings, women-centered readings, *in memoriam* readings, and so forth) generally find redemption for women only in a selective body of "feminist" or "feminine" texts, rather than finding ways of interpreting the Old Testament as a whole.[10] These strategies demonstrate the need to develop a metanarrative that satisfactorily accounts for and addresses with the problematic texts. I believe that a kind of loyalist metanarrative approach to the Old Testament with a concern to learn from the other two approaches is possible. It can help us to understand the whole of the Old Testament as authoritative and restorative for both women and men.[11]

The second acute problem with the canonical approach has to do with the fact that, for many feminist interpreters, it is precisely when the

---

her typology are Robin Parry and Todd Pokrifka (chapters 2 and 11 respectively in this volume), Cherith Fee Nordling, "Feminist Biblical Interpretation," and Jacqueline E. Lapsley, *Whispering the Word*, 3–4. Like Fee Nordling and Lapsley, I will use Osiek's third, revisionist, category in a broad sense that includes Osiek's fourth and fifth ("sublimationist" and "liberationist") categories. Revisionists in this sense all have in common a tendency to see only parts of the biblical text as authoritative rather than the biblical text as a whole. Lapsley, who considers herself a revisionist, "acknowledges the patriarchal aspects of the text, but does not view them as definitive" (*Whispering the Word*, 3).

8. The Post-Christian feminists' conclusion that the Bible is thoroughly and irrevocably patriarchal is also shared by some conservative, anti-feminist evangelicals (e.g., Haas, "Patriarchy," 321–36). The former however reject the Bible and its God (as oppressive), whereas the latter accept and seek to propagate patriarchy as God's eternal arrangement for humanity.

9. Accordingly, most loyalist feminists also tend to be very selective, choosing those texts that are more obviously "female-friendly." This is a tendency that loyalists share with the revisionists.

10. See Pamela Milne's critique of revisionism/reformism from a "structuralist" point of view in Athalya Brenner's *A Feminist Companion to Genesis*, 146–72. Milne may be regarded as a kind of "rejectionist."

11. The following quotation confirms the wisdom of going in this direction, though its authors are not concerned with feminist Old Testament interpretation in particular: "If we allow the Bible to become fragmented, it is in danger of being absorbed into whatever *other* story is shaping our culture, and it will thus cease to shape our lives as it should!" (Bartholomew and Goheen, *Drama of Scripture*, 12).

Old Testament is seen as a canonical narrative whole that it is seen as *most* patriarchal. The reason, so the argument goes, is that the canonical shape of the Old Testament is the product of the scholars and editors of the patriarchal Israelite religious and social establishment. Canonization was not a process in which the neglected voices in Israel gained a greater hearing, for the marginalized probably did not play a role in the shape of the overarching canonical narrative and its main constitutive features. Not only is the majority of the text androcentric—written by men, about men, and for men—but the general canonical shape of scripture is also patriarchal. Thus even those revisionists who admit that isolated texts of the Old Testament provide helpful resources for women would apply the hermeneutics of retrieval only in conjunction with a hermeneutics of suspicion towards the general canonical shape of Scripture.[12] While there is some initial plausibility to this view in light of the generally patriarchal and androcentric character of Israelite society and religion, this interpretation does not fit with the redemptive pattern found in the Old Testament. The biblical metanarrative that is centrally concerned with redemption and restorative justice places injustice towards women in a particular light that, in the end, breaks the back of patriarchy. In that light, the patriarchal condition of humanity is no longer seen as normative, but as a regrettable condition that God and God's human agents are working to overcome.[13]

---

12. In Richard Bauckham's description of this view (which he rejects), feminist endeavors such as reading Ruth as women's literature "would have to be an exercise in *resisting* [Ruth's] canonical 'shaping'" (Bauckham, *Gospel Women*, 5).

13. In addition, Bauckham points out that the process of canonization was not primarily an authoritarian matter settled by an elite group of men with power (Bauckham cites A. Primavesi's *From Apocalypse to Genesis* as representative of this view; see also Carol Meyers, *Discovering Eve*, 195–96), but a matter of a grass-roots process of communal use and discernment which likely included women (Bauckham, *Gospel Women*, 15–16). Even if one judges such matters as historically speculative, there are surely Christian theological reasons for saying that divine inspiration can overcome the limitations of patriarchal perspectives and concerns in the process of canonization. See Todd Pokrifka's piece in this volume for one way of viewing such matters.

THE GRAND NARRATIVE OF THE OLD TESTAMENT: AN EVANGELICAL FEMINIST VERSION

As is typical of great stories, the story of the Old Testament has a plot marked by a beginning, a middle, and an end. The beginning (or a prologue) of the Old Testament story is a glorious initial state of affairs for humanity, followed by its dissolution and the growing alienation and corruption in all of humanity's relationships.[14] The middle of the story is a conflicted story of both redemption and downfall, starting with the call and blessings of Abraham, but ending with exile. This middle part constitutes the vast majority of the Old Testament. The end of the story is marked by promises of redemption, their very partial fulfillment and hope for a greater fulfillment.

As often is the case with other great narratives, the Old Testament grand narrative starts with a beginning that anticipates the main themes and problems of the narrative to follow. As Mark Powell puts it, "the order in which a narrative relates events is important because readers are expected to consider each new episode in light of what has gone before."[15] Genesis 1–3[16] functions as the "opening violin solo" that introduces many of the fundamental motifs of the following narrative.[17] Thus, my brief overview of the Old Testament grand narrative will begin

---

14. For Bartholomew and Goheen, Creation and Fall represent acts one and two in the Bible's main storyline. The story of the patriarchs is a crucial early phase in act three, the story of "redemption initiated" in which the divine king chooses Israel (*The Drama of Scripture* and "The Story Line of the Bible").

15. Powell, "Narrative Criticism," 171.

16. Scholars have rightly noted that there is not a strong break between Genesis 1–3 and the chapters that follow, with some arguing for Genesis 2–4 as a better unit (for example, Olson, "Untying the Knot"). Many modern biblical scholars would also question whether either Genesis 1–3 or 2–4 can constitute a unit, given the presence of Genesis 2–3 (more specifically, Genesis 2:4b—3:24) as an apparently distinct unit in itself. My own sense is that there are various kinds of literary units that can be discerned for different readerly purposes, yet with some (non-arbitrary) justification in the biblical text. In that sense, Genesis 1–3 is a unit (albeit a loose one containing distinct parts) that is constituted in part by common thematic and theological themes. These themes and their treatment in Genesis 1–3 are relevant to and sufficient for my purpose in this chapter.

17. Waltke, *An Old Testament Theology*, 150. Although many scholars have seen Genesis 2–3 as marginal, disconnected from the literary flow of Genesis and unconnected with Israelite theology in the Hebrew Bible as a whole, authors such as T. Stordalen (*Echoes of Eden*) and T. N. D. Mettinger (*The Eden Narrative*) have shown quite compellingly that this is not the case, at least not in any significant sense.

with Genesis 1–3, which is best seen in the context of the wider unit of Genesis 1–11.[18]

My thematic analysis of the Old Testament grand narrative will take the following steps: (1) First, I will undertake a thematic analysis of Genesis 1–2, focusing on the three relationships of humanity. (2) Second, I will identify the antithetical thematic parallels between Genesis 1–2 and Genesis 3. (3) After that I will point out from the Genesis 3 judgment oracle the promises of the redemption of creation from the effects of sin, which point to restoration of all three relationships of humanity. In the next four sub-sections of the chapter, I will do a thematic overview of the rest of the grand narrative in light of our reading of Genesis 1–3. This will show the repetition of motifs of Genesis 1–3 and the presence of a similar pattern of reversals and a promise of future redemption in the history of Israel. Obviously there is no space for a detailed development of how those themes specifically manifest in different periods of Israel's history. We only have room for a very brief overview, while engaging those texts that raise feminist concerns. The thematic overview will start with (4) the ancestral (patriarchal) period, then turn to (5) the emergence of Israel, then address (6) Israel in the land from Joshua to the exile, and conclude with (7) the return to the land and messianic hope.

Following these steps, I will offer a brief conclusion based on my analysis, suggesting a hermeneutical approach for the intersection of biblical and feminist studies. Then I will briefly comment on how this particular way of conceiving grand narrative helps us to better interpret the evidence for "the full humanity of women" in relation to the abundant presence of androcentrism and patriarchy in the Old Testament.

Three Human Relationships in Genesis 1–2

While the creation accounts found in Genesis 1 and Genesis 2 are significantly different in terms of literary style and content, both accounts speak of the goodness of creation in relation to the three main relationships of humanity. They are (1) an "upward-looking" vertical relationship with God, (2) a horizontal relationship with other humans—the fundamental male-female relationship and parent-child and other inter-

---

18. Moberly confirms the importance of the opening chapters of the Bible. Referring specifically to Genesis 2–3, he says, "[T]he location of Genesis 2–3 at the very outset of the Old Testament . . . gives a contextual weight to the narrative that is as great as could be" (*The Theology of the Book of Genesis*, 71).

human relationships, and (3) a "downward-looking" vertical relationship with the rest of the created order—to the non-human creatures and their environment. While my primary concern is with the horizontal, inter-human relationships, all three relationships must be considered because of their immediate relevance to the questions of feminist interpretation. The text's portrayal of these horizontal relationships cannot be adequately understood apart from the two kinds of vertical relationships that are contextually interwoven with the horizontal relationships.

Accountability to God's Authority (Upward-Vertical Relationship)

In Genesis 1, as Creator, God has authority over all creation, which is utterly dependent on God for its existence. God gives life to humanity, who is made in God's image (1:28). A full life is only accessible when lived under God's authority.[19] Accordingly, God gives two authoritative mandates to humans: (1) to multiply and to thereby fill the earth and (2) to rule over the earth and its creatures (1:28). In accountability to God, human life has a mission or objective.[20] Similarly, in Genesis 2, God provides abundant food, but gives a prohibition not to eat of "the tree of the knowledge of good and evil"—together with a strong warning that death will come to the disobedient (2:17). Both the provision and the prohibition point to humanity's dependence on God and need for obedience to God.[21] Gaining the knowledge of good and evil may be understood as making a choice independent of God or deciding what is good and evil apart from God. Independence from God brings death and all kinds of sin and evil.

---

19. I recognize that hierarchical view of God's relationship to the world and to humanity that I present here might be viewed by some feminists as itself patriarchal and a vehicle of patriarchal ideology (see, for instance, proponents of the Earth Bible project). In my view, recognizing the unique authority of God over humanity helps to undermine, rather than support, the misuse and abuse of authority in human relationships, including those indicative of patriarchal social orders. But this approach requires a rethinking of the nature of divine and human authority that goes beyond the boundaries of this chapter.

20. See Christopher Wright, *The Mission of God*, 65, 425–27.

21. "Maturity readings" of Genesis 2–3 (e.g., Bechtel, in Brenner, *A Feminist Companion to Genesis*, 77–117) inappropriately minimize the seriousness of God's command, warnings, and divine authority in general. They imply that humanity is actually better off disobeying God and that this is what God is hoping that they do.

Blessed and Harmonious Inter-Human Relationships (Horizontal Relationship)

In Genesis 1:27, the juxtaposition of the singular "him" and the plural "them" and the collective "humanity" (*'ādām*) implies that the duality of humanity as male and female is not in opposition to the unity of humanity; nor does this unity require either "sameness" or the dominance of one gender/sex over the other.[22] Both male and female are equally made in God's image and likeness, which implies not only the created unity of male and female, but their equality before God. Both are equally given dominion over the rest of the earth and its creatures. Accordingly, this text affirms, in its own terms, "the full humanity of women," which Rosemary Radford Ruether calls the "critical principle of feminism."[23] Further expressions of the blessed condition of humanity in Genesis 1 are found in the divine blessing (and command) of fruitfulness (1:28), which is also given to other creatures (see 1:22; cf. 8:17; 9:1).

In Genesis 2, a harmonious relationship between man and woman is implied, as it was in Genesis 1.[24] Verses 18, 20–22 point to the need of the woman to complete humanity and to carry out the God-given mandates for humanity (Gen 1:28; 2:15). God made the woman as "a helper equal to" the man (2:18b; *'ēzer kĕnegdô*).[25] That the woman is made out

---

22. It is true that *grammatically* masculine terms are used in Genesis 1:27 (and again in 5:1) to refer to the collective unity of humanity (*'ādām* and "it"/"him" in Gen 1:27 and 5:2), but the fact that they are juxtaposed with the plural "them" and the reference to both male and female resists any facile notion that humanity is construed here in androcentric terms or in terms that make the male more important than female. How to interpret the text concerning these matters relates partly to questions about how we should translate *'ādām* in Genesis 1–5 (when is it a proper name or a collective noun?), which is discussed abundantly in feminist literature and in commentaries on Genesis (see Andrew Sloane's comments in chapter 1 of this volume).

23. Ruether, *Sexism and God-Talk*, 18–20.

24. I have found the comments of Phyllis Trible on Genesis 2 to be helpful in many respects (see *God and the Rhetoric of Sexuality* and "Depatriarchalizing in Biblical Interpretation," 30–48, esp. 35–42. However, I agree with most of the criticisms that Andrew Sloane makes concerning Trible's work (see his piece on Genesis 2–3 in this volume). Another helpful reading of Genesis 1–3 as a whole is provided by the evangelical (loyalist) Richard Hess, "Equality with and without Innocence."

25. A more literal translation of the phrase is "a helper corresponding to him." The term "helper" does not connote an inferior in this context or others. The term "helper or help" (*'ēzer*) is used twenty-one times in the Old Testament: twice for the woman in Gen 2:18, 20; three times of a (superior) human "help" that is not forthcoming (Isa 30:5, Ezek 12:14, Dan 11:34); and sixteen times of God the "helper," the deliverer (Exod 18:4;

of the man points to her essential unity with him, rather than subordination of the woman to the man.[26] Furthermore, the man's praise of the woman in the superlatives as "bone of my bones and flesh of my flesh" (2:23)[27] is his recognition that God has indeed provided him with one who is essentially like him. Accordingly, in the state of being "one flesh," there is no "shame" between woman and man in their nakedness, only an elation in being "one" with another (see 2:24–25).

Unlike Genesis 1, there is no direct divine benediction on human fruitfulness in Genesis 2, but the reference to the institution of marriage and the sexual union that belongs to it (2:24) provides the context for childbearing. It is notable that the language of Genesis 2:24 suggests a matrilocal arrangement in which the man leaves his own family to be with his wife and (apparently) her family. Even if this passage does not reflect or encourage a fully matrilocal familial structure, it runs contrary to the more common ancient Near Eastern model of a patrilocal family unit in which the woman is owned or controlled by her husband and his father with a view to ensuring patrilineage.[28] As with the rest of the language of Genesis 2, 2:24 points to recognition of the woman's fundamental likeness, mutuality, and equality with the man.

Dominion (Downward-Vertical Relationship)

Humanity, both male and female, is given the privilege, responsibility, and power to have dominion "over every living creature that moves

---

Deut 33:7, 26, 29; Pss 20:2; 33:20; 70:5; 89:19; 115:9, 10, 11; 121:1, 2; 124:8; 146:5; Hos 13:9). That the woman is created to be a *helper* does not mean that she is superior to the man. She is created to be a helper who is like the man, which means they are equal. As Trible puts it, "God is the helper superior to [humans]; woman is the helper equal to man" ("Depatriarchalizing in Biblical Interpretation," 36).

26. I realize that the formation of the woman from the man's side (a better translation than "rib") in 2:21–22 can be read as supporting androcentrism, since the man is the source of the women. In light of an ancient Near Eastern emphasis on primogeniture, this order might be significant. But this scene needs to be juxtaposed with the text's earlier attribution of the ground as the "source" of the man (2:7), a "counter-text" which points to the humble origins of humanity and/or the male human (depending on how 'ādām is understood here).

27. See Sloane, chapter 1 in this volume, for his discussion of Trible's treatment of the issue of whether or not this verse includes a naming formula.

28. Carol Meyers believes Israel followed this patrilineal descent pattern (*Discovering Eve*, 183–84). For some reason, Meyers does not comment on the significance of Gen 2:24 in resisting this pattern, perhaps because she believes the "archetypal" character of the Eden story counts against the view that this verse speaks of marriage (ibid., 109–10).

upon the ground" and over the whole earth (1:28; cf. 1:26).[29] God created humans in his image to be like God and one aspect of that likeness relates to having dominion. God delegates humans as the rulers and stewards of the earth as God's representatives. In this context, God provides humanity with the earth as a luxuriant and pleasant dwelling place. The mandate to have dominion (1:28) finds an immediate application in Genesis 2. Yahweh commands the man to "till" and to "guard" (*šāmar*, 2:15)[30] the ground of the Garden.[31] The use of the term "guard" (*šāmar*) anticipates the intrusion of the "serpent" into the Garden to tempt the humans, and the use of the expression "helper corresponding to him" implies that the woman will successfully help the man to obey Yahweh, fulfill the call to till and guard, and therefore resist the serpent's temptations.[32] Both sexes are involved in fulfilling the constitutive tasks of the proper human relationship to the non-human creation.

In keeping with the summarizing divine declaration that all is "very good" (1:31), Genesis 1 and 2 both present human life as it should be in terms of humanity's three main relationships. Even the initially "not good" state of the man's life (2:18a) is remedied by the formation of the woman as the equal partner. The man's praise of woman (2:23), the couples' union and unity in marriage (2:24), and the declaration of the absence of shame (2:25) confirm that male-female relations are good, in keeping with God's intentions for humanity.

---

29. Again, I recognize that many feminists, especially ecofeminists, regard any notion of authority or dominion as inherently problematic and oppressive, Again, in my view, authority can be legitimate if kept within the proper, God-given boundaries.

30. The verb *šāmar*, variously translated as "keep" (NRSV) or "tend" (JPS Tanakh), also can mean "watch," "guard," or "protect," which is more appropriate in this context. Humans are instructed to guard the Garden.

31. Although the text does not explicitly state that the woman was to "till" and "protect" the ground, it is implicitly present in the text. First of all, Gen 2:5 (in the expression "there was no human [*ʾādām*] to cultivate the ground") shows that it is a human responsibility to "till" the ground. Secondly, if the woman is to be an equal partner, then she is an equal partner in all that he is called to do. With the creation of the woman, the humankind can multiply and "till" and "guard" the Garden. Read in the light of Genesis 1, this cultivation of the ground would be part of what is involved in having dominion over the earth.

32. Yahweh's assessment that "It is not good for the man to be alone" and the resolve to "make him a helper suitable for him" (2:18) immediately follows his commandment to the man, which supports the view that the woman is created to help the man to obey God's commandment and effectively resist the serpent's temptation. The implication is that they would help each other in fulfilling the dominion mandate.

Three Relationships and Parallel Themes in Genesis 3

If there is a harmonious thematic parallelism between Genesis 1 and Genesis 2, there is also an antithetical parallelism[33] between the creation accounts of Genesis 1–2 and the "Fall story" of Genesis 3–11.[34] In the words of Dennis Olson about Genesis 3, "We suddenly shift from the divinely intended and positive portrait of the human couple that emerges from the end of Genesis 2 to a dramatic shattering and distortion of what God hoped for in these relationships."[35] In this discussion of the parallel themes in Genesis 3, I will sometimes draw from Genesis 4–11 as well, since these chapters powerfully illustrate the damaging effects of sin on human life in all its major relationships that are summarized in Genesis 3 (especially the poetic oracle of 3:14–19).

Rebellion against God's Authority

God's authority is contravened by human disobedience. God's words are disobeyed and there are divine words of judgment as a result. The judgment is nothing less than alienation and exile from the life-giving and

---

33. In speaking of "antithetical parallelism" here I am speaking broadly and analogically of thematic reversal within a story line, not the narrow sense in which this term is used in discussing Hebrew poetry. By using this term, I intend to emphasize both the continuity and discontinuity of Genesis 3 with Genesis 1–2 in different respects. As part of the same Garden story that began in Gen 2:4b, there is clearly literary and linguistic continuity with chapter 2 as well as thematic continuity with chapters 1–2. The discontinuity in Genesis 3, and especially in 3:14–19, has to do with the disruption and alienation in the three relationships noted above.

34. Among the authors who deny that there is anything like a "Fall" (in the traditional Jewish or Christian sense) in Genesis 3 are James Barr (*The Garden of Eden*, 87–93) and feminist interpreters Lynn Bechtel and Carol Meyers (see their chapters in Brenner, *A Feminist Companion to Genesis*, 77–141, and Meyers, *Discovering Eve*, 95–121). For a defense of the notion of a "Fall," but in a way that appropriately modifies aspects of traditional interpretation, see Moberly in *The Theology of the Book of Genesis*, 70–87. Mediating positions (between anti-Fall and pro-Fall readings) are found in the work of Terence Fretheim ("Is Genesis 3 a Fall Story?") and Goldingay (*Israel's Gospel*, 144–48). My own approach retains the notion and language of a Fall, like Moberly, but incorporates some of the modifications that he and others have suggested. For one thing, sin and its consequences are not merely a theme of Genesis 3, but of the larger unit of Genesis 3–11. Also, the "Fall" is not primarily a falling down, but a "falling out" (alienation) from proper relationship with God.

35. Olson, "Untying the Knot?," 78. Olson prefaces this comment by saying, "Genesis 3 marks one of the most drastic and unexplained disjunctions in the whole Bible"—a comment that stands in contrast with James Barr's denial of any cataclysmic Fall story in Genesis 3 (*The Garden of Eden*, 91–93).

life-sustaining presence of God in the Garden. Away from the immediate presence of God and the "tree of life," all creation and human life is subject to curse, corruption, and death.[36] Yahweh is manifested as a just judge, who pronounces the coming consequences of sin.[37]

Disharmony and Inequality in Inter-Human Relationships

Disobedience to God's word introduces guilt, shame, and blame, which not only alienate humans from God but also alienate the man and the woman from each other. There is now a contentious relationship between the man and the woman ("He will rule over you" in 3:15), which implies that the origin of patriarchy and male domination[38] are found in human rebellion against God and God's commands (2:17–18). Furthermore, the fracturing and distortion of male-female (husband-wife) relationships speaks of contention among humans in general, which soon escalates into Cain's fratricide and Lamech's murder in Genesis 4.[39]

One way of interpreting inter-human alienation and violence is to see it as a twisting or misapplication of the dominion mandate in Genesis 1:27. Human dominion over the now cursed and thus hostile creatures and ground is frustrated. Unfulfilled dominion finds its distorted outlet in human-to-human dominion. This begins in marriage (3:15; cf. 2:24),

---

36. In light of what happens in Genesis 3 and the following chapters, it may be best to understand the warning in Gen 2:17 ("in the day that you eat from it you will surely die") as a kind of metaphoric death, a loss of the abundant life that God had intended for humanity (see Moberly, *The Theology of the Book of Genesis*, 83–87).

37. The stories of the flood (Gen 6–9) and the tower of Babel (Gen 10), confirm that God will not tolerate extreme evil forever and that God's judgment can be extreme and final.

38. Carol Meyers reads this text quite differently as an observation about the predominant control of males over sexual reproduction, with a view to patrilineal descent (*Discovering Eve*, 113–17). Meyers believes she has social scientific and historical evidence that early, pre-Monarchical Israel was basically non-hierarchical and egalitarian, without patriarchy in any strong sense (e.g., ibid., 180–81 and 187–88). See also Meyers' comments on the challenge of defining words like "patriarchy" appropriately for use in reference to the social realities of ancient Israel, which are so different from those in the modern West (ibid., 24–46).

39. See James Hamilton's *God's Glory*, 82–83, for an account of "gender conflict" in the rest of Genesis (see also his preceding treatment of inter-human "seed conflict" between "the seed of the serpent" and "the seed of the women" in ibid., 80–81). Although I find much of Hamilton's work helpful, I disagree with his complementarian or hierarchical view of what ideal gender relations should be like, based upon the alleged "created order" (see ibid., 72–74).

which is supposed to be the paradigm of inter-human unity and love. Humanity "falls" into a sorry state of alienation, shame, aversion, and male-domination.[40] Society continues to break down in a thoroughgoing descent into violence that culminates in Noah's time (see 6:11–12).

Alienated from the giver of life, there is also frustrated procreation—another basic feature of inter-human relationship. This is indicated by the statement in Genesis 3:16 that the woman will bring forth children in "distress" (*'iṣṣābôn; eṣeb*)[41] and "groaning" *(hērôn).*[42] These expressions refer not merely or even primarily to "labor pains" but to anything that hinders the fulfillment of the divine blessing of fruitfulness—both in terms of having children and raising them.

Frustrated and Corrupted Dominion

The consequence of human failure to exercise dominion over the serpent and resist its temptation is the reversal of the proper dominion order between humanity and the non-human creation. God curses the human domain of the ground and the plants and animals associated with it (Gen 3:17–19). As with the realm of procreation, there is now intense labor or "toil" in food production, which will also make it more difficult to survive.

Frustrated dominion is also evident in the way in which the creatures (associated with the ground) now resist humanity. The serpent especially is not only hostile to humanity (3:15), but gains power over humanity through deceptive temptation (3:1–7). The serpent is called a "living creature" (Heb *ḥayyâ* 3:1; 3:14), the same term used for creatures in the dominion mandate in 1:28. This expression is a painful reminder that humans originally had power and authority over the serpent, but

---

40. We see further evidence of the alienation between the man and the woman in the blame-shifting during the dialogue between God and the man (3:12; see also 3:13).

41. The Hebrew term *'iṣṣābôn* is usually translated into "pain" in relation to the woman in 3:16 and into "toil" or "painful toil" in relation to the man in 3:17, but both are unusual translations for the term *'iṣṣābôn*. The more usual translation would be "distress" or "sorrow."

42. The Hebrew term *hērôn* is not the typical word for childbearing or conception. The proper word for "childbearing" or "conception," which occurs in Hos 9:11 and Ruth 4:13, is *hērāyôn*. See Cassuto's comments in support of this in his *Commentary on the Book of Genesis*, 164ff., and Meyers, *Discovering Eve*, 102–3. A better and more literal translation of *hērôn* is given by the Septuagint, *stenagmon*, which means "sighing" or "groaning."

did not use it.[43] Cain, too, is told to rule over sin (4:7), but succumbs to its temptation to kill his own brother. The flood account laments over humanity that is completely dominated by sin.

Evil has now corrupted the goodness of every aspect of the once "very good" creation. There is now "evil" experienced in humanity's relationship to God, to creation, and to itself. In this way, Genesis 3 (and, more loosely, chapters 3–11 as a whole) represents a complete antithetical parallelism to Genesis 1–2. This strong narrative reversal has the effect of powerfully evoking in the reader a sense of tragedy over the loss of paradise and exile in the cursed land due to human disobedience of Yahweh God.[44] Therefore, even without the explicit language of a "fall," the text's themes and structure point to the reality of a dark transition from "before sin" to "after sin."[45]

Hope for the Restoration of Comprehensive Goodness

While the "Fall stories" of Genesis 3–11 represent an antithesis to Genesis 1–2, they are not completely hopeless, as there are some hopeful indications. Most notably, the judgment oracle of Genesis 3 contains two statements of a redemptive "overcoming," which correspond to the two curses.[46]

---

43. One could argue that the reverse is now true, that the serpent has dominion over humanity. The serpent now has destructive power over human life, even as the term "dust" in 3:14 and 3:19 shows. The serpent's "food" is the "dust" of the ground, which ironically refers to humanity, over whom the Lord solemnly declares "you are dust" (Gen 3:19). The story of the serpent (representative of evil and sin) seeking to control and destroy human life continues in the story of Cain's murder of his brother (see esp. 4:7).

44. In the terms of narrative criticism, this is the proper and expected effect of the narrative of Genesis 1–3 upon its implied readers.

45. Accordingly, readings that regard Genesis 2–3 as an account of the maturation of humanity (such as Lynn Betchel, in Brenner's *A Feminist Companion to Genesis*, 77–117) seem to miss important elements of the text and its theology.

46. The poetic oracle in Gen 3:14–19 has typically been studied as having three distinct parts made up of three divine speeches given to the three addressees, the serpent, the women, and the man. Although such an approach has a number of benefits, it fails to adequately recognize the logical and rhetorical relationship between the penalties spoken by God. A careful consideration of the symmetrical structure of the poetry shows that the judgment oracle has a two-part structure 3:14–16 and 3:17–19. Each part contains four main elements: an indictment, a curse, a description of the outworking of the curse, and a statement of "overcoming" that curse. See H. J. Pokrifka, "Understanding the Poetry in Gen 3:14–19."

Within the context of Genesis 3, the first statement of overcoming relates to the woman's descendant or descendants "striking" the head of the serpent (3:15c), often interpreted as "messianic" by Jews and Christians.[47] This is a rich theological statement of a future redemptive victory over of the baneful effects of primeval rebellion against Yahweh.[48] Through childbearing, the woman and her descendants will prevail over the serpent that is antagonistic to the woman, to her descendants, and to childbearing itself (3:16).[49] This overcoming is significant, since it holds out the hope that all the expressions of the serpent's hostility will not ultimately prove decisive for women or men. In the literary context of 3:14–15, this suggests that pernicious hindrances to fruitful and pleasant childbearing will be removed, and the pattern of male-domination of women ("He will rule over you") will come to an end.[50] Although God's words to the woman focus on the negative consequences of sin upon inter-human relationships, they also contain hope that these consequences can be undone.

The second expression of overcoming is found in the statements, "You will eat the plants of the field" and "you will eat your food" (3:17 and 19). That is, while the ground is relatively unyielding and hostile to

47. What Christians have called the *proto-euangelian* (proto-gospel) in Gen 3:15 points to hope in the context of a cosmic struggle between good and evil, between Christ and Satan. Christians have said that the church reaps the benefits of Christ's triumph over Satan as prophesied in Genesis 3. But in this chapter, I begin to show that the promises of redemption in 3:15 is already partly fulfilled in the context of Yahweh's covenant with Israel, showing that the "seed of the women" here can also refer collectively to the corporate people of God as well as to a personal messianic figure.

48. This makes the most sense if the serpent is seen not only as an ordinary earthly creature, but also as symbolic of evil or evil power or the evil one.

49. This overcoming through childbearing is specifically highlighted in the concluding prose section following the poetic oracle in chapter 3, where the women is called Eve because she is the "mother of all living" (3:20). This overcoming and its relation to divine aid are further confirmed by Eve's words in 4:1 "I have produced a man with the help of the Lord."

50. This interpretation is evident if we see that the judgment oracle of Genesis 3 has a two-part structure, the first part being 3:14–16 and the second 3:17–19. As noted above, each part contains an indictment, a curse, a description of the outworking of the curse, and a statement of "overcoming" that curse. Interpreted this way, God's word to the woman is part of the description of the outworking of the curse to the serpent. The cursed serpent is hostile to the woman. The serpent's hostility toward the woman finds its expression in its struggle against the woman's childbearing and against the woman's equal partnership with the man, since it is through the woman and her seed that the serpent will be conquered.

humanity, man and woman will overcome this resistance and still obtain food, which is essential for their survival. While food is obtained in "distress and sorrow" (*'iṣabôn*, the same word used to describe childbearing in 3:16[51]), the ongoing production of food and sustained life is a sign of overcoming the cursed ground.[52] The human relationship to the non-human creation (the earth and its creatures) is frustrated, but there is implied hope for the restoration of a proper relationship that gives mutual benefit to both humans and the creatures they rule.

In summary, the promises of redemption give hope for a restoration of a comprehensive goodness in all three major relationships. If so, the judgment oracles in Gen 3:14–19 are *not* mandates or divine prescriptions,[53] but something to be overcome—especially through the divine redemptive work.[54]

The Ancestors of Israel

Yahweh's intention to redeem all creation and restore the original comprehensive goodness is clearly expressed in Yahweh's call of and promise to Abraham. The call to go to a promised land and the comprehensive set of promises to Abraham move the narrative toward the recovery of Eden. The Land of Canaan is "flowing with milk and honey"—exceedingly fertile, like Eden.[55]

Toward Restored Accountable Relationship with God

Following the scattering of the people from Babel, God initiates a redemptive relationship with Abraham. Through various trials and tests,

---

51. This is a linguistic marker that further points to the two-fold structure of the poetic oracle.

52. In my view, the fulfillment of the second overcoming is dependent on the fulfillment of the first overcoming. That is, the defeat of the serpent through the women's seed will end its hostile influence on the ground as well.

53. Trible, "Depatriarchalizing in Biblical Interpretation," 41. This statement presupposes that the divine oracle of judgment in chapter 3 is descriptive in nature, rather than prescriptive, that is, God is describing how things will be, rather than how things ought to be at all times.

54. If so, the mandates for humanity from Genesis 1 (procreation and dominion) remain in force rather than being fundamentally compromised.

55. See Hamilton, *God's Glory*, 79, for how the blessings of Gen 12:1–3 answer the "curses" of 3:15–19, plus the related correspondences between Eden and the people and land of Israel.

Abraham learns to trust and obey God to the point of nearly sacrificing his promised child Isaac. Based on Abraham's extreme obedience, God makes an oath ("By myself I have sworn") to fulfill all the divine promises made to Abraham—and indirectly to Sarah (Gen 22:16–18; 17:16).[56] If Adam and Eve fall from innocence to disobedience with the result of losing paradise, Abraham and Sarah mature from doubt to obedience with the result of securing divine promises for their descendants, who are likewise required to obey God by keeping the covenant sign of circumcision.[57]

Toward Harmonious Inter-Human Relationships

Ultimately, the promises are given, so that all the families of the earth (including all their women!) will be blessed in and through Abraham and Sarah (Gen 12:3; 17:16).[58] But the stories of Israel's ancestors are deeply marked by androcentric and patriarchal culture, making the blessings themselves appear androcentric. Men generally have center stage, with women typically in the periphery.[59] When women's stories are told, women are often presented in a negative light.[60]

---

56. One could say that it is only now that promises of God to Abraham become unconditional, because the prior condition of obedience has been completely satisfied ("because you have done this and have not withheld your son, your only son, I will surely bless you" Gen 22:16–17 ESV). Although the text of Genesis does not say directly that God's promises to Abraham prior to the sacrifice of Isaac are conditional, the fact of testing in Genesis 22 and its result imply that they were. For how the Lord's covenant with Abraham includes both conditional and unconditional aspects, see Wright, *The Mission of God*, 205–8.

57. The expectation is that those who violate the covenant requirement will be cut off from Israel—unless God shows mercy.

58. On how, in the Old Testament, Israel is chosen for the good of all humans, see Wright, *The Mission of God*, 222–43. Although I follow the dominant interpretation of Gen 12:3 that Abraham and his descendants are the channels of blessing the nations, there are other viable interpretations, such as that Abraham and his descendents are honored as blessed by the nations (Moberly, *The Theology of the Book of Genesis*, 148–61), or that "people will take [Abraham's] own good fortune as the desired measure when invoking a blessing on themselves" (Nahum Sarna, in his commentary on *Genesis*).

59. See especially Cheryl Exum's treatment of the "matriarchs" of Genesis 11–35 in *Fragmented Women*, 94–147.

60. There is a fierce female rivalry between Sarah and Hagar. Hagar is abused and rejected by Sarah and Abraham. See Trible, *Texts of Terror*, 9–35. Rachel and Leah are treated unjustly by their fathers. See Lapsley's insightful treatment of Rachel's words in Genesis 31, and how they can be interpreted theologically as "whispering" a divine

While there is not an abundance of evidence for restoration of the unity and equality of men and women or other inter-human relationships in the patriarchal period, there are stories that nevertheless surprise us for their favorable way of treating women and their concerns. In particular, God elevates and honors Sarah as the mother of many nations and kings (Gen 17:16). The Lord also directly appears to Hagar and gives her a historic promise of innumerable descendants (Gen 16:10).[61] Empowering revelation and promises are not given only to men, but also to the women as active carriers and fulfillers of divine purposes and destiny.[62]

There is another important way in which women are an integral part of the covenant promises and fulfillment, namely, childbearing. Childbearing is viewed as of paramount importance for the fulfillment of God's mandate of fruitfulness (Gen 1:28) and the fulfillment of all the promises to Abraham.[63] Over time, obstacles to fruitfulness are overcome through God's sovereign acts and blessings.[64] Read in light of the

---

word of disfavor upon the patriarchal abuses of Laban (*Whispering the Word*, 21–34). Dinah is raped (Gen 34) and the text does not appear to condemn it. However, see Robin Parry's perceptive treatment of this text and how it might be read (chapter 2 of this volume).

61. Even Hagar, despite being an oppressed and rejected Egyptian slave-woman, is portrayed as "a pivotal figure in biblical theology." In the context of the metanarrative of the Hebrew Bible, she is "the first person in Scripture whom a divine messenger visits," "the only persons who dares to name the deity," and the only woman "to receive a divine promise of descendants" (Trible, *Texts of Terror*, 28).

62. In addition, there are hints that husbands, even patriarchs, are not to have unilateral authority over their wives (against the view that Gen 3:16 is prescriptive), as when Abraham is told to obey (šĕmaʿ bĕqôlâ) Sarah in Gen 21:12. Such things are surely evidence of God redeeming broken, patriarchal inter-human relationships among the people of Israel.

63. In her *Kinship and Marriage in Genesis*, Naomi Steinberg argues rightly that the main function of marital arrangements in Genesis is to ensure the establishment of an Israelite line of descent.

64. The story of Abraham and Sarah in particular stands out, since their struggle was not simply against trouble in pregnancy but against the complete impossibility of getting pregnant due to old age. God's supernatural intervention in their situation is nothing less than a demonstration of God's supreme power to give life even to the "dead." Such an astounding start gives credence to God's extraordinary promises of a great nation (Gen 12:2), countless descendants like "the stars in heaven and sand on the seashore" (Gen 16:10), and multitude of nations and kings (Gen 17:16), which all seem out of reach for this original family of two.

Also, the story of Sarah and Hagar establish for Israel that "heirship to the covenant promises is to be based on an exclusive matrilineal principle" (Sarna, *Genesis*, 126).

judgment oracle of Genesis 3, the matriarchs' struggles in childbearing can be viewed as expressions of the cosmic struggle against the hostile serpent who resists proliferation of God's people, the "seed of the women." Women experience victory over this evil through God's sovereign acts and sometimes even through imperfect human means.[65] Instances of the divine elevation of women and the divinely-helped victories of women represent a movement toward the full humanity and authority of women.

Toward Restored Dominion

A related movement toward a restoration of dominion is evident on two levels. First, there is an implied dominion over animals that enables Abraham and his descendants (especially Jacob) to be rich in livestock (Gen 13:2; 26:13). Second, the chosen people are protected from their enemies and even have power over others.[66] God will bless those who bless Abraham and his descendants and curse those who curse them (12:3), and Abraham's seed will possess the gate of their enemies (Gen 22:17). God appears to validate such dominion in the regal promises given to Abraham and Sarah. Although God's original call to dominion only concerned the non-human creation, the sin-corrupted, post-Fall situation appears to involve a legitimate (yet temporary and imperfect) rule of some humans, especially God's chosen people, over others.[67] This can be interpreted as an inter-human expression of the conflict between the two "seeds" mentioned in Gen 3:15, the seed of the women and the seed of the serpent.[68] The divine election of the seed of the women and the resulting legitimation of human-to-human dominion, however, is presumably for the ultimate purpose of blessing all peoples and nations (Gen 12:3).[69]

---

65. Such as resorting to polygamy as a means for having more children and gain greater social prominence.

66. Specifically, Abraham has military victory over other kings, and Abraham and Sarah are rescued from kings who could have taken their lives.

67. Later, in the book of Judges and beyond, human kingship (a form of inter-human dominion) is sometimes elevated as a partial solution to the problem of sin, i.e., of humans "doing what is right in their own eyes."

68. See Hamilton, *God's Glory*, 80–82.

69. Unfortunately, this is certainly not the case for many nations (e.g., the Canaanites) in their relation to Israelites, which gives initial plausibility to the notion (held by some feminists) that all human rule over other humans is inherently evil. The

The patriarchal or ancestral period portrayed in Genesis 12–50 shows the beginnings not only of the Israelite people, but of a redemptive overcoming of the effects of sin. In a manner that is patient and tolerant of the failures of humans in a patriarchal world, Yahweh lays the groundwork for blessing all the peoples of the earth.

The Emergence of Israel

A new phase in biblical history begins with the Egyptian oppression of the Israelites. Yahweh overcomes this apparent setback in the divine plan for Israel by rescuing oppressed Israel through Moses (Exod 3:9–10). Then, God reveals the divine will to create a theocratic society, through which to bless other nations (Exod 19:4–6). To this end, Yahweh empowers the Israelites to conquer the Promised Land.

Accountability to God

The descendants of Abraham are brought into an accountable and redemptive relationship with Yahweh through the events of the exodus and the subsequent giving of covenant laws to Israel. Through obedience to laws of the covenant, Israel can maintain holiness and its covenant relationship with the Lord and fulfill its mission as a priestly kingdom that will bless all nations (Exod 19:5–6; cf. Gen 12:1–3). Israel's national well-being and the quality of all human relationships within Israel depend on obedience to God.

The story of exodus is not only about human liberation but (even more importantly) about establishing monotheism through Yahweh's revelation and rule. God judges all the gods of Egypt (Exod 12:12) and overcomes a political super power, demonstrating that there is no other God like Yahweh. Yahweh's unmatched power and holiness are plainly displayed in the eyes of Israel and Egypt—so that they will know who Yahweh is.[70] Yahweh alone is to be worshipped, feared, obeyed, and loved. In a fashion parallel to what occurred in the exodus, Yahweh later empowers Israel to occupy Canaan, further solidifying the fact that Yahweh alone is true God.

---

canon of the Old Testament points to a "middle way" between radical egalitarianism (or even anarchism) and authoritarianism, in which ultimately only God has dominion over humanity, yet God delegates to some responsibility to rule over others with a view to maximal justice and good for all.

70. See Hamilton, *God's Glory*, 88.

Read against Genesis 1–3, the events of exodus and conquest are interpreted as God's sovereign overthrowing of the hostile and controlling power of the serpent, manifested in and through oppressive political power and false, polytheistic religion.[71] The serpent's hostile power to influence humanity to turn away from Yahweh or to thwart Yahweh's plans is decisively vanquished by Yahweh's sovereign and gracious acts. The reestablishment of Yahweh's sovereign rule and authority is of paramount importance for women, as women's plight (as stated in Genesis 3) can be traced directly back to the serpent and his power over human life. Where the serpent and his seed rule, there is hostility, injustice, and death. Where Yahweh rules, there is hope for a restored comprehensive goodness and justice for women.

Unfortunately, the period from the Exodus to the Conquest, like other periods of Israel's history, is not marked by Israel's seamless obedience. Quite to the contrary, it is marked by heinous sins such as the golden calf episode and the rebellion of Numbers 13–14. Thus, while there is God's call to and expectation of obedience from the covenant partner Israel, because the Israelite covenant partner is imperfect and sinful, God's ultimate way of dealing with Israel is going to be one of compassion and grace.[72]

Toward Harmonious Inter-Human Relationships

Despite distinct tribal identities, the people of Israel have unity under God as God's special, chosen people. Restored covenant relationship with the Lord implies unity, harmony, and equality among all God's people.[73] No doubt, this egalitarian ideal is not fully enshrined within Israelite law, nor is its actualization in any way complete in Israelite culture. Still, Israelite unity and standards of justice often serve as harmoni-

---

71. That non-Israelite nations are "demonized" in this way is deeply problematic for many feminists, who understand this tendency as another instance of the xenophobic violence inherent in patriarchy and its deity. In my view, the canon urges a different way of reading the Exodus and the Conquest, though perhaps not one that is agreeable to contemporary Western sentiments. At the least, we can say that the biblical canon has a way of identifying God's denunciation and judgment of evil at work in other nations without minimizing God's similar work in Israel—as we will see below.

72. Thus instead of annihilation of unfaithful Israel, a remnant is preserved at the time of exile and a future restoration is promised.

73. This unity is concretely (and temporarily) expressed in the account of a new generation of Israelites coming together in unity under Joshua's leadership and beginning to enter and conquer the Promised Land.

ous parallels to the horizontal unity among Adam and Eve in the Garden (Gen 1–2), in some contrast to the extreme alienation, domination, and violence that emerged in Genesis 3–11.

Israel's laws approximate an egalitarian ideal in certain important ways. There is a just and relatively equitable distribution of the land among the tribes and families within them (Num 33:54). There are Jubilee laws that aim to maintain and protect this state of affairs—with all of its redemptive economic benefits for the poor and vulnerable (Lev 25). Should there be poor, orphans, widows, or aliens, the laws of Israel restrain wickedness and injustice toward them (Exod 22:21–27; Deut 27:19) and promote compassion and generosity, based on God's compassion and generosity toward Israel (Deut 14:29; 16:11, 14; 24:19–21; 26:12–13). These laws shows a certain underlying concern for justice and equality, even though it was imperfectly expressed in relation to the status of women in Israel. While the legal code reflects a certain inequality between the male and female status at times, it still shows some concern for giving a fair trial and justice to women, instead of leaving women to unrestrained androcentric legal procedures. In addition, respect for women is found in the commandments that honor both mothers and fathers as the teachers of the law and guardians of the religion of Israel (Exod 20:12; Deut 6:7).[74]

Besides these redemptive aspects of the law, the narratives of Exodus portray how God uses women as redemptive agents. The women are supernaturally fruitful even under the most adverse conditions.[75] Israelite midwives (like Shiphrah and Puah) fear God more than Pharaoh and thus preserve Israel's posterity (Exod 1), mediating and foreshadowing the Lord's own values and acts, especially the deliverance of the vulnerable from oppression and death.[76] Other female redemptive agents are Jochebed, Miriam, and Pharaoh's daughter—all of whom partner together in saving Moses, the primary leader God used to redeem Israel.

---

74. See the chapters by Briggs and Williams in this volume (3 and 4 respectively) for reflections on the relationship of feminist concerns to certain laws (and related narratives) in the Torah.

75. In the Sinai Covenant, the covenant blessing of fruitfulness of the womb that was already at work among the Hebrews is reconfirmed to the people of Israel, but is clearly articulated as contingent upon covenant obedience (Exod 23:26; Deut 28:4).

76. Lapsley, *Whispering the Word*, 86–87.

Therefore, women play an essential role in advancing God's redemptive work, a telling sign of the full humanity of women.[77]

Dominion

Later in Exodus, Israel is called "a kingdom of priests," which points to the calling of God's people to be a vehicle of divine blessing to other nations (Exod 19:6; cf. Gen 12:3). However, the biblical portrayal of "post-Fall" dominion is one of God's people over and against others that are hostile to God and God's people—not primarily as human dominion over the earth or its creatures (contra Gen 1:27). This dominion is paradigmatically expressed in the Conquest of Canaan. No doubt susceptible to ideological and nationalist distortions, theocratic Israel's rule is portrayed as an extension of divine dominion, which involves dominion over human enemies, who from a theological point of view are idolaters and agents of evil.

The theme of dominion is relevant to feminist concerns about male domination of women. If a people are given divine authorization to dominate other peoples, then one wonders whether this opens the door to other forms of inter-human domination, including of men over women (as in Gen 3:16). The grand narrative of the Old Testament helps us to formulate a hermeneutical response that addresses such feminist concerns. Read in light of Genesis 3, the Conquest and related texts supporting Israelite rule over other nations can be viewed as an extension of a violent and bloody struggle between the "serpent's seed" and the "woman's seed" (see Gen 3:15), which culminates in the triumph of the women's descendants. In this interpretation, the post-Fall humanity divides into two groups based upon their relationship to God.[78] Just as Adam and Eve's failure to take dominion over the serpent resulted in the serpent's hostile domination over them, if Israel fails to take do-

---

77. There are a number of thematic parallels between the Genesis 1–3 and Exodus. Unlike Eve, who is tricked by a highly crafty serpent and fails to guard her inheritance, these women face and overcome even the threat of death and thus ensure a future redeemer for the whole nation Israel. In other words, they fulfill their identity as "helpers" (see Gen 2:18) of the weak and oppressed and their calling to have dominion by overcoming even the most formidable enemy Pharaoh. In relation to Genesis 3, Pharaoh's ruthless genocide campaign against the people of God is an extension of the serpent's hostility against the "seed" of the woman. Further, the Israelite women's redemptive acts and God's employment of Moses in judgment of Egypt parallel the "seed" of the woman "striking" the serpent's head.

78. See Hamilton, *God's Glory*, 80–81, 90, 145, and 155.

minion over those who represent the serpent's rule, then the latter will dominate Israel (which is what actually happens in Israel's history). Although many questions still remain, these reflections resist the idea that the Conquest reflects an oppressive, nationalist ideology (as many post-colonial interpreters might say).[79] Moreover, the idea that in the Conquest (and other times) Israel is used as an agent of divine justice against evildoers contradicts any justification of oppression of women or other groups of people. Rather, it confirms that justice and judgment of evil—in one form or another—are central features of Yahweh's character and revelation[80] and that God will sometimes use his people as an instrument of his justice.[81]

The stories of exodus and conquest further demonstrate that the restored vertical relationship with God is the proper basis for the flourishing of all other human relationships. Conversely, when the "upward vertical" relationship of humanity with God is broken or distorted, it negatively determines the originally horizontal inter-human relationships, introducing into them the dominion that originally belonged only to the "downward vertical" relationship of humanity with the non-human creation.

Israel's Covenant Life in the Land

In the period of Joshua, Israel begins to have dominance over their hostile and powerful enemies to possess the Promised Land. The story of Israel in the land is lengthy and varied, starting with the anarchical period of the judges, rising to the partial "golden age" of the United Monarchy, and then spiraling downwards into national division and exile from the land. As I did with earlier epochs in Israel's story, I will analyze this epoch of Israel in the Promised Land through the lens of the three human relationships (and related themes) that I identified Genesis 1–3. I will draw heavily upon the language of the covenant blessings and curses found in Leviticus 26 and Deuteronomy 28, which thematically correspond to Genesis 1–3.

---

79. For a further reflections on the problem of the Canaanites, see Wright's *Old Testament Ethics*, 472–80 and *The God I Don't Understand*, 76–110.

80. Indeed, God severely judges Israel for her sin, not least her injustice, thus showing that the other nations are not treated "unfairly," but justly for their sin.

81. It is also important to realize that the concept of *ḥerem* is limited to an early period of Israel's history.

Accountability to Yahweh

After the death of Joshua, Israel enters into a period of lawlessness and anarchy, in which "everyone did what was right in his own eyes" (Judg 21:25). They live in a cycle of idolatry and sin, divine discipline in a form of onslaught from enemies, temporary repentance, and a season of divine deliverance through judges. "With each cycle of rebellion, though, the situation gets worse. The book ends with two stories that illustrate Israel's foul rebellion and with Israel's repeated cry for a king to deliver them from this mess (Judg 21:25)."[82]

Eventually, Yahweh as King is rejected and a human king is installed in Israel. The books of Samuel, Kings, and Chronicles evaluate the history of the monarchy through the "Deuteronomic" lens of national retribution; the nation prospers when its leader—and by implication the rest of the nation—follows God, and the nation wanes when its leader rebels against God. Saul is rejected for his rebellion against God, while David's heart is after God and thus David is ultimately blessed by God, paving the way for a period of unprecedented national blessing (economic prosperity, political power, and international reputation and influence) during the time of Solomon's reign. But Israel's glory does not last long, due to Solomon's ruthless policies (1 Kgs 12:4), violation of God's commands for kings (1 Kgs 11:11; Deut 17:16–17), and spiritual apostasy (1 Kgs 11:9–10). There is an internal rebellion and the kingdom divides into two.[83]

In the Divided Kingdom, the kings of both Israel and Judah typically demonstrate unfaithfulness to God and injustice in relation to their people. Instead of realizing a redeemed life and becoming an agent of divine redemption to the rest of the world, Israel (used for Israel and Judah) succumbs to idolatry, injustice, and other forms of rebellion against God and the Torah. Israel incurs divine punishment according to covenant curses delineated especially in Lev 26:14–39 and Deut 28:14–68. Ultimately, Israel ends up in an exile. Nothing less than the "death" of the nation will atone for her sins and allow her return to the land (Isa 22:14; 27:9; 40:2).[84]

---

82. Bartholomew and Goheen, "The Story-Line of the Bible," 3. See also Nicholas Ansell's treatment of Judges 19–21 in chapter 5 of this volume.

83. See Bartholomew and Goheen, "The Story-Line of the Bible," 3–4.

84. For the image of death and resurrection applied to Israel, see Gowan, *Theology of the Prophetic Books*.

Human Inter-Relationships

The period of anarchy and lawlessness recorded in the book of the Judges manifests godlessness in the form of devastating cultural sexism and misogyny (with notable exceptions like the story of Deborah). Two striking negative examples of the treatment of women in Judges are Jephthah's daughter[85] in Judges 11 and the Levite's concubine/wife[86] in Judges 19.

A few comments are in order. Far from tolerating the atrocious violence against these unnamed women as the divine will, the larger narrative context denounces it as an extreme expression of human sin and wickedness. Much like the escalation of sin and violence from Genesis 3 to Genesis 6, the book of Judges concludes with the grim story of the Levite's woman and how it leads to a bloody aftermath in virtually all of tribal Israel (Judg 20–21). Also, as Deuteronomy 28 indicates, sexual sins like rape are signs of living in a cursed situation of escalated sin and divine judgment.[87] While the themes and canonical placement of the Book of Judges may present this event simply as an expression of the anarchy that ensues without a (Davidic) king,[88] they clearly see these events as something of which Israel should be ashamed.

Moreover, Phyllis Trible draws attention to how the shapers of the canon convey another response, more comprehensive and women-friendly, to the woman of Judges 19. That is, by placing this book in a certain place in the canon,[89] the woman's story is juxtaposed with themes that are more hopeful for women. This point applies to both the Jewish order, in which the story of Hannah (1 Sam 1:1—2:21) immediately follows the story of the concubine, or the order of the Greek Bible, in which the book of Ruth follows it. Either way, the story of the Levite's concu-

---

85. Among the important feminist treatments of Jephthah's daughter are those of the "revisionist" Trible (*Texts of Terror*, 93–118) and the moderate "rejectionist" Exum (*Fragmented Women*, 16–21).

86. Some helpful feminist treatments of the rape and murder of the Levite's concubine or wife are found in pieces by Lapsley (*Whispering the Word*, 35–68) and Trible (*Texts of Terror*, 65–92; see my comments below). See also chapter 5 in this volume by Nicholas Ansell.

87. For example, Deut 28:30 says, "You shall betroth a wife, but another man will violate her," and other verses confirm hostility among families (see Deut 28:54: "The man who is refined and very delicate among you shall be hostile toward his brother and toward the wife he cherishes and toward the rest of his children who remain").

88. Trible, *Texts of Terror*, 84.

89. Ibid., 84–85.

bine and its aftermath is followed by stories marked by an "absence of misogyny, violence, and vengeance," which, in effect, "speaks a healing word in the last days of the judges."[90] With such stories, the canonical shapers "counsel redemption" from God as the hope for women like the Levite's concubine or Jephthah's daughter—a hope that was tasted by Hannah, Ruth, and Naomi and which, in the canonical prophets, will be the inheritance of all God's people in a future world of justice and peace.

Also set in the time of the Judges, the book of Ruth is the only book in the Old Testament that is pervaded by a predominantly gynocentric perspective.[91] Ruth and Naomi and their women associates see the blessing and redemption of God amidst a fallen and unstable people of Israel, and offer a unique theological perspective on life that the "male perspective" cannot convey.[92]

During the period of united monarchy, especially during the reign of David and Solomon, there is general improvement in human-to-human relationships on the public macro-level. But this period is also marked by some striking practices of sexism and oppression.[93] As Trible summarizes, "David pollutes Bathsheba; Amnon rapes Tamar . . . and Absalom violates the concubines of his father."[94] The monarchy obviously is not free of the problems of human sin, including the sexist misuse of power against women.[95]

90. Ibid., 85.

91. See Bauckham's "The Book of Ruth as a Key to Gynocentric Reading of Scripture" in *Gospel Women*, 1–16. For comments on the hermeneutical significance of Bauckham's work on Ruth, see Robin Parry's piece in this volume (chapter 2). Song of Songs is also an exception to the androcentric perspective, for which see Grenville Kent's discussion in chapter 8 of this volume.

92. For a detailed and helpful treatment of the Book of Ruth, see Lapsley (*Whispering the Word*, 89–108).

93. In Meyer's view, the transition from early Israel to monarchical Israel marked a decline in the social power of women and an increase of a kind of patriarchy (*Discovering Eve*, 181–96). In her words, "The locus of power moved from the family household, with its gender parity, to a public world of male control" (ibid., 190). In my view, there is some plausibility to Meyer's view that women had more overall power in a village-based social order in which the household had greater prominence, but in the end her overall perspective relies too heavily on speculative historical and social-scientific judgments and too little upon a careful reading of the final form of the Old Testament and its metanarrative.

94. Trible, *Texts of Terror*, 84. For Trible's helpful treatment of Tamar as a paradigm of wisdom violated, see ibid., 37–64.

95. Trible offers an in ironic alteration of the refrain of Judges to describe the

Without minimizing the horror of stories of sexist atrocities, the Old Testament metanarrative helps us to read them in a way that ultimately promotes justice for women. First, the stories of Bathsheba and Tamar demonstrate the horrific corporate effects of sin on those in power, thereby denouncing such sin. David's adultery and violence lead to the consequent escalated sexual sins and violence that destroy his family. While the God of Israel stands with Bathsheba in solidarity,[96] God lets David reap the terrible consequences of his sins. It follows that the rape of Tamar and Absalom's adulteries and the apparent divine silence reflect not divine will against women, but rather the natural process of David's sowing sin and necessarily reaping its evil fruits in his family.[97] Lack of divine intervention is itself a form of divine punishment of sin. This means that sexist atrocities are not inevitable features of human life that God has no answers for, but are evils that God seeks to root out and deter through a public exposé of both sin and its consequences. Second, various texts show evidence that the general covenantal blessing principle is also at work in monarchical Israel. Accordingly, there is greater peace and justice among all Israelites, including women, when Israel is in right relationship with Yahweh.[98] Several texts from the Monarchial period and onwards speak of positive male-female relationships in Israel or offer a positive portrayal of women. A couple of examples from Proverbs and Song of Songs will suffice.

To begin, wisdom is strikingly personified as a woman (Prov 8).[99] "Woman Stranger" (associated with adultery) is matched by "Woman

---

Davidic monarchy: "In those days there was a king in Israel, and royalty did right in its own eyes" (*Texts of Terror*, 84).

96. Although Cheryl Exum is right that David's crime is largely portrayed as a crime against Uriah in 2 Samuel 12, the wider context of the metanarrative points to how God also stands with vulnerable ones like Bathsheba—the lamb in Nathan's story (Exum, *Fragmented Women*, 184–85). One could say that the liberating "spirit" of the narrative as a whole should cause one to reassess the patriarchal or androcentric "letter" of certain texts and their conventions.

97. For a detailed discussion of 2 Samuel 13, see Miriam Bier's discussion in chapter 6 of this volume.

98. The formal covenant blessings (in Lev 26 and Deut 28) do not stress wholesome human inter-relations, but assume them—since the covenant curses speak of a destruction of good familial relations (Deut 28:30, 53–57).

99. While virtually all of Proverbs is written from a male perspective for males and much of Proverbs is clearly expressive of a patriarchal or even misogynist culture, its canonical shaping does not silence elements that are positive for women.

Wisdom" (associated with ideal and lasting life).[100] Then, in Proverbs 31, there is a mother's instruction to her royal son (31:1–9) and the portrayal of a woman who embodies the kind of wisdom the entire book has stressed (31:10–31).[101] "The husband appreciates his good fortune, in no way sees himself diminished" and is able to praise his wife's excellence and success in the city gates.[102] The woman and the man respect, value, trust, and benefit each other—exemplifying a model of the restored and mutually empowering husband and wife relationship.[103] Despite some expressions of patriarchal public culture in Israel in this text,[104] the text points to much improvement over the post-sin situation of male dominance epitomized in Genesis 3:16 ("he will rule over you"). In light of the wider metanarrative, this example relates to God's covenant blessings on the obedient and the redemption of women and men from the evil effects of sin.[105]

The Song of Songs, traditionally ascribed to Solomon, portrays a pleasant and loving relationship between a woman and a man.[106] Desire to love and to be loved is reciprocal. The lovers praise each other with sheer delight. "In the Song of Songs we see suggestions of the restoration

---

100. Day, "Women and the Feminine," 121.

101. She is prosperous, valued, favored, industrious, independent, courageous, kind, generous, and (in summary) wise.

102. Le Cornu, "Proverbs," 339.

103. See Branch, "Women," 921–22.

104. "Her husband is known at the gates when he sits among the elders of the land" (Prov 31:23). Even the glowingly redemptive portrait of the woman in Proverbs 31 remains set in the context of a patriarchal culture in which the woman's role is primarily domestic and men are the primary public decision-makers (i.e., among the elders at the city gate). However, as Carol Meyers has pointed out, the domestic sphere is a significant realm of social power and influence—despite common contemporary assumptions (see *Discovering Eve*, 40–45). Also, contrary to the notion that a woman should have power and authority *only* in the private, domestic sphere, the ideal woman in this chapter maintains some public roles, such as involvement in trade and business transactions (31:16–18). Accordingly, the concluding line of the poem calls for public praise of the woman: "let her works praise her in the gates" (31:31).

105. Even as those under covenant blessing are expected to have abundance of food and bless others in need (Deut 28:12), the wise woman of power in Proverbs 31 is exceedingly successful in everything she does, not only providing for her household, but also for the poor and needy of her society (Prov 31:20).

106. Whiteley, "Song of Solomon," 348. For further comments on Song of Songs, see the piece by Grenville Kent, chapter 8 in this volume.

of that harmony, which had been destroyed in the Fall."[107] Contrasting with the typical patterns of the Israelite family structure, the paradigmatic love relationship portrayed in Song of Songs is more in keeping with the original Edenic marital norm from Genesis 2:24, in which the man leaves his parents and cleaves to his wife. The woman brings her beloved to her mother's house, to the very chamber where she was conceived (Song 3:4; 8:1). As in the Garden of Eden, love and procreation (hinted at in Song 3:4) is free of patriarchal concerns, demands, and negative effects.[108]

Unfortunately, the ideal life as portrayed in Proverbs and Song of Songs remains largely unrealized in the wider history of monarchical Israel. This is due to the increasing and persistent covenant unfaithfulness and injustice in Israel, as reflected in numerous prophetic invectives. The breakdown of the vertical relationship with Yahweh also means the breakdown of inter-human relationships and proper stewardship and dominion over the land. Thus, instead of peace, unity, harmony, justice, and love, there is much evidence of extortion, robbery, bribes, violence, contemptuous treatment of parents, and oppression of the under-privileged of the society—the poor, orphans, widows, and aliens (Ezek 22:7–13, 29; Jer 7:9). Women are typically among those who are particularly vulnerable to oppression. In keeping with the covenant curses for disobedience (Lev 26; Deut 28), Israel experiences an increasing measure

---

107. Whiteley, "Song of Solomon," 349. The connections between Genesis 2–3 and Song of Songs are also stressed by Trible in "Depatriarchalizing in Biblical Interpretation," 42ff.

108. Another hint of God's blessing on procreation in particular is found in Psalm 113, a text that speaks of God's liberation of the poor and oppressed. It concludes with this description of God's paradigmatic actions towards barren women: "He makes the barren woman abide in the house as a joyful mother of children" (v. 9). The blessing of the fruit of the womb is evident not merely in the number of children but also in the quality of life and relationship they enjoy, such as the enjoyment of respectful and honoring parent-child relationships (cf. Prov 31:28). In parallel with the Edenic blessing and mandate to "be fruitful and multiply" (Gen 1:28), the fruitfulness of the womb is among the explicit covenant blessings given to Israel (Lev 26:9 and Deut 28:4)—a reversal of the curses and the evil effects of sin, including toil and distress in childbearing (cf. Gen 3:16). It is impossible to know to what extent the Israelites experienced relief from barrenness, sterility, miscarriage, stillborn children, and premature deaths. But since there is evidence that the Israelites experienced other covenant blessings at one time or another, we can assume that they experienced this blessing as well in their times of blessing.

of fruitlessness and foreign aggression.[109] Once numerous, Israel eventually becomes few in number with only a few survivors left (Deut 28:62; Isa 1:9). The land becomes inhabitable, and gets its Sabbaths while it lies desolate after the removal of the people from the land (Lev 26:43).

Dominion

In keeping with the covenant retribution principle (blessings for obedience and curses for disobedience), Israel during the time of Judges goes through a cycle of being dominated as a form of judgment or else employing dominion as a form of deliverance—when Israel has military victory over her foes (Deut 28:7; Lev 26:7–8).[110] Also, when the people are faithful to God, they have dominion over the land and its creatures through divine empowerment and protection; savage beasts are removed from their land (Lev 26:6). Consistent with Gen 1:28, women are counted among the military heroes and judges of Israel who establish Israel's dominion in the land. Women can act on behalf of God's redemptive purposes even in the context of a sinful, unjust, and largely patriarchal society. Most importantly, Deborah is a prophet, a judge (or ruler), governing Israel for twenty years during a Canaanite oppression, then for another forty years after a decisive victory (Judg 4:3; 5:31).[111] Her rule over Israel is presented as an extension of the Yahweh's reign over Israel.[112]

---

109. Disobedient people under covenant curses cannot multiply (Hos 4:10). Children are killed by invaders (Isa 47:9) and are sacrificed to idols (Ezek 16:20–21; 20:31). If they survive, the children go into exile (Deut 28:41; Mic 1:16). In extreme circumstances, people even resort to cannibalism, even eating their own children (Lev 26:29; Deut 28:53–57; Jer 19:9; Lam 2:20; 4:10; Ezek 5:10).

110. In light of Genesis 1–3, the proper dominion of humans was originally supposed to be concerned with humanity's relation the ground and non-human plants and animals. Although not a focus of the book of Judges, the principles governing this relationship remain in effect. Insofar as the people are obedient, God's blessing removes savage beasts from the land (Lev 26:6), but under divine curses they return (Lev 26:26). But in a sinful social world, dominion is also attained through violence against human foes.

111. There are a number of ways in which Deborah and her song of victory in Judges 5 are parallel to Moses and his song of victory in Exodus 15 (cf. Deut 32), which highlights Deborah's exalted status as a leader within the perspective of the final canonical shape of the Old Testament.

112. It goes without saying that she led all the people, including the men. The Israelites sought her out for divine judgment (4:5). Deborah takes the initiative of summoning and commanding Barak (4:6). When the military leader Barak fails to demonstrate courage and strength, Deborah becomes a commander of the Lord's army to fulfill the divine word and purpose for her people.

Jael is a less prominent woman who nonetheless plays a crucial military role by killing king Sisera (Judg 4:17–22). True, Jael is presented—in good "androcentric" fashion—as "the wife of Heber" (4:17, 21; 5:24), but in the narrative's plot and in poetic celebration (Judg 5:6, 24), she is a key player and a hero—a true "seed of the woman" who crushes the "seed of the serpent."[113]

Israel extends its dominion over its neighbors during David's reign. David's covenant faithfulness is met by divine favor, which enables him and his men to gain dominance over Israel's foes and peace for Israel. But as noted above, this dominance and peace gained by David is not long lived. After David, there is a general downward cycle of covenant unfaithfulness, judgment (in the form of famine or foreign aggression, corresponding indirectly to the hostile cursed ground and hostile cursed serpent of Genesis 3). Until the eventual disintegration of both kingdoms of Israel and Judah, this pattern is resisted by only occasional reform.[114] One of the most notable spiritual reforms and related political independence occurs during the reign of Josiah of Judah. The authoritative and prophetic leadership of a woman prophet Huldah is instrumental in Josiah's massive reform.[115] King Josiah assumes Huldah's authority over him as a spiritual leader and as God's spokesperson.[116] Set in the context of a largely androcentric culture, the examples of Deborah and Huldah are indicative of how God's redemptive work transcends culturally limited understandings of dominion, authority, and leadership and how women are called, along with men, to partner with God in extending the divine dominion, authority, and leadership originally given to humanity in the garden.

---

113. Hamilton, *God's Glory*, 158.

114. Instead of exercising proper dominion over the earth and its creatures and over hostile human foes, Israel is dominated by others. Under covenant curses, Israel is powerless and defeated before her enemies (Lev 26:17, 19; Deut 28:25; Jer 20:4; 24:10). If there is any sowing and reaping, the enemies take it away (Lev 26:16; Hos 8:7). The land is devastated (Lev 26:31–32). The cursed, disobedient people also experience plagues, madness, and diseases until they are destroyed by them (Lev 26:16, 25; Deut 28:27, 60–61; Jer 32:24; Ezek 14:21). Beasts devour children and cattle (Lev 26:22; Ezek 5:17; 14:15, 21), and the land becomes desolate (Lev 26:33, 43; Isa 1:7; Ezek 14:21).

115. Huldah validates the authority of a document found during Josiah's time, making a major contribution to the process of the formation and canonization of the Bible. Huldah spoke with prophetic authority.

116. For a more detailed treatment on Huldah, see H. J. Pokrifka, "Huldah the Prophet."

Just as the contrast between life in Eden and life outside Eden is vast, the contrast between the blessed life and the cursed life of Israel is enormous. The exile from Eden and the exile from the Promised Land show that life outside God's immediate and favorable presence is harsh, precarious, destructive, and corrupt for both women and men. The obstinate Israelites reap an intensified outworking of the curses of Genesis 3 as an expression of divine covenantal curse. Yet, as a measure of divine grace, a remnant is preserved even in exile and a measure of hope remains (Jer 30:11).

Whatever hope remains is only found in God, not in human ability. Also, the full humanity of woman cannot be sought apart from the recovery of true humanity as a whole. This restoration of humanity can be established only in the context of a faithful covenant relationship with the creator God who wills to restore all of creation to its full glory. In that future world, women will be blessed alongside men and the whole creation.

Messianic Expectations and the Future Reign of God

After the death of Israel, there is a resurrection that takes place within the gracious purposes of God.[117] The resurrection occurs in two ways. On one level there is an initial "restoration of Israel to the land" after the exile, as recorded by books like Ezra and Nehemiah. This resurrection, if one can call it that, is rather underwhelming. Sin continues to plague the people after their partial restoration to the land (e.g., the complaints of the poor of Jerusalem in Nehemiah 5). On a second level, though, there is a far greater hope for the resurrection of Israel in the context of the hope of eschatological, creational redemption—which is announced by the prophets (e.g., Ezek 36–37). As attested in the prophets, this resurrection of Israel ultimately has positive and redemptive implications for

---

117. This is perhaps the main point of Gowan's *Theology of the Prophetic Books*, where he summarizes the transition from death to resurrection like this: "God determined to do a new thing—in effect, to start over. The little kingdoms of Israel and Judah would lose their political existence forever, but out of the death of Judah, God would raise up a new people, who would be able to understand about God what most of their preexilic ancestors had never been able to comprehend and who would commit themselves to obeying his will to an extent their ancestors had never done" (ibid., 9–10). From the perspective of Christian theological interpretation of the Bible, there was a partial resurrection in the remnant of Judah, but a fuller resurrection in the coming of Jesus.

people of all nations—in fulfillment of the Abrahamic covenant (Gen 12:3). God and the divinely-sent Davidic Messiah will reign with justice and righteousness, overcoming the pretensions of the powerful and lifting up the cause of the marginalized and weak (Ps 72)—including women. The earth itself will be renewed and its Edenic qualities restored. I will use texts concerning each of the three main human relationships to show the complete overcoming of the curses of Genesis 3 and the complete restoration of God's creational intentions expressed in Genesis 1–2.

God's Supremacy Universally Recognized

All evildoers in heaven and earth will be judged (Isa 24:21–22; Mal 4:1) and God's universal rule will be established. The messianic government of peace, justice, and righteousness will be everlasting (Isa 9:6–7; 11:4–5; cf. Ps 72:8–10). All will dwell in God's glory (Isa 60:19–20; cf. 24:23). The world will come to know God and all will worship and serve the Lord (Isa 11:9; 24:15–16; 45:23; Zeph 3:9). God will make a covenant of peace that is everlasting and will dwell with the chosen people forever (Ezek 37:26). The people of God will have a new heart, have the Spirit of God within them, and will be obedient to God (Ezek 36:26–27).

Peace among Humanity

God's eschatological judgment will come upon all kinds of people, having democratizing effects (Isa 24:2ff.) that ultimately leave only God on the throne (Isa 24:23). In God's kingdom where the divine King reigns and all worship the Lord, there is also peace between all peoples (Isa 2:4; 11:9; Mic 4:3; Zech 9:10). There is a reconstitution of God's people, which includes all those formerly excluded or considered inferior—such as gentiles and eunuchs (Isa 54:4–6). There is no more oppression, strife, violence, division, devastation, or destruction within God's kingdom (Isa 54:1; 60:18). The poor and needy will be blessed and given justice under the Messianic ruler (Ps 72:2, 12–13). While there is no specific mention of the liberation of woman from male domination and oppression, it should be seen as included in the universal shalom, unity, justice, and equity that God will establish (see Pss 96:10, 97:2, 99:4).[118]

---

118. There is hope of the people of God once again becoming massive in number and power due to longevity and exceeding fruitfulness in childbirth (Isa 60:22; Ezek 37:26; Zech 8:4–50). Isaiah envisions God as overcoming the curse of barrenness in the ideal future (Isa 54:1). Supernatural blessing will overturn unfruitfulness and replace it with fruitfulness—both on physical and spiritual levels. Such fruitfulness makes dominion over the land and its peoples possible (Isa 54:3).

Dominion

Isaiah foresees a time when all hostility among the animals and humans will be overcome. Human beings and animals will again live in peace, as in Eden (Isa 11:6–9). The enemies of God will be destroyed, God's people will be healed (Mal 4:3), and death itself will be overcome (Isa 25:8).[119]

In the final reign of God, God's creational intention is fully restored. All aspects of life in the new creation, the new Garden of God, are indeed blessed (cf. Isa 11:6–9; 65:17; 66:22). In fact, the new Garden of God is actually greater than merely a recovery of the Garden of Eden. In Eden, two humans live in a kind of ignorant bliss, yet with the serpent lurking around for an opportunity to deceive them; disobedience and death are a possibility. The new Garden is a place where all evil has been overcome, where everyone in a much-multiplied family of humanity worships the one true God, and where all live in peace with one another and with all creatures. There is ultimate justice for Zion and beyond (Isa 1:26–27; 14:32; Ezek 34:15–16). That justice includes justice for women.

The hope of future justice is emphasized for good reason by many religious feminists, since it is a hope that resists oppression in any form, including that of fallen patriarchal cultures—and this hope is fully in keeping with the shape of the canonical metanarrative.[120] For the most

---

119. Humanity's relationship to (and experience of) the land will also be restored. In the ideal future, the wilderness and barren land will become exceedingly fruitful and luxuriant like Eden, like the Garden of the Lord (Isa 51:3; Amos 9:13–15). The heavens will give rain and the ground is fruitful (Zech 8:12). There will no longer be famine or hunger (Isa 49:10; Ezek 36:29–30), but joyful celebration and thanksgiving feasts with choicest foods (Isa 51:3; Isa 25:6). The righteous people of God will possess the land and enjoy the goodness and beauty of God manifested in the land (Isa 60:21; Zech 8:12; 9:17).

120. For example, see Ruether's treatment of the "prophetic principle" in her *Sexism and God-Talk*, 22–27. The danger in Ruether's version of a revisionist hermeneutic, however, is that she employs this "prophetic-liberating tradition" in Scripture as a "canon within the canon" that allows her to critique and even reject other portions of Scripture. In her own words, "Feminist readings of the Bible can discern a norm within Biblical faith by which the Biblical texts themselves can be criticized . . . On this basis, many aspect of the Bible are to be frankly set aside and rejected" (ibid., 23). Despite the problems with this approach for evangelicals, one could say that the importance of the prophetic-liberating aspect of Scripture is emphasized by Scripture itself. One can understand the main point of the Old Testament as the ultimate divine victory over the effects of sin, which is something that the prophets announce. According to N. T. Wright (*Evil and the Justice of God*, 45), for example, "the Old Testament as a whole . . . is written to tell the story of what God has done, is doing and will do about evil." One could say that this is true of the Bible as a whole, for, as Bauckham says, "The Bible is a

part, prophets do not directly spell out the liberating implications for women of God's work in the eschaton, but they do provide a framework of understanding that the injustices of sexism are something that God will one day overturn. Since the rule of women by men and other expressions of sexism are portrayed in the protological texts as expressions of the Fall (see Gen 3:16), we can expect that the eschatological texts about the end of the story will also involve overcoming these effects of the Fall. Our analysis of the future messianic age shows an expectation that all the evil effects of the Fall will be completely vanquished. This implies that there is no room for patriarchy or androcentrism, even if they or their demise are not explicitly mentioned by the prophets.

CONCLUSION

From the foregoing discussion, I would like to draw out several important theological and hermeneutical implications concerning how to understand women and gender issues in the Bible.

First of all, the grand narrative of Old Testament is marked and shaped by a thematic pattern that emphasizes redemption from sin and its evil effects. God purposefully acts to ensure that the consequences of sin found in Genesis 3 are overcome and the creational intentions found in Genesis 1–2 are restored. This way of reading the Old Testament accentuates the fact that sexism and patriarchy (as attested in Gen 3:16) are not the divine intention for humanity as a whole and certainly not for the covenant people of God. Sexism and patriarchy are neither inevitable nor desirable. God offers an alternative, redeemed life for the people of God. It is true that the idyllic life that the Sinai Covenant blessings offer is only occasionally fulfilled in the history of Israel, due to Israel's disobedience. For our purposes, this means that much of the Old Testament testifies to life within a largely unredeemed, patriarchal culture and society. But human failures do not nullify the validity and vivacity of divine intentions and will. On the contrary, the examples of both failures and successes of the past invite, encourage, and instruct

---

kind of project aimed at the kingdom of God, that is, towards the achievement of God's purposes for good in the whole of God's creation" (*Bible and Mission*, 11). This metanarrative "had a definite goal towards which it moves"—the coming of the kingdom of God—a goal that is portrayed "in a rich variety of narrative metaphors and images" (ibid., 16). Within the Old Testament, the hope of the just reign of God is especially depicted in the prophets.

succeeding generations to embrace redemption fully. The narrative framework of the Old Testament urges its readers to see patriarchy as a regrettable result of human sin and God as one who consistently, albeit gradually, resists patriarchy until it is ultimately overturned. God's sovereign grace is able to overcome what human effort could not.

Secondly, biblical scholarship needs to increasingly emphasize a grand narrative approach to the so-called "women's issue." We can no longer seek to understand women's place in God's reign solely based on atomistic exegesis of isolated "women's passages"—whether positive or negative in character—without seeing how they fit into the metanarrative of the Old Testament (or two-testament Bible) as a whole. When a loyalist tries to prove that a given text is not as patriarchal or sexist as it appears or when a revisionist critiques the patriarchal structures in the Bible in light of certain more "retrievable" texts, they can both easily neglect the place of the texts they are considering within the grand, canonical story. Those evangelicals and others who regard Scripture as authoritative need to interpret all biblical passages in light of the big picture. In my view, this means reading all texts, whether "patriarchal" or prophetic-liberating, in terms of the overarching redemptive patterns in the Bible. When a woman's identity, status, strength, and calling are considered in light of the overarching patterns of redemption and blessing, one has no theological basis for denying "the full humanity of women." Indeed, women are some of the greatest heroes of the biblical metanarrative who face and overcome great dangers and bring about the great goals of redemption and justice for all.

Thirdly, this metanarrative way of reading the Bible stresses the importance of holistic redemption. Approaching the "women's issue" in a narrowly-defined way that studies only select passages that directly deal with women will in the end fail to promote the full humanity and full redemption of women. The reason is that what is good for women is bound up with what is good for all humanity. Therefore, consideration of apparently gender-neutral spiritual issues such as covenantal obedience to God and "material" issues (such as God's provision of abundant food through a proper human dominion/stewardship over the earth and God's concern for the physically poor) are of obvious relevance to the redemption of women. On a practical level, a woman who is starving (whether in Israel of the past or Sub-Saharan Africa in the present) is not going to be concerned with any interpretation of women's rights that ignores the fact that she needs food for herself and her children to survive. All of the features of a blessed and redeemed life must be present in order for a woman to live a fully restored human life. This point is supported by how the three relationships of humanity are themselves mutually related, as shown in the examples from the various phases of the Old Testament's metanarrative.

Lastly, when we employ a hermeneutic that gives proper weight to the redemptive biblical metanarrative, the entire Old Testament and all the books within it are regarded as both useful and beneficial for woman and as the inspired and authoritative Word of God. Even the texts that reflect and appear to uphold patriarchy remain the authoritative word of God. The reason is that, when read in light of the main themes of the Old Testament narrative as a whole as introduced in Genesis 1–3, such "problem texts" are either relativized or exposed as part of God's indictment of human sin in all of its forms. Read as a grand narrative, the Old Testament authoritatively confronts, exposes, corrects, and dismantles patriarchal and sexist elements of the biblical world, and furthermore offers hope in God's progressive redemptive work in and through redeemed women and men of God, which is ultimately consummated by God's own matchless power and supreme grace.

BIBLIOGRAPHY

Barr, James. *The Garden of Eden and the Hope of Immortality*. Minneapolis: Fortress, 1993.

Bartholomew, Craig, and Michael Goheen. *Drama of Scripture: Finding our Place in the Biblical Story*. Grand Rapids: Baker Academic, 2004.

———. "Story and Biblical Theology." In *Out of Egypt: Biblical Theology and Biblical Interpretation*, edited by Mary Healy et al., 144–71. Grand Rapids: Zondervan, 2004.

———. "The Story-Line of the Bible." Online: http://www.biblicaltheology.ca/blue_files/The%20Story-Line%20of%20the%20Bible.pdf.

Bauckham, Richard. *Bible and Mission: Christian Witness in a Postmodern World*. Milton Keynes, UK: Paternoster, 2003.

———. *Gospel Women: Studies of the Named Women in the Gospels*. Grand Rapids: Eerdmans, 2002.

Branch, R. G. "Women." In *Dictionary of the Old Testament: Wisdom, Poetry, and Writings*, edited by Tremper Longman III and Peter Enns, 916–25. Downers Grove, IL: InterVarsity, 2008.

Brenner, Athalya, Editor. *A Feminist Companion to Genesis*. Sheffield, UK: Sheffield Academic, 1993.

Cassuto, Umberto. *Commentary on the Book of Genesis*. Translated by Israel Abrahams. Jerusalem: Magnes, 1961.

Day, Linda. "Women and the Feminine in the Hebrew Bible." In *Engaging the Bible in a Gendered World*, edited by Linda Day and Carolyn Pressler, 114–27, Louisville, KY: Westminster John Knox, 2006.

Exum, Cheryl. *Fragmented Women: Feminist (Sub)versions of Biblical Narratives*. Valley Forge, PA: Trinity, 1993.

Fretheim, Terence. "Is Genesis 3 a Fall Story?" *Word & World* 14.2 (1994) 144–53.

Goldingay, John. *Israel's Gospel: Old Testament Theology, Vol. 1*. Downers Grove, IL: InterVarsity, 2003.

Gowan, Donald G. *Theology of the Prophetic Books: The Death and Resurrection of Israel*. Louisville, KY: Westminster John Knox, 1998.

Haas, Gunther. "Patriarchy as an Evil that God Tolerated: Analysis and Implications for Authority of Scripture." *Journal of the Evangelical Theological Society* 38.3 (1995) 321–36.

Hamilton, James M., Jr. *God's Glory in Salvation through Judgment: A Biblical Theology*. Wheaton, IL: Crossway, 2010.

Hess, Richard. "Equality with and without Innocence." In *Discovering Biblical Equality: Complementarity without Hierarchy*, edited by Ronald W. Pierce and Rebecca Merrill Groothius, 79–95. 2nd ed. Downers Grove, IL: InterVarsity, 2005.

Lapsley, Jacqueline E. *Whispering the Word: Hearing Women's Stories in the Old Testament*. Louisville, KY: Westminster John Knox, 2005.

Le Cornu, Alison. "Proverbs." In *IVP Women's Bible Commentary*, edited by Catharine Clark Kroeger and Mary J. Evans, 319–26. Downers Grove, IL: InterVarsity, 2002.

Lyotard, Jean-François. *The Postmodern Condition: A Report on Knowledge*. Translated by Geoff Bennington and Brian Massumi. Minneapolis: University of Minneapolis Press, 1984.

Mettinger, Tryggve N. D. *The Eden Narrative: A Literary and Religio-Historical Study of Genesis 2–3*. Winona Lake, IL: Eisenbrauns, 2007.

Meyers, Carol. *Discovering Eve: Ancient Israelite Women in Context*. Oxford: Oxford University Press, 1988.

Moberly, R. W. L. *The Theology of the Book of Genesis*. Old Testament Theology Series. Cambridge, UK: Cambridge, 2009.

Nordling, Cherith Fee. "Feminist Biblical Interpretation." In *Dictionary for Theological Interpretation of the Bible*, edited by Kevin Vanhoozer, 228–30. Grand Rapids: Baker, 2005.

Olson, Dennis. "Untying the Knot." In *Engaging the Bible in a Gendered World*, edited by Linda Day and Carolyn Pressler, 76–86, Louisville, KY: Westminster John Knox, 2006.

Osiek, Carolyn. "The Feminist and the Bible: Hermeneutical Alternatives." *Religion and Intellectual Life*, 6.3–4 (1989) 96–109.

Pokrifka, H. Junia. "Huldah the Prophet: Commentary on 2 Kings 22:14–20; 2 Chronicles 34:22–28." Wynkoop Center for Women in Ministry, WIM Resources, 2006. Online: http://www.wynkoopcenter.org/images/articles/u2s3.pdf.

———. "Understanding the Poetry in Genesis 3:14–19 in its Narrative Context." Unpublished Paper presented at the Annual Meeting of the Society of Biblical Literature in Toronto, Canada, 2002.

Powell, Mark A. "Narrative Criticism." In *Methods of Biblical Interpretation*, edited by Douglas A. Knight. Nashville, TN: Abingdon, 2004.

Ruether, Rosemary Radford. *Sexism and God-Talk*. Boston, MA: Beacon, 1983.

Sarna, Nahum M. *Genesis*. The JPS Torah Commentary. Philadelphia, PA: Jewish Publication Society, 1989.

Steinberg, Naomi. *Kinship and Marriage in Genesis: A Household Economics Perspective*. Minneapolis: Fortress, 1993.

Stordalen, T. *Echoes of Eden: Genesis 2–3 and Symbolism of the Eden Garden in Biblical Hebrew Literature*. Leuven: Peeters, 2000.

Trible, Phyllis. "Depatriarchalizing in Biblical Interpretation." *Journal of the American Academy of Religion* 41.1 (1974) 42–47.

———. *God and the Rhetoric of Sexuality*. Minneapolis, MN: Fortress, 1978.

———. *Texts of Terror: Literary-Feminist Readings of Biblical Narratives*. Philadelphia, PA: Fortress, 1984.

Waltke, Bruce K. *An Old Testament Theology: An Exegetical, Canonical and Thematic Approach*. Grand Rapids: Zondervan, 2007.

Whiteley, Raewynne J. "Song of Solomon." In *IVP Women's Bible Commentary*, edited by Catharine Clark Kroeger and Mary J. Evans, 346–55. Downers Grove, IL: InterVarsity, 2002.

Wright, Christopher J. H. *Old Testament Ethics for the People of God*. Downers Grove, IL: InterVarsity, 2004.

———. *The God I Don't Understand: Reflections on Tough Questions of Faith*. Grand Rapids: Zondervan, 2008.

———. *The Mission of God: Unlocking the Bible's Grand Narrative*. Downers Grove, IL: InterVarsity, 2006.

Wright, N. T. *Evil and the Justice of God*. Downers Grove, IL: InterVarsity, 2006.

11

Can Our Hermeneutics Be Both Evangelical and Feminist?

Insights from the Theory and Practice of Theological Interpretation

TODD POKRIFKA

INTRODUCTION

EVANGELICAL HERMENEUTICS SEEKS TO interpret and use the Bible in a way that retains its supreme authority. Feminist biblical hermeneutics seeks to interpret and use the Bible in a way that "promotes the full humanity" of women.[1] Is it possible for a hermeneutic to be both evangelical and feminist? Yes, it is. In fact, we can have a hermeneutic that is feminist *because* it is evangelical, a hermeneutic that appropriately handles the patriarchal and androcentric features of the biblical text as an expression of reverent submission to the authority of the Bible. I wish to sketch the elements of such a hermeneutic in this chapter.

A hermeneutic that is both evangelical and feminist stands stands in contrast to other possible theological interpretations or hermeneutics, which often regard evangelical and feminist hermeneutics as essentially contradictory. For example, evangelicals often regard feminist hermeneutics as inimical to a full affirmation of the Bible's authority. They

---

1. This is Rosemary Radford Ruether's influential statement of "the critical principle" of feminist theology in *Sexism and God-Talk*, 18–20.

see feminists as elevating an experience-based extra-biblical norm over Scripture and then imposing it upon Scripture. Conversely, feminist interpreters often regard an evangelical approach to Scripture as an obscurantist enterprise that sides with and legitimates traditional patriarchal and androcentric social ideals and realities. Though we could find many examples that would support these mutually-oppositional portrayals of what it means to be evangelical or feminist, they are ultimately oversimplifications that ignore other possible ways of interpreting the Bible in an evangelical or feminist way. This chapter will propose one way of bringing together evangelical and feminist hermeneutics.

The scope of this chapter is wide ranging, since it involves bringing together three webs of discourse concerning biblical interpretation and hermeneutics: evangelical theology and biblical studies, feminist biblical and theological scholarship, and the theological sub-discipline of the theological interpretation of Scripture. Because of its vast scope, this chapter is relatively theoretical in character, rather than being directly concerned with close engagement of biblical texts. That said, I hope and trust that close readings and exegesis, such as those found in the other chapters in this volume, would provide concrete support for and expression of the claims I make here.

This chapter will follow the following pattern. First, I will provide some definitions and explanations of the four main terms in the title of this chapter. Second, I will sketch the main contours of what an evangelical feminist theological hermeneutic would look like. Third, I will present and then critically examine the contribution that William Webb's theological hermeneutic might make to an evangelical feminist hermeneutic. Finally, I will ask the question of which readers or reading communities should have the priority in an evangelical feminist hermeneutic.

DEFINITIONS

Defining "Hermeneutics" and "Hermeneutic"

I want to offer some preliminary definitions of the terms "hermeneutics" and "hermeneutic" as I will use them. Following Anthony Thiselton, hermeneutics is "critical reflection upon processes of interpretation and understanding, especially the interpretation of biblical texts or texts that originate from other cultures."² In my view, hermeneutics considers four main factors: the author (and the author's world), the text, the reader, and the reality or subject matter to which the texts refers.

A hermeneutic is more specific than the practice of hermeneutics. Simply stated, a hermeneutic is a specific way of interpreting, using, and reflecting upon Scripture. As a "way" of interpreting and using Scripture, a hermeneutic will imply certain methodological and substantive commitments, although these may be implicit and *ad hoc* in character.

Defining "Evangelical Hermeneutics"

What would it mean for a person or group to advocate and practice an *evangelical* way of interpreting and using Scripture? Recognizing that there is some debate about the historical and sociological contours of the evangelical movement, I would like to use a theological definition of "evangelical" that I believe would be accepted as a normative self-description by most self-professed evangelicals. In the realm of biblical hermeneutics, to be evangelical means, at a minimum, to be concerned to *interpret and use the Bible in a way that retains its primary authority for Christian faith and practice*.[3] As such, an evangelical hermeneutic is not, at least not directly or primarily, a general hermeneutic for all texts and readers. Rather it is concerned with how a particular community, the Christian church, should interpret and employ a particular book, the Bible. An evangelical hermeneutic is therefore a special *theological* hermeneutic that makes theological assumptions about God, Scripture, and the church as a reading community.

Evangelicalism shares with Roman Catholicism, Eastern Orthodoxy, and much of Protestantism the view that the Bible is authoritative and canonical.[4] More distinctively, however, the evangelical regards the

2. Thiselton, "Hermeneutics." Of course, "hermeneutics" can also be used as a simple plural of "hermeneutic" as in the phrase, "the androcentric and feminist *hermeneutics*, respectively."

3. Of course, there are several other factors that make evangelicals evangelical, not least their adherence to the Christocentric and soteriological "gospel" message, but I am emphasizing the "formal principle" of Protestantism, the supreme authority of Scripture, due to its obvious hermeneutical importance. For a helpful, five-fold description of evangelical theology and its methods, see Stackhouse, "Evangelical Theology Should Be Evangelical."

4. As such, evangelicalism is a part of a larger body of Christians that are committed to orthodoxy and who adhere to the "Great Tradition." See McGrath, "Engaging the Great Tradition," and Olson, *The Mosaic of Christian Belief*, 320–39.

Bible, understood as a canonical whole, as the primary and therefore decisive authority for Christian faith and practice.[5] It is the primary or supreme authority because it has a place of pre-eminence or supremacy among the typical sources and norms to which Christians may appeal—including tradition, experience, reason, imagination, culture, or ecclesiastical authority.[6] If there appears to be a conflict between Scripture and another alleged norm, then Scripture trumps all alternatives,[7] including those favored by the interpreter and her community. An evangelical Christian does not believe it is legitimate to reject the plain sense of Scripture, when rightly interpreted, at least as it bears on important matters of Christian belief or practice.[8]

Although the evangelical convictions I have noted allow for a diversity of hermeneutical approaches, evangelicals would need to reject some hermeneutical approaches. For example, the radically "postmodern" notions that texts are entirely unstable in their meaning or that "meaning" is created completely by the readers of texts would probably conflict with the capacity of the Scriptures to function as the primary and decisive authority on matters of belief or practice. So too, a hermeneutic that interpreted biblical texts atomistically, without concern for their relationship to each other or to a canonical whole, would be inimical to the evangelical notions of the unity and authority of Scripture. Yet, ruling out some hermeneutical approaches like these still allows for considerable diversity.

---

5. This stands in contrast to traditional Roman Catholic and Eastern Orthodox hermeneutical approaches that assume that Scripture and aspects of sacred (ecclesiastical) tradition are equal in authority and unable to contradict each other (McGrath, "Engaging with Tradition," 152–58).

6. For an account of how Scripture's priority operates in Karl Barth's work, especially in relation to tradition and reason, see Todd Pokrifka, *Redescribing God*.

7. Stackhouse, "Evangelical Theology Should Be Evangelical," 47ff. Olson, *Mosaic*, 99–109.

8. The final phrase is meant to allow for the fact that some evangelicals do not believe that the Bible is inerrant on all matters (including factual details of history or science), but continue to uphold its infallibility for all essential matters of Christian faith (doctrine) and practice. If one believes in biblical inerrancy on all matters, then infallibility on the most important matters follows. "Although debate about inerrancy . . . remains, there is universal agreement about infallibility" (Osborne, "Evangelical Biblical Interpretation," 224; see also Olson, *Mosaic*, 101–5).

Defining "Feminist Hermeneutics"

I have indicated some of the main concerns of evangelical hermeneutics. The next question is: "What is *feminist* biblical hermeneutics?" Although there is a great diversity among those who call themselves feminists, I believe that it is reasonable to say that every feminist affirms and "promotes the full humanity of women" in one way or another.[9] With respect to Scripture, then, a feminist biblical hermeneutic aims to interpret and use Scripture in a way that affirms and promotes the full humanity of women. This definition is by necessity rather broad in order to acknowledge the differences among feminist approaches to the Bible. For the purposes of this chapter, intra-feminist diversity involves two main issues: (1) what does promoting the full humanity of women *mean* in the realm of biblical hermeneutics?; and (2) to what extent does the Bible, rightly interpreted, promote the full humanity of women? I will briefly examine each of these in turn.

First, what does it mean to promote the full humanity of women? At the very least it means that women cannot be considered to be less human than men or inferior to men.[10] For many, it means the full equality of men and women. Male-female equality does not appeal to all feminists, however, since equality could be seen to imply interpreting women in terms of men.[11] A related conflict exists between feminists who minimize the perceived differences between men and women and those who are trying to accentuate them. The latter group would include those that Radford Ruether calls the "Romantic" (often separatist) feminists[12] as well as most poststructuralist and postmodern feminists. But I suspect

---

9. Ruether, *Sexism and God-Talk*, 18–20.

10. From the standpoint of typical Christian theology, the humanity of women is centrally concerned with their being made in the image of God (Gen 1:26–31).

11. The question of equality also raises the question of the extent to which men and women are different, yet still equal. This is important within the intra-evangelical debate between complementarians or hierarchalists on the one hand, and biblical feminists or egalitarians on the other. A number of leading egalitarians have recently clarified that they are quite happy to speak of significant differences between men and women (beyond obvious differences in sexual physiology), so long as they are not regarded in hierarchical terms. See especially Pierce and Groothius, *Discovering Biblical Equality*, which is appropriately subtitled *Complementarity without Hierarchy*. On the complementarian side, there are those whom William Webb identifies as proponents of "ultra-soft patriarchy" and who accept some of the egalitarian arguments. See Webb's *Slaves, Women and Homosexuals*.

12. Ruether, *Sexism and God-Talk*, 44.

that even such feminists would affirm the concept of the full humanity of women, if "humanity" is defined in a way that acknowledges the uniqueness of women.

Second, to what extent does the Bible promote the full humanity of women? There is a radical divergence in the answers that feminists give to this question. Carolyn Osiek, a feminist New Testament scholar situated in the Roman Catholic tradition, offers an influential five-fold taxonomy of the possible hermeneutical alternatives that feminists have employed.[13] She identifies rejectionists, loyalists, revisionists, sublimationists, and liberationists.[14] Since Robin Parry's piece in this volume (chapter 2) explains these five options admirably, I do not need to repeat them again here. However, I do wish to add a sixth feminist hermeneutical option to Osiek's five approaches.

Since Osiek's article was written, what we might call a postmodern approach to feminist hermeneutics has taken on an increased importance. Although notoriously difficult to define, "postmodern" refers to a diverse group of approaches that rejects "modern universal theories, seeks to destabilize power relations . . . and questions the notion of 'scientific' positivist knowledges and singular meanings by stressing particularity, difference and heterogeneity."[15] Growth of postmodern ways of thinking alongside modern modes of thought has lead to an increased reticence to regard texts, including scriptural ones, as stable in meaning.[16] Despite a change in emphasis, there are many ways in which postmodern feminists are merely developing hermeneutical and ethical considerations that modern interpreters had already begun to identify. As a consequence, much postmodern feminist interpretation overlaps somewhat with the five broadly "modern" hermeneutical options out-

---

13. Osiek, "The Feminist and the Bible" Also, a seven-fold taxonomy is supplied by David Scholer "Feminist Hermeneutics."

14. Despite the differences among liberationist thinkers, they all regard human liberation from oppression as an important or central message of the Bible. Scholer, "Feminist Hermeneutics," regards "the hermeneutic of the prophetic, liberating tradition" as probably "the foundational feminist hermeneutic" (409; cf. 408). Likewise, Pamela Cochrane identifies the related theme of justice as a "common theme" shared in some form by all feminists ("Scripture, Feminism, and Sexuality," 264).

15. Fiorenza, *Wisdom Ways*, 213. Postcolonial feminist interpretation shares much with postmodern interpretation, but is more specifically directed against the dark legacy of colonialism and imperialism and how these social realities have harmed women, from biblical times until the present.

16. See Andrew Sloane's comments on these phenomena in his piece on Genesis 2–3 in this volume.

lined by Osiek. Examples of themes present in modernity but given greater prominence in postmodernity are "difference" and otherness,[17] social location, ideology, and power dynamics in the creation and interpretation of texts.[18]

Whatever their specific school of interpretation, feminist critics typically employ the interpretative tools of suspicion and retrieval. The hermeneutic of suspicion views the text and its interpretations with a suspicious eye towards the ways that it could serve the interests of those in power, including the ways it could oppress women. As such, feminist interpreters may draw from ideological and post-colonial hermeneutical approaches. Loyalists tend to restrict the application of this suspicion to interpretations of the text (although there may be some exceptions), while those following other approaches feel free to be suspicious towards the text itself and to reject it as necessary. The degree to which the hermeneutic of suspicion can be compatible with evangelical theology is a challenging question to which I will return.[19]

The hermeneutic of retrieval aims to retrieve or recover what is redemptive and beneficial for the oppressed and marginalized, including the voices of women (in the text and among its readers) that have been inappropriately neglected in biblical interpretation. The hermeneutic of retrieval is relatively uncontroversial, although evangelicals would say that it needs to be used in a way that is sensitive to the whole Bible and not just selective "retrievable" texts.

Finally, proponents of feminist hermeneutics typically identify "patriarchy" as the main problem that they aim to overcome. In keeping with the predominant usage in feminist interpretation, patriarchy refers not merely to "the rule of the father," but more widely to any expression of male dominance that oppresses and devalues women. Some feminist scholars regard this as a misuse of the term,[20] but it can serve as a way

---

17. Although not directly concerned with biblical interpretation, the work of Luce Irigaray is especially provocative on such issues. See Storkey's treatment of Irigaray and related "postmodern" thinkers in *Origins of Difference*, 51–60. Irigaray's goal is not to argue for the equality of women and men, but for women to speak their own language as women, rather than being constantly represented by men in male terms.

18. Musa W. Dube of Botswana is a leading postcolonial feminist interpreter. See her *Postcolonial Feminist Interpretation of the Bible*.

19. See especially the concluding section of this chapter, which is entitled "Which Reading Community Should Have Priority?"

20. See especially the insightful reflections of Meyers in *Discovering Eve*, 24–46.

of identifying the main problem that most feminists are concerned to address.

Defining "Theological Interpretation"

In order to answer the question of whether a hermeneutic can be both evangelical and feminist, I also need to clarify what I have in mind when I refer to the theory and practice of the "theological interpretation of Scripture," especially as it has been characterized in recent scholarly discussion.[21] What is theological interpretation? The authors of *The Handbook of Biblical Criticism* define it as "any approach to understanding the Bible whose central concern is knowledge of and communion with God."[22] According to Kevin Vanhoozer, theological interpretation is "characterized by a governing interest in God, the word and works of God, and by a governing interest to engage in what we might call 'theological criticism.'"[23] Seeking as its ultimate aim true, transforming knowledge of God and God's word, this theological criticism is more likely to be critical of readers than of the text or its authors.[24] Proponents of theological interpretation claim, I think persuasively, that only this kind of God-centered reading "ultimately does justice to the subject matter of the text itself."[25] This assertion is important to evangelicals because they desire for their theology to follow Scripture rather than having Scripture interpretation being determined by a foreign, extra-biblical theology. In other words, while theological interpretation allows the use of theological presuppositions, it can be done in a way that draws

---

21. While the self-conscious effort to consider the theological questions and concerns of the text in one's interpretation has always been a part of the interpretation of the Bible, there has been a growing scholarly attempt to retrieve and develop this mode of interpretation in the last couple of decades.

22. Soulen and Soulen, "Theological Interpretation."

23. Vanhoozer, "Introduction," 21.

24. Ibid., 22. This point and others in this paragraph relate to the assumption that the Bible's central subject matter (the reality to which it points) is the Triune God and God's words and deeds (an assumption that I believe most evangelicals would welcome) along with theological interpreters such as Karl Barth and Brevard Childs.

25. Vanhoozer, "Introduction," 22. A similar perspective is found in Karl Barth's definition of "theological exegesis," which is essentially interchangeable with my use of "theological interpretation." For Barth, theological exegesis is exposition of Scripture that occurs "within the pale of the Church" and which asks the question "To what extent is there given to us, here in this text, witness to *God's word*?" in Barth, *Credo*, 177. See Pokrifka, *Redescribing God*, 64–65.

those presuppositions themselves from Scripture or at least holds them accountable to Scripture.[26]

Theological interpretation is not bound to either modern or postmodern problematics or modes of interpretation.[27] Both approaches are reductionistic and can miss the properly theological task of relating to God through the text.

I also wish to clarify the relationship between the theological interpretation of Scripture and "theological hermeneutics." Theological hermeneutics is either (1) a theological way of pursuing general hermeneutics (i.e., reflections on how any text is or ought to be interpreted), (2) an account of the relationship between Christian theology and biblical interpretation (special hermeneutics), or (3) some connection between the two.[28] I would emphasize the importance of the second description, which speaks of an attempt to reflect on the practice of theological scriptural interpretation. It is true that theological hermeneutics ultimately involves some presuppositions about general hermeneutics (such as the adequate stability of the meaning or meanings of the text), although this need not be construed in a systematic manner. More decisive are presuppositions drawn from its distinctive Christian context and subject matter, including assumptions concerning God, humanity, and the inspiration of the Bible.

A SKETCH OF AN EVANGELICAL FEMINIST HERMENEUTIC

Is it possible to for Christians to have a hermeneutic that is both evangelical and feminist? Yes, I believe it is. If so, what would or should such a hermeneutic look like? In my view, only a robustly theological mode of biblical interpretation is able to understand adequately the right relationship between being evangelical and feminist.[29] This hermeneutical

---

26. This approach represents a kind of "middle way" of construing the "hermeneutical circle" (or "hermeneutical spiral"). In one of its main meanings, the term "hermeneutical circle" refers to the way in which one's presuppositions (or preunderstanding) and one's encounter with the text exist in a mutually-dependent relationship with one another. On the one hand, the circle cannot be eliminated (we do not interpret with neutral or empty minds), nor is it a vicious circle in which the text is incapable of correcting the interpreter's presuppositions (see Thiselton, "Hermeneutical Circle").

27. Vanhoozer, "Introduction," 18–20.

28. Treier, "Theological Hermeneutics," 787.

29. Part of the reason is that theological interpretation is necessary for helping evangelicals break out of certain atomistic or rationalistic approaches to interpretation that have prevailed in modernity, yet also avoid an equally problematic postmodern

necessity is in large measure because theological interpretation allows the reader to bring Christian theological presuppositions to bear upon our interpretation, rather than forcing the interpreter to try to answer questions that cannot be answered on secular terms amenable to non-Christians. A theologically-driven evangelical feminist hermeneutic will treat the Bible according to its unique capacity to bear the word of God and will promote a basically God-centered and God-honoring interpretation of the Bible. Since the God of the Bible is a God of justice who opposes oppression, a theological hermeneutic that uncovers and opposes oppression that would make sense.

For evangelicals, Scripture speaks with authority about women, but evangelicals have reached a wide variety of conclusions about what Scripture actually teaches about women and what the best methods are to find out what that teaching is. As we saw above, feminist hermeneutics is also marked by great diversity, depending in large measure on how the feminist reader construes Scripture and responds to its authority. How, then, would an evangelical approach to Scripture relate to the six kinds of feminist interpretation described above?[30] The evangelical interpreter can learn something from all six of them. Most naturally finding themselves in the loyalist camp, evangelicals could not espouse the rejectionist option—even though they could still learn something from the observations of rejectionist scholars. Evangelicals could employ qualified versions of the other approaches.[31] While upholding the authority of Scripture, an evangelical could prioritize some texts or themes over others for the purpose of promoting the full humanity of women. How to make such determinations is fraught with challenges,

---

hermeneutic that gives up on the stability and authority of the text and its theocentric metanarrative (which is in many ways a natural development of certain modern approaches).

30. Excluding the rejectionist hermeneutic, I do not believe that the remaining four hermeneutics (loyalists, revisionists, sublimationists, and liberationists) are mutually contradictory feminist hermeneutics, but could be employed by the same person or community (in this respect, I believe I differ from Osiek; rather, I agree with Parry; see chapter 2 in this volume).

31. For example, evangelicals could employ the hermeneutics of retrieval with revisionists and listen carefully to postmodern or postcolonial critiques of patriarchy and sexism in biblical texts and their modern interpretations, while resisting those readings would undermine the Bible's authority. Later in this chapter, I will draw attention to the insights of the "liberationist" approach and how they cohere with an evangelical stance on Scripture.

but I believe it is worth facing these challenges rather than settling with what might be called a naïve loyalist stance (keeping in mind that it is possible to be a loyalist and not be naïve).

I now wish to move beyond these hints by sketching main contours of a theologically-driven evangelical feminist hermeneutics. I will begin stating briefly how this approach would relate to the four factors or elements of hermeneutics that I mentioned in the definition of hermeneutics above.[32]

(1) *Author.* The evangelical approach to the author of a biblical text or texts would necessarily include the notion of a divine author who in some way speaks in and through the human authors (a term that I use to include narrators, editors, collectors and redactors). Although evangelicals could legitimately understand the relationship between divine and human authors or speakers in various ways,[33] evangelicals doing feminist interpretation would stress that there are times when the perspective of the divine author diverges from, yet without necessarily contradicting, the limited perspective of the human author of a particular part of Scripture. This observation requires the reader to attend to the relationship between a part of Scripture and Scripture as a whole, discerning the difference between the limited (and often culturally relative) expressions of Scripture's humanity and the authoritative expressions of its divine Source or Author.[34]

---

32. My comments on feminist hermeneutics in this section are drawn partly from Cherith Fee Nordling's helpful description of the common presuppositions of feminist interpreters ("Feminist Biblical Interpretation," 228–29).

33. See Wolterstorff's *Divine Discourse* for an extensive exploration of these issues in a way that is friendly to evangelical concerns, yet moves beyond traditional discussions of inspiration. The insights of the school of theological interpretation show that a faithful Christian interpreter need not be restricted to the standard conservative evangelical appeals to original authorial intention (in which human and divine authorial intentions are often seen as identical), a single textual meaning, and the grammatico-historical method. (For examples of this dominant evangelical approach see Kaiser, "Evangelical Hermeneutics," 167–80, and Osborne, "Evangelical Biblical Interpretation," 224–26. Also, Felix critiques a certain kind of evangelical feminist hermeneutics from the standpoint of its perceived violations of the "the grammatical-historical method of exegesis" in "The Hermeneutics of Evangelical Feminism," 161.) Theological interpretation rightly denies the Enlightenment epistemology that is often associated with the grammatico-historical method, including the view that this method can lead to objective knowledge on the part of unbiased interpreters.

34. For helpful theological reflections on the divine and human character of

(2) *Text.* Related to the first point, evangelical views of the biblical text would be concerned to speak of it as being the written by human authors yet inspired by God.[35] Feminist approaches can operate within the circle of evangelical hermeneutics by attending to how biblical texts both convey elements of patriarchal cultural order and also (under divine inspiration) transcend the limits of that culture. In addition, because it is the final form of the text that is inspired, and not the various (speculative) stages of its prehistory or the communities that lay behind the text, the final canonical form of the text would be the focus of evangelical feminist interpretation.[36]

(3) *Reality.* Due to their embrace of inspiration, evangelicals tend to emphasize that the relationship between text and reality (subject matter) is one of truth and trustworthiness. Understood rightly, the inspired texts truly and faithfully (inerrantly or infallibly) bear witness to the realities with which they are concerned, whether they are the divine character and divine actions or various aspects of human life and experience. At the same time, evangelicals drawing from feminist biblical scholarship would draw partly from the social constructivist view of language that is prevalent among feminists. By this I mean that evangelical feminists would emphasize how language of the text both expresses and shapes (constructs) the social world inhabited by the biblical writers and their communities. In other words, this approach would acknowledge that patriarchal and androcentric social conventions both shape the text and are shaped by it. But evangelical theological assumptions would emphasize that God, the main subject matter of the Old Testament, is truly revealed through the text, not merely human religious or social realities. The reality of the biblical God of justice and mercy transcends and critiques the sin-corrupted society in which the Old Testament was written. Fortified by frequent divine commands in Scripture to seek justice

---

Scripture and how it parallels the analogous reality of the incarnation of Christ, see Enns, *Inspiration and Incarnation.*

35. As noted above, inspiration and its implications are variously understood in evangelical circles.

36. Evangelicals would agree with Brevard Childs (e.g., *Biblical Theology*) on this point, and would typically be cautious about feminist interpretation that gives a great deal of attention to historical reconstructions (e.g., Carol Meyers, *Discovering Eve* and Elizabeth Schüssler Fiorenza, *In Memory of Her*).

and overturn injustice, readers ought to read the text in a way that puts into practice these commands.

(4) *Reader*. Evangelical hermeneutics understands the reader fundamentally as a believer—a person of faith—who is under the authority of the text and who is part of a readerly community—the church—that shares a common recognition of the Bible's authority. In addition, the reader is not neutral but is shaped by the interests that arise from other aspects of her social location (e.g., gender, race, economic class or condition, etc.). Accordingly, evangelicals can embrace the typical feminist conviction that "[a]ll interpretation is 'interested' and must necessarily be critiqued according to whose interests are being served by existing systems."[37] Aware that all human interpreters are fallible and influenced by sin, evangelicals may freely reject traditions of interpretation that compromise the full humanity of women. At the same time, they need rigorous, God-graced self-critique to ensure that they are not themselves drawing up interpretations that manifest power-seeking and selfish motives.

As we have seen, many of the hallmarks of feminist hermeneutical approaches to the Bible should be embraced by evangelicals precisely because they are a natural outflow of biblically-based evangelical theological convictions about God (especially God's justice), about humans (sinfulness and fallibility as writers and readers) and about God's work (redemption). That is, an evangelical hermeneutic not only is compatible with much of feminist hermeneutics, but it may spur one to adopt feminist hermeneutical convictions and approaches.

The intersection of evangelical theological interpretation and feminist hermeneutics I am urging here involves making several theological claims that can be summarized and organized in the following argument:

1. The Bible (at least in many of its parts) attests to a God who liberates and brings justice and redemption to the oppressed and the vulnerable.

2. Simply by virtue of their gender, women should typically be included among the oppressed and vulnerable, whether or not the text states this directly.

---

37. Nordling, "Feminist Biblical Interpretation," 229. See also the section near the end of this chapter entitled "Which Reading Community Should Have Priority?" and Cochrane, "Scripture, Feminism, and Sexuality," 264–65.

3. According to 1 and 2, the biblical God promotes the full humanity of women and promotes justice for women.

4. God is the central figure and subject matter of the Bible.

5. In the Bible, what God does and promotes is the standard for humans. Unless told otherwise, humans are to imitate the character and actions of God.

6. God, the God of justice and redemption, has inspired the whole Bible.

7. Therefore, the Bible as a whole[38] promotes the full humanity of women and authoritatively calls its interpreters to do the same.

In making these points, I am advocating a particular "canonical construal" or "canonical narrative"—namely, "an interpretative instrument that provides a framework for reading the Christian Bible as a theological and narrative unity."[39] As many Christian scholars have argued, the unity of the Bible is first and foremost a *narrative* unity, for both the Old Testament and the two-testament Bible are united mainly by a great story or metanarrative.[40] Traditionally, this metanarrative is made up of four main parts: creation, fall, redemption, and consummation. The bulk of the Scriptures are concerned with the third of these four "phases," namely, "redemption."[41] This is not to say that most biblical texts are explicitly concerned with salvation or redemption, but merely that they fit into the framework of God's mission to bring redemption.

One advantage of understanding the unity of the Bible in terms of a redemption-oriented narrative rather than in terms of a straightforward doctrinal or ethical consistency is that a focus on narrative better

---

38. By referring to "the Bible as a whole" and other similar phrases, I wish to emphasize two related points: (1) that the two-testament Bible possesses a kind of canonical, theological unity and that it should be interpreted as such; and (2) that, when it is interpreted rightly as a whole, it communicates God's will to promote the full humanity of women, even if this would not seem to be the case when it is interpreted in an atomistic manner. See Marshall, "An Evangelical Approach," 51.

39. R. Kendall Soulen, *The God of Israel*, 13.

40. See the chapter by Junia Pokrifka in this volume (chapter 10 above).

41. Since consummation constitutes a distinct ending to the biblical story, I prefer the fourfold scheme including "consummation," rather than the more typical threefold scheme of creation, fall, and redemption. Yet, consummation can be seen as the completion of redemption.

handles the theological and ethical diversity of the Bible.[42] A narrative lens is important for an evangelical feminist hermeneutic, for it allows the reader to recognize that *while not all biblical texts and themes directly and independently promote the full humanity of women, all texts and themes fit into single overall metanarrative that indirectly promotes the full humanity of women.*[43] In this way, one can see that even texts that appear to present contradictory perspectives on women on the surface level do not represent fundamental contradictions in their portrayal of God's ultimate will toward women.[44] In the following two sections, I will present and critically appropriate one version of a redemptive-oriented evangelical hermeneutic that confirms the points I have made in this section and is therefore amiable to feminist concerns.

THE CONTRIBUTIONS OF WILLIAM J. WEBB'S REDEMPTIVE-MOVEMENT HERMENEUTIC

A "redemptive movement" hermeneutic has been developed by William J. Webb in his 2001 book *Slaves, Women, and Homosexuals: Exploring the Hermeneutics of Cultural Analysis.*[45] In this book, Webb uses three

---

42. Saying that the unity of the Bible is a narrative unity is not incompatible with saying that it is in some sense a Christocentric unity, a traditional Christian assertion. For Christians who believe that Jesus Christ is the ultimate revelation of God, then theological interpretation, at least when it is done with the entire two-testament canon in view, should be Christocentric in some way. This christocentrism would arguably include not only the soteriological import of Christ's death and resurrection (a typical evangelical emphasis), but also the "hermeneutical" emphases and approaches that Christ demonstrated in his use of the Old Testament, including his employment of a "prophetic interpretative grid." For support of this claim, see Stassen and Gushee, *Kingdom Ethics*, 97.

43. This is one of the main points supported by Junia Pokrifka's chapter in this book.

44. John Goldingay offers a helpful account of the four different kinds of possible contradictions that might be thought to exist in the Bible: formal, contextual, substantial, and fundamental (*Theological Diversity*, 15–25). In my view the Old Testament texts related to women involve formal and contextual contradictions, but no substantial or fundamental contradictions. Many of the tensions between different texts can be explained as instances of contextual contradiction, "a difference reflecting the variety in circumstances which different statements address" (ibid., 19). In such cases, one cannot say what the two speakers or authors would say if they encountered similar circumstances, nor do these differences necessarily represent a change in divine will.

45. See especially pages 36–41. Like many biblical scholars, Webb may not self-consciously regard his work as an instance of evangelical theological interpretation, but I expect that he would not be offended by such a characterization.

"case studies"—those of slaves, women, and homosexuals—to develop an approach to evangelical hermeneutics. His main concern is to address the question of "application," of how the Bible can be authoritatively applied to the present, despite the fact that our culture is often very different from the culture of the biblical text and its writers.[46] My treatment of Webb will be selective, focusing on his theological notion of "redemptive movement" and how it relates to the Bible's treatment of women.

Essential Features of Webb's Hermeneutic

According to Webb, there is a redemptive-historical movement both within the biblical canon and in its relationship to extra-biblical history and culture, including our own. This redemptive movement is especially evident in the transition between the Old Testament and the New Testament, although Webb notes that there also can be "movement" within a single testament (e.g., the oft-claimed development from the Law to the Prophets).

What is the redemptive movement to which Webb refers? It is a movement from a "less redemptive" revelation and ethical-theological realization to a "more redemptive" revelation and realization. Although there may be times of "devolution" in which history moves toward a less redemptive outcome (see below), Webb appears confident that God's governance of history is redemptive and thus generally moves toward a more redemptive direction *en route* to a glorious eschaton. This "redemptive movement" is progressive (not static nor regressive) in a twofold sense; it concerns both revelation and realization. For our purposes, the progressive *revelation* applies to how the authoritative divine intention for women is communicated (directly and indirectly) in a manner that develops over time. The progressive *realization* applies to the way that the women described in the text (or in its social world) are actually viewed and treated.[47]

Webb believes that although scriptural revelation about women reached its completion by the end of the New Testament, the realization

---

46. With his concern for the application of an authoritative Bible, Webb writes as an evangelical. Accordingly, he does not interact extensively with non-evangelical writers, although some of his points have a wide-ranging relevance.

47. See Webb's "The Limits of the Redemptive-Movement Hermeneutic," 328–30, for his distinction between revelation and realization.

of the revealed ethical ideals for women had not yet reached its completion within the communities described or alluded to within the canon. To some extent that realization awaits those who would apply the Bible in post-biblical times, including the present. Good interpretation and application, then, would involve distinguishing (a) what is authoritatively revealed about how women should be viewed and treated (i.e., what expresses the divine intention or will) and (b) what merely reflects the current level of human realization of the divine will for women by fallen humans in an imperfect and temporary phase of cultural and religious life. Accordingly, finding God's perspective on women requires that we look for the "redemptive spirit" in (and behind) the text, not merely the "letter" of its explicit statements.[48]

How would Webb's framework relate to the four factors of interpretation that I have appealed to above? In the briefest terms, I can make the following observations. In relation to the factor of *authorship*, Webb's approach relies on the possibility of a fairly strong distinction between the divine author, whose perspective would convey the "redemptive spirit" of the Bible, and the human authors, whose temporary and perhaps problematic perspectives are often expressed in the "letter" of isolated texts.[49] Accordingly, the *text* usually cannot be interpreted in a static way that assumes it contains unchanging truths that apply to all times. Rather, it sometimes needs to be understood as the expression of a limited moment that can be transcended by the better future to which other texts witness. The reality to which the text points is two-fold, like its two-fold divine and human authorship. That is, the subject matter of biblical texts are both (a) "culturally specific," concerned with matters relative to particular people at a particular time with a limited, temporal perspective, and (b) "culturally transcendent," concerned with God's ultimate purposes, which reveal ideas that have enduring, authoritative

---

48. Webb, *Slaves, Women, and Homosexuals*, 33. Traditional Christian hermeneutical use of the distinction between the Spirit and the letter has a long history, including Paul (2 Cor 3), Origen, and Luther.

49. According to Nicholas Wolterstorff, one should be cautious to distinguish between the meanings of divine and human discourse in Scripture. He believes that when God speaks in Scripture by means of appropriating human discourse, we should take God's appropriating discourse to be saying *the same thing* as the human appropriating discourse, "unless there is good reason to do otherwise" (*Divine Discourse*, 204). When exactly there is good reason to do otherwise is of course the important question, as is the question of how we can avoid having God and God's discourse in Scripture to mean what we *want* it to (see esp. *Divine Discourse*, 236–39).

significance. Finally, the role of the *reader* is to wisely discern what is culturally relative and what is not, by noting the ways in which the text is situated in relation to its cultural background[50] and in relation to God's progressive redemptive work in history—a work that is clear only when the Bible is understood as a narrative whole.[51]

The Benefits of Webb's Hermeneutic for Evangelicals with Feminist Concerns

What are the benefits of this approach for addressing feminist concerns and questions? Perhaps most importantly, it involves recognizing that Scripture has a "multi-level ethic," since "not everything within Scripture reflects the same level of ethical development."[52] I would add that Scripture has a multi-level *theology* as well. Scripture is not "flat," but has peaks and valleys.[53] Whether on the level of practice (ethics) or belief (theology), the Bible encompasses texts that reflect greater or lesser degrees of humanity's redemption from sin and its effects. Texts therefore vary in their level of prescriptive force for the contemporary reader. Accordingly, texts on women involve (1) varying levels in the revelation of the divine will and (2) varying levels of human realization of that divine will.[54]

---

50. Webb points to many biblical texts of various genres that improve upon or "redeem" the ethics and theological anthropology of the culture in which they were written—and this redemptive movement is not least evident in texts concerning women. Of course, some feminists (especially "rejectionists") would point out instances when this does not appear to be the case.

51. In this way, Webb's approach provides further evidence for Trible's claim that there is "a depatriarchalizing principle at work in the Hebrew Bible" ("Depatriarchalizing in Biblical Interpretation," 48). For Trible, this principle (to which we can compare Webb's "redemptive spirit") "is a hermeneutic operating within Scripture itself" (ibid., 48).

52. Webb, *Slaves, Women and Homosexuals*, 41.

53. Stassen and Gushee, *Kingdom Ethics*, 97. Stassen and Gushee go on to say that Jesus himself is the "the peak and centre" of Scripture—both his life and his teachings (ibid.). This stands against the tendency among many evangelicals to assume that, due to inspiration, all texts in Scripture stand on the same level of normativity.

54. The points I have made in this paragraph are stated in terms that go beyond what Webb says directly although I believe they are faithful to "the spirit" of his text. A similar approach is outlined by evangelical New Testament scholar I. Howard Marshall, "An Evangelical Approach," 45–60.

What specifically would this redemptive-movement hermeneutic do to help interpreters respond to the hermeneutical concerns of feminists? I would suggest that it offers two main contributions:

1. First, the redemptive-movement hermeneutic would acknowledge (with virtually all feminists) that at least when considered independently, some texts do not promote the full humanity of women. Either they offer little concerning the divine perspective on women, simply describing the actions of people within a sinful, broken, patriarchal culture (low level of ethical realization), or they involve a provisional divine accommodation of revelation to a patriarchal culture (a low level of communication of ultimate revelation). The controlled application of the hermeneutics of suspicion can uncover the sexism and oppressive potential that are found in the human, cultural dimensions of the text and its social world.[55]

2. Second, however, the wider witness of Scripture shows that such "patriarchal" texts (those that do not promote the full humanity of women) do not represent God's ultimate perspective on women. Therefore, such texts do not function in isolation from other texts, nor do they represent the epitome of God's authoritative word on women.[56] The potentially contrasting perspectives of individual texts need to be placed within the Bible's complex narrative unity, a unity that is ordered in large measure by God's redemptive-historical purposes. Therefore, the structure and content of the canon can determine the guidelines for an appropriate, non-atomistic use of the hermeneutic of retrieval that promotes the full humanity of women.

---

55. One can be "suspicious" of texts that only express a limited and temporal view of how women should be viewed or treated. This need not imply suspicion of God and God's intentions for women, but speaks of the sinfulness and limitations of the male-dominated culture that is reflected in Scripture despite its inspiration. These claims can be related to the idea that God accommodates human culture in God's mode of revelation and redemption. The theological principle of divine accommodation can be traced at least to John Calvin, especially as developed in his *Institutes of the Christian Religion* 1.14.3 and 2.11.14. See also Enns, *Inspiration and Incarnation*.

56. Watson says that such texts are not God's first or last word on women (*Text, Church, and World*, 191).

Within this approach, then, evangelical feminists can learn to appropriately employ the hermeneutics of suspicion and retrieval in ways that allow Scripture as a whole to retain its primary and decisive authority.

Apparent Biblical Support for Webb's Hermeneutic

For evangelicals, who want Scripture to function as supreme authority, it is not enough to say that Webb's approach offers pragmatic benefits for women and their readerly concerns. Rather, evangelicals want to ask whether this hermeneutical approach is actually encouraged by Scripture. I believe that there is evidence that it is.

First, we find that biblical intertextuality—the use of Scripture within Scripture—confirms the multi-level character of the Bible's ethics and theology. This approach is most obvious when we consider the New Testament's use of the Old Testament, which is relevant to Christian theological interpretation of the Old Testament.[57] But since this chapter is in a volume concerned especially with Old Testament interpretation, I will focus on how the use and reuse of texts and themes in the Old Testament itself reflects a "canonical shape" that emphasizes some themes over others. In fact, it "self-corrects" or "reinterprets" the standpoint of texts that might be interpreted as expressive of a limited or temporary perspective. For example, consider how Isaiah uttered words about eunuchs that transcended what the law said about eunuchs, based upon authoritative divine action and speech in his new, post-exilic context (Isa 56:1–7l; cf. Lev 21:18–20 and Deut 23:1). Seeing the present situation in light of God's ultimate future, Isaiah enlarges the scope of those included in

---

57. Jesus and Paul interpret and use Old Testament in a manner that makes some Old Testament texts primary and others secondary in prescriptive force and relevance, while still affirming the authority of the Scriptures as a whole. In particular, Jesus often appeared to employ "a prophetic hermeneutic" that leads him to emphasize the moral aspects of the law over its cultic aspects, which could be contravened or regarded as no longer in force (Stassen and Gushee, *Kingdom Ethics*, 91–98). Insofar as this is true, it offers partial vindication of the tendency of many feminists to see the prophetic-messianic stream of Scripture to be central to God's revelation in Scripture, as in Ruether, *Sexism and God-Talk*, 22–27. The difficulty is that Ruether and others harden a legitimate emphasis on the prophets into a "canon within a canon" (see below).

On another note, I wish to recognize that there is a debate—not least among evangelicals—about whether inner biblical interpretation is to be seen as exemplary for contemporary interpreters. In relation to the New Testament's use of the Old Testament, see G. K. Beale's edited volume *Right Doctrine from Wrong Texts?*

temple worship beyond the temporary restrictions found in the law. In a similar way, we naturally hope and expect that indications of restriction and devaluation of women in the law (e.g., their inability to come into the temple during menstruation due to ritual uncleanness or the lesser value of female slaves) will be one day overturned in the glorious future reign of God that the prophets foresaw and that the New Testament writers declared to have been inaugurated. Old Testament "anticipatory texts" provide a foretaste of this "new and improved" eschatological situation of women, by breaking out of the prevailing cultural undervaluation of women that the law often expressed and only partly overturned.

Determining what the main theological or ethical message of the Old Testament canon is on a given subject is not merely a matter of the quantitative emphasis given to a certain point (e.g., how many times a woman is portrayed in a patriarchal manner), but also the qualitative emphases that are evident from certain texts being placed at "structurally significant" junctures in the canon and its narrative.[58] For example, since Genesis 1–3 function as the "opening movement" of the narrative that will follow, it is disproportionately significant in understanding God's revealed intentions for women.[59]

Second, in addition to the support we have from biblical intertextuality, we have much indirect support for Webb's general approach in the Old Testament's portrayal of God and God's relation to Israel. One of the main theological understandings that lies behind this is that God is an accommodating God, who transforms Israel (and through Israel, all humanity) through gradual, rather than abrupt, modes of transformation.[60] God's accommodating nature is related to divine mercy towards sinners (itself an aspect of redemption) as well as God's wisdom (God knows what would be a suitable way of transforming free agents of the kind that we are). Accordingly, we would not expect God to declare the fullness of the divine will concerning any matter in a single text, nor would God enforce ultimate ethical ideals too soon in the history of redemption. Many texts in the Old Testament show a way of navigating through a world of patriarchy and other social sins; they show a way of living faithfully

---

58. Watson, *Text, Church and World*, 191.

59. See Junia Pokrifka's chapter in this volume.

60. Webb explains this point under the rubric of the wisdom of God, which includes pastoral, pedagogical, evangelistic and other components (*Slaves, Women, and Homosexuals*, 57–66).

before God in the time before the eschaton. This phenomena is in keeping with a God who is patient, and yet who is unswervingly committed to the ultimate divine purposes for creation.

RESPONDING TO POTENTIAL CRITIQUES OF THE REDEMPTIVE-MOVEMENT HERMENEUTIC

I have outlined some of the advantages of the kind of Webb's hermeneutical approach. What are some of the main critiques that could be lodged against this approach from an evangelical point of view, and how should one respond to them? I will consider three criticisms or objections to Webb.

Objection 1: Webb Over-Historicizes the Various Levels of Scripture

First, some would argue, I think rightly, that Webb over-historicizes the multi-level character of the scriptural canon. That is, he thinks of the levels of Scripture being ordered almost exclusively within a linear, temporal progress within real time.[61] To begin with, we need to recognize that most "historical" biblical texts are not ordered by simple chronology. Further, while God is certainly working to bring about redemption in history, there are sometimes cases of "regression" in history, in which a later generation loses the memory of an earlier more positive revelation or state of affairs. For example, Carol Meyers marshals evidence that women generally fared better in the more-egalitarian household-oriented life of early Israel than in the more hierarchical social orders of the centralized monarchy.[62] Also, a number of feminist writers have pointed out how aspects of the New Testament's treatment of women (e.g., several Pauline texts) are more problematic than that of the Old Testament's treatments of women.[63] As a corrective to Webb, then, it would be helpful to draw on modes of theological interpretation and biblical theology that are not bound to such a view of one-way historical

---

61. To clarify, I do not believe Webb states that the multi-level character of Scripture is *exclusively* ordered in terms of temporal progress. However, using "redemptive-movement" as his dominant model does sometimes create that impression, and he does not adequately qualify the degree to which the redemptive movement concept should be applied to history or to the texts of Scripture.

62. Meyer, *Discovering Eve*, 189–94.

63. See Ruether, *Sexism and God-Talk*, 35.

progress. I believe one can still accept the assumption that the Bible's narrative is *broadly* progressive in its treatment of women, but that allows for evidence of significant and lengthy periods of regression as well. As such, the notion of God's redemptive work in Israel and the nations is freed from simplistic modern notions of history and progress that are foreign to the Bible.[64]

Objection 2: Webb Indirectly Appeals to a Canon outside the Canon

A second criticism of Webb is that he does not offer sufficient resources to guard against creating a "canon outside the canon," an extra-biblical canon that determines how to interpret, apply, or assess the contents of Scripture.[65] Clearly, Webb is not intentionally affirming a canon outside the canon. Instead, in keeping with his stated evangelical convictions, he enunciates no less then thirteen intra-scriptural criteria for evaluating which texts have trans-cultural force and which are culturally specific or relative.[66] This does not mean, however, that it is obvious how one should use such criteria, nor whether one can do so without indirectly appealing to extra-biblical criteria. In fact, Webb recognizes that there

---

64. Some specific correctives to the historicism in Webb's approach to theological interpretation are found in: (1) Brevard Child's notion of "synchronic" relationships of canonical texts to their ultimately christological subject matter (*Biblical Theology*, 16–18, where he identifies several problems with *Heilsgeschichte* or a progressive "History of Redemption" as a model for Biblical Theology); and (2) Nicholas Wolterstorff's concepts of detecting different kinds of divine speech in different texts and of discerning between texts that fully manifest "divine discourse" and those that do not (*Divine Discourse*, 37–57, 204ff.).

65. I suspect that some conservative evangelicals would regard Webb's views on women as expressing something like a liberationist feminist hermeneutic that appeals to an extra-biblical canon. For example, Robert Yarborough identifies liberation theology as a modern (or postmodern) school of thought that "reifies a given worldview that is foreign to that of the biblical writers, and then interprets (some of) the biblical writer's words in terms of that worldview" ("The Hermeneutics of 1 Timothy 2:9–15," 177). Whether or not all forms of liberation theology (including their feminist versions) would fit this description (I do not believe they would), this quotation describes a mode of hermeneutics that would not be appropriate for evangelicals. I believe Webb would agree.

66. Webb, *Slaves, Women and Homosexuals*, 73–184. Webb therefore stands against non-evangelical feminists who openly advocate a standpoint outside the text, such as that of "women's experience," as the primary basis for determining what is helpful in the Bible.

are relevant extra-biblical criteria for determining whether a text or a feature of a text is transcultural or cultural in character, but regards such criteria as secondary and as only sometimes relevant.[67] Webb claims to argue for what is "redemptive" or "transculturally relevant" *primarily and decisively* on the basis of intrabiblical evidence, which would be consistent with evangelical commitments to Scripture. But is his work consistent with this claim? I believe it is, but to show this requires that we move beyond his own hermeneutical categories. Specifically, we need to distinguish between two kinds of intrabiblical evidence for determining what is "redemptive" in Scripture. One kind of evidence is found in texts that *explicitly* relativize or recontexualize the teachings of other texts, and the other kind is found in texts that do so *indirectly*. I will take each in turn.

Examples of texts that *explicitly* relativize or recontextualize other texts can be found in several parts of the Christian Bible. For example, Gal 3:28 states that distinctions between men and women that were a part of the law (as were distinctions between Jew and Greek/Gentile and slave and free-person) are no longer to hinder the unity or equality of men and women in Christ. At some level the gospel relativizes and even contradicts the social and religious distinctions between men and women that were present in the law.[68] Furthermore, such ways of relativizing laws and principles are found already in the Old Testament, as in the example I gave earlier about Isaiah's comments on eunuchs (Isa 56:1–7). When such texts relativize or even correct another text, this does not mean that the relativized text was wrong in its original context. Rather, the relativized texts can be wrong if they are understood as an abiding norm within a historical or theological context that God did not intend

---

67. See Webb, *Slaves, Women and Homosexuals*, 209–36, where he speaks of the criteria of "pragmatic basis between two cultures" and "scientific and social-scientific evidence" respectively. Wolterstoff makes a good case that some appeals to extrabiblical criteria or rules of interpretation—such as the assumption that "God speaks consistently"—are inevitable and to be welcomed (*Divine Discourse*, 206–8). In my view, it may be possible to regard even such explicitly extra-biblical claims as indirectly authorized or supported by Scripture as a whole (e.g., the biblical testimony to God's faithful, truth-speaking character).

68. Webb rightly regards Gal 3:28 as providing a crucial "seed idea" that has significant social implications for men and women (not only an affirmation of eternal salvation), beyond what were worked out and realized in the first century (Webb, *Slaves, Women and Homosexuals*, 85–87). He also finds support for this in other texts and themes in the New Testament. For example, Col 2:16–17 says that the once-obligatory feasts, new moon celebrations, and Sabbath days are matters of "indifference" in Christ, who is the substance to which these things were pointing.

for them. Accordingly, the interpreter can maintain the inspiration and authority of all texts, while recognizing that the degree and manner of their functional normativity may change over time.[69]

There are also less-obvious texts that *indirectly* relativize or recontextualize other "less-redemptive" patriarchal or androcentric texts. Such texts are likely much more abundant than the explicit texts noted above, though identifying them is obviously more open to the subjective dimensions of interpretation. Even so, I believe that such texts can corroborate that Webb is not appealing primarily to extra-biblical sources for his convictions. For example, any of the many texts that portray or point to God's ethical and theological ideals indirectly relativize texts that do not depict those high ideals. Within the "internal logic" of the canonical narrative, among the texts that are most likely to display God's will for humanity are those that concern protology and eschatology, i.e., original, pre-fall creation and final redemption and consummation.[70] Although the number of texts that speak of women under the condition of fallen creation and culture may be great, they would not have the same capacity to speak of God's ultimate desires for women as do the protological and eschatological texts.[71] Although even these protological and eschatological texts may also reflect elements of androcentrism or patriarchy (e.g., in Gen 1–2),[72] they provide strong support for the full humanity of women and sketch the contours of the canonical shape within which other texts ought to be read.

---

69. On the distinction between the authority of a text given its inclusion in Scripture as a whole and its potentially temporary normativeness, see Scholer, "Feminist Hermeneutics," 412–13. Similarly, Phyllis Trible says that "feminism might claim the entire Bible as authoritative, though not necessarily as prescriptive" (cited by Phyllis A. Bird in Day and Pressler, *Engaging the Bible*, 224).

70. By referring to "final redemption *and* consummation," I wish to refer to eschatology in a broad sense that includes realities that were inaugurated in the First Coming of Jesus and which will only be consummated in the Second Coming of Jesus or the eternal state to follow. It is worth noting that Webb includes both "basis in original creation" (protology) and "basis in new creation" among his "moderately persuasive" intrascriptural criteria for determining if a text has transcultural force (Webb, *Slaves, Women, and Homosexuals*, 123–52).

71. See Watson, *Text, Church and World*, 191.

72. Webb rightly points out that even "creation patterns contain cultural components within them" (*Slaves, Women and Homosexuals*, 120; cf. 122–31), and those cultural patterns may be partly negative for women.

Indications of a women-friendly canonical trajectory are found in what we may call anticipatory texts and restoration texts. *Anticipatory texts* anticipate or foreshadow a final, blessed, eschatological state of women.[73] *Restoration texts* speak of a restoration of the ideal (pre-fall) protological situation. Both kinds of texts (and sometimes a single text falls into both categories) involve examples of women who break out of the typical androcentric modes of fallen life in the "time between the times" of glorious beginning and ending. For example, Phyllis Trible speaks of the restoration of an Edenic kind of male-female mutuality and equality in Song of Songs.[74] Other examples are provided in the narratives of Deborah, Huldah, or Ruth.[75] Far from being trivial or arbitrary "exceptions" to that rule that God's overall intention is male-domination and androcentrism, these examples speak of partial progress on a trajectory out of fallen life and towards complete redemption. Their presence in the canon shows that oppressive patriarchy is not God's unchanging intention for women. Rather, God's intention is to move humans away from the lingering sexism of ancient Israel and its environment. Texts that are restorative, anticipatory and gynocentric (such as the book of Ruth) invite readers to read the whole canon in a different way.[76]

Much of my defense of Webb above depends on the notion that some biblical texts can provide "indirect authorization" for theological beliefs and ethical practices that go beyond those that are spelled out within Scripture.[77] If one could only appeal to biblical texts that directly and explicitly relativized any biblical text that did not appear to promote the full humanity of women, then one would often be disappointed and

---

73. There are few texts that explicitly speak of the eschatological state of women, but there is no reason that women should be excluded from texts about the glorious state of God's people. For example, women and men together will enjoy the conditions of a new heaven and new earth, conditions that recall (and perhaps surpass) life in Eden (Isa 65:17–25).

74. Trible, "Depatriarchalizing in Biblical Interpretation," 42–47. In earlier sections of this ground-breaking article, Trible identifies several "themes disavowing sexism" in the Old Testament (ibid., 31–35) and engages in an exegesis of Gen 2–3 (ibid., 35–42). See also Grenville Kent's piece on Song of Songs, chapter 8 in this volume.

75. See the comments on these stories in Junia Pokrifka's chapter in the volume.

76. See Bauckham's treatment of Ruth in *Gospel Women*, 12–16, and Parry's comments in chapter 2 of this volume.

77. For an account of the dynamic of indirect authorization in Karl Barth's doctrine of God, see Todd Pokrifka, *Redescribing God*, especially 65–68.

would feel pressure to turn primarily to extra-biblical criteria to support the feminist cause. However, such an approach is unnecessary. Rather, looking for indirect (rather than merely direct) authorization of theological ideas and ethical principles is a basic and longstanding Christian practice, and is surely not unique to feminist concerns. It is difficult to provide direct authorization for a multitude of Christian doctrines and practices.[78] Just as Christians have only indirect biblical authorization for the doctrine of the Trinity,[79] so also Christians could argue that Scripture provides indirect authorization for the claims that women are (and should be treated as) fully human and that patriarchy is an instance of social-structural sin that can and should be resisted.[80] Saying that the authorization that Scripture provides is often indirect in character is fully compatible with saying (against some postmodern claims) that the text itself exercises a kind of decisive pressure on our theological interpretations, rather than leaving them primarily in the realm of the imaginative judgments of readers and reading communities.[81] Even though feminist interpretation may be making some novel claims that were not directly made by Scripture, it remains possible for these claims to be indirectly accountable to and supported by Scripture.

To summarize my response to the objection that Webb appeals to a canon outside the canon, I have defended Webb's approach as a serious and subtle attempt to be faithful to Scripture's own authoritative testimony. But a further objection remains.

Objection 3: Webb Appeals to a Canon within the Canon

A third and final potential criticism of Webb's redemptive-movement hermeneutic is that is involves setting up a "canon within the canon." Some revisionist and liberationist feminists self-consciously set up such

---

78. See Kelsey, *Proving Doctrine*, 139–40.

79. See Pokrifka, *Redescribing God*, 113–16.

80. In support of this, one could claim that both Gen 1:27 and the contemporary statement that "women are fully human" make the same theological judgment, even though they obviously use different terms to do so. For the distinction between judgments and conceptual terms in the context of the theological exegesis, see Yeago, "The New Testament and Nicene Dogma," 152–64. Cf. Pokrifka, *Redescribing God*, 67–68.

81. On this point, I side with Brevard Childs in his "Toward Recovering Theological Exegesis," 17, over David Kelsey, *Proving Doctrine*, 197–201. For Kelsey, Scripture is "relevant . . . but not decisive" (ibid., 201) to the ways theological readers construe Scripture and bring it to bear on theology. Cf. Pokrifka, *Redescribing God*, 10–13.

a canon within the canon,[82] but evangelicals have not generally approved of such a move. Yet much of the evidence cited under the second criticism treated immediately above might look like evidence for a canon within the canon, as does the very notion of the multi-level character of Scripture.

There are several important questions here. One question is whether it might be legitimate in some sense to have a canon within the canon. To begin with, we need to recognize that there is clearly a gap between the theoretical views of many interpreters on this subject and their actual practice. Can anyone deny that he or she *functions* with a canon within the canon, in the simple sense of emphasizing and prioritizing some texts more than others? This point raises a second question, the question of the purpose for which a feminist would claim that some texts ought to exercise privilege over others. As Richard Bauckham argues, it is quite possible to privilege certain parts of Scripture *for a certain purpose* without saying that we ought to privilege them in *every respect*; only the latter would involve having a "canon within a canon."[83] For Bauckham, gynocentric canonical texts like Ruth "have the role not of relativizing the androcentric texts in every respect, but of relativizing or correcting precisely their androcentrism."[84] Along these lines, an evangelical like Webb would be able to say that *for the purpose of discerning authoritative theology and ethics for women today*, there are (a) certain texts that are clearly more relevant than others, and (b) among the relevant texts, some ought to be given priority over others because they declare God's will with respect to this purpose. For a different purpose—say the purpose of finding an authoritative historical portrait of how women were treated in a given period of the history of Israel—another set of texts would take precedence. In this way, evangelical feminists would be able to avoid having a canon within the canon, at least in the strong sense of giving the same texts priority in every respect and for every purpose.

Another question is whether there is really an appropriate line that can be drawn between saying (a) that some parts of Scripture relativize

---

82. See Upton, "Feminist Theology as Biblical Hermeneutics," 100–101. For Ruether on the "prophetic principle" in the Bible and its uses for feminist theology, see *Sexism and God-Talk*, 22ff.

83. Bauckham, *Gospel Women*, 15.

84. Ibid., 15. See Parry's relevant comments on Bauckham's work in his chapter in this volume.

or recontextualize others, and saying (b) that some parts of Scripture *oppose* others in a way that would deny their truth or validity altogether. This is a difficult question that deserves further consideration. My sense is that evangelicals want to say that there is such a line (in God's mind at least), but at the same time need to admit that it is difficult for us fallible and sinful humans to identify or draw it. Therefore, evangelicals can and should learn from all kinds of feminists, including those that use some Scriptures to "read against" others or even those who "read against" Scripture based upon an extra-biblical criterion. At the same time, evangelicals will ultimately want to interpret the tensions and relations between various biblical texts in terms that do not claim that one text can decisively trump another in every respect. That is, evangelicals can interpret the relations between texts in terms of the "relativising or recontextualizing" (the language I have used above)—rather than fundamentally contradicting—of one text or texts by another text or texts. This approach would be consistent both with long-standing evangelical theological convictions about the unity of Scripture and the related hermeneutical notion of "the analogy of Scripture" in which "Scripture interprets Scripture" or "Scripture interprets itself."

I have considered how Webb's redemptive-movement hermeneutic might respond to three criticisms, namely, that it super-historicizes the canon, that it turns to a canon outside the canon, and that it appeals to a canon within the canon. While not always leaving Webb's approach unqualified, I have provided an initial defense of his approach against these charges and a further indication of the benefits of his hermeneutic for evangelical feminist theological interpretation.

WHICH READING COMMUNITY SHOULD HAVE PRIORITY?

In addition to the diversity that exists within Scripture, there is clearly a diversity of readers and reading communities. I wish to conclude this chapter by commenting on whether particular readers should have priority in evangelical, feminist biblical interpretation, and if so, who they should be.

To begin with, I believe that Christians, members of the church, should have priority over other readers. The priority I have in mind does not imply social or political privilege, but simply the conviction that Christians are more likely to understand the Christian Bible. The reasons are somewhat straightforward, if one accepts the main elements of the project of theological interpretation outlined above. This interpretative approach rejects the modern Enlightenment ideal of the neutral objectivity and detachment of the biblical interpreter and the claim heard in some postmodern circles that, although there are a multitude of different interpretations, all of them are somehow equally legitimate within their own contexts.[85] In other words, some "biases" or interpretative presuppositions, such as Christocentric ones, are more appropriate than others for the Christian theological interpretation of the Bible.

Accordingly, I join Jacqueline E. Lapsley and Donald Gowan in saying that, for a Christian interpreter, a "hermeneutic of trust" is decidedly more appropriate than a "hermeneutic of suspicion" as one's primary interpretative disposition.[86] Approaching Scripture theologically with a view to knowing and following its God is suitable only for people of faith who aim to submit their wills to God's will.[87] Since the Bible is written by people of faith, it naturally solicits the readers' trust and allegiance to God. Therefore, secular modes of interpretation that give overall priority to the hermeneutic of suspicion and leave no room for divine authority being mediated through the biblical text cannot be appropriate for evangelicals, even if they offer something from which evangelicals can learn.

In addition to faith and involvement in the Christian community as important qualities of the ideal reader of Scripture, Scripture also calls for readers who have solidarity with the oppressed and seek justice for them. This point is more challenging for many evangelicals, for it indicates that those best suited to interpret biblical texts about women are women who have been oppressed or those who voluntarily stand with such women. Further, the ideal reader will be marked by a life of discipleship, faith, and obedience that enables her (or him) not only to stand in solidarity with the oppressed but to be committed to resisting situations of oppression.[88] This is reading the Bible "from the underside" rather than from a standpoint of entrenched power and comfort.

---

85. A large number of readings can be illuminating and helpful for different purposes, but some readings are clearly misleading and problematic in any context because they contradict or misapply the text.

86. Lapsley, *Whispering the Word*, 18–19 (she refers to a "hermeneutic of informed trust"). Gowan, *Theology in Exodus*, xiv.

87. Gowan, *Theology in Exodus*, xiv.

88. On this point and others in the paragraph, see Escobar, "Liberation Theologies and Hermeneutics," 454–55.

By making this point, I am in some measure aligning myself with a hermeneutics of liberation, and especially of feminist liberation hermeneutics. I am also drawing from ideological criticism and from aspects of postcolonial biblical interpretation. But my reason for doing so remains "evangelical," namely, a belief that the message of *Scripture* as a whole (and not merely a contemporary ethical stance) calls its readers to adopt a stance of solidarity with the oppressed or the marginalized.[89] Not only are there a massive number of texts that would point in this direction (the quantitative support), but the texts and themes that speak of God as deliverer from oppression occur at crucial moments in the canonical narrative (qualitative support). For example, Ron Sider points out how divine speech and action in relation to three central points of redemption history (the exodus, the exile of Israel and Judah, and the incarnation of Jesus Christ) testify to God's partiality for the poor and disadvantaged.[90] I do not mean to say that deliverance from oppression is the *primary* biblical theme or motif,[91] but simply that it is an important one. This importance is adequate for claiming that when oppression is apparent in the text—as it often is in texts about women—we should follow the divine directive to expose and resist oppression as a reader.

The kind of reader that one is can either prevent or enable seeing and embracing the Bible's theological trajectory of God's liberating justice.[92] Being a certain kind of reader—such as one who is engaged

---

89. See my brief argument for this conclusion above in the section entitled "A Sketch of an Evangelical Feminist Hermeneutic."

90. Sider, "An Evangelical Theology of Liberation." For further exegetical support for many of the ideas in this paragraph, see Tamez, *Bible of the Oppressed*, and Hanks, *God so Loved the Third World*. Evangelical interpreters should avoid both modern and postmodern errors that have been associated with liberationist hermeneutics. Against the *modern* liberationist tendency to see the Bible and all of reality through a basically Marxist worldview and mode of analysis (a reductionistic, materialistic account of history), evangelicals strive to let Scripture determine how and when to critique such ideas and to replace them with others. Against the *postmodern* and post-colonial tendency to say that "truth" in interpretation is merely a product of ideological constructions used to support those in power, evangelicals need to assert that truth has an objective, stable character that can be adequately discerned.

91. In my view the best candidate for a single concept that embraces the whole Bible is that of the kingdom or reign of God.

92. This is similar to Francis Watson's observation that, while there are standpoints within the biblical texts that critique patriarchal ideology, these internal standpoints "are only attainable because contemporary feminist analysis enables us to discover facets of the texts which are otherwise concealed" (*Text, Church and World*, 201). I think Watson overstates his case (are these internal canonical standpoints really *only*

with the plight of oppressed women and informed by feminist analysis—helps one to discover real features of the text that other readers find hard to see. The reader does not create meaning, but the reader's context, qualities, and interests do effect what meaning the reader finds in the text. This perspective allows for the evangelical conviction that the text (rather than one's own interpretative interests and ideals) must remain authoritative and decisive in practice, yet at the same time it highlights the need for readers to have the appropriate interpretative interests for a given reading purpose.

Accordingly, I believe evangelicals need to ask the hard questions posed by "ideological criticism." For example, what if our social location and our "friendliness" with dominant culture prohibit us from hearing the uncomfortable truth that God proclaims through the text? What if we fail to stand and side with those whom God stands and sides with? Alleged neutrality does not help an interpreter to "get it" when it comes to texts involving the oppressive misuse of power.[93]

I wish to return one more time to the question of the extent to which the feminist use of the hermeneutic of suspicion is compatible with evangelical theological interpretation. As Robin Parry argues, since the human heart is sinful and deceitful (e.g., Jer 17:5), suspicion "has its hermeneutical role in a fallen world, although the elevation of suspicion to the driving seat of interpretation is problematic."[94] Particularly, suspicion can be applied to the patriarchal or other oppressive or colonial ideologies that are in some way present in the text and its interpretations. Such ideologies do not represent God's ultimate will for the people of God. Reflecting or describing the fallen culture in which the text was written, the presence of ideology in the biblical text can be understood as what God allowed or tolerated in Israel or the church *en route* to God's ultimate revelatory and redemptive purposes (*a la* William Webb's work). The ideal reader's qualified suspicion toward the text must be matched with an even greater suspicion towards the text's interpreters, including oneself as the reader. This allows the Bible to be

---

accessible due to contemporary feminist analysis?), but he draws our attention to the significance that the interpreter has on interpretation, especially when issues of justice or power are at stake.

93. Similar points are made by others in this volume, such as Sloane, Parry, Briggs, and Bier.

94. Parry, "Ideological Criticism," 315. See also Parry's chapter (chapter 2) in this volume.

the vehicle of on-going divine correction and training of readers (see 2 Tim 3:16–17), including feminist readers.

Interpretation that is both faithful to the text and beneficial to oppressed groups, including women, requires readers who: (1) understand Scripture as a canonical, authoritative, narrative whole, and (2) are sensitive to the plight of the oppressed and eager to join God in resisting and ultimately overcoming that oppression. The first quality prevents the second from becoming a "special interest" that causes one to lose sight of the whole of Scripture—which is authoritative as a whole. The need to distinguish between the essential, redemptive message of Scripture and the limited cultural elements must be itself constrained by the structure and content of the canonical text as a whole. The second readerly quality prevents the first from becoming a merely theoretical endeavour that misses the subversive features of the Bible and allows one to be overly smug about one's own privileged social location in the present. Readers from marginal communities help other readers to recapture the biblical message of restorative and delivering justice. When the Scriptures are read even and as a whole, they promote the full humanity of women.

CONCLUSION

In this chapter, I have shown how it is possible to have a hermeneutic that is both evangelical and feminist. When understood rightly, evangelical hermeneutics may rightly lead evangelicals to adopt many of the hallmarks of feminist hermeneutics. Recent work in the theological interpretation of Scripture helps to provide the parameters for an evangelical hermeneutic that is capable of learning from feminist interpretation and yet remains faithful to its evangelical commitments. William J. Webb's work, when appropriately critiqued and qualified, provides the groundwork for a promising evangelical feminist theological hermeneutic. In this approach, the divine author of Scripture as a whole speaks authoritatively through human authors who themselves variously give evidence of fallen, patriarchal culture or of a perspective that transcends that culture. When read as a whole, careful readers recognize the multi-level character of Scripture and allow some texts to take precedence over others for certain purposes. Enriched by the interpretative voices of women and other oppressed groups, evangelicals will be equipped to affirm that God's normative perspective, as revealed in Scripture, supports the full humanity of women and the liberation of women from unjust gender relations. This kind of theological reading glorifies God, the main subject of Scripture, for this biblical God is a God of justice and redemption.

BIBLIOGRAPHY

Barth, Karl. *Church Dogmatics*. I/2. Translated by G. T. Thompson and H. Knight. Edited by G. W. Bromiley. Edinburgh: T. & T. Clark, 1956.

———. *Credo*, Translated by J. Strathhearn McNab. London: Hodder & Stoughton, 1935.

Bauckham, Richard. *Gospel Women: Studies of the Named Women in the Gospels*. Grand Rapids: Eerdmans, 2002.

Beale, G. K., ed. *Right Doctrine from Wrong Texts? Essays on the Use of the Old Testament in the New Testament*. Grand Rapids: Baker, 1994.

Childs, Brevard S. *Biblical Theology of the Old and New Testaments*. Minneapolis: Fortress, 1992.

———. "Toward Recovering Theological Exegesis." *Pro Ecclesia* 6 (1997) 16–26.

Cochrane, Pamela D. H. "Scripture, Feminism, and Sexuality." In *Christian Theologies of Scripture*, edited by Justin S. Holcomb, 261–81. New York: New York University Press.

Day, Linda, and Carolyn Pressler, eds. *Engaging the Bible in a Gendered World: An Introduction to Feminist Biblical Interpretation in Honor of Katharine Doob Sakenfeld*. Louisville, KY: Westminster John Knox, 2006.

Dube, Musa W. *Postcolonial Feminist Interpretation of the Bible*. St. Louis, MO: Chalice, 2000.

Enns, Peter. *Inspiration and Incarnation: Evangelicals and the Problem of the Old Testament*. Grand Rapids: Baker Academic, 2005.

Escobar, Samuel. "Liberation Theologies and Hermeneutics." In *Dictionary for Theological Interpretation of the Bible*, edited by Kevin Vanhoozer et al., 454–55. Grand Rapids: Baker, 2005.

Felix, Paul W. Sr. "The Hermeneutics of Evangelical Feminism." *The Master's Seminary Journal* 5.2 (Fall 1994) 159–84.

Fiorenza, Elizabeth Schüssler. *In Memory of Her: A Feminist Theological Reconstruction of Christian Origins*. New York: Crossroad, 1983.

———. *Wisdom Ways: Introducing Feminist Biblical Interpretation*. Maryknoll, NY: Orbis, 2001.

Goldingay, John. *Theological Diversity and the Authority of the Old Testament*. Grand Rapids: Eerdmans, 1987.

Gowan, Donald. *Theology in Exodus*. Louisville, KY: Westminster John Knox, 1994.

Hanks, Thomas. *God So Loved the Third World: The Biblical Vocabulary of Oppression*. Eugene, OR: Wipf and Stock, 2000.

Kaiser, Walter C. Jr., "Evangelical Hermeneutics." *Concordia Theological Quarterly* 42.2–3 (1982) 167–80.

Kelsey, David. *Proving Doctrine: The Uses of Scripture in Modern Theology*. Harrisburg, PA: Trinity, 1999.

Lapsley, Jacqueline E. *Whispering the Word: Hearing Women's Stories in the Old Testament*. Louisville, KY: Westminster John Knox, 2005.

Marshall, I. Howard. "An Evangelical Approach to 'Theological Criticism.'" In *The Best in Theology*, vol. 3, edited by J. I. Packer. Carol Stream, IL: Christianity Today, 1989. Online: http://www.biblicalstudies.org.uk/article_criticism_marshall.html.

McGrath, Alister. "Engaging the Great Tradition: Evangelical Theology and the Role of Tradition." In *Evangelical Futures: A Conversation on Theological Method*, edited by John G. Stackhouse, 139–58. Grand Rapids: Baker Academic, 2000.

Meyers, Carol. *Discovering Eve: Ancient Israelite Women in Context*. Oxford: Oxford University Press, 1988.

Mollenkott, Virginia Ramey. *The Divine Feminine: The Biblical Imagery of God as Female*. New York: Crossroad, 1988.

Nordling, Cherith Fee. "Feminist Biblical Interpretation." In *Dictionary for Theological Interpretation of the Bible*, edited by Kevin Vanhoozer et al., 228–30. Grand Rapids: Baker Academic, 2005.

Olson, Roger E. *The Mosaic of Christian Belief: Twenty Centuries of Unity and Diversity*. Downers Grove, IL: InterVarsity, 2002.

Osborne, Grant. "Evangelical Biblical Interpretation." In *Methods of Biblical Interpretation*, edited by Douglas A. Knight. Nashville: Abingdon, 2004.

Osiek, Carolyn. "The Feminist and the Bible: Hermeneutical Alternatives." *Religion and Intellectual Life*, 6.3–4 (1989) 96–109.

Parry, Robin A. "Ideological Criticism." In *Dictionary for Theological Interpretation of the Bible*, edited by Kevin Vanhoozer et al., 314–16. Grand Rapids: Baker Academic, 2005.

Pierce, Ronald W., and Rebecca Merrill Groothius, eds. *Discovering Biblical Equality: Complementarity without Hierarchy*. 2nd ed. Downers Grove, IL: InterVarsity, 2005.

Pokrifka, Todd B. *Redescribing God: The Roles of Scripture, Tradition, and Reason in Karl Barth's Doctrines of Divine Unity, Constancy, and Eternity*. Eugene, OR: Pickwick, 2010.

Ruether, Rosemary Radford. *Sexism and God-Talk*. Boston: Beacon, 1983.

Sider, Ronald. "An Evangelical Theology of Liberation." *Christian Century* (March 19, 1980) 314–18. Online: http://www.religion-online.org/showarticle.asp?title=1757.

Scholer, David M. "Feminist Hermeneutics and Evangelical Interpretation." *Journal of the Evangelical Theological Society* 30.4 (1987) 407–20.

Soulen, Richard N., and R. Kendall Soulen. "Theological Interpretation." In *Handbook of Biblical Criticism*. 3rd ed. Louisville, KY: Westminster John Knox, 2001.

Soulen, R. Kendall. *The God of Israel and Christian Theology*. Minneapolis, MN: Fortress, 1996.

Stackhouse, John G. Jr., "Evangelical Theology Should be Evangelical." In *Evangelical Futures: A Conversation on Theological Method*, edited by John G. Stackhouse, 39–58. Grand Rapids: Baker Academic, 2000.

Stassen, Glen, and David Gushee. *Kingdom Ethics: Following Jesus in Contemporary Context*. Downers Grove, IL: InterVarsity, 2003.

Storkey, Elaine. *Origins of Difference: The Gender Debate Revisited*. Grand Rapids: Baker Academic, 2001.

Tamez, Elsa. *Bible of the Oppressed*. Reprint. Eugene, OR: Wipf and Stock, 2006.

Treier, Daniel J. "Theological Hermeneutics." In *Dictionary for Theological Interpretation of the Bible*, edited by Kevin Vanhoozer et al., 786–93. Grand Rapids: Baker Academic, 2005.

Thiselton, Anthony C. "Hermeneutical Circle." In *Dictionary of the Theological Interpretation of the Bible*, edited by Kevin Vanhoozer et al., 281–82. Grand Rapids: Baker Academic, 2005.

———. "Hermeneutics." In *Dictionary of the Theological Interpretation of the Bible*, edited by Kevin Vanhoozer et al., 283–87. Grand Rapids: Baker Academic, 2005.

Trible, Phyllis. "Depatriarchalizing in Biblical Interpretation." *Journal of the American Academy of Religion* 41.1 (1974) 42–47.

Upton, Brigette Gilfillan. "Feminist Theology as Biblical Hermeneutics." In *The Cambridge Companion to Feminist Theology*, edited by Susan Frank Parsons, 97–113. Cambridge: Cambridge University Press, 2002.

Vanhoozer, Kevin J. "Introduction: What is Theological Interpretation?" In *Theological Interpretation of the Old Testament: A Book-by-Book Survey*, edited by Kevin J. Vanhoozer, 15–28. Grand Rapids: Baker Academic, 2008.

Watson, Francis. *Text, Church, and World*. Grand Rapids: Eerdmans, 1994.

Webb, William J. "The Limits of the Redemptive-Movement Hermeneutic: A Focused Response to T. R. Schreiner." *Evangelical Quarterly* 75.4 (2003) 327–42.

———. *Slaves, Women and Homosexuals: Exploring the Hermeneutics of Cultural Analysis*. Downers Grove, IL: InterVarsity, 2001.

Wolterstorff, Nicholas. *Divine Discourse: Philosophical Reflections on the Claim that God Speaks*. Cambridge: Cambridge University Press, 1995.

Yarborough, Robert. "The Hermeneutics of 1 Timothy 2:9–15." In *Women in the Church: A Fresh Analysis of 1 Timothy 2:9–15*, edited by Andreas J. Köstenberger, Thomas R. Schreiner, and H. Scott Baldwin, 155–96. Grand Rapids: Baker, 1995.

Yeago, David S. "The New Testament and Nicene Dogma: A Contribution to Theological Exegesis." *Pro Ecclesia* 3.2 (1994), 152–64.

Concluding Reflections

Seeing Tamar's Tears

W E HAVE COME A long way from seeing a conflict between being evangelical and being feminist. Through terrain both disturbing and delightful we have seen that evangelical and feminist biblical interpretation can engage in a fruitful conversation; indeed, that we can speak as both evangelicals and as feminists in that conversation. That conversation prompts reflections on what it means to read the Bible as evangelicals and feminists, some challenging, others encouraging.

One challenging observation is just how blind we as interpreters can be, and how distorted our vision. Such distortion is clear when we see women as the source of sin and temptation; when we let poor Dinah take the blame for her rape; when we think that Ezekiel justifies violence against women or ignore its confronting message. Such blindness is seen when we fail as evangelicals or feminists to engage with the theological issues in Numbers; when we uncritically praise the "egalitarianism" we think we see in Deuteronomy's vision; when we ignore the voice of the nameless "concubine" or abused Tamar; when we fail to hear Lamentation's passionate pleas for justice, or the Song of Song's celebration of (woman's) sexual agency. If that is how they have been taught to read their Bibles, no wonder many feminists reject it. Our aim was to try to do a little better, and so suggest that there is a more excellent way.

It is also striking that there's a lot of sexual violence here. That is not, we would claim, representative of the Bible, but it does reflect a focus of feminist engagement with it; it also reflects an absence in evangelical scholarship. The question of violence directed against women—be that metaphorical (and at the hands of God) as in the case of Ezekiel or actual (and at the hands of men) as in the case of Judges 19 or 2 Samuel 13—is not one evangelical interpreters have attended to. Indeed, evangelicals have not engaged in much constructive conversation with feminist hermeneutics and the issues it raises. We see evidence of defence of themselves or Scripture against perceived attacks, but little of constructive engagement. That is both interesting and problematic and shows, we believe, that a project such as this one is worth pursuing. And as we have seen, engaging with these issues both allows and requires that we address fundamental issues of the nature of Scripture as the word of God and its authority and, indeed, of the theological task itself. Of course, for many evangelicals these questions just do not arise, be they the questions posed by feminist interpreters or the deeper questions of theology and hermeneutics that they generate. That may be because they are comfortably ensconced in their evangelical (scholarly) enclaves, or barricaded in their evangelical fortresses, or locked in their evangelical ghettoes, trapped into thinking that even to ask these questions is to betray the gospel. We believe that broader inquiry is required if we are to be faithfully engaged in our intellectual culture; and, furthermore, we think that this volume demonstrates that the fruit of such engagement includes a richer and more (self-)critical evangelicalism and a richer and more (self-)critical feminism.

One area we see as being particularly fruitful for both evangelicals and feminists is a commitment to reading the texts canonically. As a number of us have pointed out, while not drawing the sting of either problematic texts or their feminist critics, placing such texts in their canonical context allows us to see how theirs is at best a partial witness; and that where they leave women in a vulnerable position or one of neglect or abuse, theirs is not the final word on God's character or God's purposes for women (or the human community). This is one area where our work has shown the need for further development of a friendly critical conversation between evangelical and feminist interpreters of Scripture.

Another is in the appropriate use of the hermeneutics of suspicion—an issue on which the contributors disagree. All of us recognise that the hermeneutics of suspicion needs to be (rigorously) applied to our interpretations and uses of texts (particularly in exposing the ways we have distorted or abused the texts in our own oppressive programs). Some of us also see it as appropriately directed towards the texts themselves, seeing some as encoding a problematic patriarchal agenda which is only relativized in the context of the canon as a whole and its redemptive trajectory. Others do not, believing that while such texts may reflect a problematic patriarchal agenda, they do not endorse it, particularly when understood in the context of the overall witness of Scripture. We would, nonetheless, agree that "suspicion" can be helpfully used as a guard against excessive credulity—that suspicious readings prompt us to ask fresh questions of the text, that our initial questions are called into question, enabling us to see the text afresh.

We would, however, make haste to note that we see no need to gloss over these and other points of difference and disagreement that arise from the discussion. That is, in fact, part of the genius of the project—that, amongst other things, it gives "worked examples" of different properly evangelical responses to feminist OT scholarship and provides a lived example of an evangelical pluralism arising out of and expressive of a high view of Scripture and its authority. On such issues friendly conversation both amongst evangelical interpreters and between evangelical and non-evangelical feminists can only be fruitful.

And so we engage with Scripture, knowing it to be the word of a God of freedom and fidelity, a God of love and justice, struggling to see it as such in the face of Tamar's tears. And yet we must. For with feminists we can no longer turn away from Tamar and her tears, keeping her in safe seclusion in the palace of evangelical neglect. We see Tamar's tears, we hear the unnamed concubine's cries, just as we see the claims of daughter Zion and hear the Songs of delight of a woman in another garden. And with evangelicals we cannot turn away from Scripture and the God who speaks through it, quarantining it by theory and ideology as a dangerous product of an oppressive past. For, however astringent it might be, we know that Scripture brings to us the word of the God who brings us freedom, who gives us life, who calls us from the bondage of our ideologies; we know that, however we see them, our ideologies of liberation or control bind us to interests that constrain human flourishing and thwart the purposes of God, and only the God who speaks through Scripture, who is enfleshed in the person of Jesus Christ, can set us free. And so we see Tamar's tears, and often we are overcome by them. But we see them, knowing that our God is the one who has promised to wipe them away, and every other tear along with them. And for that day we wait and we long, striving to be better hearers of the word of God, being grateful for the hard lessons that feminist OT interpreters have taught us, even as we seek to negotiate a faithfully evangelical future.

Index

Aalders, G., 36, 45, 61
Aaron, 66, 71–73
Abduct/abduction, 39–40, 115, 130, 133, 139, 152
abhor/abhorrent, 116, 205, 208
Abraham, 24, 91, 103, 114, 129, 276, 279, 290–94, 308
Abraham, J., 3, 5–9, 21, 24
Absalom, 84, 104, 117, 176, 178–81, 183–84, 187–88, 301–2
abuse/abused/abusive, 25, 42, 59, 84, 96, 100, 102, 106, 112, 114, 136, 139, 159, 163, 172, 174, 177, 191, 194, 198–99, 206–7, 211–12, 214, 218, 221, 228, 251–53, 255–56, 259, 268–69, 281, 291–92, 352–53
Achsah, 125–26, 130, 133–37, 139, 141, 146–47, 151, 153, 162, 166–67
Ackerman, S., 73, 82, 138, 165
Acshah, 147
Adam, 2–4, 25–26, 86, 143–45, 169, 241, 291, 296–97
Adultery/adulterous, 64, 74–75, 90, 93, 95, 101, 103, 100, 110, 182, 192, 200, 203, 209, 213, 302
agrarian, 13, 48
Ahijah, 135, 156
Ahithophel, 154
Akkadian, 43, 148, 150
alienate/alienation, 4, 23, 31, 184, 241–42, 279, 285–87, 296
aliens, 262, 296, 304

allegory/allegorical, 13, 26, 142, 161, 214, 235, 241
Allen, R., 76, 82
Alter, R., 167, 179, 189
Amit, Y., 179, 181, 184, 189
Amnon, 53, 104, 117, 175–87, 301
Anderson, G., 178, 189
annihilation, 112–13, 131, 163, 295
Ansell, N., 59, 119, 124, 129, 133, 140, 144–45, 154, 161, 165, 299–300
Ashley, T., 73, 75–76, 82
atrocity, 116–17, 127, 176, 302
autonomy/autonomous, 23, 41, 50, 54, 231–33, 236–37

Babbington, G., 37, 61
Babel, 286, 290
Bach, A., 26, 34, 59, 61–62, 64, 75, 82, 179, 189–90
Bakhtin, M., 237, 257
Bal, M., 3, 14–17, 19, 24, 26, 133–34, 165, 192, 213, 230, 232
Baldwin, J., 6, 24, 351
Balentine, S., 4, 24
Bar-Efrat, 181, 183, 189
Barak, 44, 305
Barker, 20, 24
Barr, J., 1, 16, 24, 204, 213, 285, 313
barren, 304, 308–9
Barry, P., 249, 271
Barth, K., 248, 271, 318, 322, 340, 349–50
Barthes, R., 235
Bartholomew, C., 143, 165, 275, 277, 279, 299, 313

Barthélemy, D., 148, 150, 165
Barton, J., 248, 271
Bass, D., 217, 241
Bathsheba, 117, 162-63, 179, 182, 301-2
battered, 192, 216, 252, 257
Bauckham, R., 54-55, 57-58, 61, 123, 165, 275, 278, 301, 309, 313, 340, 342, 349
Baumann, G., 268, 271
Beale, G., 334, 349
beast, 218, 236, 238, 241, 305-6
beaten/beating, 228, 232, 236
beauty/beautiful, 166, 176, 180, 183, 218, 220, 229-30, 234, 236, 238, 241-43, 309
Bechtel, L., 2, 16, 24, 41, 61, 281, 285, 288
bedroom, 104, 177
Bekkenkamp, J., 235, 241
Bellinger, W., 73, 75-76, 79, 82
Bellis, A., 4, 12-14, 24, 110
Benedict, H., 121, 165
Benjamin, 113-18, 129-30, 132-33, 135, 161
Bergant, D., 224, 241
Berlin, A., 179, 189, 271
Bernard of Clairvaux, 36-37, 61
Besançon Spencer, A., 2, 24
Bethel, 130, 132
Bethlehem, 113, 118, 128, 138, 152, 157
betray/betrayal, 115-16, 124, 134, 153, 158-59, 164, 353
betroth/betrothal, 90, 93, 101, 105, 300
bias, 9, 31-32, 172, 190, 198, 201, 225, 227, 239, 253-55, 344
Bier, M., 54, 56, 104, 172, 189, 302, 346
Bilezikian, G., 2, 6, 24
biology/biological, 103, 145, 196, 203, 249

Bird, P., 3, 9, 24, 33-34, 48, 61, 68, 104, 110, 172-73, 189, 192, 208, 213, 218, 241, 339
birth, 66, 71, 83, 140, 145, 203, 207, 213, 220
Black, F., 218, 229, 235-39, 241
blame, 10, 12, 14, 36, 43, 46-47, 113, 199, 211, 252-53, 286-87, 352
Bledstein, A., 16, 24, 48, 61
Blenkinsopp, J., 85, 102, 107, 110
bless/blessing, 103, 118, 132, 143, 145, 163, 219, 261, 282, 287, 291, 293-94, 296-97, 299, 301-9, 308, 310-12, 340
blind, 152, 234-35, 352
blindness, 352
Block, D., 116, 152, 165, 192, 204, 207, 209, 213
blood, 90, 142, 158-59, 161-62, 171, 297, 253, 300
Blyth, C., 38, 43, 50-52, 61
Boaz, 143, 163
body, 18, 49-50, 94, 116, 124, 126, 134, 139, 155, 159, 164, 195-96, 200, 205, 229, 232-38, 245, 256-57, 277, 317
Boer, R., 19, 24, 238, 241
Bovati, P., 260, 262, 264, 268, 271
Braiterman, Z., 265, 271
breasts, 238, 244
Brenner, A., 12-13, 24, 26-27, 55, 61-63, 71, 82-83, 110, 165, 167-69, 192-98, 200-201, 203-6, 209-14, 216-17, 224-27, 230, 232, 239, 241-44, 250, 271, 277, 281, 285, 288, 313
Brett, M., 13, 24
Brettler, M., 141, 152, 165
bribes, 261, 304
bride, 91, 97, 135-36, 138, 146, 215
Briggs. R., 76-77, 82, 101, 165, 296, 346

Index

Bronner, L., 66, 82
brother, 37–38, 41, 46, 49, 51, 72, 89, 104, 115, 128, 130, 171, 176–78, 180–84, 186, 188, 204, 221, 223, 225, 288, 300
Brown, C., 162, 165
Brown, J., 20, 24,
Broyles, C., 150, 166
Brueggemann, W., 16, 24, 146, 166, 181, 183, 189, 266–67, 271
brutal/brutality, 59, 112, 209, 229
Budd, P., 69, 73, 75–76, 82
Long, B., 189
Burns, R., 71–72, 82
Burrus, V., 238, 242
Butting, K., 235, 242

Cain, 245, 286, 288
Cainion, I., 235, 242
Caleb, 125, 130–31, 133–35, 137, 139, 141, 146–47, 151
Callahan, J., 17, 24
Calvin, J., 36–37, 61, 169, 248, 271, 333
Camp, C., 172, 189
Canaan/Canaanite, 42, 46, 128–31, 152, 290, 293–94, 297–98, 305
Carmichael, C., 91, 110
Carr, D., 19, 24
Carroll, R., 168, 204–5, 210, 213
Carson, D., 204, 213
Cassuto, U., 8, 25, 287, 313
Castelli, E., 258, 271
Catholic, 203, 317–18, 320
child/children, 9–10, 12–15, 24, 26, 29, 53, 88, 101, 103, 115, 130, 140, 156, 192, 206–7, 215–16, 223, 257, 265, 280, 287, 291, 293, 304–6, 312, 337
childbearing/childbirth, 10, 12, 18, 23, 220, 283, 287, 289–90, 292–93, 304, 308

Childs, B., 80–81, 276, 322, 326, 341, 349
Christ, 2, 6, 25–26, 142, 164, 289, 326, 329, 338, 345, 354
Christensen, D., 84, 110, 143, 166
Christocentric, 125, 317, 329, 344
Christological, 57, 79337
circumcision, 195, 291
Clines, D., 4, 7–8, 25, 33, 61, 173, 189, 227, 232, 235
Cochrane, P., 320, 327, 349
code, 54, 69, 85–86, 108, 225, 231, 261, 276, 296
Coleson, J., 203, 207, 213
Collins, C. J., 2, 25
colonial, 9, 298, 320–21, 345–46
command, 10, 15–16, 57, 104, 112, 114, 183, 200, 281–82, 284, 286, 296, 299, 305, 326–27
communication, 19–20, 22, 186, 198, 202, 333
compassion, 112, 116–19, 121, 155, 159–60, 164, 265, 295–96
complain/complaint, 40, 42, 59, 67, 71–73, 88, 253, 264–65, 267, 307
complementarian, 1, 21, 34, 286, 319
complementarity, 2, 27, 194–95, 215, 313, 319, 350
complicit, 177, 182–87, 251, 255
concubine, 59, 84, 113–18, 121–22, 125, 127, 136–37, 147, 150–52, 155, 159, 169, 300–301, 352, 354
conquest, 215, 233, 295, 297–98
Conroy, S., 183–84
consent, 33, 39–40, 93–94, 98, 102–3, 105–6, 183
conservative, 31, 60, 162, 211, 277, 325, 337
Cooper, L., 209, 213
Cooper-White, P., 181, 189

covenant, 37, 54, 62, 86, 99–101, 103, 108, 129, 131, 136–39, 145, 165, 203–4, 209, 214, 260, 262, 266, 268, 289, 291–92, 294–96, 298–99, 302–8, 310–11
Craig, K., 16, 25
creation, 1–2, 4–7, 18, 21, 2324, 26–27, 29, 35, 48, 55, 105, 124, 140, 144–45, 165, 268, 220, 251, 253, 260–61, 266–68, 275, 279–81, 284–88, 290, 293, 298, 307–10, 321, 328, 336, 339
Creator, 23, 281, 307
creature/creaturely, 5–7, 15, 21, 147, 204, 281–83, 286–87, 289–90, 297, 305–6, 309
Crenshaw, J., 141, 160, 166
Crime/criminal, 36–38, 41–42, 50–54, 75, 86, 101, 107, 110, 115, 118, 165, 262, 302
cross, 125, 164
cult, 31, 34, 43, 66, 75, 80, 86–87, 95, 102–3, 105, 107, 172, 186, 211–12, 218, 237–39, 248, 259, 261, 287, 320, 334, 341, 343
curse, 2, 16, 23–24, 48, 61, 75, 182, 192, 209, 214, 219–21, 239, 286–90, 293, 298–99, 302, 304–8
Cushite, 71–72

Daly, M., 33, 49
Darr, K., 192, 213
David/Davidic, 84, 104, 117, 128, 147, 163, 176–82, 185–87, 189–90, 299, 300–302, 306, 308
Davidson, E., 125, 166
Davidson, R., 224, 242
Davies, E., 12, 20, 25, 181, 184, 189
Davis, E., 79, 82

Davis, J., 126, 166
Day, J., 141, 166
Day, L., 3, 25
Day, P., 209, 213
dead/death, 9, 16–17, 23, 28, 44, 62, 66, 71, 74, 77, 81, 83, 91, 97, 113–15, 129, 132–34, 136, 149, 151, 156–59, 161–62, 164–65, 169, 178, 180, 213–14, 219–21, 276, 281, 286, 292, 295–97, 299, 307, 304, 309, 313, 329
Deborah, 126, 141, 300, 305–6, 340
Decalogue, 57, 102, 110, 123
deceit/deceive, 132, 221, 253, 287, 309, 346
deconstruct, 17–20, 27, 106, 161, 222, 231
degrade/degradation, 51, 125, 198–99, 249, 251
delight, 4, 21–23, 217, 219–20, 242, 303, 352, 354
Delilah, 133
deliver/deliverance, 141, 282, 296, 299, 305, 345, 347
demean, 41, 205
Dempsey, C., 192, 214
desire, 2, 18, 20, 25, 36, 39, 51, 76, 95, 105, 110, 120, 125, 138, 142, 145, 157, 161–62, 194–96, 198–99, 204–5, 207, 213–45, 253, 260–61, 272, 291, 303, 310, 322, 339
desolate, 104, 178, 184, 305–6
Deuteronomic, 53, 63, 85–87, 92, 94–95, 99–102, 106, 108–11, 128, 133, 141, 146, 156, 167–68, 170, 262, 299
Deuteronomist, 99–100, 114, 168
devastate/devastation, 9, 21, 158–59, 199, 300, 306, 308
van Dijk-Hemmes, 192–95, 197, 199–201, 203–6, 209–13, 216, 225, 235, 241–42, 244

Index

Dinah, 30–64, 96, 128, 151, 163, 169, 177, 189, 292, 352
discourse, 7, 20, 29, 56, 64, 73, 122–23, 154, 202, 216, 225, 230, 247–49, 251, 254–55, 258, 264, 268–69, 316, 325, 331, 337–38, 351
disgrace, 41, 50, 53, 90, 96, 177
dismember, 112, 116, 130, 135, 153, 159, 234
disobedience, 23, 89, 104, 220, 281, 285–86, 281, 288, 291, 304–6, 309–10
disorder, 2, 9, 101, 236, 266
distress, 49–50, 115, 147, 176, 259, 264–67, 287, 290, 304
diverse, 48, 68, 86, 105, 110, 246, 267–68, 276, 318–20, 324, 329, 343, 349–50
division, 135, 159, 298, 308
divorce, 2, 44, 49, 84, 89, 91–92, 97, 105
Dobbs-Allsopp, F., 229, 242, 265, 271
doctrinal, 328
doctrine, 17, 20, 28, 318, 328, 334, 340–41, 349–51
domestic, 34, 125, 212, 303
dominance, 14, 31, 47–48, 87, 145, 177, 217, 220, 222, 282, 288, 297–98, 303–6, 321
dominion, 8, 220, 282–84, 286–88, 290, 293–94, 297–98, 304–6, 308, 311
Dorsey, D., 126, 166
Dragga, S., 16, 25
drama, 17, 20, 28, 33, 63, 120, 190, 208, 215, 227, 277, 279, 285, 313
Driver, G., 150, 166
Driver, S., 165
Dube, M., 321, 349
Dumbrell, W., 128, 166
Durham, J., 158, 166

earth, 4, 6–7, 15, 21, 48, 105, 191, 260, 266, 281–82, 284, 290–91, 294, 297, 306, 308, 311, 340
earthly, 260, 261, 263, 272, 289
economic, 10, 18, 40, 63, 68, 89, 92, 107, 122, 201, 203, 229–30, 296, 299, 314, 327
Eden, 1, 6–8, 16, 23–28, 62, 64, 145, 205, 216, 220–21, 224, 241, 279, 283, 285, 290, 304, 307–9, 313–14, 340
Egalitarian, 6, 26, 240
egalitarian, 1, 3–6, 12, 19, 21, 26, 105, 108, 217, 221, 230, 234, 239–40, 286, 294–96, 319, 336, 352
Egypt, 60, 131, 142, 153, 159, 199, 206–7, 292, 294, 297, 313
Ehud, 126
Ekron, 130
Eleazar, 67
elected, 173, 252, 262, 293
Eli, 118
Elihu, 147
Elkanah, 118
Emerson, G., 110
Emmaus, 82
emotional, 49, 103, 187, 225–28, 262
empower, 228, 266, 276, 292, 294, 303, 305
encode, 4–5, 11–12, 201–2, 353
enemy, 53, 63, 147, 199, 262, 264, 293, 297–99, 306, 309
Enlightenment, 41, 325, 344
Enns, P., 74, 82, 326, 333, 349
Ephraim, 113–14, 126, 134, 138, 152, 156–57, 159
epistemology, 202, 325
equality, 1–7, 16, 21–23, 25, 27–28, 86, 94, 101, 104–5, 108, 172, 201, 205, 215, 218–19, 222, 225, 230–32, 234, 239–40,

equality (*cont.*)
    246–47, 249, 262, 282–83,
    292, 295–96, 313, 319, 321,
    338, 340, 350
Erlandsson, S., 150, 166
erotic, 44, 62, 220, 229, 231–33,
    235, 241, 245
eschatology/eschatological, 1–2, 35,
    62, 145, 165, 307–8, 310, 330,
    335–36, 339–40
Escobar, S., 344, 349
essentialism, 222, 250, 257, 259
Esther, 57, 139, 143
eternal, 38, 43, 50–52, 61, 277, 239,
    338–39, 350
ethics, 1, 27, 29–31, 35, 41–42, 54,
    62–63, 70, 119–23, 159–60,
    170, 191–92, 202, 209, 212,
    214, 216, 243, 247, 271, 275,
    298, 314, 328–35, 339–42,
    350
Ethiopia, 39, 72
ethnicity, 9, 229, 246, 259
Euphrates, 156
Evans, M., 2, 6, 9, 23, 25, 105, 110,
    250, 259, 269, 271
Eve, 2–10, 12–16, 21, 24–26, 29,
    32–34, 47–48, 61–62, 86–87,
    110, 143–45, 169, 173, 189,
    192, 216, 278, 283, 285–87,
    289, 291, 296–97, 301, 303,
    314, 321, 326, 336, 350
evil, 9, 12, 14, 24, 26, 29, 31, 100–
    101, 119, 129, 161, 178, 214,
    216, 219, 281, 286, 288–89,
    293, 295, 297–98, 302–4,
    309–10, 313–14
exile/exilic, 25, 44, 99, 131, 142,
    145, 162, 196, 208–11, 253,
    257, 263, 279–80, 285, 288,
    295, 298–99, 305, 307, 334,
    345
exodus, 131, 142, 153, 294–95, 298,
    345

exogamy, 39, 51, 53
exploitation, 31, 84, 207, 224, 251
Exum, C., 32, 34, 53, 61, 136, 166,
    192, 209, 214, 218, 221, 227,
    229–36, 239, 241–43, 291,
    300, 302, 313

faith, 28, 30, 59–60, 64, 69, 77,
    79–80, 118–19, 122–23, 136,
    142, 150, 166, 168–69, 172,
    216, 254, 256, 258–59, 267,
    309, 314, 317–18, 327, 344
faithful, 77–79, 118, 120, 136, 195,
    259, 263–64, 305, 307, 325,
    332, 338, 341, 347
faithfulness, 120, 131, 260, 266, 306
faithlessness, 199
Fall, 8–9, 26–27, 279, 285, 288, 293,
    297, 304, 310, 313, 349
fallen, 48, 107, 145, 219, 301, 309,
    331, 339–40, 346–47
family/familial, 10–11, 31, 37,
    39–40, 42, 51, 67, 64, 84–89,
    93–99, 102–10, 180–81, 203,
    216, 283, 292, 296, 300–302,
    304, 309
famine, 306, 309
fantasy, 19, 24, 51, 193–97, 200, 227,
    232–33
Farley, M., 33, 35, 62
fate/fateful, 51, 71, 97, 104, 118,
    133, 136, 160, 186, 246
father, 41–42, 46–47, 49, 53–54,
    63, 67–68, 88–93, 95–100,
    102–4, 107, 113–17, 125, 127,
    130, 133–34, 137–39, 144,
    146–47, 151–53, 162, 176,
    181–83, 205, 212, 220, 223,
    257, 259, 283, 291, 296, 301,
    321
Felix, P., 325, 349
fertile, 136, 290
festal, 139, 143
festival, 86, 115, 130, 139

Index

Fewell, D., 3, 15, 25, 37–38, 50, 62, 113–14, 126, 128, 132–34, 137, 147, 166, 218, 244
Fiorenza, E., 31–32, 49, 189, 247, 249, 271, 320, 326, 349
Firth, D., 181–82, 186–87
Fischer, G., 39, 62
Fischer, I., 73, 82
Fleishman, J., 39, 62
Flesher, L., 250, 254–55, 258–60, 269, 271
Foh, S., 2, 25
folly, 46, 50–51, 133, 177
Fontaine, C., 141, 166, 226, 243, 250, 271
food, 15–16, 176–77, 281, 287–90, 303, 309, 311–12
force, 6, 8, 16, 39, 53, 60, 73, 76, 84, 95, 100, 130, 133, 174, 183, 199, 201, 207–8, 211, 253, 264–65, 269–70, 290, 332, 334, 337, 339
foreshadow, 114, 142, 296, 340
forgive, 211, 214, 251, 264–65
formal, 47, 129, 302, 317, 329
formalist, 68, 71
Foucault, M., 235
Francisco, 168
free/freedom, 4, 12, 14, 19–20, 23, 44, 59, 71, 101, 105, 122, 147, 186–87, 201, 223, 225, 232, 239, 301, 304, 321, 335, 337–38, 354
Freedman, D., 128, 167
Fretheim, T., 6–7, 16, 25, 133, 167, 285, 313
Freud, S., 80, 83
fruit, 3, 28, 79, 219, 265, 304, 353
fruitful, 20, 31, 225, 282–83, 287, 289, 292, 296, 304, 308–9, 352–54
Frymer-Kensky, T., 85, 87, 94–102, 104–5, 108–10, 266, 271
Fuchs, E., 54, 62, 184, 218, 222, 243

functional, 7, 90, 228, 339

Gafney, W., 71–72, 82
Galambush, J., 201, 204, 210–11, 214
Gammie, 141, 167
Garden, 3, 6–8, 10–11, 16, 24–28, 145, 219–20, 224, 228, 239, 243, 272, 284–86, 296, 304, 306, 309, 313–14, 354
Gardner, A., 6, 25,
Garnder, E. C., 247, 260–62, 271
Gaza, 130
Gellman, J., 6–8, 25
gendered, 24–25, 27, 110, 138, 140, 142, 145, 195–97, 199, 213, 216, 232, 241–42, 244, 313–14, 349
Gibeah, 114–15, 117–18, 127–29, 134, 136, 138, 152, 159
Gideon, 126–27, 129, 141–42
Ginzberg, L., 74, 82
girl, 38–40, 46, 53, 90–94, 97–98, 102–4, 107, 111, 113, 121, 152, 227
glory/glorious, 145, 152, 256, 286, 279, 290, 293–94, 297, 299, 306–8, 313, 330, 335, 340
goal, 17, 222, 247–48, 254, 274, 276, 310–11, 321
gods, 131, 262, 294
Goheen, M., 275, 277, 279, 299, 313
Goldingay, J., 3, 25, 86, 105, 107, 110, 178, 182, 189, 285, 313, 329, 349
gone, 45, 145, 222, 279
Gooding, D., 126, 167
goodness, 21, 100, 261, 266–67, 280, 288, 290, 295, 309
gospel, 56, 142, 162, 165, 278, 285, 289, 301, 313, 317, 338, 340, 342, 349, 353
govern/government, 11, 15, 31, 79, 201, 305, 308, 322, 330

Gowan, D., 299, 307, 313, 344, 349
grace, 28, 76, 110, 128, 168, 170, 196, 203, 207, 220, 295, 307, 311–12
Gray, M., 35, 62, 186, 189
Greek, 145, 149, 151, 163, 169, 300, 338
Greenberg, M., 203, 207, 214
Greidanus, S., 20, 25, 179
Groothius, D., 313, 319, 350
grossly, 38
grotesque, 59, 236–41
ground, 48, 106, 133–34, 218, 247, 267, 283–84, 286–90, 305–6, 309, 340
grounded, 58, 266–67
Grudem, W., 1–2, 8, 25, 27
Grushcow, C., 75, 82
Guest, D., 192, 214, 250–56, 259–60, 266, 269, 271
Guinness, O., 211, 214
Gundry, R., 163, 167
Gunn, D., 3, 15, 25, 37–38, 50, 62, 127, 151, 167
Gushee, D., 329, 332, 334, 350
gynocentric, 54–55, 225, 231, 301, 340, 342

Haas, G., 277, 313
Hagar, 8, 291–92
Hahn, S., 204, 214
Hamilton, V., 7–8, 16, 25, 45, 62
Hamilton, J., 290, 293–94, 297, 306, 313
Hamlin, E. J., 134, 138, 167
Hammurabi, 43
Hamor, 55
hamstrings, 60
Hankore, D., 39–40, 62
Hanks, T., 345, 349
Hannah, 118, 161, 163, 300–301
harlot, 24, 110, 113, 136, 148, 150, 162, 208, 213
harmful, 30, 173, 193, 255, 269

harmony, 4, 6, 21, 56, 219, 282, 285, 295, 304
Harris, R. L., 167
harsh, 47, 76, 239, 307
Hartley, J., 7, 25
hate/hatred, 148, 150, 177–78, 180, 249–50
Hatton, P., 156, 167
Hays, R., 79, 82
Hayter, M., 2, 6, 25
headship, 2, 27, 102, 106
heal/health, 84, 101, 107–8, 161, 229, 259, 265, 269, 301, 309
Heart, 119, 216
heart, 34, 50, 61, 113, 116–19, 123–24, 129, 138, 151, 153–55, 160–64, 178, 216, 233, 246, 263, 299, 308, 346
heaven, 101, 145, 241, 292, 308, 340
helper, 6, 28, 144, 282–84
helpmates, 4, 12–14, 24, 110
Henry, M., 36–37, 62
hero, 24, 110, 274, 276, 305–6, 311
heroines, 54, 62
Hess, R., 2, 7, 16, 23, 25, 282, 313
hierarchy/hierarchical, 1–9, 19, 21, 23, 27, 47, 86–87, 93–94, 99, 105, 194, 215, 235, 281, 286, 313, 319, 336, 350
Hilliers, D., 139, 167
Hivite, 37, 51, 54–55, 58
Hoggard Creegan, 173, 189
Hoglah, 66, 77
Holladay, W., 204, 207, 214
Holocaust, 258, 271
holy/holiness, 30, 82, 132, 186, 235, 244–45, 251, 262, 263, 294
Honor, 96
honor, 32, 35, 38–40, 43, 54, 62, 83, 85, 91, 96–98, 101, 104, 162, 166–67, 169, 187–88, 210, 213–14, 222, 236, 242–43, 291–92, 349, 296

hope, 14, 31, 35, 77, 107, 122, 133, 135, 165, 184, 212, 245, 255, 264, 267, 275, 279–80, 288–90, 295, 301, 307–10, 312–13, 316, 335
Horeck, T., 121, 167
horror, 37–38, 112, 114, 117, 208–10, 212, 237, 256, 302
hospitality, 113–14, 118, 134, 138, 152
hostile, 114, 152, 154, 228, 286–87, 289–90, 293, 295, 297–98, 300, 306, 309
household, 10, 63, 88–93, 95–97, 99, 101–2, 104, 108, 138, 156, 159, 249, 301, 303, 314
Hugenberger, G., 37, 54, 62
Huldah, 306, 314, 340
humiliate, 39–40, 115, 163–64, 170, 177–78, 180–81, 193, 199, 210, 251
humility, 163, 170
Hunter, A., 141, 167
Hurley, J., 2, 26
hurt, 97, 102, 107, 259
husband, 10–12, 18, 45, 53–54, 66, 68, 74, 84, 89–93, 97, 99, 101–2, 108, 114, 118, 125, 134, 136–37, 193, 195, 197–99, 203–4, 220, 257, 283, 286, 292, 303
Huwiler, E., 224, 243

ideal, 4, 6, 85, 105, 126, 142–43, 147, 169, 195, 222, 230, 234, 286, 295–96, 303–4, 308–9, 316, 331, 340–46
Identity, 24, 189, 243
identity, 5, 41–42, 72, 297, 311
ideological, 3, 10–14, 20, 63, 67, 190, 199–203, 211, 214–15, 297, 321, 345–46, 350
ideology, 10–11, 13, 18, 35, 37, 49, 52, 54, 96, 173, 197–98, 200–201, 203, 205, 209–11, 221–22, 230, 234, 250–51, 281, 298, 321, 345–46, 354
idolatry, 126–28, 156, 207, 299, 305
Illegitimacy, 163, 169
illocutionary, 6, 8, 16, 56
image, 9, 48, 95, 147, 156, 193, 204, 208, 224, 229–30, 235, 251–52, 256–57, 269, 281–82, 284, 299, 319
imaged, 194
imagery, 138–41, 163, 198–99, 208–9, 215, 232, 235–36, 243–44, 255–59, 269, 350
imagination, 19, 55–56, 58–59, 82, 166, 225, 228, 239, 244, 250, 318, 341
immoral, 16, 29, 46, 186, 251
immortality, 14, 103, 313
incarnation, 9, 140, 143, 164, 326, 333, 349, 345
inclusive, 5–6, 19, 117, 262
indictment, 117, 175, 184–87, 196, 210, 212, 266, 288–89, 312
individualism, 42, 71, 222
inequality, 249, 251, 296
inequity, 76
inheritance, 32, 47, 67, 69, 89–90, 95, 99, 100–101, 103, 106–7, 225, 297, 301
injustice, 59, 72, 188, 237, 249–51, 254, 260, 270, 278, 295–96, 298–99, 304, 310, 327
innocence, 22, 25, 206–7, 282, 291, 313
innocent, 74–75, 162, 175, 182–83, 185, 253
inspiration, 57, 162, 278, 323, 325–26, 332–33, 339, 349
inspired, 56–57, 59, 121, 125, 143, 174, 223, 259, 312, 326, 328
integrity, 49–50, 69, 128, 139, 183, 187–88, 222–23, 264

intended, 21, 39–42, 89, 98, 122, 127, 131, 137, 140, 155, 157, 180, 198, 234, 236–37, 247, 260–61, 275, 285–86, 228
intention, 7, 34–35, 40, 49, 87–88, 116, 138, 171, 185, 206, 227, 232, 290, 309–10, 325, 330–31, 340
interests, 10–12, 15, 21, 58–59, 179, 184, 188, 193, 201–2, 206, 211, 223–25, 227, 230, 232, 321, 327, 346, 354
intertextual, 40, 57, 59, 122, 125, 128, 145–46, 152, 158–59, 235, 244, 276, 334–35
intimacy, 4, 23, 86, 90, 228–29
irony, 117, 126, 128, 132–36, 146–47, 167
Isaac, 114, 159, 276, 291
Isherwood, K., 17, 26

Jabesh-gilead, 115, 118, 130, 133
Jacob, 36, 41–43, 45, 50–51, 53, 55, 66, 103, 128, 219, 276, 293
Jacobs, M., 7, 16, 26
Jael, 44, 306
Jameson, F., 11, 201, 214, 216
Jeansonne, S., 37, 62
Jebus, 114, 130
Jephthah, 42, 115, 126, 133, 160, 300–301
Jericho, 112, 163
Jeroboam, 156–57
Jerome, 37, 151
Jerusalem, 25, 112, 114, 116, 130, 138, 145, 165, 169, 191, 201, 204, 207–11, 213–14, 217, 251–53, 255–57, 259, 262–63, 271, 307, 313
Jesus, 1, 17, 56, 101, 105, 108, 124–25, 142, 154, 161, 163–65, 169, 307, 329, 332, 334, 339, 345, 350, 354

Jew/Jewish, 32, 36, 43, 45, 63, 67, 72, 74, 82, 86, 108, 110, 145, 170, 244, 251, 264, 271, 285, 289, 300, 314, 338
Jezebel, 60
Jobling, D., 15, 26
Jobling, J., 3, 12–15, 17–19, 26, 221–22, 243
Jochebed, 66, 296
Jonadab, 176
Jonathan, 149–50
Jones, S., 35, 62
Josephus, 143, 151, 166–67
Josiah, 306
Jubilee, 70, 123, 242, 296
Judah, 97, 115, 130–32, 135, 138, 157, 162–63, 264, 266, 272, 299, 306–7, 345
judgment, 23, 68–71, 76–78, 88, 97, 101, 104, 118, 123, 131, 133, 136, 150, 155, 157, 183, 200, 208, 210–12, 214, 218, 220, 263, 268, 280, 285–86, 288–90, 293, 295, 297–98, 300–301, 305–6, 308, 313, 341
judgments, 23, 68–71, 76–78, 123, 183, 220, 301, 341
justice, 12, 47, 54, 58, 70, 73, 79, 84–85, 92–93, 117, 136, 161, 172, 186, 188, 191, 201, 246–49, 253–54, 256–57, 260–70, 278, 294–96, 298, 301–2, 304, 308–9, 311, 320, 322, 324, 326–28, 344–48, 352, 354
justify, 6, 12, 16, 42, 141, 180, 184, 210, 224, 252, 265

Kaiser, W., 325, 349
Kass, L., 45, 62
Kawashima, R., 6, 26

Index

Keefe, A., 42, 50, 53, 62, 205, 211, 214
Kelsey, D., 341, 349
Kennedy, J., 11–13, 26, 201, 214
Kent, G., 243, 301, 303, 340
Kermode, F., 167
Keys, G., 181, 189
Kimelman, R., 21, 26
king, 10–13, 61, 100, 103, 115, 117, 127–29, 132, 140, 144, 147, 154, 156, 160, 163, 166, 176–78, 181–82, 238, 241, 243, 279, 292–93, 299–300, 302, 306, 308
kingdom, 294, 297, 299, 308, 310, 329, 332, 334–45, 350
kingship, 117, 127–29, 144, 178, 217, 293
kinship, 47, 63, 128, 181, 190, 203–4, 225, 292, 314
Klein, L., 126, 128, 133–34, 136, 146–47, 167
Klein, R., 209, 214
know, 19, 23, 28, 46, 78, 108, 114, 142, 144, 162, 171, 243, 262, 294, 304, 308, 354
knowledge, 11, 124, 162, 222, 267, 281, 322, 325
Kock, M., 41, 62
Korsak, M., 16, 21, 26
Kroeger, C., 105, 110, 250, 259, 269

Laban, 292
lamb, 158, 159, 163, 185, 302
Lamech, 286
Lament, 151, 266–67, 273
lament, 36, 63, 131, 160, 169, 265–69, 273, 288, 352
land, 14, 27, 36, 45–46, 54, 63–64, 67–68, 70, 74, 77, 101, 117, 129–31, 133–34, 137, 147, 153, 156, 159, 167, 174, 189, 203, 216, 261–62, 280, 288, 290, 294–96, 298–99, 303–9

Landy, F., 224, 243
Lanser, S., 6, 8, 16, 26
Lapsley, J., 113, 115, 123, 132, 167, 211, 214, 277, 291, 296, 300–301, 313, 344, 349
law, 31, 37, 43, 48–49, 53–54, 62–63, 69–70, 76, 84–110, 113, 117, 123, 137, 161, 165, 214, 261–62, 294–96, 330, 334–35, 338
Le Cornu, A., 303, 313
lead, 17, 55, 67, 71, 73, 124, 153, 164, 172, 183, 194, 199, 225, 302, 320, 325, 347
leader, 66–67, 69, 72, 253, 296, 299, 305–6
leadership, 32, 71, 74, 145, 253, 295, 306
Leah, 42, 44–45, 54, 58, 128, 291
Lee, G., 167
Lee, N., 253, 271
legal, 47, 66, 69–70, 79, 84, 86, 88, 91–93, 95, 100–101, 106, 108, 121, 158, 167, 261, 271, 276, 296
legislation, 66, 74, 77, 95, 99, 102, 108
Levine, E., 84, 110
Levinson, B., 158, 167
Levite, 59, 112–16, 119, 127, 132, 134–35, 137–38, 147–48, 151–54, 157–60, 162, 169, 300–301
liberate/liberating, 13, 22–25, 30–33, 62, 85, 105–6, 172–73, 249, 275–78, 245, 249, 302, 309–11, 320, 327, 344–45, 349–50, 353
liberation, 20, 22, 31, 35, 41, 108–9, 164, 201, 228, 249, 294, 304, 308, 320, 337, 345, 347, 354
liberationist, 34–35, 277, 320, 324, 337, 341, 345

linguistic, 6, 28, 34, 140–41, 153, 196, 204–5, 244, 285, 290
Lipka, H., 75, 82, 101, 110
literal, 115–17, 136, 143, 149, 209, 235, 282, 287
liturgy/liturgical, 139, 168–69, 241, 251
logic, 75, 88, 153, 221, 251, 254, 265, 267, 269–70, 288, 339
Long, B., 181, 189
Longman, T., 143, 167, 313
LORD/Lord, 69–70, 132, 185, 253, 260, 264–68, 288–89, 291–92, 294–96, 305, 308–9
love, 9, 14–19, 24, 28, 37–39, 50, 61, 85, 110, 116, 119, 121, 124, 138, 141, 143, 162, 164–65, 168, 170, 172, 176–77, 180, 190, 196, 201, 213–29, 232–36, 238–39, 241–42, 244, 260, 263, 287, 294, 303–4, 345, 349, 354
lover, 124, 141, 221–25, 229, 232–38, 243, 303
loyalist, 33, 35, 276–77, 282, 311, 320–21, 324–25
loyalty, 116, 195, 203, 235
lust, 39, 177, 180–82, 207
Luther, M., 36–37, 62–63, 331
Lyotard, J-F., 274–76, 313

MacDonald, N., 248, 271
MacIntyre, A., 247, 271
Magdalene, 192, 209, 214
Mahlah, 66, 77
Maier, C., 138–39, 167, 250, 254, 256–57, 268–70, 272
Manasseh, 67, 126
Mandolfo, C., 250, 254, 257–60, 268–70, 272
Manoah, 141
Marah, 74

marginalize, 9, 30, 38, 51, 73, 156, 196, 230, 247, 278, 308, 321, 345
marriage, 10, 22, 31, 37–41, 45, 47, 50, 53–54, 62–63, 68, 76, 89–90, 92, 97, 99, 100, 102–8, 111, 115, 130, 133–34, 145, 151–52, 161–62, 172, 192, 195, 203, 214–16, 241, 258, 283–84, 286, 292, 304, 314
Marshall, I. H., 328, 332, 349
martyrdom, 79, 82
Marxist, 11, 202, 216, 345
Mary, 163
masculine, 18, 27, 140, 197, 201, 203, 251, 253, 255, 259, 265, 282
masculist, 3, 25
Masoretic, 139, 143, 145, 149, 162, 169
massacre, 36, 42, 52
matriarchs, 291, 293
matrilineal, 225, 292
matrilocal, 283
matristic, 225
Matthews, V., 168
maturation, 2, 14, 16, 24, 288
McCall, R., 218, 243
McCann, J. C., 134, 168
McConville, J. G., 128, 168, 261, 263, 272
McFague, S., 206, 214
McGrath, A., 317–18, 349
McKeating, H., 100, 110
McPhillips, K., 17, 26
Megillot, 139, 143, 146
members/membership, 47, 76, 92, 94, 159, 225, 343
memoriam, 59, 218, 277
Memory, 18, 71, 118, 166, 168, 196, 247, 249, 271, 326, 336, 349
mercy, 77, 162, 267–68, 291, 326, 335
Merkin, D., 226, 234, 243

messenger, 152, 200, 292
Messiah/messianic, 163, 280, 289, 307–8, 310, 334
metanarrative, 48, 60, 120, 274–78, 292, 301–3, 309–12, 324, 328–29
metaphor, 28, 35, 63, 103, 108, 138, 191–216, 223, 235, 250, 252, 258, 286, 310, 352
methodology, 3, 12, 17, 31, 62, 149, 192, 196–97, 211, 317
Mettinger, T., 1, 16, 26, 279, 313
Meyers, C., 3, 15, 26, 32–34, 44, 47–48, 62, 66, 83, 87, 110, 157, 168, 243, 246, 272, 278, 283, 285–87, 303, 314, 321, 326, 336, 350
Michal, 44
Mickelson, A., 6, 26
Middlemas, J., 264, 266, 272
Middleton, R., 48, 60, 64, 119–20, 122–23, 160, 168
Midian/Midianite, 66, 127
midrash, 45, 58, 60, 66, 72, 83
midwives, 296
Milcah, 66, 77
Military, 192, 209, 214, 293, 305–6
Miller, P., 265–66, 272
Milne, P., 3–4, 26, 174, 189, 277
Miriam, 66–67, 71–74, 77–80, 296
misogyny/misogynist, 14–15, 87, 191–93, 199, 201, 203–5, 211–12, 249–50, 276–77, 300–302
misread, 58, 135, 162, 208, 210, 232
mission, 1, 29, 171, 275, 281, 291, 294, 310, 313–14, 328
misuse, 22, 87, 182, 281, 301, 321, 346
Mizpah, 115, 130, 132
Moab, 66
mob, 114, 127, 134, 152, 159, 163
Moberly, R. W. L., 16, 26, 280, 285–86, 291, 314

Modern, 75, 83, 169, 179, 349
modern, 20, 25, 48, 50–51, 71–72, 75, 78, 83, 97, 102, 107, 113, 139, 169, 179, 198, 200, 226, 256, 275, 279, 286, 320, 323–24, 337, 344–45, 349
modernist/modernity, 210, 321, 323
Moi, T., 248–50, 272
monarchy, 10–13, 117, 127–28, 160, 205, 286, 298–99, 301–2, 304, 336
Moore, G., 121, 158, 168,
Moore, S. D., 238, 241–42, 244, 258
Moore, S., 168
moral, 2, 9–10, 16, 23, 27–28, 36, 40, 45, 52, 55, 70, 77, 86, 99, 101–3, 123, 136, 142, 175–76, 183–85, 206, 214, 216, 334
Mosaic, 37, 79, 317–18, 350
Moses, 36, 61–62, 66–68, 70–74, 76–77, 82, 114, 129, 158, 161, 168, 243, 294, 296–97, 305
mother, 10, 15, 16, 27, 42, 66, 86, 88, 99, 139–45, 167, 208, 222, 225, 243, 254–57, 264, 269, 272, 289, 292, 296, 303–4
motherhood, 15, 34, 145, 218, 220
mouth, 127, 147, 217, 237, 262–63
murder, 32, 38, 59, 61, 112, 172, 180, 184, 286, 288, 300
Murphy, R., 124, 141, 156, 168
mutuality, 21, 23, 105, 219–20, 228, 233, 237, 283, 290, 340
myth, 18, 24–27, 132, 177, 194
Müllner, I., 115, 168

naked, 192, 195, 206, 209, 214, 220, 251, 271, 283
naming, 5, 7–8, 12, 15, 27, 144, 283
Naomi, 46, 118, 143, 301
Nathan, 182, 185–86
nation, 34, 204, 207, 262, 292–99

nations, 100, 106, 129, 131, 260–63, 272, 291–95, 297–298, 308, 337
needy, 6, 207, 303, 308
Negev, 134
Nemesis, 133, 165
neoliberal, 222, 243
Neusner, J., 43–44, 62
neutral, 38, 55, 263, 311, 323, 327, 344, 346
Nicene, 341, 351
Niditch, S., 3, 26, 44, 62, 110, 150, 168
Nineveh, 157
Noah, 66, 77
Noble, P., 37, 50, 58, 62
Noegel, S., 224, 244
Nordling, C., 277, 314, 325, 327, 350
norm, 17, 40, 47, 49, 54–55, 185, 231, 238, 250, 304, 309, 316, 318, 338
normative, 5, 31, 49, 56–57, 75, 229, 262, 278, 317, 332, 339, 347
Noth, M., 70, 83

Oates, J., 121, 168
oath, 101, 115, 291
obey/obedience, 68, 80, 88, 104, 129, 281, 284, 291–96, 303, 305–8, 311, 344
objectifying, 205, 233
O'Connor, K., 250, 254–56, 258–60, 265, 268–70, 272
O'Donovan, O., 2, 27, 260–61, 272
Odell, M., 211, 214
Olson, D., 3, 16, 27, 66, 80–81, 83, 141, 168, 279, 285, 314
Olson, R., 317–18, 350
Olthuis, J., 123, 164, 168
omniscient, 175, 178–79
ontological, 90, 99

oppress, 32–33, 85, 177, 199, 259, 275, 292, 294, 297, 304, 321, 327, 344–50
oppression, 4, 13, 31, 35, 49–50, 87, 106, 164, 246, 249–50, 252–53, 274–75, 294, 296, 298, 301, 304–5, 308–9, 320, 324, 344–45, 347
oppressive, 9, 10, 13, 18, 30–33, 47–49, 85, 119–120, 172, 191, 197, 252–53, 275–77, 284, 295, 298, 333, 340, 346, 353–54
oppressors, 121, 275
oracle, 132, 141, 154, 253, 280, 285, 288–90, 293
order, 2, 4, 6, 13, 20, 34, 40, 48, 56, 58, 65–67, 87, 90, 98, 101, 105, 113, 117, 124, 139, 157, 159, 172, 176, 178, 181, 195, 197, 199–200, 211, 224, 236, 260–61, 266–68, 279, 281, 283, 286–87, 300–301, 312, 319, 322, 326
Origen, 331
orphan, 85, 120, 296, 304
Ortlund, R., 2, 27, 192, 204, 215
Osborne, G., 17, 20, 27, 204, 215, 318, 325, 350
Osiek, C., 3, 27, 33–35, 63, 172, 189, 276–77, 314, 320–21, 324, 350
Ostriker, A., 235, 244
otherness, 18–19, 321
Othniel, 125–26, 130, 134–36, 139, 141, 146–47, 151, 162
Otwell, J., 8, 27

pain/painful, 10, 14, 18, 23, 50, 75, 220, 252–53, 255, 257, 287
paradigm/paradigmatic, 17, 25, 54, 100, 133, 135, 139, 141, 146–47, 151, 153, 162, 224, 287, 301, 304, 237, 297

paradise, 220, 243, 288, 291
Pardes, I., 3, 27, 223, 244
parent, 36, 88, 93, 97–98, 102, 138, 171, 280, 304
Parker, K., 3, 27
Parry, R., 40, 63, 96, 172, 179, 183, 189, 201, 218, 277, 292, 301, 320, 324, 340, 342, 346, 350
passion, 136, 191, 207, 214, 227, 245, 352
Passover, 158–59
patrilineal, 41, 47, 90, 94, 283, 286
patrilocal, 162, 283
Patte, D., 227, 244
Patton, C., 203, 208, 210–11, 215
Paul (apostle), 14, 37, 56, 74, 76, 108, 110, 169–70, 331, 334, 336
peace, 105, 130, 239, 261, 263, 301–2, 304, 306, 308–9
peasant, 10–13, 26, 47, 201, 214
penalty, 75, 91–92, 97, 101, 288
penis, 195
Pentateuch, 45, 82–83, 128, 141, 144, 169, 204, 262
Perdue, L., 140–41, 168
performance, 121, 141, 222
Perizzites, 130
perlocutionary, 50
Perriman, A., 88, 110
Perry, T., 141, 168
Persian, 13, 157
person, 38, 40, 51, 89, 91, 99–100, 108, 154, 226, 233–34, 255, 260, 292, 317, 324, 327, 338, 354
personal, 14, 49, 54, 86, 186, 200, 226–27, 238, 244, 289
personhood, 18, 101, 108
persons, 3, 23–24, 33–34, 48, 61, 74, 86, 101, 106, 110, 172–74, 189, 213, 252, 259, 292
perverse, 10, 199, 236
Peshitta, 151

phallacy, 34, 42, 63
phallocentric, 18, 222, 224
Pharaoh, 245, 296–97
Phillips, A., 86, 91, 100, 110,
Phillips, G. A., 258, 271
Philo, 74
philosophical, 29, 64, 106, 145, 202, 216, 247–48, 250, 268, 351
philosophy, 80, 83, 85, 87, 95, 110, 162, 165, 206, 215–16
Phinehas, 66
piece, 2, 10, 12, 66, 74, 89, 91, 99, 134, 278, 282, 301, 303, 320, 340
pieces, 71, 116, 127, 135–36, 156, 164, 300
Pierce, R., 1, 27, 201, 215, 319, 350
pierce, 196, 204
Piper, J., 1, 27
plague, 66, 306–7
pleasure, 27, 36, 61, 64, 104, 185, 190, 220, 232–33
plight, 7, 115, 124, 187, 211, 295, 346–47
plot, 51–52, 57, 112, 121, 178, 181–87, 238, 279, 306
pluralism, 226, 249, 354
plurality, 17, 237
Poetics, 37, 41, 56, 58, 63, 179, 187, 189–90, 193–94, 197–98, 200, 202, 213, 215
poetry, 197, 232, 242, 247, 251, 253, 255, 264–65, 267–69, 285, 288, 313–14
Pohl, C., 173, 189
Polak, F., 149, 169
Polaski, D., 235, 244
political, 10–13, 26, 106, 117, 122–23, 127, 165, 181, 186, 194, 196–97, 199–202, 214, 216, 246, 249–51, 257–58, 272, 294–95, 299, 306–7, 343
politics, 10, 19, 24, 26–27, 37, 48, 50, 53, 63, 122–23, 165, 178,

politics (cont.)
    184, 186, 212–13, 222–26,
    243, 253, 272
pollution, 100–104, 117, 301
polygamy, 293
polygyny, 104
polytheistic, 295
polyvalence, 23, 257
Polzin, R., 114, 168
poor, 84, 104, 106, 191, 262, 296,
    303–4, 307–8, 311, 345, 352
Pope, M., 192, 215
porn, 182, 184, 186
Porno, 191
pornography, 191–216, 238,
    241–42, 244
pornoprophetics, 191–216, 271
positivist, 320
postcolonial, 320–21, 324, 345, 349
postmodern, 64, 168, 210, 221, 231,
    234–35, 241, 246–47, 271,
    274–75, 277, 313, 318–21,
    323–24, 337, 341, 344–45
poststructuralist, 222, 319
Potiphar, 62
Powell, M., 179, 189, 279, 314
power, 7–8, 10–13, 20, 22–23, 31,
    47–48, 84, 92, 97–98, 101,
    112, 119, 123–24, 162, 174,
    177, 180–82, 184, 186, 188,
    193, 196–98, 201, 203, 206,
    219–20, 222, 225, 228, 233,
    258, 266, 275, 278, 283, 287–
    89, 292–95, 299, 301–3, 308,
    312, 320–21, 327, 344–46
powerful, 18, 31, 38, 42, 79, 96, 131,
    147, 211, 266, 275, 298, 308
powerless, 84, 233, 262, 306
praise, 143, 218, 231, 238, 267, 273,
    283–84, 303, 352
prayer, 163, 254, 256, 261, 264–70,
    272
preaching, 123, 169, 212, 237, 243

prescriptive, 219, 290, 292, 332,
    334, 339
presence, 6, 11, 66–67, 118, 124,
    132, 139–40, 143–47, 157–58,
    161–62, 186, 188, 260,
    274–75, 277, 279–80, 286,
    307, 340, 346
Pressler, C., 53–54, 63, 84–110, 116,
    168, 339, 349
presuppositions, 17, 202, 227,
    322–25, 344
priest, 24, 67–75, 82, 102, 112, 115,
    118, 154, 158, 253, 262–65,
    294, 297
privilege, 20, 45, 197, 226, 265, 283,
    304, 342–43, 347
procreation, 7, 24, 287, 290, 304
prohibit, 346
prohibition, 11, 92, 281, 346
promiscuity, 43–46, 193–94, 200
promise, 37, 115–16, 129–33, 137,
    156, 230, 279–80, 289–95,
    347, 354
propaganda, 193–94, 198–200
property, 47, 53–54, 69–70, 86, 91,
    116, 136, 203
prophecy, 71, 135, 154, 197
prophet, 35, 72, 85, 123, 128, 135,
    141–42, 154–57, 182, 185–87,
    191–92, 195, 198, 203, 207,
    211–12, 253, 257–59, 262–63,
    265, 268, 301–10, 334–35
prophetess, 72, 74
prophetic, 35, 55, 71, 108, 138, 154,
    156, 186, 193–96, 198, 200,
    208, 270, 304, 306, 309, 311,
    320, 329, 334, 342
Propp, W., 158, 168, 181, 190
prostitute, 43–46, 50, 90, 95, 104,
    194–95
protection, 90–91, 94, 96, 104, 113,
    139, 195, 204, 305
protest, 187–88, 253, 256, 266
Protestant, 33, 64, 172–73, 190, 317

protological, 310, 339–40
provocative, 36, 160, 231, 239, 321
psychoanalytic, 34, 42, 63
psychological, 103, 107, 193, 225–26
Puah, 296
punishment, 15–16, 71–73, 76, 136, 181–82, 187, 195–96, 208–9, 252–53, 256, 262–64, 299, 302

Queer, 238, 243

Rachel, 45–46, 291
von Rad, G., 8, 27
Rahab, 162–63
Ramsey, G., 8, 27
rape, 36–43, 46, 49–54, 59, 61, 92–93, 98, 101–2, 104–5, 107–8, 114–18, 121, 127–28, 133, 136, 139, 159, 161, 163, 174, 177, 179–81, 186, 194, 208, 251–52, 255, 292, 300–302, 352
rapist, 38, 46, 49, 103–4, 107, 121
Rashi, 45
Rashkow, I., 34, 41–43, 53, 63
rationality, 247, 249, 254, 271
readerly, 3, 7, 12, 17, 20, 56, 58–59, 176, 235–36, 279, 327, 334, 347
Rebecca, 46
rebellion, 36, 42, 67, 88, 192, 207, 263, 286, 289, 295, 299
redeem, 119, 125, 161–62, 22, 290, 296–99, 310, 312, 332
redemption, 18, 49, 118–21, 161–62, 277–80, 289–90, 299, 301, 303, 307, 310–11, 327–28, 332–33, 335–36, 339–40, 345, 348
reign, 117, 276, 299, 301, 305–6, 308–11, 335, 345

relativize, 57–58, 60, 312, 338–42, 353
religion, 31, 211, 278, 295–96
religious, 32, 49, 75, 101, 122, 147, 193–94, 196, 199–200, 202, 211, 228, 256, 278, 309, 326, 331, 338
Rendsburg, G., 224, 244
Renkema, J., 262–64, 272
Renz, T., 203, 207–11, 215
repent, 22, 118, 119, 131, 259, 299
resistant, 201, 231, 234–35, 239, 253, 255–58, 270
restitution, 38, 86
resurrection, 17, 299, 307, 329
retrieval, 119, 278, 321, 324, 333–34
revelation, 32, 124, 132–33, 147, 154, 275, 292, 294, 298, 329–30, 332–34, 336, 346
revenge, 38, 180
reversal, 144, 164, 220, 224, 263, 285, 287–88, 304
revisionist, 34–35, 222, 276–78, 300, 309, 311, 324, 341
rhetoric, 172, 208, 212, 252, 266
Rhetorical, 189, 203, 207–11, 215
rhetorical, 11, 34, 116, 198, 208–9, 221, 266–67, 269–70, 288
Richter, D., 250, 272
Ricoeur, P., 80, 83
Riggs, P., 202, 215
righteous, 162, 187, 193, 199, 260, 262, 266, 309
righteousness, 85, 174, 191, 260, 262, 308
rights, 69–70, 86, 91, 93, 95, 99, 105, 108, 203–4, 249, 262, 266, 311
Ringgren, H., 150, 166, 168
ritual, 76, 101, 158, 335
Rodd, C., 54, 63
roles, 2, 12, 15–16, 86, 88, 99, 108, 193, 203, 230, 233, 257, 269, 303

Rooke, D., 15, 27
Rost, L., 180–81, 190
royal, 10–12, 31, 59, 117, 127, 144, 156–57, 262, 302–3
Ruether, R., 32, 35, 63, 119, 140, 165, 168, 172, 282, 309, 314–15, 319, 334, 336, 342, 350
rule, 1, 3, 5, 7, 9–11, 13, 15, 17–19, 21, 23, 25, 27, 29, 52–54, 100, 127, 129, 155–56, 220, 261–62, 281, 286, 288–90, 293–95, 297–98, 303, 305, 308, 310, 321, 340
Russell, L., 31, 33, 35, 63, 172
Ruth, 28, 44, 46, 54–55, 57–58, 61, 116, 118, 128, 139, 141, 143, 146, 152, 161–63, 165, 168, 278, 287, 300–301, 340, 342

sacred, 106, 124, 157–58, 163, 173–74, 176, 193, 256, 318
Sailhamer, J., 141, 143–44, 169
Sakenfeld, K., 3, 27, 31–33, 63, 67–68, 71, 74, 80, 83, 85, 110, 143, 169, 172–73, 190, 201, 215, 242, 246–47, 249, 272, 349
Salkin, J., 45, 63
salvation, 131, 133, 160, 207, 328, 338
Samaritan, 45, 96, 112
Samson, 126, 133, 141
Samuel, 24, 53, 56, 59, 99, 118, 128–29, 165, 171, 180–83, 185, 187, 189–90, 208, 299, 302, 349, 352
Sandel, M., 248, 272
sapiential, 141, 145
Sarah, 291–93
Sarna, N., 43–44, 63, 291–92, 314
Satan, 147, 289
Saul, 114, 117, 128, 135, 147, 299
Scalise, P., 74, 83

Schaberg, J., 163, 169
Schenker, A., 149, 169
Schneider, T., 16, 27, 126, 169
Scholer, D., 173, 190, 201, 215, 320, 339, 350
Scholz, S., 37–39, 50, 63, 151
Schottroff, 33, 48, 59
Schroeder, J., 36, 63, 151, 169
Schroer, S., 33, 48, 59, 141, 169
Schüngel-Straumann, H., 16, 27
seduction, 38, 93, 98
seductive, 138, 228, 232
seductress, 138, 165
seed, 146, 286, 289–90, 293, 295, 297, 306, 338
seeds, 146, 293
Seerveld, C., 160, 164, 169
Seidman, N., 250–51, 253–54, 256, 259, 266, 272
sensitivity, 21, 121–22, 160, 232
Septuagint, 118, 169, 287
Serach, 66, 82
serpent, 124, 144, 220, 284, 286–90, 293, 295, 297–98, 306, 309
servant, 114, 134, 163–64, 178
Setel, T. D., 197–98, 215, 238, 244
sex, 16, 45, 67, 90, 95, 100, 102–4, 106, 178, 228, 231, 282
sexism, 218, 222, 225, 234, 300–301, 310, 324, 333, 340
sexist, 102, 172, 222–23, 234, 301–2, 311–12
sexual, 15, 21–22, 36, 39–40, 43–46, 49–50, 53–54, 59, 84, 91, 93–96, 98–104, 106–8, 114, 136, 139, 145–46, 148, 163, 176–77, 182, 193, 195–96, 198–200, 205–8, 210–12, 220, 224, 228, 232, 249, 283, 286, 300, 302, 319, 352
sexuality, 5, 12, 22, 40, 53, 87–91, 94–95, 98–100, 108, 193–94, 196–200, 204–6, 209–10, 212, 228

Index

shalom, 35, 308
shame, 39, 96, 101, 125, 177–78, 210–11, 220, 259, 283–84, 286–87
Shechem, 36–39, 42, 46, 49–51, 53–55, 59, 61–63, 127–28, 156, 177
Shemesh, 40, 63, 68–71, 83
Sheppard, G., 141, 169
Shields, M., 192, 208, 215
Shiloh, 115, 118, 130, 152, 161
Shimeah, 176
Shiphrah, 296
shocking, 59, 192, 207–9, 211
Shulamite, 226, 235, 238, 241, 244
Sider, R., 345, 350
sign, 2, 71, 104, 140, 290–91, 297
signal, 140, 257
silence, 19, 41, 49–50, 53, 56, 73, 185–88, 258, 302
silenced, 51, 59, 121, 181, 187–88, 270
silent, 88, 122, 134, 178, 182, 185, 187–88, 195, 265
Simkins, R., 3, 27
sin, 2, 4–5, 7, 9, 14–16, 21–23, 36, 48–49, 57, 100, 108, 161, 181–83, 186–87, 191, 199, 208, 210–12, 252–53, 258, 263–64, 268, 276, 280–81, 285–86, 288–89, 293–94, 298–304, 309–12, 326–27, 332, 341, 352
Sinai, 296, 310
sinfulness, 107, 207, 252, 327, 333
Sisera, 44, 306
sister, 41–42, 66, 72, 141, 176–78, 180–81, 184
situated, 125, 129, 260, 320, 332
slander, 86, 88, 91, 93–94, 97, 101–2, 266
slaughter, 127, 159, 211, 256, 265
slave, 86, 99, 104, 108, 262, 292, 330, 335, 338

Sloane, A., 5, 12, 14, 17, 27, 48, 95, 99, 186, 202–3, 215, 282–83, 320, 346
Smelik, W., 150, 169
Smith-Christopher, D., 29, 208–10, 215–16, 243, 281, 314
snake, 9, 12, 124
Sodom, 152, 191
Soggin, J. A., 158, 169
solidarity, 163, 252, 302, 344–45
Solomon, 100, 157, 180, 217, 224, 237–39, 241–45, 299, 301, 303–4, 314
sons, 50–51, 55, 67–68, 89–90, 99, 127, 140, 145, 181, 186–87, 225
Sotah, 75–77, 82
soul, 217, 226
sovereign, 107, 132, 270, 292–93, 295, 311
sovereignty, 270
spiritual, 49, 74, 122, 299, 306, 308, 311
spirituality, 124, 137
Stackhouse, J., 317–18, 350
Stassen, G., 329, 332, 334, 350
Steinberg, N., 47, 63, 86, 94, 292, 314
Sternberg, M., 37, 50, 53, 55–56, 58, 62–63, 179, 187, 190, 202, 215
Sterring, A., 69, 83
stewardship, 304, 311
Stiebert, J., 211, 215
Stitzinger, M., 2, 8, 28
Stiver, D., 206, 215
Stordalen, T., 1, 16, 28, 279, 314
Storkey, E., 321, 350
Story, 24–25, 27, 40–42, 60, 62–63, 99, 111, 121–22, 168–70, 215, 275, 279, 285, 299, 313
stranger, 84, 120, 152

strategies, 3, 11, 13, 20, 33, 35, 45, 52, 120–21, 197, 206, 228, 230, 235, 276–77
structural, 106, 219, 230, 341
structuralist, 3, 15, 29, 277
structure, 31, 49, 87, 93, 96, 100, 105, 108, 126–27, 180, 188, 203, 238, 248–49, 255, 283, 288–90, 304, 333, 347
struggle, 23, 32, 70, 180–81, 289, 292–93, 297
Stuart, E., 17, 28
subjectivity, 18, 121–22, 161, 217, 231, 267
subjugation, 38, 249, 251, 253, 258
subordinate, 14, 87–88, 224
subversion, 17, 19
subversive, 49, 347
subvert, 18, 34, 49, 54, 60, 219, 258
succession, 180–81, 186
Sugirtharajah, R. S., 83, 245
superior, 148–49, 151, 282–83
superiority, 220, 225, 227
suspicion, 20, 30–31, 59–60, 71, 76–77, 80, 118, 120, 202–3, 274, 278, 321, 333–34, 344, 346, 353–54
suspicious, 19, 76, 78, 222, 234, 321, 333, 354
Swanepoel, M. G., 203, 209, 215
symbolic, 11, 13, 95, 135, 137, 142, 147, 153, 195, 205, 289

Talbert-Wettler, B., 172, 190
Tamar, 40, 51, 53–54, 59, 97, 104, 117, 162–63, 171, 174–89, 301–2, 352, 354
Tamez, 345, 350
Targum, 74, 149–50, 169
temple, 127, 157–58, 255, 335
temporal, 5–6, 21, 331, 333, 336
temptation, 174, 219–20, 284, 287–88, 352
temptress, 10–12

testimony, 251, 258, 262–63, 265, 338, 341
theocentric, 22, 260–61, 266, 324
theocratic, 294, 297
theodicy, 251–54, 258, 265
Thiselton, A., 49, 63, 123, 169, 201–2, 215, 316–17, 323, 350
Thompson, A., 116–17, 169
Thompson, J. B., 201, 215
Thompson, J. L., 151, 169, 201, 215
threshold, 114, 134, 155–59, 162, 270
Tiemeyer, L-S., 209, 211, 215, 258–60, 263, 269–70, 272
Tirzah, 66, 77
Tolbert, M., 33, 64, 172–73, 190, 247, 273
Torah, 45, 63, 85–86, 99, 111, 122, 128–29, 170, 296, 299, 314
tort, 100, 102, 104
totalizing, 120, 222, 275–76
Tov, E., 149, 158, 169
tradition, 13–17, 22, 31, 33–36, 39, 47, 59–62, 65, 67, 71–74, 82, 110, 112, 120, 138, 145, 148–49, 153, 162, 167, 170, 172–73, 201, 204, 209, 227, 235, 241, 251, 253, 256, 271–72, 309, 317–18, 320, 327, 349–50
traditional, 1, 6, 9, 12, 17, 32, 44, 55–56, 60, 94, 100, 139, 145, 149, 201, 220, 223, 285, 316, 318, 325, 329
traditionalist, 46, 232
tragic/tragedy, 23, 115, 117, 182, 219, 288
trajectory, 99, 108, 272, 340, 345, 353
transgressive, 18, 236
treaty, 192, 209, 214
tree, 11, 80, 82, 141, 165, 168, 220, 281, 286
Treier, D., 323, 350

Trevett, C., 72, 83
tribe/tribal, 67–68, 113, 115–17, 126, 128–30, 133, 135, 161, 164, 295–96, 300
Trible, P., 3–9, 16, 21–22, 24, 26, 28, 33, 48, 64, 68, 71–72, 83, 112–14, 116–22, 124–25, 128, 132, 136, 146, 159, 161–62, 169, 172, 176, 180, 185, 190, 201, 215, 218–25, 239, 244, 249, 273, 282–83, 290–92, 300–301, 304, 314, 332, 339–40, 350
Trinity, 322, 341
Trueman, C., 248, 271
trust, 3, 30, 59, 77, 80, 82, 110, 120, 123, 153–54, 179, 183, 203, 291, 303, 316, 344
trustworthiness, 267, 326
truth, 2, 8, 25, 33, 48, 60–61, 107, 119–20, 123, 142, 151, 160, 162, 165, 168, 222, 326, 331, 338, 343, 345–46
Tucker, R., 2, 6, 28
typology, 32–33, 74, 125, 172, 277

unfaithful, 75–76, 113, 136, 148, 162, 194, 204, 208, 215, 295, 299, 304, 306
unjust, 73, 75, 247, 249–51, 258–59, 266, 268–69, 305, 348
unnamed, 66, 112–13, 118–19, 121–23, 125–26, 129, 132–38, 146–48, 151–56, 158–64, 272, 300, 354
unstable, 14, 17–19, 221, 301, 318
Upton, B., 342, 351
Ur, 271
Uriah, 163, 302

vagina, 207, 237
valiant, 141–43, 146, 162, 170
Vamp, 121, 165

Van Leeuwen, M., 23, 28, 62, 205, 216
Van Leeuwen, R., 124, 140, 170
Vanhoozer, K., 17, 20, 28, 202, 216, 314, 322–23, 349–51
Vawter, B., 8, 28
Veenker, R., 3, 28
vengeance, 116, 184, 301
victim/victimize, 37–38, 40, 42, 50, 53, 59, 77, 84, 91–92, 101–4, 107, 121, 139, 174–75, 181–83, 188, 206, 211, 252, 265
victory, 115, 130–32, 137, 289, 293, 305, 309
vindicate, 184
vindicates, 268
vindication, 101–2, 163–64, 184, 251, 268, 334
violate, 7, 10, 42, 49–50, 50, 104, 107–8, 152, 163, 167, 177, 181, 199, 209–10, 252, 291, 299–301, 325
violence, 27, 39, 50, 53–54, 59, 63, 93, 108, 112–18, 121, 127, 132, 139, 158, 162–63, 168–69, 174, 184, 186, 188–89, 191–94, 195, 199–200, 208–16, 236, 251–52, 257–58, 260, 286–87, 295–97, 300–302, 304–5, 308, 352
virgin/virginity, 86–88, 90–91, 93–98, 100–103, 110, 114–15, 121, 127, 130, 133, 136, 139, 152, 163, 165, 176, 178, 225
virtue, 82, 104, 184, 247, 327
virtuous, 72–73, 82, 91, 248, 263
Vogels, W., 6–7, 16, 28
voice, 11, 16–18, 22–25, 34, 38, 50–51, 55, 67, 75, 121, 128, 133, 144, 153–54, 158, 161, 165, 175, 173, 177, 183–84, 187–88, 192, 195, 197, 213, 216–18, 225–29, 231–35, 239,

voice (*cont.*)
242–46, 250, 254–60, 264–66, 268–70, 278, 321, 347, 352
voiceless, 61, 183
vow, 62, 80, 115, 130, 133
voyeurism, 182, 208–9, 233
Vulgate, 113, 149–51, 158
vulnerability, 47, 84–85, 94, 96, 99, 162, 275, 296, 302, 304, 327, 353

Wacker, M-T., 33, 48, 59
Walhout, C., 202, 216
Walsh, B., 48, 60, 64, 119–20, 122–23, 160, 168
Walsh, C., 228, 245
Waltke, B., 170, 314
Walton, J., 85, 110
wantonness, 117, 258
war, 31, 42, 62–63, 91, 110, 114–15, 127, 130, 132, 135, 139, 209
Ward, T., 20, 28
ware, 169
warrant, 6, 20, 238, 266
warrior, 119, 138, 142, 165
Washington, H., 192, 209, 214
watchmen, 221, 223, 228, 236–37, 243
water, 44, 46, 74–75, 134, 136–37, 146, 150, 220
Watson, F., 30, 48–49, 60, 64, 333, 335, 339, 345, 351
weak/weakness, 7–8, 16, 18, 43, 50, 56, 65, 94, 125, 151, 161, 202, 205, 254, 262, 275, 297, 308
Webb, B., 126, 128, 136, 170
Webb, W., 70, 83, 315–51
wedding, 38, 97, 102
Weems, R., 192, 208, 216, 227–30, 239, 245
Wegner, P., 149, 170
Weinfeld, M., 86, 94, 111, 141, 170
Wengst, K., 163, 170

Wenham, G., 8, 29, 43, 64, 69, 73–74, 76, 83, 91, 99, 111, 122, 170
Westermann, C., 21, 29, 145, 167, 170, 266–67, 273
Western, 41–42, 50–51, 62, 68, 93, 107, 200, 275, 295
Whiteley, R., 303–4, 314
whore/whoredom, 43, 45, 136, 192, 203–4, 208–10, 214–15, 257
Whybray, R. N., 16, 29
wickedness, 133, 296, 300
widow, 84–85, 89, 120, 296, 304
wife, 7, 54, 57, 62, 66, 72–75, 82, 84, 86, 89–92, 95, 99, 101–2, 104, 108, 113–16, 125–26, 130, 136–38, 141–43, 156–57, 163, 169, 192–94, 195, 197–98, 203, 208, 214–15, 255, 257, 283, 286, 292, 300, 303–4, 306
Wilcox, M., 138, 170
wilderness, 65, 67, 70, 72, 74, 83, 116, 309
Williams, J., 37, 54, 174, 296
Wisdom, 3, 19, 25, 86, 124, 133, 139–47, 151–56, 158–62, 164–69, 241, 276, 303, 313, 320, 349
wisdom, 18, 46–47, 59, 99, 122–24, 128–29, 131–32, 140–48, 153–55, 160–62, 169, 175, 261, 277, 301–3, 335
witness, 22, 33, 76–79, 88, 96, 109, 120, 136, 149, 150–51, 158, 161, 169, 253, 255–56, 313, 322, 326, 331, 333, 353
van Wolde, E., 3, 29
Wolf, H., 126, 166
Wolters, A., 141, 149, 164, 170
Wolterstorff, N., 5, 12, 17, 20, 28–29, 56, 64, 197, 202–3, 215–16, 325, 331, 337–38, 351

womanist, 218, 227–28, 243, 245–46, 258, 271
Wootton, J., 17, 29
worldview, 17, 51–53, 194, 221–22, 228, 252, 337, 345
worship, 44, 67, 140, 262, 267, 294, 308–9, 335
wounded, 162, 181, 189, 257
wounded, 162, 257
Wright, C., 1, 29, 54, 64, 192, 203, 211, 216, 281, 291, 298, 314
Wright, N. T., 173–74, 190, 309, 314
Wudel, B., 4, 29

Yahweh/YHWH, 14–16, 67–69, 72, 100–101, 115–16, 124, 129–32, 135–37, 147, 153, 157, 182, 193, 203–4, 208, 210–11, 214, 224, 242, 252, 261–63, 276, 284, 286, 288–90, 294–95, 298–99, 302, 304–5

Yahwist, 11, 27, 100, 147
Yarber, A., 238, 245
Yarborough, R., 337, 351
Yeago, D., 341, 351
Yee, G., 3, 9–13, 29, 192, 216
Yehuda, 241

Zelophehad, 66–67, 69–71, 83
zenû, 148, 150
Zimmerli, W., 209, 216
Zion, 138–39, 155, 163, 167, 252–59, 262, 265–66, 268–69, 272, 309, 354
Zipporah, 66, 72, 82

CPSIA information can be obtained
at www.ICGtesting.com
Printed in the USA
LVHW081401220920
666792LV00008B/110